As the American colonies grew more restive, and a break with the mother country ceased to be unthinkable, John Adams was forced to spend less and less time with his beloved family. Although burdened by ever-expanding responsibilities in the Second Continental Congress, he found time for an amazing amount of correspondence.

The majority of his letters were written to secure the facts that would enable this duty-ridden man to decide and act effectively on the issues being debated. Military affairs, a source of never-ending concern, provide some of the most fascinating subjects, including several accounts of the Battle of Bunker Hill, assessments of various high-ranking officers, and complaints about the behavior of the riflemen sent from three states to the southward to aid the Massachusetts troops. The heated question of pay for soldiers and officers early strained relations between New England and southern colonies. By refusing to confront the issue of slavery when it was raised by several correspondents, Adams sought to avoid exacerbating regional sensitivities further.

When the question of independent governments for former colonies arose, at the request of several colleagues Adams sketched a model: *Thoughts on Government*, three versions of which are included here. His optimistic republicanism, however, was balanced by fear that a "Spirit of Commerce" would undermine the virtue requisite for republican institutions.

Adams' important committee work included his draft in 1775 of rules for regulation of the Continental Navy, which have remained the basis for the governance of the United States Navy down into our own time, and his plan of treaties, which would guide American diplomatists up to World War II. Both were derivative, but he skillfully adapted his materials to American needs and circumstances.

These volumes reflect the spirit of those tumultuous years when the leaders emerging in America confronted each other, and exciting new ideas, as they tried to resolve the issues of a revolutionary period.

The Adams Papers

ROBERT J. TAYLOR, EDITOR IN CHIEF

SERIES III

GENERAL CORRESPONDENCE
AND OTHER PAPERS
OF THE ADAMS STATESMEN

Papers of John Adams

Papers of John Adams

ROBERT J. TAYLOR, *EDITOR*
GREGG L. LINT, *ASSISTANT EDITOR*
CELESTE WALKER, *EDITORIAL ASSISTANT*

———————— ☆ ————————

Volume 3 · *May 1775 – January 1776*

THE BELKNAP PRESS
OF HARVARD UNIVERSITY PRESS
CAMBRIDGE, MASSACHUSETTS,
AND LONDON, ENGLAND

1979

Funds for editing *The Adams Papers* were originally furnished by Time, Inc., on behalf of *Life*, to the Massachusetts Historical Society, under whose supervision the editorial work is being done. Further funds were provided by a grant from the Ford Foundation to the National Archives Trust Fund Board in support of this and four other major documentary publications. In common with these and many other enterprises like them, *The Adams Papers* has continued to benefit from the guidance and cooperation of the National Historical Publications and Records Commission, chaired by the Archivist of the United States, which now also provides this enterprise with its major financial support.

Library of Congress Cataloging in Publication Data (Revised)

Adams, John, Pres. U. S., 1735–1826.
    Papers of John Adams.
    (The Adams papers : Series III, General correspondence and other papers of the Adams statesmen)
    Vols.
    Includes bibliographical references and index.
    1. United States—Politics and government—Colonial period, ca. 1600–1775 —Sources. 2. Massachusetts—Politics and government—Colonial period, ca. 1600–1775—Sources. 3. United States—Politics and government—Revolution, 1775–1783—Sources. 4. United States—Politics and government—1783–1809—Sources. 5. Presidents—United States—Correspondence. 6. Adams, John, Pres. U. S., 1735–1826. I. Taylor, Robert Joseph, 1917– II. Title. III. Series.

E302.A26 1977   973.4'4'08   77–4707
ISBN 0–674–65441–2 (v. 1–2)
ISBN 0–674–65442–0 (v. 3–4)

This edition of *The Adams Papers*
is sponsored by the MASSACHUSETTS HISTORICAL SOCIETY
to which the ADAMS MANUSCRIPT TRUST
by a deed of gift dated 4 April 1956
gave ultimate custody of the personal and public papers
written, accumulated, and preserved over a span of three centuries
by the Adams family of Massachusetts

The Adams Papers

The acorn and oakleaf device on the preceding page is redrawn from a seal cut for John Quincy Adams after 1830. The motto is from Cæcilius Statius as quoted by Cicero in the First Tusculan Disputation: *Serit arbores quæ alteri seculo prosint* ("He plants trees for the benefit of later generations").

Contents

Descriptive List of Illustrations

Published in the *Columbian Magazine* for July 1787 to illustrate a brief account of the State House, where the Federal Convention was then sitting. This building earlier housed the Second Continental Congress. In 1781 the wooden steeple rising above the brick tower was removed because it was badly decayed. Trenchard did his engraving from a detail in Peale's portrait of M. Conrad Alexandre Gérard, first French minister to the United States (Edward M. Riley, "The Independence Hall Group," Amer. Philos. Soc., *Trans.*, 43 [1953]:pt. 1, 23–24).
Courtesy of the Massachusetts Historical Society.

Romans' inscription on his battle scene continues: "In which an advanced party of about 700 Provincials stood an Attack made by 11 Regiments and a Train of Artillery and after an Engagement of two hours Retreated to their Main body at Cambridge Leaving Eleven Hundred of the enemy Killed and Wounded upon the field." This may be the earliest published picture of the battle, a version of it being advertised in the *Pennsylvania Gazette*, 20 Sept. 1775. Despite Romans' claim, the relative positions of Charlestown, Boston, and Breed's Hill are inexact.

Romans, born in the Netherlands, was an engineer, surveyor, cartographer, naturalist, and author, who had worked for some years in Georgia and Florida. In the 1770's he moved to the north, settling in Connecticut. He supervised construction of fortifications for the army in several places (P. Lee Phillips, *Notes on the Life and Work of Bernard Romans*, Publication of the Florida State Historical Society, 2 (1924):83–85; *DAB*).
Courtesy of the Massachusetts Historical Society.

Distant relative of Abigail Adams, old friend of John, and father of "the patriot" Josiah Quincy Jr., Col. Josiah Quincy was a Braintree citizen with trading interests in Boston. He was much concerned about the control of Boston Harbor while the British occupied the town. He sent Adams long letters detailing the means by which the harbor could be blocked up, ideas that Adams passed on to others. But action was delayed and Quincy's schemes came to naught.

Courtesy of the Dietrich Brothers Americana Corporation (Photograph by Will Brown).

Second in command under Washington after the Battle of Bunker Hill, Ward was soon the focus of much discontent. Adams' friends wrote about his incompetence and wondered how the Massachusetts delegation could have supported his candidacy as first major general. Within less than a year he was complaining of bad health and seeking to retire. Despite all the complaints and invidious comparisons with generals like John Thomas, Ward stayed on; Washington had no replacement for him, and Adams was pleased to see him made commander of the Eastern Department. He was relieved in March 1777.

Courtesy of Harvard University.

Although Adams and Dickinson had worked closely together in the First Continental Congress, the latter's moderation and insistence upon taking every step toward reconciliation alienated Adams and others who supported vigorous measures of opposition to Great Britain. An open breach between the two men was caused by Adams' reference to Dickinson (although unnamed) as a "piddling Genius" in his letter to James Warren of 24 July 1775 (below), which was intercepted by the British.

In 1779 Du Simitière sent from Philadelphia to France a set of fifteen profile drawings done from life, which he wanted engraved to sell as a set. Fourteen of the drawings were of Americans whom Du Simitière considered "eminent"; the fifteenth was of Conrad Alexandre Gérard, who carried the drawings with him on his return and was to arrange for their engraving. Apparently only fourteen engravings were made, each likeness being numbered. Dickinson's was No. 11. Some of the engraved sets were captured by the British on their way to America and were pirated by two British publishers, William Richardson and R. Wilkinson. These unauthorized engravings are readily identifiable, for the publishers did not hesitate to have their names inscribed (Edna Donnell, "Portraits of Eminent Americans after Drawings by Du Simitière," *Antiques*, 24:17-21 [July 1933]). For Du Simitière see *DAB*.

Courtesy of the Boston Public Library, Print Department.

Printed by John Haine and written from the British point of view, this account underestimates the number of British losses. Gage reported the number of officers and men killed as 249. The estimate of Americans killed is reasonably accurate, but American strength

in the battle was about 1,000, not three times the British strength of 2,000. This broadside is almost certainly that called by James Warren a "pompous account" and a "lying paper" (to JA, 7 July, below).
Courtesy of the Massachusetts Historical Society.

7. JOHN THOMAS (1724–1776), BY BENJAMIN BLYTH, 1775   120

Thomas was universally regarded as one of the ablest of the early American generals. During the siege of Boston he commanded the troops at Roxbury, and his efficiency and spirit were often compared to General Ward's to the detriment of the latter. On Washington's orders Thomas commanded the troops that fortified Dorchester Heights. Just before his fortifications compelled the British to evacuate Boston, the General was ordered to take charge of the discouraging siege of Quebec, but the situation there was past saving. Thomas died of smallpox after leading a retreat (*DAB*). Letters between Thomas and Adams are formal and correct. That Adams respected his judgment is obvious. He counted on the General to keep him informed regarding Canada.

Benjamin Blyth was a Salem limner who did pastel portraits of a number of important Americans, including young John Adams and his wife. For the Thomas portrait, Blyth presented a bill for £6 3s, which is signed and dated 15 February 1777 and is now in the Massachusetts Historical Society (Henry Wilder Foote, "Benjamin Blyth, of Salem: Eighteenth-Century Artist," MHS, *Procs.*, 71 [1953–1957]:64–107).
Courtesy of the Massachusetts Historical Society.

8. TITLEPAGE FOR *Rules for the Regulation of the Navy*, 1775   146

Using two British sources, Adams as a member of the Naval Committee drafted the rules for the Continental Navy. Meant as a handbook, this now extremely rare pamphlet does not include all the regulations that the congress passed in 1775; moreover, it was rushed into print before the congress had made an important change in wording. See John Adams' Service in the Congress, 13 September – 9 December 1775, No. VIII, notes 2 and 10 (below).
Courtesy of the Beinecke Rare Book and Manuscript Library, Yale University.

9. A PLAN OF THE TOWN AND HARBOUR OF BOSTON, BY J. DE COSTA, 1775   165

Done from an actual survey and dedicated to Richard Whitworth, M.P., this map was completed almost a month and a half after the Battle of Bunker Hill; yet it takes no notice of that event. Besides the islands in the harbor, which are placed with more than usual accuracy, the mapmaker shows the position of troops under the command of Generals Thomas and Putnam. Nothing is known of De Costa (Emerson D. Fite and Archibald Freeman, *A Book of Old Maps*, Cambridge, 1926, p. 255). The plan has been cropped here.
Courtesy of the John Carter Brown Library.

For a short time riflemen were deemed by Adams the men of the hour, and he was pleased to notify his friends that ten companies from Pennsylvania, Maryland, and Virginia would go north to aid in the siege of Boston. The great accuracy of their weapon, compared to the more commonly used musket, promised devastation among the outposts of the British. But soon Adams was receiving from correspondents tales of disorderliness, refusal to obey orders, and even the arrest of some of the riflemen. Their arrogance and the praise at first heaped upon them angered New Englanders.

This print is reproduced from Walker's *Hibernian Magazine*, April 1776. It is a largely fanciful creation, designed, as were supposed portraits of American generals and statesmen, to appeal to a market eager for knowledge about the revolutionaries. The decoration on the soldier's cap is a skull and crossbones with the words "or Liberty" under it. A glaring error is that the rifle is fitted with a bayonet, a weapon used with the musket. Because the rifleman's lack of a bayonet put him at a severe disadvantage in mass attack, his role became that of flanker, who picked off such advancing enemies as he could before those armed with muskets fired their volleys and engaged in hand-to-hand combat. Moreover, unless the rifleman depicted is grossly above normal height, the length of his weapon falls well short of the five feet or more typical of the American rifle (Warren Moore, *Weapons of the American Revolution and Accoutrements*, N.Y., 1967, p. 59–60).

Courtesy of the New York Public Library.

Howe arrived in America in May 1775, senior among the general officers sent to aid Gen. Thomas Gage, and commanded the British forces ordered against Charlestown. When Gage left Boston on 10 October 1775, Howe took his place as commander of all British troops except those under Sir Guy Carleton in Canada. It was Howe who ordered evacuation of Boston in March 1776. With his older brother, Admiral Richard, Viscount Howe, he led the peace commission through which Great Britain hoped to gain the submission of the colonists by offering pardons. Americans found the attached conditions unacceptable (DNB). This picture is reproduced from *An Impartial History of the War in America between Great Britain and Her Colonies from Its Commencement to the End of the Year 1779*, London, 1780.

Courtesy of the Massachusetts Historical Society.

Even before the congress acted to name a committee to collect authenticated information on the damage inflicted by British troops and ships, Adams saw the propaganda value such statistics would have, for he wrote James Warren on 12 October, urging the collection of such data "to facilitate Reprizals." After Adams, George

Wythe, and Silas Deane had been named to a committee on 18 October to gather information, Adams wrote Warren again that "This will be an usefull Work for the Information of all the colonies of what has passed in Some—for the Information of our Friends in England—and in all Europe, and all Posterity. Besides it may pave the Way to obtain Retribution and Compensation, but this had better not be talked of at present" (19 Oct., 1st letter, below). Adams kept up a constant pressure by writing to many of his friends on this subject. The broadside was Massachusetts' response to the action of the congress.

Courtesy of the Massachusetts Historical Society.

Introduction

1. JOHN ADAMS IN THE CONGRESS

During the months covered by these volumes, John Adams spent very little time in Braintree, for he was attending the sessions of the Second Continental Congress. When he did enjoy a respite from his labors in Philadelphia, he spent much of his time in Watertown as a member of the Massachusetts Council, or upper branch of the legislature, which also exercised executive powers in the absence of a royal governor. Away from home in Pennsylvania, Adams was eager for news of Boston and the province. Men like James Warren, Joseph Ward, and William Tudor were his eyes and ears in Massachusetts. He wanted to know about former law clerks, about the performance of generals, about the operations of the Massachusetts government, and about dozens of other matters. His thirst for information was unquenchable. But he also had things to tell concerning which he wanted advice. Although his constant complaint was that he was borne down by ever-expanding responsibilities—I have a minute when I need an hour, he protested—he managed to keep a surprising volume of correspondence flourishing. In a single day he sometimes wrote a half-dozen letters full of detail, none of them merely repetitive. If one considers that he had also begun to keep a letterbook, his labors command even more respect. He wrote to friends, political associates, generals and lesser officers, aspiring young lawyers, and colleagues absent from Philadelphia, soaking up information from everyone and pleading for more. Some sought him out first, perhaps to complain or beg, often to find that they had initiated a correspondence.

Beginning with the Battle of Bunker Hill, military affairs became a source of never-ending concern, partly because of his committee responsibilities, but probably even more because of his temperament. Adams was duty-ridden. If he was to be effective in the congress, he had to know who in the field was handling his allotted tasks and who was being overwhelmed by them. Thus he wanted to know about the tactics at Bunker Hill and the casualties on each side. Volume 3 contains five or six accounts of that bloody battle, with conflicting estimates of the killed and wounded. In addition, the two volumes include assessments of General Artemas Ward, who was responsible for Boston's defense after its evacuation, and of other officers like Richard Gridley, Henry Knox, David Wooster, Philip Schuyler, and men less well known to history. Adams was much concerned about the defense of his beloved Massachusetts and pleased when he could tell correspondents that expert riflemen were being sent northward to support the troops. Before long he was receiving reports of the obstreperousness of the riflemen, their refusal to obey orders, and the disruption they were causing. Adams took an interest not only in tactical and strategic matters but in the education of officers, compiling a list of authorities that should be read and that he felt should be added to Harvard's library. When officers were considered for promotion, his constant query was, How well were they educated? What were their erudition, presence, and family background? Were they men of reflection? After the British evacuated Boston, Adams wrote letter after letter urging proper measures for the security of the harbor and relaying plans for defense sent to him by Josiah Quincy Sr. The news that British naval vessels lingered on to prey upon American shipping wounded his pride. Correspondents kept him well informed of the bungling that preceded the warships' ultimate removal.

In this period one of the major issues had to do with soldiers' pay. In the opinion of southern officers and delegates to the congress, New England did not make a sufficient distinction between the pay of officers and men. Several of Adams' correspondents attributed to the essentially aristocratic temper of southern life the desire of southerners to reduce soldiers' pay. The letters are dotted with revealing comments on the distinctions between New England "equality" and southern emphasis on class distinctions. Adams shared the convictions of his correspondents, even to the point of believing that his ideas on government would never find acceptance among the southern colonies because his principles were too "popular" for them, although not popular enough for New England. He was, however, anxious to prevent such differences from becoming divisive. He felt that nothing could be done about soldiers' pay if raising it and reducing that of officers would jeopardize cooperation among the colonies. And when northern jealousy of alleged favoritism in promotions for southern officers flared up, he sought to mollify the aggrieved.

Adams' wish not to confront issues that would hinder united effort probably accounts for his apparent lack of interest in the slavery question. He received two anonymous letters urging abolition, one carefully reasoned and suggesting that freed blacks be established on land in

Canada, the other semi-literate but compelling in its simplicities. He also preserved an anti-slavery letter addressed to his colleague Thomas Cushing and a proposal sent to himself by Jonathan Dickinson Sergeant which would have let slaves win their freedom by serving in the army. Apart from telling Sergeant that South Carolina would vehemently oppose such a measure, Adams confined himself to asking generals how many blacks there were among New England troops. His concern arose from charges that northern forces had too many blacks and old men. Abigail's condemnation of slavery as inconsistent with the cause of liberty drew no recorded response from him. Indeed, Adams seems not to have seen the Revolutionary crisis as a time for social change. He and John Winthrop agreed that institutional alterations in 1776 would be like making repairs on a burning house.

What Adams wanted was the establishment of independent governments for each of the colonies. These could be a long step toward the independence that many of the members of the congress were so reluctant to accept.[1] The kind of interim government, based on the charter, that Massachusetts had settled for, Adams saw as a politically acceptable rather than satisfactory arrangement. Thus he welcomed from James Warren, John Winthrop, Joseph Palmer, and others who had firsthand knowledge any information about the workings of the province government. Adams helped to settle the quarrel between the House and the Council over the right of the lower branch to participate in the choice of field officers, a constitutional issue that threatened the very functioning of a wartime government. He supported the claims of the House.

Once the congress had finally resolved to urge the formation of new governments, and Adams had written a stirring preamble to the resolve, he was eager for Massachusetts to proceed to elections for a governor. But he was dismayed when talk of a new constitution led some correspondents and newspaper writers to suggest extending the right to vote, reconstituting the legislature, and creating more probate courts and offices for the registering of deeds. To one of these would-be reformers, Adams explained at length why a property qualification for the franchise should be continued with encouragement for more widespread propertyholding and why women should not have the vote.[2] A leveling spirit and changes proposed by ignorant amateurs could only do harm to the cause that still had to be fought for.

[1] The precise time of JA's firm commitment to independence is hard to pinpoint. See JA to James Warren, 6 June [i.e. July] 1775, first letter, note 6, and Robert J. Taylor, "John Adams: Legalist as Revolutionist," MHS, *Procs.*, 89 [1977]:67–71.
[2] To James Sullivan, 26 May 1776.

It is well known that, at the request of several colleagues, Adams sketched out a form of government that might be used as a model by colonies emerging into states. Actually he wrote four versions, only one being printed in his own day, of what came to be called *Thoughts on Government*.[3] He kept pretty much to forms familiar to him, recognizing that regional differences would have to be taken into account by those drafting state constitutions. In this as in other matters, one could go no further than the people were ready to follow. Notwithstanding Adams' belief, widely shared by political thinkers of the time, that man had a great propensity for evil behavior, a kind of optimism characterizes his outline of government. He asserts that if the right form is established, one that separates the functions of government and allows the legislature, the executive, and the courts to check and balance each other, republicanism and the virtue upon which it must depend can be preserved and encouraged. Such optimism is not surprising, for when Adams wrote, he was devoting much of his energy to promoting independent governments. The congressional resolve on the subject came a month and a half after he composed *Thoughts on Government*.

When Adams wrote in private to Mercy Otis Warren, however, he sounded a different note.[4] His earlier optimism gave way to pessimism about the future of republicanism in America. He assailed the "Spirit of Commerce" as a grave threat to domestic relations and a promoter of turbulence in government. Having penetrated even New England, this spirit was "incompatible with that purity of Heart, and Greatness of soul which is necessary for an happy Republic." The immediate occasion for these thoughts may have been the opening of trade on 6 April, a measure long debated in the congress.

Adams' fears were not new, only newly aroused. In the fall of 1775 he had exchanged ideas with several correspondents on the wisdom of opening up trade. The discussion was conducted by both sides largely in strategic terms. Despite the obvious risks, would opening up trade help the American cause and strike a blow at Britain? Even though this was the determining question, Adams was obviously attracted by the stratagem of a complete embargo. He was convinced that self-sufficiency was possible if the people would give up luxuries and switch from export products like indigo and tobacco to those like flax and wool that could be consumed entirely in the domestic production of clothing and cloth. He equated trade with acquired tastes in

[3] Ante 27 March–April 1776.
[4] 16 April 1776.

dress, furniture, architecture, and the like. The sacrifice of luxuries would be giving up "Trifles in a contest of Liberty."[5] Although Adams recognized the economic impact on many that would result from cutting off all trade, he saw the problem largely in moral terms: "the Question is whether our People have Virtue enough to be mere Husbandmen, Mechaniks and Soldiers? That they have not Virtue enough *to bear it always*, I take for granted. How long then will their Virtue last? Till next Spring?"[6] The italicized phrase is significant. Adams was not writing about the virtue of only a temporary sacrifice; for him, contentment with simple ways and work, the eschewing of all luxuries made possible by trade, was a key to virtue. The baleful influence of the "Spirit of Commerce" was a theme taken up by later generations of Adamses, some of whom were punished by their failure adequately to meet its demands.

However much Adams delighted in explicating the abstract principles underlying free governments, and however often he saluted the logic of events that was sweeping the colonies toward independence, he remained a consummate politician with a lively sense of the possible and a willingness to use his influence. To those who wrote from Massachusetts in the spring of 1776 asking impatiently why independence was not being declared, he acknowledged that "vast majorities" saw the need for the decisive step, but "patience, patience" was needed—and instructions from each of the colonies. Later he told Warren that "we cannot march faster than our Constituents will follow us."[7] He tried to placate not only the impatient but those angered by the release of the traitor Benjamin Church on parole. He had ideas about political strategy also. When it came time to think of choosing a governor for Massachusetts (Adams thought the decision was imminent), he cautioned against factionalism. He wanted his friends, who were among the leading politicians in the province, to caucus and to reach a consensus on the man who should have the job so that public disagreements would be avoided.

Adams did not hesitate to use his position to advance the career of others. With some justice, he would have described his recommendations to Washington and other commanders for preferment of friends and acquaintances and their sons and of former law clerks as ways of advancing the common cause. He knew a good man when he saw one, and the country needed good men. Given the situation that America

[5] To James Warren, 20 Oct. 1775, first letter.
[6] To James Warren, 19 Oct. 1775, third letter; italics supplied.
[7] To James Warren, 22 April 1776; to Mercy Otis Warren, 16 April 1776; to James Warren, 18 May 1776.

faced, Adams' use of influence can be seen as a service. An army was being built out of men unknown for the most part beyond their own communities. Commanders needed help in selecting officers, and delegates in the congress like Adams could provide information about candidates from their own areas. That is why Adams actively sought recommendations for preferment from correspondents he trusted, and why he was so impatient with the Massachusetts government for naming men to high rank without bothering to tell its delegation in the congress what qualifications the appointees had. Adams was not just a servant of a cause; he formed warm attachments, and, humanly enough, he wanted advancement of those for whom he felt affection and respect. It is to his credit that he was circumspect; he often replied that it would not be fitting for him to act through the congress, that he should not interfere with the chain of command. Moreover, he stood to gain nothing personally from the recommendations that he made. Adams was not unique, of course, in pressing consideration of the merits of men he knew something about, and he received at least as many requests for preferment as he made himself. One instance of his exercise of influence tells something about not only his attitudes but also the assumptions of his day. When it was learned that the elder son of former Governor Ward of Rhode Island had enlisted and his younger brother had obtained a commission, Adams successfully urged rectification of this unseemly situation. Charles Ward promptly became an ensign.

Besides his political acumen, Adams showed a capacity for and skill in committee work that placed him on several of the most important committees in this period. Besides serving as the president of the Board of War and Ordnance, he was directly responsible for producing two reports which were accepted by the congress with little alteration and whose influence was long lasting. As a member of the Naval Committee in the fall of 1775 he drafted rules for regulating the Continental Navy.[8] Although the body of rules was largely a compilation from British regulations, Adams kept in mind the character and needs of Americans, adapting and rejecting with care, so that his work has remained the basis for the governance of the United States Navy down into our own time. He was also a member of the committee charged with drawing up a declaration of independence, but he contributed almost nothing to its language; rather, his energies were devoted to securing the passage of the resolution of indepen-

---

[8] JA's Service in the Congress, 13 Sept. – 9 Dec. 1775, No. VIII.

dence on 1–2 July.[9] Colleagues testified afterward that his efforts were critically important. Soon after the Declaration of Independence was adopted, Adams produced a draft of a plan of treaties for the committee assigned that responsibility. The plan laid down the principles that with few exceptions would guide American diplomatists up to World War II.[10] Adams strongly favored treaties of commerce in preference to military alliances.

The picture of Adams that emerges in these two volumes is of a man punishing himself with committee work, yet somehow thriving on the demands made upon or readily assumed by him, despite his complaints of exhaustion and bad health and of the disgust he felt with some of his colleagues. It was an exciting, lively world Adams dwelt in, with its ups and downs of boredom and discouragement, achievement and triumph. He yearned for home and family, agonizing over his helplessness when friends wrote of Abigail's or the children's illnesses; yet he stuck it out month after month. When the Battle of Long Island loomed, he wrote to Warren: "I thought it would not be well to leave my Station here.... It will be necessary to have Some Persons here, who will not be Seized with an Ague fit, upon the Occasion."[11] He knew that he was at the center of great events. Vanity, however humble its guise, duty, and a sense of history kept him at his tasks.

2. NOTES ON EDITORIAL METHOD

To the description of the editorial method set forth in the *Papers of John Adams*, 1:xxxi–xxxv, some additions need to be made. As promised there, we have begun to be more rigorous in our selection of documents. For the period covered in Volumes 3 and 4 (May 1775– 28 Aug. 1776), we have omitted thirty-seven, all but two being letters. Most of those not printed repeat what is said in the letters included, or they are routine—letters of transmittal, thank-you notes, and the like. More than half of the documents not printed are referred to or, occasionally, quoted from, with their location indicated. The number of such omissions is certain to grow as the volume of materials increases.

Earlier volumes of *The Adams Papers* sought to make a distinction between endorsements and docketings on correspondence. The former were said normally to be written by the addressee "at or near the time

[9] JA's Copy of the Declaration of Independence, [ante 28 June 1776].
[10] Plan of Treaties, 12 June – 17 Sept. 1776.
[11] To James Warren, 17 Aug. 1776.

of receipt"; the latter usually by other than the addressee at a later time, often for purposes of filing.[12] The editors had so much difficulty trying to maintain this distinction that they abandoned it in favor of the single term "docketed." It proved impossible in many instances to state with certainty whether on letters received John Adams noted the writer's name and the date at the time of receipt or weeks or months later. Only after long lapses of time, when his handwriting had changed, could a distinction be made. For addressees outside the Adams family, the task was in most instances virtually impossible. When the lapse of time is obvious, however, or when the handwriting is clearly not that of the addressee, such facts are noted.

One or two other routine procedures can be usefully mentioned. Cross references omit mention of the year in dates if it is the same as the document being annotated. The location of letters mentioned as received or sent is not given if the writer furnishes an exact date ("yours of the 6th ultimo") and if such letters are included in these volumes. If the writer refers merely to "my last letter" or "your recent letter," such references are clarified in a note. Documents dated on the same day are arranged as follows: letters by John Adams, alphabetically by recipient, followed by official communications that he wrote or contributed to; letters to Adams, alphabetically by sender, followed by communications addressed to him (and others) in his official capacity. After these categories come third-party letters and official documents (credentials to the congress, and so on).

By checking standard reference works, the editors have made a reasonable effort to identify the quotations that occasionally embellish the letters of Adams and his correspondents, although a number remain unidentified. All but the most obvious Latin phrases have been translated in the notes, with or without the source being named. In these two volumes there is only one document in French, but in subsequent volumes there will be many more. To satisfy both scholars and general readers, we have decided to follow each document that is in a foreign language with a translation, so labeled and set in smaller type.

[12] *Adams Family Correspondence*, 1:xlvi, note 70.

Acknowledgments

Most of those mentioned in the Acknowledgments in Volume 1 of the *Papers of John Adams* have continued to extend courtesies and offer help and advice, but a few persons need particular recognition here. Professor John W. Zarker of Tufts University kindly checked our translations of Latin tags in these volumes, and Paul H. Smith of the Library of Congress suggested a revised date for an Adams letter. Stephen Kalkus, Director of the Navy Department Library, lent for use in our office a rare compilation of the regulations of the British Navy. Two experts on the bibliography of military manuals and other works for the eighteenth century gave us important guidance in evaluating Adams' knowledge of such books—Alan C. Aimone, Military History Librarian at the United States Military Academy, and Robert K. Wright Jr., historian, Organizational History Branch, Department of the Army. Marc Friedlaender, adjunct editor of the Adams Papers, read the entire manuscript carefully and critically, offering numerous suggestions for improvement. Elizabeth Breuer and Katherine Oppermann, editorial assistants, worked diligently at verifying notes, typing, and helping with proofreading and indexing.

Guide to Editorial Apparatus

In the first three sections (1–3) of the six sections of this Guide are listed, respectively, the arbitrary devices used for clarifying the text, the code names for designating prominent members of the Adams family, and the symbols describing the various kinds of MS originals used or referred to, that are employed throughout *The Adams Papers* in all its series and parts. In the final three sections (4–6) are listed, respectively, only those symbols designating institutions holding original materials, the various abbreviations and conventional terms, and the short titles of books and other works, that occur in volumes 3 and 4 of the *Papers of John Adams*. The editors propose to maintain this pattern for the Guide to Editorial Apparatus in each of the smaller units, published at intervals, of all the series and parts of the edition that are so extensive as to continue through many volumes. On the other hand, in short and specialized series and/or parts of the edition, the Guide to Editorial Apparatus will be given more summary form tailored to its immediate purpose.

1. TEXTUAL DEVICES

The following devices will be used throughout *The Adams Papers* to clarify the presentation of the text.

[. . .], [. . . .]	One or two words missing and not conjecturable.
[. . .] [1], [. . . .] [1]	More than two words missing and not conjecturable; subjoined footnote estimates amount of missing matter.
[ ]	Number or part of a number missing or illegible. Amount of blank space inside brackets approximates the number of missing or illegible digits.
[roman]	Editorial insertion or conjectural reading for missing or illegible matter. A question mark is inserted before the closing bracket if the conjectural reading is seriously doubtful.
⟨*italic*⟩	Matter canceled in the manuscript but restored in our text.

2. ADAMS FAMILY CODE NAMES

First Generation

JA	John Adams (1735–1826)
AA	Abigail Smith (1744–1818), *m.* JA 1764

Second Generation

AA2   Abigail Adams (1765–1813), daughter of JA and AA, *m.* WSS
           1786
WSS   William Stephens Smith (1755–1816), brother of Mrs. CA
JQA   John Quincy Adams (1767–1848), son of JA and AA
LCA   Louisa Catherine Johnson (1775–1852), *m.* JQA 1797
CA   Charles Adams (1770–1800), son of JA and AA
Mrs. CA   Sarah Smith (1769–1828), sister of WSS, *m.* CA 1795
TBA   Thomas Boylston Adams (1772–1832), son of JA and AA
Mrs. TBA   Ann Harrod (1774–1846), *m.* TBA 1805

Third Generation

GWA   George Washington Adams (1801–1829), son of JQA and LCA
JA2   John Adams (1803–1834), son of JQA and LCA
Mrs. JA2   Mary Catherine Hellen (1807–1870), *m.* JA2 1828
CFA   Charles Francis Adams (1807–1886), son of JQA and LCA
ABA   Abigail Brown Brooks (1808–1889), *m.* CFA 1829
ECA   Elizabeth Coombs Adams (1808–1903), daughter of TBA and
           Mrs. TBA

Fourth Generation

LCA2   Louisa Catherine Adams (1831–1870), daughter of CFA and
           ABA, *m.* Charles Kuhn 1854
JQA2   John Quincy Adams (1833–1894), son of CFA and ABA
CFA2   Charles Francis Adams (1835–1915), son of CFA and ABA
HA   Henry Adams (1838–1918), son of CFA and ABA
MHA   Marian Hooper (1842–1885), *m.* HA 1872
MA   Mary Adams (1845–1928), daughter of CFA and ABA, *m.*
           Henry Parker Quincy 1877
BA   Brooks Adams (1848–1927), son of CFA and ABA

Fifth Generation

CFA3   Charles Francis Adams (1866–1954), son of JQA2
HA2   Henry Adams (1875–1951), son of CFA2
JA3   John Adams (1875–1964), son of CFA2

3. DESCRIPTIVE SYMBOLS

The following symbols will be employed throughout *The Adams Papers* to describe or identify in brief form the various kinds of manuscript originals.

D   Diary (Used only to designate a diary written by a member of
           the Adams family and always in combination with the short form
           of the writer's name and a serial number, as follows: D/JA/23,
           i.e. the twenty-third fascicle or volume of John Adams' manu-
           script Diary.)
Dft   draft
Dupl   duplicate
FC   file copy (Ordinarily a copy of a letter retained by a correspond-
           ent *other than an Adams*, for example Jefferson's press copies

	and polygraph copies, since all three of the Adams statesmen systematically entered copies of their outgoing letters in letterbooks.)
Lb	Letterbook (Used only to designate Adams letterbooks and always in combination with the short form of the writer's name and a serial number, as follows: Lb/JQA/29, i.e. the twenty-ninth volume of John Quincy Adams' Letterbooks.)
LbC	letterbook copy (Letterbook copies are normally unsigned, but any such copy is assumed to be in the hand of the person responsible for the text unless it is otherwise described.)
M	Miscellany (Used only to designate materials in the section of the Adams Papers known as the "Miscellany" and always in combination with the short form of the writer's name and a serial number, as follows: M/CFA/32, i.e. the thirty-second volume of the Charles Francis Adams Miscellany—a ledger volume mainly containing transcripts made by CFA in 1833 of selections from the family papers.)
MS, MSS	manuscript, manuscripts
RC	recipient's copy (A recipient's copy is assumed to be in the hand of the signer unless it is otherwise described.)
Tr	transcript (A copy, handwritten or typewritten, made substantially later than the original or than other copies—such as duplicates, file copies, letterbook copies—that were made contemporaneously.)
Tripl	triplicate

4. LOCATION SYMBOLS

BM	The British Museum, London
CSmH	Henry E. Huntington Library and Art Gallery
CtHi	Connecticut Historical Society
DLC	Library of Congress
DSI	Smithsonian Institution
ICHi	Chicago Historical Society
M-Ar	Massachusetts Archives
MB	Boston Public Library
MHi	Massachusetts Historical Society
MeHi	Maine Historical Society
MiU-C	William L. Clements Library, University of Michigan
NHi	New-York Historical Society
NHpR	Franklin D. Roosevelt Library, Hyde Park
NN	New York Public Library
NNPM	Pierpont Morgan Library
Nc-Ar	North Carolina State Archives
NjP	Princeton University Library
OClWHi	Western Reserve Historical Society
PHC	Haverford College Library
PHi	Historical Society of Pennsylvania
PPAmP	American Philosophical Society
PPRF	Rosenbach Foundation, Philadelphia
P.R.O.	Public Record Office, London
TxDaHi	Dallas Historical Society

5. OTHER ABBREVIATIONS AND
CONVENTIONAL TERMS

Adams Papers

> Manuscripts and other materials, 1639–1889, in the Adams Manuscript Trust collection given to the Massachusetts Historical Society in 1956 and enlarged by a few additions of family papers since then. Citations in the present edition are simply by date of the original document if the original is in the main chronological series of the Papers and therefore readily found in the microfilm edition of the Adams Papers (see below). The location of materials in the Letterbooks and the Miscellany is given more fully, and often, if the original would be hard to locate, by the microfilm reel number.

Adams Papers, Adams Office Files

> The portion of the Adams manuscripts given to the Massachusetts Historical Society by Thomas Boylston Adams in 1973 and retained in the editorial office of the Adams Papers.

Adams Papers Editorial Files

> Other materials in the Adams Papers editorial office, Massachusetts Historical Society. These include photoduplicated documents (normally cited by the location of the originals), photographs, correspondence, and bibliographical and other aids compiled and accumulated by the editorial staff.

Adams Papers, Fourth Generation

> Adams manuscripts dating 1890 or later originally part of the Trust collection together with Adams manuscripts acquired from other sources, administered by the Massachusetts Historical Society on the same footing with its other manuscript collections.

Adams Papers, Microfilms

> The corpus of the Adams Papers, 1639–1889, as published on microfilm by the Massachusetts Historical Society, 1954–1959, in 608 reels. Cited in the present work, when necessary, by reel number. Available in research libraries throughout the United States and in a few libraries in Europe and Canada.

The Adams Papers

> The present edition in letterpress, published by The Belknap Press of Harvard University Press. References between volumes of any given unit will take this form: vol. 3:171. Since there will be no overall volume numbering for the edition, references from one series, or unit of a series, to another will be by title, volume, and page; for example, JQA, *Papers*, 4:205. (For the same reason, references by scholars citing this edition should not be to *The Adams Papers* as a whole but to the particular series or subseries concerned; for example, John Adams, *Diary and Autobiography*, 3:145; *Adams Family Correspondence*, 6:167.)

PCC

> Papers of the Continental Congress. Originals in the National Archives: Record Group 360. Microfilm edition in 204 reels. Usually cited in the

present work from the microfilms, but according to the original series and volume numbering devised in the State Department in the early 19th century; for example, PCC, No. 93, III, i.e. the third volume of series 93.

Thwing Catalogue, MHi
> Annie Haven Thwing, comp., Inhabitants and Estates of the Town of Boston, 1630–1800; typed card catalogue, with supplementary bound typescripts, in the Massachusetts Historical Society.

6. SHORT TITLES OF WORKS
FREQUENTLY CITED

AAS, *Procs.*
> American Antiquarian Society, *Proceedings.*

Samuel Adams, *Writings*
> *The Writings of Samuel Adams,* ed. Harry Alonzo Cushing, New York and London, 1904–1908; 4 vols.

T. R. Adams, *American Independence*
> Thomas R. Adams, *American Independence: The Growth of an Idea. A Bibliographical Study of the American Political Pamphlets Printed Between 1764 and 1776 . . . ,* Providence, R.I., 1965.

Adams Family Correspondence
> *Adams Family Correspondence,* ed. L. H. Butterfield and others, Cambridge, 1963–   .

AHR
> *American Historical Review.*

Alden, *General Charles Lee*
> John Richard Alden, *General Charles Lee: Traitor or Patriot?,* Baton Rouge, La., 1951.

Allen, *Mass. Privateers*
> Gardner Weld Allen, *Massachusetts Privateers of the Revolution* (Massachusetts Historical Society, *Collections,* vol. 77), Boston, 1927.

Amer. Philos. Soc., *Memoirs, Procs., Trans.*
> American Philosophical Society, *Memoirs, Proceedings,* and *Transactions.*

Appletons' Cyclo. Amer. Biog.
> James Grant Wilson and John Fiske, eds., *Appletons' Cyclopædia of American Biography,* New York, 1887–1889; 6 vols.

Austin, *Gerry*
> James T. Austin, *The Life of Elbridge Gerry. With Contemporary Letters,* Boston, 1828–1829; 2 vols. [Vol. 1:] *To the Close of the American Revolution;* [vol. 2:] *From the Close of the American Revolution.*

Biog. Dir. Cong.
> *Biographical Directory of the American Congress, 1774–1949,* Washington, 1950.

Black, *Law Dictionary*
> Henry Campbell Black, *A Law Dictionary Containing Definitions of the Terms and Phrases of American and English Jurisprudence Ancient and Modern,* 2d edn., St. Paul, Minn., 1910.

Bostonian Society, *Pubns.*
　Bostonian Society, *Publications.*

Boston Record Commissioners, *Reports*
　City of Boston, Record Commissioners, *Reports*, Boston, 1876–1909; 39 vols.

Braintree Town Records
　Samuel A. Bates, ed., *Records of the Town of Braintree, 1640 to 1793*, Randolph, Mass., 1886.

Burnett, ed., *Letters of Members*
　Edmund C. Burnett, ed., *Letters of Members of the Continental Congress,* Washington, 1921–1936; 8 vols.

Catalogue of JA's Library
　Catalogue of the John Adams Library in the Public Library of the City of Boston, Boston, 1917.

Clark, *Washington's Navy*
　William Bell Clark, *George Washington's Navy*, Baton Rouge, La., 1960.

Conn. Colonial Records
　J. Hammond Trumbull and Charles J. Hoadly, eds., *The Public Records of the Colony of Connecticut*, Hartford, 1850–1890; 15 vols.

Conn. Hist. Soc., *Colls.*
　Connecticut Historical Society, *Collections.*

DAB
　Allen Johnson and Dumas Malone, eds., *Dictionary of American Biography*, New York, 1928–1936; 20 vols. plus index and supplements.

Deane Papers
　Papers of Silas Deane, 1774–1790, in New-York Historical Society, *Collections, Publication Fund Series*, vols. 19–23, New York, 1887–1891; 5 vols.

Dexter, *Yale Graduates*
　Franklin Bowditch Dexter, *Biographical Sketches of the Graduates of Yale College, with Annals of the College History*, New York, 1885–1912; 6 vols.

Dict. of Americanisms
　Mitford M. Mathews, ed., *A Dictionary of Americanisms on Historical Principles*, Chicago, 1951.

DNB
　Leslie Stephen and Sidney Lee, eds., *The Dictionary of National Biography*, New York and London, 1885–1900; 63 vols. plus supplements.

Early Amer. Atlas
　Lester J. Cappon and others, *Atlas of Early American History*, Princeton, 1976.

Evans
　Charles Evans and others, comps., *American Bibliography: A Chronological Dictionary of All Books, Pamphlets and Periodical Publications Printed in the United States of America* [1639–1800], Chicago and Worcester, 1903–1959; 14 vols.

Evans Supplement
　Roger P. Bristol, *Supplement to Charles Evans' American Bibliography*, Charlottesville, Va., 1970.

Force, *Archives*
[Peter Force, ed.,] *American Archives: Consisting of a Collection of Authentick Records, State Papers, Debates, and Letters and Other Notices of Publick Affairs*, Washington, 1837–1853; 9 vols.

Franklin, *Papers*
The Papers of Benjamin Franklin, ed. Leonard W. Labaree, William B. Willcox (from vol. 15), and others, New Haven, 1959– .

Freeman, *Washington*
Douglas Southall Freeman, *George Washington: A Biography*, New York, 1948–1952; 6 vols. Vol. 7, by John Alexander Carroll and Mary Wells Ashworth, New York, 1957.

French, *First Year*
Allen French, *The First Year of the American Revolution*, Boston, 1934.

Frothingham, *Siege of Boston*
Richard Frothingham, *History of the Siege of Boston*, 6th edn., Boston, 1903.

Gage, *Corr.*
The Correspondence of General Thomas Gage with the Secretaries of State, 1763–1775, ed. Clarence E. Carter, New Haven, 1931–1933; 2 vols.

Gipson, *Empire before the Revolution*
Lawrence Henry Gipson, *The British Empire before the American Revolution*, Caldwell, Idaho and New York, 1936–1970; 15 vols.

Heitman, *Register Continental Army*
Francis B. Heitman, comp., *Historical Register of Officers of the Continental Army during the War of the Revolution*, new edn., Washington, 1914.

Hist. Soc. Penna., *Memoirs*
Historical Society of Pennsylvania, *Memoirs*.

Hoefer, *Nouv. biog. générale*
J. C. F. Hoefer, ed., *Nouvelle biographie générale depuis les temps les plus reculés jusqu'à nos jours*, Paris, 1852–1866; 46 vols.

JA, *Diary and Autobiography*
Diary and Autobiography of John Adams, ed. L. H. Butterfield and others, Cambridge, 1961; 4 vols.

JA, *Legal Papers*
Legal Papers of John Adams, ed. L. Kinvin Wroth and Hiller B. Zobel, Cambridge, 1965; 3 vols.

JA, *Papers*
Papers of John Adams, ed. Robert J. Taylor and others, Cambridge, 1977– .

JA, *Works*
The Works of John Adams, Second President of the United States: with a Life of the Author, ed. Charles Francis Adams, Boston, 1850–1856; 10 vols.

JCC
Worthington C. Ford and others, eds., *Journals of the Continental Congress, 1774–1789*, Washington, 1904–1937; 34 vols.

Jefferson, *Papers*
The Papers of Thomas Jefferson, ed. Julian P. Boyd and others, Princeton, 1950– .

Johnston, *Campaign around New York and Brooklyn*
Henry P. Johnston, *The Campaign of 1776 around New York and Brooklyn* (Long Island Historical Society, *Memoirs*, vol. 3), Brooklyn, 1878, repr. N.Y., 1971.

Madison, *Papers*
The Papers of James Madison, ed. by William T. Hutchinson, William M. E. Rachal, Robert A. Rutland (from vol. 8), and others, Chicago, 1962–

Mass., *House Jour.*
Journals of the House of Representatives of Massachusetts [1715–], Boston, reprinted by the Massachusetts Historical Society, 1919– . (For the years for which reprints are not yet available, the original printings are cited, by year and session.)

Mass., *Province Laws*
The Acts and Resolves, Public and Private, of the Province of the Massachusetts Bay, Boston, 1869–1922; 21 vols.

Mass. Provincial Congress, *Jours.*
William Lincoln, ed., *The Journals of Each Provincial Congress of Massachusetts in 1774 and 1775, and of the Committee of Safety*, Boston, 1838.

Mass. *Soldiers and Sailors*
Massachusetts Soldiers and Sailors of the Revolutionary War, Boston, 1896–1908; 17 vols.

Mayo, *Winthrop Family*
Lawrence Shaw Mayo, *The Winthrop Family in America*, Boston, 1948.

Md. *Hist. Mag.*
Maryland Historical Magazine.

MHS, *Colls., Procs.*
Massachusetts Historical Society, *Collections* and *Proceedings*.

Miller, ed., *Treaties*
Hunter Miller, ed., *Treaties and Other International Acts of the United States of America*, Washington, 1931–1948; 8 vols.

Naval Docs. Amer. Rev.
William Bell Clark, William James Morgan (from vol. 5), and others, eds., *Naval Documents of the American Revolution*, Washington, 1964–

NEHGR
New England Historical and Genealogical Register.

NEQ
New England Quarterly.

N.H. Hist. Soc., *Colls.*
New Hampshire Historical Society, *Collections*.

NYHS, *Colls.*
New-York Historical Society, *Collections*.

OED
The Oxford English Dictionary, Oxford, 1933; 12 vols. and supplement.

Parliamentary Hist.
The Parliamentary History of England, from the Earliest Period to the Year 1803, London: Hansard, 1806–1820; 36 vols.

Paullin, *Navy of Amer. Rev.*
> Charles Oscar Paullin, *The Navy of the American Revolution: Its Administration, its Policy, and its Achievements*, Cleveland, 1906.

Penna. *Archives*
> *Pennsylvania Archives. Selected and Arranged from Original Documents in the Office of the Secretary of the Commonwealth*, Philadelphia and Harrisburg, 1852–1935; 119 vols. in 123.

Penna. *Colonial Records*
> *Pennsylvania Colonial Records*, 1683–1790, Philadelphia and Harrisburg, 1851–1853; 16 vols.

PMHB
> *Pennsylvania Magazine of History and Biography.*

Josiah Quincy, *Josiah Quincy, Jr.*
> Josiah Quincy, *Memoir of Josiah Quincy, Junior, of Massachusetts: 1744–1775*, 2d edn., ed. Eliza Susan Quincy, Boston, 1874.

Sabine, *Loyalists*
> Lorenzo Sabine, *Biographical Sketches of Loyalists of the American Revolution, with an Historical Essay*, Boston, 1864; 2 vols.

S.C. Hist. Soc., *Colls.*
> South Carolina Historical Society, *Collections.*

Shurtleff, *Description of Boston*
> Nathaniel B. Shurtleff, *A Topographical and Historical Description of Boston*, 3d edn., Boston, 1890.

Sibley-Shipton, *Harvard Graduates*
> John Langdon Sibley and Clifford K. Shipton, *Biographical Sketches of Graduates of Harvard University, in Cambridge, Massachusetts*, Cambridge and Boston, 1873– .

Stark, *Loyalists of Mass.*
> James H. Stark, *The Loyalists of Massachusetts and the Other Side of the American Revolution*, Boston, 1910.

Thorpe, *Federal and State Constitutions*
> Francis N. Thorpe, ed., *The Federal and State Constitutions, Colonial Charters, and Other Organic Laws of the States, Territories and Colonies Now or Heretofore Forming the United States of America*, Washington, 1909; 7 vols.

VMHB
> *Virginia Magazine of History and Biography.*

Warren-Adams Letters
> *Warren-Adams Letters: Being Chiefly a Correspondence among John Adams, Samuel Adams, and James Warren* (Massachusetts Historical Society, *Collections*, vols. 72–73), Boston, 1917–1925; 2 vols.

Washington, *Writings*, ed. Fitzpatrick
> *The Writings of George Washington from the Original Manuscript Sources, 1745–1799*, ed. John C. Fitzpatrick, Washington, 1931–1944; 39 vols.

Wharton, ed., *Dipl. Corr. Amer. Rev.*
> Francis Wharton, ed., *The Revolutionary Diplomatic Correspondence of the United States*, Washington, 1889; 6 vols.

WMQ
  William and Mary Quarterly.

Wroth and others, eds., *Province in Rebellion*
  L. Kinvin Wroth, George H. Nash III, and Joel Meyerson, eds., *Province in Rebellion*, Cambridge, 1975.

VOLUME 3

Papers

May 1775 – January 1776

Papers of John Adams

To Joseph Palmer

Dr Sir   Hartford[1] May 2, 1775

We are very anxious to know the State of Things at Boston, Cambridge, Watertown and Roxbury.[2] The Accounts We have here are very confused and uncertain. I hope the News Papers, will come now.

Our Accounts from N. York are very well. That Province is getting into a Train, which will Secure the Union of the Colonies, and Success to their Efforts. The little, dirty, ministerial Party there, is humbled in the Dust.[3]

Certain military Movements of great Importance, and with the Utmost Secrecy have been set on foot in this Colony of Connecticutt,[4] which I dare not explain in writing, but refer you to Coll. Foster, Danielson and Bliss.[5]

I know very well the Multiplicity of your Business, but as it is of great Consequence that We should be minutely informed of every Thing, I must beg you to write as often as possible and perswade others to write me. Mr. Cooper, Mr. Ward, any Body that can write Facts.[6] The Letters will follow us and reach us, at last. I am sensible you must have a Multitude of Applications. But I am advised by Coll. Hancocks just to hint to you a Request in Behalf of my Brothers, if Either of them should have an Inclination to engage in the Army.[7] I have never Said any Thing to them, because I choose to leave them, in a Case of such interesting Importance, to their own Inclination and Discretion. I am your Friend and sert   **John Adams**

RC (ICHi); addressed "To Coll Joseph Palmer Braintree"; docketed: "John Adams Esqr. 1775."

[1] On his way to the Second Continental Congress, JA arrived in Hartford on 29 April. He had left Braintree probably on 26 April, riding in a sulky and attended by a mounted young servant (JA to AA, 30 April, *Adams Family Correspondence*, 1:188–189; JA's list of expenses from 26 April, *Diary and Autobiography*, 2:162). None of JA's extant correspondence for this period refers to the Battles of Lexington and Concord, but in his Autobiography he mentions his visit to Generals Ward, Heath, and Warren, the confusion he found in Cambridge, and his journey to the scenes of battle, where he talked to people about what had occurred (*Diary and Autobiography*, 3:314).

[2] The Second Provincial Congress, which had begun its meetings in Cam-

I

bridge, had moved to Concord on 22 March and from there to Watertown on 22 April (Mass. Provincial Congress, *Jours.*, p. 108, 147). Part of the hastily gathered army that had arisen to oppose Gage had been stationed in Roxbury under the command of Dr. John Thomas with the mission of keeping the British from moving from Boston via the Neck (Arthur B. Tourtellot, *Lexington and Concord*, N.Y., 1959, p. 221).

³ In a letter to AA, also dated 2 May, JA described the situation in New York, mentioning the flight of Myles Cooper, president of Kings College and an ardent loyalist, to board a British warship (*Adams Family Correspondence*, 1: 191).

⁴ No doubt a reference to the scheme of Samuel Holden Parsons to send a Connecticut force aided by Massachusetts men to capture Fort Ticonderoga, a stronghold of the north possessing cannon that Americans desperately needed. Parsons had probably exchanged ideas with Benedict Arnold. Arnold won the approval of the Committee of Safety of the Massachusetts Provincial Congress, which on 2 May voted to furnish him with ammunition, horses, and £100 (French, *First Year*, p. 149–150; Mass.

Provincial Congress, *Jours.*, p. 530, 531).

⁵ Col. Jedediah Foster, Timothy Danielson, and John Bliss were members of a committee sent by the Provincial Congress to Connecticut to report on measures being taken for defense by Massachusetts and to urge that colony to contribute troops for the general defense of New England. Similar committees were sent to Rhode Island and New Hampshire (Mass. Provincial Congress, *Jours.*, p. 135–137).

⁶ Pleas for information about events in Massachusetts became regular features of JA's letters while he was at the congress. His reference here is to Rev. Samuel Cooper, pastor of the Brattle Street Church, and Maj. Joseph Ward, both of whom exchanged several letters with JA later in 1775.

⁷ As a member of the Committee of Safety of the Provincial Congress, Palmer had influence over the appointment of officers (same, p. 89–90). In a letter to AA, JA advised his brothers to apply to Col. Palmer and Dr. Warren if they wanted commands. AA applied to Joseph Warren in behalf of JA's brother Elihu on 13 May (*Adams Family Correspondence*, 1:191, 196).

From Edward Dilly

Dear Sir   London May 3d 1775

I have only One Moments opportunity of acknowledging your favor of the 30th of Decr¹ and of informing you that the Packet inclosed was sent agreeable to direction. Every friend of Liberty and the English Constitution rejoice to hear of the Firmness and unanimity of our Brethren in America. By your own Virtue, Valor and Perseverance you are to expect a deliverance from the Yoke. Every attempt from the City of London has proved ineffectual.² I have sent you an Answer to Dr. Johnson's Pamphlet Taxation no Tyranny with the News Paper of this Day.³ Wishing you all success. I am most cordially Yours &c.

RC (Adams Papers); addressed: "To Mr John Adams   Boston"; docketed by Dilly(?): "London   May 5th 1775."

¹ Not found.

² Londoners submitted two petitions to Parliament stressing the paramount

nature of commercial relations with the American colonies, the second objecting to referral of their first petition to an inappropriate committee (*Parliamentary Hist.*, 18:168–171, 184–185).

[3] Lawrence H. Gipson lists seven answers in 1775 to Samuel Johnson's *Taxation No Tyranny: An Answer to the Resolutions and Address of the American Congress*, London, 1775 (*Empire before the Revolution*, 14:79–80). We have no way of knowing which of the answers Dilly sent to JA.

From James Warren

My Dear Sir   Watertown May 7th: 1775

After I had Executed my Commission at Providence,[1] I Returned Home set Mrs. Warren down in her own Habitation, made the best provision I could for the security of our Family, and some of our Effects which we considered to be not very safe at Plymouth, and Immediately hastened to this place in order to contribute my mite to the publick Service in this Exigence of affairs. Here I have been near a week every day resolving to write to you without beginning to Execute such a resolution till now. And Indeed every thing seems to be in such Confusion that I hardly know where to begin, and perhaps I shall be at as great a Loss to know where to End. I find our own Body Extreamly weakened by the several detachments (to use the stile of the Times) made from it.[2] When I see the seats of many of my Friends on whom I used to place my principal dependance empty, and feel the want of them as I do, at a Time when they are more wanted than ever, I am almost discouraged: however as I was Born to Struggle with difficulties, shall Endeavour to answer the End of my Creation as well as I Can. The Congress since I have been here has generally been full, Unanimous, and Spirited, ready and willing to do every thing in their power and frequently animated by the most agreable News from the other Colonies. The principal objects of our attention, have been the regulation and officering of the army, and arming the men and devising ways and means to support the Enormous Expence Incured under our present Situation,[3] and these I dare say you can easily Conceive to be attended with many difficulties under the present Circumstances of our Government in which recommendations are to supply the place of Laws, and destitute of Coercive power Exposed to the Caprice of the People, and depending entirely on their virtue for Success.[4]

We have Voted to Issue Notes for 100,000£ and to request your aid in giving them a Currency.[5] The Committee of Ways and means to sit again. We are Embarrassd in officering our army by the Establishment of minute men, I wish it had never taken place, and the necessity of haveing our Field officers appointed is every day seen and

Indeed in my opinion that should have been the first thing done. As to the army itself it is in such a shifting, fluctuating state as not to be capable of a perfect regulation. They are continually going and Come-ing. However they seem to me to want a more Experienced direction. I could for myself wish to see your Friends Washington and L[ee] at the Head of it and yet dare not propose it tho' I have it in Contempla-tion. I hope that matter will be Considered with more propriety in your Body than ours. If you Establish a Continental army of which this will be only a part, you will place the direction as you please.[6] It is difficult to say what numbers our army Consists of. If a return could be had one day it would by no means answer for the next. They have been so reduced at some times that I have trembled at the con-sequences that might take place. Our new Levies are coming in and by that means I hope they will be in a more permanent state. I be-lieve there are about 6,000 in Camp at present. They are Employed at Cambridge in heaving up Entrenchments, somewhere about Phip' Farm. I have not seen them. The Extream want of the Exercise of a fixt settled Government is sufficiently felt here at this time, and has produced the assignment of a Time to take that matter under Con-sideration. Next Tuesday is the time.[7] What will be done I know not. I am Inclined to think they will Vote to assume a Government, but who is to form this Constitution, who is to rigg the Ship I cant tell. It appears to me a Business of such a nature, so Important, and in which an Error once Committed, will probably be as lastn. as the Constitution itself, that I am afraid to meddle, it is sufficient for such a Genius as mine to know the places and use of the several ropes after the Ship is rigged. However we have a Chance. Success is the Criterion that generally determines the Judgement. If we should either by accident or by the force of our great abilities Build up a Grand Constitution with the same ease we could a Bird Cage, we shall be equally Clever fellows. If I dont Tire your patience now you shall have more of this in my next.

The Infatuation of the Inhabitants of Boston has reduced us and themselves to the precise state I have Expected it would do. We have been obliged for their sakes to pass some votes that we did not well relish.[8] We have admitted the refugees to send out for their Effects, tho I dont Expect any advantage from it. In short I voted for it more to gratifie my friend Warren than from any other motive. There is no Guard against the Generals Treachery. He will find some pretenses for the base arts practiced to abuse that People, and will finally keep a large number of them there. When he lets them out at all it is very slowly. When the Tories, and Tory Effects are in, and his Reinforcement arrives I presume no more of them will come out. They are to be pitied tho' this is the Effects of their own folly. The misery they are already reduced to in the Town is great, and may be seen described in the Joy of the Countenances of those who get out. By the way I have Just heard that Edes has stole out. I wish his partner was with him.[9] I called on Mrs. Adams as I came along. Found her and Family well. Your being out of health when you left us gives me some Uneasiness. Shall be glad to hear that you are well and happy. I shall make no apology for this Letter. Not because I think it stands in need of none, but because I know your Friendship will Cover, and Excuse a Multitude of Faults. My regards to all my Friends perticularly H[ancock] and A[dams] I have no time to write to either of them. I am with great Sincerity Your Friend &c,   Jas. Warren

I think they go on Charmingly and Swimmingly at York.[10]

Inclosed are a Letter from Mrs. Adams, and an Extract of a Letter from ⟨*your Friend*⟩ Hutchinson found among a Curious Collection of Letters now in the hands of our Friends.[11] I am well assured of the authenticity of it, and send this particular Extract more because it seems to be especially Calculated to be used where you are than because it shows a greater degree of wickedness than many others.

RC (Adams Papers); docketed: "Warren   May 7 1775."

[1] On 10 April, Warren was chosen as an additional member of a committee composed of Col. Timothy Walker and Dr. Richard Perkins to go to Rhode Island to seek cooperation in the defense of New England (Mass. Provincial Congress, *Jours.*, p. 136–137). The committee probably returned about 26 April, when a reference is made in the Journals to information "just now received from Rhode Island by Doct. Perkins" (same, p. 156).

[2] A large number of committees and individuals were sent on missions outside the congress. The largest of these "detachments" was the Committee of Safety, which was meeting at Cambridge, the site of the main army.

[3] There was no standing army nor even an established procedure for creating an army on extended service. Although the Lexington battle brought large numbers of men into the field, they were unorganized and soon began to disperse. To counter this dispersal and to seize the opportunity to create a large army from men already present, the Committee of Safety on 21 April voted to establish an army of 8,000 men. On 23 April the Provincial Congress enlarged the number to be immediately raised to 13,600 and set the total strength for defense of the colony at 30,000. None of these measures had a lasting effect, for as the war went on and enthusiasm diminished, the problem of getting and keeping men intensified (same, p. 520, 148). See also Jonathan Smith, "How Massachusetts Raised Her Troops in the Revolution," MHS, *Procs.*, 55 (1921–1922):345–370.

[4] Royal government ceased to function effectively in Massachusetts in 1774. The courts were closed, and the Provincial Congress as an extralegal body depended solely upon its recommendations to the towns. On 5 May the con-

gress formally repudiated Gov. Gage, sweeping away the last vestige of traditional authority. The congress then sought advice from the Continental Congress on how legal government could be reconstituted (Mass. Provincial Congress, *Jours.*, p. 192–193, 229–231). It was a continual source of wonderment in Massachusetts that men could conduct their affairs so peaceably with the dissolution of traditional forms, but it was a question how long men could go on without a formal legal structure.

[5] The expense of supporting an army was far more than Massachusetts could pay from current funds. On 25 April the treasurer reported that of £20,000 in taxes due in 1773, only £5,000 had been collected. Recognizing the hardships facing the province, legislators defeated a resolution to identify the delinquent towns (same, p. 151). As a result, on 3 May the Provincial Congress directed the receiver general to borrow £100,000 and issue securities at 6 percent annual interest payable on 1 June 1777. The Continental Congress was asked to recommend the acceptance of these bills by other colonies, just as Massachusetts had agreed to accept those of Rhode Island and Connecticut (same, p. 185–189, 530).

[6] There was nothing original about Warren's suggestion that the army be taken over by the Continental Congress; the idea was on many minds, and, indeed, the Provincial Congress made such a formal request on 16 May (same, p. 231). Even his suggestion of Washington and Charles Lee was not unique, although he made it early. Elbridge Gerry mentioned their names in a letter to the Massachusetts delegates on 4 June, in which he noted that Warren agreed with him (James T. Austin, *The Life of Elbridge Gerry*, Boston, 1828, 1:79). Washington was much discussed for commander well before the nomination was made, although apparently not so early as the first week in May (Freeman, *Washington*, 3:432–433). JA's role in the selection of Washington is described in his Autobiography in a passage often cited (*Diary and Autobiography*, 3:321–323). When JA was a member of the First Continental Congress, he had come to know Lee fairly well, but according to his autobiographical account, JA opposed Lee for second in command because such a choice would humiliate Artemas Ward, commander in Massachusetts. Thus, Lee was ranked after Ward.

[7] That is, 9 May, but the matter was postponed until 12 May, action not being completed until the 16th, when the letter to the Continental Congress was approved (Mass. Provincial Congress, *Jours.*, p. 208, 219, 229–231).

[8] Gov. Gage permitted citizens to leave Boston on condition they took no firearms or ammunition among their possessions. In response, the Provincial Congress resolved to permit those wishing to live in Boston to do so on the same condition and even to send out for their effects later. The congress further resolved that those too poor to pay for their leaving and resettlement (estimated at 5,000) should be assisted by the towns among which they were apportioned, reimbursement to come from the provincial treasury (same, p. 172–173, 176–177, 184).

[9] Benjamin Edes, partner with John Gill in publishing the *Boston Gazette*. Edes secretly brought out his press and type and set up an office in Watertown. Gill remained in Boston, where he was arrested on 4 Aug. for "printing treason," but freed on 2 Oct. (*DAB*).

[10] That is, New York, where the loyalists were being ousted.

[11] The letter from AA probably was the one of 4 May, or possibly that of 7 May (*Adams Family Correspondence*, 1:192–195). The extract from Hutchinson's letter has not been found, but it was made from the letterbooks seized from Hutchinson's house in Milton, which are now in the state archives (Mass. Provincial Congress, *Jours.*, p. 224–225, note). Some of Hutchinson's letters were printed in the newspapers of the day.

John Adams' Service
in the Continental Congress

10 May – 1 August 1775

Editorial Note

The first session of the Second Continental Congress began on 10 May 1775 and ended officially on 1 August. What went on at the congress, apart from the actions recorded in the printed journal, remains a matter for some conjecture. For the First Congress, one of the best sources is Adams' Diary, but from April to September 1775 the burden of business apparently kept Adams from getting down his impressions and recording debates; there are no entries for this period. Adams' attitude toward the various measures actually adopted by the congress can be gleaned from his letters, but his views while measures were being debated are unrecorded. The number and content of his letters make them a valuable mine of information, long recognized. Of the members' letters printed by Burnett for this session, approximately 21 percent are by Adams (*Letters of Members*, 1:89–186). His Autobiography contains what are really the only accounts of his position on the appointment of George Washington as commander in chief, on the necessity for the colonies to take over the powers of civil government, and on the monumental dispute with John Dickinson over the second petition to the King and the whole question of reconciliation (*Diary and Autobiography*, 3:314–325, 351–354). The Autobiography, however, suffers somewhat from hindsight, for these sections were written in 1805.

Adams served on nine committees during the first session. Because no evidence has been found to determine the exact role he played on these committees, his service can most usefully be presented in tabular form, showing the dates of appointment, the members with whom he served, and the dates and availability of reports.

Committee Assignments
3 June – 31 July 1775

3 June. James Duane, William Livingston, Samuel Adams, JA (*JCC*, 2:80).
To report an address to the people of Ireland.
Reported 21 July (same, p. 194); Dft not found.
Report adopted: 28 July (same, p. 212).
PRINTED: same, p. 212–218.

7 June. William Hooper, JA, Robert Treat Paine (*JCC*, 2:81).
To bring in a resolve for a fast day.

Reported and report adopted: 12 June (same, p. 87); Dft, following Editorial Note.
PRINTED: same, p. 87–88.
See JA to James Warren, 11–23 July (below).

8 June.   JA, Silas Deane, Thomas Mifflin (*JCC*, 2:82).
To examine the papers of Philip Skene and report.
Reported and a resolution adopted: 10 June (same, p. 86); Dft not found.
See JA to James Warren, 21 June, and JA to Joseph Palmer, 5 [July] (below).
Some of Skene's papers are in PCC, No. 51, I:1–7.

16 June.   Richard Henry Lee, Edward Rutledge, JA (*JCC*, 2:92–93).
To draft a commission and instructions for General Washington.
Reported commission and commission adopted: 17 June (same, p. 96); Dft not found.
Reported instructions and instructions adopted: 20 June (same, p. 100–101); Dft not found.
PRINTED: same, p. 96, 100–101
See JA, *Diary and Autobiography*, 3:321–323 and JA to AA, 17 June, *Adams Family Correspondence*, 1:215.

19 June. Patrick Henry, Thomas Lynch, JA (*JCC*, 2:98).
To meet with General Lee to find out whether he will accept his appointment.
Reported and report accepted: 19 June (same); Dft not found.
PRINTED: same.

19 June.   Richard Henry Lee, Edward Rutledge, JA (*JCC*, 2:99).
To draft commissions for major and brigadier generals.
Reported and report adopted: 19 June (same); Dft not found.
Commission for Artemas Ward, dated 19 June, in MHi:Ward-Perry-Dexter Papers.

23 June.   JA, John Rutledge, James Duane, Benjamin Franklin, James Wilson (*JCC*, 2:106).
To get engraved plates, paper, and printers for paper currency.
No report found.

22 July.   Benjamin Franklin, Thomas Jefferson, JA, Richard Henry Lee (*JCC*, 2:202).
To report on the House of Commons resolution of 20 Feb. 1775.
Reported: 25 July (same, p. 203); Dft in Jefferson, *Papers*, 1:225–230.
Report adopted: 31 July (*JCC*, 2:224).
PRINTED: Jefferson, *Papers*, 1:230–233.

31 July.   John Langdon, JA, Stephen Hopkins, Silas Deane, George Clinton, Stephen Crane, Benjamin Franklin, Caesar Rodney, Thomas Johnson, Patrick Henry, Joseph Hewes, Christopher Gadsden, Lyman Hall (*JCC*, 2:234–235).

During recess to inquire in all colonies about lead and lead ore and the processes for obtaining and refining it; also to make similar inquiry into the cheapest and easiest method for making salt.

No report found. The congress simply urged the colonies to procure lead, and the Secret Committee was empowered to import salt (same, 3:456; 4:290, 413; 5:522).

In addition to his committee work, Adams signed along with other members of the congress the second or Olive Branch petition to the King of 1 Sept. 1775, although he thought the gesture futile, even inimical to the colonies' best interests. Adams' major role was played on the floor of the congress in the debates over the state of America that began on 16 May. The outbreak of fighting in Massachusetts had convinced him that the congress would have to take supportive action. Specifically, he wanted it to assume responsibility for the army at Cambridge and to increase defensive measures. He held that negotiation with Great Britain from a position of strength made much more sense than attempted reconciliation through petition and addresses. Impatient as he was for firm measures, he recognized that the congress would move slowly, for it reflected the mood of the people (JA to James Warren, 6, 11 July, below). Adams' opposition to reconciliation and his support for resistance made him one of the leaders of the group that would ultimately push for independence.

Draft Resolution
Appointing a Fast-Day

[ante 12] June 75

Resolved that it be and hereby it is recommended to the Inhabitants of the united Colonies in America of all Denominations That Thursday the 20th day of July next be set apart as a day of public humiliation fasting and prayer, that a total Abstinence from servile labor and recreation be observed and all their religious Assemblies solemnly convened to humble themselves before God under the heavy Judgments felt and threatened, to confess ⟨those manifold⟩ our manifold[1] sins ⟨that have brought them upon us,⟩ to implore the forgiveness of Heaven, ⟨that a sincere repentance and reformation may influence our future Conduct, that the⟩ and that a[2] Blessing ⟨of Heaven⟩ may descend on the husbandry, Manufactures and other lawful Employments of this people and especially that the Union of these American Colonies in defence of their Just Rights and priviledges ⟨(for which hitherto we thank God)⟩ may be preserved, confirmed and prospered, that the ⟨Continental and Provincial⟩ Congresses may be inspired with Wisdom and ⟨prudence⟩ Concord ⟨and firmness,⟩ that Great Britain

9

and its Rulers may have their eyes opened to discern the things that shall make for the peace and Happiness of the Nation and all its Connections And that America may soon behold a Gracious interposition of Heaven for the redress of her many Grievances, the restoration of her invaded Liberties, a reconciliation with the parent State upon terms Constitutional and Honourable to them both and the Security of them to the latest posterity.[3]

Dft (Adams Papers); in an unidentified hand, but not that of any of the three committee members—Hooper, Paine, or JA; docketed in an unidentified hand: "75—Dilly June." The reference to Dilly, possibly the London bookseller Edward Dilly, remains obscure.

[1] The words "our manifold" are interlined, possibly in JA's hand.
[2] The words "and that a" are interlined, possibly in JA's hand.
[3] This draft lacks the preamble of the congressional resolution as adopted, and the wording is different except for the passage beginning "and that America ... to the latest posterity," which was copied into the final version almost verbatim. The last paragraph of the congressional resolution is modeled on the first three clauses of the draft's first sentence (JCC, 2:87–88).

From Joseph Warren

Dear Sir   Cambridge May. 20th. 1775

Having wrote fully upon several Subjects to Mr. Hancock and Mr. Adams, upon several Matters which they will communicate to you,[1] I can only add here that I Yesterday heard from your Family at Braintree were all in Health. A person having brought me a Letter from your Lady to me recommending one of your Brothers to be a Major in one of the Regiments, I am sorry the Letter did not arrive sooner, but I shall do all in my Power to obtain such a place for him yet, as he is the Brother of my Friend, and I hear is a worthy Man.[2] I am Dear Sir most sincerely, Your Friend & Humble Servt.

Joseph Warren

RC (Adams Papers); addressed: "To John Adams Esqr. in Philadelphia"; docketed: "Joseph Warren   May 20 1775."

[1] In all likelihood Warren wrote in his capacity as president pro tempore of the Second Provincial Congress, an office which he assumed on 2 May (Mass. Provincial Congress, *Jours.*, p. 178). He probably wrote about a Massachusetts letter of 16 May, in which the Provincial Congress requested advice from the Continental Congress on constituting government for Massachusetts and urged the congress to take over control of the military forces.
[2] See AA to Joseph Warren, 13 May (*Adams Family Correspondence*, 1: 196).

To James Warren

My dear Friend   Phyladelphia May 21. 1775

I am vastly obliged to you for your Letter. It was like cold Water to a thirsty Soul. We Suffer, greatly for Want of News from you and Boston.

I am very unfortunate, in my Eyes, and my Health. I came from home Sick and have been so ever Since. My Eyes are so weak and dim that I can neither read, write, or see without great Pain.

Our unweildy Body moves very Slow. We shall do something in Time, but must have our own Way. We are all secret. But I can guess that an Army will be posted in New York, and another in Massachusetts, at the Continental Expence.

Such a vast Multitude of Objects, civil, political, commercial and military, press and crowd upon Us so fast, that We know not what to do first. The state of fifteen or sixteen Colonies, to be considered, Time must be taken.[1]

Pray write me by every Opportunity and intreat all my Friends to do the Same. Every Line from you, any of you does good.

One half the Group is printed here, from a Copy printed in Jamaica.[2] Pray send me a printed Copy of the whole and it will be greedily reprinted here. My friendship to the Author of it.

The martial Spirit throughout this Province is astonishing. It arose all of a Sudden, Since the News of the Battle of Lexington. Quakers and all are carried away with it. Every day in the Week sundays not excepted they exercise—in great Numbers. The Farmer is a Coll—and Jo Reed another.[3] Their officers, are made of the People of the first Fortune in the Place.

Uniforms, and Regimentals are as thick as Bees.

America will Soon be in a Condition to defend itself by Land against all Mankind.

RC (MHi:Warren-Adams Coll.); addressed: "To the Hon. James Warren Esqr   Plymouth"; docketed: "Mr. J.A. Lettr   May 1775."

[1] JA is probably including Quebec and some of the West Indian colonies, like Jamaica, in his count. Americans were particularly hopeful that Quebec could be brought to support their cause.

[2] The Philadelphia reprinting of Mercy Otis Warren's play *The Group* lacked scenes ii and iii of Act II; that is, it included merely what had appeared in the *Boston Gazette* (Evans, No. 14613).

[3] John Dickinson and Joseph Reed were colonel and lieutenant colonel respectively in the Pennsylvania Military Association, a volunteer organization that preceded the organization of militia (*DAB*; Charles J. Stillé, *The Life and Times of John Dickinson*, Phila., 1891, p. 175; Arthur J. Alexander, "Pennsylvania's Revolutionary Militia," *PMHB*, 69:15-25 [Jan. 1945]).

To James Warren

Dr sir   Phyladelphia May 26. 1775

The Bearers of this are two young Gentlemen from Maryland, of one of the best and first Families in that Province.[1] One of them is a Lawyer, the other a Physician. Both have independent Fortunes. Such is their Zeal in the Cause of America, and Such their fellow Feeling for the People of our Province, that they are determined to Spend the Summer, in our Camp in order to gain Experience and perfect themselves in the Art military. They are soldiers already. Their name is Hall.

It will be of great Importance that these Gentlemen should be treated with the Utmost Delicacy, and Politeness. Their Letters to their Friends will have a great Influence on the Southern Colonies.

I Should take it as a favour if you would introduce these Gentlemen, to all our best Friends, and to the Knowledge of every Thing that can Serve the Cause.

I can not inform you of any Thing, passing here that is worth knowing. I hope We shall give Satisfaction. But it must be a work of Time. I am your Friend,   John Adams

RC (MHi:Warren-Adams Coll.).

[1] This is one of a series of four extant letters of introduction for Aquilla Hall and Josias Carvell Hall written between 26 and 29 May. See JA to AA, 26 May, *Adams Family Correspondence*, 1:206–207; JA to Joseph Palmer, 29 May (CSmH), not printed; JA to John Winthrop, 29 May (below). Aquilla was the lawyer, his brother, the physician. The latter served in the 9th Infantry, Maryland Line in 1776 (Henry J. Berkley, "Maryland Physicians at the Period of the Revolutionary War," *Md. Hist. Mag.*, 24:8 [March 1929]). Besides introducing the two men, these letters show JA's concern to maintain good relations between the northern and southern colonies in the common effort against Great Britain.

To John Winthrop

Dr Sir   Phyladelphia May 29. 1775

The Bearers of this are two young Gentlemen from Maryland. Aquilla Hall and Josias Carvill Hall, both of one of the best Families in Maryland, and both of independent Fortunes.

Their Errand to Cambridge, is to join our Army as Volunteers, against the Enemies of their Country in order to gain Experience, in the Art of War, in which they have already made good Proficiency.

As it is of importance that they should be treated with Politeness and Respect, I have taken the Freedom to give them this Letter, and to beg the favour of you to shew them, Harvard Colledge.

The Congress, Sir, have great Objects before them indeed. All is Secret but what you will see in the News Papers. If the Ministry, upon receiving Intelligence of the Battle of Lexington, dont receed all Ceremony will be over. At present We shall be fully United, and I hope shall do well.

My respectfull Compliments to all Friends. News of every Kind will be told you by the Bearers. Yr huml sert,   John Adams

We Suffer, excessively for Want of Letters and Intelligence from Cambridge. I must beg you would do me the Honour to write me, and desire all our Friends to do the same.

RC (MHi:JA-John Winthrop Corr.); addressed: "To the Honble. John Winthrop Esq L.L.D. Cambridge"; docketed: "29 May 1775." On the verso, using many abbreviations, Winthrop copied, except for the postscript, his letter to JA of 21 June (below).

From Philopattria

Honour'd Sir   Eastown,[1] June 1st: 1775

An ancient, and accounted a long headed Man, in these parts, has drop'd some words devising a scheme of reconciliation between the Colonies and Mother Country; which I think worthy of notice; and I am persuaded your zeal to a reconciliation is such that you will lend an ear to healing propositions, let it come from what quarter it may. Otherwise you would be unworthy of that eminence of character, which you profess, for republican candour of sentiment. He observed, suppose the Congress were to offer as much to the crown, as all the duties amount to, by a proper estimate, meaning all such duties, which we agree they have a right to lay as regulators of trade, and that exempt from all imposition on the Crown called runing;[2] which might be easily assess'd on each Province, by having recourse to their books of entry, and making at the same time, a proper allowence for what are run, which it is thought have been nearly as much again. And besides this to offer a number of forces well disciplin'd, in case of requisition, as was the case the two last wars; — so many thousands or hundreds, from each Province according to their importance and ship, Victual, Pay and cloath the same; some or all, as best judged of by the wisdom of the Congress; and the same to continue for a certain season, or during the expedition, as was the case in the attack last Wars, upon Carthagenia and the Havannah.[3] At least, the most strenious endeavours ought to be used, to some how or other effect an accommodation, considering what lamentable confusion and distress

13

must attend the quarrel if continued any space of time; and that of aiming at independency at present, affords the most frightful of all aspects, whilst the Mother Country has such power over the Ocean.

So hoping that these hints, may have their due weight, tho' communicated unknown, by the old Gentleman that dropt them; at the same time not doubting, every salutory scheme will be thought of, by yourselves; yet, that nothing may escape commemoration, which seems of a beneficial nature, in order, somehow to effect a speedy reconciliation; I hope you will not be offended at the Contents hereoff, from Sir, Your unknown Friend, & humble Servant,   Philopattria[4]

PS: I had like to have forgot that the venerable Sage would have insisted that all the obnoxious acts of Parliament should be repealed at the same time that the above mentioned offers were made, the one to be the inseperable condition of repealing the other, and in the space of ten, fifteen or twenty year, as the Provinces flourish and trade increases, an additional quantity both in money and troops, according to pressing requisitions from home, but still the mode of raising, as well as the quantity also, to be wholly left in the power of the different Assembly's.

And to confess the truth, the within letter on account of your reputed eloquence in the Congress, I direct to you, as it is thus more likely thereby you will have a due influence on that august Assembly altho your under no constraint but may still pursue your own opinion.

RC (Adams Papers); addressed: "To John Adams Esqr. one of the Delligates in the Honble. Congress"; docketed in a hand that may be Rev. William Gordon's: "Philopatria   June 1. 1775." See *Adams Family Correspondence,* 1:229–230, note.

[1] Perhaps Eastown, now Easton, Penna.

[2] That is, smuggling (*OED*).

[3] In 1741 Gen. Thomas Wentworth commanded an attack on Cartagena, seaport in Colombia, in which hundreds of Americans, recruited for the purpose, took part. The expedition was a disaster, only a fraction of the American troops coming out alive. An attack later on Cuba was equally fruitless (Howard H. Peckham, *The Colonial Wars*, Chicago, 1964, p. 91).

[4] Philopatria has not been identified.

From Alexander McDougall

Sir   New York June 5th 1775

While you are anxiously engaged to preserve the rights of your Country, I cannot entertain the least doubt, but you will readily excuse this address, when I assure you, I am induced to it, from a Sincere desire to promote the common cause of America in this City. The Delegates of this Colony who are in Trade, can inform you, I have no private interest, in the Subject on which I now Sollicit you. Since the commencement of the Non-importation in 1768, to the dissolution of the last continental Congress, the Tea Traders to Holland, were not only countenanced, but greatly Stimulated by the friends of Liberty, to import that Article; to enable us to defeat the Ministerial project of Subjecting us to the payment of the Duty on Tea imported from Great Britain. Before the Congress was convened, or any act or advice from them was announced to the Public, large orders were sent for this Commodity, and a very considerable quantity was imported. When their proceedings came out, those Traders immediately countermanded their orders, altho they were not directed to do it. Previous to this, there was a great quantity arrived, and then on its passage, as it was sometime before those orders had effect; so that when the Non-Consumption of it took place, there remained unsold near the Value of £100,000, Currency. Many of the proprietors of this Article, have the greatest part of their fortunes locked up in it; and more than one of them to the amount of £7,000: and many of the Sufferers are Zealous friends to the Country. They complain, that no order, or advice was given to them, before the dissolution of the Congress, to restrain or Countermand their Orders, and yet they are deprived of disposing and Consuming an Article, which they imported upon the Faith of Public encouragement; and they conceive their case singularly hard, as the Merchants Trading to Great Britain are allowed, (altho they were directed to countermand their orders,) to dispose of the Goods imported within the time limited by the Congress.[1] As the consumption of the Tea on Hand, will not affect the manufactorers of Great Britain or Ireland, so as to engage them in our favor, or induce the Ministry to redress our Greivances; the proprietors think they might be at Liberty, without any injury to the Common Cause, to Vend what is unsold; Especially when the British and Irish Traders are allowed this priviledge, *even with such Goods* as materially concern the Trade of those Countries. Notwithstanding those hardships and this Claim, from a regard to the union of the Colonies, and the respect they bore to the last Congress, they chearfully submited to close their Sales on the first of March, as the association directs;[2] relying on the Justice and Wisdom of the next Congress to give them releif. If I might be permitted as a Citizen of New York, fully acquainted with the State of this matter, and as a friend to the present interesting Struggle, to give my opinion, it would be; that the Congress give them Liberty to dispose of what they have on hand. I am Confident, such a resolution would tend to Establish, rather than to diminish the Power of the Congress in this City. I could adduce many Reasons in support of this opinion, but shall not trespass any longer on your Patience than while I mention the Following. These Gentlemen are great Adventurers, who would have risqued a considerable part of this property, in importing Arms and Ammunition; but were prevented by their having so great a part of their Capitals unexpectedly locked up; and they did not think it prudent to risque any other part of their property, when they were so much embarrass'd in their affairs, by the state of their Tea; which they were in danger of loosing. Nor will they be enabled to engage in the importation of those Articles for some time, even if they should be indemnified by the Public, for the loss of it, as it will be sometime before this can take place. Upon the whole of this matter, Sir, permit me to say, I think it is not a Time for us to Sink £100,000, when we shall in all probability have occasion to make the most prudent use of our common Stock; nor to discourage or impede the importation of Ammunition, which is already attended with very great risque; and especially when so much depends on our being possessed of a Sufficient quantity of that necessary Article. I hope you will excuse the Liberty of this Communication, as my sole motive in doing it, is a regard to that Cause, which I am perswaded you have above all Earthly Considerations most at Heart. I am Sir, Respectfully, Your very Humble Servant   Alexr McDougall[3]

RC (Adams Papers); addressed: "To John Adams Esqr at Philadelphi[a]"; docketed: "Mr. McDougall   June 5–75."

[1] That is, by 1 Dec. 1774 (JCC, 1:76–77).

[2] In Article 3 of the Association (same, p. 77).

[3] For McDougall, see JA, *Papers*, 2:414–415. No mention of JA's reaction to this letter has been found, but on 31 July the congress did receive petitions from New York and Philadelphia merchants regarding tea imported before the Association was adopted (JCC, 2:235). It was not, however, until 13 Oct. that these petitions were referred to a committee, of which JA was a member, the report and recommendations of which were ultimately defeated (same, 3:294, 388–389; see also JA's Service in the Continental Congress, 13 Sept.–9 Dec., No. IX, below).

The issue was a difficult and divisive one, for granting permission for the sale of the tea might have brought charges of favoritism and would certainly have raised policing problems. Moreover, the merchants' request was considered at a time when the whole question of opening trade was under debate and splitting the membership into factions for and against modification of the Association. Judging from the letters that Adams wrote to friends, he favored throwing the ports open to foreign traders if Americans could provide proper defense for their harbors, and he believed that American ships should venture forth in the winter when seizure by the British was less likely. Nonetheless, he saw the dangers and difficulties in his solution; his mind was far from closed on the subject of trade (JA to James Warren, 7 Oct., and to Charles Lee, 13 Oct., both below).

To James Warren

Dear Sir   Phyladelphia June 7. 1775

We have been puzzled to discover, what we ought to do, with the Canadians and Indians. Several Persons, have been before the Congress who have lately been in the Province of Canada, particularly Mr. Brown and Mr. Price, who have informed us that the French are not unfriendly to us. And by all that we can learn of the Indians, they intend to be neutral.[1]

But whether We Should march into Canada with an Army Sufficient to break the Power of Governor Carlton,[2] to overawe the Indians, and to protect the French has been a great Question. It Seems to be the general Conclusion that it is best to go, if We can be assured that the Canadians will be pleased with it, and join.

The Nations of Indians inhabiting the Frontiers of the Colonies, are numerous and warlike. They seem disposed to Neutrality. None have as yet taken up the Hatchet against us; and We have not obtained any certain Evidence that Either Carlton or Johnson,[3] have directly attempted to persuade them to take up the Hatchet. Some Suspicious Circumstances there are.

The Indians are known to conduct their Wars, So entirely without Faith and Humanity, that it would bring eternal Infamy on the Ministry throughout all Europe, if they should excite these Savages to War. The French disgraced themselves last War, by employing them. To let loose these blood Hounds to scalp Men, and to butcher Women and Children is horrid. Still it [is] Such Kind of Humanity and Policy as we have experienced, from the Ministry.[4]

RC (MHi:Warren-Adams Coll.); docketed: "Mr. J A Lettr   June 1775."

[1] John Brown (1744–1780), of Pittsfield, Mass., brought the news of the capture of Fort Ticonderoga, arriving in Philadelphia on or about 18 May (E. W. B. Canning, "Col. John Brown," *Book of Berkshire: Papers by Its Historical and Scientific Society*, Pittsfield, Mass., 1891, p. 312–319). James Price was a Montreal merchant sent by the other English merchants of that city to tell the Continental Congress about the conditions existing in Quebec. The substance of his report, derived from correspondence rather than from the report itself, which has not been found, was that although the French peasants would probably not act against the colonies, the French upper classes were hostile and were making efforts to raise the Indians against New England, but that their efforts had thus far met with limited success (the Committee of Connecticut to the General Assembly of New York, 23 May 1775, in Mass. Provincial Congress, *Jours.*, p. 707). This analysis accords with a letter from Montreal inhabitants to the Massachusetts Committee of Safety, 28 April 1775 (same, p. 751–752).

[2] Sir Guy Carleton (1724–1808), governor of Quebec (*DNB*).

[3] Guy Johnson (1740?–1788), superintendent of Indians in the northern department (same).

[4] Five days after JA made this statement, Gen. Gage, in a letter to Lord

Dartmouth, said that he had information that "the Rebels after Surprizing Ticonderoga, made Incursions and committed Hostilities upon the Frontiers of the Province of Quebec; which will Justify General Carleton to raise both Canadians and Indians to attack them in his turn, and we need not be tender of calling upon the Savages, as the Rebels have shewn us the Example by bringing as many Indians down against us here as they could collect" (Gage, *Corr.*, 1:403–404).

The Second Provincial Congress contacted the Stockbridge Indians to enlist them as minutemen and made overtures to the Mohawks and the Eastern Indians, seeking their military support against the British. These efforts the congress was determined to keep secret (Mass. Provincial Congress, *Jours.*, p. 114–116, 118–120, 225–226).

From Unknown

Sir   Fredericksburg June 9th 1775

The great Character he hath heard of you, induces a private Man to offer to your Consideration the following Hints, with an Assurance, that your Regard for your Country, will improve upon them for the general Good of all America.

When one Colony is declared to be in actual Rebellion, when all the others are anounced to be accessary to, and Favourers of that Rebellion, when the Sword is drawn, and a civil War actually commenced.

Every palliative Measure will be found ineffectual, and nothing will be more likely to restore Peace and a happy Union between Great Britain and America, or so effectually preserve the Liberty of the latter; as bold, daring, and strenuous Exertions of Force in the Beginning of the Contest.

In such a Situation of Affairs; Is it not impolitic to suffer the different Governors to exercise their several Functions, to drain from the People by their large Salaries, part of the Means of Defence, to restrain the Colonists from defending themselves, and to furnish Government with Intelligence, how they may most effectively divide weaken and subdue them?

Is it not still more so, to act the same pusillanimous Part with Regard to the Custom House and other Officers of the Revenue? Doth not common Sense dictate to Americans, the Necessity of strengthening their Hands, by reassuming all the Powers of Government, by seizing upon all the Revenues of the Crown, and by securing the Persons of all the Governors, and other Officers attached to Great Britain thro' out America?

It will be needless to say any Thing of the Necessity of striking a very large Sum of Money, of making it current all over America, and of pledging the Faith of the whole Continent for its Redemption.

Is not Holland our natural Ally upon the present Occasion, to supply us with Arms, Ammunition, Manufactures and perhaps Money? Ought not an advantageous Treaty of Commerce to be immediately offered her, upon her repaying that Assistance against the Oppressions of Britain, which our Ancestors in the Reign of our glorious Queen Elizabeth afforded them against the Tyranny of Spain?

To proclaim instant Freedom to all the Servants that will join in the Defence of America, is a Measure to be handled with great Delicacy, as so great, so immediate a Sacrafice of Property, may possibly draw off many of the Americans themselves from the common Cause.

But is not such a Measure absolutely necessary? And might not a proper Equivalent be made to the Masters, out of the Large Sums of Money which at all Events must be struck, in the present Emergency?

If America should neglect to do this, will not Great Britain engage these Servants to espouse her Interest, by proclaiming Freedom to them, without giving any Equivalent to the Masters? To give Freedom to the Slaves is a more dangerous, but equally necessary Measure.

Is it not incompatible with the glorious Struggle America is making for her own Liberty, to hold in absolute Slavery a Number of Wretches, who will be urged by Despair on one Side, and the most flattering Promises on the other, to become the most inveterate Enemies to their present Masters? [1]

If the Inhabitants of Quebec should assist Great Britain, would not true Wisdom dictate to the other Colonies, to lead their Slaves to the Conquest of that Country, and to bestow that and Liberty upon them as a Reward for their Bravery and Fidelity?

Might not a considerable Quit Rent reserved upon their Lands, and a moderate Tax upon their Labours, stipulated beforehand, in a Course of Years, sink the Money struck, and refund to the Colonies the Price of the Slaves now paid to their Masters for their Freedom?

RC (Adams Papers); addressed: "To John Adams Esq. of the Masachusets Bay now in Philadelphia"; in red ink: "1/4," probably the postage, and beside this in black ink: "N 8"; on the opposite side from the address and in the same hand as "N 8," docketed: "Dumfrus June 14 1775"; docketed in a different hand: "anonymous X   Fredericksburgh June 9th"; docketed in yet a different hand, possibly that of Rev. William Gordon: "Dumfrus June 9. 1775." On Gordon, see *Adams Family Correspondence*, 1:229–230, note.

A check with the Virginia Historical Society, the Historic Fredericksburg Foundation, and the Kenmore Association of Fredericksburg brought the suggestion that "Dumfrus" was Dumfries, a town north of Fredericksburg, where the letter might have been posted. No one has yet any clue to the authorship of this interesting letter. It was probably written to JA because he had already gained a reputation as a vigorous proponent of strong measures in dealing with Great Britain.

[1] The issue of slavery was and continued to be a problem as the colonies moved closer to independence. The author's belief that liberty for slaveholders and denial of liberty to slaves were in conflict was not uncommon, as is indicated by even a cursory examination of the writings of whig leaders, both northern and southern. The writer of this letter was unusual, however, because he not only states the problem, but offers a solution.

His plan did not arise wholly from perception of an abstract, if obvious, injustice, but also from events in Virginia in 1774 and 1775. By 9 June 1775, Virginia and the other southern colonies labored under a growing fear that the British, in the event of revolution, would free the slaves and use them against their former masters. These apprehensions were well grounded, for loyalists and their sympathizers had contemplated this possibility for some time (Benjamin Quarles, *The Negro in the American Revolution*, Chapel Hill, 1961, p. 21). In letters exchanged between James Madison and William Bradford in Nov. 1774 and Jan. 1775, reference is made to attempts to incite the slaves and to a ministerial plan to foment a slave rebellion (Madison, *Papers*, 1:129–130, 132). In April a group of slaves seeking to volunteer approached Gov. Dunmore, but he refused their services because he was not yet ready for action (Quarles, p. 22). Soon afterward, however, Lord Dunmore, according to a deposition taken from a Virginian, stated that in the event of rebellion, he would be able to count on the slaves for support ("Virginia Legislative Papers," *VMHB*, 13:49 [July 1905]). According to Lord Dartmouth, Dunmore in a letter to him of 1 May stated essentially the same thing (Force, *Archives*, 4th ser., 3:6). By 15 May news of Dunmore's plans had spread outside Virginia, for Gen. Gage noted the anxiety raised among the insurgents by Dunmore's design to free the slaves (Gage, *Corr.*, 1:399–400). From the warship on which he took refuge, Dunmore continued his efforts to raise forces among Negroes until in Nov. 1775 he issued his proclamation freeing the slaves (Force, *Archives*, 4th ser., 3:373, 1385). The author was, therefore, not so much anticipating Dunmore's final action as he was reacting to an existing situation and proposing a plan to avoid its consequences.

His solution to the problem was unique; no other reference to this or a similar plan has been found. In proposing to use Canada as a home for freed slaves and as a source of funds to pay the slaveholders, he obviously was responding to the American desire to take Canada. Beyond being of strategic importance, Canada could become the means to end a conflict between the ideals and realities of the American struggle and forestall the horrors of a slave insurrection.

To Moses Gill

Dr Sir [1]   Phyladelphia June 10. 1775

It would be a Relief to my Mind, if I could write freely to you concerning the Sentiments Principles, Facts and Arguments which are laid before us, in Congress: But Injunctions, and Engagements of Honour render this impossible. What I learn out of Doors among Citizens, Gentlemen, and Persons of all Denominations is not so sacred. I find that the general Sense abroad is to prepare for a vigorous defensive War, but at the Same Time to keep open the Door of

Reconciliation—to hold the sword in one Hand and the Olive Branch in the other—to proceed with Warlike Measures, and conciliatory Measures Pari Passu.

I am myself as fond of Reconciliation, if We could reasonably entertain Hopes of it upon a constitutional Basis, as any Man. But, I think, if We consider the Education of the Sovereign, and that the Lords the Commons, the Electors, the Army, the Navy, the officers of Excise, Customs &c., &c., have been now for many years gradually trained and disciplined by Corruption to the System of the Court, We shall be convinced that the Cancer is too deeply rooted, and too far spread to be cured by any thing short of cutting it out entire.

We have ever found by Experience that Petitions, Negociation every Thing which holds out to the People Hopes of a Reconciliation without Bloodshed is greedily grasped at and relyed on—and they cannot be perswaded to think that it is so necessary to prepare for War as it really is. Hence our present Scarcity of Powder &c.

However, this Continent is a vast, unweildy Machine. We cannot force Events. We must Suffer People to take their own Way in many Cases, when We think it leads wrong—hoping however and believing, that our Liberty and Felicity will be preserved in the End, tho not in the Speedyest and Surest Manner.

In my opinion Powder and Artillery are the most efficacious, Sure, and infallibly conciliatory Measures We can adopt.

Pray write me, by every opportunity—and beseech my Friends to write. Every Letter I receive does great good. The Gentleman to whom most Letters from our Province is addressed, has not Leisure to make the best use of them.[2]

There are three Powder Mills in this Province—two in New York but no Nitre—cant the Mass. begin to prepare both?[3] Pray write me, minutely the State of the People of Boston, and our Army &c. Pray let me know if Mrs. Gill and Mr. Boylstone are out of Prison.[4] I have never heard and have sufferd much Anxiety on their Account. My best Respects to them if they are to be seen by you.

RC (M-Ar:193, p. 349–350); addressed: "To Mr Moses Gill Chairman of the Committee of Supplies Cambridge"; docketed: "⟨Anonymous⟩ John Adams Letters, June 10th 1775 Philadelphia."

[1] Moses Gill (1734–1800), elected councilor when Massachusetts resumed its charter upon the advice of the Continental Congress, served continuously as councilor both under the charter and the constitution of 1780. In 1795 he became lieutenant governor, serving until June 1799, when he became acting governor until his death on 20 May 1800 (Francis Everett Blake, *History of the Town of Princeton*, 2 vols., Princeton, Mass., 1915, 1:270–273).

[2] Presumably John Hancock, regarded as the leader of the delegation; his name

appears first whenever the names of the congressional delegates are listed in the Journals of the Provincial Congress.

[3] On 10 June the Continental Congress passed resolutions calling upon the colonies to collect all available powder, saltpeter, and sulfur for the use of American forces and encouraging the manufacture of gunpowder and saltpeter (JCC, 2:85–86).

[4] Rebecca Boylston Gill, first cousin

of JA's mother, left Boston sometime before 24 June 1775, but her brother, Thomas Boylston, remained in the town throughout the siege and in 1779 went to England; whether he became a loyalist is uncertain. Patriots offered to secure his release from Boston through an exchange (*Adams Family Correspondence*, 1:228; 4:342–344; Sabine, *Loyalists*, 1:248; James Warren to JA, 31 July, note 11, below).

To James Warren

Dr sir   Phyladelphia June 10. 1775

I have written a few Lines to Dr Warren to whom I refer you.[1]

It is of vast Importance that the officers of our Army should be impressed with the absolute Necessity of Cleanliness, to preserve the Health of their Men. Cleanness, is one of the three Cardinal Virtues of a soldier, as Activity and Sobriety are the other two. They should be encouraged to go into Water frequently, to keep their Linnen washed and their Beds clean, and should be continually exercised in the manual and Maneuvres.

General Lee, has an opinion of Burgoine, Clinton and How. Burgoine he says is very active and enterprizing—fond of surprizes and Night Attacks and Alarms,[2] he entreats me, to inculcate a most unremitted Vigilance. To guard against Surprizes, especially in the Night.

We have a most miraculous Militia in this City, brought into existence, out of Nothing since the Battle of Lexington.

Measures are taken here and at New York to procure Powder. But We must be Sparing of that Article. The Supineness of the Colonies hitherto concerning it, amazes me.

Genl. Lee and Major Gates are very fond of a Project of procuring Pikes and Pike men.[3] I hope We shall send you some Rifle Men. They shoot with great Exactness, at amazing Distances.

They are casting Pateraras, and making Amuzettes[4] in this City, and preparing for War, with an alacrity, which does them Honor.

RC (MHi:Warren-Adams Coll.); addressed: "To the Hon. James Warren esq. Plymouth favd by Dr. Church"; docketed: "Mr. J: A Lettr June 1775."

[1] Not found.

[2] Generals William Howe, Henry Clinton, and John Burgoyne arrived in Boston on 25 May (French, *First Year*, p. 168). Charles Lee had served under Burgoyne in 1762 during a British ex-

pedition to Portugal and at the time of this letter was still on friendly terms with him. Lee, in fact, carried on a brief exchange of letters with Burgoyne after his arrival in Boston. Each sought to persuade the other of the correctness of the side on which he was fighting (Alden, *General Charles Lee*, p. 21–22, 84–87).

[3] Horatio Gates (1728–1806) had also served in the British army, being commissioned a major in 1762. A friend of Washington, he came to the colonies in 1772 and by 1775 was a partisan of the American cause, probably in protest against the British caste system (*DAB*). On 17 June 1775 Gates was appointed adjutant general with the rank of brigadier general (*JCC*, 2:97).

Trained pikemen were seen as an answer to British bayonets at a time when gunpowder was scarce and needed to be conserved. Franklin designed a pike for Pennsylvania's Committee of Safety (Carl Van Doren, *Benjamin Franklin*, N.Y., 1938, p. 533).

[4] Peteraras (a variation of pedrero) were small guns originally designed for discharging stones and later, shot, and for firing salutes. Amusettes were light field cannon sometimes used in mountain warfare (*OED*).

To Elbridge Gerry

Dr Sir   Phyladelphia [ante 11] June 1775[1]

Mr. Gadsden of South Carolina whose Fame you must have heard, was in his younger Years, an officer, on board the Navy, and is well acquainted with the Fleet.[2] He has Several Times taken Pains to convince me that this Fleet is not so formidable to America, as we fear. He Says, We can easily take their sloops, Schooners, and Cutters, on board of whom are all their best Seamen, and with these We can easily take their large ships, on board of whom are all their impress'd and discontented Men. He thinks, the Men would not fight on board the large ships with their fellow subjects, but would certainly kill their own officers. He says it is a different Thing, to fight the French or Spaniards from what it is to fight british Americans—in one case, if taken Prisoners they must lie in Prison for Years, in the other obtain their Liberty and Happiness.

He thinks it of great Importance that Some Experiments should be made on the Cutters. He is confident that We may get a Fleet of our own, at a cheap Rate, and this would give great Spirits to this Continent, as well as little Spirits to the Ministry.

RC (NHpR:Naval MSS Coll.); addressed: "To Elbridge Gerry Esqr Marblehead"; docketed: "Philadelphia Letter J A June 1775."

[1] JA undoubtedly wrote this letter between 1 June, when he had letters delivered to him by Benjamin Church, who had carried to Philadelphia a letter from the Provincial Congress, and 10 June, when Church left Philadelphia to return to Watertown (*Adams Family Correspondence*, 1:208, 213). Church arrived back in Watertown by 17 or 18 June. James Warren, who was chairman of a committee on armed vessels whose report "was ordered to subside" on 20 June, wrote JA on 11 July that he had seen JA's letter to Gerry and added that "haveing proposed in Congress Just such a project . . . borrowed the Letter to support it" but without success (Mass. Provincial Congress, *Jours.*, p. 353, 361; Warren to JA, 11 July, below).

[2] Gadsden's naval experience consisted of two years as a purser on board a British naval vessel (F. A. Porcher, "Memoir of Gen. Christopher Gadsden," S.C. Hist. Soc., *Colls.*, 4 [1887]:1).

From James Warren

My Dear Sir   Watertown June 11. 1775

Since my last I have waited with Impatience to hear from you. I mean Individually. The public Expectation to hear from the Congress is great. They dont Complain but they wonder that the Congress should set a month without their receiveing something decisive with regard to *us*. I presume we shall have it in due time, at least that nothing will be wanting in your power to relieve the distresses of your Country. I Intended to have devoted some great part of this Day to write to you but have been diverted by Calls that I could not dispence with. Since I knew of this opportunity I have not been able to get a minute till now when the Express is Just going of[f]. You will Collect from the publick Letter by this Express our Sentiments with regard to the necessity of assuming Civil Government Constantly Increasing upon us, what we apprehend to be the strength of our Enemies, and what have been and still are the subjects of some of our Contemplations.[1] I have not time to Add any thing more with regard to our own proceedings or the state of the Army. I can only say we have difficulties enough to struggle with. I hope we shall do well at last. It is said General Howe gives out that he Intends soon to have a frolick with the Yankees. They are ready for him, and wish for nothing more. Their Grenadiers, and Light Infantry have been Exempted from duty for Ten or Twelve days. We were greatly Elated this Morning with an Account that you had voted 70,000 Men, and 3,000000 sterling to be struck of[f] in Bills for their support.[2] Our Joy was damped at 10 O'Clock by a Letter from your Brother Cushing. I wish it had miscarried that I might have Enjoyed the pleasure a little longer, of Contemplateing the dignity of your Conduct, as well as the riseing Glory of America. His Letter was dated the 1st Instant and if he had been in the Clouds for seven Years past, I think he would have had as Just Ideas of our situation and necessities as he had Expressed to his Friend Hawley.[3] He thinks a very Inconsiderable reinforcement is to be Expected, and when Arrived that Gage will not have more than 5 or 6,000 Men, and queries whether we had not better discharge part of our Army to prevent Involving ourselves in an Immense Debt. A hint that we are to Expect no support from the Continent, but at the same time talks of an Union and the Day is our own, as saith Dr. Franklin.[4] I leave him and only add, I Breakfasted with Mrs. Adams last Wednesday. She and the Family were very well. She Came to this Town with her Father, Sister, Coll. Quincey, and

Lady, and Daughter, Parson Wybart[5] &c. with me that Day, and was greatly disappointed to hear of a Letter from Coll Hancock, when I was not able to find one for her. I could wish She knew of this opportunity. I must Conclude and am with Sincere Wishes for your Happiness, and regards for my Friends—perticularly Mr. Adams. Your Sincere Friend and Humbl. Servant, Jas: Warren

RC (Adams Papers); addressed: "To The Honbl: John Adams Esqr Att Philadelphia"; docketed: "Warren June 11, 1775."

[1] On 11 June the Provincial Congress adopted an address to the Continental Congress prepared by Joseph Hawley, Walter Spooner, James Warren, and Jedediah Foster (Mass. Provincial Congress, *Jours.*, p. 318–320). It apparently arrived in Philadelphia a day or two before 19 June, when "sundry letters from the Conventions of Massachusetts bay and New York ... were read," because JA in a letter to Elbridge Gerry of 18 June (below) answers most of the questions posed by Warren in his letter (JCC, 2:97–98).
[2] The congress did not vote its first issue of bills of credit until 22 June (same, 2:103).
[3] Not found. Thomas Cushing's reluctance to use strong measures against Great Britain led to his removal as a delegate to the Continental Congress in 1776 (DAB).
[4] Franklin had advocated a union of the colonies since 1754, when he was a delegate to the Albany Convention.
[5] Rev. Anthony Wibird, minister of the First Congregational Society of Braintree (Sibley-Shipton, *Harvard Graduates*, 12:226–230).

To Elbridge Gerry

Dear Sir Philadelphia, 18 June, 1775

I have at last obtained liberty, by a vote of Congress, to acquaint my friends with a few of the things that have been done.[1]

The Congress have voted, or rather a committee of the whole house have unanimously agreed, that the sum of two million dollars be issued in bills of credit, for the redemption of which, in a certain number of years, twelve colonies have unanimously pledged themselves.[2]

The Congress has likewise resolved that fifteen thousand men shall be supported at the expense of the continent; ten thousand at Massachusetts, and five thousand at New York; and that ten companies of riflemen be sent immediately; six from Pennsylvania, two from Maryland, and two from Virginia, consisting of sixty-eight privates in each company, to join our army at Boston. These are said to be all exquisite marksmen, and by means of the excellence of their firelocks, as well as their skill in the use of them, to send sure destruction to great distances.

General Washington is chosen commander-in-chief, General Ward the first major-general, and General Lee the second, (the last has not yet accepted,) and Major Gates adjutant-general.[3] Lee and Gates are experienced officers. We have proceeded no further as yet.

I have never, in all my lifetime, suffered more anxiety than in the conduct of this business. The choice of officers, and their pay, have given me great distress. Lee and Gates are officers of such great experience and confessed abilities, that I thought their advice, in a council of officers, might be of great advantage to us; but the natural prejudices, and virtuous attachment of our countrymen to their own officers, made me apprehensive of difficulties. But considering the earnest desire of General Washington to have the assistance of these officers, the extreme attachment of many of our best friends in the southern colonies to them, the reputation they would give to our arms in Europe, and especially with the ministerial generals and army in Boston, as well as the real American merit of them both, I could not withhold my vote from either.

The pay which has been voted to all the officers, which the Continental Congress intends to choose, is so large, that I fear our people will think it extravagant, and be uneasy. Mr. Adams, Mr. Paine, and myself, used our utmost endeavors to reduce it, but in vain.

Those ideas of equality, which are so agreeable to us natives of New England, are very disagreeable to many gentlemen in the other colonies. They had a great opinion of the high importance of a continental general, and were determined to place him in an elevated point of light. They think the Massachusetts establishment too high for the privates, and too low for the officers, and they would have their own way.[4]

I hope the utmost politeness and respect will be shown to these officers on their arrival. The whole army, I think, should be drawn up upon the occasion, and all the pride, pomp, and circumstance of glorious war displayed;—*no powder burned, however.*

There is something charming to me in the conduct of Washington. A gentleman of one of the first fortunes upon the continent, leaving his delicious retirement, his family and friends, sacrificing his ease, and hazarding all in the cause of his country! His views are noble and disinterested. He declared, when he accepted the mighty trust, that he would lay before us an exact account of his expenses, and not accept a shilling for pay. The express waits.

Reprinted from JA, *Works*, 9:357–359. RC offered for sale by Parke-Bernet Gall., N.Y., Gribbel sale, pt. 1, 30 Oct. – 1 Nov. 1940.

[1] The JCC contains no reference to this vote, but it probably came on 17 June, for various letters written by members of the congress contain essentially the same information (Eliphalet Dyer to Joseph Trumbull, 17 June; James

Duane to the New York Provincial Congress, 17 June; and John Hancock to Joseph Warren, 18 June, Burnett, ed., *Letters of Members*, 1:127–130, 134–135).

[2] The formal vote of the congress was not taken until 22 June, but the committee of the whole reached agreement on 15 June (JCC, 2:103, 91). JA writes of only twelve colonies agreeing, because Georgia was not officially represented in the Congress until 20 July. On 13 May the congress had admitted a representative from St. John's Parish in Georgia, but he could not speak for the whole colony (same, p. 192–193, 45).

[3] Washington was appointed commander in chief of the Continental Army on 15 June after considerable maneuvering by various delegates and factions at the congress (same, p. 91; JA, *Diary and Autobiography*, 3:321–323). Although present in Philadelphia, Lee did not immediately accept his commission because he wanted to be assured of indemnification if he lost his Irish estate for supporting the American cause. On 19 June a committee of three, of which JA was a member, met with Lee to learn his decision, but he asked that a committee from the congress composed of one member from each of the colonies meet with him to hear his request for indemnification. After a meeting with the new committee, its recommendation to accept his condition was promptly supported by the congress. Only then did Lee accept his commission (JCC, 2:98–99; Alden, *General Charles Lee*, p. 73–77).

[4] The congress set the pay of major generals and brigadiers at $166 and $125 per month respectively, with lesser amounts for the paymaster and commissary generals (JCC, 2:93–94). On 29 April the Provincial Congress set the pay for colonels, lieutenant colonels, and majors at £12, £9 12s, and £8 respectively; these sums were a reduction by one-fifth from the original scale, the change being justified by the reduced size of regiments that had been decided upon (Mass. Provincial Congress, *Jours.*, p. 167–168). In dollars at 6s equal to one Spanish dollar, the salaries become $40, $32, and $26 2/3. The Provincial Congress left the payment of minutemen up to the several towns, but recognized that a general muster would require payment from the province (same, p. 71). Braintree established pay for its minutemen at 1s 4d for a day of exercising with their arms from two to six o'clock each week; ordinary militiamen were to receive 1s per half-day if they exercised no more than once a week from three to six o'clock (*Braintree Town Records*, p. 461, 454). No record for monthly pay for privates on general muster has been found. These rates were set at a time when the average daily wage for farm laborers was 2s per day (Jackson T. Main, *The Social Structure of Revolutionary America*, Princeton, 1965, p. 70). Connecticut, which offers fuller records on pay scales, paid privates during the French and Indian War 36s per month of 28 days; in 1776, it was paying 40s per calendar month (*Conn. Colonial Records*, 11:94, 15:297). Roughly, then, we may say that New England privates were getting between $6 and $7 per month. This estimate is confirmed by James Warren in his letter to JA, 20 Oct. (below).

From Joseph Palmer

My dear Friend   Cambridge, 19th June 1775

I thank you for your Several favors, the last of which, the 10th Inst., I just now received.[1] I have not had time to write, and thro' abundant business my health has Sometimes been reduced; I now write in Committee of Safety, a few lines at a time as I can; all the business in this Committee has been done by only 6 or 7 Members, upon whom it has fallen very heavy, public business having pressed upon us very hard.

To see the distress occasioned by the late measures of Administration is enough to melt a heart of adamant;[2] Carts are continually passing in every direction from the Sea-Coast, loaded with Beds, Chairs, Pots, Kettles, and a thousand &ca's, with Women and Children in the midst. Great part of the Sea Coast is thin'd of Inhabitants, and most people have removed their most valuable effects. Mr. Cranch'es Family, and mine, are yet at Vertchild's House; they visit Germantown now and then: I have been with my family only 2 Nights since the 20th March.

You received from Congress the particulars of the battle of Lexington; Since which the affair of Noddles Island[3] (and several other smaller Skirmishes) has taken place; in all which, we had greatly the advantage; accounts of which you have doubtless received. But on Saturday last, the 17th, the Regulars attacked us upon one of the Charlestown Hills, where we had begun to entrench, and obliged us to retreat, by means of their Ships and Floating Batterys, we having no large Cannon to match theirs; the Cannon we cou'd have had, if we had had Gunpowder enough to Spare, but we had not more than sufficient for the Field Pieces and Musquetry; however, the Enemy have not much to boast; for tho' they kept the Field, and took from us 4 or 5 pieces, 3 Pounders, yet they lost, by the best accounts we can yet obtain, about 500 kill'd and wounded, and among the former are, as we have reason to believe, several officers of distinction: our loss in numbers is not great, by the best accounts we yet have, about 60 or 70 kill'd and missing;[4] but ---- among these is ---- what Shall I say! how Shall I write the name of our worthy Friend, the great and good Dr. W-----. You will hear by others who will write tomorrow, such particulars as I am not possessed of: Soon after the Regulars landed, they Set Fire to the Town of Charlestown, and that day, yesterday and this Day they have consumed most of the Houses as far as Penny-Ferry;[5] and they have possession of all that part of Charlestown, and are encamped upon Bunker's Hill; and we are encamped upon Prospect Hill, Winters Hill, and at the Bridge leading to Inman's, Phips's &c. Yesterday and this day, they have Cannonnaded us, but to no purpose; and our people, by Small Parties have picked off some of their out Guards: We expect another action very soon. Do send us Powder, and then we Shall, by the blessing of Heaven, soon destroy this Hornets Nest. This put me in mind of Saltpetre: J Greenleaf Esqr, and Messrs. John Peck and Wm. Frobisher, are now, by encouragement from Congress, gone to Brookfield, upon Colo. Foster's Estate, where is supposed to be a very large Bed of fine Earth, such as is described to be in the E. Indies, Strongly impregnated with Nitre: The like is discovered in Several other places. I must beg you to Send the best process of making it. Adieu my dear Friend, and assure Messrs. Hancock, Adams, Paine, &c, that I shou'd be glad to hear often, how, what, and all about the Political World in which I am deeply engaged; and that I remain Your and Their Sincere Friend and very humble Servt.   J: Palmer[6]

Earth dug up from under a Stable, put into a Tub, as ashes for Lye. Filled with Water. Stand 24 Hours. Then leaked off Slowly. Then boil'd for one Hour. Then run thro another Tub full of ashes. i.e. filtrated thro the ashes a Small Quantity, not to stand. Then put into a Kettle and boiled, untill it grows yellow. Then drop it on a cold stone or cold Iron, and it will christallise for a Proof. Then set it by in Trays in cool Places. Then it will christallise. And the Salt Petre is formed.[7]

RC (Adams Papers); addressed: "To John Adams Esqr.   Philadelphia"; docketed, possibly by the Rev. William Gordon: "John Palmer   X   June 19. 1775." The recipe for making saltpeter, written in JA's hand, appears at the top of the third page.

[1] Not found.

[2] Probably a reference to Gen. Gage's having yielded to pressure and modified the agreement he had reached with the Provincial Congress regarding those wishing to leave Boston. At first, those leaving were forbidden to take out any arms or ammunition; then provisions and merchandise were added to the list. Finally, arbitrary searches were made of all containers, and sometimes passports were so drawn as to separate families (Frothingham, *Siege of Boston*, p. 96–97).

[3] A skirmish that took place on 27 and 28 May, when Americans sought to remove livestock from Noddle's and Hog islands in Boston Harbor. The British tried to prevent the removal, and in the fighting the British lost a schooner and had a sloop badly damaged. Reputedly, the British suffered far more casualties than the Americans. Israel Putnam conducted himself so well as commander that presumably the Continental Congress was the more ready to name him a general (same, p. 109–110).

[4] For figures on battle casualties, see James Warren to JA, 20 June, note 6, and Elbridge Gerry to Massachusetts Delegates, 20 June, note 5 (both below).

[5] The town was set afire by artillery rounds and by marines. The wooden houses and other buildings burned furiously, the flames driven by an east wind. The Penny Ferry, a link between the town and Boston, was at the site of the old Charles River Bridge. A full and meticulous account of the fire and the extent of its damage, including individual claims of losses, is reconstructed from contemporary sources in James F. Hunnewell, *A Century of Town Life: A History of Charlestown, Massachusetts, 1775–1887*, Boston, 1888, p. 2–15, 112–174.

[6] Palmer's letter and those of James Warren to JA and Elbridge Gerry to the Massachusetts delegates of 20 June (both below), and the Provincial Congress to the Continental Congress (Mass. Provincial Congress, *Jours.*, p. 365–366), were sent to Philadelphia on 20 June. At New York, on 25 June, the express was intercepted by George Washington, who, after some hesitation,

opened the packet and read at least the letter from the Provincial Congress to gain recent information about the situation in Boston, particularly about Bunker Hill, for which he had had only fragmentary accounts (Washington, *Writings*, ed. Fitzpatrick, 3:304; Freeman, *Washington*, 3:464–465). The express arrived in Philadelphia on 26 June or early 27 June, the date on which the letters were read to the Continental Congress, giving that body the first official word on the battle (Jefferson, *Papers*, 1:174–175; JCC, 2:109; see also JA to James Warren, 27 June, below).

[7] Neither the source of this recipe nor the date on which it was written is known. It may have been intended for Palmer, since he asked for such instructions, but it is not known whether it was ever sent to him. It may have been included in the enclosure (not found) sent to James Warren in JA's letter of 27 June (below). On 10 June the Continental Congress had appointed a committee to "devise ways and means to introduce the manufacture of salt petre in these colonies" (JCC, 2:86). A description of the process had been published in the *Pennsylvania Gazette* of 25 January.

To George Washington

Dear Sir   Phyladelphia [19 or 20] June 1775 [1]

In Complyance with your Request, I have considered of what you proposed, and am obliged to give you my Sentiments, very briefly, and in great Haste.

In general, Sir, there will be three Committees, either of a Congress, or of an House of Representatives,[2] which are and will be composed of our best Men, Such, whose Judgment and Integrity may be most relyed on. I mean the Committee on the State of the Province, the Committee of Safety, and the Committee of Supplies.

But least this should be too general, I beg leave to mention particularly James Warren Esqr. of Plymouth, Joseph Hawley Esqr. of Northampton, John Winthrop Esqr. L.L.D. of Cambridge, Dr. Warren, Dr. Church, Coll. Palmer of Braintree, Elbridge Gerry Esqr. of Marblehead. Mr. Bowdoin, Mr. Sever, Mr. Dexter, lately of the Council will be found to be very worthy Men, as well as Mr. Pitts who I am Sorry to hear is in ill Health.[3]

The Recommendations, of these Gentlemen, may be rely'd on. Our President was pleased to recommend to you, Mr. William Bant for one of your Aid du Camps.[4] I must confess, I know not where to find a Gentleman, of more Merit, and better qualified for Such a Place.

Mr. Paine was pleased to mention to you Mr. William Tudor a young Gentleman of the Law, for a Secretary to the General—and all the rest of my Brothers, you may remember, very chearfully concurr'd with him. His Abilities and Virtues are such as must recommend him to every Man who loves Modesty, Ingenuity, or Fidelity: but as

I find an Interest has been made in behalf of Mr. Trumbull of Connecticut,[5] I must Submit the Decision to your further Inquiries, after you shall arrive at Cambridge. Mr. Trumbulls Merit is Such that I dare not Say a Word against his Pretensions. I only beg Leave to Say that Mr. Tudor is an Exile from a good Employment and fair Prospects in the Town of Boston, driven by that very Tyranny against which We are all contending. There is another gentleman of liberal Education and real genius, as well as great Activity, who I find is a Major in the Army; his Name is Jonathan Williams Austin.[6] I mention him, Sir, not for the Sake of recommending him to any particular Favour, as to give the General an opportunity of observing a youth of great abilities, and of reclaiming him from certain Follies, which have hitherto, in other Departments of Life obscured him.

There is another Gentleman, whom I presume to be in the Army either as a Captain, or in Some higher Station, whose Name is William Smith: as this young Gentleman is my Brother in Law, I dont recommend him for any other Place, than that in which the voice of his Country has placed him. But the Countenance of the General, as far as his Conduct shall deserve it, which in an Army is of great Importance, will be gratefully acknowledged as a particular obligation by his Brother.

With great Sincerity, I wish you, an agreeable Journey, and a Successfull, a glorious Campaign: and am with great Esteem, Sir, your most obedient Servant. John Adams

RC (Adams Papers); addressed: "To General Washington   Present." Although the MS was folded for sending, there is no evidence that it was sealed, and it may not have been sent. JA may have communicated his suggestions orally; but the first half of the letter with its mention of province leaders is repeated in the joint letter to Washington from the Massachusetts delegates (22 June, below). It is possible JA was persuaded that a joint effort was preferable.

[1] That this letter was written before 21 June is evident from JA to James Warren, 20 June (below), in which JA says he has mentioned Warren's name to the general.

[2] JA's uncertainty here comes from his not knowing whether Massachusetts had yet acted upon the advice of the congress respecting its government. See JA to James Warren, 27 June, note 3 (below).

[3] James Bowdoin, William Sever, Samuel Dexter, and James Pitts were all elected to the Council in May 1774, but Gage rejected Bowdoin and Dexter, along with JA and ten others (Council Members Vetoed by Gage, 25 May 1774, JA, *Papers*, 2:96). Pitts had first been elected to the Council in 1766; Sever began service in the Council in 1769. Sever became a member of the Council again in 1775 and acted as president of that body in rotation with Bowdoin and James Warren until the implementation of the Constitution of 1780. Pitts refused election to the Council in 1775 and died in 1776. On Pitts and Sever, see Sibley-Shipton, *Harvard Graduates*, 9:76–81; 11:575–578.

[4] William Bant, a Boston merchant

who acted as business agent for John Hancock, was probably the son of the merchant of the same name who died in 1754 (Thwing Catalogue, MHi). The son served on a couple of town committees, but refused the office of warden (Boston Record Commissioners, *18th Report, passim; 26th Report, passim*). Bant died in early 1779, and his widow, Mary Anna, married Caleb Davis, who undertook the complicated business of handling the settlement of accounts against Bant's estate (MHi:Caleb Davis Papers, *passim*). One letter refers to him as "Colo. William Bant," but the only record of military service is his being listed as a member of a Boston independent company in 1776 (same, Ebenezer Geary to Mrs. Bant, 26 Aug. 1783; *Mass. Soldiers and Sailors*, 1:582). On Bant and Hancock, see William T. Baxter, *The House of Hancock*, Cambridge, 1945, p. 241–242, 287–288.

[5] Joseph Trumbull, son of Gov. Jonathan Trumbull of Connecticut. See Burnett, ed., *Letters of Members*, 1:128, 133. Actually, Joseph became commissary general on 19 July (JCC, 2:190).

[6] A former law clerk for JA; for a brief sketch, see JA, *Legal Papers*, 1:xcvi.

To Joseph Palmer

Dr Sir   Phyladelphia June 20th. 1775

We send you for your Comfort the Generals Washington and Lee with Commissions for Ward and Putnam: together with a Vote to Support about twenty thousand Men, for the present, fifteen Thousands in Mass. and 5000 in New York.

We have voted to issue Bills of Credit to the amount of two Million Dollars, and must, I suppose, vote to issue a great deal more.[1]

I hope a good account will be given of Gage, Haldiman,[2] Burgoine, Clinton and How, before Winter. Such a Wretch as How, with a Statue in Honour of his family in Westminster Abbey, erected by the Massachusetts to come over with a Design to cutt the Throats of the Mass. People, is too much.[3] I most Sincerely and cooly, and devoutly wish that a lucky Ball, or Bayonet may make a Signal Example of him, for a Warning to Such, unprincipled, unsentimental Miscreants for the future.

I think We shall have an ample Variety of able experienced officers, in our Army. Such as may form Soldiers and officers, enough to keep up a Succession for the Defence of America for ages. Our Camp will be an illustrious School of military Virtue and will be resorted to and frequented by Gentlemen in great Numbers, from the other Colonies as such—great Things, are in the Womb of Providence—great Prosperity or adversity, perhaps both: the latter first perhaps.

My Love and Compliments and Duty where due, especially to your Family, Mr. Cranch's and my own. I am your Friend.   John Adams

RC (PHC:Charles Roberts Autograph Coll.); addressed: "To Joseph Palmer Esqr of Braintree   at the Provincial Congress   Watertown   favoured by General Washington"; docketed: "Honble John Adams Esqr   1775."

¹ See JA to Elbridge Gerry, 18 June, note 2 (above).

² Gen. Frederic Haldimand (1718–1791), of Swiss origin and second in command to Gage, was recalled and left Boston the day before the Battle of Bunker Hill. Dartmouth feared having a foreigner take over in the event Gage was disabled (*DNB*; French, *First Year*, p. 207–208).

³ JA is referring to George Augustus Viscount Howe (1724–1758), the older brother of William and Richard Howe, who distinguished himself during the French and Indian War, and whose death in an ill-fated expedition against Fort Ticonderoga in 1758 so affected the people of Massachusetts that in 1759 the General Court appropriated £250 for a memorial in Westminster Abbey. This affection for Viscount Howe and William Howe's statement in 1774 that he would not accept a command in America left Americans ill-prepared for William's arrival to serve under Gage. JA and others in Massachusetts felt betrayed (James Austin Holden, *New Historical Light on the Real Burial Place of George Augustus Lord Viscount Howe*, repr. from *Trans. of the N.Y. State Historical Assoc.*, 10 [1911]:9–13, 67–69; Ira D. Gruber, *The Howe Brothers and the American Revolution*, N.Y., 1972, p. 51–52, 58).

To William Tudor

Dr sir   Phyladelphia June 20th. 1775

I have lamented excessively the Want of your Correspondence ever since I have been here. Not a Line from Dr. Winthrop, Dr. Cooper, Mr. Kent, Swift, Tudor, from some or other of whom I was accustomed the last Fall, to receive Letters every Week. I know not the state, the Number, the Officers of the Army—the Condition of the poor People of Boston or any Thing else.

I have taken the Liberty to mention you to General Washington, for his secretary, which is a very genteel Place—my Brothers here very chearfully and unanimously concurr'd with me in the warmest Terms. A great Interest is making however for Mr. Jos. Trumbull and for others. What the General will do I know not. I would have you wait on him respectfully, and welcome him to the Army, and enquire after my health and let him know that I desired you to call upon him. Invite him to your Fathers, and offer your service to him.¹ You will be pleased with him. He is brave, wise, generous and humane. Our Army will be the best military school in the Empire.   John Adams

RC (MHi:Tudor Papers); addressed: "To Mr William Tudor   Attorney at Law   Cambridge   favoured by General Washington"; docketed: "June 20th. 1775."

¹ For Tudor's description of his meeting with Washington see his letter to JA of 6 July (below).

To James Warren

My Friend   Phyladelphia June 20. 1775

This Letter will go by the sage, brave, and amiable General Washington,[1] to whom I have taken the Liberty of mentioning your Name.

The Congress has at last voted near twenty thousand Men in Massachusetts and New York, and an Emission of a Continental Currency to maintain them.

You will have Lee, as third in Command, Ward being the second, Schuyler of New York the fourth, and Putnam the fifth. Ten Companies of Rifle Men too, are ordered from Pensylvania, Maryland and Virginia.

Nothing has given me more Torment, than the Scuffle We have had in appointing the General officers. We could not obtain a Vote, upon our Seat for L.[2] Sam. and John fought for him, however, through all the Weapons. Dismal Bugbears were raised, there were Prejudices enough among the weak and fears enough among the timid as well as other obstacles from the Cunning: but the great Necessity for officers of skill and Experience, prevailed.

I have never formed any Friendship or particular Connection with Lee, but upon the most mature Deliberation I judged him the best qualified for the Service, and the most likely to cement the Colonies, and therefore gave him my Vote, and am willing to abide the Consequences.

I am much obliged to you for yours of June 11. Pray write me a State of the Army, their Numbers, and a List of the officers and the Condition of the poor People of Boston. My Heart bleeds for them.

We have a great Show this Morning here. Our great Generals Washington and Lee review the three Battalions of this City. I believe there never was two Thousand Soldiers created out of nothing so suddenly, as in this City. You would be surprized to behold them, all in Uniforms, and very expert both in the Manual and Maneuvres. They go through the Wheelings and Firings in sub-divisions, grand Divisions, and Platoons, with great Exactness. Our Accounts from all Parts of the Continent are very pleasing. The Spirit of the People is such as you would wish.

I hope to be nearer to you at least, very soon. How does your Government go on? If We have more bad News from England the other Colonies will follow your Example.[3] My Love to all Friends, yours,

John Adams

RC (MHi:Warren-Adams Coll.); addressed: "To the Hon. James Warren

I. A N.W. VIEW OF THE STATE HOUSE IN PHILADELPHIA,
TAKEN IN 1778, BY JAMES TRENCHARD, AFTER CHARLES WILLSON PEALE

See page ix

2. AN EXACT VIEW OF THE LATE BATTLE AT CHARLESTOWN,
JUNE 17TH 1775, BY BERNARD ROMANS
See page ix

Esq⟨ at the Provincial Congress   favoured by General Washington"; docketed: "Mr. J. A Lettr   June 1775."

[1] Washington left Philadelphia on 23 June for Cambridge, where he arrived on 2 July (JA to AA, 23 June, *Adams Family Correspondence*, 1:226; Washington, *Writings*, ed. Fitzpatrick, 3:308, note 35).

[2] What JA means is that although he and Samuel Adams supported Lee, they could not secure the majority needed among the Massachusetts delegates if the colony was to cast a vote for him.

[3] That is, in reinstituting government under charter forms, but ignoring the royal governor.

From James Warren

My Dear Sir   Watertown June 20. 1775

Since my last I have the pleasure of Several of yours. I am Extreamly obliged to you, and to continue your Attention to me in this way can assure you I dont fail to make use of anything I think will serve the publick from your Letters. I Communicated to both our Generals that Paragraph of your Letter Containing Genll. Lees Opinion of the Generals and character perticularly of Burgoine.[1] Yours per Mr. Hall I never received till the day before Yesterday. I have never seen those Gentlemen.[2] Shall Observe your recommendation when I do. You will doubtless hear before this reaches yor of another Action here on Saturday last which Terminated with less success on our side than any one that has taken place before. However they have nothing to Boast of but the possession of the Ground. You will say that is enough. It is enough to mark with Infamy those who suffered it, but they have paid very dearly for it in the loss of many Men. They Landed about 2000. I cant learn who Commanded them. Were more than once repulsed by the Bravery of our men in the Imperfect Lines hove up the Night before, who had they been supplied with Ammunition, and a Small reinforcement of Fresh men, would thus under every disadvantage have in all probability beat them to peices. Here fell our ⟨murdered⟩ worthy, and much Lamented Friend Doctr. Warren with as much Glory as Wolf on the plains of Abraham, after performing many feats of Bravery and Exhibiting a Coolness and ⟨Judgment⟩ Conduct which did Honour to the Judgment of his Country in Appointing him a few days before one of their Major Generals.[3] At once Admired and Lamented in such a manner, as to make it difficult to determine whether regret or Envy predominates. Had our Brave men posted on Ground Injudiciously at first taken, had a Lee or a Washington Instead of a General destitute of all Military Ability and Spirit to Command them it is my opinion the day would have terminated with as much Glory to America as the 19th of April. This is our great Misfortune and is remediless from any other quarter than yours. We dare not superceed him here.[4] It will come well from you and really merits your Attention. That and a necessary article which makes me tremble to Name or think of is all we want.[5] Our men were harrassed all the morning by Cannon from 2 Batteries, 2 Ships, and a Bomb Battery, and att the attack by a great Number of Armed Boats, and nevertheless made a Stout resistance. Some fatality always attends my attempts to Write you. I am called away and fear I shant be able to add another paragraph.

I must Beg you would make my acknowledgements to Mr. Cushing, and my good Friend Mr. Adams for their kind favours. I fully designed to have wrote them but this Express goes of[f] so suddenly as not to give me an opportunity. Shall Embrace the next as well as to Enlarge to you. The Hurry of our affairs can hardly be described. We have just received an account by a Man who is said to have swam out of Boston that we killed and wounded 1000 of them among the first of which is a General, Majors Sherrif and Pitcairn and 60 other officers. 70 officers wounded. The whole of the Troops landed at Charlestown were 5000.[6] This account is not Improbable to me but I cannot warrant the authenticity of it. I am your Friend. Adieu.

J: Warren [7]

Mrs. Adams and family were well when I last heard from them. I have had great pleasure in Conversing with Doctr. Church who gives me a good account of your Spirit, Unanimity &c. I am well pleased with most of your resolves. I cant however say that I admire the form of Government prescribed, but we are all Submission and are sending out our Letters for calling an Assembly.[8] I hope we shall have as good an opportunity for a good Government in some future time.

RC (Adams Papers); docketed by JA in a late hand: "Warren   June 20 1775."

[1] See JA to Warren, 10 June (above).

[2] See JA to Warren, 26 May (above).

[3] This passage dealing with the death of Joseph Warren and that giving an account of British casualties and the number of regulars involved in the battle were printed in the *Pennsylvania Gazette*, 28 June.

[4] Warren is referring to Gen. Artemas Ward, commander in chief of the forces surrounding Boston. A contro-versy developed over Ward's conduct in regard to the Battle of Bunker Hill. Obviously Warren had little respect for Ward's ability, believing that his inaction and lack of leadership had contributed greatly to the outcome of the battle, which contemporary opinion viewed privately as a serious setback to the patriot cause. Compare the views of Elbridge Gerry and Charles Lee with those of Warren (Gerry to Massachusetts Delegates, 20 June, below; NYHS, *Colls. for 1872, Lee Papers*, 2:146–

147). For a brief modern assessment of Ward's abilities, see French, *First Year*, p. 213–214.

[5] Warren may be hinting that the colonies ought to declare their independence.

[6] In his official report Gage calls the total number of British troops engaged as "something above 2000 men" (Gage to Lord Dartmouth, 25 June, in Frothingham, *Siege of Boston*, p. 387). Gage lists the killed and wounded by name and rank, showing totals of 228 killed and 828 wounded. The officers lost were 21 killed and 70 wounded. Lt. Col. Abercrombie was the highest ranking officer who suffered fatal wounds. Maj. Pitcairn, who commanded at Lexington, and Maj. Williams also died (same, p. 387–389).

The general that Warren mentions may have been Burgoyne, who was not seen after the battle and was believed by many to be dead.

[7] See Joseph Palmer to JA, 19 June, note 6 (above).

[8] The resolve of the Continental Congress passed on 9 June regarding the government of Massachusetts was received by the Provincial Congress on 17 June in the group of letters brought from Philadelphia by Josiah Fessenden, who acted as the express during this period. On 20 June the Provincial Congress voted to call on the towns to elect members to a general court that was to meet in Watertown on 19 July (*Warrens-Adams Letters*, 1:55; Mass. Provincial Congress, *Jours.*, p. 352, 358–360).

Elbridge Gerry to the Massachusetts Delegates

Gentlemen   Watertown June 20th 1775

I Received the Letters, with which you were pleased to favor me per Mr. Fessenden on Saturday last being the 18th Instant,[1] at a Critical Time for the Army posted at Cambridge. The Evening preceeding Orders were Issued in Consequence of a Consultation between the General Officers and Committee of Safety to take possession of Dorchester Hill and Bunkers hill in Charlestown which I must confess gave me most sensible Pain on hearing more especially as it had been determined about Ten Days before by the same Council and a junction of the Committee of Supplies by their desire, that it would be attended with a great expence of Ammunition by Ordinance and that therefore it was inexpedient and hazardous.[2]

As soon as it was discovered by the Enemy on saturday Morning a firing began from the Lively in Charlestown River and also from the Batteries in Boston, which was returned against the Latter by the American Forces untill it subsided on the side of the Enemy and only one Man was lost in the Morning. Our Forces exerted themselves in getting entrenched and soon discovered that a Warm engagement must take place; not withstanding which Care was not taken to place a sufficient Number of Artillery and Cannon on the Hill to defend it. At Noon the Enemy bro't in Two or Three Ships of the Line with which, the Lively, and Batteries at Boston, they endeavoured to Dislodge our Forces, soon after they landed about 3000 Regulars and a warm Engagement began, in which our Forces in the Intrenchment behaved like Heroes, but were not sufficiently provided with Artillery nor timely reinforced from Cambridge. They soon found it necessary to Abandon an intrenchment on a Hill to the Eastward of Bunker Hill and made a stand at the Lines on the Hill last mentioned. The Forces then being put in Flames by the Enemy the Enemy advanced and a Furious Fire was kept up for some time on both sides untill the Enemy Forced the Lines and depended on pushing their Bayonets. Our Forces after being overpowered in the Intrenchments left them to the Enemy who are now posted there, and retreated about 3 Quarters of a Mile toward Cambridge where they have four [cannon]³ One of which is on a high Hill opposite or near the Stone House⁴ and So situated that with good Conduct we expect an Effectual stand. Our good, our beloved Friend Doctor Warren was on Bunker Hill when the Lines were forced and is no more, he was two Days before Chosen second Majr. General, Accepted on Friday and on Saturday dyed like a Hero. We can only drop a Tear for our worthy Brother and Console ourselves with the Consideration that his Virtue and Valour will be rewarded in Heaven. The Reports relative to our loss is varient from 20 to 80 Killed and wounded but I cannot think we shall find it quite so inconsiderable and from the best judgment which I can form at present believe it will turn out about 150 or 200.⁵ This is a Matter we decline noticing here at present, Altho we dont neglect to Speak of the Loss of the Enemy which I suppose is fully equal to our own. We labour, we are retarded, we suffer for want of a General at Cambridge. Ward is an honest Man but I think Wants the Genius of a General in every Instance. Command, order, Spirit, Invention and Discipline are deficient, what then remains that produced this Choice, I know not. General Thomas is from his Character and Conduct a fine fellow, his camp at Roxbury is always in order without trouble to Congress or their Committees.⁶ The other at Cambridge ever wanting and never right. I hope We shall not suffer from this Accident. Col. Fry of Andover is in the Cabinet intended as Major General. Colo. Heath first Brigadier General and I suppose will be chosen and Commissioned this Day,⁷ but we must have the Assistance of Military skill whereever to be found on the Continent. It will I fear be difficult intirely to drop Ward. If he is superceeded by Washington and posted at Cambridge with him, and General Thomas &c. at Roxbury I cannot but think we shall be in a Good situation provided it is timely effected.⁸

General Lee must be provided for and heartily engaged in the service without being Commissioned at present. He is a stranger and cannot have the Confidence of a Jealous people when struging for their Liberty. He will soon become familiar and be courted into office, I revere him as an Officer and wish he had been born an American.

It affords Consolation that the Congress have or [are?] about taking Command of these Matters. We notice their Resolve in which the Army is Called the American Army. May the arrangement be happy and Satisfy each Colony as well as aford us good Generals.

Medicine is much wanted and Doctor Church has given us an Invoice of necessary Articles which we beg may be ordered here from Philadelphia as soon as possible. I notice what is said relative to powder, no Exertions has been wanting of in the Committee of Supplies since I have been acquainted with it, to procure this Article. Colo. Bower [9] was depended on for 200 half Barrels and were disappointed, and the plan of fortifying lines with heavy Cannon was not then in Contemplation. We must hold our Country by Musketry principally untill supplies can be got to expel the Enemy. I rejoice to hear of the Flour ordered to the army. We have an Instance of the Humanity of the Enemy after they had obtained the Hill; not satisfied with burning the other part of Charlestown they proceeded to set Fire to Houses on the Road to Winter Hill.

The Newhampshire and Connecticut Forces as well as the Massachusetts in the Heat of Battle suffered much. I suspect some of our [inferior?] Officers are wanting and one is under Arrest.[10] We have lost Four pieces of Artillery and nothing more at present. We are in a worse situation than we shall in future Experience in many Instances, and great exertions are necessary. The Committee of Supplies, have a good share at present from sunrise to 12 at Night constantly employed for several Days but we have now a little abatement. Hall of Medford [11] was excused from the Committee on Account of a Weak Constitution and the Congress Judiciously chose one of a strong Constitution to supply the place. Another Engagement is Hourly expected may the great controuler of Events order it for the Happiness of these Colonies. I have Just Received a Letter which puts it beyond Doubt that the Enemy have sustained a great Loss. Capt. Bradford is an Intelligent Man but whether the Loss is equal to 1000 I cannot say. I inclose you the Original itself.[12] Complaint from all Quarters of Disorder in the Camp at Cambridge, that it is more like an unorganized Collection of People than a Disciplined army. I cannot rest on this precipice; and engaged as the Committee is shall find time to move this Day that a Committee of Observation be immediately chosen to enquire into and assist in and Rectify the Disorders of the Camp untill they shall subside.[13] Good God that a Congress so vigilant should have chosen a lifeless F— for such an Important Trust. Will the Honorable Mr. Hancock assist the Committee in [having] the Invoice sent us forthwith. The notes of the Colony can be made as payment without delay. They Carry 6 per Cent Interest, are negotiable, and are received in all the Governments about us readily and without Hesitancy. The Committee of Supplies are greatly Obliged by his proposal relative to the Duck. Doctor Church proposes the Boston Donations[14] for this Purpose since the Notes are equal with the Cash in this Colony. I am with the most Sincere respect, Gentlemen, your most Obedt. Sert.

Elbridge Gerry

MS, contemporary clerk's copy (Elsie O. and Philip D. Sang Coll., 1960); docketed: "Copy Letter to Members of Cont. Congress   June 20 1775." Obvious errors made by the copyist have been silently corrected.

[1] The copyist's inadvertence for the 17th, which was a Saturday.

[2] The proceedings of the Committee of Safety on 15 June, when it was recommended that Bunker Hill "be securely kept and defended," are in Mass. Provincial Congress, *Jours.*, p. 569. No record of a meeting with the Committee of Supplies has been found, but see the call on 3 June for such a meeting (same, p. 561).

[3] Word editorially supplied.

[4] That is, the Powder House in present-day Somerville.

[5] Allen French, citing Frothingham, gives the total American casualties as 441, but see his note citing the varying figures given by contemporary sources, which give the highest number killed as 139 (*First Year*, p. 263).

[6] John Thomas (1724–1776), commander of the troops in the Roxbury sector, in the spring of 1776 directed the fortification of Dorchester Heights that forced the British to evacuate Boston. Considered by Washington and others as an outstanding general, he later was sent to Quebec to try to salvage that expedition after the death of Montgomery and the wounding of Arnold. Realizing that the situation was hopeless, Thomas ordered a retreat, but he died of smallpox before it was completed (*DAB*).

[7] Joseph Frye (1712–1794) was elected a major general on 21 June but was not commissioned until 23 June (*DAB*; Mass. Provincial Congress, *Jours.*, p. 370, 378). Heath's commission as first major general, dated 21 June, is given in Wroth and others, eds., *Province in Rebellion*, p. 2291.

[8] Ward did function as second in command to Washington.

[9] For a brief sketch of Col. Jerathmiel Bowers, a member of the Provincial Congress, see same, p. 2834–2835.

[10] Actually two artillery officers were charged with misconduct, Capt. Samuel Gridley and Capt. John Callender. The former was cashiered but later got himself reinstated, and Callender was finally exonerated, his false accuser being cashiered instead (French, *First Year*, p. 244 and note).

[11] Stephen Hall III. See the brief sketch in *Province in Rebellion*, p. 2862.

[12] The enclosure, Job Bradford's report, has not been found, but it was printed in the *Pennsylvania Gazette*, 28 June.

[13] On 21 June the Provincial Congress appointed a committee composed of Joseph Hawley, Elbridge Gerry, Samuel Thompson, Noah Goodman, Benjamin Lincoln, and Nathaniel Freeman to "inquire into the reason of the present want of discipline in the Massachusetts army, and to report to this Congress what is the most proper way to put said army into proper regulation" (Mass. Provincial Congress, *Jours.*, p. 370).

[14] The donations were contributions made from all over the colonies for the benefit of the Boston poor when the Boston Port Act closed the town's har-bor. What Hancock proposed to the Committee of Supplies regarding duck cloth has not been determined.

To James Warren

Dr Sir   Phyladelphia June 21. 1775

Major Mifflin [1] goes in the Character of Aid de Camp to General Washington. I wish You to be acquainted with him, because, he has great Spirit Activity, and Abilities, both in civil and military Life. He is a gentleman of Education, Family and Fortune.

C. and H. and P.[2] have given us a great deal of Trouble, in the Election of Lee, and I expect will avail themselves of all the Whims and Prejudices, of our People.

We are like to have more trouble of the like Kind in the Choice of Brigadiers General. Old Pomeroy [3] must be the first. P. to do him Justice, has renounced his Connections in this Instance. He declares he cant and wont vote for him. I had rather vote for Prebble [4] in his Bed.

I expect, our People when they come to know the Pay of the General officers and others, will grumble. Adams, Paine and I fought against it totis Viribus. But in vain. It is amazingly high. But the southern Genius's think it vastly too low. Farewell.   John Adams

RC (NHi:Misc. MSS, Adams); docketed: "Mr J A Lettr June 1775."

[1] Thomas Mifflin (1744–1800) was recognized very early by JA and others for his ability and devotion to the patriot cause. His bravery and military knowledge brought a rapid rise in rank. Appointed as Washington's aide-de-camp on 23 June, he became a colonel on 22 Dec., a brigadier general on 16 May 1776, and a major general on 19 Feb. 1777. His conduct, however, as quartermaster general, a post he held from Aug. 1775 to March 1778, brought dissatisfaction and caused him to leave the army (*DAB*).

[2] JA's Massachusetts colleagues, Cushing, Hancock, and Paine.

[3] Seth Pomeroy (1706–1777), who had played an active role in military affairs for Massachusetts since the expedition against Louisbourg. Appointed third in command of Massachusetts forces under Jedediah Preble and Artemas Ward in 1774, he was most active in raising and drilling troops in western Massachusetts during 1775 and 1776. Although appointed first brigadier general in the Continental Army on 22 June, he apparently never served in that capacity (*DAB*; Mass. Provincial Congress, *Jours.*, p. 35).

[4] Jedediah Preble (1707–1784), appointed first in command of the Massachusetts forces in 1774 (Mass. Provincial Congress, *Jours.*, p. 35; *Appletons' Cyclo. Amer. Biog.*).

43

To Joseph Warren

Dr Sir   Phyladelphia June 21. 1775

This Letter I presume will be delivered into your own Hand by the General.

He proposes to set out, tomorrow, for your Camp. God Speed him. Lee is, Second Major General, Schuyler, who is to command at N. York is the third and Putnam the fourth. How many Brigadiers general we shall have, whether five, Seven or Eight, is not determined, nor who they shall be. One from N. Hampshire, one from R. Island, two from Connecticutt, one from N. York, and three from Massachusetts, perhaps.[1]

I am almost impatient to be at Cambridge. We shall maintain a good Army for you. I expect to hear of Grumbletonians, some from parcimonious and others from Superstitious Prejudices. But We do the best we can, and leave the Event.

How do you like your Government? Does it make or remove Difficulties? I wish We were nearer to you.

The Tories lie very low both here and at New York. The latter will very soon be as deep as any Colony.

We have Major Skeene a Prisoner, enlarged a little on his Parol—a very great Tool.[2] I hope Govr Tryon, will be taken care of.[3] But We find a great many Bundles of weak Nerves. We are obliged to be as delicate and soft and modest and humble as possible. Pray Stir up every Man, who has a Quill to write me. We want to know the Number of your Army—A List of your officers—a State of your Government—the Distresses of Boston—the Condition of the Enemy &c. I am, Dr sir your Friend,   John Adams

We have all recommended Billy Tudor for a secretary to the General. Will he make a good one?

This moment informed of Powder arrived here, 500 Blls they say. We must send it along to you.

RC (MHi:Warren-Adams Coll.); docketed: "Mr J Adams Lettr to Dr. Warren"; docketed in another hand: "recd by Genl. James Warren after the Death of Genl. Joseph Warren."

[1] On 22 June the congress chose in order of rank eight brigadier generals: Seth Pomeroy of Massachusetts, Richard Montgomery of New York, David Wooster of Connecticut, William Heath of Massachusetts, Joseph Spencer of Connecticut, John Thomas of Massachusetts, John Sullivan of New Hampshire, and Nathanael Greene of Rhode Island (JCC, 2:103).

[2] Philip Skene (1725–1810) was formerly a major in the British army, colonel in the New York militia, proprietor of Skenesborough on the shores

of Lake Champlain, and, in 1775, the newly appointed lieutenant governor of Ticonderoga and Crown Point and inspector of lands for Quebec with authorization to raise a regiment. By the time he arrived in America however, Ticonderoga had been taken. Skene's mission represented to the northern colonies a threatening move by the ministry, resulting in his arrest when he landed in Philadelphia on 7 June. JA was more directly involved in this affair than he indicates in this letter. See JA's Service in the Congress, 10 May – 1 Aug.

(above). On 27 June, probably because Skene was dangerously close to the seat of government, the congress ordered him sent to Connecticut to be put under the supervision of Gov. Trumbull, where after some time in prison, he was exchanged for James Lovell on 7 Oct. 1776 (Doris Begor Martin, *Philip Skene of Skenesborough*, Granville, N.Y., 1959, p. 38–66; JCC, 2:108).

³ William Tryon (1729–1788), the former governor of North Carolina and, in 1775, governor of New York (*DAB*).

From John Winthrop

Dear Sir   21 June 1775

I received your favor of May 29 by Messrs. Halls. I was much concerned that I had it not in my power to treat those young Gentlemen with as much respect as their characters and your recommendation entitled them to. When your Letter was deliver'd me, which was but a few days ago, we were all in the utmost hurry, packing up the Library and Apparatus, for their removal to a distance in the country for safety; in consequence of an order of the Provincial Congress which was sent us that day;¹ so that the young Gentlemen could only take a transient view of things as they lay in confusion. It was then universally expected, that there would be an action in a day or two; which happened accordingly. The night following a body of our men were sent to throw up an entrenchment on a hill in Charlstown. As soon as the day light appeared, they were discovered and fired upon from the men of war, and battery on Cop's Hill. That day, the 17th instant exhibited a most shocking spectacle. About 2, afternoon, a large body of regulars were carried over to Charlestown, and at 4, in the afternoon, the men of war's boats set fire to the town in different places, which in a few hours was burnt to the Ground. When it was all in flames, they attacked our entrenchment, which was very imperfect, being only the work of a few hours; but they were vigorously opposed, and a hot engagement ensued, which lasted above an hour, in which, numbers fell. When our soldiers had fired away almost all their cartridges, and the Regulars were entring the entrenchment with their bayonets charged, and an incessant fire of artillery kept on them on all sides from the men of war and floating batteries, our people retreated and left them in possession of the hill. This advantage they probably purchased dear; tho' what their loss was, we may never know exactly. 'Tis affirm'd their dead were seen lying in heaps on the ground. Our loss was considerable; but being now above 20 miles from the scene of action, I cannot give you any particular information about it. We lost some very good officers; but none is more universally lamented than our friend Dr. Warren, who had been appointed a Major General but a day or two before. I own, I was sorry when I heard of this appointment; because I thought, a man so much better qualified to act in other capacities than most are, ought not to be exposed in this way, unless in case of necessity. But his zeal hurried him on, and he was killed in the entrenchment soon after he got there.

We are now involved in all the horrors of war, and are every moment expecting to hear of another action. Is it not necessary Sir that our army should be effectually supported, in order to bring this cruel war to a speedy and fortunate issue? especially as there is no immediate prospect of war in any other part of America; and a vigorous support here may probably prevent its spreading to the other Colonies.

I am surprised to find you have so little intelligence from hence. I thought there had been a constant intercourse kept up between the Provincial and Continental Congresses. I mentioned this hint of yours to Dr. Warren the evening before that fatal day; he promised that he would write, and put his friends on writing. But, alas!

My respectful compliments to all friends, particularly to Col. Hancock and Dr. Franklin. I wrote to the Doctor soon after I heard of his arrival, but know not whether he has received my Letter. I want much to write to some friends in England, but there is no conveyance this way. If Dr. Franklin should be able, with safety, to keep up his correspondence with England, perhaps he might be willing to send my Letters with his. If I could know this, I would send them by the way of Philadelphia. But I own, I am in great doubt whether it will be prudent or practicable.

God Almighty bless your counsels, and render them effectual for the preservation of America. Your faithful friend and humble Servt.

June 22. Since writing the above, I have received two accounts from different hands of the loss on each side. I send them as I had them.[2] I have been also told, that the Regulars acknowlege 428 killed.

Boston almost deserted by the inhabitants—Charlestown burnt down. Cambridge, Medford, Salem, Danvers and Marblehead almost deserted. 'Tis impossible at your distance to conceive of the distress.

RC (Adams Papers); docketed: "Winthrop   21st June 1775."

[1] Because of the presence of army headquarters in Cambridge, the Provincial Congress on 15 June commandeered the college buildings and ordered "that the library, apparatus, and other valuables of Harvard College, be removed" to Andover (Samuel Eliot Morison, *Three Centuries of Harvard, 1636–1936*, Cambridge, 1936, p. 148–149; Mass. Provincial Congress, *Jours.*, p. 334).

[2] Not found.

The Massachusetts Delegates to George Washington

Sir   Phyladelphia June 22. 1775

In Complyance with your Request We have considered of what you proposed to us, and are obliged to give you our Sentiments, very briefly, and in great Haste.

In general, Sir, there will be three Committees, either of a Congress, or of an House of Representatives, which are and will be composed of our best Men; Such, whose Judgment and Integrity, may be most rely'd on; the Committee on the State of the Province, the Committee of Safety, and the Committee of Supplies.

But least this Should be too general, We beg leave to mention particularly Messrs Bowdoin, Sever, Dexter, Greenleaf, Darby, Pitts, Otis of the late Council, Hon. John Winthrop Esq. L.L.D., Joseph Hawley Esqr. of Northampton, James Warren Esqr. of Plymouth, Coll. Palmer of Braintree, Coll. Orne and Elbridge Gerry Esqr. of Marblehead, Dr. Warren, Dr. Church, Mr. John Pitts all of Boston, Dr. Langdon President of Harvard Colledge, and Dr. Chauncey and Dr. Cooper of Boston. Coll. Forster of Brookfield.[1]

The Advice and Recommendations of these Gentlemen, and of Some others whom they may introduce to your Acquaintance may be depended on.

With great Sincerity, We wish you, an agreable Journey and a glorious Campaign; and are with much Esteem and Respect, Sir, your most obedient Servants.

Samuel Adams   John Hancock
John Adams   Thomas Cushing
Robt. Treat Paine

RC in JA's hand (DLC:Washington Papers); addressed in John Hancock's hand: "To the Honble George Washington Esqr.   General and Commander in Chief of all the Forces of the United Colonies   per John Hancock"; docketed: "[. . .] Ju. 22. 1775."

[1] Benjamin Greenleaf (1732–1799) of Newburyport, was a member of the Council from 1770 to 1774; John Pitts (1737–1815), a Boston selectman beginning in 1773, was active in the Sons of Liberty and a member of the Second

and Third Provincial Congresses; Rev. Samuel Langdon (1723–1797), a strong whig, became president of Harvard College by 1774 and a chaplain to the army in Cambridge, soon thereafter serving as chaplain to the Continental Army until it moved south in 1776; Col. Jedediah Foster (1726–1779) was very active in the local affairs of Brookfield, had long service in the House of Representatives, and was rejected for the Council by Gage in 1774 (Sibley-Shipton, *Harvard Graduates*, 13:86–90;

14:197–201; 10:508–526; 11:395–398).

Richard Derby Jr. (1712–1783), a Salem merchant and shipowner, saw service in the House of Representatives before 1774 and as a delegate to the Third Provincial Congress; Col. Azor Orne (1731–1796), Marblehead merchant, attended all three Provincial Congresses (Wroth and others, eds., *Province in Rebellion*, p. 2847, 2884–2885).

From William Tudor

Dear Sir   26 June 1775

You will doubtless before the Receipt of this have heard of the bloody Engagement at Charlestown. For a particular Account of it I must refer You to a Letter I last Week wrote our Friend Collins.[1] The ministerial Troops gain'd the Hill but were victorious Losers. A few more such Victories and they are undone. I cannot think our Retreat an unfortunate one. Such is the Situation of that Hill that we could not have kept it, expos'd to the mighty fire which our Men must have received from the Ships and Batteries that Command the whole Eminence. 800 Provincials bore the Assault of 2000 Regulars and twice repuls'd them, but the Heroes were not supported, and could only retire. Our Men were not us'd to Cannon Balls and they came so thick from the Ships, floating Batteries &c., &c. that they were discouraged advancing. They have since been more us'd to them and dare encounter them. The American Army are in great Spirits, and eager to recover their late Defeat. I wish we had more Discipline But Genl. Washington we hear is coming, and we expect much from his Conduct and Experience. The Colony Forces have thrown up very extensive Lines to secure Cambridge and there are four different Entrenchments in Roxbury. The Regular Troops cannot again fight under the like advantages they did at Charlestown. They have dearly paid for one Mile's Advancement, and before they get another I much doubt if they will have Soldiers enough left to maintain it.

The lower Part of the Province has been in much Confusion and Distress. It is suppos'd 20,000 People from Boston and its Environs have deserted their Habitations, yet I hear of Nobody that thinks of any Thing less than Submission. The universal Voice is, if the Continent approve, and assist we will die or be free. The Sword is drawn and the Scabbard thrown away, till it can be sheath'd with Security and Honour.

I wish I could be near eno' to my worthy Colonel, to congratulate him on his late Proscription. If anything had been wanting to secure to him and Mr. Adams the Hearts of their Countrymen, Genl. Gage's Proclamation would have amply effected it. The Man must surely have felt ridiculous to order martial Law to take Place through a Province, one Town alone of which he had any Command in.[2]

The Loss of Dr. Warren is irreparable, his Death is generally and greatly lamented. But

Dulce et Decorum est pro Patria mori.

This is the Day of Heroes. The Fall of one will inspire the surviving glorious Band to emulate his Virtues and revenge his Death on the Foes of Liberty and our Country. Yours, with great Affection and Respect   Wm. Tudor

RC (Adams Papers); addressed: "John Adams Esq   Philadelphia"; docketed by JA in a late hand: "Tudor   26. June 1775."

[1] Stephen Collins, Quaker merchant and whig, whom Tudor probably met on his trip to Philadelphia in the fall of 1774. See JA to Joseph Palmer, 5 July (below).

[2] On 12 June, Gen. Gage issued a proclamation declaring martial law and offering a pardon to anyone who would lay down his arms except for Samuel Adams and John Hancock, "whose offenses are of too flagitous a nature to admit any other consideration than that of condign punishment" (Force, *Archives*, 4th ser., 2:968–970). Gage probably held little hope for success, for in a letter to Lord Dartmouth on 12 June he mentioned only the declaration of martial law, not the offer of pardons (Gage, *Corr.*, 1:404–405).

To James Warren

My dear Friend   Phyladelphia June 27. 1775

I am extreamly obliged to you for your Favour of the 20th. of June. The last Fall, I had a great many Friends who kept me continually well informed of every Event as it occurred. But, this Time, I have lost all my Friends, excepting Coll Warren of Plymouth and Coll Palmer of Braintree, and my Wife.

Our dear Warren, has fallen, with Laurells on his Brows, as fresh and blooming, as ever graced an Hero.

I have Suffered infinitely this Time, from ill Health, and blind Eyes at a Time when, a vast Variety of great objects were crowding upon my Mind, and when my dear Country was suffering all the Calamities of *Famine, Pestilence, Fire*, and *Sword* at once.

At this Congress We do as well as we can. I must leave it to some future opportunity, Which I have a charming Confidence will certainly come, to inform you fully of the History of our Debates and Resolutions.

Last Saturday night at Eleven O Clock, an express arrived from the worthy Govr. Trumbull, informing of the Battle of Charlestown.[1] An hundred Gentlemen flocked to our Lodgings to hear the News. At one O Clock Mr. H. Mr. A. and myself, went out to enquire after the Committee of this City, in order to beg some Powder. We found Some of them, and these with great Politeness, and Sympathy for their brave Brethren in the Mass. agreed, to go that night and send forward about Ninety Quarter Casks, and before Morning it was in Motion. Between two and three O Clock I got to bed.

We are contriving every Way we can think of to get you Powder. We have a Number of Plans for making Salt Petre and Gentlemen here are very confident, that We shall be able to furnish Salt Petre and Powder of our own Manufacture, and that very Soon. A Method of making it, will be published very soon by one of our Committees.[2]

Before this reaches you, Gen. Washington, Lee, &c will arrive among you. I wish to god, you had been appointed a General Officer, in the Room of some others. Adams and Adams Strove to get it done. But, Notions, narrow Notions prevented it—not dislike to you, but fear of disobliging Pomroy, and his Friends.

Your Government was the best We could obtain for you.[3] We have passed some Resolutions concerning North Carolina, which will do a great deal of good. We have allowed them to raise 1000 Men, and to take Care of Trayters, if necessary.[4] This must be kept secret.

We are sending you, Ten Companies of Rifle Men. These, if the gentlemen of the Southern Colonies are not very partial and much mistaken, are very fine fellows.[5] They are the most accurate Marksmen in the World: they kill with great Exactness at 200 yards Distance: they have Sworn certain Death to the ministerial officers. May they perform their oath.

You will soon find that the Continental Congress are in, deep enough. The Commissions to the officers of the Army; the Vote for your Government; the Votes about North Carolina; and a Multitude of other Votes which you will soon hear of will convince you.

I have inclosed you an Hint about salt Petre.[6] Germans and others here have an opinion that every stable, Dove house, Cellar, Vault &c is a Mine of salt Petre. The inclosed Proclamation, coincides with this opinion. The Mould under stables &c may be boiled soon into salt Petre, it is said. Numbers are about it here.

RC (MHi:Warren-Adams Coll.); addressed: "To the Hon. James Warren Esqr   President of the Provincial Congress at Watertown   These"; docketed: "Mr. J.A. Lettr   June 1775."

[1] Although Palmer, Warren, Gerry, and Winthrop all wrote soon after the event describing the Battle of Bunker Hill (see their letters, 19–21 June, above), it was the dispatch from Trumbull arriving on 24 June that brought the first news and spurred JA and the rest of the delegation to action. The dispatch contained a letter from Trumbull to the congress that briefly mentioned the battle, and that was read to the members on 26 June, but more important, it also included a detailed account written by Elijah Hide of Lebanon, Conn., who had been a spectator on Winter Hill during the battle (PCC, No. 66; JCC, 2:107; *Pennsylvania Gazette*, 28 June). JA's account in his Autobiography dates the arrival of Trumbull's dispatch as 23 June, the day that Washington left for Cambridge—an indication that JA did not consult the records of the congress or a letter he wrote to AA on 23 June (*Diary and Autobiography*, 3:324; *Adams Family Correspondence*, 1:226-227).

[2] Probably the pamphlet entitled *Several Methods of Making Salt-Petre; Recommended to the Inhabitants of the United Colonies by Their Representatives in Congress*, Phila. and Boston, 1775 (Evans, Nos. 14584, 14585).

[3] On 9 June, the congress had resolved that Massachusetts owed no obedience to a Parliamentary act that illegally changed the charter of the province, and that the Provincial Congress should call for elections to a House of Representatives, which would choose a Council. Until a royal governor was willing to abide by the charter, the offices of governor and lieutenant governor should be considered vacant, the powers of governor being exercised meanwhile by the Council (JCC, 2:83–84). JA was not entirely happy with this solution. Years later he explained that "Although this Advice was in a great degree conformable, to the New York and Pensilvania System, or in other Words to the System of Mr. Dickinson and Mr. Duane, I thought it an Acquisition, for it was a Precedent of Advice to the separate States to institute Governments, and I doubted not We should soon have more Occasions to follow this Example" (*Diary and Autobiography*, 3:353-354). Still, at the time, JA remained somewhat uneasy about the advice that had been given Massachusetts. In letters to the Warrens, he pointedly asked how the government was going on (JA to James Warren, 20 June; to Joseph Warren, 21 June, above).

[4] On 26 June the congress resolved that North Carolina should be allowed to raise a body of 1,000 men that would be considered part of the Continental Army with their pay provided by the congress (JCC, 2:107).

[5] But see James Warren to JA, 11 Sept. (below). On 14 June the congress voted to raise six companies from Pennsylvania and two each from Maryland and Virginia, and on 22 June two additional ones from Pennsylvania (JCC, 2:89, 104).

[6] The enclosure has not been found, but see the recipe in JA's hand and the explanatory note written on Joseph Palmer to JA, 19 June (above).

From James Warren

My Dear Sir   Watertown June 27. 1775

I feel great reluctance in suffering any Opportunity to pass without writeing to you. I can easily suppose your Anxiety as well as Curiosity make you sollicitous to hear every thing that passes here.

Since my last nothing material has taken place. The military Operations have Consisted in a few movements and a few Shot Exchanged with very little Effect, sometimes on the side of Roxbury, and sometimes on the side of Charlestown. Our Army have taken every precaution in their power for their defence, and future operations. They are heaving up lines from Charles to Mystick River, and have them in great forwardness. They are Carried across Temples Farm, and his beautiful Groves of Locusts have fallen a sacrifice to the necessity of the Times. At Roxbury they have fortified themselves in a manner almost as Impregnable as Gage has done in Boston. We want but one Article to Enable us to Act offensively, and make a vigorous Campaigne.[1] Men in fine Spirits well provided with every thing but the one I mention. The Generals Appointed give us great satisfaction, especially the first and the third,[2] whose Characters have for a great while been such as to fix our Esteem and Confidence. Your attention must be fixed on the Article of powder, or I will say no more. I cant but Hope you will make some suitable provision for our General Thomas.[3] His Merits in the military way have surprised us all. I cant describe to you the Odds between the two Camps. While one has been Spiritless, sluggish, Confused, and dirty, I mean where Genl. Putnam, and our Friend Warrens Influence have not had their Effects. The other has been Spirited, Active regular, and clean. He has Appeared with the dignity and Abilities of a General. We have no Intercourse with Boston. Get no Intelligence from there but by those who steal out. From them we have certain Accounts of the Amazeing Slaughter made in the last Action. Thier men die of the slightest wounds, oweing to the manner of Living they are reduced to, so there will in the End be but little Odds between being killed or wounded, and we may reckon perhaps 14 or 1500 killed. I am told Genl. Howe says the Army shall not return to Boston but by the way of Roxbury, a very pretty march. It is with Confidence said that Burgoine has not been seen since the Action, and it is given out that he is gone Home. We are not without our Hopes that we shall have little trouble from his Enterprising Genius. With regard to us We are as Busy as you ever Saw Pismires on a mole hill. Our Attention is principally fixed on the Army, to Equip, regulate, quiet, and Inspirit them, and enough it is at times for us. Genls. Washington and Lee I dare say will relieve us. The Inclosed Letter I presume will tell you Mrs. Adams is well.[4] You will remember I had not a line from you by the two last Conveyances. My compliments to all that know me; perticularly to my good Friend Adams who must Excuse my not writeing. Tis not for want of Esteem or Affection. He can hardly Conceive of my hurry. I wish you every happiness, and am yr. Sincere Friend &c

James Warren

I have not been able to Obtain the pamphlet you mentioned and Indeed after seeing it advertised in a York Paper have been less solicitous, supposing you would have it from there.[5]

RC (Adams Papers); docketed by JA: "Warren June 27 1775."

[1] Compare James Warren to JA, 20 June, note 5 (above).

[2] Gens. Washington and Lee, not Artemas Ward, the second in command, whose incompetent leadership is mentioned by Warren below.

[3] Gen. John Thomas was appointed the sixth brigadier on 22 June, an appointment that caused problems in Massachusetts because Thomas was senior to William Heath in the provincial service, but Heath was made fourth brigadier in the Continental Army (*JCC*, 2:103; *Adams Family Correspondence*, 1:237–238, note 1).

[4] Presumably AA's letter of 25 June (*Adams Family Correspondence*, 1:230–233).

[5] Warren may be referring to JA's request of 21 May for a complete copy of *The Group*, since the one published in Philadelphia was incomplete. If so, Warren is referring to the edition of the play published in New York by John Anderson, which would not have met JA's needs since it was also incomplete, omitting the second and third scenes of Act II (Evans, No. 14612).

From Moses Gill

Dear Sir   Spencer July 1 1775

I am Now Acompanyg Genl. Washington and Lee from Springfield to the Camp—having been appointed by Congress with Doctr. Church to proceed to Springfield and Acompany them to the Camp aforesaid. We Meet them at Spring, lodged last Night at Brookfield and are now under the Escort of the Troop of Horse which is to Continue till we arive at Worcester—where we are to be received by an Other Troop which is to Escort us to Morelborogh [Marlborough]—where we are to be received by an other Troop of Horse which is to Land the General at the Camp—*but Now* [no] *Powder used.* I received your Kind Letters but have had no opportunity to answer them till now. Being from Home I must Omitt it till Next Opertunity—as I have Neither pen Ink nor paper here. I heartily Simperthize with you and our good friend at Phila. in the Loss of Dear Doctr. Warren. However God is wise and Holy in all hes don by us or ours. My best respects to Mr. Hancock, Cushing Adams and Paine—and except the same from your Sincere friend and Huml. Svt.   Moses Gill

RC (Adams Papers); addressed: "To the Hone. John Aams at Philadel-[phia]"; docketed by JA in a late hand: "Moses Gill 1 July 1775." The bottom edge of the sheet has been trimmed, cutting off part of the address but none of the text.

To Joseph Palmer

Philadelphia, June [i.e. July][1] *5, 1775*

The bearers of this letter, Mr. Stephen Collins and Mr. John Kaign, are of the peaceable society called Quakers or Friends, yet they are possessed of liberal sentiments, and are very far from being enemies to American principles or practices.[2] They are warm, zealous friends of America, and hearty well wishers to her councils and arms, and have contributed much to promote both in this province.

We have an infernal scoundrel here, a certain Col. S————, who comes over full of plans and machinations of mischief. He has had the most unreserved and unlimited confidence of Lord Dartmouth, during the whole of the past winter, and it seems for some time before; and together with a contemptible puppy of a parson, V————, has been contriving to debauch, seduce, and corrupt New-York. The ministry have given him a commission in the woods as surveyor, and another to be governor of Ticonderoga and Crown Point. He is permitted to roam about, upon his parole of honour not to transgress certain limits, but is doing mischief.[3]

The colonies are not yet ripe to assume the whole government, legislative and executive. They dread the introduction of anarchy, as they call it.

In this province, indeed in this city, there are three persons, a Mr. W————, who is very rich and very timid;[4] the provost of the college, who is supposed to be distracted between a strong passion for lawn sleeves and a stronger passion for popularity, which is very necessary to support the reputation of his Episcopal college;[5] and an I————P————, who is at the head of the Quaker interest: these three make an interest here which is lukewarm; but are all obliged to lie low for the present.[6]

I am greatly obliged to you for your letters, which contain the most exact accounts we have been able yet to obtain. We are to the last degree anxious to learn even the most minute particulars of every engagement.

I want an exact list of all the officers in our army, if it can possibly be obtained.

I wish I could know exactly what powder you have. We are trying our possibles to get it; but one would not have conceived it possible that the colonies should have been so supine as they have been.

A large building is setting up here to make saltpetre, and we are about trying what can be done in the tobacco works in Virginia.

This day has been spent in debating a manifesto setting forth the causes of our taking arms. There is some spunk in it. It is ordered to be printed, but will not be done soon enough to be enclosed in this letter.[7]

MS not found. Reprinted from the *New York Review and Atheneum Magazine*, 2:220–221 (Feb. 1826).

[1] See note 7 (below).

[2] This is one of several letters that were to serve in part as introductions for Stephen Collins and John Kaighn of Philadelphia. In a letter to AA of 4 July, JA gives a brief sketch of each, and AA in a letter to JA of 16 July mentions meeting Collins and Kaighn and gives her impressions of them (*Adams Family Correspondence*, 1:238, 245–251).

[3] For Col. Philip Skene see JA to Joseph Warren, 21 June, note 2 (above). Rev. John Vardill (1749–1811) was a graduate of King's College, which in 1773 appointed him a fellow and professor of natural law. A staunch tory, his writings satirizing the whigs made him the object of a parody in John Trumbull's *McFingal*. In London in 1774 Vardill was ordained a priest in the Anglican Church. He remained in England in an effort to have King's College made a university, an effort that proceeded successfully until the war intervened. Vardill, who never returned to America, served as a spy in the British service from 1775 to 1781. His most important accomplishment was the theft, in 1777, of a packet of dispatches from Silas Deane to the congress containing all of the confidential correspondence between the American Commissioners and the French Government between March and Oct. 1777 (*DAB*; Lewis Einstein, *Divided Loyalties*, Boston, 1933, p. 51–71).

JA's reference to a ministerial plot to subvert the government of New York through Skene and Vardill was probably based on documents examined by JA's committee appointed to deal with Skene. Only two such documents appear in the records of the congress, and Skene reputedly destroyed private papers relating to his mission; yet Eliphalet Dyer of Connecticut, citing private letters from London, also wrote about Skene's purpose of undermining New York's government (PCC, No. 51, I; Doris Begor Morton, *Philip Skene of Skenesborough*, Granville, N.Y., 1959, p. 39; Dyer to Joseph Trumbull, 8 June, in Burnett, ed., *Letters of Members*, 1:115). An unsigned letter dated "London, March 4, 1775," that may have been carried by Josiah Quincy Jr. on his last voyage, states that "a Major Skene, and a Parson Vardell, a native of New York, are to be sent over thither with propositions of advantages for the college, the city, and the Province, and with a list of profitable places for individuals, sufficient, as they conceive,—with the favorable disposition which they are persuaded prevails there,—to draw off that city from the common cause, and attach them to government. They are determined to spare no promises and temporary douceurs to effect their purpose" (MHS, *Procs.*, 4 [1858–1860]:229).

Although Dyer does not mention him, Vardill's involvement in such a scheme would seem plausible, his personal participation being prevented only by the war's outbreak. Indeed, in a memorial dated 16 Nov. 1783 to the Parliamentary commission formed to compensate loyalists, Vardill noted that his service to the crown had begun very early and had included an effort "to secure to Government the Interest of two Members of the Congress by the promise of the Office of Judges in America," which failed only because of the Battle of Lexington. In addition, he stated that the new charter for King's College and his appointment as Regius Professor of Divinity were intended as payment for such services "and to give the Loyalists at New York a Proof of the Attention and Rewards which would follow their Zeal and Loyalty ... and he was ordered to acquaint the President and College with this instance of Royal Patronage" (Einstein, *Divided Loyalties*, p. 409, 412).

⁴ Thomas Willing (1731–1821), a prosperous Philadelphia banker who championed colonial rights while resisting the "radical elements." A member of the Second Continental Congress, he voted against independence (*DAB*). On 23 July JA wrote to AA that "this Province [Pennsylvania] has suffered by the Timidity of two over grown Fortunes," a reference to the wealth of Willing and John Dickinson (*Adams Family Correspondence*, 1:252–253).

⁵ Rev. William Smith (1727–1803), the first provost of the College, Academy, and Charitable School of Philadelphia. In June 1775 he preached the widely published *Sermon on the Present Situation of American Affairs* (T. R. Adams, *American Independence*, No. 196). He was against independence, and because of his resulting unpopularity, he spent most of the war on Barbados but returned after the peace to resume his activities with the college, probably his chief interest. His desire for "lawn sleeves," that is, a bishop's place, was never fulfilled (*DAB*).

⁶ Israel Pemberton (1715–1779), widely known as the "king of the Quakers," although actively involved in politics, opposed any violent means for securing American rights. At the First Continental Congress he was a spokesman for Friends who met with the Massachusetts delegation and called for that colony to grant religious liberty. Refusing to support the Revolution or the constitution of Pennsylvania, he was arrested in 1777 (*DAB*; Isaac Sharpless, *Political Leaders of Provincial Pennsylvania*, N.Y., 1919, p. 212–213).

⁷ The Declaration of the Causes and Necessity for Taking Up Arms was adopted by the congress on 6 July (*JCC*, 2:127–157).

From Mercy Otis Warren

Dear sir   Watertown july 5 1775

I have had the pleasure of seeing several of your Letters in which you Complain that your friends are Rather remiss With Regard to writing you which I think inexcusable at a time when the Liberties of all America and the fate of the British Empire Depend, in a Great Measure on the Result of your Deliberating for if that Respectable Body of which you are a Member, fails, (Either from want of Early inteligence or from any other Cause at this important Crisis) to pursue the wisest Measures what but innevitable Distruction to this Country must follow.

Could I have hoped it was in my power to Give you Either pleasure or Inteligence I should Long Ere this have taken up my pen and added one more to the Triumverate of your friends for be assured there are very few who Can with more sincerity subscribe their names to the List. But as I write in Compliance with Mr. Warrens Request, I must tell you his Application to public affairs Leave him Little time to Attend to the Demands of private friendship. And Could you Look into a Certain Assembly you would not wonder his time is wholly Engrossed or that we ardently wish you may soon be here to assist in the public Counsels of your own Distressed province.

I shall not Attempt to Give you a Description of the ten fold Difficulties that surround us. You have doubtless had it from better Hands. Yet I cannot forbear to drop a tear over the inhabitants of our Capital most of them sent Naked from the City to seek Retreat in the Villages, and to Cast themselves on the Charity of the first Hospitable Hand that will Recive them. Those who are Left behind are Exposed to the daily insults of a Foe Lost to that sense of Honour, Freedom and Valour once the Characteristic of Briton, And Even of the Generosity and Humanity which has Long been the Boast of all Civilised Nations. And while the plauges of Famine, pestilence and tyrany Reign within the walls the sword is Lifted without and the Artilery of war Continually thundering in our Ears.

The sea coasts are kept in Constant Apprehensions of being made Miserable by the Depredations of the once formidable Navy of Briton Now Degraded to A level with the Corsairs of Barbary.

At the same time they are piratticaly plundering the Iles, and pilfering the Barders to feed the swarms of Veteran slaves shut up in the town. They will not suffer a poor fisherman to Cast his hook in the ocean to bring a Little Relief to the Hungry inhabitants without the pittiful Bribe of a Dollar Each to the use of Admiral Grieves [Graves].

The Venal System of the Administration appears to the Astonishment of Every Good man in the Corruption, Duplicity And meaness which Runs through Every Department, and while the faithless Gage will be Marked with Infamy for Breach of promiss (by the Impartial Historian) will not the unhappy Bostonians be Reproached with want of spirit in puting it out of their own power to Resent Repeated injuries by giving these arms into the Hand which would have been better placed in the Heart of A Tyrant. And now they are forbidden Even to Look out from thier own house tops when He sends out his Ruffians to Butcher their Brethern, And wrap in flames the Neighboring towns, but I think this Advertisement was as Great a mark of timidity as the transaction was of a savage Ferosity. The Laws of Gratitude surely Demanded that they should spare that town at Least whose inhabitants from a principle of Humanity saved the Routed troops of *George the third* from total Distruction after the Battle of Lexington.

But Nothing that has yet taken place is more Regreted than the Death of your Friend the Brave, the Humane, the Good Dr. Warren. And though he Fell Covered with Laurels and the Wing of Fame is spread over his Monument we are Almost Led to Enquire why the useful the Virtuous patriot is Cut off Ere He Reaches the Meridian of his days while the Grey Headed Delinquent totters under the Weight of Accumulated Guilt And Counting up his scores is still Adding Crime to Crime till all Mankind Detest the Hoary Wretch,[1] yet suffer him to Live to trifle with the Rights of Society, and to sport with the Miseries of Man.

The people hear are universally pleased with the Appointment of the Generals Washington and Lee. I hope the Delegates of the united Colonies will continue to act with Dignity to themselves and in a Manner which will promote the Glory Virtue and Happiness of America. Let not the indiferent Nor the sanguinary Conduct of any individual damp the ardor of such as are Ready to fly to our assistence and Generously to sacrifice the Enjoyments of Domestic Life in support of freedom, and the Inherent Rights of their Fellow Men.

Your friend Dr. Cooper has just informed me that Dr. Eliot is Confined on Board a man of War and several of the inhabitants of Boston imprisoned.[2] The Crime of the first was the praying for Congresses Continental and provincial, and that of others was wishing success to American arms. Sad Reflections on the times into which we are fallen Crowd fast upon my Mind, but I will not Longer Call of[f] your Attention from most Important Matters by Expressing them.

I have been happy Enough to spend a Considerable part of the present Week with your amiable partner who assured me a Line from me would be agreable And to whom I will show this before I Close it, and if she thinks I have interrupted you too Long I will yet suppress it and only send all my Good Wishes by Every other Hand to whom you will Condescend [to] write. Though no one would be better pleased by such a Mark of your Esteem than your unfeigned Friend,

M. Warren

P.S. The Reason of my spending a week at Watertown and Braintree is Mr. Warrens being Detaned from home a Great Number of Weeks. I hope the time is not far Distant when both you and he may Retire with Honour to the Calm Enjoyments of private Life.

RC (Adams Papers); addressed: "to the Honble John Adams Esqr   Philadelphia."

[1] Gen. Thomas Gage.
[2] The report that Mrs. Warren had that Rev. Andrew Eliot of the New North Church was confined because of his opposition to the British was erroneous (Sibley-Shipton, *Harvard Graduates*, 10:128–159).

To William Tudor

Dear Sir   Phyladelphia July 6. 1775

I have at last the Pleasure of acknowledging your Favour of the 26. June. I have mourned, week after Week, the loss of all my old Correspondents, in a Course of Time when they were of more Consequence to me and to my Errand, than ever. What is become of Tudor? Where is Tudor? Is he gone to England? Is he sick? Is he afraid to write? Is he gone into the Army, and become so intent on War, with his Enemies as to forget his Friends? These were Questions very often in our Mouths.

But the Past shall be forgiven upon Condition, that you keep an exact Journal of occurencies from day to day for the future and transmit it to me by every opportunity.

We have Spent this whole Day in debating Paragraph by Paragraph, a Manifesto as some call it, or a Declaration of the Causes and Necessity of our taking up Arms.[1] It will be printed Tomorrow, and shall be transmitted as Soon as possible. It has Some Mercury in it, and is pretty frank, plain, and clear. If Lord North dont compliment every Mothers Son of us, with a Bill of Attainder, in Exchange for it, I shall think it owing to Fear.

Surely, upon the Same Principle that he has ordered or suffered Gage, to proclaim Adams and Hancock unpardonable, he must order all of Us to be declared so—for all have now gone further than they ever did.

The military Spirit in this City, would agreably Surprize you. It breaks out into a great Variety of Forms—Rifle Men, Indians, Light Infantry, light Horse, Highlanders, with their Plaid and Bag Pipes, and German Hussars.

This Morning a Person came to the Door of the State House where the Congress Sitts, in all his Pontificalibus:[2] I went out to see him. His Errand was to shew us the Dress, and Armour of a German Hussar —a Stout Man, with an high large Cap on his Head, with a Streamer flowing from it down to his Waistband: a deaths Head painted on the Front of it, a large Hussar Cloak, ornamented with golden Cord, Lace, and Fringe, a Scarlet Waistcoat underneath, with gold Button holes and yellow Mettal Buttons, double breasted—a light Musquet, Slung over his shoulder, and a Turkish Sabre or Scymetar by his side, longer, better fortified and more conveniently shaped than an Highland broad sword—His Horse, well bridled, Saddled—Pistols in good Holsters—an active Fellow, Slinging his Firelock and sabre about and mounting with great agility—taken all together the most formidable military Figure, I ever Saw.

It Seems he has a great Inclination to See, Burgoines, light Horse. He tells us, he can inlist immediately 50 or 60, German Veterans who have long Served in Germany, and are as desirous of going in the Character of Hussars, or Troopers, as he is.[3]

This would Set before our New England People, a fine Example for their Imitation: But what is of more Moment, it would engage the Affections of the Germans, of whom there are many in N. York, Pensylvania, Maryland and other Colonies, more intensely in the Cause of America. What will be done, I know not.

Let me intreat you, as you love your Country, and your Friend write me by every opportunity. My Compliments to your Father and Mother and all Friends.   John Adams

RC (MHi:Tudor Papers); addressed: "To Mr. William Tudor Cambridge"; docketed: "July 6th 1775."

[1] See JA to Joseph Palmer, 5 [July], note 7 (above).

[2] Official or ceremonial attire (*OED*).

[3] On 11 July the delegates from Pennsylvania were given permission to "treat with and employ 50 Hussars" and send them to join Washington's army (JCC, 2:173). On 1 Aug., however, the congress reconsidered and decided that the Pennsylvania delegation should not act upon the resolve and should discharge Hussars that had been "engaged or enlisted" (same, p. 238).

To James Warren

Dear Sir   Phyladelphia June [i.e. July] 6th. 1775

Every Line I receive from you, gives me great Pleasure, and is of vast Use to me in the public Cause. Your Letters were very usefull to me last Fall. Your Character became then known, and much esteemed. The few Letters I have received from you this Time, have increased the Desire of more, and some other Gentlemen who happened to know you, particularly Governor Hopkins and Ward of Rhode Island have confirmed, every Good opinion which had been formed. I must intreat you to omit no Opportunity of Writing and to be as particular as possible.

Want of frequent Communication and particular Intelligence led us into the unfortunate Arrangement of General Officers, which is likely to do so much Hurt. We never received the most distant Intimation of any Design to new model your Army; and indeed Some of Us, were obliged to give up our own Judgments merely from Respect to What We took to be the Arrangement of our provincial Congress. I have made it my Business ever Since I heard of this Error, to wait upon Gentlemen of the Congress at their Lodgings, and else where to let them into the secret and contrive a Way to get out of the Difficulty, which I hope We shall effect.[1]

I rejoice to hear of the great military Virtues and Abilities of General Thomas.

Alass poor Warren! Dulce et decorum est pro Patria mori. Yet I regret his Appointment to such a Command. For God Sake my Friend let us be upon our Guard, against too much Admiration of our greatest Friends. President of the Congress Chairman of the Committee of safety, Major General and Chief surgeon of the Army, was too much for Mortal, and This Accumulation of Admiration upon one Gentleman, which among the Hebrews was called Idolatry, has deprived us forever of the Services of one of our best and ablest Men. We have not a sufficient Number of such Men left to be prodigal of their Lives in future.

Every Brain is at Work to get Powder and salt Petre. I hope We shall succeed: but We must be very Œconomical of that Article. We must not use large Cannon, if We can possibly avoid it.

This Letter will go by two fighting Quakers. Mr. Stephen Collins and Mr. John Kaighn. The first is the most hospitable benevolent [man][2] alive. He is a Native of Lynn—a Brother of Ezra Collins of Boston,—is rich, and usefull here. The last has been the Instrument of raising a Quaker Company in this City, who behave well, and look beautifully in their Uniforms. My Love, Duty, Respects &c where due, Adieu,   John Adams

Secret and confidential, as the Saying is,[3]

The Congress, is not yet So much alarmed as it ought to be. There are Still hopes, that Ministry and Parliament, will immediately receed, as Soon as they hear of the Battle of Lexington, the Spirit of New York and Phyladelphia, the Permanency of the Union of the Colonies &c. I think they are much deceived and that We shall have nothing but Deceit and Hostility, Fire, Famine, Pestilence and Sword, from Administration and Parliament. Yet the Colonies like all Bodies of Men must and will have their Way and their Honour, and even their Whims.

These Opinions of Some Colonies which are founded I think in their Wishes and Passions, their Hopes and Fears, rather than in Reason and Evidence will give a whimsical Cast to the Proceedings of this Congress. You will see a Strange Oscilation between Love and

Hatred, between War and Peace. Preparations for War, and Negociations for Peace. We must have a Petition to the King, and a delicate Proposal of Negociation &c. This Negociation I dread like Death. But it must be proposed. We cant avoid it. Discord and total Disunion would be the certain Effect of a resolute Refusal to petition and negociate. My Hopes are that Ministry will be afraid of Negociation as well as We, and therefore refuse it. If they agree to it, We shall have occasion for all our Wit, Vigilence and Virtue to avoid being deceived, wheedled, threatned or bribed out of our Freedom.

If We Strenuously insist upon our Liberties, as I hope and are pretty sure We shall, however, a Negotiation, if agreed to, will terminate in Nothing. It will effect nothing. We may possibly gain Time and Powder and Arms.

You will see an Address to the People of G. Britain another to those of Ireland, and another to Jamaica.[4]

You will also see a Spirited Manifesto.[5] We ought immediately to dissolve all Ministerial Tyrannies, and Custom houses, set up Governments of our own, like that of Connecticutt in all the Colonies, confederate together like an indissoluble Band, for mutual defence and open our Ports to all Nations immediately. This is the system that your Friend has aimed at promoting from first to last; But the Colonies are not yet ripe for it.[6] A Bill of Attainder, &c may soon ripen them.

RC (MHi:Warren-Adams Coll.); addressed: "To the Hon. James Warren Esqr 6th President of the provincial Congress Watertown favoured by Messrs Stephen Collins and John Kaighn"; marked: "on the public Service"; subscribed: "John Adams"; docketed: "Mr. J A. Letter June 1775."

[1] The issue was, at first, the competency of Artemas Ward as compared with John Thomas, but it soon resolved itself into what position Thomas should have among the brigadier generals appointed on 22 June. At that time the aged Seth Pomeroy had been placed first and Thomas, whom many in Massachusetts believed to be their most able general, sixth, below William Heath, his subordinate in the Massachusetts army (James Warren to JA, 20, 27 June; Gerry to Massachusetts Delegates, 20 June; JA to Joseph Warren, 21 June, all above). By 6 July, JA was aware that a mistake had been made and began efforts to rectify it. He was aided by the action of Washington, who, on reaching Cambridge and being informed of the dissatisfaction, held back the commissions until the congress could act (Freeman, *Washington*, 3:488–489). On 19 July, on Washington's recommendation, JA moved to put Thomas first among the brigadiers in the place of Pomeroy, who had not taken up his commission (JCC, 2:191; *Adams Family Correspondence*, 1:237–238). The action by the congress brought the controversy to a successful conclusion as far as Massachusetts was concerned, but problems remained in the ranking of brigadiers. See JA to James Warren, 23 July (below).

[2] MS torn here.

[3] This communication is written on p. 3 of a large folded sheet, of which the signed letter takes up p. 1 and about half of p. 2. The secret information is written in a small hand and crowded lines with such wide margins that it

takes up only a middle strip of the page.

[4] These addresses are in *JCC*, 2:163–171, 212–218, 204–206.

[5] The Declaration of the Causes and Necessity for Taking Up Arms.

[6] Perhaps this is the earliest avowal of JA's desire for something approaching independence, which he had indignantly rejected in his Novanglus letters (JA, *Papers*, 2:263, 336). In those, he had argued for separate states under a common king. Aside from this position, his "radicalism" had meant insisting upon united and firm action in dealing with Great Britain. Rather than petitions and addresses, he had preferred increased defenses and negotiations only from a position of strength. Now, in advocating the establishment of "Governments of our own, like that of Connecticutt," a nearly self-governing colony, he would seem to be rejecting the Massachusetts charter and thus with it the prerogatives of the king. Connecticut, of course, was under the king and on occasion had been forced to bow to the royal will, but with its elected governor it would have seemed to someone from Massachusetts virtually free of the royal presence. It is impossible to say whether JA meant the change he was advocating to be permanent. In a letter to Warren of 24 July (below), he writes of "Peace and Reconcilliation" and negotiation.

In revealing to Warren the actions of the congress and his own opinion of them, JA was violating for the first time the rule of secrecy imposed by the congress on 11 May (*JCC*, 2:22). Certainly the violation stemmed from JA's frustration, but it may have had a more immediate cause—his confrontation with John Dickinson, described in JA's Autobiography (*Diary and Autobiography*, 3:317–318). This event occurred during the debate on the second petition to the king, which ended on 5 July (*JCC*, 2:127). This first disregard for secrecy rules began a series of letters equally revealing of the divisions within the congress, which culminated on 24 July with the famous reference to John Dickinson as a "piddling Genius" (JA to James Warren, 11, 23, 24 July, below; to AA, 7, 23, 24 July, *Adams Family Correspondence*, 1:241–243, 252–254, 255–258).

To James Warren

Dr Sir   Phyladelphia June [i.e. July] 6th. 1775

I have this Moment Sealed a Letter to you which is to go by my hospitable, honest, benevolent Friend Stephen Collins. But, I have several Particulars to mention to you, which are omitted in that Letter. Ten Companies of expert Riflemen have been ordered already, from the 3 Colonies of P. M. and V.—some of them have marched, under excellent Officers.[1] We are told by Gentlemen here that these Riflemen are Men of Property and Family, some of them of independent Fortunes, who go from the purest Motives of Patriotism and Benevolence into this service. I hope they will have Justice done them and Respect shewn them by our People of every Rank and order. I hope also that our People will learn from them the Use of that excellent Weapon a Rifled barrell'd Gun.

A few Minutes past, a curious Phenomenon appeared at the Door of our Congress. A german Hussar, a veteran in the Wars in Germany, in his Uniform, and on Horse back. A forlorn Cap upon his Head, with a Streamer waiving from it half down to his Waistband, with a

Deaths Head painted in Front a beautifull Hussar Cloak ornamented with Lace and Fringe and Cord of Gold, a scarlet Waist coat under it, with shining yellow metal Buttons—a Light Gun strung over his shoulder—and a Turkish Sabre, much Superiour to an high Land broad sword, very large and excellently fortifyed by his side—Holsters and Pistols upon his Horse. In short the most warlike and formidable Figure, I ever saw.

He says he has fifty Such Men ready to inlist under him immediately who have been all used to the service as Hussars in Germany, and desirous to ride to Boston immediately in order to see Burgoignes light Horse. This would have a fine Effect upon the Germans through the Continent, of whom there are Multitudes. What will be done is yet uncertain. I should not myself be fond of raising many Soldiers out of N. England. But the other Colonies are more fond of sending Men than I expected. They have their Reasons, Some plausible, Some whimsical. They have a Secret Fear, a Jealousy, that New England will soon be full of Veteran Soldiers, and at length conceive Designs unfavourable to the other Colonies. This may be justly thought whimsical. But others Say, that by engaging their own Gentlemen and Peasants, and Germans &c they shall rivit their People to the public Cause. This has more weight in it. But that it may have this Effect it is necessary that all who shall be sent, be respectfully treated.

RC (MHi:Warren-Adams Coll.); not addressed but probably sent along with JA's other letter to Warren of this date, above; docketed: "Mr. J A Lettr June 1775."

[1] See JA to James Warren, 27 June, note 5 (above).

From William Tudor

Dr Sir   Cambridge July 6th 1775

I received your very kind Letter last Evening and this Morning had the Honour of being introduc'd to Genl. Washington by Majr. Mifflin, and through Your Reccommendation was very genteely notic'd.[1] I had an Invitation from the General to dine with him tomorrow, when I shall attempt making a proper Use of your Hints. I have been intirely idle ever since the Communication with the Town of Boston was interrupted. At a Time when every Nerve of every Citizen should be stretch'd in the Service of our bleeding Country it was with Pain I found I could not be useful. The Manner in which Commissions in the Army were granted, precluded me from obtaining one, and the Numbers who sought Employment in the other Departments necessitated me to wait for some more favourable Opportunity. Indeed the very little Method or Arrangement that appear'd in the Conduct of Matters, made me decline solliciting any Office.

The General has not yet settled his Family. Having only one aid de camp, and Secretary. Mr. Reed was appointed Secretary before the General reach'd Cambridge.[2] I have some Expectation of being in that Office with him. Which will make me one of the General's Family. And I shall be in the Way at least of being known. You will please Sir to make my most respectful Acknowlegements to each Gentleman who did me the Honour of mentioning me to the General.

It has given vast Satisfaction to find the Continent have undertaken the Conduct of the War. The Plans of our Provincial Congress were narrow, and very inadequate to the Great Design. We are not to cope with Great Britain without the most powerful Exertions. Our frugal Representatives have been always so careful of the Public Money, that they are confounded at the Prospect before them. It is computed the Expence of the Army is £120,000 sterling monthly.

I have heard it quoted as a shrewd Observation, that G. Britain had began this Quarrel fifty Years too late, and the Colonies fifty Years too soon, and that by the Mistake of each both would be ruin'd. The first Part of this Position I believe true, but the Colonies are not an Hour too soon. In 20 Years the Arts of Corruption would have debauch'd so many that I doubt whether a majority could have been found to have resisted the most iniquitous Measures. Massachusetts and York felt its Influence, and it would soon have found its Way through the Continent.

Our Army are in good Spirits, but still want Discipline. The Importance of implicit Obedience to the Orders of their Officers, is not yet sufficiently felt and acknowleged by the Ranks. A hardy, free Spirited Yeomanry, all their Lives unus'd to Controul cannot easily brook it. Your most oblig'd and very hum. Servt.   Wm. Tudor

RC (Adams Papers); addressed: "John Adams Esq   Philadelphia."

[1] See JA to Tudor, 20 June (above).
[2] Joseph Reed was named secretary before Washington left Philadelphia, although Reed agreed only to a temporary appointment (Freeman, *Washington,* 3:460).

From Jonathan Williams Austin

Dr Sir   Camp Cambridge July 7th: 1775

I received yours of the 20th June,[1] and am very much obliged to you, for your Kindness in mentioning my Name to General Washington. I have since waited on his Excellency and find him answer the high Character we conceived of him. General Lee has treated me with great politeness.

We are very much pleased with the continental Congress having adopted and organized the Army. There never was greater need of it. The Massachusetts Soldiers in particular are very deficient in almost every thing but Courage. The Officers and privates are so far on a Levell, that the former do not receive the Respect and Obedience which is due to their Station. Some Regiments however are much preferable to others. And since the Arrival of General Washington, things wear a quite different Aspect. He has in a manner inspired Officers and Soldiers with a taste for Discipline and they go into it readily, as they all venerate and love the General.

You have I suppose ere this heard of the action at Bunker's Hill. Posterity will with Difficulty believe that about 8 or 10,00 Provincials could make such Slaughter, of well disciplind, regular Troops. They fight like Men who are conflicting pro Aris et Focis,[2] for all that is dear to them, and ⟨*much more willing*⟩ seem to die with the Enthusiasm of martyrs. I love my Countrymen, and when I go into Battle, I go with a Band of Brothers, who seem to be animated with one Soul. Our Men were orderd on the night of, the 16th of June, to fortify a Hill a little below Bunker's Hill. They compleatd this that night. As soon as this was percieved by the Enemy in the morning they began to fire very briskly from the Ships in the Harbour and from some very heavy Cannon on Cob's Hill. About one o'Clock the Regulars came off to the Number of 5000 commanded by General How. They were cover'd by the Fire from Cob's Hill, from the Ships in the Harbour, and a number of floating Batteries, who came all around Us. One Ship was so scituated as to rake Charlestown Neck and prevent if possible any assistance going to the Hill. This however was not effectual for our Men went thro as calmly as if all was quiet, till they were stopd by some Officers, whose Conduct was very unworthy their Station. Our Men on the Hill after having stood the Enemies very heavy fire, till all their Ammunition was expended—till the Regulars had even got, some of them into the Breastwork were obliged to retreat, but not untill they had made the Enemy pay very dear for their

Advantage. The truest Return of the Enemy's Loss is the following, which was sent out of Boston, and which we think here is pretty exact: [3]

92	commission'd Officers	⎫
102	Serjants	⎬ killd
100	Corporals	⎪
753	Rank and file	⎭
1047	Total killd	
445	Wounded	
1492	Total	

Our Loss is computed to about 140 killd, 30 taken, among whom is a L. Colonel, and better than 200 wounded.[4] But what would cloud any Satisfaction we might otherwise take is the Loss of that Great and good Man Major General Warren. Regardless of himself his whole Soul seemd to be fill'd with the Greatness of the cause he was engaged in, and while his Friends were dropping away all around him, gave his orders with a surprising Calmness, till having seen the Enemy in the breast work he unwillingly left the front and then fell amid heaps of Slaughter'd Enemies. He is now gone, and closes an illustrious Life, with all the Glory those can acquire who bleed and die for the preservation of the Rights of their Country and Mankind. Col. Gardner is also dead.

We have now fortified Prospect Hill, so call'd in a very strong Manner. This is a large Hill between Cambridge and Charlestown. The Lines extend each Side of that Hill from Winter Hill to Cambridge River. The Enemy have fortified Bunker's Hill. They are very unwilling to make any further Trial of American Courage any further at present.

The Inhabitants of Boston remain there without any possibility of their coming out. We suppose there is now one Quarter part of them there. Mr. James Lovell has been in close Confinement in Goal with a Number of others. One thing I must not omit with Respect to Mr. Lovell. General Gage sent a permit to all the prisoners to have the Liberty of the Yard. All accepted but Mr. Lovell. He told them he despis'd the Favor. He was an American, was entituled to all the priveledges of a Freeman, but was deprived of them by Treachery and Injustice—and Confinement was the same thing in his Opinion.[5]

With Respect to the officers of our Army I have not had an Opportunity of informing myself particularly but will do it very soon. I should be much obligd to you if you would favor me with what passes at the Southward Camp. Intelligence is not much to be depended on. You will mention my respectfull Compliments to those Gentlemen who went from this Colony. I am with Respect, Your sincere Friend and Humble Sevt.

Jon Williams Austin

RC (Adams Papers); addressed: "The Honourable John Adams Esqr. one of the Members of the honbl. Continental Congress at Philadelphia"; docketed: "[Jon?] Williams Austin July 7th 1775 X"; docketed, probably in the hand of Rev. William Gordon: "Jonathan Williams Austin July 7. 1775."

[1] Not found.
[2] For our altars and firesides or for God and country.
[3] Compare with James Warren to JA, 20 June, note 6 (above).
[4] Compare with Gerry to Massachusetts Delegates, 20 June, note 5 (above).
[5] See the account of this incident in Sibley-Shipton, *Harvard Graduates*, 14: 37.

From James Warren

My Dear Sir   Watertown July 7th. 1775

I am much Obliged to you for your favours[1] by the Sage, Brave, and Amiable General Washington, by Major Mifflin, and by the Express, which came to hand the Night before last. I am much pleased with General Washington. He fully Answers the Character you have given of him. Major Mifflin I have not yet found out, tho' I am told he was once in the Room while I was at the Generals. I shall take perticular Care to know him soon, perhaps this day, as I am to dine with the General. General Lee I have seen but a Minute. He appears to me a Genius in his way. He had the Marks about him of haveing been in the Trenches. I heartily rejoice at the Appointment of these two Generals, and I dare say it will give you pleasure to hear that every Body seems to be satisfied with it. I have not heard a single word Uttered against it. This is more than I Expected with regard to the second, since their Arrival everything goes well in the Army. They are quiet, Busy, and forming fast to Order. Our Business lessens upon our Hands, and we find A great relief from the Generals Arrival. I am told they are very Active &c. You will have a return of the Army from the General I suppose, who will be able to give it with more Accuracy than any Body. The General Estimation of our Army is about 16 or 17000, Ten of which are at Cambridge &c. the remainder at Roxbury. We cant with any Certainty determine the Numbers of the Enemy, we suppose from the Best Grounds we have that when the York Troops Arrive which are daily Expected they will amount to 9,000 at least, perhaps more Including the Black and White Negroes Engaged in their Service in Boston.[2] The Battle of Charlestown gave them A great Shock. It is now pretty Certain that near 1500, and cheifly of their best Troops, among which were about 90 Officers were killed and wounded, about 1000 of which were killed. This is Amazeing but I belive true. I will Endeavour to get and Enclose the return Exact as we have it. Your Appointment of the Other Generals I cant Say is so well Approved of. We cant Investigate the Principle you went on tho' I think I can Trace an Influence that Marks some of them. But I will say no more on that head. You have enough of it in A Letter I wrote in Conjunction with H. and G.[3] The General was very Sorry and somewhat Embarrassed with the Neglect of Thomas. I am told Heath behaves very well, and is willing to give place to him.[4] I am much Obliged to you and my Friend Adams for thinking of me. I am Content to move in A Small Sphere. I Expect no distinction but that of an honest Man who has Exerted every nerve. You and I must be Content without A Slice from the great pudding now on the Table. The Condition of the poor People of Boston is truely miserable. We are told that Jas. Lovel, Master Leach, and others are in Goal for some trifeling offences the last for drinking Success to the American Army. Their offenses may be Capital. It is reported that Doctr. Elliot and Mather are on Board A Man of War.[5] From these Circumstances you may form an Idea of their Situation.

I am very Sorry for the trouble given you by your Companions and Eyes. I hope to hear the last are better, if not the first. I am much pleased with your doings in General, and the Prospects you hold up to me. Is it not our Duty to pray that the Infatuation of Britain may last one year more at least. The powder you sent us Arrived Yesterday and was viewed as it passed with a kind of pleasure I suppose you felt in sending it. The want of that Article is the only Obstacle I have in geting Through A project of mine for a Fleet. I made the motion early in the Sessions, and though opposed by Pickering &c. this is the only reason that prevailed.[6] We Talk of rising Tomorrow. I hope we Shall. I long to ramble in the Fields a day or two and more especially since they have been watered with delightful Showers. I met Mrs. Warren at Braintree, and spent the last Sabbath with Mrs. Adams. Cant you suppose me very Happy in the Company of two such Ladies. The Inclosed Letter will Inform you the Family is well.[7] I brought Mrs. Warren here, and Mrs. Adams and A Number of your Braintree Friends came and dined with us on Wednesday. I shall Wish to see you As soon As matters will Admit of it I am Just Informed An Express is going from the General, and therefore Conclude and am Your Friend &c.   Jas. Warren

Pray give my regards to My Friend Adams. Apologize for me. I thank him for his Letter, and will write to him very soon.

I cant Send you A List of the officers of our Army. I hope you wont make Establishments for them in proportion to what you hint is done for the Generals. High Establishments will not be relished here, and I think Bad Policy in every view, and will Lead us fast into the Sins, follys and Sufferings of our old Impolitic and unnatural Mother. There is a printed account of the Battle got out of Boston giveing A pompous account of their Victory over the Rebels With a great Slaughter made Among them, and with A Loss only of 170 on their Side. This lyeing paper I Cannot obtain for you.[8]

RC (Adams Papers); docketed by JA in a late hand: "Warren July 7 1775."

[1] JA's letters of 20, 21, 27 June (above).

[2] *Dict. of Americanisms* cites this passage from Warren's letter as an example of "white Negro" meaning "a Negro of an exceptionally light, often albinic complexion." Yet given the context, there is no reason why Warren would mention light-complexioned Negroes. More likely, the term was one of opprobrium to condemn white laborers willing to serve the British in the besieged town of Boston.

[3] "G" is probably Elbridge Gerry, and "H," Joseph Hawley. The letter may be that from Gerry to the Massachusetts Delegates of 20 June (above).

[4] See the first of two letters from JA to Warren, 6 July, note 1 (above).

[5] James Lovell (1737–1814) and John Leach (1724–1799) were both imprisoned for sending to the patriot forces information on conditions in Boston and the disposition of British troops. In Lovell's case the arrest arose directly from his letters to Joseph War- ren that were found on Warren's body after the Battle of Bunker Hill (Sibley-Shipton, *Harvard Graduates*, 14:36–39; "A Journal Kept by John Leach, during His Confinement by the British, in Boston Gaol, in 1775," *NEHGR*, 19: 255–263 [July 1865]). Neither Rev. Andrew Eliot nor Rev. Samuel Mather, the only ministers left in Boston, was arrested by the British (Sibley-Shipton, *Harvard Graduates*, 7:232–233).

[6] On 10 June, Warren had been appointed a member of a committee to "consider the expediency of establishing a number of armed vessels." The proposal was allowed to die on 20 June (Mass. Provincial Congress, *Jours.*, p. 318, 358). On Pickering see Warren to JA, 11 July, note 3 (below).

[7] AA to JA, 5 July, *Adams Family Correspondence*, 1:239–240.

[8] Probably the untitled broadside on the Battle of Bunker Hill printed by John Haine in Boston on 26 June (MHi).

To James Warren

Dr Sir   Philadelphia July 10th. 1775

I have just Time to inclose You, a Declaration and an Address. How you will like them I know not.[1]

A Petition was Sent Yesterday, by Mr. Richard Penn in one ship and a Duplicate goes in another Ship, this day.[2] In exchange for these Petitions, Declarations and Addresses, I Suppose We shall receive

Bills of Attainder and other such like Expressions of Esteem and Kindness.

This Forenoon has been Spent in an Examination of a Mr. Kirtland a worthy Missionary among the Oneida Indians.[3] He was very usefull last Winter among all the Six Nations, by interpreting and explaining the Proceedings of the Continental Congress, and by representing the Union and Power of the Colonies, as well as the Nature of the Dispute.

The Congress inclines to wait for Dispatches from General Washington before they make any Alteration, in the Rank of the Generals, least they should make Some other Mistake. But every Body is well inclined to place General Thomas in the Stead of Pomroy.

You must not communicate, without great Discretion what I write about our Proceedings, for all that I hint to you is not yet public. I am &c.,

RC (MHi:Warren-Adams Coll.); docketed: "July 1775."

[1] The Declaration of the Causes and Necessity for Taking Up Arms and the Address to the Inhabitants of Great Britain. The first was passed on 6 July, the other on 8 July (*JCC*, 2:127–157, 162–171).

[2] The Olive Branch Petition, or second petition to the King, was carried to England by Richard Penn (1735–1811), the grandson of William Penn and lieutenant governor of Pennsylvania, 1771–1773. Although he did not support the American cause, he performed his mission, answering questions about conditions in America while the petition was being considered in the House of Lords (*DAB*). The King, however, refused to give any answer to the colonists' petition.

[3] Rev. Samuel Kirkland (1741–1808), a missionary to the Oneida Indians, was instrumental in 1774 and 1775 in preventing the outbreak of a general Indian war that might have complicated the Revolution or even produced the need for British aid. In 1775 he persuaded the Oneidas to declare their neutrality and obtained a general declaration of neutrality from the Six Nations that was, however, not kept. Kirkland did manage to keep the Oneidas and Tuscaroras loyal to America, and during the war he directed Oneida scouts, who gained valuable information on the movement of British troops (*DAB*). On 18 July the congress resolved to pay Kirkland $300 for his expenses and recommended that he be employed among the Six Nations to secure their friendship and neutrality (*JCC*, 2:187).

To James Warren

Hond & Dr Sir   Philadelphia July 11th: 1775

I have the Pleasure of inclosing you, a Declaration. Some call it a Manifesto. And We might easily have occasioned a Debate of half a Day, whether, it Should be called a Declaration or a Manifesto.[1]

Our Address to the People of Great Britain, will find many Admirers among the Ladies, and fine Gentlemen: but it is not to my

Taste. Prettynesses Juvenilities, much less Puerilities, become not a great Assembly like this the Representative of a great People.

July 23

We have voted twenty two thousand Men for your Army. If this is not enough to encounter every officer and Soldier in the british Army, if they were to send them all from Great Britain and Ireland I am mistaken.

What will N. England do with such Floods of Paper Money? We shall get the Continent nobly in our Debt. We are Striking off our Paper Bills in Nine different sorts. Some of twenty Dollars, some of Eight, 7 6 5 4 3 2 1. We shall be obliged to strike off four Milliens of Dollars I fear.[2]

Secret as usual. Our Fast has been kept more Strictly and devoutly than any sunday was ever observed in this City. The Congress heard Duche in the Morning and Dr Allisen in the Evening.[3] Good sermons.

By the way do let our Friend Adams's son be provided for as a surgeon.[4]

RC (MHi:Warren-Adams Coll.); docketed: "Mr. J A Lettr   July 1775."

[1] See Julian Boyd's penetrating analysis of the Declaration of the Causes and Necessity for Taking Up Arms, in which he demonstrates that, contrary to the usual assumption, the Dickinson draft strengthened the language of Jefferson's draft and made the Declaration more "inflammatory" in some of its points (Jefferson, *Papers*, 1:187–192). JA thought that the Declaration might well be the basis for bills of attainder against members of the congress (JA to William Tudor, 6 July, above).

[2] The congress had authorized two million paper dollars in June and an additional million was ordered struck off in July. By the end of 1775, six million were issued (E. James Ferguson, *The Power of the Purse*, Chapel Hill,

1961, p. 26).

[3] For the resolution for a fast day, see JA's Service in the Congress, 10 May – 1 Aug. (above). On 15 July the congress voted to ask Rev. Jacob Duché to preach in the morning and Rev. Francis Allison to preach in the afternoon (JCC, 2:185). For an interesting analysis of the implications of the fast resolution, see Perry Miller, "From the Covenant to the Revival," in *The Shaping of American Religion*, ed. James Ward Smith and A. Leland Jamison, Princeton, 1961, p. 322–330.

[4] Samuel Adams Jr. (1751–1788) was made a surgeon in the army on or about 4 Aug. (Sibley-Shipton, *Harvard Graduates*, 17:334–336).

From Edward Dilly

Dear Sir   London July 11th 1775

Every line from you gives me much satisfaction, my Heart Sympathizes with you in your present distress. I cannot write so fully as I could Wish, may Heaven Bless, Protect, and Prosper you, I have sent you a few things per Capt. Falkner hope they will arrive safe and prove acceptable, adieu my Dear Sir. Yours affectionately   ED

The small Parcel by the Paul, Capt. Gordon which you say is not come to Hand,[1] was sent to the care of Mr. Henry Bromfield. Beg you will make enquiry about it.

RC (Adams Papers); docketed: "recd Septr. 12 the day I arrived at Philadelphia."

[1] See Dilly to JA, 13 Jan., with explanations there, and Alexander McDougall to ?, 14 April (JA, *Papers*, 2:211–212, 414–415).

From Josiah Quincy

Dear Sir   July 11. 1775

Your amiable Lady tells me, you have often complained of your Friends not writing to you. I should have wrote to you, but was unwilling to be troublesome; for I concluded, your Head, your Heart, and your Hands must be so full, so anxious, and incessantly laboring to save your Country, that a Letter, even from a Friend, would be rather a Burthen than a Pleasure; and this Sentiment (I doubt not) has caused others, besides myself, to refrain from writing to you.

Whilst we jointly mourn, the Loss of a *Warren* and a *Quincy*,[1] who have perished in the Storm of Tyranny and oppression, that almost overwhelms our american Ship of State; may that God, in whose Hands our Breath is and whose are all our Ways, graciously preserve the Lives of our remaining skilfull Pilots, and enable them to steer the shattered Bark into the *Harbor* of *Peace Liberty* and *Safety*! So well constructed a Ship, and so richly laden ought not to become the Prize of *Robbers* and *Pirates*. Before that should happen, were all the Crew of my Mind, we would maintain the *Conflict* to the last Man. However, if General Lee's Judgment may be relied upon, the Ship is in no great Danger of being finally lost; for he last year publickly gave it as his Opinion, that, if the americans gained the first Victory, it would prove decisive; Whereas, their Enemies might gain several, and be, at last, defeated. Hitherto, they have certainly failed of Success; for, altho they obliged our Troops to retreat, from the Hill in Charlestown, where they were imprudently directed to begin an Intrenchment; yet, their Valor was invincible, whilst their Ammunition lasted; and they killed and wounded so many of their Enemies, that a few more such Victories would certainly ruin them. In short my Friend, had we a sufficient Supply of Powder and battering Cannon, such is the Spirit and Intrepidity of our brave Countrymen, we should very soon, and with little or no Hazard, lock up the

Harbor and make both Seamen and Soldiers our prisoners at Discretion.

My Head has been teeming with Projects of this kind ever since you left us; and had one of them been timely seconded by the Committee of Safety, we should (I believe) happily have saved the further Effusion of human Blood. You know, my Situation gives me an Opportunity to see, and observe everything that passes up and down the Harbor.[2] About a Week or 10 Days after the Battle at Lexington, I was informed that a large Transport was ordered to take on board from the Castle a 1000 or 1200 barrels of Powder, and 20 or 30 Pieces of brass Cannon 24 and 42 pounders; with which she fell down between the Castle and Spectacle Island and there anchored under the Protection of a 70 gun Ship.[3] A few Days afterward the Man of war was ordered to Sail for New York, upon which I informed the Committee of Safety of the Situation and Circumstances of the Store Ship and her Cargo; that now was the time to secure a sufficient Supply of Powder and heavy Cannon, by seizing the Ship as soon as the *Asia* left her. They seemed to be sensible of the Importance of the Object; but such a complicated Body was too slow in its Motion to improve the lucky Minute and catch such an *inestimable Prize*: for about a Week after the *Asia* sailed, and the very Morning of the Day that the late worthy Dr. Warren, at the Head of a subcommittee came to take a View of the Transport, and determin upon the Mode of Surprizing Her, another 70 Gun Ship anchored just by her. The letting such a favorable opportunity slip unimproved, verifys a very just tho' *trite* Observation that the military Department ought always to be under one Direction; and I devoutly pray, for my dear Country's sake, we may have no further Proofs of it.

The Inconveniences, not to say Distresses, in Consequence of a total stop to our Navigation, will, I fear, soon become insupportable, unless an adiquate Remedy can be found. Permit me (with Freedom) to communicate my Thoughts to you upon the Subject.

I am unable to concieve, any Method so likely to secure our Navigation (Coastwise) as *Row Gallies*. They are calculated to go in shoal Water, and navigated with many Men, are armed with Swivels, and one large battering Cannon in the Bow of each. By this, they can keep off any Vessel of one Tier of Guns. One such Vessel (I apprehend) might securely convoy 10 or a Dozn. provision Vessels, from Harbor to Harbor, in the summer Season.

As the whole Continent is so firmly united, why might not a Number of Vessels of War be fitted out, and judiciously stationed,

3. JOSIAH QUINCY (1710–1784),
BY JOHN SINGLETON COPLEY, ABOUT 1767
See pages ix–x

so, as to intercept and prevent any Supplies going to our Enemies; and consequently, unless they can make an Impression Inland, they must leave the Country or starve.

Floating Batteries is another Mode of anoying our Enemies which (I apprehend) might be successfully carried into Execution. I have in general a clear Idea of their Construction, and intend, if I can procure a Workman, to form a Model of one; but every Scheme of this Nature depends upon a full supply of Ammunition and heavy Cannon; which I hope the Wisdom of the Continent will soon be able to provide.

I had the Pleasure, last Wednesday of waiting on Mrs. Adams Mrs. Q———— &ca [4] to Watertown where we were kindly invited, received and entertain'd by Mr. President Warren and Lady. In our Way thither we were met by Genl. Washington Genl. Lee and their two Aid D' Camps. I beg'd Leave to make my Self known to them; was very graciously received, and had the Honor of introducing them to your good Lady. Genl. Lee complaind, that he did not find Things as the Massachusetts Delagates had represented them; but, hoped all Difficulties would soon be surmounted.

Our Enemies, (since the Action at Charlestown) are quite silent, save, now and then, a Carcase,[5] or a 24 pounder. Whether, they have received some disagreable News, or their repeated Losses have discouraged them; or they are preparing to give us a direful Blast, is, at present, problematical; however, this is certain, they are diabolically oppressive, and cruel to those they have in their Power. Poor young Master Lovel, (if not already) will probably soon fall a Victim, to their insatiable Thirst for Blood; on Account of the Contents of some Letters from him, which were found in Dr. Warren's Packets and which, they say, *contain Matters of a treasonable Nature.*[6]

I have only Room to add, my respectfull Regards to good Dr. F————n, and to your worthy Brethren, the Delagates from this Colony; which please to make acceptable to them, and believe me to be, Your Affect. & faithfull hum. Servt.   an Old Friend[7]

RC (Adams Papers).

[1] His son Josiah Quincy Jr., who died in April 1775 just as he arrived in Gloucester Harbor from England. For his mission, see JA, *Papers*, 2:168, note 2.

[2] Quincy's home was at Mount Wollaston, on the shore of Quincy Bay, from which he had an excellent view of Boston Harbor.

[3] For these islands see A Plan of the Town and Harbour of Boston, illustration No. 9.

[4] Ann Marsh Quincy (1723–1805), a close friend of AA's, who became Josiah Quincy's third wife (Sibley-Shipton, *Harvard Graduates*, 8:469).

[5] Or "carcass," a round shell holding inflammable material which flames out

of the shell's three holes as it is fired from a mortar or gun; used for the destruction of wooden defenses (*OED*).

⁶ Compare this account with that in James Warren to JA, 7 July (above).

⁷ The handwriting, as well as JA's specific reply of 29 July (below), clearly identifies the author as Col. Josiah Quincy (1710–1784), prominent Braintree citizen and Boston merchant.

From James Warren

My dear Sir   Watertown July 11. 1775

I wrote you several days ago, and wrote in a hurry, Expecting the Generals Express would be along before I could finish, but he has been detained, and am told will be on his Journey this Morning. I was much Chagrined Last Evening when setting under a Tree by the Bridge Fessenden rode up from Philadelphia without a Single Letter for me. He says you Complain that you have no Letters. I have Endeavoured to do my part. I Expected we should have rose before this, and I should have got a range over the fields before our Election but I begin to despair. One thing after another continually Crouds upon us. The General thinks he should have more Men. I am of the same opinion. How to get them is our difficulty. We are now raising 1700 for the Express purpose of guarding the Sea Coasts.¹ The People are so Engaged at this Busy Season that the Militia if called would come with reluctance, and Tarry but a short time. Just long enough to put the Camp in Confusion. What Course we are to take in Consequence of an Application from the General which now only detains us, I know not. I could wish to have seen more men from the Southward. I always forgot to tell you I have seen your Letter to Gerry, Expressing Mr. Gadsden' Opinion about fixing out Armed Vessels, and seting up for a Naval power.² I thought it very happy to have so great an Authority Confirming my own Sentiments, and haveing proposed in Congress Just such a project the beginning of the Session borrowed the Letter to support it, but yet I have not been Able to Effect it. Pickering³ and his politics, the want of Faith, and Ardor in Gerry &c. and above all the want of powder has prevented it. The last is an Objection, tho I think it would be like planting Corn. Ten very good going Sloops from 10 to 16 Guns I am persuaded would clear our Coasts. What would 40 such be to the Continent. Such a determination might make a good figure on your Journals. We are still not a word of news since my last. The Troops were Crossing the Ferry Yesterday in great Numbers.⁴ Things will not remain long in this situation. I expect Another Action soon, God Grant us Success I believe he will. I have Engaged another Friend to write to you. If it gives you pleasure it will Answer my End. I received it but last Night from Braintree where it was finished.[5] The Season here is Hot and very dry. My regards to all Enquireing Friends. I assuredly yours,   Jas. Warren

RC (Adams Papers).

[1] The Provincial Congress made provision for seacoast defense in a resolution of 28 June (Mass. Provincial Congress, *Jours.*, p. 411–413).

[2] JA to Elbridge Gerry, [ante 11] June (above).

[3] John Pickering (1740–1811), brother of Timothy, was a member of the committee on armed vessels with Warren and Gerry. At the time of Warren's proposal, he opposed any such measure, but later, in a letter to Timothy Pickering, admitted that he might have been wrong (Sibley-Shipton, *Harvard Graduates*, 14:482; Mass. Provincial Congress, *Jours.*, p. 308).

[4] That is, crossing from Boston to Charlestown.

[5] By "another Friend" Warren may be referring to Mercy Otis Warren. She wrote from Watertown on 5 July (above), but she might have finished her letter in Braintree if, on returning from Watertown, she stopped by the Adams home. She had visited there on her way to Watertown earlier (AA to JA, 5 July, *Adams Family Correspondence*, 1:240). In any case, her letter went by the same express as her husband's of 7 and 11 July, all three being acknowledged by JA on 23 July (below).

From Nathan Rice

Dear Sir   Camp in Dorchester July 14th 1775

I have, since I have had the Happiness to see you become a Son of Mars. Should have done myself the Pleasure of writing before this had not I thought your Time was spent in more importance than in reading my Letters. Have been very much tyed since I Entered the Army. Mrs. Adams informs me you complain of the Remissness of your former Correspondence; wish Sir it was in my Power to make up their Deficiency.

I am much pleased with my Situation in the Army. Have formed the highest Opinion of the Gentlemen whom you have appointed our Generals. Have had but one Opportunity to be in their Company. Should be very happy were you Sir in our military Order. I dare say Sir you would find it a very agreable Situation. We are continually Saluted with the Roar of Cannon, but Familiarity breeds Contempt. Our Army has not the least apprehension from the Enemy. Our Regiment yesterday went on Long Island[1] amidst the Enemies Fire and burnd the Buildings and Hay took of[f] about an 100 Sheep and 20 Head of Cattle lost but one Man.[2] Have lately burnt Browns Building upon the Neck. Should mention many other things, but Major Morgan is waiting by whom I send this.[3] Please to excuse my haste and Errors. Mrs. Adams and little Folks well yesterday. I have entered Adjutant in Genl. Heaths Regiment. I am Sr. your very humble Servant   Nathan Rice[4]

RC (Adams Papers); addressed: "To the Honbe. John Adams Esqr. in Philadelphia   Pr Favour Major Morgan"; docketed, probably by Rev. William Gordon: "Nathan Rice   July 14. 1775."

[1] In Boston Harbor.
[2] See also William Tudor to JA, 19 July (below), and AA to JA, 16 July, *Adams Family Correspondence*, 1:245–251.
[3] Possibly Maj. Abner Morgan of Elisha Porter's Massachusetts militia regiment (Heitman, *Register Continental Army*, p. 401, 447).
[4] For a sketch of Rice, one of JA's law clerks, see JA, *Legal Papers*, 1:cviii.

From William Tudor

Dr. Sir   Cambridge 19th. July. 1775

I am much oblig'd by your Letter of 6th. Instant and will now attempt in Part to comply with your Request.[1] Things have remaind tolerably quiet between the continental and ministerial Camps for a Week past. The Beginning of last Week a Detachment was sent in the Night to take all the live Stock that was on Long Island. They succeeded and brought away not only all the Quadrupeds but 17 Fellows who were on the Island in the Service of Gage as Mowers. The next Day orders were issu'd to make another Descent and destroy the Buildings. Ten whale Boats mann'd with 12 and 15 Men At 10 o'Clock in the Day Notwithstanding a constant Fire from the Ships of War that lay near the Island, landed and set Fire to all the Buildings, destroying all the Hay &c. on the Place; on their Return they were attack'd by the Men of War's Boats, whom they fought and kept at Bay till they reach'd the Shore, and then fir'd so briskly on them that they thought it advisable to retreat. Our People lost one Man but brought off every Boat.

Since the Arrival of the continental Generals the Regulations of the Camp have been greatly for the Better. Matters were in a very poor Way before. The General was despiz'd.[2] There was little Emulation among the Officers, and The Soldiers were lazy, disorderly and dirty. The Genls. Washington, Lee and Gates are respected and confided in, and their Orders strictly and cheerfully executed and obeyed. And I hope we shall soon be able to meet British Troops on any Ground. The Freedom which our Countrymen have always been accustomed to, gives them an Impatience of Controul, and renders

4. ARTEMAS WARD (1727–1800),
BY RAPHAELLE PEALE, 1795
See page x

it extreem difficult to establish that Discipline so essential in an Army, which to be invincible, ought to be a grand Machine moved only by the Commander of it. Discipline will not inspire Cowards with Courage, but it will make them fight.

The Day after the Arrival of the Adjutant General[3] I had a Letter from him acquainting me with his having Directions from the Commander in Chief to offer me the Place of *Judge Advocate* to the Army. I immediately accepted the Post, and have every Day since been busy at Courts Martial. And Lords Coke, Holt and Hale[4] are made to give Way to your congressional military Code. There never has been a regular Court Martial before now, by Reason of their wanting some Person to methodize and conduct the Business. The Congress have not mentioned such an Officer in the Articles of War, but were they to attend a Court Martial they would see the Importance and Necessity of such an Appointment. The Office is very honorary, but the Stipend is not sufficient. Genl. Gates informs me that the Pay is equal to that of a Capt's. vizt. £6 a month. I must keep a Horse in Order to attend both Camps at Roxbury and Cambridge. A Report must be made of the whole Proceedings in every Trial to the Commander in chief which makes a great Deal of writing, and the salary is too little to pay a Clerk, who will be wanted of the Business. The Court has set for six Days running from 8 to 3 oClock. The Evidence is all taken down in writing, and then copied for the Inspection of the Generals. In so large an Army as we have, there must necessarily be much Business for Courts Martial. I find in the Regular Army, the Judge Advocate has a Stipend as such, and draws pay as an Officer in some Regiment besides. But with us—it would not do. I must beg you to set this office in a proper Light and to get such a Stipend fix'd as shall prevent my being out of Pocket at the Year's End. You know my Situation, Sir, and will therefore excuse what, would otherwise, appear mercenary in this Request.[5]

Your Declaration has been publickly read by the Chaplains through the Army and receiv'd with great Applause. The Address to the Inhabitants of G. Britain is generally approv'd, But some think, there is too much conceeded, considering the State we are now put in. The Spirit of Freedom glows with unabated ardor. As to Difficulties, we have been so us'd to them, they now occur without occasioning Concern. While the Horror of War ceases to alarm because it is familiar.   Wm. Tudor

RC (Adams Papers); addressed: "John Adams Esq   Philadelphia   By Mr. Fessenden."

[1] That Tudor report, from time to time, day-by-day occurrences.

[2] Gen. Artemas Ward.

[3] Horatio Gates (*JCC*, 2:97).

[4] Sir Edward Coke, Sir John Holt, and Sir Matthew Hale, standard English legal authorities, whose works were frequently resorted to by American lawyers.

[5] Tudor was appointed Judge Advocate on 14 July, his appointment being confirmed by the congress on 29 July. His complaints about his pay caused it to be raised in September to $50 per month. He continued in the post until 9 April 1777, having been promoted to lieutenant colonel on 10 Aug. 1776 (Sibley-Shipton, *Harvard Graduates*, 17:256–259; JCC, 2:221; 3:257; 5:645).

From James Warren

My Dear Sir   Watertown July 20. 1775

I yesterday returned from Plymouth where I had opportunity of spending only three or four days in such a hurry of private Business as would scarcely admit of a single Meditation in the Calm retirements of the Fields. I Breakfasted in the Morning with your Sensible and Amiable Lady. She showed me a Letter from you.[1] I read it with pleasure. I arrived here about 12 O Clock. You will say a late Hour for Election day. I found here two of your Letters one of them Incloseing the two pamphlets, and your Friend Mr. Collins called upon me this Morning and delivered me two more.[2] I think myself greatly Obliged to you for your Friendship, Confidence and the Marks of partiality I meet with in every Letter I receive from you. I had but an Hours Conversation with your Friend. From the best Judgment I can make, in so short an acquaintance he is worthy of your Friendship. I admire his open Frankness, and Judicious Observations, and Sentiments. He has promised to dine with me tomorrow or next day. Our New Assembly met Yesterday, and only Chose Speaker and Clerk, and postponed the Choice of Councellors till Tomorrow morning.[3] I fear with all this deliberation we shall not get such a Board as will please you. Boston is the only place to Hold Election in. I hope the next will be there, but if we might do as we would it is Astonishing how few sterling Men are to be found in so large a Province as this is. I am not able to give my opinion of the Pamphlets you sent me, not haveing had time to read them. I was late last Evening settleing the List of Councillors. This morning I had many things to do, and then to go to meeting. The Fast is Observed here with a strictness and devotion that shows the Opinion the People have of the Authority that Appointed it as well as their Reverence for him who Overules all Events, and has so signally appeared in our favour. So few Occurrences have taken place since my last in the military way that your Curiosity will not be sufficiently satisfied with an Account of them. I will Endeavour to recollect them all. The Attempt on Long Island, the takeing off all the stock and afterwards returning to Burn the Buildings (which you will have in the Papers) was certainly a Bold, Intrepid Maneuvre, and as such Astonished our Enemies. The Barges full of Armed men were Afraid to Attack our Whaleboats at a proper distance, and the Armed Vessels, either agitated with Fear or destitute of Judgment did it without Execution. The next thing that took place, was the possessing and fortifying a post by Brown House very near their Lines. This has been Effected with the loss only of one Man, and he not Employed there, tho' they work'd in open Sight of them and Exposed to an Incessant fire from their Cannon which our people treated with Extreemest Contempt, not so much as once leaving their work, or returning a Shott. No General Movements have taken place. There was an Appearance of it the day before Yesterday on Roxbury Side, but they did not venture out. General Thomas who is yet Continued in that Command made an Excellent disposition to receive them, and was disappointed. Roxbury is Amazeingly strong. I believe it would puzzle 10,000 Troops to go through it. I mean of the best in the world. I am Just Told that our Boats have this day been to the Lighthouse, and Burnt it in spite of the Fireing from a Man of War and a number of Boats. I hear it was Executed by 300 Rhode Islanders. I dont learn that they suffered any loss. It is said they are more afraid of our whale Boats than we are of their Men of War. A few Armed Vessels I am Abundantly Convinced would produce great Consequences. I want to see the Riflemen, and should be pleased to see the Hussar at the Head of his Troop.[4] You need not fear our treating them with the utmost Tenderness, and Affection. There is a strong Spirit of Love, and Cordiality for our Friends of the other Colonies prevailing here. The Finger of Heaven seems to be in every thing. I fear Nothing now so much as the Small Pox in our Army, (there is some danger of it tho' I hope it will be stopped) and proposals of a Conciliatory Nature from England. The first would be dreadful, but the last more so. I see the difficulties you have to struggle against, and the Mortification you are Obliged to submit to. I did not Expect another Petition. I hope however your Sentiments and plans will finally prevail. The Infatuation of Britain may supply the Firmness of your Brethren, and Effect what their Timidity, and ridiculous moderation would otherways prevent. If the Canadians should relish an Army of ours there, as I am told they will I think it would be a Grand Move. Capt. Darby who we sent with the Account of the Battle of the 19th of

April returned two days ago. He was there 8 days, and came away before Gages Packet arrived. He says Trade and the Stocks were Amazeingly Affected in that short time. Lord Dartmouth sent three times for him. He refused to go, and when he threatned him he decamped got on Board and came without either Entering or clearing. I shall Inclose you a Letter Brought by him from Sherriff Lee,[5] and one of the latest papers. By the Letter I fancy Genl. Gage is to Expect no other reinforcement this fall. They are very sickly, and are greatly reduced. The Tories in Boston I believe are low enough, are Bowed down with the Load of Guilt they have by their Wickedness Accumulated, and the Apprehensions of what is to come. I am concerned for your Health in this hot Season. Pray take Care of it. I have dispensed with Attendance on publick worship this Afternoon in order to write to you, haveing no other time. Coll. Read was kind enough to give me notice of this Opportunity. Pray present my best respects to all my Friends among which I presume to rank Mr. Hopkins and Ward. Your own Goodness will Induce you to Continue your favours. I shall loose no opportunity of writing as long you Continue to be pleased with it. When you are Tired with my Incorrect ramblings you will I hope very honestly tell me of it. I shall think it not strange, and shant think of resentment. I never write well. I am sure I cant here crouded with Business and surrounded with Company. Your usual Candour must be Called into Exercise, it is greatly relied on. I am as I believe I shall be your Sincere Friend,

Jas: Warren

RC (Adams Papers); docketed in JA's later hand: "Warren July 20. 1775."

[1] Probably JA's letter of 7 July (*Adams Family Correspondence*, 1:241–243).

[2] One of the two letters mentioned first was that of 10 July (above), which enclosed the pamphlets; the other has not been identified. The pamphlets were *A Declaration by the Representatives of the United Colonies of North-America, Now Meeting in General Congress at Philadelphia; Setting Forth the Causes and Necessity of Their Taking Up Arms*, Phila., 1775, Evans, No. 14544, and *The Twelve United Colonies; by Their Delegates in Congress; to the Inhabitants of Great Britain*, Phila., 1775, Evans, No. 14532. The letters brought by Stephen Collins were the two of 6 July (above).

[3] Pursuant to the resolution of the Provincial Congress on 20 June, the newly elected House of Representatives met at Watertown on 19 July and elected Samuel Freeman clerk and James Warren speaker (Mass. Provincial Congress, *Jours.*, p. 358–360; Mass., *House Jour.*, 1775–1776, 1st sess., p. 5).

[4] JA described a Hussar in the second of the two letters of 6 July (above).

[5] Enclosures not found. Capt. John Derby (1741–1812), son of Richard Derby (1712–1783), a prosperous Salem merchant, and brother of Richard Derby Jr. (1736–1787), a member of the Provincial Congress, received orders on 27 April from the Provincial Congress to proceed immediately to England with dispatches describing the American

version of the Battle of Lexington and Concord in order to anticipate Gen. Gage's own account. Arriving in London on 28 May, Derby lost no time in circulating his description of the battle, thereby scoring a propaganda coup. Returning to the province on 18 July, he gave Washington and the Provincial Congress firsthand accounts of the British reaction (Mass. Provincial Congress, *Jours.*, p. 154–156, 159, 523; *JCC*, 2:27, 28, note [both these sources incorrectly identify Capt. Derby as his brother Richard]; *DAB*; James Duncan Phillips, *Salem in the Eighteenth Century*, Boston, 1937, p. 364–369).

To William Tudor

Dr sir   July 23. 1775

We live in Times, when it is necessary to look about Us, and to know the Character of every Man, who is concerned in any material Branch of public affairs, especially in the Army.

There will be a large Number of Voluntiers in the Army perhaps. Certainly there will be many young Gentlemen from the southern Colonies, at the Camp. They will perhaps be introduced, into Places, as Aid du Camps—Brigade Majors, Secretaries, and Deputies in one Department, or another.

I earnestly intreat you to make the most minute Enquiry, after every one of these, and let me know his Character, for I am determined, I will know that Army, and the Character of all its officers.

I Swear, I will be a faithful Spy upon it for its good.

I beg you would let me know, what is become of Coll. Gridley and Mr. Burbanks,[1] and whether they have lost their Character as Engineers and Gunners—and let me know, what Engineers, there are in the Army, or whether there are none.

I want to know if there are any Engineers in the Province and who they are. I have heard the Generals were much disappointed, in not finding Engineers, and Artillery as they expected. P[lease] let me know the Truth of this, if you can learn it, and how they come to expect a better Artillery than they found.[2] All this keep to your self. I am &c.

RC (MHi:Tudor Papers); addressed: "To Mr. William Tudor Cambridge"; docketed: "July 23d. 1775."

[1] Richard Gridley (1711–1796), a former officer in the British Army, at the time of this letter was chief engineer and colonel of artillery, appointed such by the Provincial Congress in April and June. He had directed the fortification of Breed's Hill and was wounded in the battle of 17 June. In September he was appointed colonel of artillery for the Continental Army but because of age was replaced by Henry Knox in November. He did, however, retain his post of chief engineer until Aug. 1776 and, in that capacity, oversaw construction of fortifications on Dorchester Heights. From Jan. 1777 to Dec. 1780, he served as engineer general of the Eastern Department. Maj. William Burbeck (d. 1785) was second in command in Gridley's artillery regiment (*DAB*; Mass. Provincial Congress, *Jours.*, p. 157, 373–374, 378, 153;

Mass. Soldiers and Sailors, 6:874–875; 2:818; Thomas J. Abernethy, "American Artillery Regiments in the Revolutionary War," unpubl. bound typescript, MHi, p. 96–99, 38–39, 100).

[2] See comments on Gen. Lee in JA to Josiah Quincy, 29 July (below).

To James Warren

Dr Sir   Philadelphia July 23d. 1775

I have many Things to write you, which thro Haste and Confusion, I fear, I Shall forget.

Upon the Receipt of General Washingtons Letter,[1] the Motion which I made Some Days before, for appointing General Thomas first Brigadier, was renewed and carried, So that the Return of the Express will carry his Commission. I hope that this will give all the Satisfaction which is now to be given. You ask me upon what Principle We proceeded in our first Arrangement. I answer upon the Principle of an implicit Complyance with the order in which the General Officers were chosen in our Provincial Congress last Fall. Not one of us, would have voted for the Generals in the order in which they were placed, if We had not thought that you had Settled the Rank of every one of them last Fall in Provincial Congress, and that We were not at Liberty to make any Alteration. I would not have been so shackled however, if my Colleagues, had been of my Mind.[2]

But, in the Case of the Connecticutt officers, We took a Liberty to alter the Rank established by the Colony, and by that Means made much Uneasiness: so that We were sure to do Mischief whether We conformed or deviated from Colony Arrangements.

I rejoice that Thomas, had more Wisdom than Spencer or Wooster, and that he did not leave the Camp, nor talk imprudently, if he had We should have lost him from the Continental service: for I assure you, Spencer by going off, and Woorster by unguarded Speeches have given high offence here. It will cost us, Pains to privent their being discarded from the service of the Continent with Indignation.[3] Gentlemen here, had no private Friendships Connections, or Interests, which prompted them to vote for the Arrangement they made, but were influenced only by a Regard to the Service; and they are determined that their Commissions shall not be despized.

I have read of Times, either in History or Romance, when Great Generals, would chearfully, serve their Country, as Captains or Lieutenants of Single Companies, if the Voice of their Country happened not to destine them to an higher Rank: but such exalted

Ideas of public Virtue Seem to be lost out of the World. Enough of this.

I have laboured with my Colleagues to agree upon proper Persons to recommend for a Quarter Master General, a Commissary of Musters and a Commissary of Artillery, but in vain. The Consequence has been that the appointment of these important, and lucrative Officers is left to the General, against every proper Rule and Principle, as these offices are Checks upon his.[4] This is a great Misfortune to our Colony, however, I hope that you and others, will think of proper Persons and recommend them to the General.

There is, my Friend, in our Colony a great Number of Persons, well qualified for Places in the Army, who have lost their all, by the outrages of Tyranny, whom I wish to hear provided for. Many of them will occur to you. I beg leave to mention a few. Henry Knox, William Bant, young Hitchbourne the Lawyer William Tudor, and Perez Moreton.[5] These are young Gentlemen of Education and Accomplishments, in civil Life, as well as good Soldiers; and if at this Time initiated into the service of their Country might become in Time and with Experience, able officers. If they could be made Captains or Brigade Majors, or put into some little Places at present I am very sure, their Country would loose nothing by it, in Reputation or otherwise. A certain Delicacy which is necessary to a good Character, may have prevented their making any applications, but I know they are desirous of serving.

I must enjoin secrecy upon you, in as strong Terms as Mr Hutchinson used to his confidential Correspondents; and then confess to you, that I never was since my Birth, so compleatly miserable as I have been since the Tenth of April. Bad Health, blind Eyes, want of Intelligence from our Colony, and above all the unfortunate and fatal Divisions, in our own Seat in Congress, which has lost us Reputation, as well as many great Advantages which We might otherwise have obtained for our Colony have made me often envy the active Hero in the Field, who, if he does his own Duty, is sure of applause, tho he falls in the Execution of it.

It is a vast and complicated System of Business which We have gone through, and We were all of Us, unexperienced in it. Many Things may be wrong, but no small Proportion of these are to be attributed to the Want of Concert, and Union among the Mass. Delegates.[6]

We have passed a Resolution, that each Colony make such Provision as it thinks proper and can afford, for defending their Trade in Harbours, Rivers, and on the sea Coast, against Cutters and Tenders. We have had in Contemplation a Resolution to invite all Nations to bring their Commodities to Market here, and like Fools have lost it for the present. This is a great Idea. What shall We do? Shall We invite all Nations to come with their Luxuries, as well as Conveniences and Necessaries? Or shall We think of confining our Trade with them to our own Bottoms, which alone can lay a Foundation for great Wealth and naval Power. Pray think of it.[7]

I rejoice that the Generals and Coll. Reed and Major Mifflin are so well received. My most respectfull Compliments to them all.

I thank you and Mrs. Warren a thousand Times for her kind and elegant Letter.[8] Intreat a Continuance of her Favours in this Way, to your old Friend.

RC (MHi:Warren-Adams Coll.); addressed: "To the Hon. James Warren Esqr Watertown favoured by Mr. Hitchbourne"; docketed: "Mr. J A Lettr July 1775 X." If this letter had indeed been carried by Hichborn, it would have been intercepted as were JA's letters to AA and James Warren of 24 July.

[1] In Washington, *Writings*, ed. Fitzpatrick, 3:320–329.

[2] See JA's first letter to Warren of 6 [July], note 1 (above).

[3] At the outbreak of the Revolution, Joseph Spencer (1714–1789) and David Wooster (1711–1777) were brigadier and major general respectively in the Connecticut forces. When the congress on 19 June appointed Israel Putnam the fourth major general in the Continental Army over Spencer and Wooster, Putnam's superiors in their colony's service, both were outraged. Spencer left his post at Roxbury and returned to Connecticut. It took a major effort to reconcile him to his position, but eventually he returned to the army and was appointed a major general in Aug. 1776. Wooster, the only major general in the service of a colony who was not raised to his full rank in the Continental Army, did not leave the army, but his quarrels with Generals Schuyler in New York and Arnold in Quebec raised questions about his fitness for command (*DAB; JCC*, 2:99, 103; Burnett, ed., *Letters of Members*, 1:137, 142, 164, 166–170, 174, 179, 181). The actions of the congress in regard to the Connecticut officers probably created more serious problems than did those in regard to Massachusetts officers complained of by Warren, Gerry, and others.

[4] Washington appointed Thomas Mifflin quartermaster general on 14 Aug., Stephen Moylan mustermaster general on 11 Aug., and Ezekiel Cheever commissary of artillery on 17 Aug. (Washington, *Writings*, ed. Fitzpatrick, 3:419, 414, 427).

[5] On Bant, see JA to Washington, [19 or 20] June, note 4 (above). Both Benjamin Hichborn, JA's letter carrier, and Perez Morton were lawyers; on the latter see Sibley-Shipton, *Harvard Graduates*, 17:555–561.

[6] The Massachusetts delegation was divided over the appointment of generals, especially Lee; moreover, Cushing had written back to Massachusetts a very disturbing letter (James Warren to JA, 11 June, above).

[7] The resolution on defending trade which passed on 18 July was one of a series of resolves stemming from the report of the committee on improving the militia. The resolution on opening the ports was considered on 21–22 July, but was tabled and apparently no further action was taken at this session. Two draft resolutions in the hands of Benjamin Franklin and Richard Henry Lee, both calling for the closing of all customs houses and the admission of the ships

and goods of all nations duty free, are
in JCC, 2:189, 200–202.

[8] Mrs. Warren's letter of 5 July
(above).

To James Warren

Dear Sir   Philadelphia, July 24th, 1775

In Confidence,—I am determined to write freely to you this Time.[1]
—A certain great Fortune and piddling Genius[2] whose Fame has
been trumpeted so loudly, has given a silly Cast to our whole Doings
—We are between Hawk and Buzzard—We ought to have had in our
Hands a Month ago, the whole Legislative, Executive and Judicial
of the whole Continent, and have compleatly moddelled a Constitution, to have raised a Naval Power and opened all our Ports wide,
to have arrested every Friend to Government on the Continent and
held them as Hostages for the poor Victims in Boston. And then
opened the Door as wide as possible for Peace and Reconcilliation:
After this they might have petitioned and negotiated and addressed,
&c. if they would.—Is all this extravagant?—Is it wild?—Is it not the
soundest Policy?

One Piece of News—Seven Thousand Weight of Powder arrived
here last Night—We shall send along some as soon as we can—But
you must be patient and frugal.

We are lost in the extensiveness of our Field of Business—We
have a Continental Treasury to establish, a Paymaster to choose, and
a Committee of Correspondence, or Safety, or Accounts, or something, I know not what that has confounded us all Day.

Shall I *hail* you Speaker of the House, Counsellor or what—What
Kind of an Election had you? What Sort of Magistrates do you intend to make?

Will your new Legislative and Executive feel bold, or irresolute?
Will your Judicial hang and whip, and fine and imprison, without
Scruples?[3] I want to see our distressed[4] Country once more—yet I
dread the Sight of Devastation.

You observe in your Letter the Oddity of a great Man[5]—He is a
queer Creature—But you must love his Dogs if you love him, and forgive a Thousand Whims for the Sake of the Soldier and the Scholar.[6]

Addressed, To the Hon. JAMES WARREN, Watertown. Favor'd by
Mr. Hitchborne.

RC not found. Reprinted from Draper's *Massachusetts Gazette*, 17 Aug.
1775. This version is printed here because the newspaper seems to have tried
to render the text exactly as JA probably wrote it, particularly in the use of
dashes of varying length, which normally the editors treat as commas or

periods unless the dash serves the modern function of indicating a break in thought. Comparison of the newspaper version with contemporary British MS copies, listed below in note 1, shows no differences in wording with two minor exceptions: that discussed in note 4 (below), and the use of the complimentary close "yours," which occurs in all MS copies but No. 3. None of the MS copies quite manages to reproduce all the dashes of varying lengths. All the listed copies except No. 1 include the newspaper note: "N.B. This Letter was Anonymous, but wrote in the same Hand with that addressed to Abigail Adams." Adm. Graves, commander in chief of the British fleet, to whom the original was forwarded, sent only copies back to England and to Gen. Gage, but a search of his official correspondence and of his unpublished documentary memoir of his service in America has not turned up the original (Gage, *Corr.*, 1:412; P.R.O.:Admiralty 1, vol. 485; BM:Add. MSS, 14038–14039). It may have been given to the printer, who in good 18th-century fashion, saw no need to preserve it once his type had been set, but see note 4 (below).

1 This letter, a letter of JA to AA of the same date (*Adams Family Correspondence*, 1:255–256), and a letter of Benjamin Harrison to George Washington, 21–24 July, were all three printed in sequence in the *Massachusetts Gazette*. They were seized by the British when Benjamin Hichborn, the bearer, was captured on Narragansett Bay en route to Massachusetts. Hichborn had begged JA to give him letters to carry back home because as one who had apprenticed under a tory lawyer, he felt the need to prove his loyalty to the American cause (Allen French, "The First George Washington Scandal," MHS, *Procs.*, 65 [1932–1936]:461–467). Copies of JA's letters were forwarded to England by Adm. Graves, Gen. Gage, and others. Authentic contemporary copies known to the editors in British collections are these: (1) P.R.O.:C.O. 5, vol. 122:15h, originally enclosure No. 7, according to its endorsement, in Adm. Graves to Stephen Stephens, secretary to the Lords of the Admiralty, 17 Aug.; (2) same, vol. 92:250, enclosure No. 2 in Gage to Dartmouth, 20 Aug. (covering letter printed in Gage, *Corr.*, 1:412–413); (3) MiU-C:Gage Papers, English Series, FC of an enclosure in Gage to Dartmouth, 20 Aug., endorsement on FC of the covering letter states that this packet was "Sent by Mrs. Gage" and a "Duplicate by Lt. Bilkinson"; (4) BM:Add. MSS, Haldimand Papers, 21687:225r–226v, endorsement gives John Adams as writer; (5) William Salt Library, Stafford, England:Dartmouth

Papers, endorsement leaves blank the name of the writer. Many other copies, both British and American, are recorded or exist as reproductions in the Adams Papers files. The purveyor of one copy attributed the letter to Samuel rather than John Adams, despite his knowledge that others did not agree with him (T. Bruce to Thomas Bruce Brudenwell, Lord Bruce, 12 Aug., TxDaHi:Jake L. Hamon Coll.).

With the oblique reference to John Dickinson as a "piddling Genius," this letter brought to a head the conflict between him and JA over whether conciliatory or more vigorous measures should be pursued in the congress. The expression of JA's impatience and frustration was not new, for he had relieved his feelings in earlier letters to Warren and AA (to Warren, 6, 11, and 23 July, above, and to AA, 23 July, *Adams Family Correspondence*, 1:252–253). Certainly at the time the letter was written, JA did not view it as exceptionally important, but its publication identified him as a leader among those pressing for strong resistance to Great Britain.

Copies of the letters arrived in England on or about 17 Sept. and were immediately printed in *Lloyd's Evening Post and British Chronicle*, 18–20 Sept., and then in other newspapers as well (M. W. Willard, ed., *Letters on the American Revolution: 1774–1776*, Boston, 1925, p. 187–189). Their immediate impact was probably limited, for the king had already, on 23 Aug., proclaimed that the colonies were in

5. JOHN DICKINSON (1732–1808),
ENGRAVING BY BÉNOIT LOUIS PRÉVOST,
AFTER A DRAWING BY PIERRE EUGÈNE DU SIMITIÈRE, 1781
See page x

rebellion, and the Olive Branch Petition had been submitted to Lord Dartmouth on 1 Sept., in whose hands it died (Merrill Jensen, ed., *English Historical Documents: American Colonial Documents to 1776*, N.Y., 1955, 9:850–851; French, *First Year*, p. 548–550). Thus the letters at first probably confirmed ministerial views already held.

[2] Both the *London Chronicle* of 19–21 Sept., which took its version from the *Massachusetts Gazette*, and Gen. John Burgoyne identified the "piddling Genius" as John Hancock rather than Dickinson (Edward Barrington De-Fonblanque, *The Life and Correspondence of . . . John Burgoyne*, London, 1876, p. 193–194). In Britain, however, the breach between JA and Dickinson had become known by at least December, when a letter from London declared that the peace commission led by the Howe brothers sought "to sow dissensions among the Provinces, . . . of which they entertain great hopes of success, from the supposed coolness between Mr. D–k–s–n, of Pennsylvania, and Mr. J—— Ads, of Massachusetts-Bay" (Force, *Archives*, 4th ser., 4:222–223).

[3] JA resented this passage's being interpreted as his wish for harsh treatment for tories; see his explanation in *Diary and Autobiography*, 3:320.

[4] In British contemporary copies Nos. 2, 3, 4, and 5, listed in note 1 (above), this word appears as "distressful." The same form is used in the copy furnished by an officer on board the *Swan*, the vessel which seized the ferry that was carrying Hichborn from Newport to Providence. The account of the seizure was carried in the *Newport Mercury*, 7 Aug. (reprinted in *Naval Docs. Amer. Rev.*, 1:1086–1087). The *Swan* officer, writing to London on 14 Aug., two weeks after the capture, says the letters were sent on to Graves, "but I found an opportunity of copying two of them, and herewith send the copies to you" (Willard, ed., *Letters on the American Revolution*, p. 187). If the officer made his copies from the originals, his text may be more accurate in this one respect than that used by the *Massachusetts Gazette*. It is conceivable, however, that the *Swan* officer, given the passage of time, made

his copies from copies produced for Graves. In the latter case, one must assume that some copyist made the mistake of writing "distressful" for "distressed," the word that appears in both the *Gazette* and in the copy Graves forwarded to London. Of course, if "distressful" was in the original, then the newspaper was furnished with an inexact copy and Graves sent a second such copy to London. No evidence has been found that the British tampered with the wording as JA claimed (*Diary and Autobiography*, 3:319).

[5] Gen. Charles Lee, for whose reaction to this passage, see Lee to JA, 5 Oct. (below).

[6] The effect of the letter in America is difficult to assess because it was not printed in any newspaper outside of Boston; thus the extent to which a public debate occurred over its content is a question. The failure to reprint the letter suggests that leading patriots, particularly those in the congress, wanted to avoid widely publicizing a formal split in their ranks. Gilbert Barkley, a British spy in Philadelphia, reported that as of 16 Sept. JA's letters had not been printed in that city largely because great pains had been taken to suppress them and local printers feared printing anything not approved by the congress. But Barkley promised to give his own copies as wide circulation as possible (Geoffrey Seed, "A British Spy in Philadelphia," *PMHB*, 85:21–22 [Jan. 1961]). Other MS copies circulated as well.

The effect of the letters on JA personally is also hard to determine. Barkley claimed that JA met with a cool reception, that Quakers and others considered him an enemy to his country (same, p. 22–24). Benjamin Rush, writing his Autobiography years later, remarked that publication of the intercepted letters made JA into "an object of nearly universal detestation," neglected by his friends and forced to walk "our streets alone," but Rush recognized that this treatment was temporary (*The Autobiography of Benjamin Rush*, ed. George W. Corner, Princeton, 1948, p. 142). Except for mentioning his meeting Dickinson on the street when Dickinson passed without any sign of recognition, JA apparently gave little weight to the reaction to the letters (*Diary and Autobiography*, 2:173). Nor was his role in the congress notably affected. According to his own account, he continued active in the debates almost every day, and he served on as many committees between Sept. and Dec. 1775 as he had during the first session of the Second Continental Congress (same, 3:327; Adams' Service in the Congress, 13 Sept. – 9 Dec., Editorial Note, below). He received reassurance from Joseph Reed and Charles Lee that the letters were doing no harm, and when the passing months brought more repressive measures from Britain, he was in a sense proved right and enjoyed the acclaim that correct predictions, even dire ones, usually bring (*Diary and Autobiography*, 3:319–321; Lee to JA, 5 Oct., below). It is possible that his improved reputation even led to publication of his two intercepted letters as late as 1 Jan. 1776 in the *Boston Gazette*. By that date his call for genuine continental government, with open ports backed by naval power, would find more willing listeners.

The British reaction to the letters centered on the contradiction between the tone of public statements of various patriot leaders and the attitude revealed in the letters. The British officer on board the *Swan* referred to the "real intentions of those miscreants who have misled his Majesty's subjects in North America to commit acts of open Rebellion" (Willard, ed., *Letters on the American Revolution*, p. 187). Gen. Burgoyne declared the author of the letters was "as great a conspirator as ever subverted a state" and warned that "this man soars too high to be allured by any offer Great Britain can make to himself or to his country. America, if his counsels continue in force, must be subdued or relinquished. She will not be reconciled" (DeFonblanque, *Life of Burgoyne*, p. 194–195). Any significant British political use of the letters had to await the opening of Parliament and responses to the King's speech of 26 Oct. In the ensuing debate the letters were cited as evidence that reconciliation was a forlorn hope, that a rebellion was in progress which had independence as its goal (*Parliamentary Hist.*, 18:731–732). Even those friendly to America saw little possibility for improved relations on the basis of the Olive Branch Petition, which was deemed a political ploy; JA's letters reinforced their perception (French, *First Year*, p. 550–551). The climax came with the Prohibitory Act of 22 Dec., which stopped all American trade (Jensen, ed., *English Historical Documents*, 9:853), but the intercepted letters were only one among many influences that brought that act into being. Indeed, the act might very well have come even if JA's private thoughts had never become public.

From Samuel Chase

Harford Town Monday afternoon
Dear Sir   [24 July 1775][1]

I am this far arrived on my way Home. Give Me Leave to introduce to your Notice Mr. George Lux a Son of a Gentleman who is my particular Friend, a Man of the most worthy and amiable Character, he is bound for our Camp and would be glad to carry your Commands to any of your Friends. Mr. Cary, Mr. Hopkins and Smith, young Gentlemen of Balt. Town, are also for our Camp and worthy of Attention.[2]

I met the enclosed from a young Gentleman in my office. The Contents will please You.[3]

My warmest Wishes attend You and your worthy Brethren.
I beg a Line. Your Affectionate and Obedient Servant

Saml. Chase

RC (DSI:Hull Coll.).

[1] Since JA refers to Chase's mention of these men in letters of 27 and 28 July to James Warren and William Tudor (below), a Monday date of 24 July would seem reasonable.
[2] George Lux was the son of William Lux, Baltimore merchant and shipowner (JA, *Diary and Autobiography*, 2:258, note). Although Cary has been identified as Richard Cary, aide to Washington, he, according to Freeman, was from Virginia rather than Baltimore (Freeman, *Washington*, 4:124, note; *Warren-Adams Letters*, 1:93, note). Smith and Hopkins remain unidentified.

[3] The enclosure was very likely a letter of 21 July to Chase from Thomas Maddux Jr., which reported that a Liverpool ship which had salt, cheese, and dry goods on board grounded near the West River and was burned by local people before Baltimoreans could get their hands on it. The letter also reported that the ship's owner had assured the doubtful captain before he sailed for America that 10,000 troops would arrive before him to protect him against violence. Finally, the letter mentioned a rumor that Gage had been taken prisoner (Adams Papers).

The Speaker of the House of Representatives to the Massachusetts Delegates

[Watertown,] 25 July 1775. FC (M-Ar:Mass. House of Representatives Records, 57:263). As speaker, James Warren notified JA and the other members of the delegation of their election to the Council and expressed the wish that they would take their seats on the Council as soon as their duties in the congress permitted.

Their election to the Council had taken place on 21 July. JA took his seat on 10 Aug., upon his return from Philadelphia, and served until the adjournment of the General Court on 24 Aug. (Mass., *House Jour.*, 1775–1776, 1st sess., p. 6, 60; James Warren to Mercy Otis Warren, 9 Aug., MHi:Warren-Adams Coll.). JA also participated in the work of the Council for a few days at the end of August (*Adams Family Correspondence*, 1:272–273, note 2).

The Committee of Safety's Account of The Battle of Bunker Hill

A true Extract from the Minutes
Att. Saml. Freeman Secry.

(Copy)

In Committee of Safety[1]   Watertown 25th. July 1775

In Obedience to the above Order of Congress, this Committee have enquired into the Premises, and, upon the best Information obtained, find, that the Commanders of the New England Army

THIS Town was alarmed on the 17th Inftant at break of Day, by a Firing from the Lively Ship of War; and a Report was immediately fpread that the Rebels had broke Ground, and were raifing a Battery on the Heights of the Peninfula of Charleftown, againft the Town of Bofton. They were plainly feen, and in a few Hours a Battery of Six Guns, played upon their Works. Preparations were inftantly made for the landing a Body of Men; and fome Companies of Grenadiers and Light Infantry, with fome Battallions, and Field Artillery; amounting in the whole to about 2000 Men, under the Command of Major General HOWE, and Brigadier General PIGOT, were embarked with great Expedition, and landed on the Peninfula without Oppofition; under Cover of fome Ships of War, and armed Veffels.

The Troops formed as foon as landed: The Rebels upon the Heights, were perceived to be in great Force, and ftrongly pofted. A Redoubt thrown up on the 16th at Night, with other Works full of Men, defended with Cannon, and a large Body pofted in the Houfes of Charleftown, covered their Right; and their Left was covered by a Breaftwork, Part of it Cannon Proof, which reached from the Left of the Redoubt to the Myftick River.

Befides the Appearance of the Rebels Strength, large Columns were feen pouring in to their Affiftance; but the King's Troops advanced; the Attack began by a Cannonade, and notwithftanding various Impediments of Fences, Walls, &c. and the heavy Fire they were expofed to, from the vaft Numbers of Rebels, and their Left galled from the Houfes of Charleftown, the Troops made their Way to the Redoubt, mounted the Works, and carried it. The Rebels were then forced from other ftrong Holds, and purfued 'till they were drove clear of the Peninfula, leaving Five Pieces of Cannon behind them. Charleftown was fet on Fire during the Engagement, and moft Part of it confumed. The Lofs they fuftained, muft have been confiderable, from the vaft Numbers they were feen to carry off during the Action, exclufive of what they fuffered from the fhipping. About a Hundred were buried the Day after, and Thirty found wounded on the Field, fome of which are fince Dead. About 170 of the King's Troops were killed, and fince dead of their Wounds; and a great many were wounded.

This Action has fhown the Bravery of the King's Troops, who under every Difadvantage, gained a compleat Victory over Three Times their Number, ftrongly pofted, and covered by Breaftworks. But they fought for their KING, their LAWS and CONSTITUTION.

[Bofton: Printed by John Howe, 1775]

6. BROADSIDE ON THE BATTLE OF BUNKER HILL,
26 JUNE 1775
See pages x–xi

about the 14th. ultimo received Advice that Genl. Gage had issued Orders for a Party of Troops under his Command, to post themselves on Bunkers Hill, a Promontory just at the Entrance of the Peninsula of Charlestown;[2] upon which it was determined, with the Advice of this Committee, to send a Party who might erect some Fortifications upon said Hill and defeat this Design of our Enemies. Accordingly on the 16th. Ultimo Orders were issued that a Detachment of one thousand Men should march that Evening to Charlestown, and entrench upon that Hill; just before 9 oClock they left Cambridge, and proceeded to Breeds Hill, situated on the further Part of the Peninsula West of[3] Boston, for by some Mistake this Hill was marked out for the Entrenchment instead of the other; many things being necessary to be done preparatory to the Entrenchments being thrown up, which could not be done before lest the Enemy should discover and defeat the Design, it was nearly 12 oClock before the Works were entered upon. They were then carried on with the utmost Diligence and Alacrity, so that by the Dawn of the Day, they had thrown up a small Redoubt about eight Rods square; at this Time an heavy Fire began from the Enemy's Ships, a Number of floating Batteries and from the Fortifications of the Enemy on Cops Hill in Boston, directly opposite to our little Redoubt; an incessant Shower of Shot and Bombs was rained by these upon our Works, by which only one Man fell;[4] the Provincials continued to labour indefatigably till they had thrown up a small Breastwork extending from the East Side of the Redoubt to the Bottom of the Hill, but were prevented from compleating it by the intolerable Fire of the Enemy.

Between 12 and 1 oClock a Number of Boats and Barges filled with the regular Troops, from Boston, were observed approaching towards Charlestown; these Troops landed at a Place called Moretons Point situated a little to the Eastward of our Works; this Brigade formed upon their landing, and stood thus formed till a second Detachment arrived from Boston to join them: having sent out large flank Guards, they began a very slow March towards our Lines; at this instant Smoak and Flames were seen to arise from the Town of Charlestown, which had been set on Fire by the Enemy, that the Smoak might cover their Attack upon our Lines, and perhaps with a Design to rout and destroy one or two Regiments of Provincials who had been posted in that Town; if either of these was their Design, they were disappointed, for the Wind shifting on a sudden carried the Smoak another Way, and the Regiments were already removed. The Provincials within their Entrenchments impatiently waited the

Attack of the Enemy, and reserved their Fire till they came within ten or twelve Rods, and then began a furious Discharge of small Arms; this Fire arrested the Enemy, which they for some Time returned without advancing a Step, and then retreated in Disorder, and with great Precipitation to the Place of landing, and some of them sought Refuge within their Boats; here their Officers were observed, by the Spectators on the opposite Shore, to run down to them, using the most passionate Gestures, and pushing their Men forward with their Swords; at length they rallied and marched up with apparent Reluctance to the Entrenchment; the Americans again reserved their Fire untill the Enemy came within 5 or 6 Rods, and a second Time put the Regulars to Flight, who ran in great Confusion towards their Boats; similar and superior Exertions were now necessarily to be made by the Officers, which, notwithstanding the Men discovered an almost insuperable Reluctance to fighting in this Cause, were again successfull; they formed once more, and having brought some Cannon to bear in such a Manner as to rake the Inside of the Breastwork from one End of it to the other, the Provincials retreated within their little Fort; the Ministerial Army now made a decisive Effort; the Fire from the Ships and Batterys as well as from the Cannon in the Front of their Army was redoubled; the Officers in the Rear of their Army were observed to goad forward the Men with renewed Exertions, and they attacked the Redoubt on three Sides at once;[5] the Breastwork on the outside of the Fort was abandoned, the Ammunition of the Provincials was expended, and few of their Arms were fixed with Bayonets, can it then be wondered that the Word was given by the Commander of the Party to retreat? but this he delayed till the Redoubt was half filled with Regulars, and the Provincials had kept their Enemy at Bay—for some Time confronting them with the Butts of their Muskets. The Retreat of this little handful of brave Men would have been effectually cut off had it not happened that the flanking Party of the Enemy, which was to have come upon the Back of the Redoubt was checked by a Party of Provincials, who fought with the utmost Bravery, and kept them from advancing further than the Beach; the Engagement of these two Parties was kept up with the utmost Vigor, and it must be acknowledged that this Party of the Ministerial Troops evidenced a Courage worthy a better Cause; all their Efforts however were insufficient to compel the Provincials to retreat till their main Body had left the Hill; percieving this was done, they then gave Ground, but with more Regularity than could be expected of Troops who had been no longer under Discipline, and many of whom never before saw an Engagement.

In this Retreat the Americans had to pass over the Neck which joins the Peninsula of Charlestown to the main Land; this Neck was commanded by the Glascow—Man of War, and two floating Batteries placed in such a Manner as that their Shot raked every Part of it; the incessant Fire kept up across this Neck had from the Beginning of the Engagement prevented any considerable Reinforcement from getting to the Provincials on the Hill and it was feared that it would cut off their retreat, but they retired over it with little or no Loss.

With a ridiculous Parade of Triumph, the Ministerial Troops[6] again took Possession of the Hill which had served them as a Retreat in their Flight from the Battle of Concord; it was expected that they would prosecute the supposed Advantage they had gained by marching immediately to Cambridge which was distant but two Miles, and was not then in a State of Defence; this they failed to do; the Wonder excited by such Conduct soon ceased, when by the best Accounts from Boston we were told, that out of three thousand Men who marched out upon this Expedition, no less than fifteen hundred (ninety two of which were commissioned Officers) were killed or wounded, and about twelve hundred of them either killed or mortally wounded; such a Slaughter was perhaps never before made on British Troops in the Space of about an Hour, during which the Heat of the Engagement lasted, by about fifteen hundred Men, which were the most that were at any one Time engaged on the American Side.[7]

The Loss of the New England Army amounted according to an exact Return, to one hundred and forty five killed and missing, and ⟨between⟩ three ⟨and four⟩ hundred and four wounded; thirty of the first were wounded and taken Prisoners by the Enemy; among the dead was Major General Joseph Warren, a Man whose Memory will be endeared to his Countrymen and to the worthy in every Part and Age of the World, so long as Virtue and Valour shall be esteemed among Mankind; the heroic Coll. Gardner of Cambridge has since died of his Wounds; the brave Lieut. Coll. Parker of Chelmsford who was wounded and taken Prisoner perished in Boston Goal; these three with Major Moore and Major Mcclay who nobly struggled in the Cause of their Country, were the only Officers of Distinction whom we lost;[8] some of great Worth, tho' inferior in Rank were killed, whom we deeply lament; but the Officers and Soldiers in general who were wounded are almost all upon the[9] Recovery.

The Town of Charlestown, the Buildings of which were in general large and elegant, and which contained Effects belonging to the unhappy Sufferers in Boston, to a very great Amount, was entirely destroyed, and its Chimnies and Cellars now present a Prospect to the Americans exciting in their Bosoms an Indignation which nothing can appease but the Sacrifice of those Miscreants who have introduced Horror, Desolation and Havock into the happy Abodes of Peace and Liberty.[10]

Tho' the Officers and Soldiers of the Ministerial Army meanly exult in having gained this Ground, yet they cannot but attest to the Bravery of our Troops, and acknowledge that the Battles of Fontenoy and Minden according to the Number engaged and the Time the Engagement continued were not to be compared with this;[11] and indeed the Laurels of Minden were totally blasted in the Battle of Charlestown.

The Ground, purchased thus dearly, by the British Troops, affords them no Advantage against the American Army now strongly entrenched on a neighbouring Eminence.

The Continental Troops, nobly animated by the Justice of their Cause, strongly[12] urge to decide the Contest by the Sword, but[13] we wish for no further Effusion of Blood if the Freedom and Peace of America can be secured without it; but if it must be otherwise, we are determined to struggle and disdain Life without Liberty.

Oh Britons! be wise for yourselves before it is too late, and secure a commercial Intercourse with the American Colonies before it is forever lost; disarm your ministerial Assassins, put an End to this unrighteous and unnatural War, and suffer not any rapacious Despots to amuse you with the unprofitable Ideas of your Right *to tax and officer the Colonies*, 'till the most profitable and advantageous Trade of the Colonies is irrecoverably lost. Be wise for yourselves and the Americans will contribute to rejoice in your Prosperity.

J Palmer pr Order

MS copy in a clerk's hand (Adams Papers). The letter from Joseph Palmer, dated 25 July, transmitting the account of the battle to Arthur Lee in London and the resolve of 7 July of the Provincial Congress ordering the account drawn up, as well as the narrative itself, are all brought together in a sewn booklet of sixteen pages, of which six are blank. The booklet may be the copy that on 31 Oct. Palmer forwarded to JA (see below). In minor omissions and variations, some mentioned in the notes below, it differs from the versions printed by Force and Frothingham, the differences being attributable to either the copyist's errors or perhaps varying contemporary MS versions (*Archives*, 4th ser., 2:1373–1376; *Siege of Boston*, p. 382–384). A contemporary and somewhat shortened version is printed in *The Remembrancer*, London, 1775, p. 178–179.

[1] On 6 July the Committee of Safety of the Provincial Congress, in order to counteract the misrepresentations of Gen. Gage, urged the Provincial Congress to name a committee to draw up and send to Great Britain "a fair, honest and impartial account" of the Charlestown battle. When the Provincial Congress passed the responsibility back to the Committee, the latter requested Revs. Peter Thacher, William Gordon, and Samuel Cooper to perform the task (Mass. Provincial Congress, *Jours.*, p. 463, 589, 594). A draft made by Peter Thacher is in AAS, *Procs.*, 2d ser., 19 [1908–1909]:438–442.

[2] Omitted here is the clause "which orders were soon to be executed."

[3] Printed versions have here "next to."

[4] The clause "by which only one Man fell" is omitted from the version in *The Remembrancer*.

[5] For a discussion of the likelihood that the British had to storm the redoubt three times before taking it, see French, *First Year*, Appendix 23, p. 743–747.

[6] In *The Remembrancer* "Generals" is substituted for "Troops."

[7] Thacher's draft ends here.

[8] Lt. Col. Moses Parker, Maj. Willard Moore, and Maj. Andrew McClary (Frothingham, *Siege of Boston*, p. 176, 178, 186–187).

[9] Printed versions have here "in a fair way of" for "almost all upon the."

[10] Printed versions have "peace, liberty, and plenty."

[11] In 1745 at Fontenoy, where the French won an impressive victory, the combined forces of England and Hanover totaled about 16,000. At Minden, fought in 1759, the victorious English and German forces numbered around 36,000 (William Edward Hartpole Lecky, *A History of England in the Eighteenth Century*, 8 vols., N.Y., 1878–1890, 1:455; 2:552). A comparison of English casualties at Minden and Bunker Hill was printed in the *Massachusetts Spy*, 20 Oct.

[12] Force and Frothingham have "sternly."

[13] *The Remembrancer* omits the two preceding paragraphs and the opening of this paragraph through "but."

To James Warren

Dear Sir   July 26. 1775

I can never Sufficiently regret, that this Congress have acted So much out of Character, as to leave the Appointment of the Quarter Master General, Commissary of Musters and Commissary of Artillery to the General; As these officers, are Checks upon the General, and he a Check upon them: there ought not to be too much Connection between them. They ought not to be under any dependance upon him, or So great Obligations of Gratitude as these of a Creature to the Creator.

We have another office of vast Importance to fill, I mean that of Paymaster General. And if it is not filled with a Gentleman, whose Family, Fortune, Education, Abilities and Integrity, are equal to its Dignity, and whose long Services in the great Cause of America, have abundantly merited it, it shall not be my Fault. However I cant foretell, with Certainty whether, I shall be so fortunate as to succeed.[1]

I see by Edes's last Paper that Pidgeon has been Commissary for the Mass. Forces, and Joseph Pearce Palmer Quarter Master General.[2] No Body, was kind enough to notify me of these appointments or any other.

We shall establish a Post office[3]—and do what We can to make salt Petre and to obtain Powder. By the Way about Six Tons have arrived here, within 3 days, and every Kernell of it, is ordered to you.

I want a great deal of Information. I want to know more precisely than I do the Duties and necessary Qualifications of the officers. The Quarter-Master, Commissary of Stores and Provisions, the Commissary of Musters and the Commissary of Artillery, as well as the Paymaster General, the Adjutant General, the Aid de Camps, [...] Brigade Majors, the Secretaries &c.

I want to know more exactly the Characters and biography of the officers in the Army. I want to be precisely informed, when and where, and in what Station General Ward has served, General Thomas, the two Fry's, Whitcomb &c and what Colonells We have in the Army and their Characters.

I am distressed to know what Engineers you have, and what is become of Gridley and Burbanks, what service they have Seen, and what are their Qualifications.[4] yours &c.

RC (MHi: Warren-Adams Coll.); addressed: "To the Hon. James Warren Esqr.   late President of the Provincial Congress   Watertown"; docketed: "Mr. J A. Lettr   July 1775 X."

[1] James Warren was unanimously elected paymaster general by the congress on 27 July (JCC, 2:211).

[2] John Pigeon, about whom there is little information, was appointed commissary of the army by the Provincial Congress on 19 May. Joseph Pearse Palmer (1750–1797), the son of Gen. Joseph Palmer and nephew of Richard Cranch, was recommended to Gen. Ward for quartermaster general by the Committee of Safety on 30 April. Although Ward then appointed him, no record of the approval of the Provincial Congress has been found. Palmer was supplanted when Thomas Mifflin became quartermaster general for the Continental Army (Mass. Provincial Congress, *Jours.*, p. 242, 530; Sibley-Shipton, *Harvard Graduates*, 17:584–590).

[3] On 26 July the congress established a post office and unanimously elected Benjamin Franklin to the office of postmaster general (JCC, 2:208–209).

[4] JA wrote also to William Tudor on 26 July asking for this same information about army positions and persons (MHi: Tudor Papers). James Frye (1709–1776) was a second cousin to Joseph Frye (see Gerry to Massachusetts Delegates, 20 June, note 7, above) and commander of the Essex regiment at the beginning of the war and later of the 6th brigade of the army surrounding Boston (*Appletons' Cyclo. Amer. Biog.*). John Whitcomb (1720?–1812) was appointed major general by the Provincial Congress on 26 June (same; Mass. Provincial Congress, *Jours.*, p. 326, 400).

To James Warren

Dr sir   July 26. 1775

I shall make you sick at the Sight of a Letter from me.

I find by Edes's Paper that Joseph Pearse Palmer is Quarter Master General. I confess I was Surprized.

This office is of high Rank and vast Importance. The Deputy Quarter Master General whom we have appointed for the New York Department, is a Mr. Donald Campbell, an old regular officer, whom We have given the Rank of Collonell. The Quarter Master General cannot hold a lower Rank perhaps than a Brigadier.

Mr. Palmer is a young Gentleman of real Merit and good Accomplishments; but I should not have thought of a less Man than Major General Fry for the Place. It requires an able experienced Officer. He goes with the Army, and views the Ground, and marks out the Encampment &c besides other very momentous Duties.

I have written to Mr. Palmer,[1] and informed him that the Appointment of this officer is left with the General.

My dear Friend, it is at this critical Time of great Importance to our Province, that we take Care to promote none to Places but such as will give them Dignity and Reputation. If We are not very solicitous about this, We shall injure our Cause with the other Colonies. yours,

I hope before another Year We shall become more familiarly acquainted with this great Piece of Machinery, an Army.

We have voted three Millions of Dollars—six Tons of Powder are arrived, and We have ordered every Pound of it, to you.

12 O Clock July 26. 1775 this Moment 130 full Barrels making Six Tons and an half of Powder, is brought into the state House Yard in six Waggons—to be sent off to you.[2]

RC (MHi: Warren-Adams Coll.); addressed: "To the Hon. James Warren Esqr   late President of the Provincial Congress   Watertown"; docketed: "Mr J. A Lettr   July 1775."

[1] Not found.

[2] This powder arrived on 25 July and was immediately ordered to Boston, with a guard of riflemen to join it at Trenton (JCC, 2:204).

To James Warren

Dear sir   Philadelphia July 27. 1775

The Congress have this Day, made an establishment of an Hospital and appointed Dr. Church Director and surgeon[1] and have done themselves the Honour of unanimously appointing the Honourable James Warren Esqr of Plymouth in the Massachusetts Bay, Paymaster General of the Army. The salary of this officer is one hundred Dollars Per Month. It is an office of high Honour and great Trust.

There is another Quantity of Powder arrived in New Jersey about 5000 Weight from So. Carolina—and it is said that another Boat has arrived in this River with about Six or Seven Tons. It will be ordered to the Generals Washington and Schuyler.

We have voted fifty Thousand Dollars, for Powder to be got immediately—if possible.[2]

I begun this Letter only to mention to you a Number of young Gentlemen bound to the Camp. Mr. George Lux, son of a particular Friend of my Friend Chase. Mr. Hopkins and Mr. Smith all of Baltimore in Maryland. Mr. Cary is with them son of Mr. Cary of Charlestown—neither Father nor son want Letters.

Your fast day Letter to me, is worth its Weight in Gold. I had by that Packett Letters from you, Dr. Cooper Coll. Quincy, and Mrs. Adams, which were each of them worth all that I have received from others since I have been here.[3]

RC (MHi: Warren-Adams Coll.); docketed: "Mr J. A. Letter   July 1775 X."

[1] Benjamin Church held this position until 20 Sept., when he resigned because of charges made by various regimental surgeons that he was seeking to abolish their hospitals in favor of a general hospital. Hearings ultimately exonerated him. He was arrested as a British spy on 29 Sept. (JCC, 2:211; Sibley-Shipton, *Harvard Graduates*, 13:380–398; Allen French, *General Gage's Informers*, Ann Arbor, 1932, p. 171–197).

[2] On 27 July the congress voted two sums of $25,000 to merchants in Philadelphia and in New York for the purpose of importing gunpowder (JCC, 2:210–211).

[3] Warren's fast-day letter was that of 20 July (above). The letter from Samuel Cooper has not been found. Quincy's letter was that of 11 July (above), and those from AA, 12 and 16 July (*Adams Family Correspondence*, 1:243–251).

To William Tudor

Dear Sir   July 28 75

Mr. Lux, Mr. Hopkins, Mr. Smith, with Mr. Cary, all from Baltimore, are bound as Volunties to the Camp. Beg the Favour of you, to treat them complaisantly and show them all you can consistently with the Labours of your honourable tho troublesome office.

Shall endeavour to get you a Commission this day, and Such an appointment that you will not be a Looser at the Years End. I hope to get you a Clerk, that you may have some Leisure to write me Annals and Chronicles. For Chronicles I will have, of your Army, at all Hazards.

Make my Compliments acceptable to the Generals to Coll. Reed and Major Mifflin &c.

Is it practicable to lock up Boston Harbour and how can it be done. What Islands, can be fortified? Can Row Gallies be built, or floating Batteries? This city is building a Number. Dr. Franklin is Postmaster. Some Powder is arrived, more expected.   J. Adams

RC (MHi: Tudor Papers); addressed: "To William Tudor Esqr   Judge-Advocate to the American Army   Cambridge   favoured by Mr Lux"; docketed: "July 28th. 1775."

To Josiah Quincy

Dear Sir   Philadelphia. July 29th. 1775

I had yesterday the honour of your letter of July the eleventh, and I feel myself much obliged, by your kind attention to me and my family, but much more by your care of the public safety, and the judicious and important observations you have made. Your letters Sir, so far from being "a burden," I consider as an honour to me, besides the pleasure and instruction they afford me. Believe me, Sir, nothing is of more importance to me, in my present most arduous, and laborious employment, than a constant correspondence, with gentlemen of figure and experience, whose characters are known. The minutest fact, the most trivial event, that is connected with the great American Cause, becomes important, in the present critical situation of affairs, when a Revolution seems to be in the designs of Providence, as important, as any that ever happened in the affairs of mankind.

We jointly lament the loss of a Quincy, and a Warren; two characters, as great in proportion to their age, as any that I have ever known in America. Our country mourns the loss of both, and sincerely sympathises with the feelings of the mother of the one, and the father of the other. They were both my intimate friends, with whom I lived and conversed, with pleasure and advantage. I was animated by them, in the painful, dangerous course, of opposition to the oppressions brought upon our Country; and the loss of them, has wounded me too deeply, to be easily healed. "Dulce, et decorum est pro Patria mori."

The ways of Heaven are dark and intricate; but you may remember the words, which many years ago you and I, fondly admired, and which upon many occasions I have found advantage in recollecting.

> Why should I grieve,—when grieving I must bear.
> And take with guilt,—what guiltless I might share?

I have a great opinion of your knowledge, and judgment, from long experience, concerning the channels and islands in Boston harbour; but I must confess your opinion that the harbour might be blocked up, and seamen and soldiers made prisoners, at discretion, was too bold and enterprising for me, who am not apt to startle at a daring proposal; but I believe I may safely promise you powder enough, in a little time for any purpose whatever. We are assured in the strongest manner, of salt-petre, and powder, in sufficient plenty another year of our own make. That both are made in this city, you may report with confidence, for I have seen both, and I have seen a set of very large powder works, and another of saltpetre.

I hope Sir, we shall never see a total stagnation of commerce, for any length of time. Necessity will force open our ports. Trade if I mistake not will be more free than usual. Your friend Dr. Franklin, to whom I read your letter, and who desires his compliments to you; has been employed in directing the construction of row gallies for this city. The Committee of safety for this province have ordered twenty of them to be built, some of them are finished.[1] I have seen one of them, it has twelve oars on each side. They rowed up the river the first time, four miles in an hour, against a tide which ran down four miles an hour. The Congress have recommended to the Colonies, to make provision for the defence of their navigation, in their harbours, rivers, and on their sea coasts.[2] Of a floating Battery I have no idea— am glad you are contriving one. You tell me Sir, that General Lee complained that "he did not find things, as the Massachusetts Delegates had represented them." What General Lee could mean by this Sir, I know not. What particulars he found different from the representation, I do not know—nor do I know which delegate from the Massachusetts, he received a mistaken representation from. I think he should have been particular, that he might not have ran the risque of doing an injury.[3] If General Lee should do injustice, to two of the Massachusetts delegates, he would commit ingratitude at the same time, for to two of them, he certainly owes his promotion in the American army, how great a hazard soever, they ran in agreeing to it.[4] I know him very thoroughly I think, and that he will do great service in our army, at the beginning of things, by forming it to order, skill, and discipline. But we shall soon have officers enough. Your friend, and humble servant,

MS copy made by Eliza Susan Quincy, 1822–1823 (MHi:Quincy Papers).

[1] On 15 July the Council of Safety ordered the building of twelve boats (*Penna. Colonial Records*, 10:287, 295).

[2] The recommendation was made 18 July (JCC, 2:189).

[3] In a letter to Robert Morris on 4 July, Lee wrote that when he and the rest of Washington's party arrived in Cambridge, "we found every thing exactly the reverse of what had been represented." He was referring to the lack of engineers and artillery and the apparent unwillingness of the soldiers to accept officers from outside New England (NYHS, *Colls. for 1871, Lee Papers*, 1:188).

[4] A reference to JA and Samuel Adams, who were instrumental in getting Lee appointed despite the opposition of Hancock, Paine, and Cushing (JA to James Warren, 21 June, above).

To James Warren

Dear Sir   Philadelphia July 30th. 1775

For the Honour of the Massachusetts I have laboured in Conjunction with my Brethren to get you chosen Paymaster General, and Succeeded So well that the Choice was unanimous: But whether We did you a Kindness or a Disservice I know not. And whether you can attend it, or will incline to attend it I know not. You will consider of it however.

Pray, who do you intend to make Secretary of the Province? Has not our Friend deserved it? Is he not fit for it? Has any other Candidate So much Merit, or So good Qualifications? I hope his temporary Absence will not injure him.[1]

This Letter goes by my good Friend Mr. William Barrell[2] a worthy Bostonian transmuted into a worthy Philadelphian; But whether you will grasp His Letter or the Hand that writes it first, Is uncertain, both about the same Time I hope.

RC (MHi:Warren-Adams Coll.); addressed: "To the Hon. James Warren Esqr. Speaker of the House of Representatives of the Massachusetts Bay Watertown favoured by Mr Barrell." Only an unmeaningful fragment of the second page of this letter has been found, having the address on the verso.

¹ Undoubtedly Samuel Adams, who was elected permanent secretary on 10 Aug., replacing Perez Morton, who served while Adams was in Philadelphia. Adams took up his duties on 15 Aug. (M-Ar:Executive Council Records, 17: 16, 23, 26).

² William Barrell (d. 1776) began business in Philadelphia, about two years before his death, as a representative of the Boston firm of Amory and Taylor. He was a brother-in-law of John Andrews, whose letters to Barrell describing Boston under siege, taken from a collection of Barrell papers in the Massachusetts Historical Society, have been published in MHS, *Procs.*, 1st ser., 8 (1864–1865):316–412. For a brief sketch of Barrell see same, p. 318–319.

From William Tudor

Dear Sir　　　　　　Head Quarters at Cambridge July 31st. [1775]

I have this Minute your Favour of 23d. July. We have had, Saturday Night and last Night much skirmishing between the ministerial and continental Troops. The Regulars attempted entrenching on Charlestown Neck Saturday Night, which produc'd a Brush Sunday Morning. They were obliged to desist by the Fire of our ranging Parties. It is said they lost seven and we two Men. There has been a considerable Cannonade from the Entrenchments on Bunkers Hill this Morning. They have kill'd two of our People. Marblehead Men. Their Cannon were not answer'd from our Forts—because we are not yet in a perfect State of Defence.¹

Genl. Gage has again permitted the Inhabitants of Boston to come out, on the same Lay² as before 17th. June. From the best Accounts of those I have seen who came out on Saturday, the Enemy have but 5000 effective Men. The Men grumble for Pay and fresh Provission. They are distress'd, chagrin'd and confounded. They have been very sickly but are mending. The Regulars burnt the George Tavern³ on Saturday Night—and lost one Man who deserted. Last Week we had 5 Deserters come over—I expect many more.

It is now 5 oClock Afternoon and I have but just return'd from Court Martial, which sits every Day from 8 to 3 oClock. I was appointed Judge Advocate the 14th. Instant and have not had a Leisure hour since. The Duty is excessively fatiguing. I am alone in the office without a C[lerk or]⁴ any Assistance. I am ordered to go to Roxbury tomorrow and yet have Orders to attend a very important Trial here. My Duty is vastly more important and extensive than I could have imagined. One Court is no sooner dissolv'd than another is ordered to sit. The Congress I believe were not sufficiently aware of the Necessity of the Appointment of Judge Advocate and much less of his Duty, or surely they would not have Allow'd only Captain's Pay to the Man who in this Department must act as Advocate, Register, and Clerk. I must beg Sir you will make a proper Representation of this Place to the Congress, and let there be a Stipend fix'd a little more adequate to the Office.

I am now writing this Letter on the Secretary's Table at Head Quarters—and have just return'd from viewing 35 Prisoners in the Yard taken this Morning at the Light House by a Party of our Forces. Last fast Day, a Detachment from the Army burnt the Light House and Since which Our Enemies have thought it necessary to rebuild it, or at least set up some temporary Substitute. They sent down a Number of Carpenters and a Party of Marines as a Guard, consisting of 1 Lieutenant 2 Sargents 2 Corporals and 28 Privates. Our Men made a Descent in a Number of Whale Boats from Nantasket, on the Light House Rocks, this Morning—and immediately attack'd the Enemy. They gave our People one Fire, by which we lost one Man, and then surrendered. Their Lieutenant was shot through the Head and they had three other Men kill'd. Our Men made 23 of the Marines Prisoners, 11 Artificers and 1 Tory. The infamous Abijah White[5] was shot through the Back, and it is said is mortally wounded. Your very humble Servt.   Wm. Tudor

Your kind Wishes express'd in the Letter I just received demand my most grateful Acknowlegements.

RC (Adams Papers).

[1] For other accounts of this action, as well as the raid on the lighthouse described by Tudor below, see Gage, *Corr.*, 1:413; *Boston Gazette*, 7 Aug.; Washington, *Writings*, ed. Fitzpatrick, 3:393–394; and *Adams Family Correspondence*, 1:270–271.

[2] Basis or rate (OED). For the conditions, see James Warren to JA, 7 May, note 8 (above).

[3] On Boston Neck.

[4] Supplied by conjecture but in line with Tudor's expressed complaint (to JA, 19 July, above). Sealing wax has obliterated this portion.

[5] Probably Abijah White Sr., who died in Boston on 29 Oct. (Lysander Salmon Richards, *History of Marshfield*, Plymouth, Mass., 1905, 2:44; Sabine, *Loyalists*, 2:419).

From James Warren

My Dear Sir   Watertown July 31 1775

I had the pleasure of your favours of the 23d. Instant Yesterday. I am glad to find that you have appointed Thomas the first Brigadier this I think will satisfy both him and the Army. I have been Obliged to take pains to keep him in the Camp, he seldom talks Imprudently, and I believe has never done it on this Occasion. Spencer is a Man I have no knowledge of. He left the Camp on the first hearing of the Arrangement with resentment. He has since returned, and I am

told behaves very well. I am Convinced of the Necessity of supporting your own dignity, and the Importance of your Commissions. If
you suffer them to be despised they will soon depreciate, and become
of little value. While Thomas talked of leaving the Camp, I must
do him the Justice to say he Exhibited a degree of the virtue you admire. He said he would soon return, and serve as a Voluntier.[1] I have
lately felt great Uneasiness on your Account. Your want of health, and
the disorder in your Eyes yet continueing at a time when you are Engaged in such a Variety of great and Complicated Business, I should
think sufficient, without External Embarrassments, and the pain you
must feel from dissentions which Injure the General Interest of the
whole, and that of your own Colony in perticular. It seems to be the
misfortune of every Man of Enlarged Ideas, and Extended Views,
of Integrity, and disinterested Virtue to be plagued with either the
Narrow, Contracted Notions, or Interested designs of those he is Connected with in publick life. This is Exactly your Case. I have been
sensible of it a good while, and have a more perfect Idea of it than
I can Express. The Hint you give of Inviteing all Nations to Trade with
us is indeed a grand Idea and I can easily Conceive how bitterly you
regret the loss of it, such a Step would have been worthy of such a
Body. It would have been in the true Stile of a Sully, and have produced mighty Consequences. I can easily Conceive also the Narrow
Principles that Operated against, and finally destroyed them. The two
questions you Ask, to what Articles the Trade should Extend, and
what Bottoms it Should be Carried on rcquire a Nice determination.
Perhaps it would not Answer our Immediate purposes so well by being
Confined to our Own Bottoms, but if it be not and we should finally
be detached from Britain we might have some difficulty in makeing
an Alteration so Advantageous to ourselves in gaining great Wealth
and Naval Power. I hope to hear you viva voce on this Subject.

After a most profound Tranquility for a state of War, several Skirmishes of some Consequence took place last Night. The Regulars had
advanced a little without Charlestown Neck, which gave Umbrage
to our Troops. Some Fireings happened, in the Night which was dark.
A number of the Rifle Men got within their Outer Guards, and but for
an Unlucky Circumstance (they happened at that Instant to be re-
lieving their Guards) had brought of[f] their Main Guard intire. However, a smart Action Ensued. They brought of[f] 2 or 3 of them, and
several Arms, and killed several of their Men. One of ours was taken
by them supposed to have lost his way. About the same time, the regulars about 60 of them pushed out suddenly on Boston Neck, drove

back a few of our Centinels, and by the Negligence of our Main Guard, and the Cowardice of the Captain,[2] Burnt the George Tavirn, and retired without loss. This is Esteemed the greatest disgrace we have suffered. The most Capital Action was at the light House. You will recollect that we Burnt it some time ago. They had for some time been very Industrious in rebuilding it, and had it in such forwardness as Actually to shew a Light on Saturday Night. About 25 Whale Boats, and 200 Men Commanded by Majr. Tupper set off last Night, and Arrived about daylight, Attacked the Guard, and the Workmen, and one small Tender.[3] Soon Carried it after Killing 2 or 3, and wounding 4 or 5 more. They took all the rest, Burnt and destroyed the Light House, took 36 prisoners, and all their Arms. Among the Prisoners are 4 Marshfield Tories and 3 or 4 Others the rest are Marines and soldiers. One of the Whites of Marshfield is wounded it is said Mortally.

Augt. 2d.

I went Yesterday for the first time this Session to wait on the General. I had rather delayed it as you had mentioned me to him as a person he might Consult with, to see if he had any occasion to Call on me. However out of Respect to him, and to see if I could serve the persons you recommend I went. I find the Colony as you predicted will suffer by referring the Appointments you mention to him. They will I think go to the Southward.[4] I am amazed that the Impropriety of his Appointing was not sufficient to determine every one of your Body, and I should have thought both Considerations would have clearly determined your Brethren. He has not yet made the Appointments. When I was comeing of[f], I took the freedom to mention the sufferings and Abilities of a Number of Gentlemen and to ask the Liberty to mention them if he had any occasion for them even in places of no great Importance. He said there were many Gentlemen that had come some 100 miles and as we had so large a share of the places, they must be provided for and that we had among ourselves in Effect the power of supplying all Vacancies in the Army which is true but wont Aid our Friends. Ever since the Action on Sunday evening there has been a Continual Fireing with Cannon or small arms. The Rifle Men have killed several of them and among the rest An Officer who one of them shot from his Horse Yesterday at the distance of 250 yards. The Prisoners taken at the Light House were yesterday Carried through this Town in their way to the Goals in the Upper Countys.

Our Assembly are drudgeing on in the old way, Shackled with Forms and plagued with the Concurrence and Consent of several Branches. A Question was started and warmly Contested whether our Constitution Consisted of 2 or 3 Branches, and was determined in favour of the latter rather from a supposition that it was your design than from the Express words of your resolve.[5]

It was but last Evening I heard of this Opportunity and have not time to say many things I could wish for I Expect the Express, and must be ready. The General was kind enough to direct he should call.

You will remember that our Army I mean our Forces are Inlisted only to the last of Decr. We must perhaps have a winter As well as Summer Campaign. I Am Well Informed that Newfoundland is Supplied with Provisions from N. York. A late Instance A Vessel Arrived there from York, cleared out for the West Indies. This may be worth Enquiring into. You Mention Nothing of an Adjournment. From others we are made to Expect it, and to suppose you are on your way Home.[6]

Your good Lady and Family were well a few days ago. I sent a Letter to the Care of Majr. Mifflin some days ago for you perhaps from Mrs. Adams.[7] It was sent to me and so directed. He promised good Care of it. Mr. Adams Son is provided for in the Manner he wishes.[8] Pray make my regards to him. Nothing but want of time prevents my writing to him. Please to give my regards to Mr. Paine. I acknowledge the receipt of A Letter from him. Shall write him per first opportunity. I Am Your Sincere Friend   J: W——

A Treaty has subsisted for some time between the Selectmen of Boston and Gage relative to the Poor. Application was made to us. We provided for them at Salem, and Insisted on haveing the donations with them.[9] They are on their way there but without the donations. Last Fryday he took a sudden resolution to suffer the Inhabitants to come out. A number of them landed at Chelsea. The General Advised us of it. We apprehensive of the small Pox &c., sent A Committee there on Sunday.[10] Many Persons have come out. All Agree in their Accounts of the dristresses of the Inhabitants and Soldiery, that they are very sickly, and many of them dye. It is said that not less than 1800 of the Troops are unfit for Service. Jno. Brown is out and was here Yesterday. He says Gage has determined to detain about 13 till one Jones, and Hicks now in Concord Goal shall be sent in, among which are Boylston and John Gill.[11] What is to be done cant say. Have just received a Letter from Mrs. Adams which Inclose.

RC (Adams Papers); docketed in JA's later hand: "Warren   1775"; in an unknown hand: "July 31st."

[1] For Washington's attempt to persuade Thomas not to resign, see his letter to him of 23 July (Washington, *Writings*, ed. Fitzpatrick, 3:358–361).

[2] Capt. Christopher Gardner was court martialed for "Cowardice, abandoning his post, and deserting his men." He was "sentenced to be cashiered, as incapable of serving his Country in any military capacity" (same, 3:379, 383).

[3] Maj. Benjamin Tupper was commended for his action at the lighthouse in Washington's general orders for 1 Aug. (same, 3:381).

[4] See JA to James Warren, 23 July, note 4 (above). Mifflin and Moylan were from Pennsylvania, Cheever from Massachusetts.

[5] On 28 July the House of Representatives considered how the government of Massachusetts should operate in the absence of a governor or lieutenant governor and ultimately resolved to consider the Council as the governor of the province (Mass., *House Jour.*, 1775–1776, 1st sess., p. 21).

[6] The first session of the Second Continental Congress officially adjourned on 1 Aug. (JCC, 2:239). JA arrived in Watertown on 10 Aug. (James Warren to Mercy Otis Warren, 9 Aug., with postscript 10 Aug., MHi:Warren-Adams Coll.).

[7] AA's letter of 25 July. Mifflin, who apparently did not leave for Philadelphia until at least 5 Aug., carried as well Warren's letter and AA's letter to JA of 31 July, mentioned in the last sentence of Warren's letter (*Adams Family Correspondence*, 1:260–264, 269–272; Warren to JA, 9 Aug., below).

[8] Samuel Adams Jr. (JA to James Warren, 11 July, note 4, above).

[9] On the donations, see Elbridge Gerry to the Massachusetts Delegates, 20 June, note 14 (above).

[10] Meeting on Sunday, 30 July, the House appointed a four-man committee to "inspect the State and Characters of such Inhabitants of Boston, as have, or may arrive from thence" (Mass., *House Jour.*, 1775–1776, 1st sess., p. 25).

[11] Brown reported to the House on 2 Aug. (same, p. 32–33). Jonathan Hicks (1752–1826) and Josiah Jones (d. 1825), loyalists who had taken refuge in Boston after Lexington and Concord, had taken passage in May 1775 on the *Polly*, a dispatch boat bound for Nova Scotia, which was captured. By 10 June the two men had been before the Provincial Congress and were ordered to the Concord jail (Sibley-Shipton, *Harvard Graduates*, 17:388–390; Sabine, *Loyalists*, 1:592–593; Mass. Provincial Congress, *Jours.*, p. 315–317). On 5 Aug. the House resolved to deliver up Hicks and Jones for the release of John Gill, Thomas Boylston, James Lovell, Benjamin Hichborn, and others, including all the selectmen of Boston (*House Jour.*, p. 47). The resolve had little effect, for the exchange of men was never consummated.

From Thomas Young

Sir   Philadelphia 2nd August 1775

To your request that I would give you my sentiments on the important subject of your Commission [1] which so much interests the defence of these Colonies I answer.

Of all pursuits that men have yet engaged in none is more subject to misfortune, imposition, and disappointment than that of minerals. Few are, or from the mysterious and complex nature of the thing can be judges of the matter. Few have the diligence, address and œconomy suitable to carry on so many branches of business with so many men to advantage. Few have the integrity to treat the public with that strict honor that they would a private person or company, and on all occasions to make it their study to gain and to save every farthing for them that the business would throw in their way. Suffer me at once to inform your honor that it is your meeting with a person as well calculated for mineral matters as the worthy Doctor Franklin for those of the Post office that will give you any sort of chance of success.

A man must, in the first place, be a judge of the quality of ores and capable of assaying them so as to discover what heterogeneous matters they contain and how or whether they can profitably be seperated from them; he must determine pretty readily whether a certain vein or bed of ore can be carried on to advantage; whether the ore can be had easy and in sufficient plenty to bear the expence of the high wages of this Country. He should be a judge of situation, respecting wood, water and provision of every sort to carry forward every branch of the complicated business: In fine he ought to be the Philosopher, mechanic, chemist, accomptant, *indeed a judge and director of the human passions*; or so many of the meanest, as well as greatest of mankind as he will have to deal with will never be treated by him in the manner that will afford most advantage and satisfaction to his Country.

Such a man as this, if commissioned by you, will make it his business to seek and fix upon the most advantageous spot he can find, and with the least possible expence, produce you the substance now more immediately wanted. But every one knows that the researches of a skillful and honest man might discover other advantageous metals as well as lead which in our present circumstances are much needed for defence and support.

Whatever a long continued scene of reading and expensive course of experience in this way has put in my power the Committee may at all times command, and if they should judge my services in this arduous department might be beneficial to my Country, and more likely to save the public money than advertising for a miner here, an assayer there, a smelter, colier and every other inferior workman, as chance turned up the information of his being needed, I would cheerfully engage to serve them on such term as none should reasonably complain of.[2] I make this offer as I have in fact seen the business carried on, and believe I could still find the smelter with whose abilities I am thoroughly acquainted, and once had the superintendence of his operations. This workman smelted a considerable quantity of lead from an ore belonging to the late Collo. Martin Hoffman of Dutchess County; but the vein sinking perpendicular in the bottom of a valley, which could not be mined, and not being large enough to bear the expence of a fire engine³ the work was dropped. The ore that I was most concerned in working was too much embarrassed with iron to yield any profit till it got farther down than our company were disposed to carry it. I am Sir your most obdt. humble servt.

Tho Young⁴

RC (Adams Papers); addressed: "To the Honorable John Adams Esqr."

¹ JA was a member of a committee of the congress which had members from each colony, and which was to find sources of lead and the best methods for refining it (JA's Service in the Congress, 10 May – 1 Aug., Editorial Note, above). If JA put his request in a letter, it has not been found.

² No record of acceptance of Young's offer has been found.

³ That is, a steam engine (*OED*).

⁴ Young (1732–1777), a physician and ardent whig, was active in the Sons of Liberty in Boston, although he grew to manhood in New York. In 1775 he went to Philadelphia, and in 1776 he helped to frame the Pennsylvania constitution (*DAB*; Pauline Maier, "Reason and Revolution: The Radicalism of Dr. Thomas Young," *Amer. Quarterly*, 28: 229–249 [Summer 1976]).

From James Warren

My Dear Sir   Watertown Augt:9th:1775

I have very Accidentally heard of this Opportunity by Mr. Brown and have so short Notice of it that I can do little more than Acknowledge the Receipt of your favour of the 26th. July, which I Received the day before Yesterday when my Mind was tortured with Anxiety and distress. The Arrival of powder in this manner is certainly as Wonderful an Interposition of Providence in our favour as used to take place in favour of the Jews in the days of Moses and Joshua. We have very little News here, no remarkable military Events have taken place in the Army here. In short the General has been obliged from Principles of frugality to restrain his rifle men. While they were permitted Liberty to fire on the Enemy, a great number of the Army would go and fire away great quantitys of Ammunition to no Purpose.¹ Four Captains and a Subaltern were killed the beginning of last week cheifly by the rifle men, and I am persuaded they will do great Execution. There was but one Company of them here last Week. On Sunday a very fine Company came in from Virginia. Yesterday Morning went through this Town 3 Companys more as many are Expected this Morning. I never saw finer fellows. What a view does this, and the Concourse of Gentlemen from all the Colonies give us of Bernard! and Hutchinson! small Faction. Last Evening arrived here a Gentleman from Machias with an Account of their haveing taken two other Tenders. So that they now have five prizes: three Tenders, and two Sloops taken from Jones. 28 Prisoners are on the road and will be hear this day among whom is Old Ichabod Jones.[2] The rest are Lieutenants of Men of War, Midshipmen, and Seamen. Five Sloops after wood and fresh Provisions are taken by Cargill[3] and others and Carried into Penobscot this is doing great Service. They are reduced to great straits for wood as well as fresh provisions in Boston. It is said it would fetch 3 Guineas a Cord. They have already Burnt all the fences &c. All Accounts from Boston agree that they are dismantleing the Castle, and Intend to destroy the works there, which with other Circumstances Induce many to suppose they have an Intention to leave the Town. Many People have lately come out. He has restricted them to £5 sterling in Money, a small matter of furniture and absolutely forbid them bringing out plate. What the policy should be unless he designs to plunder, destroy and then leave we cant devise. Boylston, John Gill, Lovel, the Selectmen, &c to the Number of 13, are kept it is said till Jones, and Hicks two Insignificant Puppies we have in Concord Goal are suffered to go into Boston. We have resolved they shall go. The General has sent in the resolve by a Trumpet. We have no Answer yet tho' that was done last Sunday.

I am very sorry I should omit any Information you had occasion for. It is not wholly and only Negligence. Such has been the Confusion here that it was difficult to Ascertain who held many of the offices. This was the Case with Young Palmer. I often asked, and never was satisfactorily resolved whether he was Quarter Master General or his Deputy. He was however the first, and still Acts as such in the Mass. Forces, and has Expectations of being Appointed by the General. I cant learn that any of those you so Justly regret to have referred to other hands than your own are yet made. As to Pigeon I knew he was a Commissary, but his Temper is so petulant that he has been desirous of quitting for some time, and Indeed I have wished it.

I am taking pains to give you the Information you want of the Biography of the offices in the Army, &c. I have Applyed to Genl. Thomas and one Other General for that Purpose.[4] As for Engineers I wish we were in a better way. G－－－－y is grown old, is much governed by A Son of his, who vainly supposed he had a right to the second place in the Regiment that is before Burbank and Mason. The Congress thought Otherways. He was Sulkey. We had much Trouble with them, and I Understand the General has his Share yet.[5] I have not lately heard from Mrs. Adams, though have frequently Enquired of People from and through Braintree, from which I Conclude she is well. I wrote you a long letter by the Genls. Express which went on last Saturday after being detained much longer than I Expected.[6]

I hope he will be with you Tomorrow. I wish to see the return of Fessenden before I leave this Town.[7] We have a short Adjournment in Contemplation, and Expect it the latter End of this week. You will hear of the Accident which befel the Letters sent by Hitchburn. He very Injudiciously kept them when he had all the Opportunity he could wish to destroy them.[8] I wish to hear whether the Letter to me was from You or Mr. S: Adams. I lost the pleasure of it and they Boast of great discoveries made from that and the two Letters to Genl. Washington.[9] I am very Much Obliged to you for the many Instances of your Partiality and Friendship. I am Necessitated to Conclude or loose this Conveyance, and Am with every Wish for you. Your Sincere Friend,

J:Warren

My regards to all our Friends, perticularly Mr. Adams. Many of the Tories are prepareing to leave Boston. Sewal and Family and some Others are going Home, and some know not where to go.[10] I beleive they are almost ready to Call on the rocks and Mountains to Cover them. I make no Apology for Incorrectness &c. Your Candour is relied on.

RC (Adams Papers); docketed in JA's late hand: "Warren Augt. 9th 1775."

[1] Excessive shooting concerned both Washington and the General Court (General Orders, 4 Aug., Washington, *Writings*, ed. Fitzpatrick, 3:384–385; Resolution, 12 Aug., Mass., *House Jour.*, 1775–1776, 1st sess., p. 66).

[2] In June, Ichabod Jones led an expedition to Machias, Maine, where he owned a mill, to obtain firewood for the army in Boston. On 11 June, in one of the first naval actions of the Revolution, Jones was captured together with the *Margaretta*, the schooner sent by Adm. Graves to escort the expedition. On 15 Aug., Jones was sent to jail in Northampton; a few days later the General Court ordered the seizure of his property in Machias, an action that he protested in Sept. 1776, when he petitioned for a rehearing of his case (MHi:Gay Transcripts, Adm. Graves in North America, 1:133, 142, 152, 153, 182; 3:431; Mass. Provincial Congress, *Jours.*, p. 395–396, 399, 500; Mass., *House Jour.*, 1775–1776, 1st sess., p. 88; *House Jour.*, 1776–1777, 2d sess., p. 86; *Naval Docs. Amer. Rev.*, 1:655–656, 676–677).

[3] Probably James Cargill of New-

castle, Maine (Wroth and others, eds., *Province in Rebellion*, p. 1691).

[4] See replies of Gens. Thomas and Frye of 11 and 25 Aug. (below).

[5] The pretensions of Richard Gridley's son, Maj. Scarborough Gridley, did not last long, for a court martial on 24 Sept. found him "guilty of breach of orders" and ordered his dismissal from the army but did not debar him from further service (Washington, *Writings*, ed. Fitzpatrick, 3:515–516).

[6] See Warren to JA, 31 July, note 7 (above).

[7] That is, Warren hopes for another letter from JA.

[8] For Hichborn's justification of his conduct in caring for the letters, see his letter to JA of 28 Oct. (below).

[9] The only known letter to Washington in the group of intercepted letters is that from Benjamin Harrison.

[10] The Sewalls and a number of other loyalists left Boston on 21 Aug. and arrived in London on 21 Sept. (Thomas Hutchinson to Lord Hardwicke, 22 Sept., MHi:Gay Transcripts, Hutchinson-Hardwicke Letters, p. 56a–59).

John Adams' Service in the Council

10–30 August 1775

Editorial Note

After the official adjournment of the Second Continental Congress on 1 August, another meeting was held on the morning of the next day. Adams may not have left Philadelphia, then, until 3 August (*JCC*, 2:239; Burnett, ed., *Letters of Members*, 1:185, note 2). We know that he arrived in Watertown on 10 August to take his seat on the Massachusetts Council, which was then serving as both the upper house and the executive of the province (M-Ar:Executive Council Records, 17:15).

Because Adams did not keep a diary or write letters during August 1775, it is difficult to go beyond the brief references to him in the records of the Council in describing his role in that body. He is listed as being present at Council meetings on nine days between his arrival and 30 August, which are also the days for which the Council on 11 September authorized payment of his expenses (M-Ar:Executive Council Records, 17:15, 28, 29, 31, 37, 39, 61, 66, 69, the dates being 10, 16–18, 22–23, 28–30 Aug.; same, Revolution, Council Papers, 164:91). Adams may, however, have been present on two other days, 19 and 24 August. On the 19th, a report, signed by Adams, concerning the disposition of Thomas Hutchinson's captured letters was presented to the Council, and on the 24th he is recorded as participating in four votes (report, 19 Aug., following Editorial Note; M-Ar:Legislative Council Records, 33:130, 185, 196, 204). For the entire period, the only indications of his individual activity, besides the report on Hutchinson's letters, are these: carrying to the House of Representatives a draft bill on annulling commissions given by former governors and lieutenant governors (Mass., *House Jour.*, 1775–1776, 1st sess., p. 60; text in Mass., *Province Laws*, 5:420–421); concurring in 28 votes of the Council on various acts and resolves; signing with other Council members in advance printed commissions for justices and inferior court judges; and apparently initiating the appointment of a committee on 23 August to investigate sources of "virgin lead" in Massachusetts, a motion that grew out of his committee responsibility in the congress (M-Ar:33:74–204, 154; JCC, 2:234–235). On 22 August the Council authorized payment of £130 for his expenses at the congress (M-Ar:17:38). His expense accounts are in *Diary and Autobiography*, 2:162–167.

Adams' activities outside the Council are conjectural, but he certainly spent much of his time in Braintree. He was probably there on 14 August, when he settled his account with Joseph Bass Jr., and from 25 to 27

August, as is indicated in his letter to Mrs. Warren (JA, *Diary and Autobiography*, 2:167; to Mercy Otis Warren, 26 Aug., below). Accompanied by Charles Lee, he made a tour of the American positions around Boston, but on what day is unknown to the editors (JA, *Diary and Autobiography*, 3:325). When he attended the Council on 22–24 August, he took Abigail with him to Watertown, but his stay was short, for, as noted, he was back in Braintree on 25 August (same, 2:167–168 and note 1). On 28 August, he left Braintree, stopped at Watertown for three days to attend meetings of the Council, and then continued on to Philadelphia, where he arrived on 12 September (same, 2:168; for the exact day of JA's arrival, see his docket entry on his letter from Edward Dilly of 11 July, above).

Report of Council Committee Regarding Governor Hutchinson's Letters

[19 August 1775]

THE COMMITTEE [to consider what is proper to be done with the Letters of the late Govr Hutchinson and how they shall be preserv'd] [1] Report, that it is of Great Importance that the Letters and other Papers of the late Governor Hutchinson, be carefully preserved, as they Contain Documents for History of great Moment: and that Evidence, in the hand writing of a Man whose nefarious Intrigues and practices, have Occassioned the Shedding of so much innocent Blood, and brought such horrid Calamities on his Native Country, may be preserved for the full Conviction of the Present and future Generations: and therefore that such of the Letters, and Papers aforesaid, as are not now in the Custody of the Honble Saml Dexter Esqr of Dedham, be delivered to him, and together with those, already under his care, faithfully kept by him, until the further Order of this Court, and that such of them be Publish'd from time to time as he shall Judge proper. John Adams per Order [2]

Read and accepted.

Dft not found. Reprinted from Mass., *Province Laws*, 19:59.

[1] Brackets in printed version.

[2] No evidence has been found to reveal JA's contribution to this report, but the demonstrated concern for history and the conviction that Hutchinson was responsible in great part for bringing "horrid Calamities on his Native Country" are quite in keeping with JA's attitudes and thinking.

John Thomas to James Warren

Sir   Camp at Roxbury Augt. 11. 1775

I receiv'd yours of the 7th Instant, and Consider'd the Contents.[1] To comply with every part, so as to make it Inteligable so far as fully to explain every part of the duty of each of those Officers you Mention, wou'd take a small Volume, but will Endeavour to give you some General Account of their Duty—as to their Qualifications you will be able to Judge of it.

The duty of a Quartermaster General, is to Inspect the Provisions and See that they are good and wholesom, and to see that Tents for the Army, Intrenching Tools and any other Articles Necessary for the Camp are Provided, to draw them out of the Store when wanted, and return them in when done with, to pitch on proper Ground for the Incampments, to laying out the Ground in Lines, that the Tents of each Regiment be properly Pitch'd according to their Rank, and form'd in the best manner for defence, and giveing directions to the Quartermasters of each Regiment, and Camp Culler Men, that the Barracks be kept Clean, and the Streets Sweept and all Filth be remove'd, that proper Vaults[2] be Open'd for the Use of the Troops &c.

The Commasary of Provision, is to receive the Provision from the Contractors and to deliver them to the under Commasaries with directions for the delivery of them to the Troops according to the Order he may receive from the Commanding Officer, and is to be Accountable to the Publick in what way the Provisions are expended, by takeing receipts of the Commander in Chief for his Voucher.

Commassary of Muster, is to Muster all the Regiments in the Army; Usually once in two Months, that the Commanding Officer of each Regiment, may Account for his Regiment, whether Sick, on Furlough, or on Command, and the Several Cantonements must See that the Muster Rools must Contain the Names of each Man in the Regiment to be attested by said Commasary, One to be Transmitted to the War Office, one to be kept by the Muster Master, The third to be deliver'd to the pay Master, by which the said pay Master is to pay of[f] the Troops, according to their Several Ranks.

The Commasary of Artillery, is what we generally call the Director whose business it is to keep the Artillery Stores, to be deliver'd to the Train, when drawn for by an Order from the Commanding Officer— the receiver to give his receipt, which is to be a Voucher when he is Call'd to a Settlement.

119

7. JOHN THOMAS (1724–1776),
BY BENJAMIN BLYTH, 1775
See page xi

The Pay Master General receives the Cash, and pays of[f] the Muster Rools Affore mention'd, and any other Drafts that the Commanding Officer may make on him for the Use of the Army.

The Adjutant General Attends the Commanding Officer every day at orderly times, for the General Orders, and the Adjutants of each Regiment must attend him at his Office, at a certain hour that he may perfix, where he must deliver the Order to each of them, and they to their Several Regiments.

Aid-de-Camps are constantly to attend the General, are to give him information of what comes to their knowledge, and to be ready to Attend his order, to go on any Message—and what Orders they may deliver Verbally from the General carries as much authority as if written, Especially in time of Action, and many other Services too many to be enumerated.

When the Army is divided into Grand Divisions, they are call'd Brigades, and are under the more immediate command of the Brigadier General, each one has his Brigade assigned him, and a Brigade Major Affix'd to each Brigade, who is to Attend the Brigadier General, to Convey the Orders of the said General, to the Adjutants of the Brigade, and inspect the Guards when Peraded by the Adjutants; and any order Sign'd by him as Brigade Major, must carry the same force, as if Sign'd by the Brigadier General himself. He is to attend the Brigadier General in time of Action, ready to convey his Order during the Action to every part of the Brigade, whether for Attacking, retreating, or any other matter whatever.

With regard to my Services, I first enter'd as Ensign, in a Regiment Commanded by Brigadier Waldo Rais'd for an Expedition against Cannady, was sent to Anapolis Royall and Minis, Commanded Leiut. Colo. Noble, was advanc'd in 1748 in the same Regiment to a Leiutenancy, and Surgeon, Continu'd two years in that Regiment, Rank'd by Act of Parliment with the Regulars, and did duty with them part of the time Anapolis Royall. 1755 Captain Leiutenant and Surgeon in the first Battallion in Governor Shirleys Regiment. 1756 Advanc'd to a Captain in the same Battallion. 1758 Colonel of a Regiment at Noviscotia, Beau-se-Jour. 1759 Colonel of Regiment at the same place. 1760 Colonel of a Regiment in Cannady.

Fry an Ensign at Louisbourg 1745. Major in Scotts Battallion at Noviscotia 1755. Major at the Lake 1757. Colonel at Noviscotia 1759.

General Whitcomb Leiut. Colonel at Lake George 1756. Colonel at ditto 1760.

General Ward, Major at Ford Edward, in Colo. Wm. Williams Regiment 1758, and in the same year obtain'd a Leiut. Colonel with Colo. Partridge.

As to the Colonels we have in our Forces &c I will take some other Opportunity to Inform, being much Engaged at present.[3] I am Sir yr. Friend and very huml. Servant, Jn: Thomas

RC (Adams Papers); addressed: "To The Honourable James Warren Esq. Speaker to the Hon. House of Representatives and Pay Master General to the United American Army Watertown"; docketed by JA: "Sept. Gen. Thomas"; docketed later, probably by Rev. William Gordon: "Aut 11. 1775."

[1] James Warren to John Thomas, 7 Aug. (MHi:John Thomas Papers). This letter, mentioned in Warren's letter to JA of 9 Aug. (above), did not indicate that the information to be given by Thomas was ultimately to go to JA.

[2] Drains or sewers, obs. (*OED*).

[3] Warren had asked Thomas to describe "what Colonels we have in our Forces whose Character you Esteem and their Characters." The only other question that Thomas did not answer concerned the experience and qualifications of Richard Gridley and William Burbeck, about whom JA had expressed strong interest to Warren.

From Joseph Frye

Sir   Roxbury Camp Augt. 25th 1775

I have taken leave to Send you Enclos'd herewith, a brief account of the Several Stations in which I have Serv'd my Country in a Military way—as a history of all occurrences and Personal Sufferings in that Service would have been too tedious for your Patience, I presum'd not to trouble you with it.[1] Therefore Shall say no more here than that, any Notice you Shall please to take of me on your arival in the Continental Congress, will be gratefully Acknowledged by your Honrs. most Obedient and very Humble Servt., Joseph Frye

ENCLOSURE

A brief Account of the Military Services of Joseph Frye

In 1745 He was an Ensign of a Company in Colo. Robert Hales Regiment at the Reduction of Louisbourg.

In 1746, He was made a Lieutenant in Major Moses Titcombs Company in Brigr. General Waldo's Regiment, design'd to Serve in an Expedition against Canada under the Command of General St. Clare [Saint-Clair]—but as the Expedition hung in Suspence, It was propos'd by the Government of Massachusetts-Bay, That said Regiment Should Serve in the defence of the Eastern Frontiers in Stead of Impress'd men, till called for to proceed to Canada. Agreeable to which, part of the Regiment went to Casco Bay, and was Employ'd in the Defence of that part of the Country, where the said Joseph did a large Share of the hardest of the Service, till news ariv'd from England that the Expedition was laid aside.

In 1747 He was made Captain of a Company for the Defence of the Eastern Frontiers and Posted at Scarborough for that Purpose, in which Service He continued till the Latter part of 1749 when that war ended.

In 1754 He was made Major of a Regiment Commanded by Majr. Genl. John Winslow, which was Sent to Kennebeck River, when the Regiment built Fort Halifax at the Falls in said River called Tauconnock, and before He return'd to Boston, was made a Lt. Colonel.

In 1755 an Expedition was form'd, to remove the French Encroachments in Nova Scotia. A Regiment (formed into two Battalions) was Sent from Boston for that Purpose. And as His Excellency Genl. Shirly, kept said Regiment under his own Command as Colonel— General Winslow went Lt. Colonel of the first Battalion and George Scot Esqr. Lt. Colonel of the Second Battalion, The said Joseph went first Major of the Second Battalion, and was at the Reduction of Fort Beausejour, Fort de gaspereau and other Services in that Country, and continued there for the defence of those Conquests thro' the winter and Summer following, till the fall of the year 1756.

In the fall of the year 1756, as Soon as He ariv'd in Boston, He was made Colonel of a Regiment, held in Readiness to march at a minutes warning, to Reinforce the Troops at Lake George.

In 1757, He was made Colonel of a Regiment Consisting of eighteen hundred men, formed into Seventeen Companies, which was rais'd in the Province of Massachusetts-Bay for the Service on the western Frontiers, with which Regiment, He marched to Albany; from thence to Fort Edward where he lay with said Regiment and did Duty there under the Command of General Webb till the begining of August, when he was Sent with eight hundred and twenty three of them (Inclusive of Officers) to Fort William Henry, and the next morning after his arival there, Monsr. Montcalm arive'd with a Superior Force, laid Seige to the Place, and after Six Days and Seven nights' Defence, were forced to Surrender; which was done by Capitulation, but it was barbarously violated by the French and Indians, which proved a very unhappy occurrence to the said Joseph, as the Regiment was thereby, tore to peices, and many of His Papers fell into the hands of the Enemy, it took the greatest part of his Time in the year 1758 to regain Such a State of the Regiment as that, in the payment thereof, Justice might be done to the Public, and to Individuals.

In 1759 He was made Colonel of a Regiment and Sent with it into Nova Scotia for the Defence of that Province, where he continued almost two years.

Finaly, on the 21st of June 1775, The Congress of the Colony of the Massachusetts-Bay, being Desireous of his Service in the Present unhappy war, gave Him a Major Generals' Commission, and laid him under oath for the faithful discharge of his Duty agreeable to said Commission. In Pursuance whereof He entered upon his Duty and continued therein, till the Representatives of the Several Towns in said Colony, Assembled at Watertown, when that Assembly adopted what the Congress had done in that respect, and by Letter to the said Joseph, desired his Continuance in Camp, till the Continental Congress Should determine the affair with respect to Him.

RC (Adams Papers); enclosure.

[1] In all likelihood, Frye is the "Other General" to whom James Warren applied for information requested by JA (Warren to JA, 9 Aug., above).

From James Prescott

Sir   Watertown Aut 25. 1775

I have this minit received the Inclosed account[1] and Imbrace the oppertunity of Conveying it to you by Mr. Pain. I am Sir your most obediant Huml Sert.,   James Prescott

NB: I find my Brother has not Been so perticuler as I Could have wished—he has not Given any account of his former Campain—he was an officer at the reduction of the Newtrel frinch at Noviscotia in the last war about two years.

RC (Adams Papers); addressed: "To The Honble John Adams Esqr. in Brantrey"; docketed: "Aug 25 1775."

[1] William Prescott to JA, 25 Aug. (below).

From William Prescott

Sir   Camp at Cambridge August 25. 1775

I have received a Line from my Brother which informs me of your desire of a particular Account of the Action at Charlestown.[1] It is not in my Power at present to give so minute an Account as I should choose being ordered to decamp and march to another Station.

On the 16 June in the Evening I received Orders to march to Breeds Hill in Charlestown with a party of about one thousand Men consisting of 3 hundred of my own Regiment, Coll. Bridge and Lieut Breckett with a Detachment of theirs, and two hundred Connecticut Forces commanded by Capt. Nolten [Knowlton]. We arrived at the Spot, the Lines were drawn by the Enginier and we began the Intrenchmant about 12, o Clock and plying the Work with all possible Expodition till Just before sun rising, when the Enemy began a very heavy Canonading and Bombardment. In the Interin the Enginier forsook me.[2] Having thrown up a small Redout, found it necessary to draw a Line about 20 Rods in Length from the Fort Northerly, under a very Warm Fire from the Enemys Artilary. About this Time the above Field Officers being indisposed could render me but Little Service, and the most of the Men under their Command deserted the Party. The Enemy continuing an incessant Fire with their Artilary. About 2, o Clock in the afternoon on the seventeenth the Enemy began to land a northeasterly Point from the Fort, and I ordered the Train with 2 field Pieces to go and oppose them and the Connecticut Forces to support them but the Train marched a different Course and I believe those sent to their support followd, I suppose to Bunkers Hill.[3] Another party of the Enemy landed and fired the Town. There was a party of Hampshire in conjunction with some other Forces Lined a Fence at the distance of three score Rods back of the Fort partly to the North. About an Hour after the Enemy landed they began to march to the Attack in three Columns. I commanded my Lieut Coll. Robinson and Majr. Woods Each with a detachment to flank the Enemy, who I have reason to think behaved with prudence and Courage.

I was now left with perhaps 150 Men in the Fort, the Enemy advanced and fired very hotly on the Fort and meating with a Warm Reception there was a very smart firing on both sides. After a considerable Time finding our Amunition was almost spent I commanded a sessation till the Enemy advanced within 30 yards when we gave them such a hot fire, that they were obliged to retire nearly 150 yards before they could Rally and come again to the Attack. Our Amunition being nearly exausted could keep up only a scattering Fire. The Enemy being numerous surrounded our little Fort began to mount our Lines and enter the Fort with their Bayonets. We was obliged to retreat through them while they kept up as hot a fire as it was possible for them to make. We having very few Bayonets could make no resistance. We kept the fort about one hour and twenty Minutes after the Attack with small Arms. This is nearly the State of Facts tho' imperfect and too general which if any ways satisfactory to you will afford pleasure to your most obedient humble Servt.,

William Prescott

RC (Adams Papers); docketed: "Coll. Prescott. Aug. 25. 1775."

[1] Prescott's account of the Battle of Bunker Hill was another response to JA's request for information about the army and events in Massachusetts. CFA lent this letter, along with others written to JA, to Richard Frothingham, who printed it in the Appendix to his *Siege of Boston* (p. 395–396), and thus it contributed to the controversy that developed in the 19th century over who commanded the troops in the battle, Prescott or Israel Putnam. See French, *First Year*, p. 743–747.

[2] Richard Gridley became tired or ill or left to bring up cannon (same, p. 216, note 16), but he did return and was wounded in the battle.

[3] Actually, they took up a position behind a fence, in a line perpendicular to the breastwork (same, p. 219).

To Mercy Otis Warren

Madam   Saturday Evening Braintree [26] Aug. 1775

I have been, the happiest Man, these two Days past, that I know of, in the World. I have compared myself, in my own Mind, with all my Friends, and I cannot believe any of them So blest as myself.

In the first Place, Rest, you know, is Rapture, to a weary Man; and I was quite weary enough to enjoy a state of Rest for a Day or two in all its Perfection; accordingly, I have Slept, by the best Compution, Sixteen Hours in the four and twenty.

In the next Place, for the two last Days, I have been entirely free from the Persecution, of the "Fidgets, and Caprices, Vanity, Superstition, and Irritability," which are Supposed by Some, to assault me, now and then, both from within and without. This is rare Felicity indeed.

Thirdly, I have been allowed the Pleasure of rambling all alone, through the Fields, Groves and Meadows, and over the lofty Mountains, of peacefull happy Braintree, that wholesome Solitude and Nurse of sense, "where Contemplation prunes her Ruffled Wings And the free Soul, looks down to pity Kings." [1]

Fourthly and lastly, I have enjoyed the Conversation of the amiable Portia, and her little prattling Brood of Children. This is a Pleasure of which I can say no more. Mrs. Warren can conceive it: I cannot describe it.

Now taking all these Circumstances together, neither Mr. Warren nor Mr. [...], nor Mr. any Body that I can recollect, has been in a Situation equal to mine. These have been vexed with the society of

Statesmen and Heroes: I have been disturbed with no such Animal. These have been interrupted with Cares: I have banished all of them from my Habitation, from my Head and Heart. These have been wearied with Business: I would have no Business but have been wholly at Leisure. In Short I have some Idea now of the Happiness of the Inhabitants of Arcadia, Paradise and the Elisian Fields.

Why will the cruel Thought intrude itself? Is this to last only, untill Monday Morning, four O Clock?[2] Avaunt this gloomy Thought, this impertinent Intruder: I wont Suffer myself to think, that it is ever to End, untill the Moment arrives, and then I must endeavour to forget for a while, that I have ever been so happy.

I hope, Madam, I shall not be left to Stain this Paper with any Thing concerning Politicks or War. I was determined to write you before I went away and there is no other Subject, in the whole Compass of Art, Science or Nature, upon which I could have written one Line, without diminishing my Happiness.

I wish you Madam, a Speedy Return, with your worthy Partner, to your Family, and a Happiness there as exquisite as mine has been here and much more lasting. I am with unfeigned Esteem and Affection, your and Mr. Warrens Friend and humble servant,

John Adams

RC (MHi:Warren-Adams Coll.); addressed: "To Mrs. Mercy Warren"; docketed: "J. Adams Augt. 1774"; docketed later: "August 1775 Braintree."

[1] From Alexander Pope's "Satires of Dr. John Donne, Dean of St. Paul's, Versified," Satire IV, l. 186–187.
[2] The day on which JA began his return to Philadelphia, 28 Aug.

From William Tudor

Dear Sir [Aug.? 1775][1]

You was inquiring the other Day into the Office of Judge Advocate. I will now acquaint you with some Particulars in that Department which will give you an Idea of that Officer's Duty in the Continental Army.

As Judge Advocate, I have his Excellency's (the Commander in chief) Orders, in writing, "to attend every General Court Martial, not only those of the Line but of each Brigade throughout the Army: and to see that there is a fair Copy of the intire Proceedings in each Case, made out to be reported to the General." (One Reason for which, is, That as the General is to confirm, or reject the Determination of the

Court, he cannot form a competent Opinion of the Court's Judgement, without seeing the whole State of the Evidence &c.)

The Number of Offences made cognizable by a General Court Martial only; the very large Army here; the Extent of the Camp, in each Quarter of which my Duty requires my Attendance, renders my Office, arduous and difficult.[2]

I am oblig'd to issue Orders to the Adjutants of the Regiments, to see the Prisoners brought up and that the Witnesses attend—and indeed to put all Matters in such a Train that the Court may have Nothing else to do than to hear the Examination, which is all taken down in writing, and give a Judgement. In every Case where the Evidence is complicated, it is expected of me that I analyse the Evidence and state the Questions which are involv'd in it. But I will not trouble you with a tedious Detail. It is sufficient to acquaint you that I am oblig'd to act as Advocate, Register and Clerk. For the Stipend of 20 Dollars a Month. Without the least Assistance, and without a single Perquisite of Office.

In the British Army, General Courts Martial sit only in capital Cases, or when a commissioned officer is to be try'd. He is allow'd 10/ sterling a Day and draws Pay as Capt. besides. His Duty is easy—because the strict Discipline which prevails among regular Troops, render General Court Martial but rarely necessary. The Difference between the Ministerial Army and the American, is easily conceiv'd without drawing a Parralell. I will only observe the hon. Congress have granted near 2000 Commissions and that no Commissioned Officer can be try'd but by a General Ct. Martial. While two thirds of the Crimes of the Privates must come before the same Court for Trial.

Since my Appointment (14 July) I have attended twenty seven Trials, among which were two chief Colonels and Nine commissioned Officers. Every one of which has been minutely reported in Writing to the Commander in chief. And There are now a Col. and two commissioned Officers under an Arrest—who are to be try'd as soon as possible.[3] Those of the Officers have been very lengthy. I am oblig'd to set, without a Minute's Absence from 8 to three—doing the whole Labour of the Trial—and as soon as the Court is adjourn'd, to employ the afternoon in copying the Proceedings of the Morning, that the General may have early Knowlege of the issue. And that the Order of Court may be timely put into the general Orders.

Every Day for a Month past a General Court Martial has set in one or other Part of the Camp. It is impossible for me to be in two Places at once. A Court at Roxbury adjourn'd for six Days successively, because my Duty at Cambridge, forbid my leaving it. The Court cannot consist of less than 13 Members, and the Service is hurt—but it must frequently be the Case while the Judge Advocate is allow'd no Assistant.

I must beg, Sir, on your Return to Congress You would prevail on Our American Legislature, to reconsider the Stipend affix'd to this Office, and endeavour to have a Salary fix'd, more adequate to the Service. Should there be no Alteration made I shall be under the Necessity of asking Permission to resign an Employment the Duties of which, leave me without an Hour to call my own; and the Pay of which will not give me even a Maintenance. I am your most obt. Servt.

Wm. Tudor

RC (Adams Papers); addressed: "Honble. John Adams Esq. Braintree."

[1] Since Tudor wrote while JA was still in Braintree so far as he knew and since provision for pay and a clerk for Tudor was made at the opening session of the congress in Sept. 1775, a date of August seems reasonable for this letter. Moreover, examination of Gen. Washington's General Orders, which record officers tried by court martial, from 14 July, when Tudor was appointed, suggests that in terms of the number of officers Tudor mentions, he may have written this letter as early as mid-August (JCC, 3:257; Washington, *Writings*, ed. Fitzpatrick, 3:*passim*).

[2] Some 25 of the 69 Articles of War adopted by the congress call for punishment of offenses through the means of a general court martial (JCC, 2:111–122).

[3] This sentence was written in the margin and is inserted here, where the editors believe it was intended to go.

From Mercy Otis Warren

Sir   Watertown september 4. 1775

This afternoon came to Hand your Favour of August 26. May you ever have it in your power to expatiate this Largly on your own Happiness, but I would not have you Imagine when you in your sixteen hours Nap and Dreaming of the Feilds of Arcadia, and are Enraptured with the Happy Elisian and paridisaic scenes at Braintree that you are the only Happy Mortal among your Numerous Circle of Friends. I dare say had they the talent of Easey Discription they would Boast of a share of the Felicities of Life though few can pronounce themselves Compleatly happy Even for a day, either Amidst the Cares the tumults and Follies of the World or the still pleasures of Rural Life.

By your Freind Mr. Collins I thought It my Duty to Let you know I heard from Mrs Adams this day who has been a Little unwell since you left her but is much better.[1] I shall Call on her in a day or two and Endeavour to Return her kindness to me when in the same situation.

The person who Holds the first place in my heart your invariable Friend has been too unwell this day to take up the pen this Evening or you would have Received the superier pleasure of a Line from him Instead of this Interruption from me.

The ships which Arrived Last Fryday are from Halifax with a few petatoes and a Little wood. The people there are in Expectation of an Attack from a Body of troops which they hear are to be sent down under the Command of Preble and are preparing for Defence.[2] If they suffer such terrors from the Name of a Worn out American Veteran what must be their Apprehensions from the Active Vigorous spirited Heros who are Riseing up from Every Corner of the united Colonies to oppose the Wicked system of politicks which has Long Governed a Corrupt Court.

But I ask parden for touching on War politicks or anything Relative therto, as I think you gave me a Hint in yours Not to Approach the Verge of anything so far beyond the Line of my sex.[3]

The Worthy bearer of this will inform you of all the Inteligence stiring. Tranqulity still Reigns in the Camp. We scarcly hear the Distant Roar of Cannen for 24 hours past.

By a person from Boston Last saterday we Learn they are Building a Floating Batery in town in order to Bombard Prospect Hill. What a Contemptable figure do the arms of Britain make. But I Have no time to write nor have you to Read observations either Natural Moral or political, so shall ajourn any thing of that kind till your Reverie of Compleat Happiness is a Little over and you Descend to touch again in the arts and sciences.

With Great Respect (after the affectionate Compliments of your Friend) I subscribe sir your unfeigned Friend and Humble servant,

Marcia

Swift of Boston is Really Dead.[4]

RC (Adams Papers); addressed by James Warren: "To the Honbl. John Adams Esqr. Member of Congress att Philadelphia per Favr. Mr. Collins"; readdressed: "Favd pr Sol. Southwick N. Port." At Newport, Collins put this letter into other hands, perhaps because he feared capture by British vessels. Beneath the seal, he added a note to JA:

Newport Sepr. 15th 1775
Having taken passage by water to N. York, thought best to forward this by Post. Thy Friend. Step: Collins
NB We are wating for a fair wind. We sal'd once, got as far as Point Judah [Judith] and was oblig'd to put Back with a Head Wind.

[1] AA, TBA, and several other members of the household contracted dysentery soon after JA's departure for Philadelphia. The disease reached epidemic proportions, causing many deaths, including that of AA's mother, Elizabeth Quincy Smith, on 1 Oct. (*Adams Family Correspondence*, 1:276–280, 284–285, 287–289).

[2] No expedition under Jedediah Preble, who at 69 years of age had turned down general's commissions from the Provincial Congress and from the Continental Congress, was contemplated. The Americans were, however, planning an attack on Canada, with one force going up the Kennebec River and another proceeding from New York. The commanders were respectively Benedict Arnold and Philip Schuyler (French, *First Year*, 431–432).

[3] Mrs. Warren misread JA's meaning. His own relaxed mood kept him from discussing serious matters like these. See his rejoinder in his letter to James Warren, 26 Sept. (below).

[4] Samuel Swift, who had been caught in Boston at the outbreak of war and was by August confined to his house under surveillance, died on 30 Aug. (Sibley-Shipton, *Harvard Graduates*, 9:580–583).

John Adams' Commission as Justice of the Peace in Suffolk County

Watertown, 6 September 1775. Printed form with spaces filled in appropriately (Adams Papers); signed by Perez Morton, Deputy Secretary, and fifteen Council members; on the verso in an unidentified hand: "J. Adams Esq."; docketed in later years by JA: "Commision."

This commission, listed in Council records under the date of 8 September, was approved at the same time as similar ones for John Hancock and Samuel Adams (Records of the States, Microfilm, Mass. E.1b.c, Reel No. 2, Unit 2, p. 464–465). The commissions made them "of the Quorum," a distinction reserved for only the more prominent justices in a county. The appointments followed past patronage practice of handing such commissions to members of the Council and the House, a practice that was vigorously protested a few months later by the Berkshire Constitutionalists (Robert J. Taylor, *Western Massachusetts in the Revolution*, Providence, 1954, p. 28, 83). No evidence has been found, however, that JA ever made use of his commission.

From James Warren

My Dear Sir   Watertown Sepr 11th 1775

I please myself with the probability that before this you are safely arrived at Philadelphia, after having fine weather for Journeying.[1] I hope you will not be disappointed in your wishes with regard to the Spirit and Temper of the Congress. I should have wrote you before if I had been well, but from A Cold I took in the long storm we had here, have been much Indisposed since you left us. Am now better.

Nothing very material has Occurred. The Military Operations are much in the same way as when you was last here. The works on

Ploughed Hill² are thought to be Impregnable. They fired at them and Roxbury till they Tired themselves and have now in a manner ceased. We seldom hear A Cannon tho' the natural Effusions of Resentment and disappointment now and then give us an Instance, harmless enough for they never Injure us. All seems to be in a Tranquil state for a war. The greatest difficulty seems to be to govern our own Soldiery. I may say the rifle Men only for I hear of no other. Yesterday the General was Obliged to order no less than 24 of them under Guard. They are the most disorderly part of the Army if not alone so. I have not been at head quarters since Saturday but am told that for some Crime one of them was ordered under Guard. An Attempt was made by a Number to rescue him, upon which they were also ordered to be put under Guard, upon which a whole Company undertook to rescue them, and the General was Obliged to Call out a large detachment from the Rhode Island Troops to Apprehend them, who though prepared for resistance thought proper to submit, and the Ringleaders are now in Custody. I believe he will Choose to make Examples of them. I should were I in his place.³

We have in a few days past a great deal of foreign News, and all seems to agree that both England, and Ireland are in great Confusion. It is said the Irish Parliament have resolved that no more Troops, or Provisions for Troops shall come from there to America, and that several of the Recruiting parties there have been killed. That the whole Kingdom is in an Uproar, and in such an Opposition to Administration as will Intitle them equally with the Americans to the Character of Rebels. The Vessel that brings this Account has been stoped by the Men of war at Rhode Island in her way to Providence, and perhaps many other perticulars Smothered.⁴ Callihorne⁵ is Arrived at Boston, and several Letters have been received, and some of them sent out of Boston giveing Assurances that no more Troops will be sent to America, and that the dispute will be soon settled. Oliver Wendal⁶ told me he had seen one to that purpose from a Man whose Intelligence he could depend on. Other Letters I hear of, which say the People had Obliged the King to promise not only to send no other Troops out, but to recall the Fleet and Army Already here. If all this be true how seasonably will your last Petition arrive to serve as a Mantle to Cover the Nakedness of the Ministry, and to Screen them from the Shame of being forced to a retreat by the Virtue of the Americans. Depend on it they will Catch at it, like a hungry Fish at a Bait, and we must be Content with a Harvest Blasted with Mildew, Cut before it is ripe, and Consequently of little value. Does no Powder Arrive. I wish we may be able to give them at least one Blast more, that they may leave us thoroughly Impressed with a Sense of American Bravery and Prowess. If they do go, I know you won't fail to do every thing in your power to furnish us. Money if possible grows scarcer than powder. The last dollar perhaps will be gone Tomorrow, and then I Expect we shall be all din'd with Clamours, and Complaints. We have enough of them Already from the largeness of the Bills.[7] 1200 Men March this afternoon and Tomorrow under Coll. Arnold for Newberry Port to Embark for Kennebeck in their way to Quebec. I wish they may not be Intercepted, in their passage. Were I to Conduct the matter I think I should march them all the way by Land. Two frigates and a Number of Schooners I am told left Boston Yesterday. Probably to Intercept them. A few deserters come over to us, and several of our rifle men have deserted to the Enemy.

A Ship from Piscataqua for the West Indies owned by Mr. Langdon was taken by the Lively and has been retaken by An Armed Vessel from Beverly and Carried into Cape Ann.[8] The Prisoners were Brought to Head quarters on Saturday. I don't find your Friend P: Henry in the List of Delegates from Virginia. How does it happen. It gives me Concern, you know I have a great Opinion of him.[9]

Our Council are yet seting tho' they Talk of An Adjournment Tomorrow. They seem to have been very Busy. I can hardly tell you what has been done since you left us. Coll. Prescot Sherriff of this County, Coll. Dwight Worcester, Dr. Winthrop Judge of Probate his Son Register, Foster Appointed for Worcester. No Appointments for the Superior Court.[10] They seem as much at a loss as ever. I Inclose A Letter left at my Lodgings.[11] I Suppose from Braintree and so will give you an Account of your Family. I have been much Concerned about them. Mrs. Adams and almost the whole Family I hear have been Sick. I had the pleasure of hearing last Evening that She was better, and all the rest Except One of the Maids and little Tommy who I don't learn are dangerous. You will please to make my regards to All Friends perticularly Mr. Adams, and believe me to be with great Sincerity Your Friend,   J W

Six regulars put of[f] from Boston in A Boat and were unable to row back against the Wind which blew hard at N:W they say. They drifted on Dorchester and were taken.[12]

RC (Adams Papers); docketed in an unknown hand: *"Warren   Sept. 11th 1775."*

[1] JA arrived in Philadelphia on 12 Sept., the day before the first meeting of the 2d session of the Second Continental Congress, which had been

scheduled for 5 Sept. but had been postponed for lack of a quorum. He had left Watertown on 1 Sept. in the company of Samuel Adams (JA, *Diary and Autobiography*, 2:168–169; Samuel Adams, *Writings*, 3:226; JCC, 2:240).

[2] Washington had taken Plowed Hill on 26 Aug., a site that commanded the Mystic River, and kept control despite British artillery (French, *First Year*, p. 481).

[3] On 12 Sept., 33 members of Col. William Thompson's regiment of Pennsylvania riflemen were found guilty of "disobedient and mutinous Behavior" and were fined, the money to go to the support of Dr. Benjamin Church's hospital (Washington, *Writings*, ed. Fitzpatrick, 3:490–491). For an eyewitness account of this episode, see *Penna. Archives*, 2d ser., 10:8–10.

[4] This foreign news is taken from the *Boston Gazette*, 11 Sept. Compare Force, *Archives*, 4th ser., 3:168–169.

[5] The reference remains obscure.

[6] Oliver Wendell (1733–1818), Boston merchant and officeholder (Sibley-Shipton, *Harvard Graduates*, 13:367–374).

[7] Warren writes here as paymaster general. On 1 Aug. the congress had ordered that $500,000 be sent to the army in Massachusetts (JCC, 2:235–236). By the date of Warren's letter, only $172,520 had reached the province. Washington urged speed and described the army's state as "not far from mutiny" (*Writings*, ed. Fitzpatrick, 3:482, 512–513). On 13 Sept. the congress ordered that $527,480 be sent at once; it arrived on the 29th (JCC, 2:245; Warren to JA, 1 Oct., below).

[8] The *Unity*, commanded by Capt. Flagg, was seized by the British warship *Lively* and retaken by Nicholson Broughton of the schooner *Hannah* on 7 Sept. (*Naval Docs. Amer. Rev.* 2:36, 92–93; Allen, *Mass. Privateers*, p. 163).

[9] See JA's explanation to Warren, 19 Sept. (below).

[10] Appointments were not made until October.

[11] Probably AA's letter of 8–10 Sept. (*Adams Family Correspondence*, 1:276–278).

[12] Reported in the *Boston Gazette*, 18 Sept.

John Adams' Service
in the Continental Congress

13 September – 9 December 1775

Editorial Note

In the fall of 1775 Adams worked in the congress to the point of exhaustion; by December he asked permission to leave to restore his energies. He served on thirteen committees, and judging from the fragmentary evidence that has been found, he gave full measure. He was not exaggerating when he told Mercy Warren he was "engaged in constant Business. . . . Every Body is engaged all Day in Congress and all the Morning and evening in Committees." The workday began at seven in the morning and ended at ten at night (JA to Mercy Warren, 25 Nov., below). Adams' intense activity contradicts the assessment of Benjamin Rush, who saw Adams as a man shunned because of the intemperate remarks about Dickinson disclosed in the intercepted letter (JA to James Warren, 24 July, note 6, above).

Adams arrived in Philadelphia on 12 September, just in time for the official opening for business the next day. Actually, the congress had tried to begin on the 5th, but for lack of a quorum had had to wait eight days for enough members to arrive. In contrast to the preceding spring, Adams found time to record in some detail debates taking place during one month's period, 23 September through 21 October (*Diary and Autobiography*, 2:178–180, 183–187, 188–217). Among the subjects discussed were the mode of dispensing supplies to soldiers, the gunpowder contract with the firm of Willing & Morris, the wisdom of arresting royal officers and shutting down the royal postal service, the mode of appointment of officers, and, most important, the desirability of modifying the Continental Association by opening the ports and encouraging trade and the establishment of an American fleet.

Although Adams records the positions of many of his colleagues on these issues, he records his views only twice: as making a motion to consult Washington and as making a point of order (same, 2:185, 198). It is mainly from his letters to close friends and associates, James Warren in particular, that one must learn where he stood. And these are not wholly satisfactory, for the congress continued to operate under a rule of secrecy that was reaffirmed on 9 November. Adams and other members at that time signed a formal statement carrying a penalty of expulsion and condemnation as an enemy to American liberties for divulging congressional secrets without authorization (Jefferson, *Papers*, 1:252–253; photostat of MS in MHi). Another source for Adams' positions is his recollections written down in 1805 in his Autobiography, but the evidence is plain that with the lapse of time his memory, even when stimulated by research in the Journals of the congress, confused the facts, and hindsight caused him to claim more than he should have.

In later years Adams was proudest of his contribution to the establishment of an American navy. His pride was justified, despite his oversimplifications. The naming of a committee on 5 October to plan for the interception of two British vessels carrying arms and ammunition to Canada was the first congressional step toward creating a navy (JCC, 3:277). Adams is the only source for identifying the makeup of the three-man committee, but his recollection was not disputed by his correspondent and former colleague John Langdon (JA, *Works*, 10:27, 28). Besides himself, the committee was composed of Langdon and Silas Deane. Seen now as a first step, the committee was not considered as such then, and much was to occur before the congress clearly saw where it was heading. No great effort was required to turn Adams' mind to the possibilities the sea offered. He had grown up on the coast, his legal business had acquainted him with merchants and seamen, and he got letters from Josiah Quincy urging upon him schemes for bottling up shipping in Boston harbor (Quincy to JA, 11 July, above, and 22 Sept., 25 Oct., both below). Yet he was not appointed to the committee named on 13 October to prepare an estimate of the expense of fitting out and contracting for two armed vessels for the purpose of the interception. He was not called upon until this new committee was enlarged by four on 30 October and ordered to fit out two additional ships. The enlarged committee gradually became known as the Naval Committee, not to be confused with a standing committee of later origin called the Marine Committee. The membership of the Naval Committee included Silas Deane, John Langdon, Stephen Hopkins, Christopher Gadsden, Joseph Hewes, Richard Henry Lee, and John Adams (JCC, 3:293–294, 311–312; Burnett, ed., *Letters of Members*, 1:217, note, 273, note).

Any account of the emergence of a Continental navy that confines itself to the actions of the congress overlooks the independent action of General Washington, who before word of armed vessels was received from the congress had set about hiring several to intercept British transports supplying Boston (Clark, *Washington's Navy*, p. 3–17). One can argue, of course, that a real navy could be the creation only of the congress, but certainly Washington saw the need for action at sea given the situation he found—a besieged town supplied through its harbor. A recent scholar would go back even further to find the origin of a Continental navy—back to the congressional resolution of 18 July 1775 which urged each colony to fit out armed vessels for its own defense. In so resolving, the congress may have been swayed by the action of Massachusetts' Third Provincial Congress, which on 7 June appointed a committee to consider the feasibility of arming small vessels to cruise along the coast to protect trade and annoy enemies (Raymond G. O'Connor, "Second Commentary" in *Maritime Dimensions of the American Revolution*, Washington, 1977, p. 27; Mass. Provincial Congress, *Jours.*, p. 308–309).

Formal proposals for an American fleet actually came to Philadelphia from Rhode Island on 3 October and provoked vigorous debate (JA, *Diary and Autobiography*, 2:198–199, 201). As the instructions from that colony put it, the best way to achieve peace based upon constitutional principles was to fight a "just and necessary war . . . to a happy issue," and an American fleet would greatly contribute to that end (JCC, 3:274). Although in the ensuing debate Adams does not record anything he said beyond his raising a point of order, he unquestionably supported the establishment of a fleet, and probably from the first. According to Samuel Ward, the initial attitude of many members was that a fleet was "perfectly chimerical," but opinions gradually changed until a favorable vote was achieved to create a committee made up of one delegate from each colony that was charged with "furnishing these colonies with a naval armament" (Burnett, ed., *Letters of Members*, 1:256; JCC, 3:420). This was the Marine Committee, named on 11 December and reconstituted on the 14th, that Adams in his Autobiography confused with the Naval Committee, and that gradually absorbed the functions of the other.

By 11 December, however, Adams had departed from Philadelphia. Still, he had been able to advance the cause of a navy through his membership on the Naval Committee. His duties involved him in recruiting likely men to serve as officers, a responsibility that caused him to write to correspondents for suggestions. (For his list of possibilities, see *Diary and Autobiography*, 2:221.) The Naval Committee was ordered to prepare commissions, to purchase ship supplies, to engage with Captain Stone for the seizure or destruction of Lord Dunmore's fleet, and to see to it that ships violating the nonexportation agreement were detained (JCC, 3:316, 392–393, 395–396, 406). This committee prepared Rules for the Regulation of the Navy of the United Colonies (No. VIII, below), which continued in use under the Constitution. These were adapted by Adams mainly from existing British regulations, but listing them in formal fashion with a care for the needs of the colonies was an argument that a naval service would be no casual or temporary thing. The congress was making a commitment not unlike that made when it decided to remodel the army. John Adams' industry gave the congress a nudge.

The accompanying documents and calendared item reflect the work of those committees for which some evidence exists of JA's role in their deliberations and reports or in which he had a particular interest. Following these is a synopsis of his membership on committees for which there is no record of his influence on their actions. The listing gives the names of members in the order in which they appear in the Journal, the responsibilities assigned, and the dates, locations, and authorship, when known, of reports and subsequent resolutions.

The weeks Adams spent in Philadelphia in the fall of 1775 were trying ones. Important decisions whose consequences could not be fully foreseen pressed for action. Although Adams stood with those who saw no hope of reconciliation, he did not minimize the dangers of the course on which America was embarked. He was bold in his recommendations, but he sought constantly the nourishment he could get from the letters of those in Massachusetts. Occasionally, he even had to explain to them why the colonies could not press on faster. He operated always within the political realities that confronted him in the congress.

I. Resolutions of the Congress on Intercepting British Vessels

Thursday, October 5, 1775

Resolved,[1] That a letter be sent by Express to Genl Washington, to inform him, that they [Congress] having received certain intelligence of the sailing of two north country built Brigs, of no force, from England, on the 11 of August last, loaded with arms, powder, and other stores, for Quebec, without a convoy, which it being of importance to intercept, that he apply to the council of Massachusetts bay, for the two armed vessels in their service, and despatch the same,[2] with a sufficient number of people, stores, &c. particularly a number of oars, in order, if possible, to intercept said two Brigs and their cargoes, and secure the same for the use of the continent; Also, any other transports laden with ammunition, cloathing, or other stores, for the use of the ministerial army or navy in America, and secure them in the most convenient places for the purpose abovementioned; that he give the commander or commanders such instructions as are necessary, as also proper encouragement to the marines and seamen, that shall be sent on this enterprize, which instructions, &c., are to be delivered to the commander or commanders sealed up, with orders not to open the same until out of sight of land, on account of secresy.

That a letter be wrote to said honble council, to put said vessels under the General's command and direction, and to furnish him instantly with every necessary in their power, at the expence of the Continent.

Also that the General be directed to employ said vessels and others, if he judge necessary, to effect the purposes aforesd; informing the General that the Rhode Island and Connecticut vessels of force will be sent directly after them to their assistance.

That a letter be wrote to Govr Cooke, informing him of the above, and desiring him to despatch one or both the armed vessels of the

colony of Rhode Island on the same service, and that he take the precautions abovementioned.[3]

Also that a letter be wrote to Govr Trumbull, requesting of him the
largest vessel in the service of the colony of Connecticut, to be sent
on the enterprize aforesaid, acquainting him with the above particulars, and recommending the same precautions.[4]

That the encouragement recommended by this Congress to be given
shall be, on this occasion, that the master, officers and seamen, shall
be intitled to one half of the value of the prizes by them taken, the
wages they receive from the respective colonies notwithstanding.[5]

That the said ships and vessels of war to be on the continental risque
and pay, during their being so employed.

Reprinted from JCC, 3:278–279; Dft not found.

[1] These resolutions grew out of the report (not found) of a committee appointed on 5 Oct., which, according to JA, was composed of himself, Silas Deane, and John Langdon. The Journals do not give the names of the members (same, 3:277). As JA recalled the episode, the question of whether to try intercepting the ships caused sharp debate, for the attempt was thought by some to be imprudent and potentially destructive of the morals of American seamen because it might put their minds upon plunder. JA and others argued that success would bring needed supplies and would be an encouraging stroke at the enemy. JA added that it would be the beginning of "a System of maritime and naval Opperations." Because he wrote these recollections long after the event (in 1805) and because he showed some confusion about his own role at this early stage in bringing naval operations into being, one must be cautious about accepting JA's account. He says nothing about his contribution to the report which led to these resolutions (*Diary and Autobiography*, 3:342–343).

[2] Actually Washington had decided on recruiting two armed vessels before he received these orders from the congress (Instructions to Col. John Glover and Stephen Moylan, 4 Oct., *Writings*, ed. Fitzpatrick, 4:6–7). For the outcome, see Benjamin Hichburn to JA, 25 Nov., note 9 (below).

[3] The published records of Rhode Island do not give the colony's action on the request of the congress.

[4] For the action taken by Connecticut, see *Conn. Colonial Records*, 15:131.

[5] "On the margin of the 'corrected Journal' the words '2. this particularly' were written against this paragraph" (ed. Worthington C. Ford's note).

II. Committee Report on Gunpowder
Sent to the Northern Army

[post 16 Oct. 1775][1]

The Committee appointed to enquire, what Powder has been Sent
to the Army in the Northern Department, have attended that service
and beg Leave to report

That five Thousand Weight of Powder, sent from
South Carolina, has been forwarded to the said Army.   5000 wt.

That Two Thousand one hundred and thirty six
Pounds Weight have been forwarded to the Same 2136
Army from the City of Philadelphia.

That Seventeen hundred Weight have been forwarded from New York. 1700

That Eight hundred Weight has been forwarded
from Connecticutt. 800

That Thirteen hundred Weight has been forwarded at another Time from the City of Philadel- 1300
phia. 10936

In Addition to which Two thousand Weight has
been lately ordered to New York and from there to the 2000
same Army.[2] 12,936

MS in JA's hand (Adams Papers, Microfilms, Reel No. 346, filmed under
date [1776–1778]).

[1] On 16 Oct. a committee composed of John Langdon, Eliphalet Dyer, and JA was ordered to make a survey of the amounts of gunpowder sent to the northern army and by whom. The Journals do not record any report made or accepted (JCC, 3:296).

[2] Pres. Hancock informed Gen. Schuyler of the shipment of powder in his letter of 11 Oct. (Burnett, ed., *Letters of Members*, 1:228).

III. Form Letter Requesting
Information on British Depredations

Sir   Philadelphia, 19 Oct. 1775

The continental congress having been pleased to appoint us a committe[1] for collecting an account of the hostilities committed by the
ministerial troops and navy in America, since last March, with proper
evidence of the truth of the facts related, the number and value of
the buildings destroyed, and of the vessels inward and outward
bound seised, by them as nearly as can be ascertained, and also the
stock taken by them from different parts of the continent, as you may
see by the resolve inclosed; we entreat the assistance of the convention
of your colony in this business, that we may be enabled to perform
what is required of us, in the manner and with the expedition congress expects; and, to that end you will be pleased to furnish us with
the necessary materials sending to us clear distinct full and circum-
stantial details of the hostile and destructive acts, and the captures

or seizures and depredations in your colony, and accurate estimates of the loss and damage with the solemn examinations of witnesses, and other papers and documents officially authenticated. We are, Sir, Your obedient humble servants,

Silas Deane
John Adams
George Wythe

MS (PHi:Sprague Coll.).

[1] This letter was the work of the committee formed on 18 Oct. to obtain "a just and well authenticated account of the hostilities committed by the ministerial troops and navy in America since last March" (JCC, 3:298–299).

For JA's comments on the committee and its purpose, see his letters to James Warren of 12, 18, and 19 (1st) Oct. (below). No indication of when or whether this committee reported to congress has been found.

IV. Resolution of the Congress on New Hampshire Government

3 November 1775. Dft not found. PRINTED: JCC, 3:319. Based on a report (not found) from a committee appointed 26 October composed of John Rutledge, JA, Samuel Ward, Richard Henry Lee, and Roger Sherman, which reported on 3 November (same, 3:307, 319).

On 18 October the delegates from New Hampshire laid before their colleagues instructions from their province which asked the advice of the congress "with respect to a method of our administering Justice, and regulating our civil police" (same, 3:298). The congress recommended the calling of "a full and free representation of the people" and the establishment of a government that would promote the people's happiness and secure good order during the dispute with Great Britain.

In his Autobiography JA recalled that when the New Hampshire delegates presented their instructions, he took the opportunity to harangue "on the Subject at large" and to urge the congress "to resolve on a general recommendation to all the States to call Conventions and institute regular Governments" (*Diary and Autobiography*, 3:354–357). The congress was deeply divided on the issue, but according to JA, some began to come around. If he spoke as he claimed, he was anticipating by some seven months his motion for independent governments offered in May 1776. Again, JA's recollection may very well have been inaccurate. At any rate, moderates saw to it that the advice to New Hampshire was to be operative only until the dispute was settled. In private correspondence, where the need for circumspection was less, JA saw more than temporary possibilities (JA to Elbridge Gerry, 5 Nov., note 4, below; see also his first letter to James Warren of 6 July, note 6, above).

V. Naval Committee to Silas Deane

To Silas Deane Esqr.   Philadelphia November the 7th 1775

You are desired to repair immediately to the City of New York, and there purchase a Ship suitable for carrying 20 nine pounders upon one deck, if such a Ship can there be found. Also a Sloop, suitable to carry ten guns, which we would choose should be Bermudian built if such a one can be had. If you succeed in purchasing both, or either of these Vessels, you will use all possible expedition to procure them to be armed and equipped for the Sea. For this purpose you will apply to, and employ such persons as can carry this business into the most speedy execution. Should there be danger in fitting these Vessels at New York from the Kings ships, you may then send the Vessels eastward thro the Sound to New London or Norwich in order to be armed and fitted. Should this be the case you will repair immediately to the place where the Ships are to be fitted, and there use every means in your power to procure this to be done with the utmost expedition. In the Colony of Connecticut you are to procure powder for both these Vessels, and such other Military Stores as can there be had. You will procure the Cannon and other Stores at New York or any other place where it can be done in the best and most expeditious manner. You will also procure Officers and Men suitable for these Vessels. As soon as these Vessels can possibly be fitted for the Sea, you will order them immediately into Delaware Bay. You will by every opportunity give us the most exact intelligence of all your proceedings by conveyances the most safe and secure that can be obtained. You are empower'd to draw on Governor Hopkins for such sums of money as may be necessary for the above business.

Step Hopkins
Chris Gadsden
Richard Henry Lee
Joseph Hewes
John Adams
Jno. Langdon[1]

PS. In the course of your Journey at New York, or elsewhere you are to employ proper Persons to engage experienced and able-bodied seamen to man the ships now fitting out who must repair to Philadelphia with all possible dispatch.

RC in Lee's hand (CtHi:Deane Papers).

[1] This commission was signed by all members of the Naval Committee ex- cept, for obvious reasons, Silas Deane. It is printed as a sample of the kind of

commissions that the committee sent out. On 6 Nov. Stephen Hopkins had written his brother Esek regarding the command of the fleet which the committee had offered to Esek on the day before (CSmH:Harbeck Coll., in JA's hand but signed by Hopkins). Hopkins said in part, "they have pitched upon you to take the Command of a small Fleet, which they and I hope will be but the Beginning of one much larger." See also S. Adams to JA, 22 Dec., note 2 (below).

VI. Committee Report on Petition from Nova Scotia

Proposals.[1]   [ante 9 Nov. 1775]

That two Battallions of Marines be raised consisting of one Collonell, two Lt. Collonells, two Majors &c. (officers as usual in other Regiments) that they consist of five hundred Privates each Battalion, exclusive of Officers.

That particular Care be taken that no Persons be appointed to office or inlisted into Said Battalions but such as have actually Served in the Merchant Service as seamen, or so acquainted with maritime Affairs as to be able to serve to advantage by sea, where required.

That they be enlisted and commissioned to be held for and during the present War, between G. Britain and the Colonies, unless regularly dismissed by orders of the Congress.

That they be distinguished by the Name of the 1st. and 2d. Battalion of American Marines.[2]

That a Sufficient Number of Vessels be taken up, and provided at Newbury Port, or Portsmouth by the 1st. day of December next for transporting Said two Battalions and three Months Provisions, and other Necessaries.

That Said two Battalions be raised and marched to said Place of Rendezvous, by the 1st. of December, and in Case they are not easily raised or there is likely to be delay, that the General Draught out of the Forces under his Command to make up, any such Deficiency, of those who have been employed at sea if such are to be had.

That Said Battalions, shall be armed in the following Manner. vizt. a light Fusee,[3] fitted for Slinging, a large Hatchet with a long Handle, and a Spear, with thirty two Rounds per Man of Ammunition.

That a Number of Men be immediately Sent into Nova Scotia, to inform themselves of the Temper and Disposition of the Inhabitants of that Colony with respect to the Present Struggle between G. B. and these Colonies, and how far they may be willing or able to take an active Part in the present Dispute.[4]

That two swift Sailing Boats be employed constantly to ply between Minas and Portsmouth or Newbury to bring Intelligence of the State and Situation of the Province, in general, but most minutely of every Thing, respecting the Town and Harbour of Hallifax.

That as soon as the Said two Battallions, shall be arrived, at either of Said Ports and the situation of that Colony and the Town of Hallifax shall be known the Said Battallions embark for Minas and make their Voyage with all possible Dispatch.

That previous to their Arrival, Horses and Carriages, be privately engaged for their Use, and that on their Landing they immediately make a forced March for Hallifax and possess themselves of that Town and of the naval and other Stores there and if practicable of the Shipping.

Note. Coll. Arnolds Expedition was Supposed in Boston to have been against this Place, which caused the General to send thither Shipps, and Troops, but not enough to make Resistance to two Such Battallions. Further the Country are intirely in our favour, a few Scotch Traders and renegade Tories excepted.

Should this Expedition by any Accident be found impracticable, these would be two Battallions of the Utmost service, being capable of Serving either by sea or Land.

Should the Expedition succeed, the Consequences will be of the Utmost Importance, nothing less than the greatest Distress, if not the Utter Ruin of the ministerial Navy in America. The Naval Stores in that Place are Said to be of vast Value, the Docks and Barracks and Yards cost the Nation more than one Million sterling, and is the only Place at which Shipps of War can refitt in America.

These Battalions Should consist of Ten Companies each of fifty privates in a Company. The Reason for this is, that in fitting out any Ship of War one of these Companies would compleatly man a Small Vessell and two of them make a large Proportion of Marines for the largest.

Should this Expedition succeed, which it most unavoidably will, if prudently managed, the Destruction of the Docks and Yards, and the Stores, which may be brought off,[5] will be an immense affair, and a Retreat can ever be made with Safety.

But if a ship or two of Warr, should be taken, in the Harbour, of which you may be certain, and the Place by Reinforcements held, untill a force Superior can be brought from G. B. it will unavoidably destroy, and defeat every operation of our Enemy for the next Campaign, as all their Transport Ships may by a few Armed Vesells from this Port be intercepted before they can have Intelligence to avoid them.

MS in JA's hand (Adams Papers, Microfilms, Reel No. 345, filmed under date [ante 1 Dec. 1775]).

[1] On 2 Nov. the congress took cognizance of a petition from the inhabitants of Passamaquoddy, Nova Scotia, who had chosen a committee of safety and asked for admission into "the association of the North Americans, for the preservation of their rights and liberties." To determine what steps should be taken in response, the congress named a committee of five: Silas Deane, John Jay, Stephen Hopkins, John Langdon, and JA (JCC, 3:316). The Journals note that the committee's report was considered on 9 Nov. but give nothing of its substance. The next day the congress acted on the report by adopting three resolutions (same, 3:343–344, 348). It is possible, of course, that the proposals here printed were only JA's preliminary suggestions for a committee report; if so, they must have made their way into it, for some of the language appears in the congressional resolutions.

[2] These first four paragraphs constitute the third resolution adopted by the congress, most of the wording being taken verbatim from JA's MS. There are three substantive differences: the congress ruled that the size of the battalions should be the same as others; it called for good seamen, omitting mention of service in the merchant marine; and it added that the two battalions should constitute part of the authorized strength of the Continental Army.

[3] A light musket (*OED*).

[4] This paragraph was the basis for the first resolution adopted by the congress, which again borrowed some of JA's phrasing. But the congress settled on two persons for the mission and listed several additional subjects for their inquiry: fortifications, docks, military stores, and the like. In short, the mission was to gather more than political information.

[5] The second congressional resolution called for the seizure of military stores and the destruction of installations if Gen. Washington deemed such an expedition practicable. The congress tempered JA's enthusiasm with more caution than he felt, and it insisted upon seeing such an expedition as an integral part of a total effort. The congress preferred to leave the details of mounting an attack to the General's judgment.

VII. Naval Committee to Dudley Saltonstall

Sir [1]   Philadelphia Nov. 27th. 1775

The Congress are now preparing two Ships and two Brigantines to be fitted out as soon as possible to cruise against our common enemy. They have thought of you as a proper person to take the command of one of those ships as Captain. If you enter into this service, which we take to be the service of your country, you will give us the earliest information and repair to Philadelphia as soon as your affairs will possibly admit, and bring with you as many officers and seamen as you can procure at New London and between that place and Philadelphia. Those who may not be able to come with you, leave proper persons to encourage and conduct along after you.

If money should be necessary for the performance of this service

RULES

FOR THE

REGULATION

OF THE

NAVY

OF THE

UNITED COLONIES

OF

NORTH-AMERICA;

Eſtabliſhed for Preſerving their RIGHTS
and Defending their LIBERTIES, and
for Encouraging all thoſe who Feel
for their COUNTRY, to enter into its
Service in that way in which they
can be moſt Uſeful.

———————————————

PHILADELPHIA:

Printed by WILLIAM and THOMAS BRADFORD, 1775.

8. TITLEPAGE FOR
Rules for the Regulation of the Navy, 1775
See page xi

you may draw on Mr. Eleazur Miller Merchant in New York who has money in his hands for that purpose.

In a day or two after you receive this, you will receive by the Messrs. Mumfords[2] the Conditions and encouragement offered to the Seamen. We are, Sir, Your humble servant

Signed by Order of Comme.

Step. Hopkins
Christ. Gadsden
John Adams
Joseph Hewes
Silas Deane

Facsim. of MS in unidentified hand (*Magazine of History*, 29 [1926]:242 [Extra No. 116]).

[1] Dudley Saltonstall (1738–1796) commanded the ship *Alfred* under Como. Esek Hopkins, with John Paul Jones as his first lieutenant (*DAB*).

[2] One of these Mumfords was prob-ably Thomas, of Groton and New London, an active whig (Charles R. Stark, *Groton, Conn., 1705–1905*, Stonington, Conn., 1922, *passim*).

VIII. Rules for the Regulation of the Navy of the United Colonies

[28 November–December 1775][1]

ART. 1. The Commanders of all ships and vessels belonging to the THIRTEEN UNITED COLONIES, are strictly required to shew in themselves a good example of honor and virtue to their officers and men, and to be very vigilant in inspecting the behaviour of all such as are under them, and to discountenance and suppress all dissolute, immoral and disorderly practices; and also, such as are contrary to the rules of discipline and obedience, and to correct those who are guilty of the same, according to usage of the sea.[2]

ART. 2. The Commanders of the ships of the Thirteen United Colonies, are to take care that divine service be performed twice a day on board, and a sermon preached on Sundays, unless bad weather or other extraordinary accidents prevent it.

ART. 3. If any shall be heard to swear, curse or blaspheme the name of God, the Captain is strictly enjoined to punish them for every offence, by causing them to wear a wooden collar or some other shameful badge of distinction, for so long a time as he shall judge proper: If he be a commissioned officer, he shall forfeit one shilling for each offence, and a warrant or inferior officer six pence: He who is guilty of drunkenness (if a seaman) shall be put in irons until he is sober, but if an officer, he shall forfeit two days pay.

ART. 4. No Commander shall inflict any punishment upon a seaman beyond twelve lashes upon his bare back with a cat of nine tails; if the fault shall deserve a greater punishment, he is to apply to the Commander in Chief of the navy in order to the trying of him by a court martial, and in the mean time he may put him under confinement.

ART. 5. The Captain is never by his own authority to discharge a commission or warrant officer, nor to punish or strike him, but he may suspend or confine him; and when he comes in the way of a Commander in Chief, apply to him for holding a court-martial.

ART. 6. The officer who commands by accident of the Captain's absence (unless he be absent for a time by leave) shall not order any correction but confinement; and upon the Captain's return on board, he shall then give an account of his reasons for so doing.

ART. 7. The Captain is to cause the articles of war to be hung up in some public places of the ship, and read to the ship's company once a month.[3]

ART. 8. Whenever a Captain shall enlist a seaman, he shall take care to enter on his books the time and terms of his entering in order to his being justly paid.

ART. 9. The Captain shall before he sails make return to and leave with the Congress, or such person or persons as the Congress shall appoint for that purpose, a compleat list of all his officers and men, with the time and terms of their entering; and during his cruise, shall keep a true account of the desertion or death of any of them, and of the entering of others; and after his cruise, and before any of them are paid off, he shall make return of a compleat list of the same, including those who shall remain on board his ship.

ART. 10. The men shall (at their request) be furnished with slops that are necessary, by the Captain or Purser, who shall keep an account of the same; and the Captain in his return in the last mentioned article directed to be made, shall mention the amount delivered to each man in order to its being stopped out of his pay.[4]

ART. 11. As to the term inferior officers the Captain is to take notice, that the same does not include any commission or any warrant officer, except the second master, surgeons mates, cook, armourer, gun-smith, master at arms, and the sail-maker.

ART. 12. The Captain is to take care when any inferior officers or volunteer seamen are turned over into the ship under his command from any other ship, not to take [5] them on the ship's books in a worse quality or lower degree of station, than they served in the ship they were removed from; and for his guidance, he is to demand from the commander of the ship from which they are turned over, a list under his hand of their names and qualities.

ART. 13. Any officer, seaman or others entitled to wages or prize-money, may have the same paid to his assignee, provided the assignment be attested by the Captain or commander, the master or purser of the ship, or a chief magistrate of some county or corporation.

ART. 14. The Captain is to discourage the seamen of his ship from selling any part of their wages or shares, and never to attest the letter of attorney of any seaman until he is fully satisfied; the same is not granted in consideration of money given for the purchase of his wages or shares.

ART. 15. When any inferior officer or seaman dies, the Captain is forthwith to make out a ticket for the time of his service and send the same by the first safe conveyance to the Congress or agents by them for that purpose, appointed in order to the wages being forthwith paid to the executors or administrators of the deceased.[6]

ART. 16. A convenient place shall be set apart for sick or hurt men, to be removed with their hammocks and bedding when the surgeon shall advise the same to be necessary: and some of the crew shall be appointed to attend and serve them and to keep the place clean. The cooper shall make buckets with covers and cradles if necessary for their use.

ART. 17. All ships furnished with fishing tackle, being in such places where fish is to be had, the Captain is to employ some of the company in fishing, the fish to be distributed daily to such persons as are sick, or upon recovery, if the surgeons recommend it; and the surplus by turns amongst the messes of the officers and seamen without favour or partiality, and *gratis*, without any deduction of their allowance of provisions on that account.[7]

ART. 18. It is left to the discretion of the Commander of squadrons to shorten the allowance of provisions according to the exigence of the service, taking care that the men be punctually paid for the same. The like power is given to Captains of single ships in cases of absolute necessity.

ART. 19. If there shall be a want of pork, the Captain is to order three pounds of beef to be issued to the men in lieu of a two pound piece of pork.

ART. 20. One day in every week shall be issued out a proportion of flour and suet in lieu of beef for the seamen; but this is not to extend beyond four months' victualling at one time, nor shall the purser receive any allowance for flour or suet kept longer on board than that time. And there shall be supplied once a year, a proportion of canvas for pudding bags, after the rate of one ell for every sixteen men.

ART. 21. If any ships of the Thirteen United Colonies shall happen to come into port in want of provisions, the warrant of a Commander in Chief shall be sufficient to the agent or other instrument of the victualling to supply the quantity wanted; and in urgent cases where delay may be hurtful, the warrant of the Captain of the ship shall be of equal effect.

ART. 22. The Captain is frequently to order the proper officer to inspect into the condition of the provisions, and if the bread proves damp to have it aired upon the quarter deck or poop, and also to examine the flesh cask; and if any of the pickle be leaked out, to have new made and put in and the cask made tight and secure.[8]

ART. 23. The Captain or purser shall secure the cloaths, bedding and other things of such persons as shall die or be killed, to be delivered to their executors or administrators.[9]

ART. 24. All papers, charter parties, bills of lading, pass-ports and other writings whatsoever, found on board any ship or ships which shall be taken shall be carefully preserved, and the originals sent to the court of justice for maratime affairs, appointed, or to be appointed by Congress for judging concerning such prize or prizes; and if any person or persons shall wilfully or negligently destroy, or suffer to be destroyed, any such paper or papers, he or they so offending, shall forfeit their share of such prize or prizes, and suffer such other punishment, as they shall be judged by a court-martial to deserve.[10]

ART. 25. If any person or persons shall embezzle, steal or take away any cables, anchors, sails, or any of the ship's furniture, or any of the powder or arms, or ammunition or provisions of any ship belonging to the Thirteen United Colonies, he or they shall suffer such punishment as a court-martial shall order.[11]

ART. 26. When in sight of a ship or ships of the enemy, and at such other times as may appear to make it necessary to prepare for an engagement, the Captain shall order all things in his ship in a proper posture for fight, and shall, in his own person, and according to his duty, heart on and encourage the inferior officers and men to fight courageously, and not to behave themselves feintly or cry for quarters on pain of such punishment as the offence shall appear to deserve for his neglect.[12]

ART. 27. Any Captain or other officer, mariner or others, who shall basely desert their duty or station in the ship and run away while the enemy is in sight, or in time of action, or entice others to do so, shall suffer death or such other punishment as a court-martial shall inflict.[13]

ART. 28. No person in or belonging to the ship shall utter any words of sedition and mutiny, nor endeavour to make any mutinous assemblies upon any pretence whatsoever upon such punishment as a court-martial shall inflict.

ART. 29. Any officer, seaman or marine, who shall begin to excite, cause, or join in any mutiny or sedition in the ship to which he belongs on any pretence whatsoever, shall suffer death, or such other punishment as a court-martial shall direct.[14]

ART. 30. None shall presume to quarrel with, or strike his superior officer, on pain of such punishment as a court-martial shall order to be inflicted.[15]

ART. 31. If any person shall apprehend he has just cause of complaint, he shall quietly and decently make the same known to his superior officer, or to the Captain, as the case may require, who will take care that justice be done him.[16]

ART. 32. There shall be no quarreling or fighting between ship mates on board any ship belonging to the Thirteen United Colonies, nor shall there be used any reproachful or provoking speeches tending to make quarrels and disturbance on pain of imprisonment, and such other punishment as a court-martial shall think proper to inflict.[17]

ART. 33. If any person shall sleep upon his watch, or negligently perform the duty which shall be enjoined him to do, or forsake his station, he shall suffer such punishment as a court-martial shall think proper to inflict, according to the nature of his offence.[18]

ART. 34. All murder shall be punished with death.

ART. 35. All robbery and theft shall be punished at the discretion of a court-martial.[19]

ART. 36. Any Master at Arms who shall refuse to receive such prisoner or prisoners as shall be committed to his charge, or having received them, shall suffer him or them to escape, or dismiss them without orders for so doing, shall suffer in his or their stead, as a court-martial shall order and direct.[20]

ART. 37. The Captain, officers and others, shall use their utmost endeavours to detect, apprehend and bring to punishment, all offenders, and shall at all times readily assist the officers appointed for that purpose in the discharge of their duty on pain of their being proceeded against, and punished by a court-martial at discretion.[21]

ART. 38. All other faults, disorders and misdemeanors which shall be committed on board any ship belonging to the Thirteen United Colonies, and which are not herein mentioned, shall be punished according to the laws and customs in such cases used at sea.[22]

ART. 39. A court-martial shall consist of at least three Captains and three first Lieutenants, with three Captains and three first Lieutenants of marines, if there shall be so many of the marines then present, and the eldest Captain shall preside.[23]

ART. 40. All sea officers of the same denomination shall take rank of the officers of the marines.

ART. 41. Every Member of a court-martial shall take the following oath, viz. "You   swear that you will well and truly try, and impartially determine the cause of the prisoner now to be tried according to the rules of the navy of the United Colonies; so help you God." Which oath shall be administered by the President to the other members, and the President shall himself be sworn by the officer in said court next in rank.

ART. 42. All witnesses, before they may be admitted to give evidence, shall take the following oath, viz. "You swear, the evidence you shall give in the cause now in hearing, shall be the whole truth and nothing but the truth; so help you God."

ART. 43. The sentence of a court-martial for any capital offence shall not be put in execution until it be confirmed by the Commander in Chief of the fleet; and it shall be the duty of the President of every court-martial to transmit to the Commander in Chief every sentence which shall be given, with a summary of the evidence and proceedings thereon by the first opportunity.[24]

ART. 44. The Commander in Chief of the fleet for the time being, shall have power to pardon and remit any sentence of death that shall be given in consequence of any of the afore mentioned articles.[25]

There shall be allowed to each man serving on board the ships in the service of the thirteen United Colonies, a daily proportion of provisions, according as is expressed in the following table,[26] viz.

Sunday, 1 lb. bread, 1 lb. beef, 1 lb. potatoes or turnips.

Monday, 1 lb. bread, 1 lb. pork, 1/2 pint peas, and four oz. cheese.

Tuesday, 1 lb. bread, 1 lb. beef, 1 lb. potatoes or turnips, and pudding.

Wednesday, 1 lb. bread, two oz. butter, four oz. cheese, and 1/2 pint of rice.

Thursday, 1 lb. bread, 1 lb. pork, and 1/2 pint of peas.

Friday, 1 lb. bread, 1 lb. beef, 1 lb. potatoes or turnips, and pudding.

Saturday, 1 lb. bread, 1 lb. pork, 1/2 pint peas, and four oz. cheese.

Half pint of rum per man every day, and discretionary allowance on extra duty, and in time of engagement.

A pint and half of vinegar for six men per week.

The pay of the officers and men shall be as follows: [27]

Captain or commander,	32	dollars,	Per Calendar month.
Lieutenants,	20	do.	
Master,	20	do.	
Mates,	15	do.	
Boatswain,	15	do.	
Boatswain's first mate,	9 1/3	do.	
Ditto, second ditto,	8	do.	
Gunner,	15	do.	
Ditto mate,	10 2/3	do.	
Surgeon,	21 1/3	do.	
Surgeon's mate,	13 1/3	do.	
Carpenter,	15	do.	
Carpenter's mate,	10 2/3	do.	
Cooper,	15	do.	
Captain's or Commander's clerk,	15	do.	
Steward,	13 1/3	do.	
Chaplain,	20	do.	
Able seaman,	6 2/3	do.	
Captain of marines,	26 2/3	do.	
Lieutenants,	18	do.	
Serjeants,	8	do.	
Corporals,	7 1/3	do.	
Fifer,	7 1/3	do.	
Drummer,	7 1/3	do.	
Privates or marines,	6 2/3	do.[28]	

MS not found. Arts. 1–44 reprinted from *Rules for the Regulation of the Navy of the United Colonies of North-America*, Phila., 1775, facsim. edn., Washington, 1944, with "Introductory Note" by Adm. Joseph Strauss; material after Art. 44 from JCC, 3:383–384.

[1] These rules were reported on 23 Nov. by the committee for fitting out armed vessels, later called the Naval Committee, which had been enlarged on 30 Oct. to include four additional members, among them JA. After its reading, the report was ordered "to lie on the table for the perusal of the members." The congress considered the rules on 25 Nov. and approved them on the

28th. The order to have them printed came on 30 Nov. (*JCC*, 3:293–294, 311–312, 364, 375, 378–387, 393). As will be explained in note 2, the rules before being printed were stylistically revised to facilitate their use, and they were in the hands of fleet officers by 8 Dec. (Strauss, "Introductory Note").

² About his role in drawing up these rules, JA wrote: "They were drawn up in the Marine Committee [that is, Naval Committee] and by my hand, but examined, discussed and corrected by the Committee" (*Diary and Autobiography*, 3:350). Nothing in the Journals specifically indicates that either the original committee or the enlarged one was to draft rules for the regulation of a navy, although rules undoubtedly were necessary for ships being fitted out by the congress. Worthington C. Ford, in citing an endorsement by Charles Thomson in a letter from Washington of 5 Oct., seems to have found some authorization for the committee's rule-making, but Ford misread the MS. The endorsement reads: "That part of this letter which relates to the capture of a vessel in N. Hampshire referred to the committee appointed to bring in regulations for priv[ateers]." Ford read the final word of the endorsement as "navy." Although Washington's letter was read on 13 Oct., the part requesting "the determination of Congress as to the Property and disposal of such Vessels and Cargoes as are designed for the Supply of the Enemy and may fall into our Hands" received no action in subsequent days. In all likelihood, Thomson wrote his endorsement after a committee on disposal of prizes was established on 17 Nov., in response to a second letter from Washington urging that the congress give him guidance on prizes (*JCC*, 3: 293 and note 2, 357–358; Washington, *Writings*, ed. Fitzpatrick, 4:11, 73).

The separately printed version of the rules, of which only one copy is known to be extant, that at Yale University, differs in several respects from the version in the Journals. Only the rules regulating the day-to-day conduct of officers and men were separately printed. The rules on rations and wages and the terms of the covenant which officers and men signed upon entering into service would not have been appropriate for a handbook meant to inform them of fixed duties and rights and of penalties for infractions of the rules. Probably for this reason also, the paragraphs were numbered for ease of reference, and some stylistic changes were made (see note 14, below), although the order to have the resolutions of the congress printed does not specifically authorize such alterations. The handbook was even provided with an enticing subtitle: "Established for Preserving their RIGHTS and Defending their LIBERTIES, and for Encouraging all those who Feel for their COUNTRY, to enter into its Service in that way in which they can be most Useful."

One difference between the handbook and the Journals, however, needs another sort of explanation. Thomson's rough draft shows a change of wording in Art. 24 that was included in the transcribed or corrected Journals, but does not appear in the handbook. Obviously the change occurred after the articles went to the printer (PCC, No. 1, I, f. 248; No. 2, I, f. 130; note 10, below).

³ The first seven articles were taken virtually verbatim from Arts. I–VII under "Rules of Discipline and good Government to be observed on Board His Majesty's Ships of War" in *Regulations and Instructions Relating to His Majesty's Service at Sea*, eleven editions of which had been issued at London by 1772 (hereafter cited *Regulations*, page numbers being for the 11th edn.), p. 45–47. In these as in other articles that JA drew upon, all mention of British institutions or administrative bodies was of course omitted and the term "Thirteen United Colonies" or other such terms substituted.

⁴ Art. 10 was adapted from Art. II under "Instructions relating to the Execution of two Acts of Parliament . . ." in *Regulations*, p. 49. Slops were clothing and other necessities furnished to seamen out of the ship's stores (*OED*).

⁵ A printer's error. Both the rough and transcribed Journals have "rate" (PCC, No. 1, I, f. 246; No. 2, I, f. 128).

⁶ Arts. 11, 12, 14, and 15 are virtually verbatim from Arts. VII, X, XV,

and XVI under "Instructions relating to the Execution of two Acts of Parliament . . ." in *Regulations*, p. 50–54. Art. 11, however, does not list a schoolmaster or a corporal, which are mentioned in the British regulation. The former was meant to teach navigation, arithmetic, and writing to young volunteers on British war vessels. The corporal was an assistant to the master-at-arms (*Regulations*, p. 136–137). In the British regulation comparable to Art. 14 no mention is made of shares. Indeed, the section on prizes makes no mention of anyone sharing in prize money (same, p. 89–91).

[7] Art. 16 was based on Arts. I, II, and III, and Art. 17 is virtually verbatim from Art. IV under "Rules for the Cure of Sick or Hurt Seamen on board their own Ships" in *Regulations*, p. 55–56.

[8] Arts. 18–22 are virtually verbatim from Arts. II, VI, VII, XII, and XVII under "Of the Provisions" in *Regulations*, p. 61, 63–65, 67. Art. 18, however, neglected to include the British stipulation that when rations had to be reduced, the purser was not to supply the officers full allowance of provisions, that all were "to be equal in Point of Victualling."

[9] The comparable British article provides that the effects of those dying or killed on board should be sold at auction, the proceeds to be given "Executors or Administrators of the Deceased" (Art. XI under "Of Slop-Cloaths" in *Regulations*, p. 75–76).

[10] Except for the designation of the court which was to have jurisdiction, Art. 24 is a close paraphrase of Art. II, Sect. 7 under 22 Geo. II, ch. 33, passed in 1749 (Danby Pickering, *The Statutes at Large*, Cambridge, Eng., 1765, 19: 327 [cited hereafter *Statutes*]). Although the handbook mentions the congress as the power appointing a court for maritime affairs, the rough Journal has "Congress" stricken out and the phrase "the legislatures in the respective colonies" substituted (see note 2, above). Obviously the congress was not yet ready for a central court with this jurisdiction. In the fall of 1775 JA would have seen the original language as an important step toward unification.

[11] The *Statutes* make no mention of theft of ship's equipment or arms, but condemn any sort of robbery. See note 19 (below).

[12] Adapted from Art. II, Sect. 10, but the British provided the death penalty or other punishment by court martial for faintheartedness (*Statutes*, p. 328).

[13] This provision on desertion was briefly paraphrased from Art. II, Sect. 16 (same, p. 329).

[14] Arts. 28 and 29 on seditious speech and mutinous action were adapted from Art. II, Sect. 19 (same, p. 329–330), in which mutiny is mentioned before seditious speech in a single paragraph— just as in the Journal version (*JCC*, 3:381–382). The presumption is that this order was followed in the committee report and changed only when the paragraphs were numbered for printing. Separation into two articles gave greater emphasis to two kinds of conduct. The Americans, however, lumped together speech and attempting "to make any mutinous assemblies," behavior which could incur a penalty of less than death. The British punished by death the making of a mutinous assembly, reserving a possible lesser punishment for words alone and failing to make a distinction between assembly and joining in a mutiny.

[15] Briefly adapted from Art. II, Sect. 22 (*Statutes*, p. 330). The British penalty for striking or threatening with a weapon any officer was death.

[16] Briefly adapted from Art. II, Sect. 21 (same), which mentions "complaint of the unwholesomeness of the victual, or upon other just ground."

[17] Adapted from Art. II, Sect. 23 (same).

[18] Adapted from Art. II, Sect. 27 (same, p. 331), which mentions death as a possible penalty.

[19] Arts. 34 and 35 are comparable to Art. II, Sects. 28 and 30, respectively, except that the British rules mention death as a possible penalty for robbery (same).

[20] Adapted from the first part of Art. II, Sect. 32 (same), which, however, does not mention the guilty party's suffering in the place of the escaped or dismissed prisoner.

21 Adapted from the second part of Art. II, Sect. 32 (same).

22 Adapted from Art. II, Sect. 36 (same, p. 332).

23 The British rules require from three to thirteen officers, three of them to be captains. No mention is made of marine officers (Arts. XII and XIV, same, p. 334).

24 Adapted from Art. XIX (same, p. 336), but the British made additional stipulations, particularly when the offense (except mutiny) took place within the "narrow seas," that is, the English Channel and Irish Sea. Then approval of the death penalty had to come from the lord high admiral.

25 The pardon power for the British was the prerogative of the king. The British rules limit confinement to a maximum of two years and forbid the use of naval court martials for trying soldiers on transports (Arts. III and V, same, p. 332). But generally, the British code is harsher in that it makes the death penalty available for twenty-four offenses; the Americans specify death only for murder. The American rules make no mention of buggery (Art. II, Sect. 29, same, p. 331) nor of a number of other crimes listed in the British rules—spying, aiding the enemy, striking for arrears of wages, failing to protect convoys, wasting ammunition, sabotage of stores or equipment, negligent steering of ships, and several more.

26 Under "Of the Provisions," Art. I in *Regulations* (p. 61) sets forth a table of rations which probably inspired the American table, but the latter provides for beef or pork on every day except Wednesday; the British on only four days. Where the British provided for beer (wine and spirituous liquors being substitutes), the Americans stipulated rum. The allowances for cheese are equal, but the British allowed 6 oz. of butter per week to the Americans' allowance of only 2.

27 For officers, rates of pay are difficult to compare, since the British had six different rates for each rank. Thus a British captain, depending upon his rate, could earn from 6s to £1 per day. At 6s per Spanish dollar, the American captain could earn slightly over 6s per day; but an American lieutenant would earn slightly less than 6s per day compared to a maximum of 5s for a British lieutenant. The British able seaman earned 24s per month compared to the American wage of 40s, later raised to 48s (JCC, 3:427). All comparisons must take into account that the British paid in sterling, the Americans in lawful money, which overvalued silver by over one-fourth (*Regulations*, p. 146–149).

28 In JCC, 3:384–387, the section on pay is followed by "Orders of Congress," which consists of a covenant of seven parts entered into between the ship's commander, representing the United Colonies, and the officers and men. The latter promised to do their duty and abide by the rules, and in return were assured of pay according to schedule and a fair share of prizes, those disabled having first claim on prize money. It is not clear whether the covenant was part of the Naval Committee's report. In any case, the covenant is omitted here, for it has no apparent relation to the British regulations.

IX. Committee Assignments

14 September – 4 December 1775

14 September. Eliphalet Dyer, Thomas Lynch, John Jay, JA, Francis Lewis (JCC, 2:250).
A standing committee to devise ways and means for supplying the Continental Army with medicines. This committee left only scattered evidence of its activities and is treated here through August 1776. JA may not have been an active member for this entire period.

Thomas Heyward Jr. and Lyman Hall added to the committee: 18 June 1776 (*JCC*, 5:463).

Reported on memorial from Dr. John Morgan and report tabled: 12 July; Dft in PCC (same, 5:460–461, 556; PCC, No. 19, IV, f. 181–184).

Resolutions adopted: 17 July (*JCC*, 5:568–571).

Benjamin Rush added to the committee: 7 Aug. (same, 5:636).

Reported on petition of Dr. Samuel Stringer and resolutions adopted: 20 Aug.; Dft not found (same, 5:661, 673).

Reported on petition of Dr. James McHenry and resolutions adopted: 26 Aug.; Dft not found (same, 5:698, 705).

See also, for other references to the committee, *JCC*, 3:261, 344; 5:528, 622, 633.

25 *September*. Thomas Lynch, Richard Henry Lee, JA (*JCC*, 3:261).

To prepare an answer to letters from George Washington of 4 and 31 Aug. 1775.

Reported and report agreed to: 26 Sept.; Dft not found (same, 3:263; see John Hancock to George Washington, 26 Sept. 1775, LbC in PCC, No. 12A, I, f. 3–6).

9 *October*. JA, John Rutledge, Samuel Chase, Robert R. Livingston, Silas Deane (*JCC*, 3:284–285).

To prepare an answer to letters and enclosures from Philip Schuyler of 19 and 29 Sept.

Reported and report tabled: 10 Oct.; Dft not found (same, 3:287).

Report agreed to: 11 Oct. (same, 3:288; see John Hancock to Philip Schuyler, 11 Oct. 1775, LbC in PCC, No. 12A, I, f. 13–16).

13 *October*. John Rutledge, Samuel Adams, JA, Samuel Ward, Richard Henry Lee (*JCC*, 3:294).

To consider memorials from New York and Philadelphia merchants on tea imported before 1 March 1775.

Reported and report postponed: 18 Oct., 13 Nov., 25 Nov.; Dft not found (same, 3:298, 353, 370).

Report rejected: 28 Nov. (same, 3:388–389).

2 *November*. Thomas Lynch, John Jay, Richard Henry Lee, Silas Deane, JA (*JCC*, 3:317).

To draw up instructions for the committee to confer with Philip Schuyler.

Letter from Philip Schuyler of 21 Oct. with enclosures referred to the committee: 4 Nov. (same, 3:320).

Report agreed to and instructions printed: 8 Nov.; Dft not found (same, 3:339–341).

17 *November*. George Wythe, Edward Rutledge, JA, William Livingston, Benjamin Franklin, James Wilson, Thomas Johnson (*JCC*, 3:357–358).

To consider the portion of George Washington's letter of 8 Nov. relating to the disposal of captured ships and goods.

Reported and report tabled: 23 Nov.; Dft not found (same, 3:364–365).

Report debated and deferred: 24 Nov. (same, 3:368–369).
Resolutions adopted: 25 Nov. (same, 3:371–375).
Reported again, modifying second resolution of 25 Nov., after JA had left congress: 19 Dec. (same, 3:437).
Additional duties assigned, 25 Nov.: to consider the portion of George Washington's letter of 11 Nov. concerning a vessel captured by inhabitants of New Hampshire (same, 3:375).
Report not found.

4 *December.* JA, Thomas Cushing, Thomas McKean (JCC, 3:406).
To inquire into the facts which caused congress to give permission, on 2 Dec., to Capt. Thomas Jenkins to supply Nantucket.
Reported and report read: 8 Dec.; Dft not found (same, 3:415).
Resolutions adopted: 11 Dec. (same, 3:421–422).

To James Warren

Dr sir   Philadelphia Septr. 17. 1775

I have nothing in particular to write. Our most gracious K––– has given a fresh Proof of his Clemency, in his Answer to the City.[1] But no more of Politicks, at present—if this Scratch of a Pen should fall into the Hands of the wiseacre Gage, as long as I confine myself, to Matrimony, and Horsemanship, there will be no Danger.

Be it known to you then that two of the most unlikely Things, within the whole Compass of Possibility, have really, and actually happened. The first is the suden Marriage of our President, whose agreable Lady honours us with her Presence and contributes much to our good Humour, as well as to the Happiness of the President.[2] So much for that.

The next Thing is more wonderfull still.

You know the Aversion, which your Secretary,[3] has ever entertained to riding, on Horseback. He never would be perswaded to mount a Horse. The last time we were here, I often laboured to perswade him, for the Sake of his Health, but in vain.

Soon after We sat out, on the last Journey, I reflected that some Degree of Skill and Dexterity in Horsemanship, was necessary to the Character of a Statesman. It would take more Time and Paper than I have to Spare, to shew the Utility of Horsemanship to a Politician; so I shall take this for granted. But I pointed out the particulars to him, and likewise shewed him that Sociability would be greatly promoted, by his mounting one of my Horses.

On Saturday the second day of September 1775, in the Town of Grafton He was prevailed on to put my servant with his, into Harrisons

Chaise and to mount upon my Horse, a very genteel, and easy little Creature.

We were all disappointed and Surprized, instead of the Taylor riding to Brentford[4] We beheld, an easy, genteel Figure, upon the Horse, and a good deal of Spirit and facility, in the Management of the Horse, insomuch that We soon found our Servants were making Some disagreable Comparisons, and Since our Arrival here I am told that Fessenden (impudent Scoundrel!) reports that the Secretary rides fifty per Cent better than your Correspondent.

In this manner, We rode to Woodstock, where we put up for the Sabbath. It was Soon observed that the Secretary, could not Sit So erect in his Chair as he had Sat upon his Horse, but Seemed to be neither sensible of the Disease or the Remedy. I Soon perceived and apprised him of both. On Sunday Evening, at Mr. Dexters,[5] where we drank Coffee and Spent an agreable Evening I perswaded him to purchase, two yards of flannell which we carried to our Landlady, who, with the assistance of a Taylor Woman in the House, made up a Pair of Drawers, which the next Morning were put on, and not only defended the Secretary from any further Injury, but entirely healed the little Breach which had been begun.

Still an Imperfection, remained. Our Secretary had not yet learned to mount and dismount—two Servants were necessary to attend upon these occasions, one to hold the Bridle and Stirrup, the other to boost the Secretary. This was rather a ridiculous Circumstance Still. At last, I undertook to instruct him the necessary Art of mounting. I had my Education to this Art, under Bates, the celebrated Equerry, and therefore might be Supposed to be a Master of it. I taught him, to grasp the Bridle, with his Right Hand over the Pummell of his Saddle, to place his left Foot firm in the Stirrup; to twist his left Hand into the Horses Main, about half Way between his Ears and his Shoulders, and then a vigorous Exertion of his Strength would carry him very gracefully into the Seat, without the least Danger of falling over on [the ot]her Side. The Experiment was tryed and Succeeded to Admiration.

Thus equipped and instructed, our Horseman rode all the Way from Woodstock to Philadelphia, sometimes upon one of my Horses, Sometimes on the other. And Acquired fresh Strength, Courage, Activity and Spirit every day. His Health is much improved by it, and I value myself, very much upon the Merit of having probably added Several years, to a Life So important to his Country, by the little Pains I took to perswade him to mount and teach him to ride.[6]

Sully and Cecil were both Horsemen, and you know I would not have our American, inferiour to them in the Smallest Accomplishment.

Pray Mrs. Warren to write to me. I would to her, if I had half so much Time.[7]

RC (MHi:Warren-Adams Coll.); addressed: "To the Hon. James Warren Esqr Speaker of the House of Representatives of the Massachusetts Bay and Paymaster General to the American Army Watertown favd by Mr. Andw. Cabot"; docketed: "Mr. J. A Lettr Sepr. 1775."

[1] On 16 July the King rejected the demands contained in an "Address, Petition, and Remonstrance" adopted by the City of London on 24 June that called upon him to dismiss his present ministers and end the despotic war against the American colonies. George III replied: "I am always ready to listen to the dutiful Petitions of my Subjects, and ever happy to comply with their reasonable Requests, but while the Constitutional Authority of this Kingdom is openly Resisted by a part of my American Subjects, I owe it to the rest of my People of whose Zeal and Fidelity I have had such constant Proofs, to continue and enforce those Measures by which alone their Rights and Interests can be asserted and maintained" (*Boston Gazette*, 18, 25 Sept.). Such a reply supported JA's view that there was little to be gained by attempts at conciliation and clearly foreshadowed the fate of the Olive Branch Petition.

[2] John Hancock, president of the congress, married Dorothy Quincy at Fairfield, Conn., on 28 Aug. (same, 11 Sept.).

[3] Samuel Adams.

[4] "Taylor Riding to Brentford" was the title of a well-known puppet show (Alice Morse Earle, *Customs and Fashions in Old New England*, N.Y., 1893, p. 246).

[5] Samuel Dexter of Woodstock Hill, former Massachusetts legislator, moved to Connecticut in 1775 (Clarence Winthrop Bowen, *The History of Woodstock, Connecticut*, Norwood, Mass., 1926, 179–181).

[6] Samuel Adams wrote to Elbridge Gerry: "I arrived in this city on the 12th instant, having rode full three hundred miles on horseback, an exercise which I have not used for many years past. I think it has contributed to the establishment of my health, for which I am obliged to my friend Mr. John Adams, who kindly offered me one of his horses the day after we sat off from Watertown" (26 Sept., Samuel Adams, *Writings*, 3:226).

[7] This letter and JA's to Mercy Otis Warren of 26 Aug. (above) suggest that JA's absence from Philadelphia had really refreshed his spirit and allowed some of his old playfulness to reappear, however briefly.

To James Warren

Dear Sir   Philadelphia Septr. 19 1775

I have but a moments Time to write and nothing of Importance to say.

Mr. Randolph, our former President is here, and Sits very humbly in his Seat, while our new one, continues in the Chair, without Seeming to feel the Impropriety.[1] Coll. Nelson, a Hunter, Mr. Wythe, a Lawyer and Mr. Francis Lightfoot Lee, a Planter, are here from Virginia, instead of Henry, Pendleton and Bland. Henry is General of Virginia. The other two are old and infirm. I am well pleased that Virginia, has Set the Example of changing Members, and I hope that Massachusetts will follow it, and all the other Colonies.

I Should be glad upon a new Election to be relieved from this Service. This Climate does not agree with my Constitution, so well as our own: and I am not very well fortified you know against the Inclemencies of any.

This Congress, I assure you, feels the Spirit of War, more intimately than they did before the Adjournment. They set about Preparations for it, with Seriousness, and in Earnest.

RC (MHi: Warren-Adams Coll.); docketed: "Mr. J. A Lettr Sepr 1775."

¹ In JA's eyes, Hancock's tenure as president was temporary in that he had been elected to fill the vacancy Peyton Randolph made by returning to Virginia to preside as speaker over a session of the House of Burgesses a few days after his re-election in May as president of the Continental Congress. JA's criticism of Hancock suggests the hostility that had grown up between them (JCC, 2:12, 58–59; *Adams Family Correspondence,* 1:323).

From James Warren

My Dear Sir   Watertown Sepr 19th: 1775

I had fixed a determination in my own mind to omitt no Oppertunity of writeing either to you, or my Friend Mr. S. Adams, but I have Indeed so little to say at this time, that I should have thought it hardly worth while to trouble you with a Letter had it not been to Inclose one from Mrs. Adams,¹ who with the Children I had the pleasure Yesterday to hear were recovered. I have been much Concerned about them. I presume the Inclosed will give you the State of the Family, and make it Unnecessary for me to Add more. I have been here ever since you left us, without once hearing from you. I wrote to you a week ago, and took pains to Collect every thing I could think of as News foreign or Domestic. Your Intelligence from Abroad is so much better than ours at this Time that I Expect no Success in handing you our foreign News, and of the domestic kind we have very little. We suffer Extreamly for want of it when we meet in the Street. We have not a word more to say than to Enquire after each others Health, or make on Observation on the weather. These are Circumstances so different from what we have been used to, that we are quite out of our Element. Scarcely any one thing has happened since my last worthy of your Notice. We have frequent desertions to us, seldom two Nights without an Instance of that kind. The Night before last were four or five Sailors, by the best accounts given by Gentlemen out of Town.

The Soldiery are dispirited, by their Confinement, their want of Supplies, and above all by their vast fatigue. They Live in Continual Horror of being Attacked. Their Guards are therefore large, and must be Numerous from the Extensiveness of their works. It is supposed that frequent Shews of Attacking them would soon wear them out. I mentioned this at Head Quarters Yesterday. I hope they will take that Method to harrass them. A Servant of Genl. Howe! deserted about 10 days ago. I heard him tell the General that his Master Constantly set up till one O Clock, and then slept till Morning in his Boots and Cloaths. They seem to be makeing but little preparation for winter. It was reported that they were pulling down the Houses from the Haymarket to the Fortification in order to Erect works to retreat to if they could not hold those they now have.[2] They really have begun to pull down the Houses, but it is generally thought to be only for fuel of which they are in great want, and they Choose that place as the Clearing it would be most Convenient for new works if they should have Occasion for more. We have had scarce a Gun fired for 10 days before Sunday Morning when A Number of the Rebels Appearing without their works on Boston Neck, our People fired four Cannon on them which, drove them in, killed two, and wounded five of their Men as we have learned by deserters.[3] They returned a smart **Fire** without any Success, and Yesterday again Roxbury Side had a very heavy Canonade with as little, only one officer very slightly wounded. This is indeed very remarkable as our People Expose themselves without reserve haveing been so Enured to Shott, and shells that do no Execution that they totally disregard them. Cobble Hill is to be possessed and fortified this or Tomorrow Night. Putnam is to be gratified with the Command.[4] This must Open a warm Sceen, and will furnish us Abundantly with the Musick of Cannon, and Topicks of Conversation. The Constant Expectation I have had of receiving the Money from Philadelphia has Confined me to this place, Contrary to both my Inclinations and Interest, supposeing it would not do to be Absent when it came. It is not yet arrived. This delay is Astonishing, and I fear will Cause irreperable Injuries to the Army. The Soldiers that are not paid for the Month of August are very Uneasy. The General Can't fulfill his promise to them. The Quarter Master Genl. and Commissary Genl. are both out of money. Their Credit suffering, and their provisions for the Army at a stand, and this at a time when the Season is Approaching that Transportation from distant places will be difficult. Do Apologize to my Friend Adams for my not writeing to him. It is really Oweing to the poverty of the Times. I had no Subject without I had entered on Metaphysicks, Mathematics or some subjects foreign from Politics or News which alone Engage my Attention. I will however write him soon, Subject or no Subject. The Councill Adjourned for a week. The Assembly meets tomorrow. Whenever any thing Occurs you shall hear it, and shall on my part be glad to hear of your doings. I want to hear of high Spirited Measures. It is in my Opinion ridiculous to hesitate now, about takeing up Crown officers, and fifty other things.

You won't loose sight of powder, and Money. I wish You Health and every Happiness, and am with Great Sincerity your Friend.

Compliments to all Friends. I forgot to tell you that they are Exerciseing their Wit, and diverting themselves in Boston by versifying the Letters taken from Hitchburne as I hear. I have not been Able to get Sight of it.[5]

RC (Adams Papers); docketed: "Sept. 19, 1775   Warren."

[1] Probably AA's letter of 16 [i.e. 17] Sept. (*Adams Family Correspondence*, 1:278–280).

[2] Such a line would have protected the harbor, particularly the Long Wharf area, and thus supply lines and escape routes.

[3] Reported in the *Boston Gazette*, 25 Sept.

[4] Actually Putnam did not fortify this hill until November (Frothingham, *Siege of Boston*, p. 268).

[5] Almost certainly a broadside entitled *A Paraphrase on the Second Epistle of John, the Round-Head, to James, Prolocutor of the Rump-Parliament, in a Liberal Manner; wherein the True Spirit of the Writer Is Preserved* (Evans Supplement, No. 42918). Misdated 25 July and probably taken from the intercepted letter as it appeared in the *Massachusetts Gazette*, the letter in the broadside took the form of a series of sentences and paragraphs, ten in all, taken in order from the original and labeled "verses." After each piece of text or verse, the satirist contributed a "paraphrase" or unflattering explication.

From Josiah Quincy

Dear Sir   Sept: 22d: 1775

Under my adverse Circumstances, I stood, and still stand in great Need of your Advice; and am therefore, very sorry I had not an Opportunity to converse with you, before your Return to the Congress.

Your kind Letter of July 29th is now before me. Were my Abilities equal to my Inclination, you would be amply assisted, in giving Birth to a Revolution, which, I think with you, "seems to be in the Womb of Providence as important as any that has happened in the Affairs of Mankind."

Agreable to the Old Man's Sentiments, in this enclosed Paper, "the *Sword* and not the *Quill* is *now* to decide the Controversy;"[1] Nothing therefore, could revive my desponding Hopes more, than the assurance you give me, of a sufficient Plenty of Powder against another Year, and of our own make.

In my former Letter[2] I said, that "the Harbor might be blocked up; and both Seamen and Soldiers made Prisoners at Discretion;" which seems to you incredible. Please, to read at your Leasure this following Explanation. There are but two Channels, through which Ships of Burthen can pass to and from Boston. One of them runs between the west Head of Long Island, and the Moon, (so called) and is about a Mile across. This Channel is too shallow for any Ship of War above 20 Guns. The other runs between the east Head of Long Island, and the south Point of Dear Island; and is about a Mile and half from Side to Side. This, the only Channel through which capital Ships can pass, leads (outward bound) through the Narrows (so called) between Gallop's Island and Lovel's Island; where the Channel is not wider than the Length of a 50 Gun Ship. In the opening between Gallops Island and George's Island is Nantasket Road; where, *one*, is always, and at present, *five* Men of War are stationed, to gaurd the Narrows from being stop'd up.

Upon the foregoing Facts, I thus reason:

The Moon Island communicates with Squantum Neck, at low Water, almost dryshod. A defensible Fort, therefore, upon Squantum, may be so placed, as to secure a Retreat not only from the Moon, but from Squantum to the Main. One upon the east Head of the Moon, and another, if found necessary, upon the west Head of Long Island, secures the Passage between, and covers a Retreat from the *Latter* to the *Former*. Another upon the *Summit* in the middle of Long Island covers the Shore on each Side, so, as that no Force can land without being greatly anoyed, if not entirely prevented. Another strong Battery from 20 to 40 peices of heavy Cannon at the east Head of Long Island, commands, not only the Ship Channel, but the Narrows, and Nantasket Road, so that no Ship can remain there with Safety; and consequently, by sinking Hulks in the Narrows we might prevent any Ship of Force from going out or coming in. If the Passage thro' the Narrows is not stop'd, I am sensible, a Ship with a fresh Gale of Wind, and flood or Ebb Tide, which is rapid between Long Island and Deer Island, might run through without any great Hazard; but, after the east Head of Long Island is fortified, I can foresee Nothing to hinder, the Narrows being reduced to such a Draught of Water, as that, no Vessel of any considerable Force, can pass through there. This, being effected; as I said above, both Seamen and Soldiers, if they dont escape, by a timely Flight, must become Prisoners at Discretion.

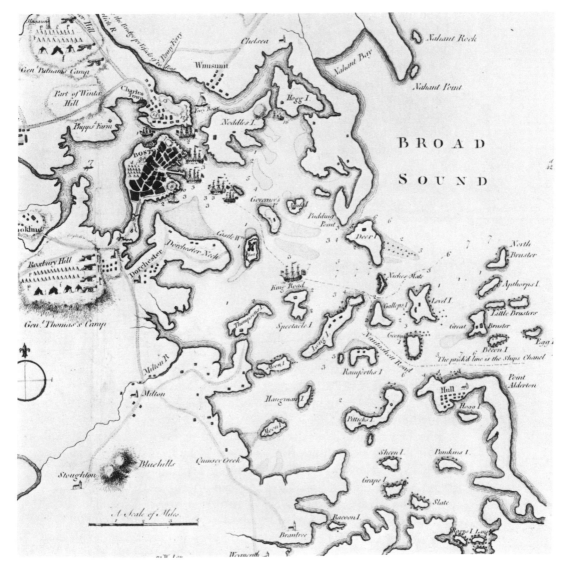

9. A PLAN OF THE TOWN AND HARBOUR OF BOSTON,
BY J. DE COSTA, 1775
See page xi

I have been told, there is in one of the English Magazines, an accurate Draft of the Harbor.[3] If you can procure it, upon Examination, you may determin, the Distance and Depth of Water between the Islands aforesaid with Precision; and consequently, whether such a Scheme is practicable or not.

I have thought, and said from the Beginning, that *Row Gallies* must be our first mode of Defence by Sea; it gives me therefore, Pleasure to hear, our worthy Friend Doctor F————n is employed in constructing some for the City of Philadelphia. I wish I had the same Employment here, for I am very sure, twenty of them, under proper Direction, would have taken or destroyed all those Cruisers and Cutters, that have infested, and done so much Damage, in, the Vineyard and Long Island Sounds in the Course of the Summer past; besides, being a safe Convoy to our Provision Vessels. When I first proposed the Scheme to our Committee of Safety, it was objected, that, we had no Body skilled in the Construction of them. Afterwards I heard of a Ship Carpenter, just escaped from Boston, who had been several Years a Prisoner in a Turkish Row Galley, and had formed a compleat three feet Model of one. It was then objected, that, heavy Cannon, and Powder were wanting. An insuperable Objection, most certainly; which I hope will soon be removed.

Several Vessels have lately arrived in Boston from England; but the News they bring is industriously secreted. The sullen Silence, and dejected Countenances of the Officers, give Rise to various Conjectures. God grant the Truth may be a Dissolution of a venal P————t, a disbanded Army, and an Order for the Ships and Troops here to return imediately Home.

A few Days since, I received a Letter from my Daughter in Norwich,[4] in which is the following Passage: "I have just heard that the Ship in which Mr. ———— sailed is arrived in England after 28 Days Passage. I have the Pleasure to hear that there is like to be an Accommodation between Great B———— and America, and that speedily." By the same Conveyance I received the Resolves Petition and Remonstrance of the City of London to *their* Sovereign. If such a Spirit of Resentment animates that powerfull Corporation upon the first News of Hostilities, what must be their Indignation, when they come to hear all the Circumstances, that have attended, and *disgraced* the *British Arms*, both by Sea and Land! Must not such accumulated Disasters, like so many Flashes of Lightning and Peals of Thunder, penetrate the Hearts of a *bloodthirsty Scotch Faction* with Dispair of ever enslaving *Americans*, who have fought with such Valor and Intrepedity as must exclude all Hope of Success in any future Attempt! Where will those Sons of Violence, H————n, S————l, [5] and others of the same Complection, hide their guilty Heads, when called to answer, for the insidious Arts they have been practicing, against their native Country; to the Ruin and Distruction, of countless Numbers of their industrious Fellow Citizens, whose *Worth* compared with theirs, is as *Diamonds* to *pebble Stones*! When I contemplate the Conduct of such *infamous Parricides*, my Nerves are braced, my Hand feels the Impulse of my Heart, is ready to drop the *Pen* and grasp the *Sword of Vengeance*! I feel my Self young again, and long to exterpate them, and the Memory of them from the Face of the Earth!

> "Is there no hidden Thunder, in the Stores of Heav'n,
> Red with uncommon Wrath, to blast the men,
> Who owe their Greatness, to their Countrys Ruin?" [6]

Oh! that kindred Flame, has ere this, inspired the Breast of every *true Briton*; and their s————d S————n [7] made to feel, what it is to alienate the Affections of the greatest Part of his Subjects, to gratifie the insatiable Avarice and Ambition, of those treacherous Sycophants, who wish to see him dethroned; and his royal Diadem encircling the Head of a *caledonian Exile*.[8] Must the *Trappings* of a M————h and his Minions, which wou'd maintain a *Commonwealth* be provided for at such an immense Expence of Blood and Treasure? Forbid it Heaven! Shall not the virtuous Part of Mankind, finally prevail over the vicious, notwithstanding the Numbers of the *Latter* and the Scarcity of the *Former*? They certainly will, if upon every Occasion, the Spirit of Party is sacrificed, to Unanimity and Perseverance. But whither does my Zeal transport Me? I forget, I am transmitting Sentiments to One, who anticipates all, and more than all I have said or can say upon such interesting Subjects. I beg Leave, therefore, to conclude, with my ardent Wishes, that, the Success of your Endeavors to restore Peace and Tranquility; the genuine Offspring of Order and good Government, may be equal to your distinguished Abilities! And that you and yours, may live long to enjoy the happy Fruits of your *patriotic Exertions*; however infinite Wisdom may see fit to dispose of Your affectionate and faithfull humble Servant,

P.S. Your good Lady is so well recovered of her tedious Indisposition, as to favour us with a short Visit with your amiable Daughter last Monday.

Be so good as to present my Affectionate Regards to good Doctor F————-n; and tell him I have wrote three long Letters to him to

London, and one since his Arrival at Philadelphia; but, having received no Answer fear they all miscarried.

Please to present my Compliments of Congratulations to Colo. Hancock and his Lady to whom I wish mutual and lasting Happiness.

RC (Adams Papers); with enclosure, for which see note 1.

[1] From an enclosure, a letter printed in the *New England Chronicle*, 24 Aug., and signed "An OLD MAN, from my cottage near Boston." Probably written by Josiah Quincy himself, it dealt with the exchange of letters between Gen. Burgoyne and Gen. Charles Lee that occurred in July.

[2] Of 11 July (above).

[3] Probably "A Plan of the Town and Chart of the Harbour of Boston, Exhibiting a View of the Islands, Castle Forts, and Entrances into the Said Harbour," which originally appeared in the *Gentleman's Magazine* for Jan. 1775 (vol. 45:facing p. 41). This map is reprinted in reduced size in *Adams Family Correspondence*, 1:following p.

240, No. 9. JA refers to the map in a letter to James Warren, 8 Oct. (below).

[4] Abigail Phillips Quincy, widow of Josiah Quincy Jr. (Josiah Quincy, *Josiah Quincy, Jr.*, p. 288–289). She may be referring to the arrival in London on 14 Aug. of Richard Penn, who carried the Olive Branch Petition from the congress.

[5] Thomas Hutchinson and Jonathan Sewall.

[6] Written in the margin and its place in the text indicated by an asterisk, this is a quotation with slight modifications from Addison, *Cato*, Act I, scene i.

[7] Sacred sovereign.

[8] The Young Pretender, Charles Edward Stuart, grandson of James II.

To James Warren

Dr Sir   Philadelphia Septr. 26. 1775

This Afternoon, and not before I received a Line from the excellent Marcia,[1] which [is] the first and only Letter I have received from the Family to which She belongs Since I left Watertown. Be pleased to thank her for this Favour, and to let her know that She must certainly have misinterpretted Some Passage in my Letter Since I never thought either Politicks or War, or any other Art or Science beyond the Line of her Sex: on the contrary I have ever been convinced that Politicks and War, have in every age, been influenced, and in many, guided and controuled by her Sex. Sometimes it is to be feared by the unworthy Part of it: but at others, it must be confessed by the amiable and the good. But, if I were of opinion that it was best for a general Rule that the fair should be excused from the arduous Cares of War and State; I should certainly think that Marcia and Portia, ought to be Exceptions, because I have ever ascribed to those Ladies, a Share and no small one neither, in the Conduct of our American Affairs.

I have nothing new to communicate. Every Thing, has been done, and is now doing, to procure the *Unum Necessarium*:[2] I wish I could give you a more agreable account of the Salt Petre Works in this City.

I fear they have chosen injudiciously a Place for their Vatts, Vaults and Buildings, a low marshy Place which was lately overflowed by the Storm. Still We have Sanguine Accounts of the Skill and Success of some operators.

Coll. Dyer[3] produces a Sample of excellent Salt Petre, made by two De Witts, one of Norwich the other of Windham, and he is confident that they can and will make large Quantities. Coll. Harrison of Virginia,[4] whose Taste in Madeira, I know, and in Girls I believe, and in Salt Petre I hope to be much Superiour to his Judgment in Men, is very confident that they are making large Quantities from Tobacco House Earth, in his Colony.

We are hourly expecting Intelligence from Canada, as well as Massachusetts, and from London.

My dear sir, Let me intreat you to do every Thing in your Power to get ready the Accounts of all that our Province has done and expended in the Common Cause, for which they expect or hope to be reimbursed by the United Colonies. It has ever appeared to me a Thing of much Importance, that We should be furnished with these Accounts as soon as possible. From present appearances, our session will not be long, and if We should not be furnished with the Necessary Papers, very soon, We shall not be able to obtain any Reimbursement this Fall: and the next Spring We may be involved in so many Dangers, as well as new Expences as to render our Chance for obtaining Justice, more precarious. You know that your Delegates have been here, almost the whole Time since the Commencement of Hostilities, and therefore can say nothing of their own Knowledge concerning your Exertions or Expences, but must depend altogether upon Information from the General Court.

This is really a Strong Reason for a Change in the Delegation. We have been absent so long from our native Country as to be a Kind of Aliens and strangers there. If it is good Policy to reelect one of the old Delegates, because he is personally knowing to what has passed here; it is equally good Policy to elect Some new ones, because they are Witnesses of what has passed with you. For my own Part, as my political Existence terminates with the Year, I Sincerely wish to be excused in the next Election. I long to be a little with you in the General Court, that I may see and hear, and feel with my Countrymen. And I ardently wish to be a little with my Family, and to attend a little to my private Affairs. To be frank and candid to a Friend, I begin to feel for my Family, to leave all the Burthen of my private Cares, at a Time when my affairs are in so much Perplexity, to an excellent Partner, gives me Pain for her. To leave the Education of a young Family, entirely to her, altho I know not where it could be better lodged, gives me much Concern for her and them.

I have very little Property, you very well know, which I have not earned myself, by an obstinate Industry, in opposition to the Malice of a very infirm Constitution, in Conjunction with the more pernicious Malice of Ministerial and gubernatorial Enemies. Of the little Acquisition's I have made, five hundred Pounds sterling is sunk in Boston in a Real Estate, four hundred sterling more is compleatly annihilated in a Library [5] that is now wholly useless to me and mine, and at least four hundred sterling more, is wholly lost to me, in Notes and Bonds not one farthing of the Principal or Interest of which, can I obtain, and the Signers are dying, breaking, flying every day.

It is now compleatly two years since my Business has been totally ruined by the public Confusions. I might modestly estimate the Profit of my Business before this Period at three hundred sterling a Year, perhaps more. I think therefore I may fairly estimate myself a sufferer immediately, to the amount of two Thousand Pounds sterling. I have purchased Lands, which these Causes have prevented me from paying for, and the Interest is running on without a Possibility of my paying it, and I am obliged to hire Labour yearly upon my Farm to no Small amount.

In the mean Time, all that has been granted me by the general Court for the sessions of this Congress last Fall and this Spring has not defreyed my necessary Expences, however strange it may appear.

The Conclusion from all this is, that I am rushing rapidly into Perplexities and Distresses in my private Affairs from which I can never extricate myself. By retreating from public Life, in some Measure I might, preserve myself and Family from a Ruin, which without it will be inevitable. I am willing to sink with my Country, but it ought not to be insisted on that I Should Sink myself without any Prospect of contributing by that Means to make it Swim. I have taken my Trick at Helm, when it was not easy to get Navigators who would run the Risque of the storm. At present the Course is plain whatever the Weather may be, and the prospect of that is much better than it was when I was called to assist in steering the ship.

RC (MHi: Warren-Adams Coll.); docketed: "Mr. J. A Lettr   Sepr. 1775."

[1] Mercy Otis Warren to JA, 4 Sept. (above).

[2] The "one necessity," that is, gunpowder.

[3] Eliphalet Dyer (1721–1807), delegate to the congress from Connecticut (*DAB*).

[4] Benjamin Harrison (1726?–1791),

delegate to the congress (*DAB*).
  [5] JA's library, given to the town of Quincy in 1822, is now housed in the Boston Public Library.

To Mercy Otis Warren

Madam   Philadelphia Septr. 26. 1775

Your Favour, by my Friend Collins,[1] never reached me till this Evening. At Newport, concluding to go by Water, he put it into the Post office, least it Should meet with a Fate as unfortunate as Some others. I call them unfortunate after the manner of Men for, altho they went into Hands which were never thought of by the Writer, and notwithstanding all the unmeaning Noise that has been made about them, they have done a great deal of good. Providence intended them for Instruments to promote valuable Purposes, altho the Writer of them, thought so little of them that he never could have recollected one Word in them, if they had been lost. The most that I care about them, is the indecent Exposure of the Name of a Lady,[2] who cannot be put to Pain, without giving me Uneasiness by Sympathy.

I boasted, Madam, of my Happiness, in my last to you, because I knew you could excuse the appearance of Vanity, and because I knew very well that the Person who so deservedly holds the first Place in your Heart, could say by Experience, that an Happiness so perfect was not merely ideal.

I am much obliged to you, for your kind Information concerning the Health of a Lady whom I esteem so highly. I presume her Indisposition has been the Cause why I have not heard from her before. I rejoice to hear she is better. I Hope, my invariable Friend, is better and that I shall receive a long Letter from him, Soon. My best Wishes attend him, as well as all His.

RC (MHi:Warren-Adams Coll.); docketed twice in two different unknown hands: "Hon: Jno Adams   Septr 26th 1775" and "J Adams Esqr   Septr 1775   Philadelphia."

[1] That of 4 Sept. (above).
[2] In the original an asterisk is inserted here to go with a note at the bottom of the page written in the hand of Mrs. Warren: "The intercepted letter alluded to was to Mrs. Adams. It was Caryed into New York and some little things said which would naturally be unpleasant both to herself and Mr. Adams."

To James Warren

Dr sir   Philadelphia Septr. 28. 1775

I write at this Time, only to remind you that I have received no Letters.

Let me intreat the earliest Attention of our Houses, to the Accounts and Vouchers of our Province. Accounts must be exact and Vouchers genuine, or We shall suffer. The whole Attention of every Member of both Houses, would be not improfitably employed upon this subject untill it is finished.

The Accounts, I mean are of Ammunition, such as Powder, Ball, Cartridges—Artillery, Cannon Field Pieces, Carriages—Camp Equipage, Cantins, Kettles, Spoons &c Tents, Canvas &c &c &c.

Provisions, Bread, Meat, Meal, Peas, every Thing in short. In fine it is idle for me to enter to detail. The Pay and Cloathing of the Troops &c &c.

But I must entreat, to have these Accounts and Vouchers. I do beseech that it may be remembered that I was importunate, on this Head with several Gentlemen, when I was with you.

RC (MHi:Warren-Adams Coll.); docketed: "Mr. J: Adams Lettr. Septr 28th. 1775."

To James Warren

Dr sir   Philadelphia Septr. 30. 1775

Mr. Lynch, Coll. Harrison, and Dr. Franklyn are preparing for a Journey to Watertown and Cambridge, one of whom will do me the Favour of taking this Letter.[1]

Mr. Lynch, you have seen before. He is an oppulent Planter of Great Understanding and Integrity and the best Affections to our Country and Cause.

Coll. Harrison, is of Virginia, and the Friend and Correspondent of the General, but it seems by a certain Letter, under some degree of Prejudice against our dear New Englandmen.[2] These Prejudices however, have arisen from Misrepresentation and may be easily removed.

Dr. Franklyn needs nothing to be said. There is no abler or better American, that I know of.

I could wish a particular Attention and Respect to all Three.

I know you will be pleased to be introduced to these Gentlemen, because it will give you an opportunity of serving your Country.[3] I am your Friend,   John Adams

RC (MHi:Warren-Adams Coll.); docketed: "Mr. J. A Lettr Septr 30. 1775."

[1] Probably Franklin; see the following calendar entry, JA to James Warren, 30 Sept.

[2] A reference to Harrison's letter to Washington of 21 July, which was intercepted with JA's two letters of 24

July and published in the *Massachusetts Gazette*, 17 Aug. (see same).

³ This was the first of a series of letters of introduction (see JA to William Sever, 2 Oct.; to John Winthrop, 2 Oct.; and to Gen. Heath, 5 Oct., all below). The committee of the congress was appointed on 30 Sept. in response to a resolution of the previous day directing that a committee go immediately to Cambridge to confer with Washington, representatives of the New England colonies, and any others who could help in determining "the most effectual method of continuing, supporting, and regulating a continental army" (JCC, 3:265, 266–267). The General Court was officially notified of the committee's mission on 14 Oct. and immediately made preparations for its reception. The committee arrived in Massachusetts on or about 17 Oct. (Mass., *House Jour.*, 1775–1776, 2d sess., p. 162–163; Artemas Ward to JA, 23 Oct., below).

To James Warren

Philadelphia, 30 September 1775. RC offered for sale by Parke-Bernet Gallery, N.Y., Gribbel sale, pt. 2, 22–24 Jan. 1941, lot 2. Addressed to James Warren as Speaker of the House of Representatives of Massachusetts, "favoured by Dr. Franklin."

After giving the names of the congressional committee members and explaining their function, JA proceeds, "I hope our Province, in every Part of it, will treat these Gentlemen with every possible Demonstration of Respect, Confidence and Affection. . . .

"Let me intreat you, Sir, to be particularly attentive to these Gentlemen, — to Coll. Harrison particularly — convince him, that the only narrow, selfish People belonging to our Province, the only ones actuated by Provincial Prejudices and Attachments, compass the Sample here.

"Will it not be excellent Politicks to make Dr. Franklin welcome by making him a grant of what is due to him from the Province?"

A quotation from Benjamin Harrison's intercepted letter to Washington of 21 July explains JA's comment: "your Fatigue and various Kinds of Trouble, I dare say are great, but they are not more than I expected, knowing the People you have to deal with by the Sample we have here" (*Massachusetts Gazette*, 17 Aug.).

On 23 Oct. the General Court resolved to pay Franklin £1,854 sterling for his services as agent from 31 Oct. 1770 to 1 March 1775 (Mass., *House Jour.*, 1775–1776, 2d sess., p. 188).

From William Tudor

Dear Sir   Cambridge 30th. Sepr. 1775

The manœuvers of the Camp have afforded Nothing important for a month past. The Works at Plough'd Hill are finish'd, but are useless, because we have not Powder to annoy the Enemy and if we had, it would be an idle Expence of it to expend it in Cannonading at such a Distance. The Enemy have fir'd from their different Works 2000 Cannon Balls and 300 Bombs, without killing ten men of ours.

When Orders were given for 1100 men under Col. Arnold to

march for Quebec, the men offer'd so readily, that 5 Times the Number might have been draughted for this laborious and hazardous march, had they been wanted. We were in anxious Suspense, during their Passage from Newbury to Kennebeck; We have Accounts since of their safe Arrival in Kennebeck River, and are now only solicitous to hear of the successful Movements of General Scuyler.

The Lovers of Turtle in the Camp are like to be indulg'd with a feast of it, by the Marbleheadmen this Week taking a Schooner belonging to Lewis Gray, bound from New Providence to Boston, loaded with Turtle and Fruit.[1] This is no very great Acquisition for Us, but will be a severe Disappointment to our ministerial besieg'd Enemy. The next Day some Boats from Cape Ann took a more valuable Prize, in the Capture of a Brig sent by Genl. Carleton to Boston from Quebec, with 45 horned Cattle and 60 Sheep on board, and the Hold full of Wheat.[2] This is but a small Retaliation for the dayly Piratical Acts of Graves's Squadron. There is scarce a Vessel that escapes the Clutches of the Cutters and Men of War that infest the Coast. The Week before last they carried eleven Sail of Vessels into Boston, where after the Formality of a Trial in an admiralty Court, they are confiscated, to the Use of Graves and his Harpies. Notwithstanding these continual Depredations, our Assembly will not be prevail'd on to fit out Privateers.[3] The Delicacy is absurd surely.

Two of the Enemy's Sentries left their Post on the Neck last Night and came over to our Camp. They are Privates of the 49th. Regiment. They say, Genl. Gage's Army, consists, sick and well, at Charlestown and at Boston of 6000 Men. That the Troops have the Scurvy very badly and generally, and that it is very sickly among them still.

The Carphenters are all at Work here, building 20 flat bottom Boats, which are to carry 50 men, and which with 250 Whale Boats, which it is said are ordered here, can carry 3000 Men. There are 3 floating Batteries which carry 1 Nine Pounder and 2 six Pounders each, besides, Swivells and small Arms. They are man'd with 30 Hands a peice. From these and some other Preparations it is conjectur'd, Some great Attempt will be made before the Winter sets in. A large Number of Hands are at Work on the Barracks, and it is expected by the End of October, the whole Army Will get into good Quarters.

To our great Astonishment the Surgeon General was this forenoon put under an Arrest for Corresponding with the Army in Boston.[4] An intercepted Letter wrote in Characters, and some other Circumstances, have made the Suspicions very strong against him. His House has been search'd and all his Papers seiz'd, by the General's Orders. I am not now acquainted with any farther Particulars. You will doubtless have the fullest Information sent the Congress from Head Quarters. Good God! Doctor C————h prove a Traitor! What a Triumph to the Tories? But I quit the shocking Subject.

We have had no Letters from any of You, since the Meeting. I must beg Sir, you would continue your friendly Letters, and oblige me with some further Communications. I am Sir your most oblig'd and very hble Servt.,   Wm. Tudor

RC (Adams Papers); addressed: "Honble John Adams Esq."; docketed: "Wm. Tudor   Sep. 30. 1775."

[1] The schooner *Industry*, commanded by Francis Butler, was captured on 27 Sept. (Mass., *House Jour.*, 1775–1776, 2d sess., p. 129–130).

[2] The brigantine *Dolphin*, commanded by William Wallace, was captured on 28 Sept. by men from Gloucester (same, p. 131, 137; Records of the States, Microfilm, Mass., A.1a, Reel No. 12, Unit 1, p. 197).

[3] Two days before Tudor wrote, the House of Representatives had appointed a committee to consider the "Expediency of fitting out a Number of Armed Vessels," which brought in a favorable report on 9 Oct. On 1 Nov. "An Act for Encouraging the Fixing Out of Armed Vessels to Defend the Sea-Coast of America, and for Erecting a Court to Try and Condemn All Vessels that shall be Found infesting the Same" was adopted (Mass., *House Jour.*, 1775–1776, 2d sess., p. 125, 151–152, 217; Mass., *Province Laws*, 5:436–441).

[4] At the time of his arrest, Benjamin Church was not only director of hospitals for the Continental Army, but represented Boston in the House of Representatives and was a member of the Committee of Safety. On 3 Oct. a Council of War consisting of Washington and his generals ordered Church confined and then referred his case to the Continental Congress and the General Court. On 2 Nov. the House expelled him from that body. On 7 Nov. the congress resolved to have him jailed in Connecticut (Mass., *House Jour.*, 1775–1776, 2d sess., p. 171, 186, 198, 200–206, 226; JCC, 3:294, 297, 334). No final determination of his case was made until Jan. 1778, when he was allowed to take passage on the sloop *Welcome*, which apparently went down with all hands in a New England coastal storm (Sibley-Shipton, *Harvard Graduates*, 13:380–398).

To William Tudor

Dr Sir   Philadelphia Octr. 1. 1775

I have at last the Pleasure to mention to you what I Suppose Mr. H.[1] has informed you of, before, vizt that the Pay of the Judge Advocate is raised to fifty dollars per Month for himself and his Clerk, and this is to be allowed from the day he entered upon the service.

There was an Expression in your Representation to the General which alarmed me much, and put me to some Pain lest it should excite a Disgust.[2] It was this "The Congress as I have been informed were wholly unacquainted with the Duties of a Judge Advocate, especially in the continental Army." If this had been true, yet it was indecent to tell them of it, because they ought to be presumed to know

175

all the Duties of this officer, but most especially in their own Army. The Construction that I put upon it, was that the Congress had never been made Acquainted with the orders of the General to the Judge to attend every general Court Martial, which made the Duty in the American Army, essentially greater than in any other. By this Interpretation, satisfaction seemed to be given and by the favourable Representation of the General, together with the friendly Notice of General Gates and some Members who had been at the Camp, this Matter was at last well understood, and Justice was done.

I am, very Sorry to learn, that you have been sick, but rejoice to hear you are better. I have this Morning received from my dear Mrs. Adams, two letters which have put all my Philosophy to the Proof.[3] Never Since I had a Family was it in such Distress, altho it has often seen melancholly Scenes. I tremble for fear my Wifes Health should receive an irreparable Injury from the Anxieties, and Fatigues, which I know she will expose herself to, for the relief of her Family in their present Sick Condition. I fear too the Contagion of such an Hospital of an House. Whether to return I know not. We expect every Hour, momentous Intelligence from England, and from Schuyler and from Washington. And altho, my Presence here is not of any great Consequence, yet some of my Constituents may possibly think it of more than it is, and be uneasy, if I should be absent. At least, if I am here, and any thing goes differently from my Wishes, I shall have the Satisfaction to reflect that I have done all I could, however little it might be. Yet if I Stay here, I shall not be happy, till I know more from Braintree. Perhaps I may receive another Letter in a day or two. My Respects to your Father and Mother, and all Friends. Pray write me if you are well enough. I am, sir, your Friend,   John Adams

RC (MHi:Tudor Papers); addressed: "To William Tudor Esqr. Judge Advocate in the American Army Cambridge favd by Major Bayard"; docketed: "Octr. 1st. 1775."

[1] Benjamin Harrison.

[2] Tudor's memorial of 23 Aug. was enclosure No. 1 in Washington's letter to the President of the Continental Congress, and can be found in PCC, No. 152, I, f. 99–101. JA's quotation is not exact, but the meaning is unchanged.

[3] Those of 8–10 and [17] Sept. describing the family's illness and the deaths of several others (*Adams Family Correspondence*, 1:276–280).

To James Warren

Dear sir   Philadelphia Octr. 1. 1775

This Morning I received your kind Favours of the 11th. and 19th. Ultimo—with the Enclosures. Drapers Paper is a great Curiosity and you will oblige me by Sending it as often as posible.[1]

The Foreign News you mention, is all a Delusion my Friend. You may depend upon it, every Measure is preparing by the Ministry to destroy Us if they can, and that a Sottish Nation is Supporting them.

Heaven helps those who help themselves, and I am happy to find a Disposition so ⟨happily⟩ rapidly growing in America to exert itself.

The Letters, by your Packett from my Family, have given me Serious Concern indeed. I am much at a Loss what Course to take. I have thoughts of returning home. I fear, my dear Mrs. Adams's Health will sink under the Burthen of Care that is upon her. I might well enough be Spared from this Place, where my Presence is of no Consequence, and my Family might derive some Advantage from my being there, and I might have an opportunity of attending a Conference between a Committee of this Congress and the Council of Mass. Where perhaps I might be of more service than I can here. However I am not determined. My Friend, your secretary[2] is very much averse to my going. I dont know what to do.

The Committee who are going to the Camp, are Dr. Franklin Mr. Lynch and Coll. Harrison, who I hope will be received with Friendship and Politeness—by all our Friends.

I assure you, sir, there is a serious Spirit here—Such a Spirit as I have not known before.

The Committee by whom this Letter will go, are determined Americans. I fear that two of them, I mean Mr. L. and H. may have received Some unfavourable Impressions from Misrepresentations, concerning our Province, but these will be easily removed, by what they will see, and hear I hope. I wish that every Civility may be Shewn them, which their Fortunes, Characters and Stations demand.

Our news from England, is, Troops from England Scotland, Ireland, and Hanover[3]—Poor old Britania! I am, your Friend,

John Adams

RC (MHi:Warren-Adams Coll.); addressed: "Coll Warren"; docketed: "Mr: J: Adams. Lettr. Octr. 1. 1775."

[1] None of the enclosures except the letters from AA has been found. Draper's paper would be a copy of the *Massachusetts Gazette.*

[2] Samuel Adams.

[3] Great Britain had decided to send some 20,000 troops to America by the spring of 1776 and to do so it was trying to hire mercenaries (Merrill Jensen, *The Founding of a Nation,* N.Y., 1968, p. 646).

From James Warren

My Dear Sir   Watertown Oct. 1. 1775

An Event has lately taken place here, which makes much Noise, and gives me much Uneasiness not only as it Affects the Character, and may prove the ruin of a Man who I used to have a Tolerable Opinion of, but as it may be the Cause of many suspicions and Jealousies and what is still worse, have a Tendency to discredit the Recommendations of my Friends at the Congress. Dr. C————h has been detected in a Correspondence with the Enemy at least so far that a Letter wrote by him in Curious Cypher and directed to Majr. Cane[1] (who is an Officer in the Rebel Army and one of Gages Family) has been Intercepted. The History of the whole matter is this. The Doctor haveing formed an Infamous Connection, with an Infamous Hussey to the disgrace of his own reputation, and probable ruin of his Family, wrote this Letter last July, and sent it by her to Newport with Orders to give it to Wallace, or Dudley to deliver to Wallace for Conveyance to Boston.[2] She not finding an opportunity very readily, trusted it with a friend of hers to perform the orders, and came away and left it in his hands.[3] He kept it some Time and haveing some suspicions, of Wickedness, had some Qualms of Conscience about Executeing his Commissions, after some Time Consulted his Friend. The result was to Open the Letter which was done. The Appearance of the Letter Increasing their Suspicions, the next question after determining not to send it [to] Boston was what should be done with it. After various Conferences at divers times they Concluded to deliver it to Genl. Washington. Accordingly the Man Came with it last Thursday. After Collecting many Circumstances, the man was Employed to draw from the Girl, by Useing the Confidence She had in him, the whole Secret but without Success. She is a suttle, shrewd Jade. She was then Taken into Custody, and Brought to the Generals Quarters that Night. It was not till the next day that any thing could be got from her. She then Confessed that the Doctor wrote and sent her with the Letter as above. Upon this the General sent a Note desireing Majr. Hawley[4] and me to Come Immediately to Cambridge. We all thought the Suspicion quite sufficient to Justify an Arrest of him and his Papers, which was done, and he is now under a Guard. He owns the writeing and sending the Letter. Says it was for Flemming[5] in Answer to one he wrote to him,[6] and is Calculated, by Magnifying the Numbers of the Army, their regularity, their provisions and Ammunition &c, to do great Service to us. He declares his Conduct tho' Indiscreet was not wicked. There are however many Circumstances new and old which Time wont permit me to Mention, that are much Against him. The Letter I suppose is now decyphering, and when done will Either Condemn, or in some measure Excuse him. Thus much for this long Story.

A Strong S.W. Wind put into Marblehead last Week a New Providence Man, with a large Number of Turtle, &c &c.[7] They Boarded took, and Carryed him to Salem, and prevented the Scoundrels from Enjoying, and feasting on Callipee, Callipach,[8] and a desert of Pine Apples &c. A Few Fisher Men also, have taken a Brigantine from Quebec[9] with Cattle, Sheep, oatmeal &c A Present from the Tory Merchants &c, to the Sick and Wounded in Boston, and some Forrage for the Light Horse. She is Carried in to Cape Ann. There are two Letters from one Gamble, An officer one to Genl. Gage, the other to Sherriff,[10] which tell them that they are to Expect no aid to Government from there. That Carlton dare not Issue his orders to the Militia supposeing they would not be Obeyed. That the Canadians poisoned from N Engld. had got in use the Damned Absurd Word Liberty. I cant recollect the Time She Sailed, her Bills Ladeing dated Sepr. 5 but the Master says that Carlton has had no Success in Recruiting. He went of[f] the Night he came away for St. Johns[11] with about 75 Raggamuffins the whole Posse he could Collect. That there were at Quebec 10,000 barrels Powder. I long for them more than Turtle, or Pine Apples. Arnold was last Monday with his detachment 60 miles up Kennebeck, every thing as it should be. We please ourselves with fine Prospects of Success. I say Nothing about St. Johns &c, presuming you know as much or more about it than I do.

The Money Arrived safe here last Fryday, and I assure you gives a New face to our Affairs which by a greater delay must have run into Confusion. I Thank you for your short Letter. Would have Thanked you more if it had been longer. I have no Letter from Braintree to Inclose. I believe they are well.

Is it worthwhile to wonder that some People cant feel Improprieties.[12] However Ambition and Vanity I think must predominate, and mark strongly the Character of a Man who can Act such a part if he has any Sense at all. I am glad to find the Congress in such a Temper. I have drawn this Epistle I know not how to An Enormous Length. Intending only to write a few Lines, and Indeed pressed for Time, what it is I hardly know. What you don't like you must Excuse. I give it to you as it is, and with Complements to all Friends, and Assurances of Friendship to Mr. Adams. I am &c

I must write General Court News, and Plans on foot for fixing Armed Vessels, Animated by our late success—in my next, which will be soon after my return from Plymouth where I go in a day or two, having never been there since you left us. I shall also talk to you about your Constitution the Climate of Philadelphia and change of delegates in Massachusetts Bay &c.

Dr. Sir   Watertown Oct 2d. 1775 [13]

When I wrote the Inclosed I Expected it would have been called for early this morning. It was not, and by that means I have an opportunity of Inclosing 2 Letters received this day I suppose from your good Family at Braintree.[14] I am sorry to hear of the Continued Afflixtions of your good Lady. I am told that her mother is very Ill. I presume the Inclosed will give you the true state of the matter. I hope to hear of her Recovery however Bad she may now be. I have Just heard that the Letter is decyphered, and is much against the writer.[15] Shall give you a full state of this matter as soon as I have an opportunity after I am possessed of it. Adieu.

RC (Adams Papers); addressed: "To The Honbl: John Adams Esq. Member of Congress att Philadelphia"; docketed by JA: "Septr. 11 Warren Oct. 1. 1775."

[1] Lt. Col. Maurice Cane, 6th Regiment (Worthington C. Ford, *British Officers Serving in the American Revolution, 1774–1783*, N.Y., 1897, p. 44).

[2] James Wallace, commander of the British sloop *Rose* at Newport (DNB); Charles Dudley, last collector of customs at Newport (Sabine, *American Loyalists*, 1:394–395).

[3] Godfrey Wainwood or Wenwood, an inhabitant of Newport (Washington, *Writings*, ed. Fitzpatrick, 4:10, note 17).

[4] Although Joseph Hawley was merely a member of the House at this time, JA's recommendation of him to Washington apparently caused the general to turn to him from time to time (E. Francis Brown, *Joseph Hawley, Colonial Radical*, N.Y., 1931, p. 153).

[5] John Fleming, printer of the *Boston Chronicle* with John Mein until 1770, was Church's brother-in-law (DAB).

[6] Fleming's letter to Church is printed in Mass., *House Jour.*, 1775–1776, 2d sess., p. 204–205.

[7] The schooner *Industry*.

[8] Calipee and calipash, considered delicacies, are gelatinous substances found near a turtle's lower and upper shells (OED).

[9] The *Dolphin*.

[10] Capt. Thomas Gamble and Maj. William Sheriff of the 47th Regiment (Ford, *British Officers*, p. 76, 160). Gamble's letters were printed by authority in the *Boston Gazette*, 9 Oct.

[11] The fort on the Richelieu River on the line of march for Gen. Richard Montgomery.

[12] See JA to James Warren, 19 Sept., note 1 (above).

[13] This portion of the letter, which was written on a separate sheet, the verso carrying the address, was clearly intended to be a continuation despite its separate date and closing.

[14] AA to JA, 29 Sept. and 1 Oct. (*Adams Family Correspondence*, 1:287–289).

[15] Church's deciphered letter is printed in Mass., *House Jour.*, 1775–1776, 2d sess., p. 202–203.

To William Sever

Dr sir [1]   Philadelphia Octr. 2. 1775

I do myself the Honour of writing to you for the sake of introducing to you Three Gentlemen, whose Characters and Embassy will render any private Introductions unnecessary. Dr. Franklyn, Mr. Lynch and Coll. Harrison, are a Committee from this Congress to consult, the General and the Council of the Massachusetts, the Governers of Connecticutt and Rhode Island, and the President of the Congress of New Hampshire, upon Points of great Consequence, concerning the Army, which they will open to you.

We are in Hopes of News, every Day, from Genl. Schuyler and from Cambridge. The last Advices from England, are rather alarming. But We expected no better. If Powder can be imported or Petre made, We need not dread their Malice. I am sir, with great Respect and Esteem, your very hml sert, John Adams

RC (MHi:Adams Papers, Fourth Generation); addressed: "The Hon. William Sever Esqr Watertown Pr Favour of Mr. Lynch."

[1] Sever was president of the Council at this time.

To James Warren

Dr sir   Philadelphia Octr. 2. 1775

I believe you will have a surfeit of Letters from me, for they will be as inane, as they are numerous.

The Bearer of this is Major Bayard a Gentleman of this City of the Presbyterian Perswasion of the best Character and the clearest Affections for his Country.[1] I have received so many Civilities from him, that I could not refuse myself the Pleasure of introducing him to you.

Our obligations of Secrecy, are so braced up, that I must deny myself the Pleasure of Writing Particulars. Not because some Letters have been intercepted, for notwithstanding the Versification of them, they have done good, tho they have made some People grin.

This I can Say with Confidence, that the Propriety and Necessity of the Plan of Politicks so hastily delineated in them is every day, more and more confessed, even by those Gentlemen who disapproved it at the Time when they were written.

Be assured, I never Saw, So Serious and determined a Spirit as I see now every day.

The high Spirited Measures you call for, will assuredly come. Languid and disastrous Campaigns are agreable to Nobody.

Young Mr. Lux desires his Compliments to you and your Lady. He is vastly pleased with his Treatment both from you and her.

Remember me to her. I have Shocking Letters from her Friend at Braintree, such as have put my Phylosophy to the Tryal. I wait only for another Letter to determine, whether I shall come home.

RC (MHi:Warren-Adams Coll.); addressed: "To the Hon. James Warren Esqr Speaker of the House Watertown favoured by Major Bayard"; docketed: "Mr. J: A: Lettr Octr. 2. 1775."

[1] John Bayard (1738–1807), who carried back to Massachusetts several of the letters written by JA during this period, was a Philadelphia merchant at this time, an ardent whig, and a major in the second battalion of the Philadelphia Associators (*DAB*).

To John Winthrop

Dr sir   Philadelphia Octr. 2. 1775

I do myself the Honour of writing you, a very few Lines, just for the Sake of introducing to you, the Gentlemen who compose a Committee of this Congress, who are to consult with your Honorable Board,[1] about a Plan for continuing the Army.

I conjecture that the Reduction of the Pay of the private Soldiers, and the Introduction of Some Gentlemen from other Colonies, into the Service as officers will be principal objects.

The Pay of the Privates is generally, if not universally thought to be too high, especially in Winter:[2] but whether a Reduction of it would not give Such a Disgust as to endanger the Service, I dont know. If The War Should continue, and their Pay is not reduced this Fall this Congress, will certainly reduce it next Spring, and in a Way that will perhaps be dangerous, at least attended with many Inconveniences. This Way will be by each Colony furnishing its Quota of Men as well as Money.

The other Thing that is wished by many, is not so reasonable. It is altogether Absurd to Suppose, that the Council of Massachusetts, should appoint Gentlemen from the southern Colonies, when Connecticutt, Rhode Island and N. Hampshire do not. But it is idle to expect it of either.

The Council, if they are Men of Honour cannot appoint Gentlemen whom they dont know, to command Regiments or Companies in their service. Nor can they pay a Regard to any Recommendation of Strangers, to the Exclusion of Persons whom they know. Besides it is certain that the Massachusetts has Numbers of Gentlemen, who have no Command in the Army at all, and who would now be glad to get in, who are better qualified, with Knowledge both of Theory and Practice than any who can be had upon the Continent. They have been more in War, and longer in the study of it. Besides can it be Supposed that the private Men will be easy to be commanded by Strangers to the Exclusion of Gentlemen, whom they know being their Neighbours. It is moreover a Reflection, and would be a Disgrace upon that Province to send abroad for Commanders of their own Men. It would Suppose that it had not Men fit for officers than which nothing can be further from the Truth.[3]

But I must desist: We have heard nothing from the Committee appointed to write to Us, as yet, nor from that about Lead and salt.[4]

I pray you sir that We may have, the Accounts and Vouchers sent Us, that our poor suffering Province, may obtain a Reimbursement. I am, with great Respect &c.

RC (MHi:JA-John Winthrop Corr.); addressed: "The Hon. John Winthrop Esqr. L.L.D. Cambridge favoured by Mr. Lynch"; docketed: "Mr. Adams 2 Oct. 1775."

[1] Winthrop was a member of the Council at this time.

[2] On pay scales, see JA to Elbridge Gerry, 18 June, note 4 (above).

[3] JA is putting himself in opposition to Washington's position that the army be truly continental and that competent officers be assigned regardless of their home colonies. Washington particularly wanted to find places for qualified officers from outside New England (French, *First Year*, p. 506).

[4] The committee named to correspond with the delegates in the congress was composed of William Sever, Jedediah Foster, and Joseph Palmer from the Council, joined by Richard Devens, George Partridge, Isaac Lothrop, and Elbridge Gerry from the House. The committee on lead and salt included Benjamin Greenleaf, Eldad Taylor, and Joseph Palmer of the Council, and Col. Nathaniel Freeman, Capt. Jonathan Greenleaf, Dr. William Whiting, and William Story of the House (Records of the States, Microfilm, Mass. A.1a, Reel No. 12, Unit 1, p. 153–154, 121–122).

To William Heath

Sir   Philadelphia Octr. 5th. 1775[1]

I never had the Pleasure of a Correspondence or any particular Acquaintance with you, which can justify the Freedom I have taken of giving you this Trouble: But as the good of our Country, which I know is your first Consideration, is my Motive, I presume you will think it a Sufficient Apology.

In the present State of America, which is so novel and unexpected, and indeed unthought of by Numbers of Persons in every Colony, it is natural to expect Misapprehensions, Jealousies and Misrepresentations in Abundance: and it must be our Care to attend to them, and if possible explain what is misunderstood and State truly what is misrepresented.

It is represented in this City by Some Persons, and it makes an unfriendly Impression upon Some Minds, that in the Massachusetts Regiments, there are great Numbers of Boys, Old Men, and Negroes, Such as are unsuitable for the service, and therefore that the Continent is paying for a much greater Number of Men, than are fit for Action or any Service. I have endeavoured to the Utmost of my Power to rectify these Mistakes as I take them to be, and I hope with some success, but still the Impression is not quite removed.

I would beg the favour of you therefore sir, to inform me Whether there is any Truth at all in this Report, or not.

It is natural to suppose there are some young Men and some old ones and some Negroes in the service, but I should be glad to know if there are more of these in Proportion in the Massachusetts Regiments, than in those of Connecticutt, Rhode Island and New Hampshire, or even among the Rifle Men.

You may depend, sir upon my Using the most prudent Caution, in the Use of your Letter, and especially of your Name but I could certainly make a good Use, of a Letter from you upon the Subject. Great Fault is likewise found in Several Parts of the Continent of the Massachusetts Officers, whom I believe, taken on an Average, and in Proportion to Numbers to be equal at least if not Superiour to any other Colony.

I must confess I had another View in giving you this Trouble which was to introduce to your Attention, Dr. Franklin, Mr. Lynch and Coll Harrison, a Committee from this Congress to consult with the General and with the New England Colonies, concerning a Plan for future Armies. Mr. Lynch is from S. Carolina, Coll Harrison from Virginia, both Gentlemen of great Fortune, and respectable Characters, Men of Abilities and very Staunch Americans. Dr. Franklyn needs no words of mine. I am, sir, with great Respect, your very huml servant,

John Adams

RC (MHi:William Heath Papers); addressed: "To William Heath Esqr Brigadier General in the American Army   Cambridge   Per favour of Mr. Lynch"; docketed: "from Jno Adams Esqr   Octr. 5th. 1775."

[1] On this same date, JA wrote a similar letter to Gen. John Thomas, introducing the committee members and asking about boys, old men, and Negroes among Massachusetts regiments. In addition, he asked particularly about the qualifications of Henry Knox and Josiah Waters as engineers (RC offered for sale, *The Collector*, March 1948, p. 57).

From Charles Lee

My Dr Sir   Camp Oct'r the 5th 1775

As you may possibly harbour some suspicions that a certain passage in your intercepted letters have made some disagreeable impressions on my mind I think it necessary to assure You that it is quite the reverse. Untill the bulk of Mankind is much alter'd I consider ⟨*your*⟩ the reputation of being whimsical and eccentric rather as a panegyric than sarcasm and my love of Dogs passes with me as a still higher complement. I have thank heavens a heart susceptible of freindship and affection. I must have some object to embrace. Consequently when once I can be convincd that Men are as worthy objects as Dogs I shall transfer my benevolence, and become as staunch a Philanthropist as the canting Addison affected to be. But you must not conclude from hence that I give into general misanthropy. On the contrary when I meet with a Biped endow'd with generosity valour good sense patriotism and zeal for the rights of humanity I contract a freindship and passion for him amounting to bigotry or dotage and let me assure you without complements that you yourself appear to me possess'd of these qualities. I give you my word and honour that I am serious, and should be unhappy to the greatest degree if I thought you would doubt of my sincerity. Your opinion therefore of my attainments as a Soldier and Scholar is extremely flattering. Long may you continue in this (to me) gratissimus error. But something too much of this.

Before this reaches you the astonishing and terrifying accusation or rather detection of Doctor Church will be reported to the Congress. I call it astonishing, for admitting his intentions not to be criminal so gross a piece of stupidity in so sensible a Man is quite a portent. And supposing him guilty, it is terrifying to the last degree—as such a revolt must naturally infect with jealousy all political affiance. It will spread an universal diffidence and suspicion than which nothing can be more pernicious to Men embark'd in a cause like ours, the corner stone of Which is laid not only on honour virtue and disinterestedness—but on the perswasion that the whole be actuated by the same divine principles. I devoutly wish that such may not be the effects.

We long here to receive some news from the Congress. Now is the time to shew your firmness. If the least timidity is display'd, We and all Posterity are ruin'd; on the contrary at this crisis courage and steadiness must insure the blessings of liberty not only to G Britain but perhaps to all Mankind. Do not go hobling on, like the Prince of Liliput, with one high heel'd shoe one low one, for you will undoubtedly fall upon your noses evry step you take. It is my humble opinion that you ought to begin by confiscating (or at least laying under heavy contributions) the estates of all the notorious enemies to American Liberty through the Continent. This wou'd lighten the burthen which must otherwise fall heavy on the shoulders of the Community—that afterwards you should invite all the maritime powers of the world into your Ports. If they are so dull as not to accept the invitation—weed yourselves from all ideas of foreign commerce—and become intirely a Nation of Plowmen and Soldiers. A little habit, and I am perswaded you will bless yourselves for the resolution but I am running into an essay, shall therefore to prevent pedantry and impertenence stop short with once more assuring you that I am most huly and affectionately yours,   C Lee

My respects to your namesake and let me hear from you.

Spada[1] sends his love to you and declares in very intellegible language that He has far'd much better since your allusion to him for He is carress'd now by all ranks sexes and Ages.

RC (Adams Papers); docketed: "Gen. Lee.   Octr. 5. 1775."

[1] The name of one of Lee's dogs.

To Josiah Quincy

Dear Sir   Octr. 6. 1775

Two days ago I had the Pleasure of yours of Septr. 22. I am very Sorry to learn from your Letter that you have occasion for any Advice of mine, and have not had an opportunity of taking it. I fully intended to have made you a visit, but my stay was so short and I had So many Engagements that it was out of my Power.

That a great Revolution, in the Affairs of the World, is in the Womb of Providence, Seems to be intimated very Strongly, by many Circumstances: But it is no Pleasure to me to be employed in giving Birth to it. The Fatigue, and Anxiety, which attends it are too great. Happy the Man, who with a plentifull Fortune an elegant Mind and an amiable Family, retires from the Noises, Dangers and Confusions of it. However, by a Train of Circumstances, which I could neither foresee nor prevent, I have been called by Providence to take a larger share in active Life, during the Course of these Struggles, than is agreable either to my Health, my Fortune or my Inclination, and I go through it with more Alacrity and Chearfullness than I could have expected. I often envy the silent Retreat of some of my Friends. But if We should so far succeed as to secure to Posterity the Blessings of a free Constitution, that alone will forever be considered by me as an ample Compensation for all the Care, Fatigue, and Loss that I may sustain in the Conflict.

I am much obliged by your kind Explanation of your opinion that the Harbour might be locked up. I must confess, altho I was born so near it, I never before understood the Course of the Channell, and the Situation of the Harbour so well. I have carefully compared your Description of Squantum, the Moon, Long Island, Gallops Island, Lovells Island, and Georges, the Narrows and Nantaskett Road, with "A Plan of the Town and Chart of the Harbour of Boston, exhibiting a View of the Islands, Castle, Forts, and Entrances into the said Harbour, which was published in London, last February."[1] This Plan I knew to be inacurate in some Particulars, and the Chart may be so in others: but by the best Judgment I can make, upon comparing your Facts with the Chart, and considering the Depths of Water marked on this Chart, I think it extreamly probable, with you that nothing but Powder and Cannon are wanting, to effect the important Purposes you mention, that of making soldiers and sailors Prisoners at Discretion.

Dr. Franklyns Row Gallies are in great Forwardness. Seven of them are compleated, manned, armed &c. I went down the River the other Day with all of them.[2] I have as much Confidence in them as you have. But the People here have made what some call Chevaux De Frize and others Vesseaux de Frize, Machines to be sunk in the Channell of Delaware River. Three Rowes of them, are phased in the River, with large Timbers barbed with Iron. They are frames of Timber sunk with stone. Machines very proper, for our Channell in the Narrows.

The News you wrote me from my Family, gave me more Pleasure than you could have imagined when you wrote it. My last Accounts from home, before I received your Letter were so melancholly, that I was very unhappy, and was on the Point of returning Home. But your Letter and the Arrival of Mr. Williams,[3] have removed my Fears and determined me to continue here in my Post.

We have favourable Accounts from Schuyler. He will have the Province of Canada.

Our Accounts from England breath nothing but War and Revenge. What Pains and Expence, and Misery that stupid People will endure, for the sake of driving the Colonies to the Necessity of a Seperation, and of alienating their best Friends.[4]

My Compliments to your good Lady and Family, Mr. Wibird and all Friends.

I must entreat your Excuse for the Haste and inaccuracy with which I am obliged to write. Every Letter you can find Leisure and Inclination to write will oblige your Friend & huml sert,

RC (MHi:Hoar Autograph Coll.); the last page of the MS is a Dft of Quincy's reply to JA of 25 Oct. (below).

[1] See Josiah Quincy to JA, 22 Sept., note 3 (above).

[2] JA, together with other members of the congress and the Pennsylvania Assembly, made this trip on 28 Sept. For JA's description of it, see *Diary and Autobiography*, 2:187–188.

[3] Mr. Williams, otherwise unidentified, brought to JA the letter which AA had written to him on 25 Sept. (*Adams Family Correspondence*, 1:295).

[4] The tone of this letter here and above clearly indicates that separation was not something that JA welcomed but something that he felt the colonies were being forced into.

To James Warren

Dr sir   Philadelphia Octr. 7th. 1775

The Debates, and Deliberations in Congress are impenetrable Secrets: but the Conversations in the City, and the Chatt of the Coffee house, are free, and open. Indeed I wish We were at Liberty to write freely and Speak openly upon every Subject, for their is frequently as much Knowledge derived from Conversation and Correspondence, as from Solemn public Debates.

A more intricate and complicated Subject never came into any Mans thoughts, than the Trade of America.[1] The Questions that arise, when one thinks of it, are very numerous.

If The Thirteen united Colonies, Should immediately Surcease all Trade with every Part of the World, what would be the Consequence? In what manner, and to what degree, and how soon, would it affect, the other Parts of the World? How would it affect G. B. Ireland, the English West India Islands, the French, the Dutch the Danish, the Spanish West India Islands? How would it affect the Spanish Empire on the Continent? How would it affect the Brazills and the Portuguese Settlements in America? If it is certain that it would distress Multitudes in these Countries, does it therefore follow that it would induce any foreign Court to offer Us Assistance, and to ask us for our Trade or any Part of it? If it is questionable Whether foreign States would venture upon Such Steps, which, would perhaps be Violations of Treaties of Peace, and certainly would light up a War in Europe is it certain that Smugglers, by whom I mean private Adventurers belonging to foreign Nations, would come here, through all the Hazards they must run. Could they be suffered to clear out for America in their own Custom houses? Would they not run the risque of Seizure from their own Custom house officers, or of Capture from their own Men of War? Would they not be liable to be visited by British Men of War, in any Part of the ocean, and if found to have no Clearances be seized? When they arrived on any Part of the Coast of N. America, would they not be seized by Brittish Cutters, Cruizers, Tenders, Frigates without Number: But if their good Fortune should escape all these Risques, have We harbours or Rivers, sufficiently fortified, to insure them Security while here? In their Return to their own Country would they not have the Same Gauntlett to run.

In Short, if We Stop our own ships, have We even a Probability that the ships of foreign Nations, will run the Venture to come here, either with or without the Countenance and Encouragement of their severall Courts or States public or private open or secret? It is not easy for any Man precisely and certainly to answer this Question. We must then say all this is uncertain.

Suppose then We assume an intrepid Countenance, and send Ambassadors at once to foreign Courts. What Nation shall We court? Shall We go to the Court of France, or the Court of Spain, to the States General of the United Provinces? To the Court of Lisbon, to the Court of Prussia, or Russia, or Turkey or Denmark, or Where, to any, one, more, or all of these? If We should is there a Probability, that Our Ambassadors would be received, or so much as heard or seen by any Man or Woman in Power at any of those Courts. He might possibly, if well skilled in intrigue, his Pocketts well filled with Money and his Person Robust and elegant enough, get introduced to some of the Misses, and Courtezans in Keeping of the statesmen in France, but would not that be all.

An offer of the Sovereignty of this Country to France or Spain would be listened to no doubt by Either of those Courts, but We should suffer any Thing before We should offer this. What then can We offer? An Alliance, a Treaty of Commerce? What Security could they have that We should keep it. Would they not reason thus, these People intend to make Use of Us to establish an Independency but the Moment they have done it: Britain will make Peace with them, and leave Us in the Lurch And We have more to dread from an Alliance between Britain and the United Colonies as an independent state, than We have now they are under one corrupted Administration. Would not Spain reason in the same manner, and say further our Dominions in South America will be soon a Prey to these Enterprizing and warlike Americans, the Moment they are an independent State. Would not our proposals and Agents be treated with Contempt! And if our Proposals were made and rejected, would not this sink the Spirits of our own People, Elevate our Enemies and disgrace Us in Europe.

If then, it will not be Safe to Stop our own Ships entirely, and trust to foreign Vessells coming here either with or without Convoy of

Men of War, belonging to foreign States, what is to be done? Can our own People bear a total Cessation of Commerce? Will not Such Numbers be thrown out of Employment, and deprived of their Bread, as to make a large discontented Party? Will not the Burthen of supporting these Numbers, be too heavy upon the other Part of the Community? Shall We be able to maintain the War, wholly without Trade? Can We support the Credit of our Currency, without it?

If We must have Trade how shall We obtain it? There is one Plan, which alone, as it has ever appeared to me, will answer the End in some Degree, at first. But this is attended with So many Dangers to all Vessells, certain Loss to many, and So much Uncertainty upon the whole, that it is enough to make any Man, thoughtfull. Indeed it is looked upon So wild, extravagant and romantic, that a Man must have a great deal of Courage, and much Indifference to common Censure, who should dare to propose it.

"God helps those who help themselves," and it has ever appeared to me since this unhappy Dispute began, that We had no Friend upon Earth to depend on but the Resources of our own Country, and the good sense and great Virtues of our People. We shall finally be obliged to depend upon ourselves.

Our Country furnishes a vast abundance of materials for Commerce. Foreign Nations, have great Demands for them. If We should publish an Invitation to any one Nation or more, or to all Nations, to send their ships here, and let our Merchants inform theirs that We have Harbours where the Vessells can lie in Safety, I conjecture that many private foreign Adventurers would find Ways to send Cargoes here thro all the Risques without Convoys. At the Same Time our own Merchants, would venture out with their Vessells and Cargoes, especially in Winter,[2] and would run thro many Dangers, and in both these Ways together, I should hope We might be supplied with Necessaries.

All this however Supposes that We fortify and defend our own Harbours and Rivers. We may begin to do this. We may build Row Gallies, flatt bottomed Boats, floating Batteries, Whale Boats, Vesseaux de Frize, nay Ships of War, how many, and how large I cant say. To talk of coping Suddenly with G. B. at sea would be Quixotish indeed. But the only Question with me is can We defend our Harbours and Rivers? If We can We can trade.

RC (MHi: Warren-Adams Coll.); docketed: "Mr. J: A   Octr. 7 1775."

[1] This letter, together with those to James Warren on 19, 20, and 28 Oct. (below), provides a valuable supplement to JA's Diary accounts of the con-

gressional debates that began on 4 Oct. and continued through December over the trade of America, that is, whether to depart further from the nonimportation stipulations of the Continental Association (JA, *Diary and Autobiography*, 2:188–194, 196–197, 204–217, 219–220). Although JA implies that the questions he raises come merely from his own thoughts or from the common talk in the coffeehouses, he was apparently summarizing, at least in part, for Warren the arguments brought out in debate by his colleagues. JA's own

solution, stated at the end of the letter, may have been the one he advanced in the debates, although nothing in his Diary indicates that he did so. His solution is not very different from that which he advocated in the first session of the Second Continental Congress. His letter to James Warren of 23 July (above) noted that the congress had had before it a proposal to open its ports to the trade of all nations but that it had "like fools . . . lost it for the present."

[2] That is, when British cruisers could not be so active.

To James Warren

Dear Sir   October the 8. 1775

You will not think your Time misspent in Perusing any Plans for the Service of your Country, even altho they may prove, upon Examination chimerical. There are two Channells only, through which Vessells of large Burthen, can pass, to and from Boston: one, is between the West Head of Long Island and the Moon: It is a mile wide, but incumbered with Rocks and too shallow for a Man of War of more than twenty Guns. The other is between Long Island and Deer Island, a mile and an half from Point to Point, the only Channell, thro which capital Ships can pass, leads through the Narrows, between Gallops Island and Lovells Island where it is not wider, than the length of a fifty Gun Ship. In the Interval between Gallops and George's, is Nantaskett Road where, five Men of War are now Stationed; for what other End, do you Suppose, than to guard the Narrows from being obstructed?

The Moon communicates with Squantum, at low Water, even without a Canoe. A Fort, therefore, upon Squantum, may be so placed as to Secure a Retreat from the Moon to Squantum and from that to the Main: one upon the East Head of the Moon, and another on the West Head of Long Island, Secures the Communication, and covers a Retreat from the latter to the former: Another, on the Summit of Long Island, covers the shore on each Side. A strong Battery at the East Head of Long Island, commands the Ship Channell, the Narrows, and Nantaskett Road. Consequently by Sinking Hulks, or Vesseaux de Frize, in the Narrows, We might prevent any Vessell of great Force from going out, or coming in.

In the Month of February last, "a Plan of the Town and Chart of the Harbour of Boston," [1] was published in London. I think in a

Magazine: I wish you would examine this Project by that Plan, and give me your opinion.

I dont trouble Washington with any of these Schemes, because I dont wish to trouble him with any Thing to no Purpose. But if I could command a Thousand Tons of Powder, and an hundred Pieces of heavy Cannon I would scribble to him till he would be weary of me. Mean Time It may not be amiss for me to amuse myself with some of my Friends, in Speculations of this kind; because Some good, may some time or other Result from them.

Can no Use be made of Rowe Gallies, with you? Eight or Ten are compleated here. Can they be used in the Vineyard Sound? Would not their heavy Metal demolish a Cruizer now and then? There is a shipwright escaped from Boston, who [has] been several Years a Prisoner in a Turkish Galley, and has a Model of one. Coll. Quincy knows him. Or I could procure you Directions from this Place, how to construct them.

We have just received by an express from Schuyler, very promising Intelligence concerning the Operations of the Northern Army. Ethan Allen are in the Heart of the Country joined by 200 Canadians. Montgomery was beginning to bombard St. Johns.[2]

If We should be successfull in that Province, a momentous, political Question arises—What is to be done with it? A Government, will be as necessary for the Inhabitants of Canada, as for those of the Massachusetts Bay? And what Form of Government, shall it be? Shall the Canadians, choose an House of Representatives, a Council and a Governor? It will not do to govern them by Martial Law, and make our General Governor. This will be disrelished by them as much as their new Parliamentary Constitution[3] or their old French Government.

Is there Knowledge and Understanding enough among them, to elect an Assembly, which will be capable of ruling them and then to be governed by it—Who shall constitute their Judges and civil Officers?

This appears to me as curious a Problem as any We shall have to solve. ⟨*There are some Gentlemen, whose rule it is to let others think, to play themselves, then claim the Honour and Merit of their Thought and [...] for them. Oh that I had been born one of this happy breed— with Meanness of Soul enough to applaud myself as they do, when all is done, for their Cunning.*⟩[4]

When I was at Watertown, a Committee of both Houses was appointed to Correspond with us. We have not received any Letter from it.

Another was appointed to enquire after Virgin Lead and leaden ore and the Methods of making Salt and acquaint us with their Discoveries. We have not heard from this Committee.

Please send the enclosed News Paper to my Wife, when you have read it.[5]

RC (MHi:Warren-Adams Coll.); docketed: "Mr. J: A Lettr Octr. 8. 1775."

[1] Closing quotation marks supplied. Obviously JA is making use of Josiah Quincy's plans without mentioning their author, for his first two paragraphs closely paraphrase Quincy's description (to JA, 22 Sept., above).

[2] The express carried letters from Gen. Philip Schuyler of 19 and 28 (bis) Sept., with enclosures including letters from Gen. Richard Montgomery, Ethan Allen, and James Livingston (PCC, No. 153, I, f. 140–175). These were read to the congress on 9 Oct., when JA was named to a committee to answer them. Montgomery's siege of St. John's began 17 Sept. and lasted till 3 Nov. (French, *First Year*, p. 421, 429).

[3] That is, the Quebec Act, which left the peasants as oppressed as they had been under the French government.

[4] These six lines of the MS are heavily crossed out. Most of the reading given here is conjectural. Within the brackets are two or three words that could not be read at all.

[5] Not found.

To James Warren

Dr Sir   Philadelphia Octr. 10th. 1775

Mr. Jonathan Mifflin, a young Gentleman of this City, a Relation of our Friend the Quarter Master General will hand you this Letter.

I believe you will have enough of my Correspondence this Time, for it has certainly been filled with mere Impertenence and contains nothing of War or Politicks which are so Agreable to your Taste.

Our Expectations are very Sanguine, of Intelligence from Schuyler that Canada is ours. Our Advises from England breath nothing but Malice, Revenge and Cruelty.[1]

Powder, and Salt Petre are Still the Cry from one End of the Continent to the other. We must, and, God willing, We will have them.

I long to hear concerning our Friends in Boston. My Friends cannot be too particular. I want to know the Condition of every Individual. I want to know also every Event however minute which Turns up in our Camp or Lines. We have most formidable Discriptions of Gages Fortifications in Boston. Ninety Pieces of Brass Field Pieces from four to Eight Pounders have certainly been cast in the Tower for America, and Carriages, Wheelbarrows, Flatbottomed Boats &c. I am &c.

RC (MHi:Warren-Adams Coll.); docketed: "Mr. J: A Lettr Octr. 10. 1775."

[1] Probably a reference to Britain's decision to raise a large army to send to America, including mercenaries. See JA to James Warren, 1 Oct., note 3 (above).

To William Tudor

Dr sir   Octr. 12. 1775

I have received yours of the first of this Instant[1] and am glad to find you have me still in Remembrance. I wrote you some time ago, and ventured to acquaint you with the appointment of fifty dollars a Month to the Judge Advocate for himself and his Clerk, to commence from his first appointment. This I hope you received. I feel more anxious about Letters than formerly as you may well imagine. The Times are so critical and there are so many Peepers, that one cant be too carefull. Indeed the horrid Story you allude to in yours of the surgeon[2] &c. is enough to make one jealous[3] of every Body, but it must not have this Effect. In the Reign of Charles the first, such Instances of Treachery and Infidelity, were not uncommon. I would fain hope however that this has turned out more favourably than was feared: yet from several private Letters received here by Gentlemen, I am Staggered. What shall We say? I think it very odd, however, that every Event which happens at the Camp should regularly come to Governors Ward or Hopkins, or to Coll. Dyer or Mr. Deane, before it comes to me. It is really astonishing. However hush Complaint.

The last Accounts from my Family were very disagreable. And yours mentions not a Word of it. I hope for the best but should be rejoiced to hear.

Three Battalions I believe will be raised in Pensilvania and the Jersies for the Defence of New York.[4] News We have none, but such as you see in the Papers.

As you are now in the military Line of Life, I presume it will not be disagreable to have your Thoughts turned to military Speculations. I want to know what Books upon Martial Science are to be found in the Army, and whether, among the many young Gentlemen in the service, any of them are studious of the Principles of the Art. It is a shame for Youths of Genius and Education to be in the Army, without exerting themselves to become Masters of the Profession. If it is objected that Books are not to be had, Measures ought to be taken to procure them. To this End I wish to collect [a] perfect List of the best Authors, and should be obliged to you if you would enquire and make up one for me. And at the same time enquire whether the following are in the possession of any Body in the Army. Dalrymples military Essay. Saxes Reveries. History of Prussia. History of Frederic 3d. Le Blonds military Engineer. History of the late War. Mullers Works Eight Volumes. Maneuvres for a Battalion of Infantry—by Major

Young. Military Guide, by Simes. Andersons Art of War. Prussian Field Regulations. King of Prussias Advice to young officers. Playdells Field Fortification. Simes's Medley. Bellidoze, Worth all the rest.[5]

RC (MHi:Tudor Papers); addressed: "To William Tudor Esqr   Judge Advocate in the American Army   Cambridge   favd. by Mr. Tracy"; docketed: "Octr. 12th 1775."

[1] No letter from Tudor of 1 Oct. has been found; JA is probably referring to that of 30 Sept. (above).

[2] Benjamin Church.

[3] That is, suspicious (*OED*).

[4] The congress reached this decision on 12 Oct. (*JCC*, 3:291).

[5] The evaluation of the following military titles has been furnished to the editors by Alan C. Aimone, Military History Librarian of the Library of the United States Military Academy, and Robert K. Wright Jr., historian in the Organizational History Branch of the Department of the Army. The former's overall assessment, given in a letter of 10 Sept. 1976, is the following: "Most of the books . . . would be among the best military science works of his age. None indicates new departures such as light infantry tactics or even basic cavalry sources. Such military writers of the time as . . . Lewis Lochée, James Wolfe and Timothy Pickering are missing . . . that would reflect a balanced military library of the John Adams era."

Campbell Dalrymple, *A Military Essay*, London, 1761. Considered current literature, this dealt with the problems of recruiting, clothing, arming, and disciplining infantry and cavalry, furnishing information basic for establishing an army. An abridgement, *Extracts from a Military Essay*, Phila., 1776, is listed in the *Catalogue of JA's Library*.

Maurice, Marechal de Saxe, *Reveries*, Edinburgh, 1759. Considered basic, this work regularly appears in military inventories of the time. Listed in the *Catalogue of JA's Library*.

W. H. Dilworth, *The Life and Heroic Actions of Frederick III* [II], *King of Prussia . . . containing All the Military Transactions of Germany from the year 1740, and including All the Operations of the Campaign of 1757*, London, 1758.

Guillaume Le Blond, *A Treatise of Artillery*, London, 1746. Translated from the French, this work was considered important along with those of Muller's listed below.

Gen. Henry Lloyd, *The History of the Late War in Germany; between the King of Prussia and the Empress of Germany and Her Allies*, London, 1763.

None of the standard catalogues lists Muller's works in eight volumes, but these titles are found in American libraries: La Mamye Clairac, *The Field Engineer*, transl. Muller, London, 1773. *The Attack and Defence of Fortified Places in Three Parts; the Third Edition . . . enlarged, . . . also Belidor's New Method of Mining; and Valliere on Countermining*, London, 1770. *A Treatise Containing the Elementary Part of Fortification*, London, 1746, 1756, 1774. *A Treatise Containing the Practical Part of Fortification*, London, 1755, 1774. *A Treatise of Artillery*, London, 1757, 1768. Muller was the leading English writer on military science.

William Young, *Manoeuvres, or Practical Observations on the Art of War*, London, 1770, 1771.

Thomas Simes, *The Military Guide for Young Officers*, London, 1772. A popular work, this contained a section on military terms arranged alphabetically. Volume 2 of the 1776 edition is listed in the *Catalogue of JA's Library*.

The next three works in JA's listing are of uncertain identity. No standard catalogue lists an art of war by Anderson. Robert K. Wright Jr. suggests two possibilities: Marechal de Puysegur, *L'art de la guerre*, Paris, 1747, or Granmaison, *La petite guerre*, Paris, 1756. The British Museum *Catalogue* lists *New Art of War*, London, 1726, which was also published under the title *The Art of War*, neither with author given. Evans lists —— deLamont and others,

The *Act of War*, Phila., 1776 (No. 14816). Conceivably JA knew of its forthcoming publication.

According to Wright, "Prussian Field Regulations" might be one of several works: *Regulations for the Prussian Infantry*, transl. William Fawcett, London, 1757; Thomas Hanson, *The Prussian Evolutions in Actual Engagements*, 2 vols., Phila., 1775; *The Prussian (Short) Exercise*, N.Y., 1757, this last probably a reprint of the Fawcett translation.

The "King of Prussia's Advice to Young Officers," again in Wright's view, seems a garbled title derived from two works perhaps: Frederick the Great, *Instructions for His Generals*, transl., London, 1762; Gen. James Wolfe, *Instructions to Young Officers*, London, 1768.

J. L. Pleydell, *An Essay on Field Fortification*, London, 1768.

Thomas Simes, *The Military Medley*, London, 1768.

Bernard Forest de Belidor, "the 18th-century Vauban of fortifications," wrote a number of widely circulated books, almost none apparently translated: *La science des ingénieurs dans la conduite des travaux de fortification et d'architecture civile*, Paris, 1729, 1739, 1754, 1775. *Le bombardier françois ou nouvelle méthode de jetter les bombes avec précision*, Paris, 1731. *Traité des fortifications*, Paris, 1735. *Nouveau cours de mathématiques, à l'usage de l'artillerie et du génie*, Paris, 1725, 1757. *Oeuvres diverses ... concernant l'artillerie et le génie*, Amsterdam, 1764.

It should be added that although JA lists authors and in some instances brief titles, he apparently knew little at this time about his selections, for later he asks Tudor who Belidor is and in what language he wrote (JA to Tudor, 14 Nov., below).

To James Warren

Dr Sir   Octr. 12. 1775

I would write often if I had any thing to communicate: But Obligations of Honour forbid some Communications and other Considerations prevent others.

The common Chatt of a Coffee house, is too frivolous for me to recollect or you to read. I have inclosed a Paper upon which I will make no Remark: But leave you to your own Conjectures.[1] Only I must absolutely insist that it be mentioned to nobody. It may gratify your Curiosity and give Some Relief to your Cares.

I most earnestly pray that all my Friends, would exert themselves to furnish me with Intelligence of a particular Nature. I mean with a List of all the Depredations committed upon our Trade. A List of all the Vessells which have been taken by the Cutters, Cruizers &c. The Names of the Vessells, Masters owners, Burthen of the ship the Nature of the Cargo's and the Value of both. Nothing will contribute So much to facilitate Reprizals, as an exact Account of our Losses and Damages. I wish our General Court would take it up—and examine it thoroughly.[2]

We have no Accounts nor Vouchers yet. Nor one Line from the Committee appointed to correspond with Us.

I am very happy—how it is I know not—but I am very happy.

ENCLOSURE

As the Article of Powder is much wanted to carry on the operations vs the ministerial Army, and as the british Ministry, have taken every Step that human Nature could divise to prevent the Americans obtaining So essential an Article; it is humbly Submitted to the Wisdom, of the cont. Congress, whether it will not be prudent to Supply yourselves with that Article at the Expence of the said Ministry, by taking it whenever you can get it. It is thus further recommended that 2 Vessells properly mann'd be sent to the Island of Antigua, one of which may anchor at Old Road on the South Side of the Said Island (where there are only a few Houses) in the Evening under Dutch Colours; passing for a Vessell bound on a forced Trade, to the French Islands; in the night you may land, and take away all the powder; there being not above one or two Persons, in the fort to prevent it. As Soon as the Powder is obtained the Vessell may proceed down to Johnsons Point Fort, at the S. W. point of the Island; and take what is there; there being only a Single Matross in the Said Fort; the other Vessell must be commanded by a prudent Man; well acquainted with the Bar and Harbour at St. Johns; if any Man of War be anchored without the Bar; it will not be prudent to attempt any Thing, but Should there be none; the Vessell may then go over the Bar, and anchor close under the fort; as is commonly the Custom. There are generally 10 or 12 Soldiers in James Fort Situated on a Point on the larboard Hand, Seven miles distant from the Town; the Magazine is in a hollow; on the Left Hand just after entering the Gate, and commonly contains from 500 to 1000 Blls of Powder, or more. 2 miles from thence to the northward is a Small fort call'd Corbresons point fort; and 2 miles from this northward is another Small fort called Dickensons bay fort, in either of which there is not above a Single Matross. All this Powder may be easily obtained, without any opposition, if conducted with Prudence; it will be necessary, that the Captain Should have Some Money, to distribute among the Soldiers, to assist in taking it away; He may go into the Fort in the Afternoon (and see how the Land lies) under pretence of Sailing that night and thereby guide his operation.

The Same Thing may be done by other Vessells at Montserrat, Nevis, Charlesfort at Sandy point, St. Kitts, also at St. Martins; without any Risque.

I would advise the continental Congress, to make a general Sweep of all the Powder, at St. Eustatius, it may first be taken and then paid for afterwards as the Dutch refuse to sell it to us;[3] I am well perswaded the whole of this Plan may be executed, that near 3000 Blls of powder may be obtained in the Course of 3 or 4 months.

RC (MHi:Warren-Adams Coll.); addressed: "To the Hon. James Warren Esqr Speaker of the House and Pay Master General Watertown favd. by Mr Tracy"; docketed: "Mr. J. A Lettr Octr 12. 1775"; with enclosure in JA's hand.

[1] The origin of the enclosure remains obscure. JA probably copied the proposal from some source. The intimate knowledge of Antigua's geography indicates that it was written by some person well informed about the West Indies. Certainly the calling for two ships to go out aggressively and seek munitions accorded with JA's sentiments, for he was a vigorous supporter of the scheme to arm vessels to intercept two British ships known to be carrying munitions to Canada (JA, *Diary and Autobiography*, 3:342–345).

It is uncertain whether the proposal was presented to the congress or to one of its committees (perhaps the secret committee on the procurement of gunpowder that had been created on 18 Sept.) and if so, when (JCC, 2:253). The plan is not mentioned in the Journal of the congress, JA's Diary, or any of the other sources examined. If it was presented, it was probably around 6 Oct., when the procurement of gunpowder was debated (JA, *Diary and Autobiography*, 2:196–197).

[2] JA is here anticipating the action of the congress on 18 Oct., when it resolved that an account of hostilities committed since March be compiled.

To implement the resolution, a committee composed of Silas Deane, JA, and George Wythe was established (JCC, 3:298–299). On 19 Oct. the committee sent form letters to Massachusetts and elsewhere, seeking information. For the form letter see JA's Service in the Congress, 13 Sept.–9 Dec., No. III (above). For JA's interpretation of the period of time to be covered, see JA to James Warren, 19 Oct., first letter, note 3 (below). The province responded on 7 Nov. by naming a committee to compile the requested information, although no record has been found that Massachusetts sent in a formal report (Mass., *House Jour.*, 1775–1776, 2d sess., p. 242).

[3] The Dutch States-General, under pressure from Great Britain, had on 20 March ordered that no munitions be exported to the North American continent for six months, an order which was subsequently renewed periodically, but which was not obeyed in the Dutch West Indies during the American Revolution (F. C. Van Oosten, "Some Notes Concerning the Dutch West Indies During the American Revolutionary War," *The American Neptune*, 36:156 [July 1976]).

From James Warren

My Dear Sir   Watertown Octr. 12. 1775

I have only a Minute to Cover the Inclosed Letters.[1] I have been on an Excursion to Plymouth for a Week and returned Yesterday with Mrs. Warren. On our way we Called a little while on Mrs. Adams as you may well suppose, have the pleasure to Inform you we left her well, and hope to see her here in a few days. The rest the Inclosed will tell you.[2] We Condole with her, and you on the great Loss sustained in her Good Mother.[3]

I Received a Letter from you Yesterday, have Observed your directions, and proposed with Earnestness the Compleating the Accounts.[4]

They are Attended with great difficulties but hope to get them along in some Shape or other. I Received before I went Home 2 Letters.[5] Can only say at present that I Observe you think me very Negligent. I dont wonder at it, but by this Time believe you are Convinced that it was more oweing to my misfortune than Negligence. They were long while in their passage. I knew [not?] of this opportunity till this minute and Mr. Randolph waits. We have no Remarkables. Adeu,

J:W

Mrs. Warren desires her Compliments you will soon here from her. She loves to Scribble to those she has a good Opinion off.

RC (Adams Papers); addressed: "To The Honbl: John Adams Esq Member of Congress Philadelphia"; docketed: "Octr 12. 1775 Warren"; docketed in a later hand: "J. Warren October 12th 1775."

[1] These have not been identified, but see note 2.

[2] Probably Mercy Otis Warren's letter that was begun on 12 Oct. but was not finished until the 14th (see below).

[3] AA's mother, Elizabeth Quincy Smith, died on 1 Oct. See AA to JA, 1 Oct., and Mrs. Smith's obituary of 6 Oct. (*Adams Family Correspondence*, 1:288–289, 293–294).

[4] JA's letter of 28 Sept. (above). The report of the House committee on Massachusets' accounts with the congress was very long in preparation and was recommitted several times (Mass., *House Jour.*, 1775–1776, 2d sess., p. 152, 155–156, 159).

[5] Probably JA's letters of 19 and 26 Sept. (above).

From Mercy Otis Warren

Watertown October 12 1775

I Write again from Waterton, where I Arrived Yesterday with your Excclent Friend who has been so much Engaged by his Necessary Attention to public affairs that he has had time since you Left us only to run to Plimouth four days ago and bring back your Correspondent to this Crouded inconvenient place, where the Muses Cannot dwell, or the Graces of Elegance Reside. Yet the feelings of Real Friendship will not Languish, nor the tender simpathy of a Compassionate Heart Decay, though within the sound of the Cares and Tumults of the more busy scenes. This I Can Attest from the Concern I have Lately felt for the suffering, of those you stand Nearest Connected With.

How fleeting are all the Joys of this precarious state, by what a slender tenure do we hold the Best Blessings of Life.

Within a few days after your agreable Discription of Domestic Happiness, and the temporary Felicity you tasted under your own quiet Roof, the Good Portia was Involved in a Variety of Affliction. But I called on Her yesterday and found the Little Flock Restored to

Health. Their Mamah perfectly Recovered and Bearing up under A stroke of Adversity with that Fortitude and Equinimity which Can only Result from the Noblest principles. But when we take a Rational survey of the Condition of Humanity and the Narrow Limits within which our Advances both to perfection And Happiness are Circumscribed, at the same time that the Hope of the Christian smooths the passage to a More Exalted state, why should the shocks of private Misfortune, the Allarms of War, or the Convulsions of states, Ruffle the soul Conscious of Its own Integrity.

Mrs. Adams has Doubtless informed you that she has the Highest Consolation under the Loss of a most Exelent parent and how much Less painful ought the temporary seperation from those we are assured are Translated to unfading Felicity to be, then to behold the Depravity of mind into which some Wretched Individuals are sunk.

I fear a Late Instance of perfidy and Baseness in one who Rancked Himself among the Friends to the Rights of society and the Happiness of the Community Will occasion many Inviduous Reflections from the Enemies of the American Cause.

I was Ever sorry that there should be one among the Band of patriots Whose Moral Character was Impeachable for when the Heart is Contaminated, and the Obligations of private Life Broken through, And the man has thrown of[f] the Restraints Both of Honour and Conscience with Regard to His own Domestic Conduct, what Dependance is to be Made on the Rectitude of His public Intentions.[1]

The Culprit Assumes an air of Inocence, and with the Confidence usual to Veterans in Iniquity Complains that He is unjustly Restraind. But I imagine when he has no further hopes, left of Imposing on the Friends of his Country, he will be mean, And abject in proportion to his affectation of Intrepidity, for no true Fortitude can subsist in a Mind Devoid of these principles which Leads to some Higher hopes. Yet when they are about to Leap the Gulph of Futurity, the Natural Intimations of an Impartial Tribunal, shakes the firmness of the sceptic And plunges him in all the Horrors of Dispair.

The two armies Remain Rather Inactive. Nothing Vigorous or Decisive on Either side.

It is Generally beleved Gage is Gone home.[2] The Communication between the town and Country is now intirly Cut off: so that no inteligence Can be Expected from Boston Except the Little by way of Desserters.

There seems to be such a spirit for Navel preperations, that I beleive it will not be many years before your Friend Gadsdens American Fleet[3] will make A very Respectable Figure on the Western side of the Atlantic. And if we Can once Gaurd our sea coasts from the Depredations of the British Bucaneers I beleive we may soon bid Deffiance to all the, Hessians Highlanders and Hanoverians, Employed by an unfeeling Arbitrary, ‒‒‒‒ Monarch.

October 14

Mr. Warren and myself are just returned from Head quarters where we had the pleasure of spending the afternoon with the Agreable Mrs. Miflin. The Annimated spirit which Reigns there seems to beat in unison with the sentiments Breathed in your Respectable Assembly, if we may Judge by your Letters just Come to Hand. We Expect Great projects are to open upon us, and that A system of politics will soon be disclosed that will do Honour to the Genius of America, and Equal to some of the Capital Characters which Compose the Grand Counsel of the Continent.

I thank you sir for a Line Received Lately,[4] and if you find a Leasure Moment shall be Gratifyed and Obliged if you Condescend at any time to write to your assured Friend,   Marcia

RC (Adams Papers); docketed: "Marcia's Letter   Octr. 12. 1775." A Tr of this letter erroneously dated 22 Oct. is in MHi:Mercy Warren Letterbook, p. 160–162. The copy was apparently made at a later date from one not now extant. The only significant difference between the two versions is her specific identification of Dr. Church, whose conduct she describes but whose name she does not mention in the letter here printed. The Tr carries this note: "This was Dr. Church recently detected of betraying the affairs of America to the British army." For comment on Mrs. Warren's "Letterbook," see *Adams Family Correspondence*, 1:93–94, note 1.

[1] Rumors, probably much exaggerated, flew around concerning Church's private immorality; but the evidence is clear that he had a mistress who carried the letter which was his undoing (Allen French, *General Gage's Informers*, Ann Arbor, 1932, p. 149–150).

[2] Gage had received orders to return to England, and on 13 Oct. the *Massachusetts Gazette* reported that he had left Boston on the 10th (Gage to Dartmouth, 30 Sept., Gage, *Corr.*, 1:417).

Gage was recalled by the King presumably to help with plans for military operations in 1776, but his recall actually was owing to political enemies in London who used the outcome of the Battle of Bunker Hill as an excuse (John R. Alden, *General Gage in America*, Baton Rouge, 1948, p. 280–283).

[3] See JA to Elbridge Gerry, [ante 11] June (above).

[4] That of 26 Sept. (above).

To Charles Lee

My dear Sir[1]   Philadelphia Octr. 13. 1775

Your obliging Favour of the fifth Inst. I this Moment received, and give me Leave to assure you that no Letter I ever received, gave me greater Pleasure. In truth sir I have been under some Apprehensions, that a certain Passage, in a very unfortunate as well as inconsiderate Letter, might have made Some disagreable Impressions on your Mind: I was indeed relieved in some Degree by Accounts which I had from Gentlemen who knew your sentiments, especially such as were present when you first heard it read. The candid, genteel and generous Manner in which it was heard and animadverted on, gave me great Satisfaction: I had thought of writing you on the Subject, but was hindered by certain Notions of Delicacy perhaps as whimsical, as any Thing alluded to in that Letter. But I rejoice exceedingly, that this incident has induced you to write.

I frankly confess to you that a little Whim and Eccentricity, so far from being an Objection to any one in my Mind, is rather, a Recommendation, at first Blush, and my Reasons are, because few Persons in the World, within my Experience or little Reading, who have been possessed of Virtues or Abilities, have been entirely without them; and because few Persons, have been remarkable for them, without having Something at the same Time, truly valuable in them. I confess farther that a Fondness for Dogs, by no means depreciates any Character in my Estimation, because many of the greatest Men have been remarkable for it; and because I think it Evidence of an honest Mind and an Heart capable of Friendship, Fidelity and Strong Attachments being Characteristicks of that Animal.

Your Opinion of my Generosity, Valour, Good sense, Patriotism and Zeal for the Rights of Humanity, is extreamly flattering to me: and I beg leave to assure you, in the Strongest Manner and I flatter myself that my Language and Conduct in public and private upon all occasions, notwithstanding the wanton Expressions in the intercepted Letter have demonstrated, that this Opinion is reciprocal. Your Sincerity, sir, I never doubted, any more than I did my own, when I expressed or implied an opinion of your Attainments as a Scholler and a Soldier. Indeed I might have expressed a much higher opinion of these than I did, with the same Sincerity. But enough of this.

At the Story of the Surgeon General I stand astonished. A Man of Genius, of Learning, of Family, of Character, a Writer of Liberty songs and good ones too, a Speaker of Liberty orations, a Member of the Boston Committee of Correspondence, a Member of the Massachusetts Congress, an Agent for that Congress to the Continental Congress, a Member of the House, a Director General of the Hospital and Surgeon General—Good God! What shall We say of human Nature?

What shall We say of American Patriots? or rather what will the World Say? The World however, will not be too severe. Indeed, Sir, We ought to expect, in a Contest like this, however we may detest, Such Examples as this. History furnishes Instances more or less, in all Quarells like this. The Doctors Brother Poet Waller[2] in the Struggle with a Stuart, was his Antitype. We cannot be too cautious of the Persons We entrust, in such Times as these: yet We ought not to let our Caution degenerate into groundless Jealousy. There is a Medium between Credulity on one hand and a base suspicious Temper on the other from which We need not be induced to deviate, even in such Times as these, and by such Examples as the Doctors.

The Nature of the Conspiracy and the Duration and Extent of it Seem as yet in much Obscurity. I hope Time, and Care will bring the whole Truth to light that exact and impartial Justice may be done, if that is possible.

Before this Reaches you, a Committee from Congress[3] will tell you News from hence. I wish, sir that I could write freely to you concerning, our Proceedings: But you know the obligations I am under to be upon the Reserve: and the danger there would be as I know not the Carrier of this Letter, if I was at perfect Liberty. But this I must Say, that I See no danger of our "displaying Timidity." This Congress, is more united, and more determined, than ever. And, if the petrified Tyrants would but send us their Ultimatum, which is expected Soon, you would see us, in Earnest.

As to confiscating Estates, that is but a Small Part of what will be done when We are engaging seriously.

You began upon a subject, towards the Close of your Letter of infinite Importance; I read with avidity your Thoughts and was much chagrin'd, that you gave me so few of them. The Intricacy and Multiplicity of the Questions involved in it, require more extensive Knowledge and a larger Mind than mine to determine them with Precision. There is So much Uncertainty too, that I believe no Man is capable of deciding with Precision: but it must be left to Time Accident and Experience, to begin and improve the Plan of our Trade.

If We Should invite "all the maritime Powers, of the World into our Ports" would any one of them come? At least, untill they should be convinced that We were able, and determined to fight it out with G.B. to the last? Are they yet convinced of this, or will they be very soon? Besides, if they should, would it be Sound Policy in Us to admit them? Would it not be Sounder to confine the Benefit and the Bargain to one or a few?

Is it not wiser to send our own Ships to all maritime Powers, and admit private Adventurers from foreign Nations, if by any Means We can defend them against Cutters and Cruizers, or teach them to elude them. I have upon this Subject a System of my own but am not bigoted to it, nor to any other. You will oblige me vastly by your Sentiments at large.

RC (MHi:Warren-Adams Coll.); docketed in an unidentified hand: "Mr. John Adams   Oct 13. 1775   X."

[1] Although James Warren was thought by Worthington C. Ford to be the recipient (*Warren-Adams Letters*, 1:136–139), and his judgment was accepted by William Bell Clark (*Naval Docs. Amer. Rev.*, 2:445), this letter was intended for Charles Lee, for it is an almost point by point reply to Lee's letter of 5 Oct. (above), and Lee replied to it on 19 Nov. (below). It may have been enclosed with JA's letter to Warren of 13 Oct. (below), but how it got back among Warren's papers remains undetermined.

[2] Edmund Waller (1606–1687), a noted poet and member of the House of Commons, who at the beginning of the struggle against Charles I, appeared to stand with the Commons, but who in 1643 was seized as the perpetrator of "Waller's plot," a scheme to seize London for Charles. In 1644 he was exiled, saving his life only because he informed on other members of the conspiracy (*DNB*).

[3] That is, Harrison, Lynch, and Franklin.

To James Warren

Octr. 13. 1775

Yours of october 1. and 2d I received this Morning with the Letters inclosed. These were from my afflicted Wife,[1] giving me Such a continued History of her Distresses, as has affected me too much to write you a long Letter.

The Misfortune, or what shall I call it of the Surgion General had been represented here in several Letters in very glaring Colours untill one arrived from the secretary to the general, couched in Terms of more Temper and Candour.[2] By your Account, and indeed by the Letter itself it appears an unaccountable Affair—Balaam praying for Leave to curse Israel, is the Emblem. A manifest Reluctance at hurting his Country, yet desirous of making a Merit, with the other Side—what shall We think! Is there reason to believe that other Letters have gone the same Way? I was so little acquainted with the World that I never heard a Suspicion to the Disadvantage of his Moral Character, untill I was lately with you at the Adjournment. I should scarcely have joined in a certain Recommendation, if I had heard before what I heard then[3]—for Honour and Fidelity violated in Such gross Instances in private Life, are slender securities in public. Be not concerned about your Friends at the Congress—their Recommendations will not be discredited by this Event. Gentlemen here have behaved universally with the Utmost Politeness, upon this occasion. They say they pitty us, for the Suspicions that there is danger may arise among us of one another, and the Hurt to that Confidence in one another which ought to be. But any Man ought to be kick'd for a Brute that shall reproach Us in Thought, Word or Deed on this account.

Our Accounts from Schuyler's Army are as agreable as yours from Arnold. We are in hourly Expectation.

Rejoice to hear of your Successes by Sea.[4] Let Cargill and Obrien[5] be put into continental service immediately I pray. We begin to feel a little of a Seafaring Inclination here. The Powder at Quebec, will place us all upon the Top of the House.

Your Letters are very usefull to me—and I cannot have too many, or too long.

I believe We shall take some of the twenty Gun ships before long. We must excite by Policy that Kind of exalted Courage, which is ever victorious by sea and land—which is irresistable—the Saracens, had it—the Knights of Malta—the Assassins—Cromwells soldiers and sailors—Nay N. England men have ever had it hitherto—they never yet fail'd in an Attempt of any Kind.

RC (MHi:Warren-Adams Coll.); addressed: "The Hon. James Warren Esq   Speaker of the House Watertown   By favour of Mr. Tracy"; docketed: "Mr J: A Lettr   Octr. 13. 1775."

[1] See James Warren to JA, 1 Oct., note 14 (above).

[2] Washington to the President of Congress, 5 Oct. (*Writings*, ed. Fitzpatrick, 4:9–13).

[3] JA had a hand in getting Church his appointment as director of hospitals on 27 July (*JCC*, 2:211).

[4] That is, the capture of the schooner *Industry* and the brigantine *Dolphin*, mentioned in Warren's letter of 1 Oct.

[5] Why JA mentioned James Cargill and Capt. Jeremiah O'Brien at this point is not clear. Warren does not name them, nor does the Journal of the House, in connection with the seizure of the two ships. Warren did mention Cargill on 9 Aug. (above), however. O'Brien had shown spirit in leading a group of men on board a sloop belonging to Ichabod Jones to pursue a royal tender, which had escorted Jones to Machias. This incident occurred in June and may have been reported to JA (Mass. Provincial Congress, *Jours.*, p. 395–396).

From The Intelligencer

Gentlemen   N. York Octbr. 16th 1775

I[1] have been here, almost ever since I had the Pleasure of seeing you at Fairfield, and have attentively observed the Conduct of these People's Leaders; and, according to the best of my slender Judgement, think that their Councils are stampt with Folly, Timidty, and Treachery. But to trace the whole Labyrinth of their Inconsistency and Perfidy, would be irksome and endless; therefore I shall only mention such as have occurred lately, leaving the Rest for a Day of more Leisure.

In the first Place, the Committee of Safety, during the Recess of the Congress, pass'd a Resolve to impress all the Arms of those who had not sign'd the Association by the 16th of Septr., the Time of passing the Resolve,[2] which was done too, only in Consequence of a Letter, or Letters, from your Body, as it is generally imagined. This was first attempted to be carried into Execution on Long Island, in Queen's County, by sending out one or two of their own Board, with 4 or 5 Citizens, who at the same Time were restrain'd from exercising any manner of Coercion whatever by private Instruction, unless endanger'd by Violence &c. According they went out on the 23rd Ultimo and were treated in the most contemptuous Manner, even to Insult and Threat; declaring they knew no Congress, neither would they sign any Association, nor pay any Part of the Expense accruing by an Opposition to the King's Troops &c. On the Contrary, that they were determin'd to support the "King's Laws" and defend themselves against all other Authority &c. Some of this happen'd within 5 or 6 Miles of the City, and some further. They got *a few worthless Arms*, from some of the most Timid, who, it was tho't, had concealed their best.[3]

After they had been out 2 or 3 Days a Report was bro't to Town that they were imprison'd, and an Order was made out for the first Battalion of Militia, with some of the Provincials, to go to their Relief. But before this could be carried into Execution, Means were devised, by mustering their whole Force and calling a Committee, to defeat the Measure. .

Oct. 16th Sub[4] 1775

The next Expedient was to appoint a Committee of that Board to wait on them, who return'd as Fruitless as the First. Since the Meeting of the Congress they have endeavour'd to pass a Censure on the whole Proceeding of the Committee of Safety in that Affair and several others.

Some of the Congress have declared that they would not receive the Bills of Credit to be emitted by themselves. Others have said that they would join the King's Standard if Troops came, in order to save their Estates &c. This was said in Congress without any Censure, as reported by a Member in full Company, within these few Days.

A few Days since some Blankets, Sheets Shirts &c. to the Amount of several thousand Pounds worth, and what was more necessary, a large Chest of Lint[5] was found in the Lower Barracks and secur'd. These were all return'd next Day by Order of Congress.

The Post being just on the Point of going obliges me to omit many Things which I intended to mention.

Finally I inclose you a Paper containing an Extract of Mr. Tryon's Letter to our Mayor, for the Perusal of the Congress.[6] I am told this Morning that his Friends had a Meeting on Saturday Night last, to a Considerable Amount, in order to defend him at all Events. I believe there is Truth in it, and shall, as soon as I have put this in the Office make Inquiry. I am also told that he has written a second Letter to the Mayor, desiring to know if [he] cannot be protected against an Order of the Continental Congress &c.[7] Both of these last I shall inquire further of, and give you such Intelligence as I receive. This Minute I am inform'd that there is a Vessel at the Hook, in a Short Passage from England, but the Viper Sloop[8] detains her, as it is said. Should you want to communicate any Thing to me, direct for the Intelligencer, and cover it to Mr. John Holt, Printer.[9] Be assur'd that Mr. Tryon is most assiduously stirring up every Coal that will catch, through the Medium of his mercenary Emissaries &c. If Something be not done very speedily he will give you some Trouble, or I am greatly Mistaken. The Gentleman who told you this Time 12 Month that all would go well here, is now exceedingly alarm'd, and told me Yesterday that we were in a most dangerous Situation. I am, with the greatest Regard, Gentlemen your very Humble Servant,   The Intelligencer

P.S. Your Candour is begg'd to this hasty Scrawl.[10]

RC (Adams Papers); directed: "To Messrs. Samuel and John Adams Esqrs."

[1] A comparison of this letter and a second from the Intelligencer of 18 Oct. (below) with letters from Hugh Hughes of 31 March and 29 May 1776 (both below) shows such a similarity in handwriting that it is almost certain that Hughes was the Intelligencer. Hugh Hughes (1727?–1802?) was an unsuccessful businessman who by recurrent financial difficulties was forced also to keep a school. An ardent patriot and member of the New York Sons of Liberty, he was assistant quartermaster general with the rank of colonel for the province of New York from May 1776 till Dec. 1781. He was the brother of John Hughes (1712–1772) of Philadelphia, friend of Benjamin Franklin (*New Jersey Archives*, 1st ser., 24:646,

note; Charles Henry Hart, ed., "Letters from William Franklin to William Strahan," *PMHB*, 35:442, note [Oct. 1911]; N.Y. *Genealogical and Biographical Record*, 47 [1916]:173; Heitman, *Register Continental Army*, p. 306).

That this letter is addressed to both Samuel Adams and JA, together with the mention of Fairfield, Conn., suggests that the author met them when they stopped in Fairfield at "Penfields" on their way to the second session of the Second Continental Congress (JA, *Diary and Autobiography*, 2:168).

[2] The New York Provincial Congress adjourned on 2 Sept. and reconvened on 4 Oct. During the recess, the Committee of Safety conducted business

(Force, *Archives*, 4th ser., 3:582, 1267). For the committee's resolve, see same, 3:898.

[3] Maj. William Williams describes conditions on Long Island and the resistance of the people to efforts to disarm them. In substance, the Intelligencer's account is almost identical (same, 3:912).

[4] Probably an abbreviation for "subsequent," indicating a break in the writing of the letter of perhaps even a day or two.

[5] Soft material for dressing wounds (*OED*).

[6] Gov. William Tryon's letter of 13 Oct. to New York Mayor Whitehead Hicks threatened New York with bombardment from warships in the harbor if he was not protected against seizure ordered by the Continental Congress. A reply came from the City Committee to Hicks and from Hicks to Tryon on 13 and 14 Oct., assuring the governor of his safety and asserting they knew of no such order from the congress to arrest him (Force, *Archives*, 4th ser., 3:1052–1053). Apparently Tryon was moved by a report that the Continental Congress had entertained a motion for his arrest on 5 Oct. Although the Journal makes no mention of the motion, it was offered and failed to carry (JA, *Diary* and *Autobiography*, 2:195).

[7] Tryon's letter of 14 Oct. to Hicks expressed his dissatisfaction with the lack of positive assurances in the replies to his first letter. The mayor and City Committee responded yet again, but Tryon, still unsatisfied, took refuge on the Halifax Packet in the harbor (Force, *Archives*, 4th ser., 3:1053–1054). On 19 Oct. the Continental Congress asked the New York Provincial Congress to forward a copy of any order from them or the city in consequence of Tryon's letter and to send an attested copy of the governor's letter (JCC, 3:300).

[8] The British sloop of war *Viper* had arrived at Boston from England in September but was ordered to proceed to New York. It was commanded by Capt. Samuel Greaves (*Naval Docs. Amer. Rev.*, 2:38, 611).

[9] John Holt (1721–1784), publisher of the *New York Journal*, a whig paper (*DAB*).

[10] Actually the MS is very clearly written. Although some phrases are interlined, a few words crossed out, and some sentences in the margin, the writer shows unusual care with word choice and placement of modifiers, as well as with punctuation and consistency of spelling.

To James Warren

Dr sir   Octr. 18. 1775

The Letter of Dr —————— is the oddest Thing imaginable. There are so many Lies in it, calculated to give the Enemy an high Idea of our Power and Importance, as well as so many Truths tending to do us good that one knows not how to think him treacherous: Yet there are several Strokes, which cannot be accounted for at least by me, without the Supposition of Iniquity. In Short I endeavour to Suspend my Judgment. Don't let us abandon him for a Traitor without certain Evidence.

But there is not So much Deliberation in many others, or so much Compassion.

The Congress declined entering into any Discussion of the Evidence, or any Determination concerning his Guilt, or the Nature of his offence. But in general they had a full Conviction that it was so gross an Imprudence at least, and was So Suspicious, that it became them to dismiss him from their Service, which they did instantly.[1]

Yesterday they chose a Successor, Dr. Morgan an eminent Surgeon of this City.[2] We, As usual had our Men to propose, Dr. Hall Jackson and Dr. Forster [Foster]. But Dr. Forsters Sufferings and services—and Dr. Jackson's great Fame, Experience and Merits were pleaded in vain.[3]

There is a Fatality attends our Province. It Seems destined to fall into Contempt. It was destined that We should make Mistakes I think, in our Appointment of Generals, Delegates, Surgeons and every Thing else except Paymaster and Judge Advocate.[4] I hope they will not turn Cowards, Traytors, nor Lubbers, if they do I shall renounce all.

Dr. Morgan will be with you soon. He is Professor of Medicine in the Colledge here, and reads Lectures in the Winter. He is a Brother [-in-law] of Mr. Duche and of our Mr. Stillman. I may write you more particularly about him another Time.

Let me close now with a Matter of Some Importance. Congress have appointed Deane, Wythe, and your servant a Committee to collect a just Account of the Hostilities committed by the ministerial Troops and Navy, in America, Since last March; with proper Evidence of the Truth of the Facts related, the Number and Value of the Buildings destroyed by them, also the Number and Value of the Vessells inward and outward bound, which have been Seized by them, Since that Period, also the Stock taken by them from different Parts of the Continent; We shall write to the Assemblies of New England and Virginia, at least, but we shall likewise write to many Individuals requesting their Assistance and to you among others. I wish you would think a little and consult with others concerning this Business, for it nearly concerns our Province to have it well done.[5]

RC (MHi:Warren-Adams Coll.); addressed: "To the Hon. James Warren Esqr Speaker of the House Watertown favoured by Captn. Mordecai Gist"; docketed: "Mr J A Lettr Octr. 1775"; above the address, probably postage: "d ster 2." It may be that Gist carried the letter as far as Dorchester and posted it from there for 2d. For biographical details on Gist, see *DAB*.

[1] On 14 Oct. (JCC, 3:294).

[2] Dr. John Morgan (1735–1789), founder of the University of Pennsylvania medical school, who despite his eminence was removed from the post in the Continental Army in Jan. 1777. His wife, Mary, was a sister-in-law of Rev. Jacob Duché (*DAB*). His sister was married to Rev. Samuel Stillman of Boston (*Adams Family Correspondence*, 1:314–316, notes 2–4). See also JA to James Warren, 25 Oct. (below).

[3] Dr. Hall Jackson (1739–1797) was a noted and innovative surgeon from Portsmouth, N.H., who, like Morgan, had studied in England. At the outbreak of the war, he joined the army, was at the capture of Ticonderoga, and ultimately became the chief surgeon for the New Hampshire troops in the Con-

tinental Army (*DAB*).

Dr. Isaac Foster (1740–1781) graduated from Harvard in 1758 and soon after the outbreak of war became deputy director in charge of the Eastern Medical Department of the Continental Army. His "sufferings" resulted from the loss of all his property in the burning of Charlestown (Sibley-Shipton, *Harvard Graduates*, 14:262–268).

⁴ JA's friends James Warren and William Tudor.

⁵ See JA to James Warren, 12 Oct., note 2 (above). On 19 Oct. JA wrote to William Cooper, then speaker pro tem of the House of Representatives, and to Joseph Palmer telling them also about the committee on depredations and requesting their assistance. He also asked each to send him a copy of the authorized account of the Battle of Charlestown, that is, Bunker Hill (25 July, above), which he had forgotten to take to Philadelphia, and which, he told Palmer, he wanted "very much" (to Cooper, MHi:Misc. Bound Coll.; to Palmer, M–Ar:194, p. 150–150a). Form letters on British depredations were sent out on 24 Oct. to James Warren, Elbridge Gerry, Samuel Cooper, and others.

From The Intelligencer

Gentlemen   New York Wednesday Evening 18th Octbr. 1775

Since I closed my last, of this Morning,[1] I have been inform'd of a most curious Motion that was made in Committee, last Evening, by a Member of our Congress, on Mr. Tryon's last Requisition.[2] It was, that they should not only protect him, and his, from any Attempt which may be made by Individuals &c. but that they should give him Notice if any Order of the Continental Congress came to Hand for that Purpose, i.e., of Seizing him and see him safe onboard one of his Majesty's Ships.[3] This is a Fact. I have heard several of the Members declare it publickly, and not one contradict it. This is New York; how do you like it? They have complimented him highly, on the Rectitude of his Administration, I understand; and let him know that, they would protect him, as far as was consistent withe the overruling Law of Self-preservation; but not a Word of the Union, or Continental Congress.

If some speedy Method be not fallen upon to remove this intriguing Courtier, he will become daily, more and more popular, and of Course, very dangerous, at such an important Post as This. If Troops are to be sent, do let them hasten along as fast as possible; the Defection becomes greater every Day, in Town and Country. Those that have been pretty hearty, are now afraid of falling a Sacrifice.

Thursday—What I only heard and conjectured Yesterday, you'l find confirm'd in the inclos'd Paper,[4] if you should not see it before this arrives. In it you will also see that our motley Council, as Dr. Church phrases it, is shortly to be dissolved.[5] I wish the next may be better, but much doubt it I assure you. There is an insuperable Ignorance predominant here, which the Enemies of our Happiness avail themselves of, by some Means or other, continually.

An Attempt was made, previous to the last Election for City Officers, to persuade the Citizens to reject those Magistrates who had discover'd an unfriendly Disposition to the Cause; but to very little Purpose. There was but one Alderman, and 3 or 4 Common Council, left out. The inclos'd Hand-bill contains some of the principal Objections to them, and will characterize the Men. If you think well of it, you may hand it to Dunlap, and Bradford;[6] for which Purpose I shall inclose a Couple, that their Infamy may be as publick as their Actions are criminal, if possible.

Do inform me, under Cover to Mr. Holt, for The Intelligencer, as mention'd in my First, when the Pensylvania and New Jersey Troops may be expected?[7] It is not possible to communicate the Necessity there is, just now, for their being here.

I took the Liberty about 8 or 10 Days ago, to mention our Situation to Col. Seymour, of Hartford,[8] begging him to lay it before Governour Trumbull, in order that he might prepare a Number of the Militia to assist us, in Case of an Arrival of foreign Troops &c. as our own were not to be depended on, in general. I wish Mr. Deane, Col. Dyer &c. would back it, if approv'd of. I made use of the same Signature, that I do to you.

Evening—Capt. Cressop, of the Rifflemen, was buried here with Military Honours, this Afternoon, in Trinity Church-yard.[9] He return'd from Camp to this Place, about 8 Days since, as I am told. The Procession was pretty well conducted, and made a considerable Appearance, allowing for the Defection of the People. But our Fondness for Parade, I imagine, made up for a Want of Zeal, in this Case.

Low, De Lancey, Walton, Kissam, Verplank[10] &c, &c, have labour'd hard in Congress to-day, that the Freemen (Freemen being excluded, they expect that the Freeholders will return none but such as will be for preserving this City at the Expense of the Liberties of America; that is, Creatures of their own Cast, and Complexion)[11] of this City should be precluded from voting for new Members, and that they should not vote by Ballot; but by Poll, as we are us'd to do.[12]

I have tho't that, if it were recommended by the Continental Congress to vote by Ballot, it might have a good Effect. I believe it would be adopted; as there has been an inkling for it here, some Time.

Another Stratagem is, that the Members of the next Congress shall serve gratis, by which Means they are in Hopes of having very few return'd, but such as are in the Pay of the Ministry already, and the others can easily be taken into Pay. But this is ridiculous, when it is only considered that the Present Congress can not bind a Future.

Friday Morn. There is a Report, by a Sloop from Connecticut River this Morning, that St. John's is taken, but whether true or not, is yet doubtful.[13]

The Viper Sloop is daily stopping the Vessels and Boats from Sea and New Jersey.

The Post is waiting, or I could add. I am, with the greatest Regard, Gentlemen, your most obedient Humble Servant,

The Intelligencer

RC (Adams Papers); directed: "To Messers. Samuel and John Adams Esqrs"; docketed by JA: "Intelligencer Oct. 1775."

[1] No other letter of 18 Oct. from the Intelligencer has been found, but see his of 16 Oct., note 4 (above).

[2] Probably Tryon's second letter to Mayor Hicks, that of 14 Oct. (same, note 7, above).

[3] The substance of this motion was not included in the letter addressed by the City Committee to Mayor Hicks on 17 Oct., but the committee did compliment the Governor on his administration and did desire him to remain and offered him protection consistent with "our safety" (Force, *Archives*, 4th ser., 3: 1053–1054).

[4] Not found.

[5] A phrase lifted from Dr. Church's intercepted letter and applied here to the New York Provincial Congress, which on 18 Oct. resolved to dissolve itself on 14 Nov. for new elections (same, 3:1295).

[6] The handbill has not been found. John Dunlap (1747–1812) published the *Pennsylvania Packet*; Thomas Bradford (1745–1838), the *Pennsylvania Journal* (DAB).

[7] On 9 Oct. the congress voted to have New Jersey raise two battalions at continental expense and on 12 Oct. Pennsylvania was requested to raise a battalion

on the same terms (JCC, 3:285–286, 291).

[8] Thomas Seymour (1735–1829), prominent in Connecticut's political affairs, was named a lieutenant colonel in 1774 (Dexter, *Yale Graduates*, 2: 378–379).

[9] Capt. Michael Cressop of Virginia, corps of riflemen, died on 18 Oct. in his lodgings (NYHS, *Colls.*, 84:123).

[10] Isaac Low (1735–1791), merchant, member of the First Continental Congress, but opponent of independence; James DeLancey (1732–1800), leader of the loyalist political faction (both in DAB). Jacob Walton, Daniel Kissam, and Philip Verplanck were all opponents of the Livingston faction, which supported the Revolution (Patricia U. Bonomi, *A Factious People*, N.Y., 1971, p. 246).

[11] This passage, given here in parentheses, was written in the left-hand margin, its place in the MS text indicated with a dagger.

[12] On 18 Oct. a motion to elect delegates to the next provincial congress by ballot was rejected (Force, *Archives*, 4th ser., 3:1294–1295).

[13] One of a number of premature reports.

To James Warren

My dear sir   Octr. 19. 1775

It was the latter End of August that I left you. All September has run away, and 19 days in Octr.—and We have had no regular Intelligence from Watertown or Cambridge. Your Goodness I acknowledge. But there was a Committee of both Houses appointed, to correspond with your Delegates; and We were to be informed of every Thing that occurred in Boston, Cambridge, Roxbury, Watertown &c especially of every Thing which passed in Either House: But have never received a single Letter not even a Scratch of a Pen from this Committee or any Member of it, unless you are one, which I don't know that you are. Should be glad to hear if this Committee, is all defunct or not.[1]

I have, in almost every Letter I have written, to any of my Friends, entreated that We might have Accounts and Vouchers sent Us, that We might obtain a Reimbursement of some Part at least of the inordinate Expence that has fallen upon Us. But have received No Answer from any one, concerning it.[2] I wish to be informed, however, what the Difficulty is, that lies in the Way, if We cannot have the Accounts &c. The Continental Money goes away So fast, that I greatly fear We shall have none left in the Treasury, before We get the Proper Evidence and Information to obtain a Reimbursement for our Province. Dollars go but little Way in Maintaining Armies—very costly Commodities indeed. The Expence already accrued will astonish Us all, I fear.

Congress has appointed a Committee Deane, Wythe and your servant to collect a Narration of Hostilities, and Evidence to prove it—to ascertain the Number and Value of the Buildings destroyed, Vessells captivated, and Cattle plundered &c every where. I hope We shall tell a true Story, and then I am sure it will be an affecting one. We shall not omit their Butchers nor their Robberies nor their Piracies. But We shall want Assistance from every Quarter. I want the Distresses of Boston painted by Dr. Coopers Pencil—every Thing must be supported by Affidavits. This will be an usefull Work for the Information of all the colonies of what has passed in Some—for the Information of our Friends in England—and in all Europe, and all Posterity. Besides it may pave the Way to obtain Retribution and Compensation, but this had better not be talked of at present.

The Committee will write to the assemblies, and to private Gentlemen—no Pains or Expence will be Spared. I hope to render the Execution of this Commission compleat. It concerns our Province very much.[3]

RC (MHi:Warren-Adams Coll.); addressed: "The Hon. James Warren Esqr Speaker of the House Watertown"; docketed: "Mr J: A Lettr Octr. 19. 1775."

[1] In his letter to Joseph Palmer of this same date, JA complained of the failure not only of this General Court committee to write but of the committee on lead and salt as well (M-Ar:194, p. 150–150a; see also JA to

Warren, 18 Oct., note 5, above). For the membership of these two committees, see JA to John Winthrop, 2 Oct., note 4 (above).

[2] JA made a similar complaint to Palmer (M-Ar:194, p. 150-150a). After JA's mention of the congressional committee on damages, he went on to tell Palmer that the congress hourly expected "Floods of Intelligence" from a variety of places and told of a British ship running aground at Egg Harbor, N.J., the crew destroying weapons and powder on board, an incident reported in the *Pennsylvania Gazette*, 25 Oct.

[3] The committee on damages done by the British was the main topic of JA's letter to Warren of 23 Oct., in which he added: "You will observe the Vote limits Us to last March. This was done without design and I dont intend to be so limited; and therefore I hope the two Houses will appoint a Committee upon a larger Scale and collect Facts at least from the Port Bill, i.e. the time when it took place" (MHi:Warren-Adams Coll., printed in *Warren-Adams Letters*, 1:159-160).

To James Warren

Dr Sir   Octr. 19th. 1775

What Think you of an American Fleet? I dont mean 100 ships of the Line, by a Fleet, but I Suppose this Term may be applied to any naval Force consisting of several Vessells, tho the Number, the Weight of Metal, or the Quantity of Tonnage may be small.

The Expence would be very great—true. But the Expence might be born and perhaps the Profits and Benefits to be obtained by it, would be a Compensation. A naval Force might be created, which would do something. It would destroy Single Cutters and Cruizers—it might destroy small Concerts or Fleets of those like Wallaces at R. Island and Lord Dunmores at Virginia. It might oblige our Enemies to Sail in Fleets—for two or three Vessells of 36 and twenty Guns, well armed and manned might attack and carry a 64 or a 70 or a 50 Gun Ship.

But, there is a great objection to this. All the Trade of Pensylvania, the Lower Counties, a great Part of Maryland and N. Jersey Sails in between the Capes of Delaware Bay—and if a strong Fleet should be posted in that Bay, Superiour to our Fleet it might obstruct all the Trade of this River.

Further the Trade of Virginia and the rest of Maryland floats into Cheasapeak Bay between the Capes of Henry and Charles where a Fleet might stop all. Besides Virginia and Maryland have no Navigation of their own nor any Carpenters to build ships. Their whole Trade is carried on in British Bottoms by British, most of it by North British Merchants.

These Circumstances distinguish them quite from New England, where the Inlets are innumerable and the Navigation all their own.

They agree that a Fleet, would protect and secure the Trade of New England but deny that it would that of the Southern Colonies.

Will it not be difficult to perswade them then to be at the Expence of building a Fleet, merely for N. England. We arc Speculating now about Things at a Distance—should We be driven to a War at all Points—a Fleet a public Fleet as well as privateers might make prey enough of the Trade of our Enemies to make it worth while.[1]

RC (MHi:Warren-Adams Coll.); addressed: "Hon. James Warren Esqr Paymaster of the American Forces   Watertown"; docketed: "Mr. J: A Lettr Octr. 19. 1775."

[1] Compare this letter with that to Warren of 7 Oct. (above) and those of 19, 20, and 28 Oct. (below). JA was almost certainly giving, in the guise of his own thoughts on the subject, the substance of the debates over trade and the creation of a navy then going on in the congress. Thus, these letters become a useful supplement to JA's Diary entries for this period.

To James Warren

Dr sir   Octr. 19. 1775

I want to be with you, Tete a Tete, to canvass, and discuss the complicated subject of Trade. I Say nothing of private Consultations or public Debates, upon this important Head.

When I write you Letters you must expect nothing from me but unconnected Scraps and broken Hints. Continual Successions of Company allow me Time only to Scrawl a Page of Paper, without Thought.

Shall We hush the Trade of the whole Continent and not permit a Vessell to go out of our Harbours except from one Colony to another? How long will or can our People bear this? I Say they can bear it forever—if Parliament Should build a Wall of Brass, at low Water Mark, We might live and be happy. We must change our Habits, our Prejudices our Palates, our Taste in Dress, Furniture, Equipage, Architecture &c. But We can live and be happy. But the Question is whether our People have Virtue enough to be mere Husbandmen, Mechaniks and Soldiers? That they have not Virtue enough to bear it always, I take for granted. How long then will their Virtue last? Till next Spring?

If We Stop all Trade, Great Britain, Ireland and West Indies will not be furnished with any Thing.

Shall We then give Permission for our Vessells to go to foreign Nations, if they can escape the Men of War? Can they escape the Men of War? How many will escape in Proportion? If any Escape, will they not venture to Britain, Ireland, and W.I. in defyance of our Association? If they do not, will not the British Dominions furnish hemselves with our Produce from foreign Ports, and thereby avoid that Distress, which We expect will overtake them? Will not the W.I. Islands especially, who cannot exist without our Provisions for 6. Months, unless G[...][1] Walker were ignorant.

If We should invite other maritime Powers, or private Adventurers from foreign Nations to come here, Will they venture? They run the risque of escaping Men of War, and the Dangers of an unknown Coast. Maps and Charts may give Strangers a confused Idea of the Geography of our Country, and of the Principal Inlets of Harbours, Rivers, Creeks, Coves, Islands &c. but without skillfull Pilots, the danger of Shipwreck will be 10 to one.

This vast object is never out of my Mind. Help me to grapple it. The W.I. Barbadoes particularly begin We are told here, by a late Vessell to be terrified out of their Wits.

RC (MHi:Warren-Adams Coll.); addressed: "Hon. James Warren Esqr Paymaster of the American Forces   Watertown"; docketed: "Mr. J: A Lettr Octr. 19. 1775 X."

[1] MS torn here. The reference remains obscure.

To James Warren

Dear Sir   Octr. 20. 1775

Can The Inhabitants of North America *live* without foreign Trade?

There is Beef and Pork, and Poultry, and Mutton and Venison and Veal, Milk, Butter, Cheese, Corn, Barley, Rye, Wheat, in short every Species of Eatables animal and Vegetable in a vast abundance, an immense Profusion. We raise about Eleven hundred Thousand Bushells of Corn, yearly more than We can possibly consume.

The Country produces Provisions of all Kinds, enough for the sustenance of the Inhabitants, and an immense Surplusage.

We have Wood and Iron in plenty. We have a good Climate as well as a fertile Soil.

But Cloathing. If instead of raising Million Bushells of Wheat for Exportation, and Rice, Tobacco, naval stores, Indigo, Flaxseed, Horses, Cattle, &c Fish, Oyl, Bone, Potash &c &c &c the Hands now employed in raising Surplusages of these Articles for Exportation, were employed in raising Flax and Wool, and manufacturing them into Cloathing, We should be cloathed comfortably.

We must at first indeed Sacrifice Some of our Appetites Coffee, Wine, Punch, sugar, Molasses, &c and our Dress would not be So elegant—Silks and Velvets and Lace must be dispensed with. But these are Trifles in a Contest for Liberty.

But is there Temperance, Fortitude and Perseverance enough among the People to endure Such a Mortification of their Appetites Passions and Fancies? Is not the Merchantile Interest comprehending Merchants, Mechanicks, Labourers So numerous, and So complicated with the landed Interest, as to produce a general Impatience and Uneasiness, under Restrictions So severe?

By a total Cessation of Commerce, [shall we not drive?] away our Mariners? Will they not go, [to other?] maritime Nations, the French, the Spaniards the Dutch? or which is worse will they not go to England, and on Board of British Men of War?

Shall We not lose a large Property in Navigation which will rot by the Wharves?

On the other Hand if We give Liberty Trade, will not most of our Vessells be Seized? Perhaps all but those of the Tories who may be priviledged.

RC (MHi:Warren-Adams Coll.); addressed: "Hon. James Warren Esq Paymaster of the American Army Watertown pr Favr of Messrs Folwell and Hart"; docketed: "Mr J: A Octr 20 1775." Small tear in MS.

To James Warren

Dr sir   Octr. 20. 1775

The Bearer of this is John McPherson Esq.[1] He is a Genius—an old Sea Warriour, Nine or ten Times wounded in Sea Fights.

He has a son in the Service—Aid de Camp to Schuyler—a very sensible Man.

Of Mr. McPhersons Errand to the Camp ask no Questions and I will tell you no false News. It will make a Noise, in Time—but for the present for Gods sake let not a Word be said.

I hope all our Friends who have Opportunity will show him Respect.

RC (MHi:Warren-Adams Coll.); addressed: "Hon James Warren Esq Watertown favoured by John McPherson Esq."; docketed: "Mr J: A Lettr Octr. 20. 1775."

[1] On 20 Oct. the congress sent McPherson to Cambridge to consult with Gen. Washington. He was the originator, according to a JA Diary entry, of a plan to "take or burn every Man of War, in America." At the camp, Washington and others who heard the plan found it to be based on unsound principles and prevailed upon McPherson to return to Philadelphia to use his energies on row galleys. The exact nature of the plan remained a secret, for those who were given its details took an oath not to divulge it (JA, *Diary and Autobiography*, 2:176; JCC, 3:296, 300, 301; Washington, *Writings*, ed. Fitzpatrick, 4:71–72; Burnett, ed., *Letters of Members*, 1:238, notes; Clark, *Washington's Navy*, p. 65–66).

From James Warren

My Dear Sir   Watertown Octr. 20th: 1775

After an Interval much longer than I ever designed should take place, I now set down to write again. The Multiplicity of Business, and the Croud of Company here must be my Excuse, every Body either Eats, drinks or Sleeps in this House, and very many do all, so that for A week past I could get no opportunity to write Morning, Noon, or Night.

The Committee of Congress Arrived here last Sunday. Coll. Harrison went through Town without my seeing him. Doctr. Franklin, and Mr. Lynch stopped at Davis.[1] I waited on them, and they came over and drank Coffee with us. The next day I dined with them all at Head Quarters, and Yesterday they and the General Officers, and the Gentleman of Character from the Southward[2] on a Visit here were Entertained by the House at Coolidges[3] on the best Dinner we could get for them, Turtle, Codfish, &c. Every kind of Civility and mark of Respect is shewn them here, and if they don't leave us better satisfied than they came, to us, it will not be our faults. From the little Conversation I have had with them, which has been as much as could be got in A Croud, I presume they will. I am much pleased with them. Doctr. Franklin who I never saw before Appears venerable in the Characters of A Gentleman, A Phylospher, and Statesman. I think Mr. Lynch very Sensible, and Judicious, and all of them firmly Attached to the good Cause, and I flatter myself their Zeal will not be Abated by this Visit.

In my last Short Billet I forgot to Congratulate you on your Appointment to the Supream Bench of Justice here, and I Expect the first Seat, as no doubts are made of it tho' they are not yet ranked. Four only are Appointed, Mr. Adams, Mr. Cushing, Mr. Read, and Mr. Sergeant.[4] The Board voted by Ballot for those that should be Nominated and with the four mentioned voted Mr. Sever, but from his Diffidence &c he prevailed not to be Nominated. Where the Next Appointment will fall I can't tell. Some of Paines Friends had it in Contemplation to have him Nominated but gave it up after you was Appointed very naturally supposeing he could not be ranked before you, and he haveing previously declared to them that he would not serve in an Inferiour Station, as every Body must know he was your Superiour. I am told they have A design to Nominate him Kings Attorney; how far his Acceptance of that place is to be reconciled to his declaration you may Judge.[5] Lowel seems to stand no Chance, at least till he has served An Apprentiship in Purgatory.[6] This appointment if you Accept it will Cooperate with your Wishes Expressed in several Letters to Leave the Congress. Indeed we want you here for this and divers other Reasons, but how to be reconciled to your leaving the Congress I cant tell. I shall certainly when such An Event takes place loose some share of my Confidence in, and Reverence for that August Body. We have passed A Bill for the Judges Holding their Commissions qua[m]diu se Bene Gesserunt but could not Compleat their Independency by Established Salaries. As for the Town of Boston it Continues in the same Miserable Situation. A few deserters come out, and of late several of the Inhabitants have stole out in Boats Among the rest our Friend Hitchburne the Night before last.[7] One Man who got out last Night has Just called on me. He says one reason of their running all hazards to get out is the Threats of forceing them to take Arms. They all give the same general Account that fresh provisions are very scarce. 1/ sterling per pound and no vegetables, the meat Excessive poor, that the Troops have not been served with it but twice dureing the Summer and Fall, that their Duty is very severe and they Continue sickly about 1500 in the Hospitals, that they suppose Canada is in our Hands, and are not Elated with any certain Expectation of reinforcements. They are Apprehensive of An Attack— were hove into great Confusion A few Nights ago by Admiral Putnam[8] who went down into the Bay with our floating Batteries &c. and fired some Shott into the Town which Interrupted their Ball and the Acting of A Play they were then Engaged in and their repose for the Night.[9] A Misfortune Attended this Expedition, which Contributed to their relief, and cost us the loss of two Men Killed and six wounded. A Gun splitt in one of the Batteries, and destroyed her also.

Gage sailed about 10 days ago, and is Succeeded by Howe. Gill, Leach & Edess Son are out of Goal.[10] Lovel still remains. It is said he refuses to come out but I doubt that. Several Armed Vessels are fixing by the General, and we have passed a Bill to Encourage Individuals to fix out others.[11] We have Just received an Account that they have been Canonadeing Falmouth Casco Bay, and that Wallace the Pirate at Newport has Insisted on the Removal of the Troops from Rhode Island, or he will destroy Newport, and shewn Instructions to the Committee there to destroy four Towns, Among which are Plymouth and Machias, the others I cant learn. This account the Govr. Cook has Just received.[12]

Please to tell Coll. Hancock I have the Honour to be ranked A damned Rebel with him. Upon hearing we were Concerned in a

Brigantine Bound to London the beginning of Sepr. they sent out A Cruiser on purpose for her, took her, Carryed her in, Condemned her and Cargo and ordered them sold. Our Accounts or rather the delay of them has given me Infinite pain. We are determined to Exert ourselves and prepare them as soon as possible. In the meantime shall forward you An Application which tho a Lumping one is not perhaps far from the Truth.[13] I wish it may have a favourable Reception. It is Impossible to describe the field of Business before us, rendered still more difficult and Embarrassing by the Multitude of New questions out of the common road. When are we to see the Resolves upon which is Grounded the Credit of your Bills. The Misers will soon be started upon that question.

I will thank you for the Establishment of my office. You wrote me it was 100 dollars per mo. Coll. Hancock had every other Establishment here but that. Our army are in much the same state they have been for some time past, as vigorous Spirited as ever, and more healthy than they have been, well secured by Impenetrable Lines. So far we are prepared for the defensive. When we are to be so for the offensive I know not. I suppose that depends much on haveing A large quantity of a certain Article with which we have never Yet Abounded.[14] We have no News from Coll. Arnold since he left Norridgwalk.[15] I flatter myself he is before this in Quebeck, where are large quantities of warlike Stores not less than 10,000 barrels powder. They would be A grand Acquisition but I can hardly hope that they will be so stupid as not to take care to prevent it by setting them A float. We have no late News from St. Johns. We begin to grow Impatient.

The 21st: The Conference I am told is to be finished this Day. I know little about it. There seems to be such a reservedness among those concerned here, that my pride wont permit me to Ask many Questions. By the way the Committee of Council are Coll. Otis, Mr. Sever, and Mr. Spooner, to whom has since been Added Bowdoin, who lately came to Town and took his Seat at the Board. I believe your Committee were very soon Convinced that the Soldiers never had less wages.[16] The Bounty given on An Average last war, I suppose might be set at £8—sometimes we gave £12—tho at first less than £8—which will make at least 20/, per mo. to be Added to 36/, the wages then given. We now give them A Coat upon An Average about 24/, which will make 3/, to be Added to 40 s.[17] A Blanket they had in both Cases. It will from these facts be easy to Infer that they then had 13/, at least per mo. more than now.

I have given you before A minute detail of Churchs Affair. I have learnt that you are furnished with a Copy of the Letter or should not fail to send one. I am Told that he Continues with great Confidence or rather Impudence to Assert his Innocence and against Common Sense and the most flagrant Evidence to pretend he was serving his Country. This is Indeed Hutchinson like, Affronting to our Understandings. I have never seen him. I never wish to again. You know I hate an Apostate. I hate A Traitor. How he is to receive An Adequate Punishment is I suppose A question for your determination. I am sensible of the deficiencies in your Code of Laws and the Objections to *post Facto* Laws, but something must be done and he made An Example of, or the People will suppose us all Traitors and loose their Confidence in what we say or do. Our House are Adjusting the Ceremonies of proceeding in order to Expulsion, and there will end our Tether.

I believe it is time to think of Concludeing this Letter, or never Expecting you to wish for Another but before I do I must, and do thank you heartily and fervently for your several Letters received by Majr. Bayard, the Gentlemen of your Committee, and Yesterday by Mr. Mifflin. Tho you Communicate no Secrets, I can see and Taste the Traces of that Extensive System of policy which always mark your way and which I hope will be Adopted. Your Last[18] has lead me into a Sea so Extensive, and deep that my small Abilities have not yet been Able either to fathom the Bottom or descry the Shore, however I shall rally them and, if I have vanity enough to suppose I can, strike out one particle of Light on so Grand, and Important a Subject shall certainly Attempt it in my next which will soon follow this if Opportunity presents. In the mean time Your Maxim, "God Helps those who help themselves" recurs to mind. We are in a Storm and must make A Port. We must Exert ourselves in some of the ways you mention. I think we must have Trade and Commerce. I see no difficulty in Admitting it in our own Bottoms consistantly with the Association if Individuals will hazard their Interest and opening our Ports to foreigners, one or more. If you could see me at this Instant you would think that the Embarrassments, and hurry of Business on hand would by no means admit of discussions of this kind. The Great Objects some of us would wish to Confine our House to are, the Manufactureing salt Petre and fire Arms, the regulateing the Militia, and fixing out Armed Vessels. The first is in a good way in Connecticut. We have sent Doctr. Whiteing[19] there to learn the process and art, and since his return have directed him to Try the Experiment here. I am not able to Inform you of his Success. The next I think we shall succeed in. The two others are under Consideration, and a Bill for the last in great forwardness so far as relates to Individuals. We have a difficulty with regard to the Militia from A Construction in our House of your resolve giveing them A power to Appoint officers. I wish it could be Explained.[20]

The 22d. We have Just heard that the Pirates on the Eastern Shore have destroyed two thirds of Falmouth burnt down, and have orders to destroy every Sea Port from Boston to Pemmaquid.[21] This is savage and Barbarous in the highest stage. What can we wait for now. What more can we want to Justifie any Step to take, Kill, and destroy, to refuse them any refreshments, to Apprehend our Enemies, to Confiscate their Goods and Estates, to Open our Ports to foreigners, and if practicable to form Alliances &c. &c.

Hitchburne was to see me last Evening. He seems distressed to Approve his Conduct to us relative to the Letters—very little of a publick kind can I learn from him more than we have from Others. He says they dread and Apprehend the Erecting Batteries on Dochester Hill, and Noddles Island. The first will drive them from their Lines on the Neck, and the other make it Impossible for Ships to Lay in the Harbour I mean above the Castle. I wish and hope we may be able to Effect it.

One peice of good News I had like to have forgot. A Vessel is arrived at Sheepscot, with a very Considerable quantity of Powder, Cannon and Arms. I believe she belongs to the Massachusetts Bay Colony. I shall Endeavour to see and form a Judgment of your Plan as soon as I can procure the Chart.[22] The Row Gallics you have at Philadelphia may be very serviceable in smooth water but if I am rightly Informed would not do in a Sea. No doubt such might be Constructed as would but I am Inclined to think that our common Armed Vessels, especially as we can be so superiour in Men, and are more used to them will Answer the purpose better, if we choose such as sail well.

I am sensible of the Importance of the question you propose about the Government of Canada. It is indeed a Curious Problem, and I am glad it is in such good hands. I never Expected you would derive any Advantages from the Committees you mention. The Spirit of Indolence is too prevalent.

There is in the western parts of this Province a Lead Mine of 3 Miles in length which Affords one half pure Lead. It is said the Country abounds with Sulphur. We want Nothing but salt petre. I trust Providence will give us that. I cannot Inclose you any of Mother Drapers Papers.[23] They are very Scarce. I think I have not seen one since that I Inclosed you. I shall Endeavour however to procure you one or two Curiosities of a like kind and Inclose without any Comment, tho' I feel somewhat Inclined to it.

Now please to Recollect, and say if you ever received or read so random a Letter before. If I thought there was occasion to produce Evidence of the Confidence I place in you I should think of this for one.

Mrs. Adams has not yet made us a Visit to Watertown. We suppose the weather has prevented. I believe and hope that She and Family are well. I have no Letter from her to Inclose. Mrs. W is here and to my great Comfort, and Consolation aiding and Supporting me in my daily Labours, for the publick Good, and Joins with me in every Wish for your Happiness. I am Yr. Friend, JW

My regards to all Friends. I would write to some of them if I could. I will write to my good Friend Mr. Adams if possible.

RC (Adams Papers); docketed in three places: "Warren   Octr. 20 1775."

[1] Probably a tavern in Watertown.

[2] Jonathan Mifflin.

[3] That is, by the House of Representatives at Coolidge's tavern in Watertown.

[4] The Council made these nominations on 11 Oct. (M–Ar:Executive Council Records, 17:128). Perez Morton officially notified JA of his appointment as chief justice in a letter of 28 Oct. (below). Although JA intended soon afterward to assume his judicial duties, he could not get free of responsibilities in the congress. He resigned the post in Feb. 1777 (JA, *Works*, 3:25, note). The other justices named with JA at this time were William Cushing, William Read, and Nathaniel Peaslee Sargeant.

[5] Actually Paine was named a justice of the Superior Court of Judicature but refused the office. His being ranked below JA exacerbated the hostility that had begun to grow up between the two men (Warren to JA, 5 Nov., below; Sibley-Shipton, *Harvard Graduates*, 12: 474–475).

[6] John Lowell (1743–1802), who had been thought by many whigs to be lukewarm to the cause. See the characterization of him in JA, *Diary and Autobiography*, 1:299–300.

[7] Benjamin Hichborn, the bearer of JA's intercepted letters, who had been imprisoned on Adm. Graves' flagship, the *Preston*, in Boston Harbor (Sibley-Shipton, *Harvard Graduates*, 17:37–38).

[8] Gen. Israel Putnam's reputation for impulsive, almost heedless action, ashore or afloat, probably led Warren to bestow the rank of "admiral."

[9] On 17 Oct. (*Boston Gazette*, 23 Oct.).

[10] John Gill, printer of the *Boston Gazette* with Benjamin Edes, John Leach, and Peter Edes.

[11] A bill on armed vessels was originally proposed on 9 Oct. in response to a resolve of the congress of 18 July permitting each colony to make whatever preparation it wished to protect itself from British depredations. It became law on 1 Nov. with the concurrence of the Council (JCC, 2:189; Mass., *House Jour.*, 1775–1776, 2d sess., p. 151, 217) .

[12] Nicholas Cooke, at this time governor of Rhode Island. Capt. James Wallace of the *Rose* made a business of harassing Newport traders (David S. Lovejoy, *Rhode Island Politics and the American Revolution*, Providence, 1958, p. 183, 185; *Boston Gazette*, 16 Oct.).

[13] See General Court to Massachusetts Delegates, 24 Oct. (below).

[14] An immediate guess is that Warren refers to gunpowder, but a few lines later without any reticence he mentions how important it would be to get powder from Quebec. Warren may be referring

to independence. Compare Warren to JA, 20 June, note 5 (above).

[15] Norridgewock, Maine, in 1775 the last settlement on the Kennebec River at which Arnold's force could stop before it set off into the wilderness for its attack on Quebec.

[16] The proper pay for army privates had long been an issue in the congress, where many southerners were apparently convinced that New England paid too high wages to enlisted men and too low to officers. Presumably the pay question was one of the major concerns of Franklin, Lynch, and Harrison, the committee from the congress. See JA to Elbridge Gerry, 18 June (above).

[17] These figures are based on eight months' service in the year, since campaigning in the winter months was very rare.

[18] That is, JA's letter of 7 Oct. (above).

[19] William Whiting (1730–1792) of Great Barrington, who apparently was the Massachusetts expert on the method for making saltpeter. He probably wrote the recipe for its manufacture that appeared in the *Boston Gazette*, 23 Oct., and he furnished an appendix for the General Court's republication of the congress' *Several Methods of Making Salt-petre*, Watertown, 1775 (Evans,

No. 14585). For a biographical sketch, see Stephen T. Riley, "Dr. William Whiting and Shays' Rebellion," AAS, *Procs.*, 2d ser., 66 (1956):119–166.

[20] The issue was whether the Council needed to consult the House on the appointment of militia officers. In its resolves of 18 July, the congress suggested that officers above the rank of captain be appointed by assemblies, but the advice of the congress on constituting government in Massachusetts seemed to leave regulation of the militia, as well as all other matters, as it had been under the charter, the governor's powers, including appointment of militia officers of high rank, being exercised by the Council (JCC 2:83–84, 188; Council to Massachusetts Delegates, 11 Nov., below). For JA's view, see his letter to James Otis, 23 Nov. (below).

[21] For contemporary accounts of the burning of Falmouth (Portland, Maine), see the *Boston Gazette*, 23 and 30 Oct., and Nathan Rice to JA, 21 Oct. (below). For a later account, see William Willis, *The History of Portland*, facsim. 1865 2d edn., Portland, Maine, 1972, p. 516–524.

[22] The plan to block up the harbor sketched in JA's letter of 8 Oct. (above).

[23] That is, the *Massachusetts Gazette*.

To James Warren

Dear Sir   Octr. 21. 1775

I believe I shall surfeit you with Letters, which contain nothing, but Recommendations of Gentlemen to your Attention, especially as you have So many important affairs to take up all your Time and Thoughts.

But the Bearers, are Gentlemen, who come so well recommended to me that I could not refuse my self the Pleasure of giving them an opportunity of Seeing my Friend Warren, of whom you must know I am very proud.

The Name of one of them is John Folwell, the other Josiah Hart, each of them a Captain of a Company of Militia in the County of Bucks in this Province. Mr. Joseph Hart the Father of one of them has exerted himself with much Success in procuring Donations for Boston.

These Travellers visit the Camp from the best Motive that of gaining Knowledge in the military Art by Experience, that their Country may have the Use of it, whenever there shall be an opportunity.[1]

You will greatly oblige them by giving them a Letter to General Thomas, and by introducing them to such Persons and Places as will best answer the honest and usefull End they have in View.

I could wish them as well as other Strangers introduced to H. Knox and young Josiah Waters,[2] if they are any where about the Camp. These young Fellows if I am not mistaken would give strangers no contemptible Idea of the military Knowledge of Massachusetts in the sublimest Chapters of the Art of War.

Salt Petre is certainly making in considerable Quantities in several Places. I wish to know what success Dr. Whiting has.[3]

You wonder, that certain *Improprieties* are not felt. Well you may. But I have done finding fault. I content myself with blushing alone, and mourning in Secret the Loss of Reputation our Colony Suffers, by giving Such *Samples* of her Sons to the World. Myself, remember the worst Sample of all. Pray change it.[4]

RC (MHi:Warren-Adams Coll.); addressed: "Hon. James Warren Esqr Speaker of the House Watertown Per Favr Messrs Follwell and Hart"; above the address: "J.A."; docketed: "Mr. J: A: Lettr Octr. 21. 1775."

[1] On this date JA also addressed to William Tudor a letter of introduction for the two men. The only significant additional information in it is the following: "The Continental association is most rigidly and Sacredly observed, throughout the Continent in all material Branches of it. Not a Vessell puts to Sea any where" (MHi:Tudor Papers).

[2] Henry Knox, later in charge of Washington's artillery (*DAB*), and Capt. Josiah Waters, who helped direct the construction of fortifications near Cambridge after the Battle of Bunker Hill (William Heath, *Memoirs*, ed.

William Abbatt, N.Y., 1901, p. 16).

[3] See Warren to JA, 20 Oct., note 19 (above).

[4] JA is referring to an earlier exchange between the two on the impropriety of Hancock's conduct. The reference to *"Samples"* is to the intercepted letter of Benjamin Harrison to Washington. In concluding, JA asks again that he be relieved of his congressional post (JA to Warren, 19 Sept.; Warren to JA, 1 Oct.; JA to Warren, 30 Sept. [calendar entry], all above).

To James Warren

Dear Sir   Octr. 21. 1775

We must bend our Attention to Salt Petre. We must make it. While B. is Mistress of the Sea, and has so much Influence with foreign Courts, We cannot depend upon a Supply from abroad.

It is certain that it can be made here because it is certain that it has been formerly and more latterly. Dr. Graham of White Plains in the Colony of New York told me, that he has made Some thousands of Pounds Weight, many years ago, by Means of a German Servant whom he bought and found to be good for nothing else.

Messrs. De Witts, one of Windham the other of Norwich have made a considerable Quantity, a sample of which has been shown me by Coll. Dyer, and they have made a large Collection of Materials for making more.

Mr. Wisner of New York,[1] informs me that his son has made a Quantity of very good, by the Method published by the Continental Congress.

Two Persons belonging to York Town in this Colony have made one hundred and twenty Weight, have received the Premium and are making more.

A Gentleman in Maryland made some last June from Tobacco House Earth.

Mr. Randolph our venerable President, affirms to me that, every planter almost in that Colony, has made it from Tobacco House Earth. That the Proscess is so simple that a Child can make it. It consists in nothing but making a Lixivium from the Earth which is impregnated with it, and then evaporating the Lixivium. That there is certainly discovered in Virginia a vast Quantity of the Rocks of salt Petre. That these are salt Petre Rocks he says all Chemists and Naturalists who have written agree. And that he was informed by many Gentlemen in Virginia, cautious, incredulous Men, of strict Honour and Veracity, that they have been to see the Rocks and tryed them and found them, by Experiment to be the very Rock of salt Petre.[2]

The old Gentleman in short, who is not credulous nor enthusiastical but very steady, solid, and grave, is as sanguine and confident as you can conceive, that it is the Easiest Thing in the World to make it, and that the Tobacco Colonies alone are sufficient to supply the Continent forever.

Every Colony My Friend must set up Works at the public Expense.

I am determined never to have salt Petre out of my Mind but to insert Some stroke or other about it in every Letter for the future. It must be had.

RC (MHi:Warren-Adams Coll.); addressed: "Hon. James Warren Esqr Speaker of the House Watertown"; docketed: "Mr. J: A Lettr Octr. 21. 1775."

[1] Henry Wisner (1720–1790), a delegate to the congress and a member of the committee for promoting the making of saltpeter (JCC, 3:296; DAB).

[2] On 26 Oct., because of the reported discovery of a mineral rich in saltpeter, the Virginia delegates were ordered to send an express to verify the discovery and bring back a sample (JCC,

3:307). The express went to Charles Lynch of Bedford co., Va., who, in two letters of 20 Nov., promised to produce the mineral in quantity and described his discovery on the "north East Side of Reed Iseland River" (Jefferson, *Papers*, 1:261–264).

From Nathan Rice

Dr. Sir   Camp in Cambridge Octr. 21t. 1775

I must acknowledge myself culpable, by a Breach of Orders, should not have neglected writing, but for an almost invincible Disorder in My Hands which has deprived me of their Use for two Months, am now almost recovered.

Many things have happened during the Season which I should have transmitted had it been in my Power. The State of our Army you doubtless Sir are as well acquainted with as myself, by Gentlemen more capable of informing you.

There have been Desertions both from the Enemy, and us; those from us were all Foreigners and of the Corps of Rifle-Men. It were to be wished none were in the Service of America, but Americans. In so large an Army as the American it cant be wondered at if there are some Judas's who will betray and Sell us; some we have found, one in an especial Manner whom I thought the best of our Frinds, has forfeited the Character. Can it be possible Sir that the great Patriotick Dr. Church could be guilty of so great Treachery, how are Men lead from their True Intrest by the False Charms of Riches and Honor. Who can we trust or confide in? Our Dependence is on that honorable Assembly of which Sir you are a Member, our Eyes are to you as to the Fathers of the People and from you we hope for Salvation.

We wait with great Impatience for News from Quebec. The Success of our Arms there will be of the utmost Importance to us, as doubtless there are large Magazines from whence we may have the one thing needful.

Our Navy has not in all Respects been so prosperous as I could wish, our Floating Batteries last Week went down the River in Order to give the Enemy a few Shot into Boston, meaning at least to interrupt their Evening Diversion, it being their first Assembly Night for the Season. Capt. Ayres[1] who commanded gave them a Dozen or fourteen with a very good Discretion and Execution as we have since learned, one entering the Chamber of Doctor Canner; another passing through 20 Tents on the Common, Several entering their Hospital &c. At length either through Badness of Mettle or Carelessness in loading, one of the Cannon burst which killed one of our Men, wounded several slightly, split of[f] a plank in the Battery between Wind and Water; by which She filled. The Water being shallow, the Guns were got out and She brought up the River.

The Enemies fireing on Bristol you have doubtless heard of and News is just arrived in Camp, of their having burnt Part, the greatest Part, of Falmouth in Casco Bay, for its Non Compliance with their Requision for Provision &c. We have now no Mercy to expect from them, nothing but Fire and Sword; our Sea Port Towns must Fall Victims to their Rage.

I rejoice however to see none disheartened or discouraged. The Field now invite us. Husbandry smiles in the interior Parts. There we defy them, let them come if they dare, but by this Time they are Sensible we shall and will Fight. *When* the Hanoverians arrive I expect perilous Times, which by Accounts is soon to take place.

The Day after the honorable Committee from the Continental Congress arrived in Town, Part of our Brigade were under Arms and reviewed by them. The Brigade is composed entirely of Troops of our Province. Those Gentlemen will doubtless give you their [opinion] of us. Many Gentlemen think our Troops not inferior to those of other Colonies; altho many things have been said against us, little Animosities and Jealousies will arise in all Societies and Armies composed of various Corps's. I hope we shall act from more noble Motives than to suffer such Trifles to break our Union or disturb our internal Happiness: It cant be wondered at if among our Officers there should be some who do not fill their Posts with that Dignity and Honour which they ought; Our Colony Sir you are Sensible laboured under the greatest Calamities, Disadvantages in distributing their Commissions; done in the greatest Hurry and Confusion, and he that was popular obtained the Commissions; good sensible Men are not all Soldiers. The greatest Fault in our Troops is having bad Officers; I could wish in the next Inlistment we might be culled. Coll. Brewer was Yesterday dismissed the Service for Fraud.[2] I am Sr. with the greatest Respect yr. very humble Servant   Nathan Rice

RC (Adams Papers); addressed: "To John Adams Esqr in Philadelphia"; docketed: "Mr. Rice's Lettr Octr. 21. 1775"; minor tear at right edge of second page.

[1] Possibly Capt. John Ayers (Washington, *Writings*, ed. Fitzpatrick, 4:303, 304).

[2] Col. David Brewer of the 9th Regiment of Foot was court-martialed for drawing the pay for his son's commission as a lieutenant while the son remained on the farm, requisitioning too many blankets, and using troops to work his farm. Washington approved his sentence on 23 Oct. (same, 4:39–40).

To James Warren

Dear Sir   Octr. 24. [i.e. 23] 1775 [1]

I have only Time to acquaint you that Yesterday, that eminent American, and most worthy Man The Honourable Peyton Randolph Esqr. our first venerable President, departed this Life in an Apoplectic Fit. He was seized at Table having but a few Moments before set down with a good deal of Company to dinner. He died in the Evening without ever recovering his senses after the first stroke.

As this Gentleman Sustained very deservedly ONE of the first American Characters, as he was the first President of the united Colonies, and as he was universally esteemed for his great Virtues and shining Abilities, the Congress have determined to show his Memory and Remains all possible Demonstrations of Respect. The whole Body is to attend the Funeral, in as much Mourning as our Laws will admit. The Funeral is to be tomorrow. [2] I am the more pleased with this Respect on account of an Impropriety, which you know was unfelt. [3]

This venerable Sage, I asure you, since he has stood upon the same Floor with the rest of Us has rose in the Esteem of all. He was attentive, judicious, and his Knowledge, Eloquence, and classical Correctness showed Us the able and experienced Statesman and senator, whereas his former station had in a great Measure concealed these and showed Us chiefly the upright and impartial Moderator of Debate.

You would have wondered more at the Want of [sensi?]bility which you remarked if you had [been] here and seen, the Difference.

Mr. Randolph was as firm, stable and consistent a Patriot as any here. The loss must be very great to Virginia in Particular and the Continent in general.

I sometimes wonder that a similar Fate does not befall more of the Members. Minds so engaged and Bodies so little exercised are very apt to fall.

This goes by Mr. Gawen Brown. [4]

RC (MHi:Warren-Adams Coll.); addressed: "Hon. James Warren Esqr Speaker of the House   Watertown   favoured by Mr. Gawen Brown Jnr"; docketed: "Mr. J: A: lettr   Octr. 24th 1775."

[1] JA states that Peyton Randolph died "yesterday"; accordingly, his letter should have been dated 23 Oct. That Randolph died on the 22d is confirmed by Samuel Ward, who refers to his death as occurring on Sunday evening (*DAB*; Ward to Henry Ward, 24 Oct., Burnett, ed., *Letters of Members*, 1:240).

[2] The funeral was held on the 24th, further evidence that JA misdated his letter (*JCC*, 3:302–304).

[3] See JA's first letter to Warren, 21 Oct., note 4 (above).

[4] Boston   clock-   and   watchmaker,

father of the portrait painter Mather Brown. Why JA tacked on "Jnr" to Brown's name in the address is unclear. Brown had a grandson named after him, the son of John, but no record has been found of a "Junior" (MHS, *Procs.*, 46 [1912–1913]:250; 47[1913–1914]: 32, 289–291; Hamilton Andrews Hill, *History of the Old South Church, Boston 1669–1884*, 2 vols., Boston, 1890, 2: 93–94 and note).

From William Heath

Dear Sir   Camp at Cambridge Octr. 23rd: 1775

I have to acknowledge the Honor of the Receipt of yours of the 5th. Instant, and shall think myself fortunate if by writeing or Otherwise, I can in the least Contribute to the Good of my Country, or Advantage of my Native Colony.

It is not Surpriseing that Jealousies do Subsist, and that Misrepresentations have been made, respecting our Colony by *some*, But Such will be despised, by the Wise the Generous and Brave, who will be rightly Informed before they Censure.

A publication in one of the Connecticut Papers Some Time Since, ascribed the Honor of the noble Resistance made at Bunkers Hill on the 17th. of June last, to a Number of Officers by name, belonging to that Colony,[1] Some of Whom as I am Informed were not on the Hill, Whilst other Brave Officers belonging to our Colony, such as Colonels Prescott, Brewer, Gardner, Parker &c. who nobly fought, and Some of whom fell, are not even mentioned. But this Account was detested by the Brave Putnam and others of that Colony.

There are in the Massachusetts Regiments Some few Lads and Old men, and in Several Regiments, Some Negroes. Such is also the Case with the Regiments from the Other Colonies, Rhode Island has a Number of Negroes and Indians, Connecticut has fewer Negroes but a number of Indians. The New Hampshire Regiments have less of Both. The men from Connecticut I think in General are rather stouter than those of either of the other Colonies, But the Troops of our Colony are Robust, Agile, and as fine Fellows in General as I ever would wish to see in the Field. We have many Good Officers also, altho Some few have been Disgraced, viz Colos. Gerrish, and Mansfield, and Major Gridley for Backwardness in Duty on the 17th. of June. Some few also have been Guilty of Peculation.

On the 15th. Instant Doctor Franklin, Mr. Lynch, and Colo. Harrison, Arrived at our Camp, the next morning Four Regiments of my Brigade (the other Two being Chiefly on Command, at Medford, Chelsea, Malden &c.) were Under Arms and Reviewed by those Gentlemen. These Regiments are Entirely of our own Colony; and those

Gentlemen can Inform you how much Inferior they were, either in appearance or Discipline to the other Troops which they Saw.

But why should we tell of the Troops of this or that Colony, we are now One; and Jealousy and Misrepresentation should be banished. In every Colony doubtless there are Some bad mixed with the Good. The Riflemen So much Boasted of by many before their arrival, have been Guilty of as many Disorders as any Corps in Camp, and there has been more Desertions to the Enemy from them, then from the whole Army Besides, perhaps Double. But these were Foreigners, and there is in that Corps as Faithfull and Brave Officers and Soldiers as in any Other. It would be Ungenerous to Characterize the Troops of any Colony, from the Conduct of a few Scounderels. In short we have a Fine Army, and no Colony has Reason to be ashamed of their own Troops as a Body, altho they may as to Some Individuals. Men who Judge wisely will not Expect *Suddenly* that Regularity in an Army (may I not say) Raised almost from Chaos, that is to be found in an Army of Veterans. We are in a fine way, one thing only is wanting, had we been furnished with it, we should e're this have presented you Some pleasing Laurels of victory. But here I must Close, requesting you to present my Best Regards to my Honor'd Friends, Hancock, Cushing, Adams, and Pain. I am your Engaged Brother in the Cause of America and very Humble Servt   W Heath

RC (Adams Papers); addressed: "To John Adams Esqr.   at Philadelphia"; docketed: "Gen. Heath.   Octr. 23. 1775."

[1] A letter to the printer signed "A Friend to Truth" (*Connecticut Courant*, 31 July). Heath's complaint is a good example of provincial sensitivity, for the letter obviously means to call attention to Connecticut officers "whose conduct in the battle . . . has not been publickly noticed." The writer begins by naming three officers mentioned in the New London newspapers, but he wants to celebrate the names of all who dis- tinguished themselves and hopes that justice will be done to others as soon as their names become known. Unfortunately, it is only by implication that the letter refers solely to Connecticut officers, and unfortunately, too, he begins with a panegyric to Gen. Putnam, who a number of Massachusetts men felt had already been given more than his due.

From Samuel Osgood Jr.

[23 Oct. 1775][1]

Without apologizing for interrupting you a short Moment I have to inform you that Genl. Frye not receiving any Intelligence respecting himself, and being informed that Genl. Washington had received Word from the Honorable Congress that the Appointment of another

Brigadier was suspended for the present, he left us about the 10th of Octr. unable to account for his not having any particular Intelligence. But when he arriv'd at Cambridge the Mistery was partly unfolded by Mr. Mifflin who had, in a Letter received a Paragraph to this Purport "In Congress we have had some warm Words respecting a Brigadier General. A southern Gentleman was put up but did not obtain some of the southern Gentlemen themselves not voting for him," from which Genl. Frye draws this Conclusion "that for Peace and Unitys sake our worthy Members would not push the Matter; after a short Suspension of the Affair a more favourable Moment might offer itself." Thus it stands in Genl. Fryes Mind who doubts not your Inclination to serve him if it may be done consistent with his above Inference otherwise he desires it not.[2]

The Army is in good Spirits and enjoys unusual Health: prospered and protected by Heaven as we have hitherto been can we but succeed when we have drawn the Sword from the purest Principles of Virtue, to defend the noblest of Causes? Forbid the Tho't that we should sink and Tyranny be indomitable.

If the Cloud thikens with impenetrable Darkness we shall have the Pleasure to fight in the Shade.

New England is the Nusery of brave and hardy Men. She alone Stems the intended rapid Progress of our unnatural Enemy, as yet, and from the Specimen we have had of the Riffle Men I can but conclude she *must* do it. Genl. Lee wishes they were all in Boston. Genl. Gates says before we have any Action let the Rifle Men be removed to a Distance from the Camp. A Number of them have deserted and gone over to the Enemy.

With the Assistance of the Wealth of the southern Governments the continental Congress will long support in the Field a numerous and brave Army. I am not insensible, that not a Tory Province upon the Continent that has been by Appearance so tho'roughly contemned as ours. It is hard to see it trampled upon by her Sisters, when every Circumstance serves to corroborate the mental Evidence that not one of them all would have received the Shock and bore it with unshaken and unyielding Bravery as ours has done.

But Sir, the Cause we are engaged in peremptorily forbids all Jealousy which is the King Demon of all Tormentors. It is an indisputable Fact that our southern Brethren have not annexed the same Ideas to the Word Liberty as yet that we have neither have we annexed the same to the Words, Honor, Politeness and Dominion which has not a Tendency to make us the most cordial and unreserved Friends: But

I hope all these Things will be winked out of Sight till Peace is established upon a solid Basis.

The famous Waters Machine from Connecticutt is every Day expected in Camp. It must unavoidably be a clumsy Business as its Weight is about a Tun. I wish it might succeed [and] the Ships be blown up beyond the Attraction of the Earth for it is the only Way or Chance they have of reaching St. Peters Gate.[3]

I am, Sir, extremely sorry it was not in Genl. Wards Power to treat the Honorable Committee from Congress with those Marks of Friendship and Politeness which would have afforded him much Satisfaction. In not doing which he cannot be tho't deficient. Very soon after their Arrival he had the Pleasure to wait upon them at the General's and asked them separately and repeatedly to afford him an Opportunity of waiting upon them at Roxbury. Genl. Ward was again called to Cambridge before they had finished their Business and then told Genl. Washington that by his other Invitation he meant to have them dine with him and renewed the Request (Genl. Washington and Family also I suppose). His Excellency told Genl. Ward after the Business was finished he would give him Intelligence of it. The Day they had about compleated their affairs I was at his Excellency's and heard him inform the Gentlemen that they were to dine with Gen. Ward the next Day. After this the Connecticutt Officers in Camp at Roxbury sent an Invitation to his Excellency and the Honorable Committee to dine with them upon Turtle the next Day. Compliments were returned and the Invitation accepted. Genl. Ward told Colo. Harrison and Mr. Lynch after they came to Roxbury he expected them to dine with him: they both told him they did not know but they were to dine with him till they had got to Roxbury. They took the Invitation to be the same. The next Day they were to set out upon their Journey.

I should be very unwilling to suppose that it was designed to place Genl. Ward in such a Light to the Honorable Committee as to make him appear deficient in Point of good Manners. These Affairs give no small Pain and Uneasiness. Was he sure the Conduct was pointed he would choose to Leave the Service. For before this his Tho'ts were employed upon the Subject of Resignation by Reason of his Ill state of Health. The Service is very Burthensome But especially the two or three first Months since which Genl. Ward has never enjoyed scarcely a tolerable State of Health and I fear it will Occasion his Resignation sooner or later doubt not but he then laid the Foundation for those consequent Disorders which will long trouble him. His Health would not permit him to tarry now was not the Cause the best that ever any Person was engaged in (Vizt.) that of preserving for himself and Family the civil and sacred Rights and Priviledges which God and Nature have bestowed upon him, and not only so but infinitely more, those of a Country extensive and formed to flourish, however it may be marked out for the Rod of Chastisment and Life and Property may be sported with as Objects of little or no Value. But an immutable Enemy to Tyrants and tyrannical Measures he is willing to Sacrifice his own Peace and Quiet and devote himself to sufferings that others may not after him inherit Chains and Slavery. I am Sir your most obedient Humble Servt.,   Samuel Osgood junr.[4]

N.B. a Week after the Gentlemen arrived Genl. Ward received your Favor. His Ill State of Health will not permit him to write in Return[5] therefor, is much obliged to you for it.

P.S. Pardon me I did not expect to write half so much.

RC (Adams Papers); docketed: "Sam. Osgoods Letter Oct. 1775"; in a later hand, the insertion, "25th."

[1] Osgood refers to his letter of the 23d when he writes to JA on 4 Nov. (below).

[2] The attempt to appoint Joseph Frye a brigadier general aroused sectional rivalries that prevented a decision when his name first came up in Sept. 1775. Col. John Armstrong of Pennsylvania had equal support. Frye did not receive his appointment until 10 Jan. 1776; Armstrong had to wait until 1 March, when the congress selected six additional brigadier generals (JCC, 3:257; 4:47, 181; Burnett, ed., *Letters of Members*, 1:204, 307 and note).

[3] Osgood had probably heard about the American *Turtle*, a submarine built by David Bushnell (1742–1824) at Saybrook, Conn., from Benjamin Franklin, who had inspected the vessel on his way north with the committee from the congress. Bushnell began building it soon after Lexington and Concord with the apparent intention of using it

against the British in Boston Harbor. By October construction and testing had been completed, but minor problems, particularly a means of lighting the interior when the vessel was submerged, prevented it from being ready for action until after Boston had been evacuated. It was tried out in 1776 and 1777 in New York and Philadelphia, but difficulty in attaching the mine that it carried to the bottoms of British ships caused it to fail. Bushnell then gave up his project, which had produced the first workable submarine (*DAB*; Frederick Wagner, *Submarine Fighter of the American Revolution*, N.Y., 1963, p. 1–47; Dr. Benjamin Gale to Silas Deane, 9, 22 Nov., 7 Dec., and 1 Feb. 1776, Conn. Hist. Soc., *Colls.*, 2 [1870]:315–318, 322–323, 333–335, 358–359).

[4] Osgood was an aide to Gen. Ward (*DAB*).

[5] But see the next document. Ward's letter from JA has not been found.

From Artemas Ward

Sir   Roxbury Camp October 23. 1775

Yesterday I Received your favour of the fifth Instant,[1] a week after the arival of Mr. Lynch, although I had been twice in his company before. I have indeavoured to treat the Gentlemen Committe with Decency and Politeness, I invited them to Roxbury twice. The day after I invited them Mr. Lynch came to Roxbury, but did not dine with me, he being Ingaged to dine with Genl. Washington as he said. The next day I was at Cambridge, and mentioned to Washington his and the Committee dining with me. He answered they could not untill they had finished their business and he would let me know when they would come and dine with me. Major Osgood informs me Genl. Washington told the Committee that I depended on their dining with me this day. This day Genl. Gates wrote to the field officers of the Connecticut forces, that the Committee did accept their invitation to dine with them, and accordingly came and dined with them. When they came I informed them I expected they would have dined with me, they said they thought till then, that accepting of the one invitation, was accepting the other; that is they were one and the same invitation. I afterward invited them to dine with me tomorrow. They told me if they did not set out on their Journey they were Ingaged to dine with Genl. Putnam. I think I have given a true state of facts, and now Judge whither, I have been deficient in inviting, and whither I have not been Ill treated. What would not some men do, to make this Colony and the Inhabitants thereof appear contemptible?

Octr. 30. 1775

They do not boast so much of the Riflemen as heretofore. Genl. Washington has said he wished they had never come. Genl. Lee has damned them and wished them all in Boston. Genl. Gates has said, if any capital movement was about to be made the Riflemen must be moved from this Camp. I am in great concern about the raising a new army, for the Genious of this people is different from those to the southward. Our people are Jealous, and are not Inclineable to act upon an Implisit faith, they Chuse to see and Judge for themselves. They remember what was said of them by some that came from the Southward last summer, which makes them backward in Inlisting or manifesting a willingness to Inlist. Its my opinion we should have began a month ago to Ingage men for another Campain. If the present armys time should be out, and no other secured I fear the Enemy will take advantage thereof. I wish Genl. Frye might be provided for. I think him a good man for the service, and am very sorry he has not been provided for by the Continental Congress before this time. Some have said hard things of the officers belonging to this Colony, and despised them, but I think as mean as they have represented them to be, there has been no one action with the enemy, which has not been conducted by an officer of this Colony, except that at Chelsea, which was conducted by Genl. Putnam.[2]

I am this moment informed, that Major Tupper of this Colony and off [of] the army hath seized two Vessels at the Vineyard loaded with oyl, Belonging to Holmes, and Coffin in Boston two Tories, and has Carried them into Plymouth he having been dispatched for that purpose. He now desires to resign his command in the army, and take the command of one of those vessels, when fitted out for a Privateer.[3]

You mentioned the scene is thickning, I hope as that thickens our deliverance approaches. I have no doubt, but we shall finally come off victorious, if we continue persevering. There has not been one action with the enemy, without a signal appearance of Divine Providence in our favour. If so what reason can we have to doubt of sucess more than when we began.

I should have wrote you before, but was prevented by Indisposition and frequent avocations of a pulick nature, and probable you may think I had better have spent my time some other way than in writing the above. I hope you will excuse all the foregoing Inaccuracies and honor me with a line, in the mean time I rest your affectionate friend and humble Servant, Artemas Ward

RC (Adams Papers); docketed: "Gen. Ward. Oct. 23. 1775."

[1] Not found, but it was probably similar to those sent on this same date to Gens. Heath and Thomas.

[2] The reference is to the burning of the British schooner *Diana* in Chelsea Creek in May. Convinced that the British had suffered heavy losses in trying to save the ship as it grounded on a bar, American letter-writers hailed a significant victory. Actual British losses were negligible (French, *First Year*, p. 190–193).

[3] On 20 Oct. Washington ordered Maj. Benjamin Tupper to seize two vessels, probably owned by Benjamin M. Holmes and John Coffin, that were then at Martha's Vineyard on their way to Boston with supplies for the British Army. Tupper's use of one of the ships for privateering was made conditional upon its being fit to sail at once for a period of four to six weeks. Tupper was later promoted to colonel in the Continental Army (*Naval Docs. Amer. Rev.*, 2:539, 608).

From Joseph Ward

Sir Camp at Roxbury 23 Octr. 1775

I have been long waiting for an opportunity to communicate some intelligence worthy of your notice, but nothing very important has taken place since you left the Camp; and every action with the Enemy has been published in the Newspapers, which has superceded the necessity of communicating those events by Letter. The general face of our public affairs both civil and military appear much as they have done for months past. By all the intelligence we receive from the *Tyrant Country*, it appears that the *Heathen still rage and the people imagine a vain thing*[1]—That they can enslave America; *but none of these things move us*, the Spirit of War and Liberty thrives by persecution, and I trust they will be invincible in this Country. I humbly conceive we have a glorious prospect before us notwithstanding the gathering Storm. We are yet in blossom, but ripen fast, and when we have done playing with petitions and making kites for George, I expect we shall exert our united vigour in a direct line to "Liberty Peace and Safety," and soon reach the summit of human happiness and glory.

That the united efforts of the free the brave and the hardy millions of independent Americans whose minds are enlightened and animated with the divine Spirit of Freedom, should ever be enslaved by British Tyrants is incredible among men! Nothing but the curse of Heaven (which we devoutly deprecate) can spread the cloud of despotism over the extensive region of America. *Fear* or *folly* only can produce our ruin; I am happy in believing that *these* do not dwell in the Great Council of America—but that Wisdom and Fortitude with a steady hand and persevering firmness will guide our political helm until we arrive at the haven of perfect Freedom.

I expect soon to hear that the Continental Congress have published the Confederacy of the Colonies—compleated the Republic of America —and formed a *commercial* Alliance with France and Spain. Such tidings will be musick in my ears, as I apprehend nothing short of such a plan will secure our Liberties; and if America should be enslaved it is probable freedom will expire thro the World. It is a great and a glorious Prize which the Americans contend for, *the happiness of all future ages, and the freedom of the World* as the Liberties of all Nations may in some degree be connected with ours.

I should not have taken the freedom to write to you, Sir, had not you condescended to request it,[2] and as I had no News to write, this is only to shew that I had not forgot my promise. I am, Sir, with the greatest Respect, yours &c.,   Joseph Ward[3]

P.S. I have had the pleasure of seeing the illustrious Doctor Franklyn, and the other American Worthies, who came from the honourable Continental Congress; we have endeavoured to pay them that respect which is due to such distinguished characters. As they are soon to set out for Philadelphia, I write in haste that my letter may go by this conveyance. Your candour, Sir, will make allowance for the inaccuracies in whatever I may write.

My best Regards to my honoured Friends the Members for this Colony. They, and the whole Congress, have the warmest good wishes, the highest esteem and confidence, and the fervent Prayers of all the wise and good in the circle of my acquaintance, and I trust through all America. The love and veneration of so great so patriotic so brave a people, Kings and Emperors may sigh for in vain. "I am not the most covetous of gold, and care not who my garments wear; but if to covet Honour, be a crime, I am the most offending soul alive!"

Henry. V.[4]

RC (Adams Papers); docketed: "Jo. Wards.   Oct. 23. 1775."

[1] Paraphrased from Psalms 2:1.
[2] JA's letter to Ward has not been found.
[3] Joseph Ward (1737–1812), Artemas Ward's second cousin once removed, was a schoolmaster, patriot, frequent contributor to newspapers, and correspondent with various Revolutionary leaders. Before the war began, Ward may not have been so strong a patriot as he seems here, for in 1772 and 1773, as the controversy over the Hutchinson letters was growing, he was corresponding with Lord Dartmouth with the hope of obtaining a position in the colonial administration. At the time of this letter, he was aide-de-camp and secretary to Gen. Ward (Charles Martyn, *Artemas Ward*, N.Y., 1921, p. 90–92; William Carver Bates, "Col. Joseph Ward, 1737–1812: Teacher, Soldier, Patriot," Bostonian Society, *Pubns.*, 1st ser., 4 [1907]:57–76).
[4] *Henry V*, Act IV, scene iii.

To James Warren

Dear Sir   Octr. 24. 1775

When it is Said that it is the Prerogative of omniscience to Search Hearts, I Suppose it is meant that no human sagacity, can penetrate at all Times into Mens Bosoms and discover with precise Certainty the secrets there: and in this Sense it is certainly true.

But there is a sense in which Men may be said to be possessed of a Faculty of Searching Hearts too. There is a Discernment competent to Mortals by which they can penetrate into the Minds of Men and discover their Secret Passions, Prejudices, Habits, Hopes, Fears, Wishes and Designs, and by this Means judge what Part they will act in given Circumstances for the future, and see what Principles and Motives have actuated them to the Conduct they have held, in certain Conjunctures of Circumstances which are passed.

A Dexterity and Facility of thus unravelling Mens Thought and a Faculty of governing them by Means of the Knowledge We have of them, constitutes the principal Part of the Art of a Politician.

In a Provincial Assembly, where We know a Mans Pedigree and Biography, his Education, Profession and Connections, as well as his Fortune, it is easy to see what it is that governs a Man and determines him to this Party in Preference to that, to this system of Politicks rather than another &c.

But here it is quite otherwise. We frequently see Phonomena which puzzle Us.

It requires Time to enquire and learn the Characters and Connections, the Interests and Views of a Multitude of Strangers.

It would be an exquisite Amusement, and high Gratification of Curiosity, this Same Mystery of Politicks, if the Magnitude of the Interests and Consequences did not interest us sometimes too much.[1]

RC (MHi:Warren-Adams Coll.); addressed: "To Mrs. Adams   Braintree To the Care of Coll Warren"; docketed by James Warren: "Mr. J: A Lettr Octr. 24. 1775."

The address is a mistake. Probably this letter is the one received by AA, read, and then returned to James Warren in her letter to Mercy Otis Warren of [ca. 5] Nov. In that, AA commented that she "could not comprehend how I came to have such a reply to a subject I had said very little upon" (*Adams Family Correspondence*, 1:322–324). Very likely JA addressed several letters on 24 Oct. and inadvertently repeated an address.

[1] This letter seems less a communication than a thoughtful coda to JA's letter to Warren of 24 [i.e. 23] Oct. (above), in which he remarks that it took some time before he got to know the several sides of Peyton Randolph.

From John Thomas

Sir   Roxbury Camp Octor. 24th. 1775

I Received your favour of the fifth Instant,[1] am Pleased to hear the Unanimity of the Colony's Increase, as the Salvation of our Country Depends on the United Efforts of the whole. Altho: our Number of men in the New England Colony's may be Sufficient to Repell any Force the Ministry may be able to Send; Yet the Expence of Such an Army as is Necessary to be kept up for that purpose, would be Intolerable for those Colony's Seperate.

I am Sorry to hear that any Prejudice Should take Place in any of the Southern Colony's with Respect to the Troops Raised in this; I am Certain the Insinuations you Mention are Injurious; if we Consider with what Precipitation we were Obliged to Collect an Army. The Regiments at Roxbury, the Privates are Equal to any that I Served with Last war, very few Old men, and in the Ranks very few boys, Our Fifers are many of them boys, we have Some Negros, but I Look on them in General Equally Servicable with other men, for Fatigue and in Action; many of them have Proved themselves brave, the Officers, the Greatest part of them Unexperienced, and in General not Equal being Unacquainted with Subordination, which to me was not Unexpected as they were Chosen by their Privates.

10. A REAL AMERICAN RIFLE MAN, 1776
See page xii

240

I would avoid all Reflection, or any thing that may Tend to give Umbridge, but there is in this Camp, from the Southward, A Number Called Riflemen, who are as Indifferent men as I ever Served with, their Privates, Mutinous and often Deserting to the Enemy, Unwilling for Duty of any kind, Exceedingly Vicious, And I think the Army here would be as well without as with them, but to do justice to their Officers, they are Some of them Likely men, but this Matter altho: Truth may not best go from me any further.

The two Gentlemen you Named to me,[2] I have had Some Acquaintance with, the first I take to be judicious, and has by Reading, Obtained a Theoretical Knowledge, in fortifications. I have been Pleased with Some of his Projections, but he has had no Opportunity of Practicing any great, as he doth not belong to the Army; but I have thought, had he Practised he would make as good a Figure as any that I am Acquainted with; here, As to Gunnery I blieve has not made that so much his Study; The Last Mentioned, I Apprehend has no great Understanding, in Either, any further than Executing or overseeing works, when Trased out, and by my Observations, we have Several Officers that are Equal or exceed him; the Next to Mr. Knox I Esteem one Lieut. Colo. Putnam,[3] who has Planed almost all our works, at Roxbury, and one Capt. Wadsworth[4] I should Prefer as the Next, for Executing, but I am Sensible we at Present are Dificient in Persons that Excell, in that Department; Colo. Gridley so famed I think falls much Short of my Expectations, [and] Appears to me to be Superanuated.[5]

Sir, you may think I make very free with Characters, but by your request, I have given myself Liberty; Supposeing to be in Confidence.

My Complements to the Honble. Mr. Hancock, Adams, Cushing, and Paine, &c. I am, Sir, with respect your most Obedient and very Hble. servt.,

John Thomas

RC (Adams Papers); addressed: "To The Honble. John Adams Esqr. Member of The Honble. Continental Congress at Philadelphia"; docketed: "Gen. Thomas   Oct. 24. 1775."

[1] Not found, but see JA to William Heath, 5 Oct., note 1 (above).

[2] Henry Knox and Josiah Waters.

[3] Rufus Putnam (1738–1824), an experienced engineer who was at this time in charge of the defensive works around Boston. Active in the American cause throughout the war, he was made a brigadier general by the congress in 1783 (DAB).

[4] Peleg Wadsworth (1748–1829), an engineer attached to Gen. Thomas. In Feb. 1776 he was appointed aide-de-camp to Gen. Ward (Sibley-Shipton, *Harvard Graduates*, 17:291–303).

[5] Richard Gridley, colonel of artillery and chief engineer of the American Army, was at this time 65 years old. He was soon removed from his artillery command and replaced by Henry Knox (DAB).

The General Court to the Massachusetts Delegates

[24 Oct. 1775]

The General Court of the Colony which you represent in Congress, now incloses you an application, made to your Honorable Assembly for a Grant of the sum therein mentioned: which application you will lay before said Congress or not, as you shall judge prudent.[1] The frequent calls this Colony has been obliged to attend to in support of the Army, together with those daily made for that purpose, renders it of the greatest importance to it, to have an immediate Grant of the Money applied for.[2] This Court therefore desires your Particular Care and attention in procuring the same, according to the best of your prudence and the true interest of your Constituents.

FC (M-Ar:Legislative Council Records, 33:288).

[1] These were the accounts which JA had been calling for since his letter to James Warren of 26 Sept. (above). They arrived in Philadelphia on 16 Nov. and consisted of two parts. The first was an itemized statement of drafts on the province treasurer made by the Provincial Congress, the Committee of Safety, the Committee of Supplies, and other bodies, which totaled £133,055 8s 3d. The amounts were certified by Henry Gardner as treasurer. The second, embodied in the General Court's letter to the congress, consisted of three sums: £65,680 in estimated wages to be paid to soldiers for service to 1 Aug., the date recommended by Gen. Washington; £16,220, the estimated cost of coats given to all enlistees; and £4,083 8s paid to soldiers defending the coastal settlements. These sums were not totaled, but they came to £85,983 8s, for a grand total of £219,038 16s 3d. Further, the General Court pointed out that it had not yet estimated the cost of removing persons from Boston (JCC, 3: 356; PCC, No. 65, I, f. 59–67).

[2] Lack of sufficient vouchers to support the claim of Massachusetts led the congress to vote only $443,333 1/3 in reimbursement (JCC, 3:402–403). In New England, lawful money meant six shillings to the dollar, or £130,000, as the sum the congress voted, even though Samuel Adams called it £133,000 (*Warren-Adams Letters*, 1:191).

To James Warren

Sir   Octr. 25th. 1775

A Method of collecting Salt Petre from the Air which is talked of here is this. Take of Lime and Ashes equal Quantities, and of horse dung a Quantity equal to both the Ashes and Lime, mix them together into a Mortar, with this Mortar and a Quantity of long Straw to keep it together build two Walls Eighteen Inches thick, and three feet high, about four feet asunder. Then make a Center and turn and [an?] Arch over cemicircularly from the Top of one Wall to that of the other, and this Arch may be made Eighteen Inches thick too. These Walls with the Arch over them, may be continued to any length you please. There must be a shed over it to keep off the Rain, and the Arch must be wett every Day with Urine. This, in summer, will collect so much salt Petre that an ounce may be extracted from every Pound of the Walls in three Months. In Winter it will make as fast provided you keep a Fire at one End of the Arch, that the Wind may blow the Fire and Smoke under the Arch, and keep it from freezing.

This is one Method as it is affirmed by Gentlemen here.

Sulphur, Nitre, and Lead We must have of our own. We must not depend upon Navigation for these. I wish the Committee of the General Court for Lead and Salt would transmit their Discoveries to me. I dont know whether you are one of that Committee or not.

Pray inform me if Obrian and Carghill[1] were or were not commissioned by some Vote of the general Court, and whether they cant be put into the Continental service. An order is gone to Genl. Washington to that Purpose if it can be done.

RC (MHi:Warren-Adams Coll.); addressed: "Hon. James Warren Esqr Speaker of the House Watertown"; docketed: "Mr. J Adams Lettr. Octr. 1775."

[1] Mentioned earlier by JA to Warren, 13 Oct. (above).

To James Warren

Dear sir   Octr. 25th. 1775

Governor Ward of Rhode Island has a son about five and twenty years old who has been so far carried away in the Absence of his Father, with a Zeal for his Country as to inlist into the Artillery as a private.[1] He never Said a Word to the Governor about, or he would have had a Commission. A younger Brother, who solicited of his father Permission to enter the service, was made a Captain.[2] Now it is a Pity, that this young Gentlemans Patriotism, should not be encouraged and rewarded, and it is a greater Pity that an Elder Brother should be a private soldier in an Army where his younger Brother is an officer and a Captain—and a greater Pity still that a Governor of a Province and a worthy Member of the Continental Congress, and the Constant Chairman of our Committee of the whole House, Should have a deserving son in the Army in the Ranks, when Multitudes of others in Commissions have no such Pretensions.

I wish you would mention this Matter at Head Quarters and see if any Thing can be done for him. The Governor had no Expectations I believe that I should interest myself in this Matter, but the Fact coming accidentally to my Knowledge, I determined to write about it immediately, and I knew not how to set the Thing in Motion.

I write every Thing to you, who know how to take me. You dont Expect Correctness nor Ceremony from me. When I have any Thing to write and one Moment to write it in I scratch it off to you, who dont expect that I should dissect these Things, or reduce them to correct Writing. You must know I have not Time for that.

RC (MHi:Warren-Adams Coll.); addressed: "Hon. James Warren Esq. Speaker of the House Watertown"; docketed: "Mr. J A Lettr Octr. 1775 X."

[1] Charles Ward (b. 1747). JA's concern that the son of a governor and member of the congress did not have a commission suggests a view of the fitness of things characteristic of the period and not unknown in our own day. Compare James Warren's response on 14 Nov. (below). On 1 Jan. 1776, Charles Ward was appointed an ensign in the 25th Continental Infantry, an appointment that pleased Samuel Ward (to Catherine Greene, 10 Feb. 1776, Samuel Ward, *Correspondence of Gov-ernor Samuel Ward, May 1775 – March 1776* [ed. Bernhard Knollenberg] *and Genealogy of the Ward Family*, comp. Clifford P. Monahon, Providence, 1952, p. 187, 214; Heitman, *Register Continental Army*, p. 568).

[2] Samuel Ward Jr. (1756–1832) was a captain in the 1st Rhode Island Regiment, and at this time was probably on his way to Quebec, where he was captured in December during the siege (*DAB*).

To James Warren

Dear Sir   Octr: 25th: 1775

Upon the Receipt of the Intelligence of Dr. [Church's] Letter, Dr. Morgan was chosen in his Room. This Letter is intended to be sent by him, and therefore probably will not go in ten days.[1]

John Morgan, a Native of this City, is a Doctor of Physick, a Fellow of the Royal Society at London; Correspondent of the Royal Academy of Surgery at Paris; Member of the Arcadian Belles Lettres Society at Rome; Licentiate of the Royal Colledges of Physicians in London and in Edinburgh; and Professor of the Theory and Practice of Medicine in the Colledge of Philadelphia.

This Gentleman Served an Apprenticeship of six or seven years under Dr. John Redman, an eminent Physician in this City,[2] during which Time he had an opportunity of Seeing the Practice of all the eminent Physicians in this City, as he attended at the Hospital, and for one year made up the Prescriptions of all. After this he devoted himself four years to a military Life, and went into the Service as a Physician and Surgeon to the Troops raised by this Colony; after this he went abroad, and Spent five years in Europe, under the most celebrated Masters in every Branch of Medicine, and visiting the principal Cities and Seats of Science in Great Britain, Holland, France and Italy.

This Gentleman in 1765, delivered a Discourse upon the Institution of Medical Schools in America, at a Commencement, which was published with a Preface, containing an Apology for attempting to introduce the regular Mode of practising Physic in Phyladelphia.[3]

Every Winter, Since he has read Lectures to the Students at the Colledge as a Professor &c.

He and our Revd. Chaplain Mr. Duche, who is now promoted to be Rector of the three United Episcopal Churches in this City, married two sisters. Mr. Stillman of Boston, the Antipœdobaptist Minister married Dr. Morgans sister.

The Doctors moral Character is very good. Thus much sir I thought myself well employed in Writing to you, who have a Curiosity after Characters. I wish I could give a Loose to my Pencil and draw Characters for your Inspection, by the Dozen. But Letters dont always go safe.

Dr. Morgan Sir, deserves particular Honour and Respect, whereever he goes.

RC (MHi:Warren-Adams Coll.); addressed: "Hon. James Warren Esqr Speaker of the House Watertown"; docketed: "Mr J A Lettr Octr. 1775."

[1] This letter arrived on the evening of 15 Nov.; see Warren's letter of 14–16 Nov. (below).

[2] Dr. John Redman (1722–1808), a noted surgeon who had studied widely in Europe, also trained Benjamin Rush (*DAB*).

[3] *A Discourse upon the Institution of Medical Schools in America; Delivered ... May 30 and 31, 1765 ...*, Phila., 1765 (Evans, No. 10082).

From William Gordon

My dear Sir   Jamaica Plain Octr 25. 75

I begin upon a half sheet, as a quarter may possibly not hold what I have to write, but should I comprehend the whole within that compass, shall dock your allowance, the times demanding the utmost frugality as well as courage. Pray how many more burnings of towns are we to be abused with by the British Barbarians, ere the long suffering of the Congress is concluded, and every manly exertion of power and wisdom is to be exercised in opposing our enemies? By a Captain arrived from one of the French ports we are told, that the French are ready to trade with us, and to defend such trade. The Buccaneers of America made a great noise in times past; let the Congress give out letters of m[arque] to take all British bottoms, and we shall soon acquire a greater reputation and a better. West India and East India ships will make good men of war. The British sailors, who might be taken, would be likely to join us upon receiving proper encouragement; the single men might be married among us; the married might go back to their [own] country after a while. The West India property belongs in general to English merchants, the planters being [to a] man over head and ears in debt to them. If the merchants will support the ministry, we have a right [to] their property when we can catch it, that we may support ourselves.

[Chu]rch that villain Church! He I suppose was the fellow that betrayed the proceedings of the [Cong]ress, for which poor Cushing was suspected and suffered in the opinion of many. I hope you will hang [him]. His crime was committed before he was a military officer; let him be tried therefore as a private person, that he may not escape his deserts, upon the common law or custom of arms, and suffer death as a spy upon proof of the facts alleged against him. I am cold, have no more time to spare, and by reason hereof can write no more than best respects to self and brother delegates, instead of brethren delegates which does not read so well, from your sincere friend,

William Gordon [1]

I had forgot a material thing I wanted to mention. The necessity of an hospital on Roxbury side must be self evident to you, and has existed almost from the first; this will make it necessary to appoint two more surgons than what the congress have allowed. Pray you to procure the establishment and continuance of Drs. Howard and Aspenall,[2] Who have given great satisfaction, and live the first on the Plain, the other at Brookline. They cannot act as mates, as that would sink them in the opinion of the neighborhood and hurt their practice, especially after having acted as surgeons. Shall inclose Dr. Howards letter.

ENCLOSURE

Sir   Tuesday Evening [24 Oct.?]

I have attended the Hospital ever since about the middle of May last by Order from Genl. Thomas, but am unable to ascertain the Number I attended or the Event till June 10th. since which Time Doctr. Willm. Aspenwall and myself have attended not less than six hundred Patients as Provincial Surgeons and out of that Number have not lost more than forty. This I have collected from the Hospital Books. Yours most respectfully   Leml. Hayward

RC (Adams Papers); addressed: "For The Honle John Adams Esqr   Philadelphia"; docketed: "Mr. Gordon   Octr. 24. 1775." The left edge of the sheet is mutilated. The enclosure is without place or date and is addressed:

"To the Revd Mr. Gordon   Present." It is microfilmed under the date Oct.? 1775 (Adams Papers, Microfilms, Reel No. 345).

¹ Rev. William Gordon had visited JA about a month earlier in Philadelphia, when JA recorded in his diary an unflattering estimate of the man — "an eternal Talker, and somewhat vain, and not accurate nor judicious. . . . Fond of being thought a Man of Influence" (*Diary and Autobiography*, 2:174).

The Appendix to JA, *Papers*, vol. 2 contains an essay entitled "Thoughts upon the Dispute between Great Britain and Her Colonies," the authorship of which is there erroneously attributed to Gordon. The editors are grateful to Prof. Robert M. Calhoon for calling their attention to the mistake. The author was the historian William Smith Jr. of New York, who wrote the piece between 1765 and 1767. See Calhoon, "William Smith Jr.'s Alternative to the American Revolution," *WMQ*, 3d ser., 22:105–118 (Jan. 1965). How Gordon was able to make a copy of an unpublished MS remains a mystery. Gordon was, however, well known to Smith's mother-in-law, who left Gordon a legacy about 1776 ("Letters of the Reverend William Gordon, Historian of the American Revolution," MHS, *Procs.*, 63 [1929–1930]:498).

² Dr. Lemuel Hayward (1749–1821) and Dr. William Aspinwall (1743–1823) were Harvard graduates. Hayward studied medicine with Joseph Warren in Boston before opening practice in Jamaica Plain; Aspinwall studied in Philadelphia and began practice in Brookline as that town's first permanent physician. The two joined the army around Boston and were appointed surgeons at Roxbury Hospital (Sibley-Shipton, *Harvard Graduates*, 17:32–34; 16:8–12).

From James Otis Sr.

Sir   Watertown October 25th 1775

I Recived your favor of the first Current¹ and Note the Contents and in answer say that I am Obliged for this first favor of the Kind Since you have Been In Congress. The Gentlemen of your Comitee have had Every Demonstration of Respect shewn them by the Councell and house of Representatives of this Province and I hope it Was agreeable to them: We have had an agreeable interview and our Conclusions are to be Laid before the Congress for your Approbation, and In the mean Time matters are kept Secret untill Their determination. Give me Leave to Say that I have the highest opinion of the Conduct of Mr. Lynch and Doctor Frankling. The other Gentleman appears to me to have some Prejudice against the northern Coloneys. Nevertheless there was a Good harmony in our meeting. The Difficulties we are under for want of Powder and the Ravages the Enemy are makeing on our Sea Coast I Presume you are and will be fully acquainted with. Sir from our Long acquaintance and former friendship I have a favor to aske which is as There is a new army to be Raised for another year my Eldest Grandson namely James Otis the third² who Took his degree Last Commencement has a Great Inclination to Enter the Army (as he Improved himself In the Military art

while at Collidge). If he Can be Properly Recomended, and the Congress will I Presume Recomend and Leave the appointment to the
Generall to whom I shall apply In a sutable Time, and your and my
Friends Recomendation will Go a Great way and I think the family
name Worthy of Notice all Curcumstances Considered. I am Sir
your very Humble sert   James Otis

RC (Adams Papers); addressed: "For the Honble. John Adams Esqr   In
Philadelphia   per favor of Doctor Franklin"; docketed: "Coll Otis   Oct 25.
1775."

[1] Not found, but it was probably similar to other letters JA wrote to introduce to prominent Massachusetts people the three committee members from the congress.

[2] No evidence has been found that he received a continental commission, but he was an adjutant in Col. Joseph Otis' regiment from Barnstable as of 29 Sept. (*Mass. Soldiers and Sailors*, 11: 712).

From Josiah Quincy

Dear Sir   Octr: 25th: 1775
     I have now before me your obliging Letter of the 6th: Instant. It
came to hand with another for your good Lady,[1] which was imediately
forwarded to her by Mr. Thaxter who was here when I received it.
At the same Time, I received a Card from our Friend Doctr: Franklin,
assuring me a friendly visit before he returns to Philadelphia. If he
can spare Time to take a View of the Harbor I hope to convince him
of the Practicability of stoping up the *Narrows*, and forcing our
Enemies to ask our Leave to return home. If you can procure, and
send me a Model, or at least a perfect Draft of the Machine you mention for obstructing the Passage of Vessels up the River Delaware,
with explicit Directions how to sink, and secure them from being
weighed or destroyed by the Enemies Ships, it would greatly facilitate
the same valuable Purposes here, not only in the Narrows, but also
in the Lighthouse Channel, which in the narrowest Part is not much
if anything above half a Mile wide. Could the Depth of Water be reduced there, so as to prevent Line of battle Ships from entering the
Harbor, we might, for the future, bid Defiance to our Enemies. But,
you shall hear more from me, after I have conversed fully with Doctr.
Franklin upon the Subject, which is, to me, of much more Importance,
than I had any Conception of 'till I read what you have wrote upon it;
and especially, since the cannonading our maritime Towns, and the
Destruction of *Falmouth* demonstrates, the malicious Purpose of our
Enemies to execute, their unrelenting Vengeance by every Means in

their Power. Good God! what savage Barbarity! Let us no longer call our Selves *Englishmen* but free *born Americans*. Let us unitedly exert every Faculty to confound the Devices, and frustrate the hostile Attempts of our Enemies! We must, or Vassalage, if not an ignominious Bondage will, inevitably be the Consequence.

But, alass! what can our Strength avail us, when such vile Apostates as H[utchinso]n, C[hurc]h, and others of the same stamp stand ready, for filthy Lucre, to betray our Councels, expose our Weakness, and advise our Enemies what Measures will most effectually secure the Conquest of Us. Pray tell me, what Punishment is due to such Perfidy as C[hurc]h has been guilty of? There are others I shrewdly suspect, but, dare not name, least I should be mistaken; for your Profession has taught me, that, "It is better ten guilty should escape, than one innocent Person suffer." But this humane Maxim shan't divert me from watching; with the Eyes of *Argos*, if I had them.

How long must the Courts of Justice remain unopened, and the Law of the Land unexecuted? Shall Criminals escape the Halter? Shall Debtors defraud and starve their Creditors, and every Species of Dishonesty be countenanced and encouraged by a Delay of Justice, which is virtually a Denial of it? I know it is said, that, "inter arma silent Leges." But will not our Enemies take the Advantage of our deplorable Circumstances, and say, Now, you see, by sad Experience, the dreadful Effects of your Zeal to get rid of the Riens of Government! Is not the Man of *Substance* reduced to a Level with those who have *none*? Have not the dishonest MANY, in every Respect, but that of being honest, the Advantage of the honest FEW? Does not the Price of every thing depend upon Quantity and Demand? If the continental Congress had opened, a Mine of Silver, and another of Gold, and coined as much Money as they have struck off paper Dollars; would not every Man of Property suffered enough, by such a sudden Plenty of Money, compared with every thing of which it is the Measure? What then, but inevitable Ruin, must be the Consequence of such a Flood of Paper Credit, without any Fund established to secure it from depreciating, especially in this Colony, where it is considered as a lawfull Tender in all Payments; so, that, if you have lent a Man a 1000 Dollars, and should be so unpolite as to ask him for the Interest of it, he will borrow of a rich paper Proprietor a 1000 *fictitious Dollars* and discharge his Debt: Should you refuse to receive them, because they were not the same you lent, you will be exposed to publick Resentment perhaps Ignominy. But what operates still more injuriously to the N. E. Colonies, especially this, is, that, it is the Seat of War; and of

Course the greatest Part of the Paper Credit, both continental and colonial, will circulate here; we must therefore, be subjected, not only to the Calamities and Horrors of a civil War, but to all the Loss resulting from a flood of depreciating Paper Bills, for which we have exchanged our Property, as if they were so many Dollars.

But suppose, what is not yet Fact, that you have repelled your Enemies, and secured your *darling Liberty*: What is become of your Property? Your maritime Towns are destroyed! Your Trade and Navigation are annihilated, and those concerned in it reduced, to Want and Beggary! The Value of your Lands, as you have no Vent for the surplus of your Produce, reduced to half its Value! Your Brethren in the southern Colonies have lent you their Credit; but what does it amount to? A Quantity of *Dollars*, stamp'd upon Paper by Order of the continental Congress, without any Security to the Possessor, for the Value, or Redemption of them in any reasonable Time? Had a continental Fund been established, and all the Money wanted been borrowed upon the Credit of it, @ :3:4: or 5 per Ct. Interest, redeemable at a certain Period, the Bills could not have depreciated; though all things might, and would have rose, in Proportion to the Quantity and Demand of each. But, under present Circumstances, we shall, from the necessary Consequence of them, soon be able to verifie the late Bishop of Cloyne's Doctrine of *Ideas*[2] for we shall have the *Idea of Money* Nomen et preterea Nihil.[3]

Suppose, an artfull insidious *Parracide* under the Mark of Friendship, to declaim pathetically upon the *Topicks* above hinted at, before a suffering Auditory: Is there no Danger of his making many Proselites? If there is, since it's foreseen, let us endeavour to prevent the Poison from entering the Body politick, where, I fear it would soon spread and prevail, so as not to be easily eradicated, by any Antidotes in our Power.

Mrs: Q. Mrs: L. Miss: B[ets]y and N[anc]y[4] desire their affectionate Regards may be joined with those of, Your Faithfull Friend &ca:

RC (Adams Papers); addressed: "To The honble: John Adams Esquire Philadelphia   Per Favour of Doctr: Franklin} Q D C"; docketed: "Coll Quincy   Oct 25. 1775." Quincy's Dft on last page of JA to Quincy, 6 Oct., MHi:Hoar Autograph Coll.

[1] Probably that to AA of 7 Oct. (*Adams Family Correspondence*, 1:294–296).

[2] The idealist philosopher Bishop George Berkeley (1685–1753) (DNB).

[3] The name and nothing more.

[4] Mrs. Bela Lincoln, the former Hannah Quincy, who had been JA's first romantic interest; Betsy and Nancy were Elizabeth and Ann Quincy, daughters of Josiah by his second and third marriages.

From William Tudor

Dear Sir   Cambridge 25th. Octr. 1775

I wrote you by the Post 3 Weeks ago but have not been honour'd with a Line since your Return to Philadelphia.[1] I should write oftener but every Thing of Importance is communicated in the Prints, and I am in no Secrets at Head Quarters, and I hate to set down to write when I can't tell You something worth reading.

About 10 Days ago two floating Batteries were ordered down Cambridge River to fire into the Enemy's Camp on Boston Common and alarm the Troops there. It had the expected Effect, but was attended with an unfortunate Circumstance. A 9 Pounder the sixth Time it was discharg'd burst, and very badly wounded 7 of the Men. It reduc'd the Batterie to a perfect Wreck. She was however brought off with her Remaining Guns &c. The Enemy never return'd the Fire. One of our Men died of his Wounds next Morning and one since.

The Enemy have been very quiet in their movements for some Time. We have 16 or 20 flat bottom Boats which carry 80 Men each finish'd, and the Carppenters are at Work on others. What they are intended for is not yet known. The Conjecture is that they are design'd for a Descent on Boston.

We had an Express yesterday from Falmouth, Casco Bay, who brings News that a Number of the Enemy's Ships were in that Harbour, the Capt.[2] of which, after informing the Inhabitants that they must deliver Up all their Arms and give Hostages for their peaceable Behaviour, and allowing them 24 Hours to comply or he should fire the Town. At the Expiration of the Time set, finding they would not comply with the Demand, began a most infernal Connonade and Bombardment on the Town which destroy'd two thirds of it. After the ships had burnt 2 or 300 Houses and drove 2000 People into the Woods they fell down, and it was suppos'd were going to Portsmouth. As they had inform'd the People of Falmouth that they were to visit that place next and make the same Requisition, a Non Complyance with which would be attended with a Bombardment. And that every Sea Port Town on the Continent was to be visited for the like kind Purpose. These being the Orders from our most gracious King. Surely it is become Time That we had a French Fleet to protect our Coasts. On Land we can defend ourselves.

The General Voice is throw open our Ports wide to all the World— and If we must be Slaves, let Us be the Slaves of France, Spain,

Turkey, rather than the Slaves of ungrateful Britain. I am Dr. Sir Yr. most obt. Servt.   Wm. Tudor

RC (Adams Papers); addressed: "To The Honble. John Adams Esq Philadelphia"; docketed: "Tudor   Octr. 25. 1775."

[1] JA had written to Tudor on 1, 12 Oct. (above) and 21 Oct. For the latter, see JA to James Warren, first letter, 21 Oct., note 1 (above).

[2] Capt. Henry Mowat, who com-manded the *Canceau*, an element of Adm. Graves' fleet (William Willis, *The History of Portland*, facsim. of 1865 2d edn., Portland, Maine, 1972, p. 516).

From John Winthrop

Dear Sir   Watertown Octr. 25. 1775
I received your Favor by Mr. Lynch. I was very sorry I had no opportunity of Shewing respect to the Gentlemen of the Congress, and was particularly concerned that I could not have more of the conversation of my excellent Friend Dr. Franklin. But they were continually sitting at Head Quarters, and the Council were every day sitting at Watertown; so that I never saw them but once, which was when they dined here at the invitation of the House of Representatives. I thought it necessary to communicate your Letter to the Committee of Council appointed to confer with the Delegates from the Congress, who were Mr. Bowdoin, Col. Otis, Mr. Sever and Mr. Spooner.

What news we have here, the Gentlemen will inform you at their return. The two armies remain in the same situation as when you left us. Ours, tis said, continues inactive, for want of ammunition. I heartily wish, any method could be devised to furnish them with a sufficient stock, without delay. I am very much afraid, if those folks are not got out of Boston before they receive reinforcements, we shall never be able to get them out afterwards.

We have just received an account, that last Wednesday two men of war and two Tenders cannonaded the town of Falmouth, and set it on fire, and that 2/3 of it is burnt down. This, without any provocation. The particulars, I suppose, you will see in the Newspapers. Tis expected they intend to treat our other Sea ports in the same manner.

The General Court is constantly sitting. A difficulty has arisen, relating to the choice and appointment of Military officers; founded on a Resolve of the Congress, which seems to leave the appointment of such officers to the *Assemblies* in the several Colonies.[1] The House think this Resolve gives them the power of appointing Military officers. The Board are of opinion, that, by the Charter, this power is lodged with them at present; and as, in the first Resolve of the

Congress, by which this Court was convened, we were advised to keep as near as possible to the Charter, the Board think themselves obliged to adhere to it. I am afraid, this will bring on an altercation which may be attended with disagreable consequences, unless the Congress should explain themselves on this head.

I have the pleasure to congratulate you on your being appointed a Judge of the Superior Court; and I add, to the universal satisfaction of the people. I hope, e'er long to see you on that Bench. In the mean time, I cannot but pity you under the load of perplexing difficulties with which I suppose you are embarrassed; but hope that by firmness and perseverence you will extricate your selves and us.

It is reported that there is a rich lead mine at South Hampton in this Colony, and another at Middleton in Connecticutt. But whether any thing is likely to be done to effect in either of them, I cannot say.

With respectful Compliments to the Gentlemen of your Company I am with great esteem Your sincere Friend and humble servt

Octr. 29. Last night I was very kindly and hospitably entertained at your Seat in Braintree, having accompanied Dr. Franklin a little way on his journey. This morning, I left your Lady and young Family in perfect health.

RC (Adams Papers); addressed: "To the Honorable John Adams Esq at Philadelphia Favord by Dr Franklin"; docketed: "Dr. Winthrop. Octr 2[5] 1775."

[1] See James Warren to JA, 20 Oct., note 20 (above).

From Henry Knox

Sir   Cambridge Oct 26 1775

Encourag'd by your kindly mentioning my name in your Letters to several Gentlemen this way [1] I now take the liberty of writing to you.

A number of the Generals desir'd me to act as engineer and said that when the delegates from the Continental Congress came here the matter should be settl'd—myself as cheif engineer with the rank and pay of Colonel and a Lt. Col. Putnam as second also with the rank of Col.— but the Gentlemen (two of them, Dctr. Franklin was of another opinion) [2] delegates did not see proper to engage for any other rank than that of Lt. Col. and I believe have recommended us in that order to your Congress.

I have the most sacred regard for the liberties of my country and am fully determined to act as far as in my power in opposition to the present tyranny attempted to be imposed upon it, but as all honor is comparative I humbly hope that I have as good pretensions to the rank of Col. as many now in the service, the declining to confer which by the delegates not a little supriz'd me. If your respectable body should not incline to give the rank and pay of Col. I must beg to decline it, not but I will do every service in power as a Volunteer. It is said and universally beleived that the officers and soldiers of the train of artillery will refuse to serve under their present Commander,[3] the reasons of which you no doubt have heard. If it should be so and a new Col. Appointed I should be glad to suceed to that post where I flatter myself I should be of some little service to the Cause. The other field officers of the regiment wish it and I have great reasons to beleive the Generals too. This would be much more agreable to me than the first and would not hinder me from being useful in that department. It ever appears to me to detract from the merit of a person when he takes the liberty to reccommend himself, nothing but the flattering Idea of being in a small measure assisting to free my country should induce me to.

I beg an answer as soon as possible and am Sir Most Respectfully Your very Hble. Servant   Henry Knox

RC (Adams Papers).

[1] For example, JA to Gen. Heath, 5 Oct., note 1, and to James Warren, first letter, 21 Oct. (both above).

[2] Parentheses and comma supplied for clarity. These words were written in the margin with an indication that they should be inserted after "Gentlemen."

[3] Knox, only 25, took over command of the artillery on 17 Nov.; Richard Gridley remained as chief engineer until Aug. 1776 (*DAB*).

To James Warren

Dr Sir   Octr. 28. 1775

Our Association, against Importations and Exportations, from and to Gr. Britain, Ireland and the British West Indies, if We consider its Influence, upon the Revenue, the Commerce, the Manufactures and the Agriculture of the Kingdom, is a formidable Shield of Defence for Us. It is Shearing of its Beams that Luminary, which in all its Glory might dazzle our feeble Sight.

But a Question arises, whether, our Association against Exportations, can be observed, so as to have its full Effect, upon Britain, Ireland, and the West Indies, unless We extend it further?[1] We have agreed not to export to B., I. and the W. Indies. Parliament has made an Act that We Shall not export to any other Place. So that Trade is entirely stopped. But will not a Smuggling Trade be opened? That is will not Adventurers push out Vessells against the Act of Parliament? If they do, when the Vessells are once at Sea, will they not go, to the Place where a Famine price is to be had. The Spirit of Commerce is mercenary and avaricious, and the Merchants will go where the Scarcity is greatest, the Demand quickest and the Price highest.

What Security then can we have that Merchants will not order their Vessells to the West India Islands British or foreign, to Ireland or even Great Britain, in Defyance of our association?

Besides is there not reason to apprehend, that the concealed Tories of whom there are many in every Colony, and especially in every maritime Town, will send their Vessells to sea, on purpose to be taken by the Enemy and sent to Supply the Army and Navy in America. It is true, their Vessells would be forfeited, and seized and condemned no doubt but they might be pleased with this, and would easily obtain hereafter Compensation or Retribution for this meritorious Sacrifice, from the Ministry.

In Short may not our association be wholly evaded and eluded, if we dont draw it closer? My own opinion upon these great Questions I may possibly give you sometime or other. But I wish to have yours.

RC (MHi:Warren-Adams Coll.); addressed: "Hon. James Warren Esqr Speaker of the House Watertown"; docketed: "Mr. J. A Lettr Octr. 1775."

¹ Off and on during October, the congress, sitting as a committee of the whole, had been debating the wisdom of opening up trade. The last of JA's notes on this debate were recorded the day before he wrote this letter (*Diary and Autobiography*, 2:219).

From Benjamin Hichborn

Dear Sir   Cambridge 28 Octr: 1775

If tears of blood were to follow my pen, they wou'd but faintly marke the distressing anxiety I have suffered for near three months past, to be betrayed into a situation which equally exposed me to the Insults of my Enemies and the Suspicions or Contempt of my Friends, by a Scoundrel whose base duplicity, I coud neither expose or counteract, excited feelings, which often proved too severe a trial for my utmost fortitude.¹ I have been a week in the Country and till now have not had resolution enough to write you a line. I have So much to communicate, that at present I shall only relieve my Mind of what I cannot contain. It was generally presumed (and I confess with the greatest apparent reason) that the discovery of those letters was owing to my imprudence—imprudence in such a Case I shoud esteem a Crime, and a crime of such a nature as, in myself, I coud never pardon. The circumstances were shortly these. When we came to New York, contrary to our expectations, we found a packet-boat waiting for Passengers, and in the opinion of every one there was not the least danger in crossing the Sound, we accordingly took passage for New-Port, and I never saw more reason for destroying your letters till the second day we had been on board the Man of war, than there was for throwing them in the River Delaware. Capt. Ayscough[2] Received us on board the Ship with the greatest politeness and Civility, making a thousand apologies for the rough treatment he had given us, said his object was the Sailors, who were in the boat with us, and was very sorry he had stopt us in our passage. This continued till the next day, when his Conduct suddenly wore quite a different appearance. I told Mr. White, that Scoundrel Stone, (a person who formerly was Clerk to Henry Lloyd,[3] and came passenger with us from New York) had given Ayscough some information which had produced this Change in his conduct, and it was time for me to secure my letters, I had before this secreted them in a part of the Ship where I thought them perfectly safe. I immediately loaded them with money of the least value I had about me intending to drop them over board in the Evening. We (Mr. White and myself) were then told that we must look upon ourselves as prisoners, and while Mr. Stone was caressed in the Cabin, we had a Centinel over us. However I had then, not the least doubt of eluding their Strictest scrutiny—my plan I thought was compleat and ensured me success; I had provided a couple of blank letters directed to General Washington and Coll. Warren, which in Case Stone shoud acknowledge himself the Informer and confront me with his declaration, I intended to deliver them up with seeming reluctance and pretend I had concealed them through fear. Just as the boat was preparing to carry our baggage on board Capt. Wallace for examination a Gentleman who came passenger with us from New York sent on board for a trunk which we thro' mistake had taken for our own, this circumstance looked so favourable that I coud not avoid seizing [it] to get the letters on shore. I opened the trunk with my own key, put the letters in the folds of the Gentlemans Linen and with some difficulty locked it again, when the trunk came upon deck the Lieutenant mistook it for mine put it into the boat with the rest of our things and rowed off immediately on board the other Ship. By such a mere accident as this did the letters fall into their Hands. The next day an Officer told Mr. White that he heard Stone giving the Capt. information of the Letters, or we shoud never have been searched or suspected. General Washington does not yet appear altogether Satisfied with my Conduct.[4] The only Satisfaction I have at present arises from the generous Reception I met with from Coll. Warren, but my anxiety to know your Sentiments of the part I have taken prevents my attention to any thing else. I am Sensible of the injustice I do you in harbouring the least diffidence of your generosity, but at the same time I know your nice feelings must receive such a shock from having your confidential observations, upon such delicate Subjects exposed, that the Reflection gives me the keenest pain. General Washington and the World, may think meanly of me, but suffer me to say without the appearance of adulation, possessed of your Confidence of favourable opinion, I can be happy under their united frowns. Nothing but a line of approbation from you can restore me to myself. Let me intreat you, if from no other motives but pity, to send me a short letter by the Post, and I will then open myself to you with the greatest freedom. Enclosed you have a rude plan of a design which I am satisfied may be carried into execution with the greatest ease.[5] I propose communicating it to the Genl. through Mr: Bowdoin. I am Sir your unhappy but Sincere Friend   B Hichborn

RC (Adams Papers); addressed: "John Adams Esq.   Philadelphia"; docketed: "Benja. Hitchbourne   Octr. 28. 1775."

[1] This letter is a first installment of Hichborn's defense of his actions and appeal for JA's forgiveness for the capture of JA's letters to James Warren and AA of 24 July. Hichborn also wrote to JA on 25 Nov., and 20 May 1776 (both below). JA's only extant response is his letter of 29 May 1776 (below).

[2] Captain of the British sloop *Swan* (Disposition of the Fleet on 30th June 1775, MHi:Gay Transcripts, The Conduct of Adm. Graves in North America, 1:132).

[3] Probably Henry Lloyd (1709–1795), the Boston merchant and loyalist (Sabine, *American Loyalists*, 2:24).

[4] Washington thought that the conduct of Hichborn and Capt. White, who traveled with him, was "imprudent" and added, "If their suffering only affected themselves, I should not think it improper that they should feel a little for their Misconduct or Negligence" (Washington, *Writings*, ed. Fitzpatrick, 3:398–399, 403).

[5] Enclosure not found. It may have concerned the placing of artillery on Dorchester Heights and Noddle's Island that Hichborn had discussed with James Warren (Warren to JA, 20 Oct., above).

From Perez Morton

Sir   Council Chamber, Watertown Octo. 28th. 1775

I am directed by the Major part of the Council of this Colony, to acquaint You, that by Virtue of the power and Authority in and by the Royal Charter in the abscence of the Governor and Lieutt. Governor lodged in them, they have seen fit to appoint You, with the Advice and consent of Council, to be first or Chief Justice of the Superior Court of Judicature &c. for this Colony. The inclosed is a List of Your bretheren of the Bench, who are to hold their Seats in the Order therein Arranged. I am further directed, to request Your Honor to signify to the board in writing Your Acceptance or refusal of said appointment, as soon as may be. In the Name and by the Order of the Council.   Perez Morton Dpy. Secre.

ENCLOSURE

Honble. John Adams Esqr.
William Cushing Esqr.
William Read Esqr.
Honble. Rob. Treat Paine Esqr.[1]
Nathl. P. Sargent Esqr.

RC (Adams Papers); addressed: "To The Honble. John Adams Esq   at Philadelphia"; docketed: "Dpty Secys. Letter.   Octr. 28. 1775."

[1] For Paine's placement in the ranking and its consequences, see James Warren to JA, 20 Oct. and notes (above).

From William Tudor

Dr Sir   Cambridge Octr. 28th. 1775

I received your Letter of the 12th. Instant by Mr. Tracy. But the One you mention to have sent me some Time before I never got.[1] I am much oblig'd by your Exertions to get my Pay augmented, which is now made fully equivalent to the Office. The Concern which you have shewn for the Advancement of my Honor and Interest in a thousand Instances, demands something more than bare Acknowlegements. If the Time should come when my Gratitude can be express'd by Actions rather than Words alone, I shall with Eagerness seize the Occasion to discharge my uncommon Obligations to your Kindness and Friendship.

Hichbourn, after 3 Months Imprisonment, luckily escap'd from his Confinement on board the Preston. He told me he should take the first Opportunity of writing you.

I am sorry to acquaint you that some of our Masstts. Officers in the Army here have disgrac'd the Country by practising the meanest Arts of Peculation. Every Subtlety which Avarice could invent, or Rascality carry on, have been used to cheat the Publick by Men who procur'd Commissions, not to fight for the Liberty of their Country, but to prey upon it's Distresses. Col. David Brewer, Lt. Col. Brown[2] and 5 Captains have been try'd for defrauding the Publick. The Colonel and 4 of the Captains have been cashier'd.[3] The Army that will soon be inlisted I hope will be better officer'd. There must be a Revision of the Articles for the Government of it. I have, by the Requirement of the General, made some Strictures on the continental Articles as they were published by Order of Congress, and which will be sent to Philadelphia. The Sooner a New Edition of the Articles of War is published the better.[4]

I must mention one Grievance we are subject to here. Persons who come from the Southward bring with them the Pensilvania Bills of an Emission long before the present Year, and pass them here at the Rate of 6/ to the Dollar. There are thousands here who don't know the Difference of the Currency and thus get trick'd. A Person told me that in receiving £8 he lost 15/ Lawfull. This Fraud is the more aggravating, as we are told, that our Colony Bills, though emitted for the Publick Safety, are refus'd in Payments at Philadelphia.

I was in the Gallery yesterday at Watertown, during the Examination of Dr. Church at the Bar of the House, respecting the intercepted Letter of his which has occasion'd so much Talk and Uneasiness. He made an artful and masterly Defence. He endeavoured to evade the Censure of the House by insisting, that as it would be before another Court that this Matter must have a final Issue, should the House proceed to expell him it would have a fatal Effect whenever a final Judgement should be given on his Conduct; and to give force to his Objection, adduc'd the Case of Wilkes, who, though accurs'd "of blaspheming his God and Libelling his King," was not censur'd by the House of Commons as a member, till he was declar'd an Out Law by the Court of King's Bench, Lest it should have had an undue Influence on the Jury. He told the Court, that the Occasion of his writing the Letter on their Table was that some Time in July he received a Letter from his Brother Fleming advising him to secure his Safety with Government by immediately quitting the Cause of Rebellion, and informing him if he would come to Boston, he (Fleming) would procure him a Pardon. This Letter the Doctor said was wrote in Cyphers and one Day having occasion to light his Pipe he burnt it. He could not tell the Name of the Person who gave it to him, nor find out (though he had been indefatigable in the Inquiry) where she lived. In the Course of his Defence, he told the House, that he was once offer'd a Guinea a Day for Life, if he would change Sides. He refus'd it, and has been long Subject to Abuse, and outrage in some Instances. And could it be thought, at a Time when he had a Promise from his Country men of a Post that would gratify Avarice itself, he should turn Traitor, with no other view than securing Pardon? (for he was promis'd no more) Such a Conduct would be more than Folly, it would be Insanity.[5] The Dr. said he let the Letter lay by him 8 or 10 Days when a Thought struck him of making it advantageous to Our Cause, by a fallacious Answer which might gull Fleming and induce him to send the Doctor some important Intelligence. He made the most solemn Appeal to Heaven that this was his only View in writing the Letter. He then pointed out the Paragraphs which he thought to Minds unwarp'd by Prejudice would evince this to have been his Design. He observ'd that there was not a single Paragraph in the Letter which contain'd Information that could have hurt Us. But that the exagerated Accounts of our Force, Strength and Unanimity, would tend to dishearten the Enemy and keep them quiet, at a Time when we were poorly able to have withstood a vigorous Attack. Those Sentences which look'd as if the Writer despiz'd or was inimical to the Cause which We are all embark'd in, were necessary to blind his Correspondent and produce the Effect he anticipated from it. He reminded the House that at the Time the Letter was wrote he enjoy'd the fullest Confidence, was possess'd of some Secrets and perfectly knew the State of our Politicks and intended Manoevres. Therefore his not communicating an Iota that could injure or betray Us was a convincing Reason, that his Views were friendly to the Cause of *our* Country. The Reason he said why he did not intrust his Scheme to a Friend, was because he waited for the Success of it when he should have certainly Communicated the advices he receiv'd, with his Project for obtaining them. He observ'd that it was Indiscretion, it was Folly, but conjur'd them not to let the Indiscretion of an Hour cancel the Services of his Life. He appeal'd to the Knowlege of all who knew him for his Principles and Conduct, and for his Uniformity and undeaviating Adherence in them. But it is impossible to write all he said. Let it suffice to acquaint You, That if the Force of Rhetorick and the Powers of Language, if the most Pathetick Arts of Persuasion, enforc'd by All the Ingenuity, Sense of Spirit of the Doctor could have made him innocent, he would have appear'd spotless as an Angel of Light. A few Days before the Doctor had petitioned the House for a Dismission. After He had gone thro' with his Defence and withdrawn, when a Debate insued in the House. Majr. Hawley was for granting him a Dismission, and leaving Censure and Punishment to another Tribunal.[6] The House after Debate chose a Committee to consider the Doctor's Case and report.

The Candid think, the Doctor was frightened at the Length to which

Matters had arriv'd, was dubious and fearful how they might terminate, and was sollicitous to secure a Retreat in Case of Necessity. But that he meant to provide for his own Safety, without Betraying the Interests of America. And that he is rather to be despiz'd for Timidity, than damn'd for Villainy.[7]

Most of the military Books You mention are at Head Quarters,[8] but not more than two of them are in any Officer's Hands in Camp. Bellidore (which General Gates tells me is worth all the rest) is not own'd by any Gentleman in the army that I am acquainted with. His Works are printed in 4 Volumes Qto. and are to be bought at New York for £12 Lawfull.[9] I am, Dr Sir Yours Sincerely   Wm. Tudor

RC (Adams Papers); docketed: "Tudor   Octr. 28. 1775."

[1] JA's letter of 1 Oct., which went by Maj. Bayard (above).

[2] Lt. Col. Abijah Brown (Washington, *Writings*, ed. Fitzpatrick, 4:19–20).

[3] In the MS the preceding two sentences are written in the left margin of the first page and are placed in the text at this point by editorial decision.

[4] Tudor's comments on the Articles of War were enclosed in a letter from Washington to Joseph Reed on 30 Oct. He told Reed that, although Tudor might have made "some observations worthy of notice," they should be "considered with some degree of caution" because "a desire of lessening his own trouble may induce him to transfer many matters from a general court martial, where he is the principal actor, to the regimental courts where he has nothing to do" (same, 4:54–55). A number of Tudor's suggestions were incorporated in the sixteen amendments to the Articles that the congress passed on 7 Nov. Worthington Ford mistakenly associated Tudor's suggestions with the revision made in Sept. 1776 (PCC, No. 41, I, f. 1–4; JCC, 3:331–334; 5:788, note 2).

[5] In the MS the preceding eight sentences are written in the left margin of the third page, their place in the text being indicated by Tudor.

[6] In the MS the preceding three sentences are written in the left margin of the fourth page and are placed in the text at this point by editorial decision.

[7] The session of the Massachusetts House described by Tudor was officially only a hearing on whether formally to expel Church or accept his letter of resignation of 23 Oct. It resulted in his expulsion on 2 Nov. but little else, for although the House returned Church to custody, it tacitly agreed to leave "Censure and Punishment to another Tribunal." The congress, to which the case had been referred on 3 Oct. by the Council of War, was no more willing to take decisive action than the House, and on 7 Nov. resolved only to send Church to a "secure gaol" in Connecticut. In the end, because of shifting political currents and because no one really knew what to do about him, no final action was taken, and Church remained imprisoned off and on in various locations in Connecticut and Massachusetts until Jan. 1778, when to be rid of an apparently insoluble problem, the congress allowed him to take passage on the sloop *Welcome*, which was lost at sea (Mass., *House Jour.*, 1775–1776, 2d sess., p. 186, 203–204, 226; Washington, *Writings*, ed. Fitzpatrick, 4:9–11; JCC, 3:334; Sibley-Shipton, *Harvard Graduates*, 13:393–397; French, *General Gage's Informers*, p. 189–201). See also Benjamin Kent to JA, 26 May 1776, note 1 (below).

[8] See JA to William Tudor, 12 Oct., note 5 (above).

[9] No record of an English translation of Belidor in four volumes has been found.

From James Warren

My dear Sir   Watertown Octr. 28th: 1775

I did not hear till Yesterday in the Afternoon that Coll. Reed had any Intention to leave us so soon and begin his Journey to Philadelphia on this day. The first reflection on this Occasion was that he would be missed here. I have formed an Excellent opinion of him as a Man of Sense, Politeness, and Ability for Business. He has done us great service. He is I might add strongly Attached to the public Cause of America, but all this you know and perhaps more of his Character than I do. I shall therefore only say that I regret his leaving us and shall wish for his return.[1] The next reflection was that I must Embrace the opportunity and write to you. For that purpose I assigned the Evening but Unluckily the House set till 8 O Clock, and prevented me. Church had a hearing before us Yesterday which took us nearly the whole day. After he withdrew there was a Motion for a Suspension of any Judgement upon him, least it might Influence his Court or Jury upon his Trial. Another Motion that we should Accept a Resignation he had made by Letter, and accompany it with a resolve that should save our honour, and not Injure him in his Trial. The End of the whole matter was Appointing a Committee to report how to proceed. I have now only time to thank you for your kind Letters by Mr. Tracy which I received a few days ago, and those by Capt. Mcpherson which came to hand Yesterday.[2] You have Obliged me Extreemly. They have Edifyed, Comforted, strengthened, and Encouraged. I feel like a New Man. I have not seen the Bearer of the last, shall try to see him this afternoon. We have no kind of News. Time wont permit me to say anything, on the Important subject of your Letters, but to Compensate for any Observations of mine I shall Inclose what I Guess will be much more Agreable. The Author has stole an hour now and then since we came to Town to proceed so far as you'll see, on purpose to Unbend your mind a little, by Amusements of a Poetical kind well knowing you have a Taste for them. You have the two Acts in Print you wrote for last Summer, and two Subsequent ones and the Epilogue. The whole are at your disposition.[3] I shall send Mrs. Adams's Letters &c. this day. I wrote you a long Scroll by Mr. Lynch, and Just as it was going received some Letters from Mrs. Adams which I Inclosed.[4] I have received none from her since. I have not Time to Add a word more, and therefore must Conclude, that you may ever be happy is the wish of your Friend,

I forgot to tell you that the powder arrived in our Vessel at the Eastward has got from 90 Tons by various Gradations to 7 1/2 which I think I gave you as the true account being what I thought I might rely on, and from thence to 15 hundred, and from thence to 6 hundred, which I believe is the true one, tho' I cant say that it wont descend to 3 ct.[5]

RC (Adams Papers); docketed: "Octr. 28. 1775 Warren." The main body of this letter takes up two pages and four lines of a third page. The final paragraph is written on a separate strip of paper, torn from what may have been an address sheet, for on the reverse appear an "Esqr" and a final "n." Why Warren should have written his concluding words on a scrap rather than using the ample space of his barely used third page is not clear. A possible explanation is that he wrote his afterthought on the back of a cover sheet carrying the address and covering this letter and others, as well as enclosures; but if this is true, he did not do so because a seal prevented him from adding his concluding words on his own letter. JA might, then, in filing Warren's letter have torn off the strip. An alternative explanation is that someone (CFA?) mistakenly attached this scrap to the wrong letter, although no other extant letter of Warren to Adams in this period is so full that it could not have accommodated these lines.

[1] Joseph Reed, Washington's secretary, did not return to Massachusetts but remained in Philadelphia, where he was elected to the Pennsylvania Assembly in Jan. 1776 and was appointed adjutant general by the congress in June 1776 (*DAB*; *JCC*, 5:419).

[2] Those of 12 and 13 Oct. carried by Tracy and the two letters of 20 Oct. carried by McPherson (above).

[3] Warren's enclosure has not been found, and his reference here is unclear. He seems to be saying that Mrs. Warren has completed two more acts and an epilogue for her poetic play *The Group*, which appeared as two acts of four scenes in the version printed by Edes and Gill in the spring of 1775 (see JA, *Papers*, 2:214, note 2). Yet that version has a concluding speech that, although it is not labeled as such, could be an epilogue. JA had complained in May that he had been unable to get a complete version of the play, the Philadelphia edition, copied from the first version in the *Boston Gazette*, containing only two scenes. In reply to JA, Warren mentioned an advertisement of the play appearing in the New York press, but the New York edition also had only two scenes (to JA, 27 June, above). It may be that Warren is confusing "acts" and "scenes" and is merely furnishing JA with a complete copy of the play, for the siege of Boston so soon after its publication may have made the Edes and Gill edition unavailable. Still, Warren's mention of Mrs. Warren's activity in Watertown suggests work on something new. If Warren did send an enclosure, JA does not acknowledge receipt of it in any extant letter to either of the Warrens.

[4] Warren had last written to JA on 20 Oct. (above) and, if Lynch did not leave at once, probably included two letters from AA to JA, those of 21 and 22 Oct. (*Adams Family Correspondence*, 1:305–308, 309–311). "Mrs. Adams's Letters," which Warren says he will send on, were probably those of JA to AA of 21 and 23 Oct. (same, 1:309, 311–312).

[5] Warren is probably referring to the arrival at Sheepscot of a "very Considerable quantity of Powder, Cannon and Arms" (to JA, 20 Oct., above). It should be understood that he is shifting from tons to pounds; that is, 1,500 pounds, etc. The "ct," very carelessly written after the 3, is arguable, but this abbreviation for hundredweight seems logical.

To Mercy Otis Warren

Octr. 31. 1775

I received, this day with great Pleasure your Favour of the Twelfth and fourteenth Instant[1]—and was the more gratified with it, because it was dated from Watertown, where I wish my excellent Friend very constantly to reside, for the good of the Public and where consequently I wish you to be, because his Happiness will be promoted by it.

The Graces and the Muses, will always inhabit with such Company, whatever Crouds may Surround, whatever Accomodations may be wanting.

MS (Adams Papers); apparently a fragment that was never finished and sent.

[1] That is, the letter of the 12th, which was finished on the 14th (above).

From Joseph Palmer

Dear Sir   Watertown, October 31st. 1775

Herewith you have a Copy of the Account of the Battle of Charlestown;[1] the other matters will be attended to as soon as possible; That there has been an unreasonable delay, is not owing to J. P.; he is employ'd in signing &c. the Bills of Credit, which takes up, as he thinks, too much of his time.

There has been a Sample of Lead-Oar, which has been assayed, and turns out 50 per cent Lead: I am endeavouring to obtain a Committee of Court, to go upon the Spot, and to have it assayed there in their presence, they to report the prospect of Quantity and Quality, Situation for working &c., &c.[2] I also send a considerable number of Samples of Oars, which I received from Mr. E. Quincy of Sto[ughtonha]m:[3] with directions to forward them to Mr. Hancock, to whom I shall therefore send them: That there are plenty of good Lead-Mines and others in this Colony, I am fully satisfied; and if the Colony, or Continent, wou'd give Such a price for the Lead and other Mettle, which shou'd involve in it a Sufficient bounty, above the common rates, and for a Sufficient length of time to encourage adventurers, I think it wou'd answer all reasonable expectations: In that case, I wou'd again write to England by the first opportunity, and hope we might Succeed so far, as to obtain both Miners and Smelters from thence, provided the Controversy between G.B. and the Cs., does not prevent it. This leads me to Say, what I have not mention'd to you before, That had not this controversy prevented, we Shou'd have had many Families from

Derbyshire Sent over hither, of both Branches,[4] last Spring; they were all engaged, and prepared to come, but were prevented by this unnatural Quarrel: This is a fact you may depend upon.

Novr: ⟨7th⟩ 11th.

Since the above, a Committee is appointed to make farther enquiry into the Lead-Oar first mention'd; of this Committee I am one, and intend to go to the Spot next Week, if possible: The result you will be acquainted with in proper time.

Mr. Revere carries from hence a Budget of Letters &c., taken in a Vessel from Ireland, little Capt. Robins of Bulls Wharf, Master;[5] I hope your Congress will think there are very important matters contained in it—a Proclamation by the King, in which we are all called Rebels—Letters mentioning a Declaration of War against us—Many Troops, 5 Regiments &c. this fall (some of these we Suppose are arrived)—Russians, Prussians, Hessians, Hanoverians, &c. in abundance next Spring! How long is this Continent to hope for a reconciliation with G B? When will be the proper time to open our Ports to one or more other Nations? How long are we to be embarrassed and plagued with our vile Monarchical Charters? And when will the Congress give leave to all the United Colonies to take any form of Government they may respectively best like, not inconsistant with the General Union, of which the Congress to judge?

Our prospect for Salt-petre rises very fast, and I think we Shall do very well with it;[6] But apprehend we Shall need further supplys, large supplys, of Powder before we shall have enough of own Manufacture.

J. Adams, W. Cushing, W. Read, R. T. Paine, and N. P. Sargeant, J[ustices] of the S[uperior] C[ourt]. J.A. must not refuse us, it wou'd hurt us greatly.

I hope to write you again after my return from the Lead-Mine. Pray exert your Selves *now* to break off the Fetters of T−−−−ny for the Colonies. I wish your whole Congress cou'd See our distress; 'twill distract us, if not liberated. Many of our Friends in Boston are likely to come out as 'tis said; I think that the expected hunger, will give them liberty. A large Canal cut across, by the Haymarket, from Sea to Sea, and a large Breastwork. Adieu, May God bless and direct you all. So Pray your   J. Palmer

RC (Adams Papers); docketed: "Palmer.   Octr 31. 1775."

[1] See the Committee of Safety's account, 25 July (above).

[2] No record of such a special committee has been found. The matter may have been referred to the existing committee on lead and salt, of which Palmer

was a member (see JA to John Winthrop, 2 Oct., note 4, above).

[3] Probably Edmund Quincy (1726–1782). Stoughtonham is now Sharon, Mass.

[4] Palmer and Cranch branches? Palmer had married the sister of Richard Cranch, bosom friend of JA. The Cranches and Palmers had emigrated from towns in Devon (JA, *Diary and Autobiography*, 1:140, note 1; 3:209). Or it may be that Palmer was referring to family connections in Derbyshire.

[5] The letters, written from Cork, Ireland, to British officers in Boston, were taken from the schooner *Two Sisters*, under Capt. Robbins, which was captured and brought into Beverly on 7 Nov. The General Court, after examining the seized papers and showing copies to Washington, dispatched them to the congress in care of Paul Revere. They were read before the congress on 20 Nov. The documents, which were extracted in the *Boston Gazette* on 13

Nov. and in the *Pennsylvania Gazette* on 22 and 29 Nov., as well as in other papers throughout the colonies, reflected both sympathy and hostility to the American cause but, in their overall effect, indicated that Britain would follow a hard line and supported JA's contention that attempts at reconciliation were useless. The King's proclamation for "suppressing rebellion and sedition" of 23 Aug. 1775, was unequivocal in its stand (James Otis to John Hancock, 11 Nov., PCC, No. 65, I; JCC, 3:360; Washington, *Writings*, ed. Fitzpatrick, 4:82; also extracts from the letters in Force, *Archives*, 4th ser., 3:167–169).

[6] Probably a reference to the action of the General Court on 31 Oct. and 1 Nov. in appointing a four-man committee to find a reliable method of manufacturing saltpeter by 15 Dec. (Mass., *House Jour.*, 1775–1776, 2d sess., p. 215, 218–219).

To James Warren

Dr Sir   Octr. 1775

What think you of a North American Monarchy? Suppose We should appoint a Continental King, and a Continental House of Lords, and a Continental House of Commons, to be annually, or triennially or Septennially elected? And in this Way make a Supreme American Legislature? This is easily done you know by an omnipotent Continental Congress, and When once effected, His American Majesty may appoint a Governor for every Province, as his Britannic Majesty used to do, and Lt. Governor and secretary and judge of Admiralty—Nay his Continental Majesty may appoint the Judges of the Supream Courts &c. too—or if his American Majesty should condescend to permit the provincial Legislatures, or Assemblies [to] nominate two three or four Persons out of whom he should select a Governor, and 3 or 4 Men for Chief Justice &c. out of whom he should choose one, would not this do, nicely?

To his Continental Majesty, in his Continental Privy Council, Appeals might lie, from all Admiralty Cases, and from all civil Causes personal at least, of a certain Value and all Disputes about Land, that is about Boundaries of Colonies should be settled by the Continental

King and Council, as they used to be by the British K. and Council. What a magnificent System?

I assure you this is no Chimæra of my own. It is whispered about in Coffee Houses, &c. and there are [those] who wish it.

I am inclined to think it is done, as one Artifice more to divide the Colonies. But in vain. It would be very curious to give you an History of the out a Door Tricks for this important End of dividing the Colonies. Last Fall the Quakers and Antipœdobaptists were conjured up to pick a Quarrell with Massachusetts.[1] Last Spring the Land Jobbers were stimulated to pick a Quarrell with Connecticutt for the same End.[2] The Quakers and Anabaptists were hushed and abashed, or rather the reasonable conscientious Part of them were convinced in one Evening. The Land Jobbers will meet no better success.

RC (MHi:Warren-Adams Coll.); addressed: "Hon. James Warren Esqr Speaker of the House   Watertown"; docketed: "Mr. J A Lettr   Octr 1775."

[1] The Massachusetts delegation met with Quakers and Baptists at Carpenters' Hall in Philadelphia on 14 Oct. 1774. For the origin of the confrontation and its outcome, see JA, *Diary and Autobiography*, 2:152–154, note 3, and 3:311–313.

[2] The dispute between Pennsylvania and Connecticut over the claims of the Susquehannah Company in the Wyoming Valley once again broke out into armed conflict in the fall of 1775. For the action of the congress and the background of the dispute, see JCC, 3:283, 285, 287–288, 295, 297, 321, 335–336, 377, 435, 439–440; Julian P. Boyd and Robert J. Taylor, eds., *The Susquehannah Company Papers*, 11 vols., Ithaca, 1962–1971, 5:xlvi–lii.

From Mercy Otis Warren

Sir   Watertown October 1775[1]

The extensive system of policy which must engross your thoughts, and the vast field of business in which you are engaged, is such that I feel some checks whenever I call of[f] your attention for a moment on anything so unimportant as a letter of mine. Yet I cannot find myself willing to give up the pleasure of corresponding with a gentleman, I hold in high estimation, both as a defender of the rights of mankind, and as the faithful friend to a very worthy person who holds the first place in my heart. I think the last consideration gives me a claim to the indulgence of my scribbling humour, and frequently a letter in return.

As I feel myself as much interested in the welfare and happiness of the community, and the honour of my country, as any individual of either sex, I cannot but express some part of my concern, that any thing should take place among ourselves, which may give our vindictive foes just cause to unbraid us, as being actuated by the same narrow[2] and principles, we have so loudly borne testimony against. A new dispute has lately arisen between the board of Consellors and the house of Representatives: a full detail thereof will be given you by Mr. Warren, the first moment of leisure he can find.[3] I fear by this, and I will presume to say by some other injudicious steps, the hands of our new goverment will be weakened, and the legislative authority perhaps in time become contemptible among us.

Shall I ask you Sir, what is the reason that *man* in general, as soon as he is a little elevated towards the pinnacle of power (by whatever means he is invested therewith) grows forgetful at once of primeval principles, and becomes so tenacious of *prerogative* that he is sore in every part that affects it, and shrinks at the approach of any thing that might injure the newborn bantling. He wishes to cherish the young embrio till it grows to a gigantic size, to a formidable monster, that endangers the choicest claims of society.

I am more and more convinced, of the propensity in human nature to tyranize over their fellow men: and were it not for the few—the very few, disinterested and good men, who dare venture to stem the tide of power, when it grows wanton and overbearing, the ideas of native freedom, and the equal liberty of man would long ee'r this have been banished the western hemisphere. The darkness, the despotism, and slavery, of the eastern world, would soon spread their sable curtain over this clearer region. But I leave every ideal object, either of peace, terror, or war, to give you some further account of what in reality exists among us.

We may look into the capital and simpathize with the miserable remnant of inhabitants yet there; they are pining for bread, emaciated by fears and watching—wasted by sickness, and daily insulted by their cruel inmates who enter and take possession where ever they please. Many convenient houses, are levelled to the ground, and still to aggravate the insolence and barbarism of the times, the sanctuaries of religion are some of them converted into stables, while others are prostituted to the most ludicrous purposes.

The desk, the pews, and other incumbrances are taken down in the old South (a church long venerated in the town) to make it convenient for the accomodation of Burgoyne's light horse;[4] while the infamous Dr. Morison[5] whose character I suppose you are acquainted with, reads prayers in the Church in Brattle street, to a set of banditti who after the rapines, robberies, and devastations of the week, dare, some of them at least, to lift their sacrilegious hands, and bow before the altar of mercy.

The troops in Boston lie on their arms every night, in expectation that the Americans will attempt to enter. I wish we had possession of the town, yet, I fear it will be a bloody scene whenever it takes place. I will breath one wish more, and that is for the restoration of peace; peace I mean on equitable terms; for pusillanimous and feeble as I am, I cannot wish to see the sword quietly put up in the scabbard, until justice is done to America: the principles both of honour and humanity forbid it.

I hope Dr. Franklin has safely arrived among you. I was pleased with an opportunity of seeing and conversing with this venerable person, whose philosophic character has long been revered, nor was I less pleased to observe the affability and politeness of the gentleman, happily united with the virtues of the patriot in this respectable man. He commanded the veneration and esteem of every one here by a dignity of deportment, which I candidly hope is the result of conscious worth.

You will permit me to go on and give my opinion of several other distinguished characters, who have an active and important part to exhibit in the American cause. From their high rank in life, their names will be handed down to future generations and I hope with deserved applause. The Generals Washington, Lee, and Gates, with several other distinguished officers from head quarters dined with us three days since.[6] The first of these I think one of the most amiable and accomplished gentleman, both in person mind and manners that I have met with. The second who I never saw before, I think plain in his person to a degree of ugliness, careless, even to unpoliteness—his garb ordinary, his voice rough, his manners rather morose,—yet sensible, learned, judicious, and penetrating; a considerable traveller, agreeable in his narrations, and a zealous indefatigable friend to the American cause, but much more from a love of freedom and an impartial sense of the inherent rights of mankind at large than from any attachment or disgust to particular persons or countries. The last is a brave soldier, a high republican, a sensible companion, an honest man, of unaffected manners, and easy deportment. You know these people: if I have made up a wrong judgement, you may correct it.

I am disappointed in not seeing Mrs. Adams here this day;[7] but I shall soon call on her, at her own house on my way to Plymouth. I expect now in a few days to set out for that place where I shall go into winter quarters. I shall think myself and family quite safe there, as one of the reconnoitering pirates has reported it *too hazardous to venture the Kings ships into that harbour.*

I am exceedingly sorry for the death of so worthy a man, and so firm a friend to America as the Honourable Mr. Randolph.[8] When I view him as the unshaken patriot, I grieve for the loss my Country has sustained. When I consider him in the light of an amiable friend, and an affectionate husband, I commiserate the affliction of his lady: I have been told they were remarkably happy in the conjugal relation.

May those of your assembly, who are both capable and disposed to do service to their country be long continued and protected; and may you Sir, when your public duties will permit be returned to your friends, family, and connexions!

My letter has already run to such a length that I will only add, that if all men were like yourself and your friend Mr. Warren, it would not have been necessary for you to have written so often, with so much importunity, and to so little purpose for certain important public accounts. But they are at present in the hands of a set of men, who if left to themselves, would not compleat them till the close of the Millenium, even if it was not to begin till many more centuries are counted up in the score of *time*.[9]

That they will soon be put into hands less indolent; and appear in some more hopeful way, is wished, and believed by your sincere friend.[10]   Mrs. Warren

November 7th 1775 [11]

The Circumstance I Mentioned with Regard to the old south Church and which you may well think Gives Great affliction to the sisterhood, Comes from Mrs. Hooper who Got out of Boston Last week with a Number of other persons. Howe Has Lately Given Liberty to many people to Come out. But still the Wretchs are Miserable, for General Washington does not think proper to suffer the Boats to Come out by way of Chelsey and the Comander in Boston will not suffer them to Come by Roxbury. Our Caution is on account of the small pox with which Many are infected.

A New Commitee of accounts are to be Appointed ⟨yesterday⟩ soon who may perhaps do something to your satisfaction.[12] Your friend thinks the airs of prerogative, and the high sense of Dignity which some New made Creatures assume is Beyond Bearing.

Human Nature is the Cause the Guilty Cause. Nothing but a Rapid Rotation will keep the sins of men within due Bounds.

It was also a Resolve of the House that the Boston people should not Come out by Chelsey.[13]

LbC (MHi:Mercy Warren Letterbook, p. 156–159); RC (Adams Papers); addressed in the hand of James Warren: "To John Adams Esqr   [M]ember of Congress att Philadelphia." The RC, a supplement to the LbC, is written on a half sheet and dated 7 Nov. at the left (here moved to the right in accord with editorial practice), as was often done when a letter was continued. This half-sheet has been trimmed at the top and bottom and on the right side, but the address on the reverse is almost complete. This fact plus comparison of the half-sheet with full sheets used in the Warren household, particularly with respect to the position of watermarks, suggest that the original letter begun in October ended at the top of a page with only a line or so and the signature. Possibly the top was trimmed off for the benefit of an autograph collector.

[1] The nature of Mrs. Warren's so-called Letterbook, which is not arranged chronologically but by correspondents, means that the letters, which are not in her hand, were copied into it well after the time of composition, probably from drafts. Comparison of her letters in the Adams Papers with those in the Letterbook shows differences in phrasing and occasional discrepancies in dating; the drafts may not always have been dated so that conjectural dates were supplied. For possibly more exact dates for the present letter, see notes 6, 7, and 8 (below).

[2] The copyist inadvertently left out a word here.

[3] See James Warren to JA, 5 Nov. (below).

[4] For a brief account of the fate of various buildings in Boston, see Frothingham, *Siege of Boston*, p. 327–328.

[5] Rev. John Morrison (1743–1782) had been a minister of Peterborough, N.H., from 1766 to 1772, when he was dismissed. In 1775 he joined the army at Cambridge but deserted to the British immediately after the Battle of Bunker Hill. In Sept. 1775 he replaced Dr. Samuel Cooper, who had fled the town, as minister at the Brattle Street Church and preached at least one sermon. He left in the evacuation and died in Charleston, S.C. (Sabine, *Loyalists*, 2: 108; MHS, *Procs.*, 60 [1926–1927]: 94).

[6] The dinner referred to is possibly that given by the House of Representatives for the congressional committee and high-ranking officers on 19 Oct. (James Warren to JA, 20 Oct., note 3, above). If this supposition is correct, then this part of Mrs. Warren's letter can be dated 22 Oct. But see the next note.

[7] That is, Saturday, 4 Nov. James Warren says she was expected on that day; thus this part of the letter must be a delayed continuation (Warren to JA, 5 Nov., below).

[8] At this point the Letterbook includes a footnote: "Mr. Peyton Randolph was the first President of the American Congress." Randolph died on 22 Oct., further proof that this part of Mrs. Warren's letter must have been written well after that date. Her husband knew of the death by 5 Nov. at least (same).

[9] Concerned about the expenses that Massachusetts was incurring in behalf of the colonies, the House on 24 Aug. had appointed a committee to draw up an account of expenditures for supplies and soldiers' wages. The committee, which was to work during the House recess from 24 Aug. to 20 Sept., consisted of Isaac Lothrop, Capt. George Partridge, William Greenleaf, and Deacon David Jeffries. On 4 Oct. two additional committee members were named: James Sullivan and William Story. The enlarged committee reported first on 9 Oct., and its report was recommitted for amendments three times. The report was accepted on 13 Oct., and the accompanying letter to the delegates in the congress, on the 20th (Mass., *House Jour.*, 1775–1776, 1st and 2d sess., p. 103, 140, 147, 152, 155–156, 159, 160, 176). The date of the actual letter sent to the congress, however, was 24 Oct. (above). Mrs. Warren might well express impatience. The committee took two months to get its request sent off to the congress, and even then the form of the accounts was recognized to be only a "Gross Sum" without sufficient substantiation (*House Jour.*, p. 138, 196).

[10] On 21 Oct. the speaker (James Warren), Elbridge Gerry, Joseph Hawley, Joseph Otis, and Benjamin Mills were named a committee to suggest to the House "a more expeditious Method of settling Accounts." On 28 Oct. the House, in accordance with the recommendations of this committee, appointed a committee on accounts to authenticate sums spent in behalf of both the congress and the General Court, but the Council nonconcurred. On 8 Nov. the House changed somewhat the makeup of the committee and changed its powers so that it could act during both sessions and recesses. It is not clear whether the Council approved before the session ended, however (same, p. 185, 208, 214, 246, 268).

[11] On 25 Nov. JA acknowledged receipt of Mrs. Warren's letter "of Novr. 4th several Days ago" (below). But her 7's look very like 4's.

[12] The words "are to be" are written in the margin, a change made necessary by the crossing out of "yesterday." The implication is that Mrs. Warren had information about a new committee before its establishment had been completed. She may have been referring to one of three new committees in the making: the committee mentioned in note 10 (above), which would keep track of expenditures in behalf of the congress in the future; a committee proposed for estimating the damages done by the British, which the House considered on 7 Nov. (*House Jour.*, p. 242, 247–248, 266–267); or a new committee appointed 9 Nov. to replace the old one that had been working on accounts of money already spent in behalf of the congress (same, p. 256–257). JA would have been pleased with any one of these developments.

[13] On 5 Oct. (same, p. 141).

From Lemuel Hayward

Honored Sir   Roxbury St Thomas's Hospital Novr 1 1775

The small Acquaintance I have had with your Honor emboldens me to write you on an Affair which has given me no small degree of Perplexity, out of which I hope your Influence, and wonted Benevolence will relieve me. What I have respect to is the fixing of Surgeons in this Hospital.[1] Ever since Lexington Battle I have been wholly engaged in the Service of my Country as a Surgeon; on that Day I waited upon the Militia in that Capacity, and afterwards by the Desire of the late Dr. Warren attended with Dr. Aspinwall almost the whole of the Army on this Side, till regular Surgeons were appointed, after which by the Desire of Dr. Warren, Church, and the Generals, was with the above Gentleman, at the Trouble of forming, supplying, and attending a Hospital without either Mate, Steward or Clerk. On the 28th June Dr. Aspinwall, and myself received Warrants as joint Surgeons to the above Hospital intended for the Reception of the Sick of this Colony. This we attended with that Diligence, and Success that we trust was satisfactory, untill Dr. Church was appointed Director General of the Hospital; when we found the Honorable Continental Congress had established a General Hospital for the Reception of the Sick of the whole Army, and as Surgeons were already appointed to it of Consequence found ourselves superceded. This we mentioned to Dr. Church who told us that as it was absolutely necessary that a Hospital should be continued in this Camp, and as the Surgeons appointed were barely sufficient to attend the Sick in the other, more Surgeons must be appointed; desired us to continue in the Hospital as Surgeons, till he could obtain Permission from the Honorable Congress to appoint more, when we should be appointed. He afterwards told us he had wrote, soon expected an Answer, and desired us to act as Continental Surgeons. Accordingly by his Order, [we] took up two more Houses, as Hospitals, and attended them. Dr. Church so assured us of our Appointment, that by his Persuasion we were at the trouble, and Expence of sending to Philadelphia for Cloth &c. to dress in Uniform with the other Surgeons.

Upon the Confinement of Dr. Church finding ourselves without Warrants as Continental Surgeons, and without much Prospect of obtaining any, we applyed to his Excellency General Washington, and made him acquainted with our Situation; he appeared not a little surprised that an Affair of this Kind was not settled before, appointed us as Surgeons for the Present, till a new Director should be appointed, when he said the Matter should be further inquired into.[2]

And now, Sir, as I am unwilling to remain an idle Spectator in the present Contest, and at the same time anticipating the disagreable Sensations (on account of its disgraceful Appearance) that a Dismission from that Hospital I have for so many Months attended, must occasion, take this Me[ans] to sollicit your Influence to our Appointment in the Hospital. That two or more Surgeons must be appointed, I am certain, the Honorable Congress will soon be sensible of as the four Surgeons already appointed are wholly taken up in attending the Hospitals on the other side. I might mention the number of Sick to shew the necessity but as your Honor is already acquainted with the State of the Army I think it needless.

I am with you a friend to the Cause of Liberty and your Honors most obedient and most humble Servant   Lemuel Hayward

RC (Adams Papers); addressed: "To The Honorable John Adams Esq: Member of the Honorable Continental Congress in Philadelphia"; docketed: "Dr. Lem. Haywards Letter.   Novr. 1. 1775   answd. Novr. 13th by Dr Morgan."

[1] See William Gordon to JA, 25 Oct. (above).
[2] See Washington's appeal on behalf of Hayward and Aspinwall in his letter to the President of Congress, 14 Dec. (*Writings*, ed. Fitzpatrick, 4:161).

From John Thomas

Sir   Camp at Roxbury Novr. 1. 1775

I wrote you some time since the Gentlemen of the Committee from the Congress and presume'd to trouble you once more on the Account of the Hospital at Roxbury.

When I had the command last Spring att this place it was found Necessary to Establish a Hospital here. I Apply'd to the Provincial Congress on the matter and was by them desir'd to Establish One. I Accordingly took the House on Jamaica Plains, where Commadore Loring formerly live'd[1] and Doctor Warren Appointed Doctor Aspinwall—A Gentleman regularly educated in the Profession, as Surgeon of said Hospital, who has conducted Extreamly Well, and I am ceartain this Hospital is under ⟨better⟩ the best regulation of any in either Camp, and I understand he is not Provided for. Now if tis Consistant I could freely recommend him for some imployment in that Way, as I am certain no one wou'd give better Satisfaction in this department. I am Sir with Very great respect, Yr honours hum Ser

John Thomas

RC (Adams Papers); addressed: "To The Honourable John Adams   Philadelphia"; docketed: "Gen. Thomas.   Novr. 1. 1775."

[1] The Loring house, commandeered from the tory Joshua Loring, is described in Francis S. Drake, *The Town of Roxbury: Its Memorable Persons and Places*, Roxbury, Mass., 1878, p. 414–415, with accompanying small engraving.

From Samuel Osgood Jr.

Camp at Roxbury Novr. 4th. 1775

I have no other excuse for troubling you with another Letter but to inform you that my other ought to have been dated at Roxbury Camp Octr. 23d. pardon me the Neglect.

Our worthy Generals have all been together this is the third Day. Tomorrow I hope will finish it marking as some are pleased to term it the black Sheep among the Officers and I suppose the white are to receive enlisting Orders and their Commissions immediately.[1] May Heaven remove from us all dangerous Altercations and verify in us the Proverb that if we are smote upon one Cheek we may disposed to turn the other. Otherwise I am perswaded our Colony will not acquiesce in the Determination respecting those that are to be field Officers in the Army to be rais'd.

As the Regiments are reduced from 38 to 26 we must necessarily have many Officers Struck out of the List and some are for dismissing as many as possible. The Courtier or something more vile appears in the tame Submission of our own Generals who not boldly asserting their just Rights yield if not favor Incroachment excepting one[2] who always seeks that repose of Mind which arises from reflecting that he has always endeavored to prevent Oppression in every Form.

I have many Observations to make upon the Method taken to raise the new Army but have not Time at present. Only poor Massachusetts is like to be cut into flitters therefore I fear we shall not have an Army so soon as it will be absolutely necessary to have one. I am Sir with the greatest Respect your most Humble Servt.

Saml. Osgood junr

RC (Adams Papers); addressed: "To The Honble. John Adams Esqr. Member of the Continental Congress in Philadelphia favd. by Capt. Price."

[1] Out of necessity Washington was in the process of implementing the decisions reached during the visit of the congressional committee in October. The maintenance of an army in the field was his prime consideration, for Connecticut enlistments ran out on 10 Dec. and others on the 31st. Moreover, he needed an army with standardized units and a regular chain of command in which personal jealousies would be minimized. To this end the congress decreed that the army be established at 20,372 men, made up of regiments of 728 men each (28 regiments less 12) rather than of 40 regiments of varying sizes (JCC, 3:321, 322; French, *First Year*, p. 509, 761). This establishment meant a significant decrease in the number of officers and the demotion of some of those that remained in service. Thus, it threatened the New England system, in which the company or regiment was the personal domain of the officer commanding it, in which generals kept their rank as colonels and colonels as captains to maintain control over regiments and companies. Washington and his generals had to decide which officers to retain and how to persuade men to re-enlist when they did not know who their officers were to be. By the end of December, only about 6,000 men had re-enlisted. Obviously reorganization was not the sole cause of this disappointing result. Homesickness, lack of activity, shortages of firewood and clothing as winter approached also had their effect. It was local tradition that one went home from a campaign when the enlistment period was up. Soldiers had not yet learned to think of themselves as fighting for a cause extending beyond their own colonies; provincial rather than nationalistic attitudes persisted (French, *First Year*, ch. 31).

[2] Osgood is probably referring to his immediate superior, Gen. Artemas Ward.

From Joseph Ward

Sir   Camp at Roxbury 4 Nov. 1775

I beg leave to recommend to your Notice Capt. Price,[1] the Bearer of this, who has commanded one of the Companies of Riflemen in this Encampment; he has supported the Character of a good Officer and a worthy Gentleman; any Services which you may have opportunity to render him, will I apprehend, be serving our Country.

We have received an account from Halifax, that great disturbances have lately happened in London, but it wants confirmation. A report is just brought into Camp, "That the Continental Congress have resolved to offer a free trade to all Nations, except the British, and never to have any future connection with Britain until she has repaired the injuries we have suffered by her tyranny." If this news is not true, I hope it is a forerunner of such proceedings. The late infernal conduct of the *Pirates* at Falmouth, I apprehend is a full answer to all American Petitions, and in its consequences will, I conceive be the best answer we have received. We wait with solicitude to know the success of the Troops which are gone to reduce Quebec and St. Johns. The Army here is now healthy, and notwithstanding our progress is slow, I trust we shall sooner or later conquer the Enemies of Freedom. The Pirates and Rebels in Boston are very busily employed in fortifying themselves, and by late accounts from them, they are very much afraid we shall attack the Town. They however flatter themselves that our Army will be greatly lessened by the cold weather, want of necessaries, &c. It appears from good authority, that the Enemy are sickly, and much distressed for want of provisions, wood, &c. I hope we shall in the course of the Winter bring them to reason, or to *ruin*. No reinforcements have lately arrived, and it is said by Persons from Boston, that none are expected before next Spring. If no reinforcement should arrive this Fall, and we can secure what troops are now in America before Spring, I apprehend the Contest would be near to an end; and therefore I hope every nerve will be exerted to sweep the Continent and secure every Enemy before they can form a Spring Campaign.

My constant wishes and prayers are for Wisdom, Prosperity Health and Happiness to the Continental Congress. I am Sir your Obedient and most Humble Servant,   Joseph Ward

RC (Adams Papers); docketed: "Jo. Wards Letter   4. Novr. 1775."

¹ Probably Thomas Price of Maryland (Heitman, *Register Continental Army*, p. 452).

To Elbridge Gerry

Dear Sir   Philadelphia November 5. 1775

I am under Such Restrictions, Injunctions and Engagements of Secrecy respecting every Thing which passes in Congress, that I cannot communicate my own Thoughts freely to my Friends, So far as is necessary to ask their Advice, and opinions concerning Questions which many of them understand much better than I do. This however is an inconvenience, which must be Submitted to for the sake of Superiour Advantages.

But I must take the Liberty to say that I think We shall Soon think of maritime Affairs, and naval Preparations: No great Things are to be expected at first, but out of a little a great deal may grow.[1]

It is very odd that, I, who have Spent my Days in Researches and Employments so very different, and who have never thought much of old Ocean, or the Dominion of it, should be necessitated to make such Enquiries: But it is my Fate, and my duty,[2] and therefore I must attempt it.

I am to enquire what Number of seamen, may be found in our Province, who would probably inlist in the service, either as Marines, or on board of Armed Vessells, in the Pay of the Continent, or in the Pay of the Province, or on board of Privateers, fitted out by Private Adventurers.

I must also intreat you to let me know the Names, Places of Abode, and Characters, of such Persons belonging to any of the seaport Towns in our Province, who are qualified for Officers and Commanders of Armed Vessells.

I want to be further instructed, what ships, Brigantines, schooners &c. are to be found in any Part of the Province, which are to be sold or hired out, which will be suitable for armed Vessells—What Their Tonnage the Depth of Water they draw, their Breadth, their Decks &c., and to whom they belong, and What is their Age.

Further, what Places in our Province, are most secure and best accommodated for Building new Vessells, of Force in Case a Measure of that Kind Should be thought of.

The Committee have returned, much pleased with what they have seen and heard, which shews that their Embassy will be productive of happy Effects. They say the only disagreable Circumstance, was that their Engagements Haste and constant Attention to Business was such as prevented them from forming such Acquaintances with the Gentlemen of our Province as they wished. But as Congress was waiting for their Return before they could determine upon Affairs of the last Moment, they had not Time to spare.[3]

They are pretty well convinced I believe of several important Points, which they and others doubted before.

New Hampshire has leave to assume a Government and so has South Carolina,[4] but this must not be freely talked of as yet, at least from me.

New England will now be able to exert her strength which a little Time will show to be greater than either Great Britain or America imagines. I give you Joy of the agreable Prospect in Canada. We have the Colors of the Seventh Regiment as the first fruits of Victory.[5]

RC (NHpR:Naval MS Coll.); docketed in an unknown hand: "Phila Letter   Hon John Adams Esq   4th Novr 1775." An extract of this letter carries a docket entry: "Mr. Speaker   Mr. Gerry   Colo. Orne" (M-Ar:207, p. 266). Apparently Gerry extracted part of the letter for the consideration of the House, which had completed action on its own bill on armed vessels on 18 Oct. (Mass., *House Jour.*, 1775–1776, 2d sess., p. 173).

[1] On 30 Oct. JA was appointed to a reconstituted committee to fit out armed vessels. For details, see JA's Service in the Congress, 13 Sept. – 9 Dec. (above).

[2] In a very similar letter sent to James Warren on this date (not printed here), JA makes a little more of his duty: he tells Warren "a secret in Confidence [that] it has become my Duty" to serve on a committee to fit out armed vessels. (*Warren-Adams Letters*, 1:174–175).

[3] The congress approved the committee's report on 4 and 7 Nov. (JCC, 3:321–325, 330–334).

[4] JA adds here in his letter to Warren of 5 Nov. (MHi:Warren-Adams Coll.): "and so will every other Colony which shall ask for it which they all will do soon, if the Squabble continues." And toward the end of his letter, he adds this: "Who expected to live to see the Principles of Liberty Spread and prevail so rapidly, human Nature exerting her whole Rights, unshackled by Priests or Kings or Nobles, pulling down Tyran-

nies like Sampson, and building up, what Governments the People think best framed for human Felicity. God grant the Spirit, success." For the action of the congress on New Hampshire and South Carolina, see JCC, 3:319 and 326–327.

[5] On 19 Oct., 83 men of the Seventh Regiment or Royal Fusileers were captured when Fort Chambly was taken. Their capture meant that St. John's on the route to Montreal could expect no relief from the siege mounted by Gen. Montgomery. Letters from Gens. Schuyler and Montgomery announcing the victory arrived in Philadelphia on 3 Nov. and were read in the congress the next day. With them came flags of the Seventh Regiment, which were hung "in Mrs. Hancocks Chamber with great Splendor and Elegance" (same, 3:320, 353; French, *First Year*, p. 428–429; *Adams Family Correspondence*, 1:319–320).

To John Trumbull

My dear Sir   Novr 5. 1775

I take an opportunity by this Express, to thank you for Mc Fingal, a Poem which has been shewn me within a few days. It is excellent, and perhaps the more so for being misterious. It wants explanatory Notes as much as Hudibrass. I cant conjecture the Characters either of Honorius or Mc Fingal.[1]

Am Sorry to learn that We are likely to loose some of our best Men. We may have better in their stead for aught I know but We shall certainly loose good ones.

There is scarcely a more active, industrious, enterprising and capable Man, than Mr. Deane, I assure you.[2] I shall sincerely lament the

Loss of his services. Men of such great daring active Spirits are much Wanted.

I shall think myself much obliged to you, if you would write me. I want to hear the great Politicks and even the Small Talk of your Colony.

For my own Part I feel very enthusiastic at Times. Events which turn up everyday are so new, unexpected and surprising to most Men, that I wonder more Heads are not turn'd than We hear of. Human Nature seems to be employed like Sampson, taking Hold of the Pillars of Tyranny and pulling down the whole building at a ⟨Time⟩ at a— Lunge I believe is the best Word. I hope it will not, like him bury itself in the Ruins, but build up the wisest and most durable Frames for securing its Happiness. But Time must determine. I am, sir, with much Esteem your Friend

RC (NjP:de Coppet Coll.); docketed in an unknown hand: "John Adams Esqr [re?] John Trumbull   Novr. 5th 1775."

[1] *McFingal: A Modern Epic Poem . . . or the Town Meeting* was written by Trumbull in the fall of 1775 and published that year by William and Thomas Bradford of Philadelphia (Evans, No. 14528). Almost certainly JA read the MS copy that Trumbull sent to Silas Deane with the admonition to reveal the name of its author to no one but JA (Trumbull to Deane, 26 Oct., *Deane Papers*, 1:86–90). Deane and other leading patriots, including JA, had probably encouraged Trumbull to write the poem to raise whig morale, ridicule tory efforts to gain control, and to exploit the talent that Trumbull had already shown in other works, such as the piece that appeared in the *Connecticut Courant* on 7 and 14 Aug. 1775 satirizing Gen. Gage's penchant for proclamations. Written in the mock-epic style of Samuel Butler's *Hudibras, McFingal* centered on the confrontation between Squire Mc-Fingal, representative of Massachusetts tories, and Honorius, traditionally identified as JA, at an imaginary town meeting after the Battle of Lexington and Concord. The poem was a success both in 1776 and after Cornwallis' defeat, when Trumbull expanded the work (Evans, No. 17750). The several American and English editions made Trumbull a major literary figure for his day (Moses Coit Tyler, *Literary History* of the American Revolution, new edn., N.Y., 1941, p. 430–450; Alexander Cowie, *John Trumbull, Connecticut Wit*, Chapel Hill, 1936, p. 145–206; see also Lennox Grey, "John Adams and John Trumbull in the 'Boston Cycle,'" *NEQ*, 4:509–514 [July 1931], in which the identification of Honorius as JA is disputed).

[2] In October, Connecticut had decided to replace Deane and Eliphalet Dyer with Oliver Wolcott and Samuel Huntington as delegates to the congress, while retaining Roger Sherman as the third member of the delegation (*Conn. Colonial Records*, 15:136). John Trumbull explained to Deane that the General Assembly believed that it was "dangerous to trust so great a power as you now have, for a long time in the hands of one Set of Men, lest they should grow too self-important and do a great deal of mischief in the end" (*Deane Papers*, 1:87). See also Trumbull's explanation to JA, 14 Nov. (below). In his often repeated plea that he be replaced and allowed to return home to replenish his estate, JA had also argued for the benefits of rotation in office, but Deane was "Confoundedly Chagrined at his recall" (Dyer to Joseph Trumbull, 1 Jan. 1776, Burnett, ed., *Letters of Members*, 1:292–293).

From James Warren

My dear Sir   Watertown Novr 5th: 1775

I must begin every Letter with Thanks for the Receipt of your Favours, haveing such Abundant reason for it, that mine would be marked with Ingratitude (a Vice I detest) if I did not. Last Sunday Coll. Reed dined with us in his way to Philadelphia. By him I wrote and Inclosed some packages[1] which I hope will reach your hand this day, since which I have not been Able to get one single Hour to write, Paying of the Regiments for Septemr., Attending the House which sets till 8 in the Evening, and some want of Health from the great fatigue I am Obliged to Submit to have prevented. I am reduced to the Necessity of denying myself the pleasure of hearing Good Doctr. Cooper in order to write this. I received yours per Messrs. Fallwell and Hart[2] one day last week, at a Time very Unlucky. They came in when I had a room full of Colonels and money. I Endeavoured to Treat them with all the Civility and politeness due to strangers, but partly from the pressure I was under, and partly from want of discretion, or a Fatality or something I can't Account for a material part of Civility was omitted. I did not open the Letters till they were gone. This however did not proceed from any Inattention to your recommendations. They certainly give me great pleasure and do me great honour. I have tryed to remedy the mistake, and hope I shall have an opportunity at least to make my Excuse. I can hope for little more as I hear they go Tomorrow. You will I dare say do it for me. Last Week was an Excessive Busy one. The Regiments to pay, and Majr. Hawley preparing for a Recess which he was bent upon the Amazeing Field of Business before us prevented but I suppose it will take place this week, tho' I think we shall leave things in a State of Confusion.[3] I have Just received yours by Mr. Brown.[4] I Lament the Death of the Good old President. I had before formed a Good Opinion of him. The Character you give him Enhances it.

I want to tell you a Thousand Things as much as you want to know them. Had I time I should Assuredly tire you with my Scribbles. I Expect little more than An Hour when Meeting will be done and Company return to Interrupt me. The Prices of European and West India Goods, are Notwithstanding our Resolves much Advanced. Trade will have its Course. Goods will rise and fall in proportion to the demand for them and the quantity at Market &c. in Spite of Laws Honour, Patriotism or any other Principle. The People however seem to have forgot their Expectations, and the Injunctions laid on the Merchant, and little is said about it.

The Non Exportation is sacredly Observed and I believe never been violated in a Single Instance, and such is the Spirit here, that it cannot be violated with any degree of Safety. Provisions are plenty and Cheap. Beef is a drugg and our People Complain much that the Commissary sends to Connecticut for all his Beef. I think it but fair that he should give this Colony a Chance in that Article at least, especially as we are to Supply the Army with Hay and wood, which our People say they can't do and keep their Cattle now fat over the winter. This has Occasioned great difficulty here. The General has offered 5/. per [ct?] for hay and 20/. per Cord for wood, and cannot be supplyed. This he Imputes to a Monopolizeing Avaritious Spirit and perhaps not wholly without foundations. The prices are indeed high, but the People have much to say, and among other things ask why that Spirit should be Confined to those Articles and why Cyder is to be had at 4/. per barrel.[5] In the mean time the Army has suffered much for want of wood, and the officers have not been able to restrain them from Cutting down the fine Groves of Cambridge and threatning to pull down Houses for fuel. The General has made repeated Applications to us.[6] We at last set ourselves seriously to remedy the Evil, which perhaps might Terminate in breaking up the Army. We spent the whole of last Fryday and Evening on the Subject. We at last Chose a Committee in Aid to the Quarter Master General to purchase those Articles, and Impowered them to Enter the wood Lotts of the Refugees, Cut, Stack, and procure Teems to Carry to the Camp wood as fast as possible and Hay as soon as they can get it.[7] The Teems are passing all day, and I hope this Step will be a radical Cure.

Your next Question is with regard to Trade a Subject Complicated vast, and Unbounded. When I Consider the great Abundance we have of the necessaries and Conveniences of Life, that we want Nothing but Salt Petre and I hope we are in a way to get that, I could wish a Total Stop was put to all Trade but when I consider the Temper, and Genius of the People, the long Habits they have been used to, I fear it would produce Uneasiness, and Bad-Consequences. I believe therefore you will find it necessary to Indulge so much as will not Endanger the Success of your Commercial Measures. If the Merchant will run the Hazard, so much may Tend to Conciliate the Affections of other Nations, and Unite them with us on Principles of Interest. The strongest of all principles in these degenerate days. I am Sensible many Important questions may arise on this head, too many and too Important for my Abilities or Opportunities to discuss at present.

I am Extreamly pleased with the Appointment of the Committee you mention, and with the Committee itself.[8] I believe this Business will produce great Consequences. You may be assured I shall Exert myself to have your Expectations and wishes Complied with both with regard to Time and manner.

Mcpherson is yet here but I dare not ask questions.[9] Nothing Transpires and whether any plan is adopted or not, can't Inform you.

We have no News here. All Things remain in Statu quo, the Enemy I mean. Their Army are quiet and we watch them. Barracks are building for our Troops, and many of them are ready to receive them. The whole will be Compleated in the Course of this Month, and indeed it is Time. The Season is rainy and Cold. The Pirates Continue to rove about, and Threaten our Seaports. They made an Attempt to go into Plymouth but were discouraged by the Appearance of the Harbour, returned and reported to the Admiral that it was not fit to receive Kings Ships. Our People are however prepareing for them if they alter their minds. Our Assembly have Established Saltpetre works at Newburyport under the direction of a Committee, Dr. Whiteing, John Peck, Deacon Baker and one Phips the last of whoom is said to be an Adept that way, and have given a Bounty of 4/. per lb to any man that shall make 50 lbs or upwards this Bounty to Continue to next June. We have also taken Care to Encourage the manufacture of Fire Arms.[10] Thus far we have done well, but our militia is still in a miserable, unsettled Situation. This principally or wholly arises from a dispute between the two Houses. We claim an equal Right with them in the Appointment of the Field Officers. This claim we ground on your Resolutions which will bear very fairly that Construction and is certainly the most Eligible Constitution, and say that if that is not the true Construction we that deserve as large privileges as any People are not on an equal footing with the other Colonies. The Board Contend for the Exclusive right, plead the Charter, and Assert the Prerogative with as much Zeal, Pride and Hauture of Dominion as if the powers of Monarchy were vested in them, and their Heirs by a divine Indefeasible right. This is indeed Curious to see a Council of this Province Contend for the dirty part of the Constitution the prerogative of the Governor. How it is to End or when I know not. I wish they had in the Exercise of Powers we dont dispute with them, made Appointments in some Instances less Exceptionable than they have. You will hardly Expect to hear after what I last wrote you[11] that Paine is Ap-

The Hon.: Sir Willm Howe K.^t of the
BATH,
Commander in Chief of all his Majesty's Forces in America —

11. WILLIAM HOWE (1729–1814)
See page xii

pointed a Judge, but so it is. At a Time when I least Expected he was Appointed, it is said by the Influence and Management of Hawley. Spooner, Foster and I believe Palmer were the principle Conductors. The Rank is thus John Adams Esqr. Chief Justice, Cushing, Read, Paine, Sargeant. Now we shall see if he will act in an Inferiour Station to his Superiour. The People at the Eastward are Apprehensive the Enemy Intend to possess themselves of an Advantageous Post at Falmouth and hold the place and secure the Harbour.

I have no Letters at present from Mrs. Adams to Inclose. She was very well a few days ago, and had an Intention to have come here Yesterday to spend Sunday and hear Doctr. Cooper. I suppose the weather prevented. My Compliments all Friends Mr. Adams especially. Adeu

Doctr. Church is Expelled by almost an Unanimous Vote.

Favourable Accounts from the Western Army. Doubtless you have the whole.[12]

Is it not Time for a Test Act. Will the Continent have one from Congress.[13] How long are we to wait for the Success of the Petition.[14]

I long to hear of the [Sweep?], a good devise to furnish the Capital Article.[15] You will see in our Papers Howes Proclamation and an Association.[16]

Nov 7th.

I now Inclose two Letters received Yesterday from Mrs. Adams.[17]

We shall rise perhaps Tomorrow or next day. We have some thoughts of comeing to a new Choice of delegates this setting. I could wish to have it put of[f] to hear from you. I cant think of a List without Your Name in it. If we make any Change who shall we get. I do not Expect to be suited.[18]

One of the Enemies vessels bound to N. Scotia with a Cargo to purchase provisions taken and Carried into Beverly. Another of them on Shore at Cape Cod with 120 Pipes of wine &c. so we get a Supply of Turtle, wine, and all the delicacies that Luxury can wish.[19]

I congratulate you on the Success at Chamblee. The Bell rings. I must go.

RC (Adams Papers); docketed: "Novbr 5 1775   Warren."

[1] See James Warren to JA, 28 Oct., notes 3 and 4 (above).
[2] See JA's first letter to Warren of 21 Oct. (above).
[3] The General Court adjourned on 11 Nov. to reconvene on the 29th (Mass., *House Jour.*, 1775–1776, 2d sess., p.

271). For the confusion, see Warren's comments below about the quarrel between the branches over military appointments.
[4] JA to Warren, 24 [i.e. 23] Oct. (above).
[5] Cider had taken a sharp decline in

price in 1774 and had rallied very little in 1775, according to figures given by William B. Weeden. In 1773 it had sold at £2 5s O.T. per barrel; in 1775, at £1 12s 2d (*Economic and Social History of New England*, 2 vols., Boston, 1894, 2:900). Warren of course is quoting not Old Tenor but lawful money prices.

⁶ Washington declared that conditions had so deteriorated that "different Regiments were upon the Point of cutting each others throats for a few Standing Locusts near their Encampments" (Washington to the General Court, 27 Oct. and 2 Nov., *Writings*, ed. Fitzpatrick, 4:47–48, 60–61).

⁷ See Mass., *House Jour.*, p. 229–230.

⁸ The committee to collect information on British hostilities, on which Silas Deane and George Wythe served with JA.

⁹ A reference to McPherson's secret scheme to destroy British warships (second letter of JA to Warren, 20 Oct., note 1, above).

¹⁰ Whiting, Peck, and Baker were appointed on 31 Oct., Jedediah Phips of Sherburn on 1 Nov. after he had appeared before the House and explained improvements in the production of saltpeter. The resolve on firearms, adopted on 2 Nov., offered a bounty of £3 on arms manufactured in the province and delivered to Watertown (Mass., *House Jour.*, p. 215, 218–219, 225).

¹¹ Warren to JA, 20 Oct. (above).

¹² The General Court responded to news of the capture of Fort Chambly by issuing a proclamation of thanksgiving on 4 Nov. (Mass., *House Jour.*, p. 232).

¹³ The congress did not pass a test act and on 9 March 1776 specifically declared that "no oath by way of test be imposed upon, exacted, or required of any of the inhabitants of these colonies, by any military officers." New York delegates were dismayed when Gen. Charles Lee imposed such a test on citizens of New York (*JCC*, 4:195, note 1).

¹⁴ The congress received news of the rejection of the Olive Branch petition on 9 Nov. (same, 3:343).

¹⁵ Probably saltpeter, about which JA wrote in several of the letters that Warren is answering.

¹⁶ Gen. William Howe's proclamation forbade anyone not in the navy to leave Boston without Howe's permission, on pain of imprisonment or even execution. The "Association" of "Loyal Citizens" arose from a request (i.e., order) on 28 Oct. for the loyalists in Boston to organize to take over some of the duties of the regular soldiers. The texts of the "Association" and the "request" were printed in the *Boston Gazette*, 6 Nov.

¹⁷ Probably AA's letter of 5 Nov. with an enclosure—the account of the Battle of Bunker Hill signed by Joseph Palmer (*Adams Family Correspondence*, 1:320–322; Committee of Safety's Account of the Battle, 25 July, above).

¹⁸ On 11 Nov. the General Court extended the commissions of the Massachusetts delegation until 31 Jan. 1776 (Mass., *House Jour.*, p. 269).

¹⁹ The first-mentioned ship, the *North Britain*, going from Boston to Annapolis Royal and carrying dry goods to exchange for provisions, was disabled in a storm and carried into Beverly. The second, owned by Thomas Salter and a victim of the same storm while bound from Philadelphia to Boston, went aground at Eastham on Cape Cod (*Boston Gazette*, 13 Nov.; Washington, *Writings*, ed. Fitzpatrick, 4:71–75; *Naval Docs. Amer. Rev.*, 2:891, 893, and notes).

From Samuel Cooper

Sir   Waltham Novr. 6. 1775

I take the first Opportunity to acknowledg the Honor I receiv'd in a Letter sign'd by you as Chairman of a Committee of the Honorable Congress for obtaining a just and well authenticated [account] of the Hostilities committed by the Ministerial Troops and Navy &c.,

and desiring me to take some Part[1] in this Business. You will be so good as to present my Compliments to the other Gentlemen of the Committee and acquaint them, that Nothing could give me greater Pleasure than to contribute all in my Power towards the Aid of my Country in its present Distress, and for facilitating in any degree any Branch of that great and important Service in which the Congress is engag'd. I wish indeed my abilities and present Situation would allow me to do more in the Matter upon which you write. What I can do, shall be done.

Your Letter mentions an Application to several Assemblies on this Point. I know not Whether Massachusett's is included in this Number. A Committee from one or both Houses here, (to whose Care in this Matter I would most readily join my own, should it be needed) would, I imagine, best answer your Intention.[2]

Devoutly wishing the Direction and Blessing of Heaven to the Congress, I am Sir, Yours and the Committee's most obedient humble Servant,   Saml Cooper

RC (Adams Papers).

[1] See JA to James Warren, 18 Oct., note 5 (above).
[2] On 7 Nov. the House of Representatives first considered appointment of a committee on British hostilities (Mass., *House Jour.*, 1775–1776, 2d sess., p. 242, 247–248, 266–267).

John Adams' Commission as Justice of the Peace in Massachusetts Counties

Watertown, 8 November 1775. Printed form with spaces filled in appropriately (Adams Papers); signed by Perez Morton, Deputy Secretary, and fifteen Council members.

This commission is identical to that received by JA dated 6 September appointing him Justice of the Peace of Suffolk County (see calendar entry, above) except that it broadened his powers to include all of Massachusetts. Like the previous commission, it was given under the patronage system, for at the same time that JA was appointed, 26 others also received commissions, including the other four members of the Massachusetts delegation to the Continental Congress (Records of the States, Microfilm, Mass. E.1, Reel No. 9, Unit 1, p. 161). No evidence has been found, however, that JA ever made use of his commission.

To Henry Knox

Dr Sir   Philadelphia Novr 11. 1775
I had the Pleasure of a Letter from you[1] a few days ago and was rejoiced to learn that you have at last determined to take a more im-

portant share than you have done hitherto in the Conduct of our military Matters. I have been impressed with an Opinion of your Knowledge and Abilities in the military Way for several years, and of late have endeavoured, both at Camp, at Watertown and at Philadelphia, by mentioning your Name and Character, to make you more known, and consequently in a better Way for Promotion.

It was a sincere Opinion of your Merit and Qualifications, which prompted me to act this Part and therefore I am very happy to be able to inform you, that I believe you will very soon be provided for according to your Wishes, at least you may depend upon this that nothing in my Power shall be wanting to effect it.[2]

It is of vast Importance, my dear sir, that I should be minutely informed of every Thing which passes at the Camp, while I hold a Place in the Great Council of America: and Therefore I must beg the Favour of you to write me as often as you can by safe Conveyances. I want to know the Name, Rank and Character of every officer in the Army. I mean every honest and able one. But more especially of every officer, who is best acquainted with the Theory and Practice of Fortification and Gunnery. What is comprehended within the Term Engineer? and whether it includes skill both in Fortification and Gunnery—and what skillfull Engineers you have in the Army and whether any of them and who have seen service and when and where. I am sir your very humble sert   John Adams

I want to know if there is a compleat set of Books upon the military Art in all its Branches in the Library of Harvard Colledge, and what Books are the best upon those subjects.[3]

RC (MHi:Henry Knox Papers); addressed: "Mr Henry Knox Cambridge To the Care of Coll Warren"; docketed: "Honble John Adams Esq Philadelphia   Novr 11 1775."

[1] Knox to JA, 26 Oct. (above).
[2] See same, note 3.
[3] No printed catalogue is available for 1775, but that of 1790 does not list a military arts category, nor do any of the books mentioned by JA to William Tudor (12 Oct., above) appear in it. Since for safety's sake the library was moved out of Cambridge in 1775 and the books stored in several places, it is unlikely that additions of military titles to the collection were practical (*Catalogus Bibliothecæ Harvardianæ*, Boston, 1790; *The Library of Harvard University: Descriptive and Historical Notes*, 4th edn., Cambridge, 1934, p. 17).

From Elbridge Gerry

Dear Sir   Water Town Novr 11. 1775

I received a Letter from the honorable Committee of Congress for collecting "a just and well authenticated Account of the Hostilities committed by the ministerial Troops and Navy in America since last March," and beg leave to inform You that Colo. Palmer, Mr. Cooper and Colo. Thomson are appointed a Committee to subserve the purpose in this Colony in the Recess of the Court, which is this Day adjourned to the 28th of the Month.[1]

I am greatly concerned to inform You, that a Dissention has taken Place between the Council and House which must be speedily remedied, or the most unhappy Consequences may be expected therefrom; It relates to the Right of appointing militia Officers in this Colony. The Council conceive that by the Resolve of the Honorable the Continental Congress for resuming Government in the Colony, they are held to observe a strict adherence to the Charter, and that a Deviation therefrom, agreable to another Resolve of the Congress for regulating the militia of the united American Colonies, would counteract the Sense of the Congress and hazard a disunion of the Colonies; and while they profess a Desire of conducting agreably to the last Recommendation and acknowledge that it is most for the Interest of the people, they rigidly oppose the Doings of the House in this Respect upon the principle that they are obliged so to do. The House impressed with the Importance of immediately regulating the Militia in the Middle of the last Session sent a Resolve to the Board for appointing a joint Committee to consider of and report a Method for choosing militia Officers which should be best adapted to promote the Interest of the Colony and warranted by the Resolves of the continental Congress, having Previously chosen a Committee to bring in a Militia Bill who could not report untill the Method of appointing Officers should be first settled and determined. This the Board most unexpectedly nonconcurred, and gave the House Reason to conclude that they inclined to retain the prerogative in their Department as *Governor*. The House notwithstanding this sent up another Resolve proposing a Conference by Committees, which accordingly took place; but without any salutory Effects. Since this Application has been made from the County of Cumberland for a General Officer to conduct the Militia and Forces stationed there Against the Enemy, and the Resolve of the House for appointing such an Officer in their distressed Circumstances was nonconcurred. Messages from each have been sent to the other, without any other Effects that I can perceive than widening the Breach. In one of those Messages the Council proposed an Application to the Continental Congress for an Explanation of their Resolves, which the House for many Reasons refused; particularly these that the Resolves were so clear and intelligible to the House that

An Application for that purpose did not appear necessary and it would imply Obscurity and Want of precission in a performance which was evidently penned with great Care and Correctness. This the Council answered, as You will probably See if Copies of the Messages should be sent, by entering into the Argument which the House has hither to studiously avoided; and altho an Officer has been this Day chosen by joint Ballot for Cumberland, yet it is expressly declared by the Board that the same is from the Necessity of the Case and not to be considered as a precedent for the future.[2] I am exceedingly sorry that at so critical a Time as this such a Controversy should be persisted in, and the more so, as I apprehend the Board will apply to the Congress for an Explanation, that shall comport with the Sentiments as it is said of some of the Delegation from this Colony, and one of the Gentlemen who was upon the Committee from the Congress, relative to this Matter. Should this be done and the Congress order the Appointment according to the Charter, it will create such a Ferment amongst the people, as well as in the House, as will divide and ruin Us. I cannot say what was the Intent and Design of the honorable Congress touching this Matter, but by the Resolve for Regulating the Militia, it is clearly recommended to the Inhabitants of *all* the united American Colonies to form themselves into Companies and choose their Captains and other Officers of the Company, and in many Towns in this Colony it is not only considered by the people as their *Right* but in Conformity to the Resolve they have actually chosen such officers and made Return to the Court that the same may be commissionated. Had it been the Design of the honorable Congress that this Government should have been made an Exception and the Rights of Appointment have been in the Council as Governor, I am certain that the people would have considered it as extremely hard and having once experienced the previlege of choosing would hardly have been prevailed on to give it up; but after having so clear and plain a Resolve of the Continental Congress and knowing from their Representatives the Sense of the House upon it, what can be expected to take place should an Explanation be obtained that will deprive them of a Right which they consider as fairly ceded, other than an Aversion to that Branch of the Legislature which has been instrumental in thus depriving them of the same. If it is proposed to commission the Captains and Subalterns agreably to the Choice of the people, it must then be apparent that the Argument of being held to the Charter in this Respect falls to the Ground and nothing can be said in favour of the Councils Appointing General or Field Officers for the Militia that can ever reconcile the House to consent thereto. The House abhor the Thought of ever having the Appointment of militia Officers revert to the Governor, they are not sure of a new Government, they conceive that once the Mode of Appointment is confirmed to and practised by the Assemblies and people thro' out the Continent it never will revert to the Governor, and altho they would not contend about the Matter so strenuously was it held by the Council as the second Branch of the Legislature, yet they are highly displeased at the Conduct of the Council in holding for a detestable Governor this precious Jewel with which he has heretofore gained such advantages over us, and the House considers it altogether needless for the Board so to conduct, for putting the Resolve for exercising Government out of the Question, nothing is more clear than that the Field Officers in this Colony ought to be appointed and commissionated by the Assembly or in their Recess by a Committee of Safety by them appointed, and the lower officers by each Company respectively; and this Resolve can never be supposed to have been intended to exclude this Colony from the Benefit of a Regulation made for all the Colonies and confessedly advantageous to the Colony, and especially as it never proposed a strict Adherence to the Charter, but only one that should be as near as may be to it. And what makes the Supposition that the Congress intended to exclude this Colony from regulating the Militia according to the Resolve made for *all* the united Colonies, less justifiable, and the Idea that the Congress did not mean to supersede the Charter in any Respect, somewhat unnatural, is the Consideration that in the last paragraph of this Resolve it is recommended to the provincial Congresses and the *Assemblies* of any Colony which are elective by the people to adopt the Resolve in whole or in Part &c., and it is also recommended to the *Assemblies* as well as Conventions of all the united Colonies to choose Committees of Safety with powers of appointing and commissionating Officers of the Militia in the Recess of such Assembly or Convention, which is evidently a Supersedeas to the Charters of each Colony now governed by an assembly. I will not trouble You further with the Sense of the House and the Arguments to be produced by it on this subject and only propose, that since Matters are come to such a Crisis, as You will find by the Express Mr. Revere, that no Terms of Reconciliation can ever be expected to take place, a Recommendation of the Congress may issue to the Council which will render them blameless, explicitly blameless for conducting agreably to the Recommendations for regulating the Militia before cited; this will serve to unite both Branches, conduce towards the Settlement of the Militia, make the People and House easy and in every Respect I hope be attended with happy Consequences, whereas a contrary Conduct would have an Effect directly the Reverse which You would have discovered at the first agitation of the Matter had We been so happy as to have had You present at that Time.

The packet which Mr. Revere will deliver You from the Board, I apprehend will convince the honorable Congress that Devastation and Slaughter fulfil the Desires of our Enemies who have already reinforced the Army with 3 or 4000 Men and propose sending in the Spring upwards of 20,000. A paragraph of one of the Letters read in the House[3] mentions the last petition of Congress as being considered by the Ministry to have discover'd an Inability On the part of the Congress to carry on the War and animated them in their Measures; whether this is the Case or not I cannot say but think it high Time for the Continent to form foreign Alliances, open all their ports, establish 50,000 more Men, order Test Acts thro'out the Colonies, order Brigadiers to each County Militia thro'out the Continent, and Saltpetre Works and powder Mills also; this by the latter End of Spring may put Us in a Situation to welcome 40,000 of our Enemies if we can tell where to find them.

I have been always attentive to the Manufactory of Salt petre and Fire Arms and I think the Art of making the first is now discovered. The Assembly has sent Hand Bills into all the Towns for obtaining both, 4/ bounty in addition to the price offered by Congress for Salt petre and 60/ for all fire arms and Bayonets manufactured in this Colony before the 1st June next is offered by this Government. An Act to encourage the fitting out of Arm'd Vessels has passed and is Published, and an additional Resolve entitling all persons whether commissioned with Letters of Marque or otherwise to prizes brot into this Colony by them hereafter and taken within 30 Leagues of the Shore.[4] Mr. Revere is to qualify himself to manufacture powder, and Mills will be soon created. I hope all necessary Assistance will be afforded him at Philadelphia. There wants now a good Settlement of the Militia and an Supply of powder and Arms by Importation and our own Manufactories; and adeiu forever tyrannical Step Mother.

The Delegates from this Colony are further impowered to represent it untill the 31st January as a new Choice could not be made at the last Session of the Court.

I hope soon to see Canada in our Hands, an Army of 30,000 Men at each extreme of the Continent and one of the same Number in the Middle, as it is too great a Hazard to put our all on the Sweep of a single Army.

We expect that the Enemy will soon make a Sally and hope they will meet with the Defeat due to their infamous Cause. I remain Sir with Tenders of Friendship and Respect to the other Members from this Colony and particularly to your good self. Your most obedient and very huml. Sert.,   Elbridge Gerry

Mr. Revere's Waiting prevents my reading the Letter and will excuse Want of Clearness which I am apprehensive You will meet with in the preceding Letter.

RC (Adams Papers); addressed: "Hona. John Adams Esqr. in Philadelphia   favd per Mr Revere"; docketed: "Mr Gerry   Novr 11 1775."

[1] See JA to James Warren, 18 Oct., note 5 (above). On 8 Nov. the House named Cooper and Thomson to the committee proposed by the Council (Mass., *House Jour.*, 1775–1776, 2d sess., p. 247–248). Actually the General Court adjourned to 29 Nov.

[2] The appointment of a general to command the forces at Falmouth in Cumberland co. illustrates the course of the dispute between the two houses. On 31 Oct. the House received Falmouth's request and on 4 Nov. appointed Joseph Frye, requesting the concurrence of the Council. In response, the Council appointed Gen. Frye on its own author-ity and informed the House that it "unanimously non-concurred" with the House resolution of 4 Nov. Finally, after much argument that covered the whole ground of the dispute, the situation meanwhile becoming desperate, Frye was appointed by joint ballot of both houses (same, p. 213, 232, 241–242, 267).

[3] Letters taken on 7 Nov. in the capture of the *Two Sisters*, under Capt. Robbins; see Joseph Palmer to JA, 31 Oct. – 11 Nov. (above).

[4] See James Warren to JA, 20 Oct., note 11 (above), and the resolve of 10 Nov. (*House Jour.*, p. 264).

The Council to the Massachusetts Delegates

Gentlemen   Watertown Novr. 11th. 1775

The Manifest Militation between the Resolve which passed the hon'ble the American Congress on the ninth June last relative to Establishing Civil Government in this Colony and the Resolve which passed the Congress on 18th of last July pointing to a method how the Militia should be regulated in the Several United American Colony's hath caused some Altercation between the Hon'ble House of Representatives, and the Council.[1] The House have claimed by Virtue of the Last resolve a right to a choice, in the Choice with the Council of the Militia Officers in this Colony. The Council have considered themselves bound to Act in conformity to the first mentioned Resolve. But such is the Prevailing sentiments of the House, that they have a right to join in the Election of Military Officers, that it will be difficult for the Council longer to Storm the Torrent of a measure so popular, unless absolutely directed thereto by the Hon'ble Congress. The Council hope an Order of that kind will not take place. They rather wish the Representatives of the people may be Gratified in this claim, as we think it will promote the peace of the Colony and the Public Cause. You will think of the matter and give us your advice, either with or without Compelling your brethren of the Congress as you shall Judge best.

FC (M–Ar:195, p. 393–394). The RC, which has not been found, was signed by James Otis (see JA to James Otis, 23 Nov., below).

[1] The dispute between the Council and the House over the appointment of militia officers had been an irritant for weeks (see James Warren to JA, 20 Oct., note 20, above).

Credentials of the Massachusetts Delegates to the Continental Congress

Watertown, 11 November 1775. (Misc. Papers of the Continental Congress, Reel No. 8). Although the credentials as passed by the house bear the date 10 November, the *Journal of the House of Representatives* (1775–1776, 2d sess., p. 269–270) indicates that they were passed on 11 November and immediately concurred in by the Council.

These credentials extended the appointments of JA, Samuel Adams, Thomas Cushing, Robert Treat Paine, and John Hancock as members of the Massachusetts delegation from 31 December 1775 to 31 January 1776. The one-month extension was an interim measure to allow the General Court, which adjourned on 11 November, to consider changes in the delegation at its next session beginning on 29 November. When new credentials, to be in effect until 1 January 1777, were adopted on 18 January 1776, the delegation was retained intact with the exception of the moderate Thomas Cushing, who was replaced by Elbridge Gerry (same, 3d sess., p. 165).

To John Thomas

Sir   Philadelphia Novr. 13th 1775

I am much obliged to you for two Letters one by the Committee:[1] the other dated Novr. 1.

The subject of the first is not yet determined in Congress, but I have no doubt your Desires will be complied with.[2]

As soon as I received the last I waited on Dr. Morgan and shewed your Letter, together with one from Mr. Gordon and a very sensible one from Dr. Hayward relative to the same subject.[3] Mr. Aspinwall was known to Dr. Morgan, and well esteemed. Of this Gentleman I know nothing but by Character. Dr. Hayward I know personally and highly esteemed.

I hope, that neither Aspinwall nor Hayward will be removed, but it will depend much on the Representations of Dr. Morgan, which I dare say will not be against Either of them. No doubt he will think two surgeons necessary at Roxbury, and represent accordingly and then Congress will probably establish them.

You may depend upon the little in my Power at all Times, to assist Merit and promote the service. As Congress has made the Postage of Letters, free[4] I hope to receive more frequent Intelligence from my Friends for the future, and you may be assured sir, that every Line from you will be peculiarly acceptable to, sir your most obedient sert

John Adams

The Sum total of all Intelligence from England is that the first Man[5] is "unalterably determined, Let the Event and Consequences be what they will to compell the Colonies to absolute Obedience." Poor, deluded Man!

RC (MHi:John Thomas Papers); addressed: "To General Thomas Roxbury   favoured by Dr Morgan"; docketed: "Mr. J. Adams   Letter 13. Nov."

[1] Thomas to JA, 24 Oct. (above), was carried by the congressional committee that had visited Massachusetts in October.

[2] Probably Thomas' desire to see Richard Gridley replaced.

[3] William Gordon to JA, 25 Oct., containing an enclosure from Dr. Lemuel Hayward, and Hayward to JA, 1 Nov. (both above).

[4] On 8 Nov. the congress had re-solved that all letters to and from a delegate should go "free of postage" (JCC, 3:342).

[5] George III. JA's contemptuous reference loses something with the passage of time, but it should be remembered that Americans still drank the health of the king and referred to "ministerial" policies and troops as a way of shifting blame away from the royal person.

To Samuel Osgood Jr.

Novr: 14. 1775

I was yesterday favoured with your agreable Letter by Captn. Price, for which as well as a former Letter I acknowledge myself much obliged to you.[1]

In such a Period as this, Sir, when Thirteen Colonies unacquainted in a great Measure, with each other, are rushing together into one Mass, it would be a Miracle, if Such heterogeneous Ingredients did not at first produce violent Fermentations. These ought to be expected, and prepared for by every Man concerned in the Conduct of our Councils or Arms.

I hope the Generals will act with Discernment and Integrity in Seperating those officers who are to be discharged from the rest. But the Reduction of the Regiments cannot be avoided. Our Province had So many more officers than other Colonies in Proportion to their Number of Men, that altho the Congress excused it for the Time passed, in Consideration of the Confusion and Distress of our Affairs when the Troops were raised, yet they will not consent that the Inconvenience should continue, now there is Leisure to correct the Error.

I am much concerned at Times on Account of the Pay of the Privates. It is thought here to be very exorbitant, and many Gentlemen are under great Concern about the Consequences. The Expence of the War will accumulate upon the Colonies a Debt, like that of our Enemies. And We have no Funds out of which even the Interest can be paid, and our People are not used to Taxes upon the Luxuries, much less upon the Conveniences and Necessaries of Life.

I shall always be obliged to you for Information, which at this distance is much wanted. You may write [with] the Utmost Freedom to me, the minutest Parti[culars]. I shall make no use of such Freedoms to your Disadvantage, [...] may improve them to the Benefit of the Public. Be careful however of your Conveyances.

My respectful Compliments to General Ward and all his Family. I am with much Respect your very humblest,   John Adams

RC (NHi:Osgood Papers); addressed: "To Samuel Osgood Jur Esqr Aide de Camp to General Ward Roxbury To the Care of Coll Warren"; dockcted: "Jno. Adams 1775." The second page of the MS is mutilated at the right edge.

¹ Osgood to JA, [23 Oct.] and 4 Nov. (both above).

To William Tudor

Dear Sir   Novr. 14. 1775

I received your kind Letter of the 28th. of Octr.—but yesterday. It was such a Letter as I wish all my Friends would write me, as often as possible—that is it was long, full of Intelligence, well written and very entertaining.

I lament the Dishonour which falls upon the Colony by the mean, mercenary Conduct of some of her Servants. But in all Events I hope no Instance of Fraud or Peculation will be overlooked, but Strictly and impartially punished, untill every Rascall is banished from the Army, whatever Colony may have given him Existence.

It behoves the Congress, it behoves the Army to Shew that nothing but a rigid inflexible Virtue, and a Spotless Purity [of] Character, can preserve or acquire any Employment.

Virtue, my young Friend, Virtue alone is or can be the Foundation of our new Governments, and it must be encouraged by Rewards, in every Department civil and military.

Your Account of the Doctors Defence at the Bar of the House is every entertaining. I should have formed no Idea of that Hearing if you had not obliged me, with an Account. I think with the Candid, that Contempt is due to him for his Timidity and Duplicity. But I cannot wholly acquit him of something worse. He mentions in his Letter [1] his having in a former Letter given his Correspondent a Hint of the Design against Bunkers Hill. Now I never can be clearly freed from Jealousy, untill I see that Letter. The *Hint* he mentions might have occasioned our Loss of that Post, and of all the Lives which were destroyed on the 17th of June. However I have hitherto kept my Mind in suspense.

I wish you would let me know who Bellidore is.[2] What Country man, and in what Language he wrote—what was his Station Employment and Character.

We must make our young Genius's perfect Masters of the Art of War, in every Branch. I hope America will not long lie under the Reproach of not producing her own officers and Generals, as England has done a long Time.

Wearing an Uniform, and receiving Pay is not all. I want to see an Emulation among our young Gentlemen, which shall be the most perfect Master of all the Languages and Arts which are subservient to Politicks and War. Politicks are the Science of human Happiness and War the Art of Securing it. I would fain therefore have both perfectly understood.

RC (MHi:Tudor Papers); addressed: "William Tudor Esqr Judge Advocate in the Army Cambridge"; docketed: "Novr. 14th. 1775."

[1] Benjamin Church's intercepted letter in cipher that led to his arrest (Mass., *House Jour.*, 1775–1776, 2d sess., p. 202–203).

[2] See JA to Tudor, 12 Oct., note 5 (above).

To Joseph Ward

Sir   Philadelphia, November 14, 1775

I had yesterday the pleasure of your letter of the 4th instant by Captain Price, for which, as well as a former kind letter,[1] I heartily thank you.

The report you mention, that Congress have resolved upon a free trade, is so far from being true that you must have seen by the public papers before now that they have resolved to stop all trade untill next March.[2] What will be done then time will discover. This winter I hope will be improved in preparing some kind of defence for trade. I hope the Colonies will do this separately. But these subjects are too important and intricate to be discussed in a narrow compass, and too delicate to be committed to a private letter.

The report that Congress has resolved to have no more connections, &c., untill they shall be indemnified, for the damages done by the tyranny of their enemies, will not be true so soon as some expect it. Verbal resolutions accomplis nothing. It is to no purpose to declare what we will or will not do in future times. Let reasoning Men infer what we shall do from what we actually do.

The late conduct, in burning towns, so disgraceful to the English name and character, would justify anything, but similar barbarity. Let us preserve our temper, our wisdom, our humanity and civility, though our enemies are every day renouncing theirs. But let us omit nothing necessary for the security of our cause.

You are anxious for Arnold. So are we, and for Montgomery too, untill this day, when an express has brought us the refreshing news of the capitulation of St. Johns, for Arnold I am anxious still. God grant him success. My compliments to Gen. Ward and his Family. I am with respect, Your very humble servant,   John Adams

Tr (DLC).

[1] Ward to JA, 23 Oct. (above).
[2] On 1 Nov. the congress voted to end exportation outside the colonies until 1 March (JCC, 3:314–315).

From Joseph Hawley, with
Notation by John Adams

Dear Sir   Brookfield Novr 14th. 1775

En passant. As Church said in his letter to the Regulars, *Remember I Never deceived you.* If your Congress don't give better encouragement to the Privates, than at present is held forth to them, You will have No Winter Army. There must be some small bounty given them on the inlistment. A Strange Mistaken Opinion Obtains among the Gentlemen of the Army from the Southward and if I mistake Not in your Congress, that our Privates have too high wages and the officers too low. Another thing I just hint, That if your Congress go About

to repeal or explain away the resolutions of the 18th of July last respecting the Method of Appointing Military officers and vest our Council solely with that power, It will throw the colony into the Utmost Confusion and end in the destruction of the Council. I have wrote Mr. S. Adams on the last head. I am with great regards your Obedt. Servt.,
                                                                 Joseph Hawley

Received this Letter at Dinner 4 O Clock Saturday November 25. 1775. Yesterday Morning i.e. Fryday Novr 24. Paul Revere, went off from this Place with my Letter to the Board,[1] in which I gave it as my opinion that the Council might give up the Point in Dispute with the House about the Appointment of Militia officers, and that the Resolution of Congress mentioned in this Letter was so clear that We need not apply to that Assembly for any Explanation.[2]

RC (Adams Papers); addressed: "To the Honble John Adams Esqr at the American Congress Philadelphia"; written in red ink above the address: "4.16"; below the address: "Poste. fees paid by the Writer"; docketed: "Major Hawley Novr 14. 1775." JA's notation is on the reverse of the first page.

[1] JA's message to the Council is contained in his letter to James Otis of 23 Nov. (below).

[2] The Council had already expressed its hope that the congress would not instruct it to act contrary to popular wishes (Council to Massachusetts Delegates, 11 Nov., above). For JA's detailed reply to Hawley, see 25 Nov. (below).

From John Trumbull

Sir   New Haven Novr, 14th 1775

I had the satisfaction last evening of receiving your very friendly Letter, which was the more agreable for being unexpected.[1] As I am setting out tomorrow on a short Tour to the eastward, I have taken the only leisure moment to answer it.

You may easily guess how much I am flattered by your approbation of the little essay, you mention in yours. As to its being mysterious, as you term it, you know Sir an affected mysteriousness is often a good artifice for exciting the Curiosity of the Public, who are always pleased to have an opportunity of applying fictitious Characters and discovering latent allusions. To you Sir I can explain my design in a few words. To expose a number of the principal Villains of the day, to ridicule the high blustering menaces and great expectations of the Tory Party, and to burlesque the atchievements of our ministerial Heroes, civil, ecclesiastical and military, was my whole plan. This could be done with more spirit in dialogue than plain narration, and by a mixture of Irony and Sarcasm under various Characters and different Styles, than in an unvaried harangue in the Author's own Person. Nor is it a small beauty in any production of this kind, to paint the manners of the age. For these purposes, the Description of a Townmeeting and its Harangues, appeared the best Vehicle of the Satire. Had there been any one grand Villain, whose Character and History would have answered exactly, I should have made use of him and his real name, as freely as I have the names of others. But I could think of no *One*, and therefore substituted a fictitious Character, of a Scotch Tory Expectant,[2] which I hope is not drawn so illy, but that the world might find hundreds perhaps to whom it might be properly applied. The other Speaker[3] has properly speaking no Character drawn, and no actions ascribed to him. He is anyone whose Sentiments are agreeable to his Speeches. The Picture of the Townmeeting is drawn from the life, and with as proper lights, shades and Colouring as I could give it; and is I fancy no bad likeness.

As to explanatory Notes, the Piece I am sensible would want many more than I have given it, in all those places, where personal Characters and particular Allusions are introduced: beyond that the Reader should for me, be welcome to his own guesses. And so much for a Piece, which tho' the Offspring of my own Brain, I do not feel sufficient fondness for, to be sollicitous about making its apology; and which, I assure you Sir, came very near following many of its former Brethren into the flames, as a Sacrifice to that Poetical *Moloch* (if such a one there be) who delights in burnt offerings of the Infants of our modern Muses; or at best was in danger of suffering perpetual imprisonment, under the Sentence of Horace's Law, *Nonum prematur in Annum*;[4] which I should have looked on as an Authority directly in Point, had I not recollected that the Piece was of so temporary a nature, that if it was of no value now, it would sink as fast as your Massachusetts old tenor Bills, and in that time become no longer passable.

And now for Connecticut Politics, which you desire an Account of. We are Sir a People of a very independent Spirit, and think ourselves as good as any Body, or on the whole a little better—wiser at least, and more intelligent Politicians. Do you wish to know Sir, what ousted Col. Dyer and Mr. Deane? The Spirit of shewing our own Power, and reminding our Delegates of their mortality, influenced us to change some of the men. Indeed so far, I cannot blame it. But the reason of dropping out those two Men was principally this, that the Congress, last spring being led away by a vain opinion of their own importance and forgetting their inferiority to the venerable Assembly of this Colony, did wickedly, wittingly and willingly of their own forethought and malice prepense, wholly pass by, disregard and overthrow the Arrangement of General Officers for the said Colony;[5] and the said two Delegates were aiding, abetting, advising and Comforting them therein; against the Appointment and Commissions of this Colony, by their Statute-law in that Case made and provided, against our Honor and Dignity &c. Add to this that Deane is a Young Man, and one who never courted Popularity by cringing to the People, or affecting an extraordinary sanctity of manners; a man, whose freedom of Speech and pointed-ness of Sarcasm has made him as many enemies, as have been raised against him by envy—and both together form a large Party. In this Colony three or four well invented lies, properly circulated and coming from the right Persons will ruin any the most Respectable Character. However, the Delegates from other Provinces have said so much in Deane's favor since he was dropped, that his Enemies have shut their mouths and adjourned their lies to a more convenient Season. I fancy in a year or two you may be sure of having him again with you: I guess sooner. And the new Delegates we have chosen are all hearty in the Cause and (one only excepted)[6] Men of very distinguished Abilities.

I will give you a story or two that may show you a little the Character of our people in this Colony.

A little while since at a Public House in this Town, one of our highest Sons of Liberty was holding forth on the occasion of our Changing our Delegates. "The Congress, said he, have too much power given them to be long intrusted to one Set of Men; and they begin to grow too selfsufficient upon it; it is high Time they were changed. The people must keep the Power in their own hands; The Resolves of the Congress are sacred so far as they do what is right and agreable to the People; but where they fail, the people must take up the matter themselves. The Congress are good men, very good Men; but then they are but Men, and so are fallible; fallible Men, said he, and we must have a special eye to them." To this you see Sir, nothing could be objected, and so I contented myself with telling him, that tho' it was true that the Congress were Fallible, I looked on it as the peculiar felicity of this Town, that we had so many Men in it who were infallible; and what added to our happiness was that these Gentlemen of Infallibility were so ready to put themselves forward, take the Charge and Oversight of Public Affairs and rectify the mistakes of our wellmeaning, but weak and shortsighted Delegates.

Sometime last Summer A Merchant in this Town had obtained licence from the Assembly of this Colony for exporting some Cattle notwithstanding an Embargo just laid upon them, because he alledged they were bought previous to it. It seems he undertook under that Color to purchase and export more. The people were called together in a summary way to stop the exportation. As I was going to the meeting I overtook a very Spirited Man, but of rather ordinary abilities and asked him the occasion of the meeting. He said it was to stop this Gentleman from sending off Cattle under a licence from the Assembly; and added, "the Sons of liberty here do not intend to allow any such doings." Aye, said I (for I knew the man) Do our Assembly presume to give licences in matters of that importance to the Town, without consulting the Sons of Liberty here, who as they are on the Spot, must be so much better able to judge of the matter? Yes, said he, they have and we do not like it at all. Indeed, said I, I think it a most extraordinary Step, that they should take so much upon them; why, by this rule, they might undo you all, if you do not put some check upon them. "Aye that we shall do, said he, and if they make such laws, the People mean to get together and repeal them; nay they shall not, one of them go Representatives next year if they do not mind better what they are about."

Can this Spirit which hardly brooks subjection to Men of its own Chusing, ever be brought to yield to the Tyranny of Parliament?

I have scarcely room left to assure you, with how much respect and gratitude I am Your Obliged Humble Servt. Compts. to Messrs. S. Adams, Cushing and Deane.

RC (Adams Papers); docketed: "Mr Trumbull.   Novr. 14. 1775."

[1] That of 5 Nov. (above).
[2] Squire McFingal.
[3] Honorious, often identified as JA.
[4] Let [your compositions] be kept in your desk for nine years.
[5] The ranking of Israel Putnam above David Wooster and Joseph Spencer. See JA to James Warren, 23 July, note 3 (above).
[6] Roger Sherman, of whom Trumbull wrote contemptuously in his letter of 20 Oct. to Silas Deane (*Deane Papers*, 1:87–88).

From James Warren

My Dear Sir   Watertown Nov 14th: 1775

I last Evening received yours by Capt. Gist, and this Morning by Fessenden.[1] It gives me great pleasure to see things in such a fine way and you in such Choice Spirits. I Congratulate you on the takeing of St. John's. This news Fessenden brings with him from Hartford. This gives us great Spirits. He says likewise that Arnold was within twelve Miles of Quebec. You must know that our Anxiety for him and his party has been great. Last Night I was at Head quarters where Accounts were received that one Coll. Enos[2] of Connecticut with three Companies he Commanded as a rear Guard had come off and left him, while Advanced thirty Miles Ahead, and perhaps at Chaudere Pond. This officer certainly deserves hanging.

It will Always give me great pleasure to be Able to give you any Information. Great Numbers of the Whalemen are gone on Voayges which we permitted after haveing taken Bonds for the landing their Oil and Bone in some Port here other than Boston, and Nantucket.[3] Some of them are in the Army, and Sea Coast Service, many of them, and the greater part of our Fishermen and Seamen at Home, and in no Service Earnestly wishing to be Employed in the Privateering Business. What Numbers might be Inlisted in that Service I cant readily Compute, but I have no difficulty in supposeing, that at least three Battalions might be raised in this Colony. The Taste for it runs high here.

As to Ships and other Vessels, I believe there are great Numbers very suitable to Arm Already on hand. Almost every Port of any Consequence could furnish more or less either great or small. Perhaps Ships might be difficult to find that could mount 20 Guns or Upwards, but Vessels to Carry from 6 to 16 Guns I think we abound in, and I think they would soon furnish us with Others. These Vessels are of all Burthens, drafts of water, and dimensions and are many of them Excellent Sailors, and may be either purchased or hired, on very reasonable Terms. I think the General gives only 5/4 per Ton per Month. I am not Acquainted at Haverhill, Newberry &c. but from what I have heard, Vessels might be Built there, safe and with great dispatch, and perhaps at Kennebeck and North River &c. &c. We have no want of the best Shipwrights. As to the Time for Compleating them, much will depend on the winter, but they may be ready as soon as wanted in the Spring if Immediately Engaged in. As for your Next Question, the Names &c. of those fit to Command I am not quite so ready to answer. You know we have not practised Privateering so much here as they have in some of the other Colonies and it is A Business I never was Concerned in, but I have no doubt that many fine Fellows can be found who have been Masters of Vessels and at some time in their Lives served on Board Men of War and Privateers. I have one Capt. Samson[4] in my Employ who has serv'd in both, and perticularly with Capt. Mcpherson the last War. Him I would venture a Vessel with. There is Souter[5] who you know. Time wont permit me to recollect many others, but from the Nature and Circumstances of this Colony there must be many. I will Endeavour to recollect some for my Next. I am glad to see the Policy of Congress turned this way, and to see you Engaged. You must know I think you qualified for anything you will Undertake.

I Congratulate So. Carolina, and New Hampshire, on the Indulgence shewn them by the Congress. I hope they will Improve it to the best Advantage. I wish for the Time when we shall all ⟨want⟩ have the same Liberty. Our Situation must be more Irksome than ever to be surrounded on all Sides with Governments founded on proper Principles and Constituted to promote the free and equal Liberty and Happiness of Mankind, while we are plagued with a Constitution where the Prerogative of the Crown, and the Liberty of the Subject are Eternally militateing, and in the very Formation of which the last is but a secondary Consideration to the first. Indeed my Friend I am sick of our Constitution, more so than ever, have seen enough lately to make me so. I hate the name of Our Charter, which fascinates and Shackles us. I hate the monarchical part of our Government[6] and certainly you would more than ever if you knew our present Monarchs, but many of them you have no Idea of. They are totally changed since you left us, divers of them I mean. They have got a whirl in their Brains, Imagine themselves Kings, and have Assumed every Air and Pomp of Royalty but the Crown and Sceptre. You might search Princetown, Brookline, Wrentham, Braintree and several Other Towns without finding a Man you could possibly know, or suppose to have been chose a Councillor here by the Freemen of this Colony no longer ago than last July, and for no longer a time than next May. I shall not trouble you with any further and more perticular Account than I have already given of a dispute the last Session between the two Houses, much to our disadvantage and disgrace haveing seen a Copy of a Letter from Gerry to you by Revere where the matter seemed to be fully taken up.[7] The Court was adjourned last Saturday to the 29th Instant after haveing Extended your Commission for one Month to the last of January. We were not ready to come to a Choice, and was afraid to postpone to the first of next setting, so near the Expiration of the Time. I shall be Utterly at a loss for three new men. Do advise me.

Nov 15th:

I expected to have had the roar of Cannon this Morning, and some News from the Army to have given you. Our Army were prepared to Intrench on Cobble Hill and on Lechmores Point last Night.[8] I suppose the Weather has prevented. I hear Nothing of it this stormy

Morning. What Number of the new Recruits are Arrived we can't learn. It is generally thought not many of them, though there has been Appearances of Fleets in the Bay. I wish this Storm may put some of the Transports upon the Rocks and Quicksands.

You will learn by Revere the General State of things here, the Movements and Success of our Land, and Naval Force, perticularly an Account of the several prizes made. A Number of Letters, and the Kings Proclamation taken in one of them,[9] will give you a General view of their whole System with regard to America. I think your Congress can be no longer in any doubts, and hesitancy, about takeing Capital, and Effectual strokes. We shall certainly Expect it. It is said that the delicacy of modern Civilization will not Admit of foreign powers while you Continue to Acknowledge A dependency on Britain or Britains King, haveing any Connection with you. Let us so far Accomodate ourselves to their small policy as to remove this obstacle. I want to see Trade (if we must have it) open, and a Fleet here to protect it in opposition to Britain. Is the Ancient policy of France so lost or dwindeled that they will loose the Golden Opportunity.

We must have a Test, that shall distinguish Whiggs from Tories &c. &c. I have a Thousand Things to say to you. I want to see you. I want you there, and I want you here. What shall I do without you and my Friend Adams at Congress, and yet you are both wanted here. I believe you must stay there. I mean belong to that Body once more. I thank him for his kind Letter, will write to him as soon as I can, propose to go Home Tomorrow. Mrs. W⟨arre⟩n grows homesick. She wants to see her Boys haveing been Absent 5 weeks. She sits at the Table with me, will have a paragraph of her own. Says you "should no longer *piddle* at the Threshold. It is Time to Leap into the *Theatre* to unlock the Barrs, and open every Gate that Impedes the rise and Growth of the American ⟨*Empire*⟩ Republic,[10] and then let the Giddy Potentate send forth his puerile Proclamations to France, to Spain, and all the Commercial World who may be United in Building up an Empire which he cant prevent."

> At Leisure then may G– – –ge his Reign Review
> and Bid to Empire, and to Crowns Adeu
> For Lordly Mandates and despotic Kings
> are Obsolete like other quondam things
> Whether of Ancient or more modern date
> Alike both K– –gs and Kinglings I must Hate
> Extempore

I have but this Evening received several of your Letters of the latter End of Octr.[11] I cant tell you how much I am Obliged to you. I
admire the Character you give Dr. Morgan. I think it will do honour
to the Station he is to fill. You need not fear a proper regard will be
paid to him. I love to see Characters drawn by your pencil. The
more dozens you give me the more Agreable. I have a great Respect
for Governor Ward, and his Family. I will agreable to your desire
mention his Son at Head Quarters Tomorrow.

The method of makeing salt petre you mention, if to be depended
upon is simple and easy in the moderate Seasons. I could wish to hear
more of it, and also of the Rocks. I am not of the Committee for Sulphur &c. I will look them up and urge them to forward their discoveries
to you. I believe Obrian is Commissioned, and Carghill in a Sort
Commissioned. There will be no difficulty in haveing them in the
Service of the Continent. The General may easily execute his Order.
I am very sensible of the Mercenary Avaritious Spirit of Merchants.
They must be watched. We oblige all to give Bonds, but how to
Guard against throwing themselves in the way to be taken has puzzled us, but such is the spirit here for preserving inviolate the Association, that a Man must have Indisputable Evidence, that his being
taken was unavoidable, or never show his Head again, upon this I at
present rely. However very few Vessels except Whalemen are gone, and
very few have any Intentions to go, unless to the Southern Colonies,
and their Characters must be so well Established as to Obtain Certif-
icates from our Committees who are not yet Corrupted. I apprehend
more danger from Other places. I think the Association cant be too
Close drawn. We had better have no Trade than suffer Inconveniencies from the Interested Tricks of Tories, or even Merchants who
pretend to be well principled, and yet are governed by Interest alone.
I Believe you have a Curious set of Politicians in your Coffee Houses.
The System you Mention is an Instance of it, a Magnificent one Indeed, too much so for you and I, who I dare say will ever be
Content to be Excused from the two most Superb Branches, the first
more especially. I hope the Tricks of these people will never Answer
their purposes. The Union is everything. With it we shall do everything without it Nothing. My good wife sends her Compliments and
says I must Conclude and so says my Paper, Adeu

Nov 16.

No News this Morning. I think all things on our side look well,
and pleasing. I can't however but feel a little uneasy, till our Army
has got settled on the new plan. The General has many difficulties

with Officers and Soldiers. His Judgment and Firmness I hope will Carry him through them. He is certainly the best Man for the place he is in Important as it is, that ever lived. One Source of Uneasiness is that they are not paid four weeks to a Month.[12] There are some grounds for it. I believe they Inlisted here in Expectation of it, as it has been at all times the Invariable Custom of our Armies and Garrisons. I could wish the Congress had settled it so. Where are the Articles of Confederation. I want to see some settled Constitution of Congress. My regards to all Friends, and among the rest to Governor Ward, and your Friend Collins. To the last I wrote some time ago. I have never heard from him since. My Compliments to Coll. Reed.

RC (Adams Papers); docketed: "November 14 1775   Warren."

[1] See JA to Warren, 18 Oct., and to Elbridge Gerry, 5 Nov., note 2 (both above).

[2] Lt. Col. Roger Enos (1729–1808) commanded the fourth division of Arnold's expedition against Quebec. He returned because his troops were out of provisions and in danger of starvation. He was acquitted in a court martial on 1 Dec., the decision of the court being that he "was by absolute necessity obliged to return with his division." Despite the court's decision, the military remained hostile, and in Jan. 1776 he resigned from the army (*Appletons' Cyclo. Amer. Biog.*, 2:359; Enos to Washington, 9 Nov., enclosed in Washington to the President of Congress, 19 Nov., PCC, No. 152, I; French, *First Year*, p. 437–438; Washington, *Writings*, ed. Fitzpatrick, 4:131–132, 139; for the proceedings of Enos' court martial, see Force, *Archives*, 4th ser., 3: 1708–1711).

[3] This island off the coast of Massachusetts was vulnerable to British raids.

[4] Simeon Samson in 1776 captained the brigantine *Independence*, one of the first ships built for the Massachusetts State Navy (Allen, *Mass Privateers*, p. 185).

[5] Daniel Souther in 1776 captained the brigantine *Massachusetts* of the State Navy (same, p. 218).

[6] Warren's opposition to the Council's attempt to assert the prerogative had something in common with that of the Berkshire Constitutionalists (Robert J. Taylor, *Western Massachusetts in the Revolution*, Providence, 1954, p. 78–79).

[7] Elbridge Gerry to JA, 11 Nov. (above).

[8] The fortifications on Cobble Hill were put up on 22 Nov., those on Lechmere's Point, on the 29th (*Boston Gazette*, 27 Nov. 1775; Frothingham, *Siege of Boston*, p. 268–269; Washington, *Writings*, ed. Fitzpatrick, 4:116, 131).

[9] See Joseph Palmer to JA, 31 Oct., note 5 (above).

[10] The substitution of "Republic" for "Empire" suggests how far the thinking of the Warrens had gone. The term "Empire" just before the poem may be used in the sense of an economic one that would join America and other countries.

[11] The second letter of 21 Oct., the three letters of 25 Oct., and those of 28 Oct. and [?] Oct. (all above).

[12] Traditionally New England had paid its troops by lunar rather than calendar months. On 2 Oct. the congress resolved that "where months are used, the Congress means calendar months by which the men in the pay of the Continent are to be regulated." This change caused Washington much trouble in his effort to enlist New England men, who were naturally unhappy at the prospect of losing one month's pay per year (*JCC*, 3:272; French, *First Year*, p. 518).

To Richard Henry Lee

Dear Sir   Philadelphia Novr. 15th 1775

The Course of Events, naturally turns the Thoughts of Gentlemen to the Subjects of Legislation and Jurisprudence, and it is a curious Problem what Form of Government, is most readily and easily adopted by a Colony, upon a Sudden Emergency. Nature and Experience have already pointed out the Solution of this Problem, in the Choice of Conventions and Committees of safety. Nothing is wanting in Addition to these to make a compleat Government, but the Appointment of Magistrates for the due Administration of Justice.

Taking Nature and Experience for my Guide I have made the following Sketch, which may be varied in any one particular an infinite Number of Ways, So as to accommodate it to the different, Genius, Temper, Principles and even Prejudices of different People.[1]

A Legislative, an Executive and a judicial Power, comprehend the whole of what is meant and understood by Government. It is by ballancing each of these Powers against the other two, that the Effort in humane Nature towards Tyranny, can alone be checked and restrained and any degree of Freedom preserved in the Constitution.

Let a full and free Representation of the People be chosen for an House of Commons.

Let the House choose by Ballott twelve, Sixteen, Twenty four or Twenty Eight Persons, either Members of the House, or from the People at large as the Electors please, for a Council.

Let the House and Council by joint Ballott choose a Governor, annually triennially or Septennially as you will.

Let the Governor, Council, and House be each a distinct and independant Branch of the Legislature, and have a Negative on all Laws.

Let the Lt. Governor, Secretary, Treasurer, Commissary, Attorney General and Solicitor General, be chosen annually, by joint Ballott of both Houses.

Let the Governor with seven Councillors be a Quorum.

Let all Officers and Magistrates civil and military, be nominated and appointed by the Governor, by and with the Advice and Consent of his Council.

Let no Officer be appointed but at a General Council,[2] and let Notice be given to all the Councillors, Seven days at least before a General Council.

Let the Judges, at least of the Supream Court, be incapacitated by

307

Law from holding any Share in the Legislative or Executive Power, Let their Commissions be during good Behaviour, and their Salaries ascertained and established by Law.

Let the Governor have the Command of the Army, the Militia, Forts &c.

Let the Colony have a Seal and affix it to all Commissions.

In this Way a Single Month is Sufficient without the least Convulsion or even Animosity to accomplish a total Revolution in the Government of a Colony.

If it is thought more beneficial, a Law may be made by this new Legislature ⟨giving⟩[3] leaving to the People at large the Priviledge of choosing their Governor, and Councillors annually, as soon as affairs get into a more quiet Course.

In adopting a Plan, in some Respects similar to this,[4] human Nature would appear in its proper Glory asserting its own real Dignity, pulling down Tyrannies, at a single Exertion and erecting such new Fabricks, as it thinks best calculated to promote its Happiness.

As you was last Evening polite enough to ask me for this Model, if such a Trifle will be of any service to you, or any gratification of Curiosity, here you have it,[5] from, sir, your Friend and humble servant,

John Adams

RC (Kevin D. Harrington, Tiburon, Calif., 1977); addressed: "Richard Henry Lee Esqr. Present"; docketed: "Mr. Adams plan of Government." Tr in the hand of William Cranch (Adams Papers). Cranch notes that the Tr was made on 7 April 1827 from the original, then in possession of Edmund Jennings Lee, son-in-law of Richard Henry Lee.

[1] What follows is the germ of JA's *Thoughts on Government*, written in the spring of 1776. It anticipates the later call for a government in which the legislative, executive, and judicial branches balance each other. What it lacks is any general discussion of the purpose of government and the meaning of representation, as well as provisions for the franchise, education, and the militia, all included in the later effort (see Thoughts on Government, ante 27 March–April 1776, below).

[2] The appointment of officers at a "General Council" was the practice in Massachusetts. In 1776 such a council met usually on Thursdays. What distinguished it was advance notice of the day it would act upon specific business.

[3] JA was firm in his conviction that privileges and rights were not given to the people; they were theirs inherently. It was they who gave powers to their government. He repeatedly stressed to later correspondents that what the people wanted should be accepted.

[4] Comma supplied here.

[5] Lee circulated copies of this letter and probably made it into a handbill with some modifications. At least one copy of the letter found its way to England. The handbill was printed in Purdie's *Virginia Gazette* on 10 May 1776 and had some influence on the form the Virginia constitution took (John E. Selby, "Richard Henry Lee, John Adams, and the Virginia Constitution of 1776," *VMHB*, 84:387–400 [Oct. 1976]; P.R.O.:C.O. 5, vol. 93: 395, via DLC:British Reproductions; Jefferson, *Papers*, 1:334–335).

To Samuel Osgood Jr.

Novr. 15. 1775

Your first Letter to me is now before me.[1]

The true Cause why General Frie, has not received from me, any particular Intelligence, is that the Matter has been hitherto Suspended, and that I am under Such Engagements of Secrecy,[2] that I could not in Honour acquaint him with any Thing that has pass'd in Congress.

As Soon as I arrived in Philadelphia, I made it my Business to introduce General Fries Name and Character into Conversation in every private Company where it could be done with Propriety, and to make his long services and Experience known. But I found an Interest making in private Circles in Favour of Coll. Armstrong of Pensilvania, a Gentleman of Character, and Experience in War, a Presbyterian in Religion, whose Name runs high for Piety, Virtue and Valour. What has been done in Congress I must be excused from Saying, but nothing in my Power has been omitted, to promote the Wishes of our Colony or the Honour and Interest of General Frie. It is Sufficient to say, that nothing has as yet been determined. But it will be settled soon. And let it be decided as it may, every good American, will acquiesce in the Decision.

New England, as you justly observe is the Nursery of brave and hardy Men, and has hitherto Stemmed the Torrent of Tyranny, and must continue to do it, but the other Colonies are making rapid Advances in the military Art, and We must be cautious that we dont hold our own Heads too high, and hold up invidious Distinctions. The other Colonies are capable of furnishing good Soldiers, and they Spare no Pains to emulate New England herself.

You observe that no Tory Province has been So contemned as ours. There may be Some ground of Complaint, but have not our People aimed at more Respect than was their due? No other Colony I am fully sensible could have born the shock as ours has done and it is possible that this Circumstance may have made our people expect more than their due.

It is certainly true that some of our Southern Brethren have not annexed the Same Ideas to the Words Liberty, Honour and Politeness that we have: But I have the Pleasure to observe every day that We learn to think and feel alike more and more.

I am Sorry that the Committee did not dine with General Ward, but am convinced there was no unfriendly Design. The Gentlemen politely told me that the only disagreable Circumstance in their Journey was that they had not Time to cultivate an Acquaintance, with Gentlemen in Camp and at Watertown, as they earnestly wished.

Am very Sorry for General Wards ill State of Health, and that this has made him entertain Thoughts of resigning. I cannot think that the Acceptance of the Invitation from the Connecticutt officers, was pointed, or intended as a Slight to General Wards. Perhaps the Connecticutt Gentlemen might send a Card, which General Ward might omit, or it might be mere Inadvertence or Accident. *A Card is an Engine of vast Importance in this World*. But even if it was designed it is not worth regarding. These Little things are below the Dignity of our glorious Cause, which is the best and greatest that ever engaged the human Mind.

It has been an inexpresible Mortification to me, to observe in So many Instances, the Attention of Gentlemen in high Departments both civil and military, to the little Circumstances of Rank and Ceremony, when their Minds and Hearts ought to have been occupied, by the greatest objects on this side of Heaven.

I have been sufficiently plagued with these Frivolisms myself, but I despise them all, and I dont much revere any Man who regards them.

I wish you to write me often and with Freedom. But you must not be too punctilious in waiting for my Answers for I assure you I have more things to do than I am fit for, if I had three Hours where I have one. I am &c.,
John Adams

RC (NHi:Osgood Papers); docketed twice: "Jno Adams" and "From Jno Adams '75 to Samuel Osgood."

[1] See Osgood to JA, 23 Oct. and note 1 there (above).
[2] A reference to an agreement of secrecy signed by members of the congress on 9 Nov. (JCC, 3:342–343; see also JA's Service in the Congress, 13 Sept. – 9 Dec., Editorial Note, above).

From Samuel Chase

My Dear Sir[1]   Baltimore Town. Nov. 16th. 1775

I am well assured that a Supply of Powder is arrived at Statia,[2] so writes Captain Waters on 10th. October. A Dutch Vessell bound to Surrinam has contracted with a Captain of this place for twenty five Tons, if he comes for it by Xmas.

I have seen several of the principal Gentlemen here. They are wishing for the Destruction of Lord Dunmore and his fleet.[3] Inclosed You receive the Terms on which two Vessells can be procured here.[4]

The first I am well assured is very reasonable. The province have 15–6 pounders, and the Merchants here will furnish a Ton of Gunpowder for that Expedition. If either of the Vessells should be accepted, write to Robert Alexander Esqr. of this town. My Compliments to your worthy Colleagues. Yr. obedt. Servt.   S Chase

RC (Adams Papers); addressed: "To John Adams Esquire   One of the Delegates of the Congress   Philadelphia"; postal markings: in red ink, "2/5," in black ink, "1N4"; stamped: "Baltimore   Nov. 18"; docketed: "Mr Chase Nov 16. 1775."

[1] Chase probably wrote to JA in the latter's capacity as a member of the committee for fitting out armed vessels (JA's Service in the Congress, 13 Sept. – 9 Dec., Editorial Note, above).

[2] St. Eustatius, a Dutch possession in the West Indies, was the major conduit for trade between Europe and the American colonies, particularly in arms and ammunition. This trade, which continued relatively unabated from 1774 through 1780 despite vigorous British objections, was a major reason for the declaration of war between the United Provinces and Britain on 20 Dec. 1780. The British ambassador to the Hague reported that between January and May 1776 eighteen Dutch vessels had cleared for St. Eustatius carrying arms, obviously for the American market (J. Franklin Jameson, "St. Eustatius in the American Revolution," *AHR*, 8:683–708 [July 1903]).

[3] After Gov. Dunmore had taken refuge with the British navy, he made raids on Virginia in the fall of 1775. Americans estimated the number of blacks under his command at up to one hundred (*Naval Docs. Amer. Rev.*, 2: 630, 994).

[4] Not found.

From Charles Lee

My Dr Sir   Camp Nov'r the 19th 1775
I receiv'd your obliging letter[1] and cannot express the pleasure I feel in standing so high in your opinion as without flattery I esteem you a Man of excellent judgment and a singular good heart. Some of the queries You offer to my consideration are perhaps above my sphere, but in a post or two I shou'd endeavour to answer 'em, had I not hopes of conversing with You soon in propria persona. I think it absolutely necessary for the service of your Country that You or your name-sake or both shou'd without delay repair to this Province, the affairs of which are really in a most alarming if not frightfull situation. There seems to be a dearth or at least a total stagnation of all public virtue amongst your Countrymen. I do assure you that this assertion is no discharge of a splenetick humour but a most melancholly truth. Little malice little intrigues and little pecuniary jobbs prevail amongst all orders of men; the officers are calumniating and pulling at each other. Your Assembly is benumb'd in a fix'd state of torpitude. They give no symptoms of animation unless an apprehension of rendering them-

selves unpopular amongst their particular constituents by any act of vigor for the public service deserves the name of animation. In short They seem to dread losing their seat in a future assembly more than the sacrifice of the whole cause. Perhaps my idea may be idle, and unjust, but it is not singular. We have indeed no other way of accounting for their inconsistent and timid conduct. To what other principle can We ascribe their taking out of the Quarter Master General's hand the business of supplying the Army with necessaries and failing us in the articles of supply which We were taught to expect from 'em.[2] In consequence of this torpor narrow politics, or call it what You will, the Army has been reduc'd to very great distress, particularly in the article of wood. The uncomfortableness of the soldiers situation has of course given a most dreadfull check to the ardor of inlisting. If You therefore or some good Genius do not fly and anticipate the impending evil, God knows what may be the effects. I conjure You therefore. We all conjure you to come amongst us. You and your Friend Samuel have ever been their prime conductors —and unless they have from time to time a rub of their prime conductors no electrical fire can be struck out of 'em. The game is now thank God and the elements in our hands, nothing but the most abominable indolence cowardice or want of virtue can make us lose it. If You are enslav'd You richly deserve it. You have, My Dear Sir, liberallity of mind and zeal sufficient in the great cause of the human race (for it is the cause of all mankind to bear truths, be they ever so grating)=in this persuasion I venture to unbosom myself. There are most wretched materials in the composition of your Officers and People. Every day furnishes us with some fresh instance of mutiny faction and disaffection amongst the former, and cowardice amongst the latter. You will have heard before this of the astonishing desertion of Colonel Enos from a service on which the whole fate of America depended, and the cowardice of the People of Falmouth who with at least two hundred fighting Men and powder enough for a battle cou'd suffer with impunity twenty five marines to land and set their Town in flames. In short You must come up and infuse vigor spirit and virtue into evry part of your community. Your presence cannot be so importantly necessary in the congress as it is here, for the love of Heaven therefore and that fairest gift of Heaven let us see one of the Adams's. I intreat You will consign this letter to the flames, the instant you receive it and believe that it proceeds alone from the irresistible zeal of, Dr Sir, yours most sincerely[3]   C Lee

RC (Adams Papers); docketed: "G. Lee.   Novr. 19. 1775."

[1] That of 13 Oct. (above).

[2] Washington complained to the General Court about what he believed was an artificial shortage of wood and hay and expressed his fear that soldiers would begin pulling down houses for firewood (*Writings*, ed. Fitzpatrick, 4: 47–48, 60–61). The sentiments of Lee were quoted virtually verbatim by William Gordon in *The History of the Rise, Progress, and Establishment of the Independence of the United States of America*, 2d edn., 3 vols., N.Y., 1794, 1:418. The quotation is strong evidence that Gordon had access to JA's papers and made use of them. See Lemuel Robinson to JA, 30 Nov., note 3, and Samuel Adams to JA, 15 Jan. 1776, note 6 (both below); compare with *Adams Family Correspondence*, descriptive note, 1:229.

[3] On 2 Dec., Gen. Lee wrote in similar vein to one of the Lees, urging the necessity of the return to Massachusetts of either John or Samuel Adams (Adams Papers). Lee was quick to criticize, but his professional background and air of assurance impressed many besides JA (*DAB*).

To James Otis Sr.

Sir   Philadelphia Novr. 23. 1775

I had the Honour of your Letter of Novr. the Eleventh,[1] by Express, and am very Sorry to learn that any Difference of Sentiment has arisen between the two Honourable Houses, respecting the Militia Bill, as it is so necessary at this critical Moment, for the public Service.

If I was of opinion that any Resolution of the Congress now in Force was against the Claim of the Honourable House, as the Honourable Board have proposed that We should lay the Question before Congress I should think it my Duty to do it; But it appears to me that Supposing the two Resolutions to clash, the last ought to be considered as binding. And as, by this, it is left in the "Discretion of the Assembly either to adopt the foregoing Resolutions, in the whole or in Part, or to continue their former, as they on Consideration of all Circumstances shall think fit," I think it plain, that the Honourable Board may comply with the Desire of the Honourable House if, in their Discretion they think fit.[2]

I am the more confirmed in the opinion, that it is unnecessary to lay this Matter before Congress, as they have lately advised the Colonies of New Hampshire, and one more, if they think it necessary, to establish such Forms of Government, as they shall judge best calculated to promote the Happiness of the People.

Besides the Congress are So pressed with Business, and engaged upon Questions of greater Moment that I should be unwilling, unless in a Case of absolute Necessity to interrupt them by a Question of this Kind, not to mention that I would not wish to make known So publickly and extensively, that a Controversy had so soon arisen, between the Branches of our new Government.

I have had frequent Consultations with my Colleagues, since the Receipt of your Letter, upon this subject; but as we are not unanimous, I think it my Duty to write my private sentiments as soon as possible, If either of my Colleagues shall think fit to propose the Question to congress, I shall there give my candid opinion, as I have done to you.

I have the Honour to be with great Respect to the Honourable Board, Sir, your most obedient and very humble Servant

John Adams

RC (DLC:J. P. Morgan Coll., Signers of the Declaration of Independence); docketed: "In Council Decr 30th 1775 Received and ordered to be entered in the files of Council Perez Morton Dpy Secry."

¹ That is, the letter of the Council to the Massachusetts delegation signed by Otis (above).

² JA's circumspect reply closely paralleled Samuel Adams' answer of 23 Nov. to Otis' letter (*Writings*, 3:242–243). Both men not only opposed presenting the question to the congress but rejected the Council's position. John Hancock and Thomas Cushing, apparently the colleagues to whom JA later refers, stated in a joint letter to the Council dated 24 Nov. that "we dare not venture our opinions what would be the sentiments of Congress upon such a measure as the House proposes, and therefore are clearly of opinion the matter ought to be laid before the Congress" (Force, *Archives*, 4th ser., 3:1662–1663). On 29 Nov., after consulting with other members of the congress, Hancock and Cushing wrote again to advise the Council that most members were against presenting the issue to the full congress. They added that although the Council might be on solid ground in its dispute with the House, it should, in the interest of harmony at a difficult time, give the House a voice in the appointment of militia officers (same, p. 1705). In a far more candid opinion of the controversy, expressed to Joseph Hawley in a letter of 25 Nov. (below), JA attacked Cushing for his obstructionism.

To Perez Morton

Sir   Philadelphia Novr. 24. 1775

I had the Honour of receiving your Letter of the Twenty Eighth of October last,¹ by Mr. Revere; in which you acquaint me that the Major Part of the Honourable Council, by Virtue of the Power and Authority, in and by the Royal Charter of the Massachusetts Bay, in the absence of the Governor and Lieutenant Governor lodged in them have Seen fit to appoint me, with the Advice and Consent of Council, to be a Justice of the Superior Court of Judicature, &c. for that Colony, inclosing a List of the Honourable Gentlemen, who are to hold Seats on the Same Bench, and requesting me to signify in Writing my acceptance or Refusal, of Said Appointment as Soon as might be.

I am deeply penetrated, sir, with a sense of the high Importance of that office; at all times difficult, but under those Distresses in which

our Country is involved, exposed to greater Hazards and Embarrassments, than were ever known, in the History of former Times.

As I have ever considered the Confidence of the Public the more
honourable, in Proportion to the Perplexity and Danger of the Times,
So I cannot but esteem this distinguished Mark of the Approbation
of the honourable Board, as a greater Obligation, than if it had been
bestowed at a season of greater Ease and Security: Whatever discouraging Circumstances, therefore may attend me, in Point of Health,
of Fortune or Experience I dare not refuse to undertake this Duty.

Be pleased, then to acquaint the Honourable Board, that as soon
as the Circumstances of the[2] Colonies, will admit an Adjournment of
the Congress, I shall return to the Honourable Board and undertake,
to the Utmost of my Ability, to discharge the momentous Duties, to
which they have seen fit to appoint me.[3]

Although I am happy to see a List of Gentlemen appointed to the
Bench, of whose Abilities and Virtues I have the highest Esteem,
and with whom I have long lived in Friendship;[4] yet the Rank in
which it has pleased the Honourable Board to place me, perplexes me
more than any other Circumstance but as I ought to presume that this
was done upon the best Reasons,[5] I must Submit my private opinion to
the Judgement of that honourable Body, in whose Department it is to
determine.

With the most devout Wishes for the Peace and Prosperity of the[6]
Colonies, and of the Massachusetts Bay in particular and with the
greatest Respect to the Honourable Board I am, sir, your most obedient, humble servant   John Adams

RC (M–Ar:194, p. 162–164); addressed: "Perez Morton Esqr Depty
Secy to be communicated to the Honourable Board"; docketed: "In Council
Decr. 1st 1775 Read and ordered to be entered on the files of Council
Perez Morton Dpy Secry." Dft (Adams Papers) shows variations, some noted
below.

[1] In the draft "two days ago" follows
here.

[2] The draft has "united" lined out
before "Colonies."

[3] JA never served. See James Warren
to JA, 20 Oct., note 4 (above).

[4] In the draft the first clause, not introduced by "although," comprises the
whole paragraph. The second part of
the present paragraph was separately
written on the blank page following the
signature in the draft. JA probably had
in mind the hard feelings the ranking
produced in Robert Treat Paine.

[5] The draft has "done upon the most
enlarged View of the whole subject."

[6] The draft has "thirteen united" lined
out before "Colonies."

To Joseph Hawley

My dear sir   Philadelphia Novr. 25. 1775

This afternoon at five o Clock, I received your kind Letter of November the 14. dated at Brookfield—which was the more agreable because such Favours from you short as this is are very rare.

You tell me, Sir, "that We Shall have no Winter Army, if our Congress dont give better Encouragement to the Privates than at present is held forth to them"—and that "there must be Some Small Bounty given them, on the Inlistment."

What Encouragement is held forth, or at least has been, I know not, but before this Time no doubt they have been informed of the Ultimatum of the Congress. No Bounty is offered. 40 shillings lawfull Money Per Month, after much altercation, is allowed.[1] It is undoubtedly true, that an opinion prevails among the Gentlemen of the Army from the Southward, and indeed throughout all the Colonies, excepting New England, that the Pay of the Privates is too high and that of the officers too low. So that you may easily conceive the Difficulties We have had to surmount. You may depend upon it, that this has cost many an anxious Day and Night. And the utmost that could be done has been. We cannot Suddenly alter the Temper, Principles, opinions or Prejudices of Men. The Characters of Gentlemen in the four New England Colonies, differ as much from those in the others, as that of the Common People differs, that is as much as several distinct Natures almost. Gentlemen, Men of sense, or any Kind of Education in the other Colonies are much fewer in Proportion than in N. England. Gentlemen in the other Colonies, have large Plantations of slaves, and the common People among them are very ignorant and very poor. These Gentlemen are accustomed, habituated to higher Notions of themselves and the Distinction between them and the common People, than We are, and an instantaneous alteration of the Character of a Colony, and that Temper and those sentiments which, its Inhabitants imbibed with their Mothers Milk, and which have grown with their Growth and strengthend with their Strength, cannot be made without a Miracle. I dread the Consequences of this Dissimilitude of Character, and without the Utmost Caution on both sides, and the most considerate Forbearance with one another and prudent Condescention on both sides, they will certainly be fatal. An alteration of the Southern Constitutions, which must certainly take Place if this War continues will gradually, bring all the Continent nearer and nearer to each other in all Respects. But this is the Most Critical

Moment, We have yet seen. This Winter will cast the Die. For Gods sake therefore, reconcile our People to what has been done, for you may depend upon it, that nothing more can be done here—and I should shudder at the Thought of proposing a Bounty. A burnt Child dreads the fire. The Pay of the officers is raised that of a Captain to 26 dollars and one third per Month Lieutenants and Ensigns in Proportion.[2] Regimental officers not raised. You then hint, "that if Congress should repeal or explain away the Resolution of 18 July respecting the appointment of military officers, and vest the Council with the sole Power, it would throw the Colony into Confusion and end in the Destruction of the Council."

The Day before Yesterday I wrote a Letter to the Honourable Board in answer from one from their President by order to us upon that Subject, which Letter Revere carried from this City yesterday Morning.[3] Therein I candidly gave my opinion to their Honours that our Resolution was clear and plain, that the Colony might Use their own Discretion, and therefore that they might yield this Point to the House—and that the Point was So plain that I did not see the least occasion for laying the Controversy before Congress. But my dear Friend I must, take the Freedom to tell you that the same has happened upon this occasion which has happened on a thousand others, after taking a great deal of Pains with my Colleague your Friend Mr. Cushing, I could not get him to agree with the rest of us in Writing a joint Letter, nor could I get him to say what opinion he would give if it was moved in Congress.[4] What he has written I know not. But it is very hard to be linked and yoked eternally, with People who have either no opinions, or opposite opinions, and to be plagued with the opposition of our own Colony to the most necessary Measures, at the same Time that you have all the Monarchical superstitions and the Aristocratical Domination, of Nine other Colonies to contend with.

Dft? (Adams Papers); docketed in an unknown hand: "Mr John Adams Novr 27. 1775." That this document is a Dft rather than an RC seems probable because of its presence in the Adams Papers and the absence of any address or closing. Hawley replied on 18 Dec. (below).

[1] On 29 July the congress voted $6 2/3 per month; it confirmed its decision on 4 Nov. (JCC, 2:220; 3:322).

[2] Lieutenants and ensigns were to get $18 and $13 1/3 per month respectively (same, 3:322).

[3] JA to James Otis, 23 Nov. (above).

[4] Samuel Adams expressed himself similarly about Thomas Cushing in a letter to James Warren on [5] Dec. (*Warren-Adams Letters*, 1:191–192). Cushing lost his place in the delegation to Elbridge Gerry when new appointments were made by the General Court on 18 Jan. 1776 (Mass., *House Jour.*, 1775–1776, 3d sess., p. 165).

To Mercy Otis Warren

Madam [1]   Philadelphia Novr. 25. 1775

I had the Pleasure of yours of Novr. 4th several Days ago.[2]

You know Madam, that I have no Pleasure or Amusements which has any Charms for me. Balls, Assemblies Concerts Cards, Horses, Dogs, never engaged any Part of my attention or Concern. Nor am I ever happy in large and promiscuous Companies. Business alone, with the intimate unreserved Conversation of a very few Friends, Books, and familiar Correspondences, have ever engaged all my Time, and I have no Pleasure no Ease in any other Way. In this Place I have no opportunity to meddle with Books, only in the Way of Business. The Conversation I have here is all in the ceremonious reserved impenetrable Way. Thus I have sketched, a Character for myself of a morose Philosopher and a Surly Politician, neither of which are very amiable or respectable, but yet there is too much truth in it, and from it you will easily believe that I have very little Pleasure here, excepting in the Correspondence of my Friends, and among these I assure you Madam there is none, whose Letters I read with more Pleasure and Instruction than yours. I wish it was in my Power to write to you oftener than I do, but I am really engaged in constant Business of seven to ten in the Morning in Committee, from ten to four in Congress and from Six to Ten again in Committee. Our Assembly is scarcly numerous enough for the Business. Every Body is engaged all Day in Congress and all the Morning and evening in Committees. I mention this Madam as an Apology for not writing you so often as I ought and as a Reason for my Request that you would not wait for my Answers.

The Dispute you mention between the House and Board, I hope will be easily settled. Yet I believe the Board acted with great Honour and Integrity and with a wise Design and a virtuous Resolution to do nothing that should endanger the Union. But I am clear that it is best the two Houses should join in the Appointment of officers of Militia, and I am equally clear that the Resolve of Congress was intended to leave it to the Discretion of the Colony to adopt such a Mode as should please themselves and I have done myself the Honour to write these Sentiments to the Board, who were pleased to write to us upon the occasion.

Am obliged to you for your Account of the state of Things in Boston, I am ever anxious about our Friends who remain there and nothing is ever more acceptable to me than to learn what passes there.

The Inactivity of the two Armies, is not very agreable to me. Fabius's Cunctando³ was wise and brave. But if I had submitted to it in his situation, it would have been a cruel Mortification to me. Zeal, and Fire and Activity and Enterprize Strike my Imagination too much. I am obliged to be constantly on my Guard. Yet the Heat within will burst forth at Times.

The Characters drawn in your last entertained me very agreably. They were taken off, by a nice and penetrating Eye. I hope you will favour me with more of these Characters. I wish I could draw a Number of Characters for your Inspection. I should perhaps dawb on the Paint too thick—but the Features would be very strong.

The General is amiable and accomplished and judicious and cool; you will soon know the Person and Character of his Lady.⁴ I hope she has as much Ambition, for her Husbands Glory, as Portia and Marcia⁵ have, and then the Lord have Mercy on the Souls of Howe and Burgoigne and all the Troops in Boston.

Dft (Adams Papers); addressed: "Mrs Warren"; docketed in a late hand by JA: "J. A to Mrs Warren Nov. 25 1775."

¹ This letter was probably never sent. Its presence in the Adams Papers, the absence of a closing, and the docketing by JA all suggest it was retained, perhaps for completion later. On 8 Jan. 1776 (below) JA wrote another letter to Mrs. Warren, apologizing for not writing and commenting once again on the "three Characters [Washington, Lee, and Gates] drawn by a most masterly Pen, which I received at the southward."

² Mercy Otis Warren to JA, [?] Oct. (above), which includes a later addition. See note 11 there.

³ Delaying. A reference to the Roman general Fabius, nicknamed *Cunctator*, or delayer, for his avoidance of pitched battles with the Carthaginians and his preference for harassing action (*Dict. of Americanisms; Century Cyclo. of Names*).

⁴ Washington asked his wife to join him at headquarters partly to remove her from the danger posed by Lord Dunmore's activities in Virginia. She arrived in Philadelphia on 21 Nov. and remained there until the 28th, during which time JA undoubtedly met her (Washington, *Writings*, ed. Fitzpatrick, 4:28; Freeman, *Washington*, 3:580–581).

⁵ Intimate names used by AA and Mercy Otis Warren respectively.

From Samuel Chase

Pheasant Hall. Fred. Coty. Maryland

Dear Sir   Nov. 25. 1775. Saturday

I did Myself the Pleasure to write to You from Baltimore Town,¹ relative to two Vessells, which could be procured there, and that I was informed and beleived the Brigg was reasonable. The Owner is waiting your Answer, I therefore beg You to send the Determination of the Committee to Mr. Robert Alexander of that Town.²

I this Evening learn the Capture of Quebec. Montreal would gloriously close the first Years War.[3]

I am alarmed at the Instructions to the Deputies of Pennsylvania. I heartily condemn them. I think them ill timed, timorous and weak, they were not drawn by Men fit to conquer the world and rule her when she's wildest. How are they received by the Members of Congress? They suit the Palates of the persons instructed, and were probably drawn by themselves.[4] But I may censure too rashly. I am young and violent.

I return to Annapolis on tomorrow Week, and shall always be glad to hear from You.

I beg a Tender of my most respectful Compliments to your Brethren. Your Affectionate and Obedient Servant   Saml. Chase

Connolly is seised. I examined him. The proceedings are sent to Colo. Hancock.[5]

RC (Adams Papers); addressed: "To John Adams Esquire   Philadelphia"; endorsed: "Mr Chase   Nov 20 1775" [an obvious misreading].

[1] 16 Nov. (above).

[2] None found.

[3] It was Montreal that had fallen, not Quebec.

[4] The instructions for the nine-man Pennsylvania delegation, which included John Dickinson and Benjamin Franklin, were drawn up by a committee headed by Dickinson and adopted by the Assembly on 9 Nov. The delegates were ordered to exert themselves to the utmost to secure a redress of grievances in order to restore "Union and Harmony" between the colonies and Great Britain. The most controversial provision instructed the delegates to "dissent from, and utterly reject, any Propositions, should such be made, that may cause, or lead to, a Separation from our Mother Country, or a Change of the Form of this Government" (*Penna. Archives*, 8th ser., 8:7347, 7350, 7352–7353).

[5] Dr. John Connolly (ca. 1743–1813), an acquaintance of Washington, was captured with two others on his way to recruit a regiment, the Loyal Foresters, in the western lands and Canada under a commission from Lord Dunmore. Connolly's examination took place on 23 Nov. before the Fredericktown Committee of Safety, and its results, together with seized documents, were immediately sent to the congress. On 8 Dec. Connolly was ordered brought to Philadelphia for imprisonment. On 22 Dec. the results of the examination and the captured documents were printed. They appeared in the *Pennsylvania Gazette* of 27 Dec. Connolly apparently remained in prison for the duration of the war (*DAB*; Clarence Monroe Barton, "John Connolly," AAS, *Procs.*, 20 [1909–1910]:70–105; Force, *Archives*, 4th ser., 3:1660–1662; JCC, 3:394, 415, 445; PCC, No. 78, XI).

From Benjamin Hichborn

Dear Sir   Cambridge Saturday Eveng. Novr. 25 1775

From my last,[1] you may form some judgment of the disagreeable state of mind I have suffered from the Commencement of my late misfortunes. Anticipating your approbation, I have so far overcome the

restraint I have long labour'd under, as to attempt again to write you.
My first interview with Ayscough, after his discovery of the Letters, I
think worth relating—(if I had been subject to fits, I am sure he
wou'd have thrown me into the most violent Convulsions)—"Oh the
damn'd, black, hellish, bloody Plots contained in these Letters! Pray
Capt. Ayscough what do they contain? Oh too shocking to relate!
Treason! Rebellion! Massacre! (then beating his breast, with the most
unnatural distortions of his face and body) O my God! It makes my
blood run cold to think on it. For God's sake, Capt: Ayscough, if you
have any compassion for my feelings, tell me what you mean. Oh!
(beating his breast again) it chilled the very blood in my veins when
I read them. There is a plan laid to seize and massacre all the Officers
and Friends of Goverment and all the Churchmen upon the Continent in one Night. Pray Gentlemen is it a fair question, to ask if you
are Churchmen? (Mr. White said he was, I told him I was not.) Such
cruel, black designs, never before entered the heart of Man! But Capt.
Ayscough, are you not mistaken? Oh I read them over and over again.
I am not disposed to question your veracity, but if I had read it myself I woud not believe it. Pray Sir, whose signature do they bear?
They are all signed John Adams." I imagine at this time, he had no
thoughts of their being published, and was determined to make the
most of them. This may account For the apparent Chagrin and disappointment of our Enimies at Boston upon their appearing in Print.
They had been taught to believe the most infernal plots would be disclosed with these Letters, but to their great mortification, were obliged
to confess (to use their own terms) that they were very sensible and
consistent, and discovered the author to be a capable, determined,
finished Politician. This had a very good effect upon my Spirits, and
I must own I felt no small degree of pride in being the Bearer of them.
Poor Ayscough in the height of his zeal against your Letters, dropt, or
rather bolted out, what I think in justice to his Friend, he ought to
have kept a secret. He said they were fully acquainted with all the
proceedings of the Congress not withstanding their fancied security;
and then went on railing at our Members, who he said were pushing
matters to extremes against the general opinion of the Body. He asserted that upon a motion made by one of the Adams's, leading to independence, Mr. Randolph the then President, and one of the New
York Members, were so much disgusted, that they took their Hats and
left the Congress in resentment; and that Randolph was determined
not to meet them again. Upon our appearing to doubt the authenticity
of his information, he declared he had it from the New York Member

himself. He spoke highly in the praises of this New Yorker, and added with a good deal of rancour, that the Congress were much disunited, and the *appearance of uninimity*, which was all they had been able to preserve, was owing to the damned artful, unfair management of our Members.

Lexington Decr. 10th. 1775

Being interrupted by Company, on the Eveng I had devoted to this Letter, I rose early the next morning intending to fill this sheet, at least, and send it by Mr. Revere. I had wrote to the bottom of the preceding page, when a Gentleman called me aside and whispered that he had the day before been in a large Company, among whom were Collel. Otis, Doct: Winthrop and his Lady. That Mrs. Winthrop censured my Conduct respecting the letters very highly; in which she was joined by her Husband and Col. Otis. One of the Company suggested that I had satisfied General Washington, but was answered by Colel. Otis, with a good deal of warmth, that *he knew* neither the General nor any of the Officers about him, were in any degree satisfied with my Conduct.[2] This story induced me to postpone writing till I shoud hear from you. Your most welcome Letter of the 6th ultimo[3] did not reach me till yesterday. This delay happen'd by my taking a different hous in the Country, to what my Friend (who took it out of the Post Office) expected. I assure you Sir, nothing cou'd have come more opportunely, no event cou'd have given me equal satisfaction; it contained everything I coud wish for, so far as respected myself and is full of sentiments, that are certainly just, independent and liberal.

One thing only, I must dissent from you in, because I know you are mistaken. You suppose, the accident that threw your Letter into their possession, has exposed you to the ridicule of our common Enimies. Believe me Sir, it is directly the reverse. They all dread (and many of them were ingenuous enough to aknowledge that they respected) your firmness in a system of Politics that must prove fatal to their Schemes. The incidental Remarks upon private Characters and occurrences, they found themselves so little interested in, and so much qualified by other observations, that I scarcly heard them mentioned. Even the humorous anecdotes of H————[4] (at which I believe the G————l is so much disgusted) they called a Boyish performance and it hardly provided a smile.

You are a better Judge of the Effect it may have upon *private Friends*, than I can pretend to be; but I am certain it will have but *one bad tendency*, among *many good ones*, with your adversaries. Till this Event, your political Character has been so blended with your

Name-Sake's, in the Minds of those who had not a personal Acquaintance with you, that he has been saddled with a great share of your political Crimes; but since your treasonable designs have been convey'd to his Majesty under your own Hand, you may possibly have the *Honor* of an *Exception*, in the next tender of a general Pardon.[5] You are pleased to say you shoud *be glad to have my whole Story*. I woud with pleasure give it to you, but as it is very long, and I am yet weak and but poorly provided with every material for writing, I must beg leave for the present to omit it.

From an expression in your Letter, I imagine you presume I was discharged by Graves and Gage. The fact is this—my very ill State of Health preventing my Swiming away while the water was mild enough for such an enterprise, I had constructed a vehicle of two kegs and a strip of pine board, which I coud put together in two minutes, and was determined to set off on it the first favourable opportunity: but fortune made better provision for me than I was able to make for myself. On a very stormy day a small Canoe belonging to the Capt: was fastened to the Stern of the Ship. An exceeding dark night succeeding and the Storm continuing, afforded a season exactly suited to my purpose. From long confinement, miserable diet and a disorder which had not then entirely left me, I was quite feble: but anticipating the pleasures I have since realized with my Friends, I felt superior to every difficulty and hazzard. About ten o'Clock that Eveng: I stole out of the Gun-room-port and by the rudder Chains, let myself down (not without some danger as the sea run very high) into the Canoe. After being upon the Water about two hours and an half I reach'd Dorchester Neck, half drowned but completely happy.

As I find you are upon a Committee for collecting Evidence of the Hostilities committed by the British troops and Navy, I cannot omit the following anecdote, as a remarkable Instance of their Savage barbarity. One Drew[6] now a Lieutenant of the Scorpion or Viper, I am uncertain which, and Bruce a private belonging to the Preston, landed on Bunkers Hill, soon after the battle of the 17th of June. Drew, after walking for some time over the bodies of the dead, with great fortitude, went up to one of our wounded Men, and very deliberately shot him through the Head. Bruce advanced further over the Hill, and meeting with a forlorn wretch, begging *Mercy for Gods Sake!* he advanced and with a "damn ye, you Bugger you! are you not dead yet?" instantly demolished him. In a day or two after, Drew went upon the Hill again opened the dirt that was thrown over Doctr: Warren, spit in his Face jump'd on his Stomach and at last cut off his Head and committed every act of violence upon his Body. I had this Story from two Gentlemen belonging to the Preston who were eye Witnesses of the facts. In justice to the officers in general I must add, that they despised Drew for his Conduct, the other was below their notice.

I am very happy to find that your zealous Efforts in promoting so important a Matter as the better regulation of the Army have not been altogether without effect. Knox is in a station that I think he is fit for, and dare say, he will make a figure in. I am pleased to find Tudor so agreeably circumstanced, but must own I shoud be much more happy to see him in a station that wou'd give him greater military Consequence, and more extensive advantages for improvement in the Art of War. For my own part, I can truely say, as I never had a view seperate from the interest of my Country in wishing to be concerned in public affairs, I can be not merely *contented*, but *happy* in a path of private life, among a few Friends whose Confidence I am sure to possess without bounds and whose esteem it is my greatest ambition to merit. However I have done, and ever shall do everything in power consistent with the Character of a man of honor, to alleviate the distresses and promote the happiness of my Country.

The speculation you were so partial as to call ingenious, I must confess I was so much engaged in, that I feel no small disappointment in not finding it encouraged.[7] I wou'd not propose a Plan, which I was afraid to execute, and therefore offered to rest my life upon it's Success. It would be illiberal in me, to suppose it was rejected merely because it was a proposal of mine; I must, therefore presume there were some good reasons against it, tho I am not able to fathom them.

Many People have been much alarmed at the backwardness of the Soldiers to enlist for another year, but this disposition I think, may be accounted for very easily, without attributing to them an indifference to the Cause; indeed I can say from my own knowledge, that the People are as warm and annimated to support the Contest as ever they were; and the ready supply of 7,000 minute-Men upon a late Demand of the General, appears to me full evidence of it.[8]

Our privateers have made so many Captures that it is impossible for me to be particular, most of those from Europe I am informed have considerable quantities of Coal in them. Capt: Broaton who in Company with another, (I think Capt. Selmon)[9] were ordered to cruise in the Mouth of the River St. Laurence have done a feat which seems to meet with general disapprobation. In their way home, they called in at the Island of St. Johns and by force brought off Mr. Calbeck who married N. Coffins Daughter and Capt. Higgins who married a

Daughter of Job Princes. Higgins had just arrived from Europe and I believe had not been on shore. Higgins told me he expected to be released, with his Vessel and Cargo immediately. Capt: Broaton may perhaps deserve censure for going counter to his orders, but I think in justice to ourselves we ought to seize every officer in the service of Goverment wherever they may be found. For the propriety of this observation, we need only observe the Effects of our politeness to Lord Dunmore, and I am much mistaken if we don't soon see a Tryon immitating that malevolent Genius.

I never was more shocked than when I saw an article in the Instructions for the Pensilvania Delegates enjoining them "to dissent from, and utterly reject any proposition that shoud be made, that may Cause, or lead to a separation from the Mother Country" &c. &c. How long shall we torture all language to reconcile inconsistencies, and court insult, by cringing to our determined foes? As if the terror of our arms were owing to accident, shall we meanly relinquish the field, at the very Eve of Victory?

Suffer me Sir, to enquire what can we expect from a patched-up truce with Men, who have made their Salvation to depend upon our ruin? What terms can we expect to make for our Brethren at Canada, to whom we have pledged our honor and our Religion for their Security? In short, what a figure must we make, in the Eyes of every Power, whose influence and Commerce we wish to engage in our favour, while we have not Resolution enough to fight, but under the Banners (tho' by a fiction) of the very Tyrant we are contending with?

I find the People in general here, breathing the same sentiments, and seem on tip-toe for Independence as their only security against total ruin. I wish an unreasonable moderation, might not abate their ardour.

It is not easy to conceive the advantages that now instantly arise, upon a Continental Declaration of Independence. Many thousands of our Merchants and Mechanics who are now idle in the Country, woud repair to the Sea Coast and begin a Commerce that must be constantly encreasing; a very numerous Body who are now a burthen upon the Community, woud be thrown into employment, the Laws woud be rendered respectable and every one woud wear a cheerful Countenance.

As we may expect our Coast to swarm with Transports and Men of War next Spring, I hope the Congress will take the precaution of having some ships of considerable force prepared to receive them. Two or three Frigates of two and thirty Guns, woud be of incredible Service, with Such a naval force, we might venture among a fleet of Transports and perhaps captivate the greatest part of their mighty armament. Shoud any thing of this kind be in agitation, I woud beg leave to mention Mr. Natl. Tracy[10] as a Person every way qualified to undertake the building and fitting such Vessels for the Sea, and I think his zeal and service to the Publick in providing transports for Coll. Arnold's Expedition, without the least consideration, (tho he advanced large sums of Money, which he has not yet received) may entitle him to some notice. But I presume you are too well acquainted with his Character and disposition, to need any thing I can say by way of Recommendation.

I am under a necessity of omitting many Matters which I wish to mention, but you may expect to be troubled with a series of Letters, unless you forbid it in Season. Please to accept in Return for your kind endeavours to promote my happiness and success in every laudable pursuit, the warmest wishes of my heart for yours. I am Sir, with great Truth, your Friend & Servt. Benja. Hichborn

An Extract of (what I called) a State of facts, drawn up by the direction of the Admiral.

Scene, in Mrs. Yards House[11] in Company with some Members of the Continental Congress.

The Conversation turned upon a variety of topicks. The only Matter of a political kind that engaged my attention, was the probability of a Reconciliation between great Britain and her Colonies.

From implication only I learnd that in a late Address to his Majesty which is not yet made publick, they had ceded in *essence*, if not in *form*, every thing that the Parliament coud pretend to demand. But the difficulty lay in this: his Majesty wou'd have the Same Reasons to treat this address with Contempt that he had the former ones they had sent him—that they coud address him in no other manner, because in no other way, cou'd the Sentiments of the whole be jointly collected—that Goverment, while they held out proposals in one hand, presented a dagger in the other, even before any hostilities had been commenced, or they coud possibly have known it, had they taken place —that the proposals themselves were *partial*, and instead of *conciliating*, were evidently calculated to *divide* the Colonies, and thereby make them, seperately an easier prey—that these Considerations led them to conclude; there was a Systematical design in the Ministry to reduce them to a State of Vassalage and as they had openly boasted of Success from the Impotence and pusilinimity of the Continent, they were determined to exert every Power in their possession, to make a desparate Resistance. This they were sensible, must issue in a total reduction of the Colinies or their Independence; either of which, was so little the object of their wishes, that nothing short of necessity, wou'd induce them to place the Controversy upon that footting; and therefore they were always ready to Submit to an *equal* Administration, under those strong ties of mutual Interest and affection, which had so long and happily united them with Great Britain.

The admiral enquired where I lodged, and what Company I kept at Philadelphia, and insisted upon my giving him a particular account of the Conversation of the Adamses and other Members of the Congress. I believe the above is pretty just, and cou'd not conceive of its' having a bad tendency or I shou'd not have given to him. I hope it will not meet your disapprobation.

RC (Adams Papers); docketed: "B. Hichborn   Novr 25. 1775."

[1] 28 Oct. (above).

[2] For Washington's opinion of Hichborn, see same, note 4.

[3] Not found.

[4] Benjamin Harrison, whose letter to Washington was also seized at the same time as JA's letters.

[5] As Samuel Adams and John Hancock had been excepted from Gage's pardon on 12 June.

[6] James Drew was first lieutenant on the sloop *Scorpion* (Philip Stephens to Vice Adm. Graves, 27 Sept., The Present Disposition of His Majesty's Ships and Vessels in Sea Pay, 1 Dec., *Naval Docs. Amer. Rev.*, 2:736–737; 3:1400).

[7] See Hichborn to JA, 28 Oct., note 5 (above).

[8] Hichborn is probably referring to the militia force of 5,000 men, 3,000 from Massachusetts and 2,000 from New Hampshire, that Washington called out in early Dec. 1775 to replace the Connecticut forces whose enlistments ran out on 10 Dec. (French, *First Year*, p. 521; Washington to Gov. Jonathan Trumbull, 2 Dec., *Writings*, ed., Fitzpatrick, 4:137–138).

[9] Ordered on 5 Oct. by the congress to capture two ships headed for Canada, Washington directed Nicholson Broughton, commander of the *Hancock*, and John Selman, captain of the *Franklin*, to undertake the mission. Although they failed to capture the ships, they did manage to create confusion around Nova Scotia and particularly in the Gut of Canso. In the process, however, they largely ignored their orders, and Washington was forced to free their prizes and their prisoners—Philip Callbeck, Thomas Wright, and a Mr. Higgins (Clark, *Washington's Navy*, p. 19, 46–57, 75–79; Washington to Nicholson Broughton, 16 Oct., and to the President of Congress, 7 Dec., *Writings*, ed. Fitzpatrick, 4:33–34, 152).

[10] Nathaniel Tracy (1751–1796), a Newburyport merchant who entered into partnership with his brother John and Jonathan Jackson shortly before the Revolution began. In Aug. 1775 he sent out his first privateer and during the war sent out 23 others, a few of which made satisfactory profits. Soon after the war's end bad luck with his merchant ships caused his early retirement from trade (Sibley-Shipton, *Harvard Graduates*, 17:247–251; Benjamin W. Labaree, *Patriots and Partisans: The Merchants of Newburyport, 1764–1815*, Cambridge, 1962, p. 218–219).

[11] Mrs. Sarah Yard, at whose boardinghouse JA stayed in Philadelphia (*Diary and Autobiography*, 2:115, note 4).

From Samuel Osgood Jr.

Sir   Camp at Roxbury Novr. 30th. 1775

I have to acknowledge your Favors of the 14th and 15th Novr. and now Sir I think myself sufficiently happy since you have authorized me to write with Freedom and no advantage will be taken of my Simplicity. I flatter myself that the most triffling Intelligence from Camp if sometimes there is interspersed any Thing of Importance will not be disagreeable to you in your present Situation. Their Motions Feelings, general Sentiments, Immoralties, general Supply of Necess[aries], Hopes and Fears, Success and Disappointment may all in their Turn afford Matter worthy of Contemplation.

The Conduct of our General Officers is such with Regard to raising a new Army that many suppose we have a Specimen of a small Degree of Tyranny concealed in the Heart. All the Colonies are to be united. All Distinctions are to be thrown aside. No Difference of sentiment, no Regard or Attachment a Soldier has to this or that Officer of his own Colony to be respected—but on the contrary despised. And is the faithful obedient Soldier to be contemned because he says I know my own Colony Men, I choose to be commanded by them? Is it not opening a Door for needless Altercation? And besides does it not destroy a grand Stimulus that has always actuated different Bodies of Men most powerfully? Allied Armies of different Nations have found Honor and Reputation as strong an incentive to Action as self Preservation and perhaps much more so.

This same kind of emulous Ambition has and will subsist between the Several Colonies, and the same Argument that will prove it best to intermix the Colonies, will also convince me that it is best to loose all that noble Ambition which fires the manly Breast and raises a just Indignation at being second when it is possible and equitable to be first. Can anything, Sir, fire upon us a more infamous Name, than that we are able to raise Men, but cannot officer them! Alas, Sir, we may do the Drugery, but must not share the Honor. I heard an Officer of the first Rank say, soon after his Arrival in Camp, that the Men were very good, but by --- we must send to the southward for Officers. Now, Sir, Jealousy will look out with a Sharp Eye, and predict hard Things. Southern Gentlemen are some how or other to be introduced to command nothern Men, for they are sufficiently sick of their own. (A Number of them have deserted and one about three Nights Since being placed as one of the most advanced Sentries before Midnight deserted and the Camp might have been sacrificed as he undoubtedly carried in the Countersign). The nothern Men are determined not to be commanded by them. If our Notions in some Respects are different from our Brethren, yet by Heavens we are not destitute of common Sense and Feelings; for if Oppression only makes wise Men mad, I believe, Sir, we have sufficiently proved ours to be the wisest Colony the Sun blesses with its Rays.

I never mean to intimate that we are to be revered and adored upon that Account; neither are we to be oppressed for it. We are, Sir, nearly all of us Freeholders in this Colony, which emboldens us to look any Man in the Face. We are not accustomed to any other Treatment than such as a Freeholder may receive, which creates a Kind of Equality, that we shall always highly prize. But I fancy Sir it is not so in all the Colonies.

The above motly Plan (I mean the Plan of mixing the Officers of the different Colonies and also the several Regiments belonging to this Colony. The Officers are so ranged that if they belong to the Colony they do not belong to the same County and are entire Strangers to each other which is disagreeable to the privates)[1] was opposed by two worthy Generals—only *two*, Sir! Generals W--d and Sp-----r.[2] The first opposed it with as much Firmness as was prudent with Peace and Quietness; desiring them to observe he was against it. Genl. Sp-----r has an open upright and honest Mind. Knowing our Situation is peculiar, he is loth even to try an Experiment, but choses to travel in the Road that has been so often trod with pleasing Sucess and crowned with Honor.

I can but think some other Plan might have been adopted that would have given general Satisfaction. Genl. Spencer observes, that their Colony always was able to raise, and always did without Fail, the Number of Men they were calld upon for; but this Day, Sir, the General Officers are all call'd together to consult, and find out (if possible) what Step is best to be taken now, for the Connecticutt Soldiers Time has expired, or does the beginning of next Week, and none are raised to supply their Place, and they at present appear to be determined to Leave the Camp, at Least a great Majority of them. Genl. Spencer exerts himself like a good Man among his Troops, but it is a hard Task to force Men to act contrary to their Inclination.

I fear Sir (and therefore dread to have the Time arrive) that our province Men will dance to the same Tune when their Time is ended. It was so in the last *War* and altho this is infinitely Different from *all* others: yet they neither Reason civilly or politically; they Doubtless are possessed of cogitative Powers; but like Gold in the Ore, which is scarcely perceived till refined, the Commonalty always will be. I hope, Sir, it will prove to be the best that the Generals were obliged to take those Officers that have served this Season: yet Sir you will readily conclude we might get much better Men in the Colony for Officers, now we have got Government to assist us, than when we were all in Chaos. Pray Sir, (if Time and Opportunity Serves) unfold to me the disadvantages in calling upon each Colony, that I trust now joyfully supply Men to oppose our blood thirsty Tyrants, for their Quota of Men. I fancy our Colony would have its Quota ready being allowed a proper Time. And now Sir I doubt not but the generals will all agree, it is of the last Importance to keep a sufficient Army together, and will therefore be obliged to call upon our Colony, for the Militia which will not be vastly agreeable.

But Sir when I consider how apparent it is thro' the whole Season that Providence has been on our Side I dispel the Gloom and forget my Fears. You gave me Leave to write freely. I fancy you will imagine me now sufficiently free. I am, Sir, with the Greatest Respect, your most Humble Servant   Samuel Osgood junr.

RC (Adams Papers).

[1] Parentheses supplied. The sentences within parentheses were written in the margin, and the text was marked to indicate where they should be inserted.
[2] Artemas Ward of Massachusetts and Joseph Spencer of Connecticut.

From Lemuel Robinson

Dear Sir   [30 Nov. 1775]
These Lines are to inform you of my Situation[1] which in the Multaplicity of your Business is undoubtaley far from your Mind. Let it Suffice to Say an Army is Raising in which I have no part. As to the part I have taken for Several Years past to prepare for the Last Appeal is not unknown to You. At the Battle of Concord, So Called, You was there When we took post On Roxbury Hill. I was obliged to Act the part of General Till Genll. Thomas took Command and he Being a Stranger the Burden Lay upon me for a Considerable Time. The Intercepted Letters in May Mention me as the First in Command at Roxbury Camp.[2] I Mention this as proff that I was not Idle. At the Time the Committee of Safety were Giving out their Orders to Raise Regiments. I was then Ordered To Marshfield with 1100 Men to dislodge the Enemy who it was Said were Strongly Reinforct. On my Return I met A Gentleman who informd me that the Committee of Safety had Determind There Should be but one Regiment in the

County of Suffolk and that his, upon which I Continued in Camp and Did my duty Acting as 2d. To Genll. Thomas. The Officers at this Time Left the Camp to Raise Men and Men went off to List and fix for the Campaign, Till the Daily Returns wer Less then 700 Men 300 of which were of my Regiment and Relievd Every 3d. day. The duty you must be Sensable Lay hard upon me. At this Time for 9 days and Nights I Never Shifted my Cloths nor Lay down to Sleep bing obliged to do the duty Even Down to the Adjutant. And no officer of the Day, I was obligd to Patrole the Guards Every Night which was a Round of 9 Miles.[3] This Took up my time So that I never Saw the Committee of Safty in Order to know the Truth, of the One Regiment Only bing Raisd. The Committee bing So Imbarast at this time that Although they Had me principally in view yet Gave out their Orders So fast that they overan their Complment before they were aware and desird me to Continue in Service Assuring me of a Regiment.[4] In the Meun while Appointd me Muster and Pay Master. Thus I Continued Till Goverment took place when I was Assurd of Regiment. Several Vacancys then Hapning, the Councill Applied to Gell. Washington for a Return of Vacancis but he never made any upon which the Concill Sent him a Recommendation, in my Favour. But the Generall Saith that he is Tied up By Instructions and Cannot Admit any person who Has Not been Commissiond[5] thus I am entirely Left out of the Army Although I have the Voice of Both Civil and Military in my favour. The Modcling the Army out of the Old one intirely, with Submison and Raising the pay of the officers will be Attended with many bad Consequences. The Men through the Course of the Summer Have had oppertunity to know the Officers. Those few who have behavd well will get their men. The Others Never will And as all the Officers are appointed by the Generall To Each Regiment I believe there will not be One full Regiment. The Camp is this Moment in Alarm. The Coneticut Forces whose Time is out Universally going home. No Intreaty Can Stop them. If this Should be the Case of the Rest God Only knows what will Become of us. I Expect if nothing more favourable Turns up the Militia must be Called in. I believe I Can Collect frinds Enough to hold them in on Roxbury Side once more. A Store Ship is Carried in to Cape Ann Loaded with warlike Stores Valud at £10000 Sterling.[6] If you Can procure an Exeption for me with Respect to the Resolve that no officer be Admitted into the Army you will Lay me under the Greatest Obligation. I Can Assure you that my inclination to the Service is Such that I Cannot any way Content myself out of the Same.

The Inclosd is Signd as you will See by the Committee of Safety Which gave out the Orders. I Remain Your Hue. Sert.

Lemuel Robinson

ENCLOSURE

Colony of the } Massachusetts-Bay }

To all whom it may concern   Watertown, Novem. 30th 1775

We the Subscribers, Members of the late Committee of Safety of this Colony, do certify, That Colo. Lemuel Robinson of Dorchester has exerted himself in his Countrys cause, perhaps, as much as any other Man in the Government, and so as, in our opinion, to merit much of his Country, and said Committee did all in their power to obtain the Command of a Regiment for him, in the Colony Service, but thro' an unhappy mistake, some misrepresentations of Facts prevented its taking place.

J. Palmer
Azor Orne
S Holten
Benjan. White
Abram. Watson
Nathan Cushing

RC (Adams Papers); addressed: "To the Honbl. Jno Adams Esqr. at the Congress in Philadelphia   Free"; docketed: "Lem Robinson 1775   Nov 30th"; and enclosure.

[1] Lemuel Robinson (1736–1776) of Dorchester was the proprietor of the Liberty Tree Tavern, where, on 14 Aug. 1769, 350 Sons of Liberty, including JA, met to celebrate the fourth anniversary of the founding of "the True Sons of Liberty." Robinson was elected to the First and Third Provincial congresses and at the beginning of the war was lieutenant colonel in Col. Heath's Suffolk co. Regiment. Despite the problems described in the letter, perhaps because of them, Robinson was appointed by the General Court on 23 Jan. 1776 colonel of a new regiment to be raised out of Suffolk and York cos. He died soon after of smallpox (*Boston Gazette*, 21 Aug. 1769; JA, *Diary and Autobiography*, 1:341; *NEHGR*, 39:83 [Jan. 1885]; 49:341 [July 1895]; Mass. Provincial Congress, *Jours.*, p. 7, 273; *Mass. Soldiers and Sailors*, 13:458).

[2] These may have been letters examined and ordered printed by the Provincial Congress on 1 May 1775. The excerpts printed, however, do not mention Robinson (Mass. Provincial Congress, *Jours.*, p. 173; *New-England Chronicle*, 2 May).

[3] Robinson's account of his activities at Roxbury as second in command to John Thomas was quoted virtually verbatim by William Gordon in his history under the date 28 April (*The History of the Rise, Progress, and Establishment of the Independence of the United States of America*, 2d edn., 3 vols., N.Y., 1794, 1:337). Gordon, who neither cited his source nor mentioned Robinson's reference to Thomas, gives the impression that Robinson was in sole command. This treatment led Allen French to criticize Gordon for his handling of this episode (*First Year*, p. 719). Although

the light shed on Gordon's inaccuracies is interesting, of some significance is this further evidence that Gordon, barring the unlikely possibility that Robinson kept a copy of his letter, made use of JA's papers. Compare Charles Lee to JA, 19 Nov., note 2 (above).

[4] Robinson had failed in June 1775 to raise the necessary number of men for his commission as colonel. It was William Heath that was competing with him in Suffolk co. (Mass. Provincial Congress, *Jours.*, p. 339, 342, 563; Wroth and others, eds., *Province in Rebellion*, p. 2502, 2706).

[5] According to the instructions of the congress, colonels and officers of lesser rank had to be commissioned by the colonial governments (JCC, 2:100–101).

[6] The brig *Nancy* out of London was taken by Capt. John Manley of the *Lee*, a privateer, on 28 Nov. The capture of this ship was of great importance to the American Army, for it was loaded with ordnance for the British Army in Boston. Among other things, the Americans gained 2,000 muskets, 100,000 musket flints, 62,500 pounds of musket shot, 75 carbines, 11 mortar beds, and one complete 13-inch brass mortar that with its bed weighed over 5,000 pounds. This mortar, described as "the noblest piece of ordnance ever landed in America," arrived in Cambridge on 2 Dec. and was christened by Israel Putnam "The Congress." It exploded during the bombardment of Boston in March 1776 (*Boston Gazette*, 11 Dec.; Clark, *Washington's Navy*, p. 60–64, 74, 122).

From Joseph Palmer

My dear Sir   Watertown, Decemr. 2d. 1775

Yesterday Mr. Revere returned, and brot your acceptance,[1] which was truly acceptable to our Friends. Since mine by Revere,[2] I have been exploreing some of the Mountains of North and Southhampton; and in the former we examined a Lead-Mine which has been worked, and in which, much loss has been Sustained.[3] The circumstances of this Mine I will now give you, as near as I can recollect, but shall be able to do better, perhaps, after we have prepared our Report. The present Proprietors of it, are Colo. Ward 6/15ths, Mr. Hedge 3/15ths, and Mr. Bowdoin 6/15ths; These, or former Proprietors, have pursued the Vein of ore about 30 feet deep, and the Clerk[4] says, that it grows richer, as they go deeper. The Clerk keeps a Tavern about 4 or 5 Miles distant from the Mine, and boards the workmen; what days work were done, and who had the profit, may be easily conjectured. It has not been work'd for some time past. The best pieces of the ore produced 75 per Cent Lead, in their Essays; others 50 per Cent; and some coud hardly be called ore. But when they came to work it in the large way, not knowing what Fluxes to use, or how to discharge the oar of the Sulphur, they burnt it all up, and obtained no Lead. At the Mine, they have brot a Stream of Water which drives a Wheel, that works the Pumps, which empties the Water [out of] the Mine. This Mine is near the Summit of the Mountain, at the foot [of] which runs a Small River; and the owners of the Mine have 200 Acres of Land bounding about 1/2 a Mile upon the river, and running up to the Summit of the Hill, or near it; besides which, they have a long Lease, for 999 Years for 25 Acres more adjoining; upon condition of delivering a certain part of the Ore dug (how much I don't know) from thence. Near the Mine, they have a Small Store, with a Chimney. And from the Mine is a Cartway, about 3/4 of a Mile, Slanting down to the River, which has there an Elbow, across which is brot a Stream which drives the Stampers; at this place is their Stamping-Mill, Washing Troughs, and Smelting House. They Stamp and Wash the ore, which, without Smelting, produces very good Lead for the Potters, and is much used for the purpose of Glazeing their Ware. The Proprietors ask £1000 Sterling for all their Interest there; but wou'd probably be glad to sell for £1000 Lawful money.[5] Their Works are all much ruined. Their Land is worth about £200 Lmo. This leaves 800 for the Supposed Riches in the Mine, with their Works; which Works are worth nothing for any other purpose; and if applied to this, will not be worth more than *one or £200 Lmo.* 'Tis not unlikely but that other rich Mines in the vicinity, will hereafter be discovered, especially if this is worked; for that wou'd naturally lead to farther discoveries. We found, in other Lands, about 20 Rods distant from the Mine, a very rich Rock of ore; and it has been traced, with short intervals, Several Miles upon the Mountains. There will be 12 or 14 Miles Cartage from the Mine to good Water-Carriage; unless it shou'd be found practicable to remove Some obstructions so as to carry the Lead upon Rafts, or Floats down the river runing near the Mine; but of this I am wholly ignorant. The vein is seen in the Summer time where it crosses a river. Shou'd the Continent, or Colony, purchase of the Proprietors, and give £1000 Lmo.; it will cost as much more to purchase other Lands to secure the full benefit of the Streams, to accomodate the workmen, to command Wood and Roads, and especially to command all the Summit of the Hill, so as to have all the Mines in that Mountain; and it will probably take £1000 Lmo. more to set the Works all in proper order, and carry it on so far, as to produce the first Ton of Lead. After this, 'tis probable, it will prove profitable, but far from certain, because there may not be a Quantity equal to the prospect, which is doubtless very promising. I do not think that it will do for either the greater or lesser public to work it upon their own account; but if either will purchase and Supply, as above, then Sell to AB the Land, which Shall be Mortgaged as Security for the whole without Interest so many Years; AB to give

Bond to deliver all the Lead produced for such number of Years, he to have Security that the public will receive it, at Such a price, at Such a place, and at all times within said Term; said Price to be so large as to involve in it some considerable bounty: Then, if the public do not make a mistake in their Man, they will be well served; and AB will have a fair chance for making somthing hansome for himself: But the public must be careful who this AB is. We went also to the Summit of another Mountain, in So.hampton, where we found some ore; but as the ground had not been opened, and near Night, we cou'd not inspect so closely into that, but left directions for opening a Suspected place. The ore we brot down will be assayed next Week; after which if time and opportunity permits, I intend to send you the result. If any thing is done, I will, if possible, send four of my Derbyshire Friends.

Whether the Study of Mineralogy naturally produces *Dreamers,* or not, I shall not take upon me to say; but certain it is, that smatterers in it often *dream.* Whatever was the cause, upon my tour, I dreamt more of Political matters, than of Gold and Silver; and of the latter only as subservient to the former. Whether in company, or alone, my mind was constantly possessed with a notion that the American Congress had, or very soon wou'd, publish a Manifesto to the [world] [6] purporting, That in Such a Year, the British Ministry made such and such unconstitutional claims upon some one or other of these Colonies, &c. &c.; giving an Historical account of matters, up to the present day: Then adducing these Facts, as Sufficient reasons for Declareing themselves the United Colonies, absolutely independant of GB. But, in order to put a stop to the effusion of human Blood; from naturel affection &c., &c., offer'd to treat with her upon terms of Commerce, provided She withdrew all her forces on or before Such a day, and then accepted to treat, on or before Such a day; but if She neglected to *withdraw,* or neglected or refused to *treat,* as aforesaid, then declared themselves no farther bound by this *tender*: and no cessation of hostilities, until such *withdraw.* Then it held up to the [world], in clear and Strong terms, that this tender contained, all that GB *ever* had any equitable right to, from the Colonies. That the appointment of Crown-Officers here, was no benefit to GB, but an infinite evil to both them and the Colonies; and that the Colonies will never more submit to it, be the consequences what they may; and that this is the last offer will ever be made to 'em; and which, if refused, or neglected, on the part of GB, Their Ports are thereby declared free to all the World excepting GB only, after such a day, and such refusal. I had tho't of this matter, and talked of it so much, that I had almost persuaded myself that I shou'd meet with such a Manifesto by Revere's return. 'Tho I have not yet met with it, my enthusiasm works so strong, that I cannot persuade myself but I shall soon see it: The deep-vaulted Chemist never more earnestly expected the Philosopher's stone. This general affair, which respects the whole Union, leads me to ask, what is there now in the way, that can possibly prevent a Congress-Declaration, of liberty to each Colony to take up such form of Government as they may respectively most approve of? I think, the sooner the better, particularly for this Colony; I long to be more free; but only so, as best to promote the Union of the whole; and I think, that if we were Set entirely free from the Charter, we shou'd act with more vigour and expidition. I had like to have said, that I knew we shou'd. A Representative body, equal and frequent, with their Committees will do better, and more business, in like time, than 3 Branches. I freely own that I do not wish for any Governor or Council, not even if chosen by ourselves. But why do I, who am so tired of public business, and wait only for a favourable opportunity to withdraw myself, project Schemes for future Ages? 'Tis the love of liberty! 'Tis Heaven its Self that points out liberty!

Two critical experiments have been made in the Saltpetre way, one by Colo. Orne, the other by Colo. Lincoln;[7] the former of these I have, and have the promise of the latter; when possessed of them, I intend to transmit 'em to you; or if they permit, publish 'em for public Use: They are short, plain and Simple, so that Dick, Tom, and Joan, may understand 'em, so as to practice upon it with certain success. I intend to propose farther encouragement upon that Article: Now is the critical time, and we may now establish it, so as to make it a perminant article in our Manufactures.

The General has sent you an Account of the Store-Ship carried into Cape-Ann. 2000 Stand of Arms, a Brass 13 In. Morter, with a Thousand Military &ca's to the value of £20000 Stg., as 'tis Said, makes our Army rejoice; the Genl., Washington, Shew'd me the Invoice, and appeared much pleased.[8] There is, Since the Store Ship, a Small Vessel with Wood &c., brot into Salem; and another Vessel into Plymouth.[9]

There is a farther account of the Storm at Nfd. Land;[10] all their Vessels so damaged, that it was tho't not one of 'em wou'd be able to return loaded; 4000 Men lost; 1000 dead Bodies draged on Shore with Nets; A Lieutenant who had been there to enlist Men for the

Army at Boston, when the Fishery was finished, had enlisted many, but such an unusual Storm, carrying such amazing destruction with it, pointed to him so plainly the hand of Providence against these oppressive measures, that he openly declared, that he *"beli'ved God almighty was against 'em, and that he wou'd no longer bear his Commission, or act against his Brethren in the Colonies."* This, and more, is Said and believed; but I am not possessed of the particular evidence. As was said in another case, "Seeing &c. – – – –, what manner of Persons ought we to be &c." It is also Said, that the Vessell in which Mrs. Borland &c. went passengers to England, is lost, and all perished.[11] One Vessel in the Bay was lately burnt, supposed by Lightening; Frank Green (at the Lines) said that it was a Ship, the Juno, from England, with Hay; by circumstances, I suspect she had Powder.[12] 'Tis supposed that the Enemy are watching our motions, and hope to find a weak moment in the change of the Army, that may favour an Attack upon us; but we are taking measures to prevent their Success: 2000 Men from Hamshire, and 3000 from our Colony, to be at Head Quarters the 10th. Instant; besides all the Militia in the vicinity of Cambridge and Roxbury (who do not furnish any part of the 3000) to be in readiness on the shortest notice. I hope much, from the goodness of our Cause; and firmly believe that Heaven will be with us: The short remainder of my life, I am willing to devote in support of this righteous Struggle; and in such a way as the public may direct; but it may be, I would rather retire, and give way to some one firmer in Body and Mind. My affectionate regards attend all our Friends, may the path of your duty be made, as the riseing light, more and more plain to all the Congress, every day and every Hour.

The last I heard from Braintree, all was well; but I have not had opportunity to see Mrs. Adams for several Weeks past. Adieu my dear Sir, may every blessing be Yours, and believe me to remain Your Affect. Frd. and Hble. Servt.   J. Palmer

PS. Decr. 3d., 8 o'Clock PM, this Moment received the News of a Brig from Britain, with Coals and Bale Goods, carried into Beverly.[13]

RC (Adams Papers); docketed: "Mr Palmer   Decr 2. 1775"; outside edges of the MS are mutilated.

[1] JA's acceptance of his appointment as chief justice of the superior court (JA to Perez Morton, 24 Nov., above).

[2] Palmer to JA, 31 Oct. (above).

[3] This mine, located about six miles from the center of Northampton, had been worked periodically, with limited success, since 1679. In 1769 William Bowdoin, brother of James, bought the mine in partnership with two others and began operations. By 1775 operations had stopped, probably because of lack

of profits (J. R. Trumbull, *History of Northampton*, 2 vols., Northampton, Mass., 1898, 1:359, 361, 364–365). On 17 Feb. 1776 the Joint Committee on Virgin Lead, of which Palmer was a member, presented its report, which closely followed the facts of this letter, clearly stating the expense involved in returning the mine to operation, but which came to no conclusions about continuing operations (Mass., *House Jour.*, 1775–1776, 3d sess., p. 304–305). The congress, to which the report was forwarded, finally resolved on 5 July 1776 that immediate steps be taken to procure lead from the mine (JCC, 4:185–186; 5:522). None of these actions had much effect, for the land was ultimately sold for about two dollars an acre and mining was not resumed until 1807 (Trumbull, *Northampton*, 1:366).

[4] The clerk was a Mr. Clap, called Maj. Clap by James Russell Trumbull (Mass., *House Jour.*, 1775–1776, 3d sess., p. 304–305; Trumbull, *History of Northampton*, 1:365).

[5] Lawful money was about 29 percent less valuable than sterling, for it valued an ounce of silver at 6s 8d instead of 5s 2d.

[6] "World" is represented in the text with a sign: ☉. In the Library of Congress facsimile edition of *Two Rebuses from the American Revolution* (Washington, 1973), the symbol of a snake holding its tail to form a circle is translated "unity" as an alternative to the ancient meaning "eternity." But in a later passage Palmer crosses out "rest of the ☉" and substitutes "all the world." It is impossible to tell whether Palmer intended a snake or merely a circle, but the line is thickened where a snake head might be.

[7] Azor Orne and Benjamin Lincoln (1733–1810), latter in *DAB*.

[8] The *Nancy* (see Lemuel Robinson to JA, 30 Nov., note 6, above).

[9] The *Boston Gazette* of 4 Dec. reported that in the previous two weeks two vessels had been brought into Cape Ann, one into Portsmouth, and several small vessels into Plymouth.

[10] Palmer's account of the storm that hit Newfoundland on 9 Sept. was taken from the same issue of the *Gazette*. The newspaper put the loss at £140,000 sterling and noted that the fifteen or sixteen transports that had sailed to pick up the men who were to enlist in the army at Boston were destroyed in the same storm.

[11] Probably Anna Vassall Borland (1735–1823), widow of the Boston merchant John Borland (Edward Doubleday Harris, "The Vassalls of New England," *NEHGR*, 17:119–120 [April 1863]).

[12] The ship's destruction was described in the *Boston Gazette* of 4 Dec.

[13] The *Concord* (same, 11 Dec.; Clark, *Washington's Navy*, p. 61–62).

To James Warren

My dear Sir   Philadelphia Decr. 3. 1775[1]

I have only Time to acquaint you that Congress have ordered the arrears of Pay to be discharged to the soldiers and one Months Advance Pay to be made. No Bounty nor any allowance for Lunar Months.[2]

I have a Thousand Things to say—But no Time. Our Army must be reconciled to these Terms, or We shall be ruined for what I know. The Expenses accumulating upon the Continent are so vast and boundless that We shall be bankrupt if not frugal.

I lately had an opportunity, suddenly, of mentioning two very deserving officers, Thomas Crafts Junior who now lives at Leominster and George Trot who lives at Braintree to be, the first a Lt. Colonel the second a Major of the Regiment of Artillery under Coll. Knox.[3] These are young Men under forty, excellent officers, very modest, civil, sensible, and of prodigious Merit as well as suffering in the American Cause. If they are neglected I shall be very mad, and kick and Foume like fury. Congress have ordered their Names to be sent to the General, and if he thinks they can be promoted without giving Disgust and making Uneasiness in the Regiment, to give them Commissions. Gen. Washington knows neither of them. They have too much Merit and Modesty to thrust themselves forward and solicit, as has been the Manner of too many. But they are excellent officers, and have done great Things both in the political and military Way. In short vast Injustice will be done if they are not provided for. Several Captains in the Artillery Regiment were privates under these officers in Paddocks Company.[4] Captain Crafts who is I believe the first Captain, is a younger Brother to Thomas.[5] I believe that Burbeck, Mason, Foster &c. would have no objection.[6]

The Merit of these Men from the Year 1764 to this day, has been very great tho not known to every Body. My Conscience tells me they ought to be promoted. They have more Merit between you and me than half the Generals in the Army.

RC (MHi: Warren-Adams Coll.); docketed: "Mr J Adams. Decr 1775."

[1] This and one to AA of the same date are the last known letters written by JA from Philadelphia in 1775. On 8 Dec., "worn down with long and uninterrupted Labour," JA successfully requested the congress for permission to return to Massachusetts. On 9 Dec. he began his journey, arriving in Braintree on 21 Dec. (JA to AA, 3 Dec., *Adams Family Correspondence*, 1:331; *Diary and Autobiography*, 3:350; 2: 223–224 and notes).

[2] The congress took this action on 1 and 3 Dec. (JCC, 3:394, 400; compare James Warren to JA, 14 Nov., note 12, above).

[3] On 2 Dec. the congress established the organization of the artillery regiment and recommended that Crafts and Trott be appointed field officers (JCC, 3:399). When Washington offered them commissions, however, Trott chose not to serve and Crafts' "ambition was not fully gratified by the offer of a Majority" rather than a lieutenant colonelcy (Washington, *Writings*, ed. Fitzpatrick, 4:161; see also James Warren to JA, 11 Dec. and Thomas Crafts Jr. to JA, 16 Dec., both below).

[4] For a partial listing of the officers and men of Capt. Adino Paddock's artillery company, see Thomas J. Abernethy, American Artillery Regiments in the Revolutionary War, unpubl. bound typescript, MHi, p. 4–5.

[5] Capt. Edward Crafts (*Mass. Soldiers and Sailors*, 4:64).

[6] William Burbeck, David Mason, and Thomas Waite Foster, all officers under Richard Gridley and later Henry Knox (Heitman, *Register Continental Army*, p. 133, 383, 234).

From William Tudor

Dr Sir   Head Quarters. Cambridge 3d. Decr. 1775

Long before the Receipt of this You will have heard by Express from the General, of the important Prize we have made in the Capture of the Brig Nancy loaded with Ordnance Stores for the Army at Boston. Orders were given that she should be unloaded with all possible Expedition, and we have now the greatest Part of her Cargo safely hous'd in the Laboratory here.[1] The Loss must be very great to the Enemy, but the Acquisition is immense to Us. Col. Barbeck assured me that it would have taken eighteen Months to have prepar'd a like Quantity of Ordnance Materials, could they have been furnish'd with every Thing requisite to make them. There are many Things which Money could not have procur'd Us. I heard Col. Mason say that, had all the Engineers of the Army been consulted they could not have made out a compleater Invoice of military Stores, than we are now in Possession of. We want Nothing now but a Ship Load of Powder, to raise such a Clatter in the Streets of Boston, as to force George's Banditti to seek Protection in his Ships, or fly to his Ministers for Security.

We have had much Disturbance in The Camp here, by the Connecticut Troops insisting upon returning home at the Expiration of their Enlistment which was the 1st. Instant.[2] Every Act of Persuasion was used to prevail with them to reinlist, but to no Purpose. Numbers of them refused staying only till the Militia could be called in to man the Lines. When Intreaty fail'd, force was used, and the greatest Part of them have at Length consented to stay Ten Days longer. Orders have been issu'd for 5000 Militia to come down immediately and join the Camp. The Massachusetts Soldiers shew as much Backwardness in inlisting as the others. They complain of a Poll Tax being laid on them; that the Province is in arrears to them; they want bounty money, and lunar Months instead of Calendar ones. In short they expect to be hir'd and that at a very high Price to defend their own Liberties, and chuse to be Slaves unless they can be bribed to be freemen. Quid facit Libertas, cum sola Pecunia regnat?[3] The mecernary Disposition of our Soldiery, made a Gentleman observe, that had Lord North sent over Guineas instead of Cannon Balls, New England would have been conquer'd in a Twelvemonth. This was an illnatur'd Remark, but similar to others which are daily made by a certain Set of Gentlemen, who affect to think that neither Patriotism or Bravery is the principal Motive of Action in any Man born and educated to the Northward of New York.

At a General Court Martial held last Friday, Lt. Col. Enos was try'd, "for leaving the Detachment under Col. Arnold (on the Canada Expedition) and returning home without Permission from his commanding Officer" and after a full Hearing acquitted with Honour. It fully appear'd that absolute Necessity was the Cause of his Retreat, and had he not return'd his whole Division must have perish'd for Want of Provision. The News of his Return at first rais'd a prodigious Ferment and excited much Indignation; the Instant he arriv'd he was put under an Arrest, but has since been honorably discharged.

Bellidore was a Lt. General in the Emperor's Service, and the first Engineer in Europe. The Work I mentioned is the compleatest System of Fortification and Gunnery extant. It was originally wrote in French, but there is an indifferent English Translation of it.[4] The great Number of valuable Plans which are inserted in the Books make them very dear.

Sunday Evening

We have just had an Express from Marblehead which informs Us that the same Privateer, which took the Brig Nancy, has taken a large Scotch Ship of 250 Tons, with a Cargo of 350 Chaldrons of Coals and £5000 Sterlg. of dry Goods bound to Boston.[5] The Letters are brought up some of which I have just read at the General's. They contain Denunciations of British Vengeance against the rebellious Colonies, and Effusions of Scotch Loyalty. None that I saw had any Thing very material. Both these Vessels were taken by Capt. Manley, who You may recollect—When told he was your Client formerly in an Action brought against him by Vernon.[6]

I was particularly obliged by your very kind Letter of 14th. Novr. and intreat a Continuance of your Favours. I will make no other Reply to your Partiality than in the Words of Tully Laetus sum laudari a *Te laudato Viro.*[7] It was ever my Ambition to meet your Approbation, as it is now my Pride to be distinguish'd by your Friendship. I am with the highest Esteem and Respect your most obliged and very hble Servt.

Wm. Tudor

RC (Adams Papers); addressed: "The Honble. John Adams. Esq Philadelphia P Post Free"; docketed: "Tudor Decr. 3. 1775."

[1] That is, at Harvard College.

[2] The Connecticut enlistments actually ran out on 10 Dec., although even Washington believed they ran out on the 1st (French, *First Year,* p. 514; *Writings,* ed. Fitzpatrick, 3:506).

[3] Freely, how can there be freedom when money alone rules?

[4] See Tudor to JA, 28 Oct., note 9 (above).

[5] The *Concord;* see Joseph Palmer to JA, 2 Dec., note 13 (above).

[6] See JA, *Legal Papers,* 3:344.

[7] I am delighted to be praised by one who is praised by all men.

From Joseph Ward

Sir   Camp at Roxbury 3 Decr. 1775

I had the honour some time since to receive your Favour of the 14 Ultimo which I am now to acknowledge. The Enemy have not made any important movements for a considerable time. Last week Genl. Howe sent 300 of the poor inhabitants of Boston to be landed near Point Shirley,[1] which was such a distance from any Houses where they might receive entertainment and many of them being in very poor circumstances, without provisions, that several persons died before assistance could be had! Such barbarity might well make a Savage blush—and the Brute creation cry out with indignation and astonishment. But I hope Americans will, be their trials ever so great, "preserve their temper, their wisdom, their humanity, and civility—tho' our Enemies are every day renouncing theirs;" as you Sir, have with great propriety and justice observed.[2] I would not be enthusiastic but I cannot believe that *Heaven* will smile upon that cause which is supported by such infernal means and measures as our Enemies make use of. The good success of our Privateers, which you will hear before this reaches you, is very encouraging, and I hope it will stimulate the seafaring Gentlemen to greater exertions in that way. I think we have a prospect of important advantages from exertions by Sea; and I hope, with you Sir, this will be done by the Colonies separately,[3] as, for many reasons, greater advantages will arise thereby to the great Cause of America.

Altho' I repose high Confidence in the Great Council of America, I fear they will too long delay (in hopes of reconciliation with Britain) those important and decisive steps necessary for the independence and compleat Freedom of America.[4] Such a *false hope* has already given the Enemy advantage against us. May *Heaven* guide where human wisdom fails.

The Army is healthy, and many happy circumstances attend us here; but our success in raising a new Army is not equal to our wishes, however I hope we shall surmount all difficulties. Unhappily, as I humbly conceive, the best plan was not adopted to raise the new Army, for the sake of greater advantages, the old experienced path which has conducted our Fathers with safety and glory 150 years, was neglected, and a new one chosen. But I will not charge it as a *fault* upon any man as I believe all acted with a sincere regard to the public interest; and perhaps, notwithstanding appearances, it may eventually terminate for the best. I think these times require great caution in remarking upon public men and measures; and wish that the distinctions of *Southern* and *Northern* were lost in the glorious Name of *American.* Certain necessary distinctions between Colonies, in raising men, and money, may I conceive, always subsist with advantage to the great Republic. To preserve *union and harmony* among our American Brethren of the different Colonies will be the study of every good man; my small influence has and shall be exerted for this purpose in the Army.

You justly observe, Sir, "verbal resolutions accomplish nothing, it is to no purpose to declare what we will or will not do in future times," unless we carry our Resolves into *execution*—which we ought punctually to do. It is said Caesar's *Name conquered,* and I hope it will be said in future time, the *Name of Americans,* made the wicked tremble and submit, and the virtuous rejoice and triumph. Scarcely anything is so important to an individual as a good Name, and it is vastly more interesting to a Community. If the Americans should uniformly maintain the Character of humane, generous, and brave, we shall be invincible to all the tyrants in the world, and even our Enemies will at once fear and reverence the guardians of Liberty. Nothing gives me so much pain as any appearance of the *Demon Discord,* among our American Brethren, the Farmer never said a wiser thing nor gave a more important caution to his Countrymen than this, "United we stand, divided we fall."[5] Every spark of contention ought to be carefully extinguished, and harmony cultivated as the vital springs and Lamp of Life. I cannot say that I have not some times been grieved and astonished by observing *private interest and self honour* occupy some minds which ought to be wholly employed to promote the honour and interest of their Country; it is the lot of humanity to meet with such mortifications, but I pray that such vile things may be rare in America, and the love of Virtue and Freedom may extinguish every ignoble and inferier passion in the Breasts of our Countrymen. Nothing can be more vile and base in this great Day of contest, for all that is sacred and glorious in this world, than to forget or neglect the Public in a *mean regard to little self.* Altho' there may be an inequality among the Colonies, in numbers in riches in strength and in wisdom, yet I conceive it will in general be wise for the greatest to claim no more than an equality with their brethren. Mankind will bear with equals who only share with them in honour, but they hate to be eclipsed and thrown into the shade by haughty Superiors. To preserve Union, being the highest point of Wisdom, I hope every American whether in Senate or the Field will steadily pursue it.

As my duty often calls me to attend a Flagg of Truce when Letters are sent into Boston, or a Conference is permitted between people in Boston and those who belong to different parts of the Continent, I have an opportunity to observe the Air of the Tories and the Regular Officers, and of late they are more complaisant than formerly and discover an earnest desire (particularly the Officers) that the grand Controversy might be amicably settled; and some of them say it will be settled next Spring; but *their* information is not at all to be regarded.

But very few Vessels have arrived at Boston from Britain for a long time, and by the best accounts, not more than 250 of the great reinforcement which the Enemy have so long talked of. I believe 2300 is the most that they expect this Fall. The Troops in Boston continue sickly, and it is said they are not in so good Spirits as they were in the Summer. If we can obtain a supply of Powder I trust we shall give a good account of them before Spring; if it be possible we must subdue the Ministerial Fleet and Army which is in America this Winter, otherwise we may expect a strong reinforcement in the Spring. Should we conquer what are here I apprehend the Ministry would not hazard another expedition, but if they should we might be able to resist all their force. I think we have nothing to fear but ourselves, and if we do our duty we may gain every political advantage the heart of Man can desire.

I have just seen the *Instructions* of the Pennsylvania Assembly to their Delegates in Congress.[6] I am astonished and mortified to see at this day such *wretched* instructions from an American Assembly! May Heaven inspire them with more wisdom! I am Sir with great Esteem your obedient and most Humble Servant   Joseph Ward

P.S. The Small Pox is now spreading in Boston by inoculation; I conceive that the Enemy have a design to spread it into our Army, but I hope our precautions will defeat all their malicious designs.

December 20. Last Sunday we began a work on Lechmeers point, the nearest land to Boston, on Cambridge side, where we intend to have a Bomb Battery; the Enemy seem much disturbed at this movement of ours, and have been cannonading and bombarding our people who are employed in the new works every day and night since we began, but by the good hand of Providence, not one man has yet been killed, and but one slightly wounded! Heaven, my honoured Friend, is certainly for us—our Enemies who boasted of superiour and unequalled skill in the art of war, have thrown about forty shot and shells to one shot that we have thrown and we have done more execution than they—is not this a demonstration that the "God of our Fathers" regards our cause and guides our hands?

Of late the Army for the next year fills up faster than at first, and I hope it will be compleated in good season.

RC (Adams Papers); docketed: "Jo. Ward. Dec. 5. 1775."

[1] The point of land across the gut north of Deer Island in the present town of Winthrop (Shurtleff, *Description of Boston*, p. 437). Although the Americans were sympathetic to the plight of those expelled from Boston, they were more concerned that the refugees might spread smallpox to the American Army (*Boston Gazette*, 27 Nov.; French, *First Year*, p. 493–495). Their fears were increased by reports that "a Number of Persons who had been Innoculated, were to be sent out of Boston by Gen. Howe, with a Design to spread the Small-Pox among the Troops" (Mass., *House Jour.*, 1775–1776, 3d sess., p. 13). Washington forbade any of the refugees' going to Cambridge. On 6 Dec. the General Court allowed the removal of those certified to be free of the disease while continuing to quarantine the rest and making some provision for their care (Washington, *Writings*, ed. Fitzpatrick, 4:118; *House Jour.*, p. 19, 35).

[2] This and a second quotation below are from JA to Joseph Ward, 14 Nov. (above).

[3] JA had already committed himself with other members of the congress to Continental privateers and a navy (JA's Service in the Congress, 13 Sept. – 9 Dec., Editorial Note, above).

[4] JA had already received calls for independence from Mercy Otis Warren, Benjamin Hichborn, and Joseph Palmer (James Warren to JA, 14 Nov.; Hichborn to JA, 25 Nov.; Palmer to JA, 2 Dec., all above).

[5] John Dickinson, *The Liberty Song*, 1768: "By uniting we stand, by dividing we fall" (*The Writings of John Dickinson*, ed. Paul L. Ford, Hist. Soc. Penna., *Memoirs*, 14 [1895]:421–432). This song was widely reprinted in the newspapers and sung at patriotic gatherings.

[6] See Samuel Chase to JA, 25 Nov., note 4 (above).

From James Warren

My Dear Sir   Watertown Decr. 3. 1775

I Returned from Plymouth last Wednesday after An Absence of about 10 days. In my way I called on Mrs. Adams and found her pretty well, having recovered her Health after a Bad Cold which threatoned A fever. From her I received the Inclosed Letter,[1] which I presume will give you A full Account of herself and Family. I came to Watertown with full Expectation of receiving several of your favours. You may Guess my disappointment when I found not One. Doctr. Morgan who with his Lady had lodged in my Chamber the Night before had left a Packet Containing Letters &c. to your Friend, which I have taken proper Care off. This Gentleman I have not yet seen. He was Attended next day by the Surgeons of the Army, and Escorted to head quarters, in state. I propose to see him Tomorrow, and shall look on him with all the reverence due to so Exalted A Character as you give him.

Revere returned here on Fryday. No Letters by him from you or my Other Friend at Congress. I have run over my Sins of Omission and Commission, to see if they were Unpardonable and at last presumed to Account for it from the Nature, and Magnitude of the Business you are Engaged in, and the Constant Application it requires.

I Congratulate you on the success of our Northern Army. We have no late Accounts from Arnold, but have sanguine Expectations that before this the whole Province of Canada is reduced. You will no doubt have heard before this reaches you that A Lieutenant Colonel and A Considerable Number of Men had come of[f] from Arnolds detachment and returned here.[2]

Our Army here have taken possession of and fortified Cobble Hill, which the Enemy seem to view without any Emotion not haveing fired A Gun. It is said they Confidently rely on our Army's dispersing when the Terms of their Inlistment Ends, and leaving the Lines defensless, and an easy Conquest to them. Howe I believe has received such Intelligence and Assurances from One Benja. Marston[3] who has fled from Marblehead to Boston. This fellow is A Cousin of mine. Had ever any Man So many rascally Cousins as I have. I will not presume any danger of that kind tho' I own My anxiety is great. Our Men Inlist but slowly and the Connecticut Troops behave Infamously. It was with difficulty the General prevented their going of[f] in great Numbers last Fryday. However they Consented finally to return to their duty till the Army could be Reinforced.

The General on the first day of our meeting had Represented to the Court the difficulties he laboured under and the dangers he Apprehended, and desired A Committee to Confer with him and the other General Officers. A Committee went down. The result of the Conference was that 5000 Men should be immediately raised in this and New Hampshire Colony and brought into Camp by the 10th. Instant, to supply the deficiencies in the Army by the going off, the Connecticut Troops, and the Furlows the General is Obliged to give the New Inlisted men by way of Encouragement. Genl. Sullivan Undertook to raise 2000 of them, and we reported that the rest should be raised in several parts of this Colony, and Yesterday sent off, more than 20 of our Members to Effect it,[4] knowing no Other way as our Militia is in a perfect state of Anarchy some with, and some without Officers. If they don't succeed I know not where I shall date my next letter from, but I have such An Opinion of my Countrymen as to believe they will. The only reasons I know of that are Assigned by the Soldiers for their Uneasiness, or rather backwardness to Enter the service again are the Increase of the Officers wages lately made and the paying them Contrary to their Expectation, and former usage by Calender instead of Lunar Months. The last I have given you my opinion of in a former Letter,[5] and the first I think was very Unluckily timed. I have till lately thought it A favourable Circumstance that so Many Men were raised in these Goverments. I begin to think Otherways and many reasons operate strongly to make me wish for more Troops from the Southern Goverments.

I Pity our Good General who has A greater Burthen on his Shoulders, and more difficulties to struggle with than I think should fall to the Share of so good A Man. I do every thing in My power to releive him, and wish I could do more. I see he is fatigued and worried. After all you are not to Consider us as wholly Involved in Clouds and darkness. The Sun shines for the most part, and we have many Consoleing Events. Providence seems to be Engaged for us. The same Spirit and determination prevails to Conquer all difficulties. Many Prizes have been taken by our Cruisers, and A Capital one last week carried into Cape Ann, of very great value perhaps £20,000 sterling. A Brigantine from England with a A Cargo Consisting of Almost every Species of Warlike stores except powder and Cannon. 2,000 very fine small Arms with all their Accoutrements, four Mortars one which Putnam has Christened and Called the *Congress* the finest ever in America, Carcases, Flints Shells, Musket Balls, Carriages &c. &c. These are principally Arrived at head quarters and the great Mortar is a Subject of Curiosity. I hope we shall be Able to make good use of them before Long. A small Cutter has since been taken loaded with provisions from Nova Scotia to Boston and Carried into Beverly the first by a Continental Vessel, the second by A private one.[6] All serves to distress them and Aid us.

The Reinforceing the Army has Engrossed the whole Attention of the General Court since their Meeting. The Manufactory of Salt Petre proceeds but slowly, tho it is made in small quantities. Our General Committee seem to me too much Entangled with perticular Systems, and general Rules to succeed. In practice they have done nothing. Coll. Orne and Coll. Lincoln have made tryals in the recess and succeeded According to their wishes. They Affirm the process to be simple and easy and that great quantitys may be made. They shew Samples of what they have made, and it is undoubtedly good. No Experiments with regard to Sulphur have yet succeeded. We have good prospects with regard to Lead. Coll. Palmer has promised me to write you on that Subject.[7]

I hope soon to hear from you. The Confidence in the Congress prevailing among all ranks of People is Amazeing, and the Expectation of great Things from you stronger than ever. It gives me great pleasure to see the Credit, and reputation of my two perticular friends, Increasing here.[8] Their late disinterested Conduct, as it is reported here does them much Honour. A certain Collegue of yours has lost or I am mistaken A great part of the Interest he Undeservedly had.[9] Major Hawley is not yet down.[10] What he will say to him I know not. Paine I hear is gone to Gratify his Curiosity in Canada.[11] A good Journey to him. He may possibly do as much good there as at Philadelphia tho' I find some People here would not have pitched on him for the Business we suppose he is gone on, and perhaps there are some who would not have done it for any. Many men you know are of many Minds.[12] My regards to my Friends. I thank Mr. Adams and Mr. Collins for their kind Letters. Shall write Mr. Adams first opportunity. I am yr. Sincere Friend, Adieu   JW

The Great Loss at Newfoundland of Men &c. I think may be Considered as An Interposition of Providence in our favour.[13]

Doctr. Adams has Just called on me to Acquaint Me that Mr. Craige who has been Apothecary to the Army is like to be superceeded, and Mr. Dyre Appointed in his room.[14] As he Appears to me a very clever fellow and such Changes do us no good I could wish it might be prevented.

RC (Adams Papers); docketed in an unidentified hand: "Warren   Decr 3. 1775"; also "Mr Gerry."

[1] AA to JA, 27 Nov. (*Adams Family Correspondence*, 1:328–331).

[2] See Warren to JA, 14 Nov., note 2 (above).

[3] Benjamin Marston (1730–1792) fled Marblehead on the night of 24 Nov. and ultimately followed the army to Nova Scotia in March 1776 (Sibley-Shipton, *Harvard Graduates*, 12:439–454).

[4] The resolve to raise 3,008 men was adopted on 1 Dec., and the committee to put it into effect was appointed the next day (Mass., *House Jour.*, 1775–1776, 3d sess., p. 7, 9–10; see also John Sullivan to JA, 21 Dec., below).

[5] Warren to JA, 14 Nov. (above).

[6] The *Nancy*, a brig not a brigantine, and the sloop *Polly* were captured by Capt. John Manley of the *Lee* on 28 and 27 Nov. (Clark, *Washington's Navy*, p. 60–61).

[7] Joseph Palmer to JA, 2 Dec. (above).

[8] This and the following seven sentences were copied by Thomas Cushing and given to Robert Treat Paine; a copy of them in Cushing's hand is in the Robert Treat Paine Papers (MHi). Paine himself explained how Cushing was able to make the copy. After JA had read Warren's letter he returned it unsealed to the bearer with instructions, according to the bearer's story, to deliver it to the other Massachusetts delegates. JA had intended it to be delivered to Samuel Adams, but the bearer, not finding him, handed it to Cushing, who,

because it was unsealed, thought it was simply news from the province (Paine to Joseph Hawley, 1 Jan. 1776, Dft, MHi:Robert Treat Paine Papers). Cushing could not resist copying out the jibe at Paine and himself.

⁹ That is, Thomas Cushing.

¹⁰ Hawley, a good friend of Cushing's, arrived at Watertown for the General Court on 15 Dec. (Hawley to JA, 18 Dec., below).

¹¹ Paine had been named with Robert R. Livingston and John Langdon as a committee to confer with Gen. Schuyler at Ticonderoga; in fact, JA was on the committee that drafted instructions for the guidance of the three men (JA's Service in the Congress, 13 Sept. – 9 Dec., No. IX, 2 Nov., above). Warren shows his pique by implying that Paine's trip was a junket.

¹² This whole passage underlines the growing dissatisfaction among the leadership in Massachusetts, at least as represented by Warren and JA, with the moderate positions of Cushing and Paine. Cushing was replaced in Jan. 1776, and Paine, although he retained his seat in the congress, broke with Warren and became more embittered with JA (Mass., *House Jour.*, 1775–1776, 3d sess., p. 165; Paine to Warren, 5 Jan. 1776, enclosed with Warren to JA, 31 Jan., below). Paine's ranking below JA on the bench of the superior court became known to Paine when he returned from Ticonderoga. For comments on the ranking, see Warren to JA, 20 Oct. and 5 Nov. (above). There is no reason to think that Paine saw these comments, but he needed only to

see the positions to feel aggrieved. JA was a major figure in these disputes, but how much he was directly involved is unclear. He had not yet taken his seat on the Council when the election of delegates took place (Perez Morton to JA, 19 Jan. 1776, note 1, below). Joseph Palmer and Warren, however, kept him informed of the correspondence passing between Paine and others (for example, Tr of Paine to Palmer, 1 Jan. 1776, below). Yet there seems to have been no violent public dispute between the two men at the congress, perhaps because Hawley advised Paine by letter that for the good of the country he "Stifle every private resentment, incompatable with the public good" (24 Jan. 1776, MHi:Robert Treat Paine Papers). Hawley may also have talked with JA in Watertown. AA, however, was not willing to let the friction subside; she told JA that Paine's attack on Warren had caused Paine to become "an object of contempt" (*Adams Family Correspondence*, 1:350–352 and note 2).

¹³ See Joseph Palmer to JA, 2 Dec., note 10 (above).

¹⁴ Dyre remains unidentified. Andrew Craigie (1743–1819) remained Apothecary to the American Army, a post to which he had been appointed by Benjamin Church in response to the resolve of the congress on 27 July creating the position (*JCC*, 2:209–210, 211). Craigie was named Apothecary General in 1777 and remained in that position for the rest of the war (same, 7:232; 15:1214; *DAB*).

From Elbridge Gerry

Dear sir   Water Town Decr. 4. 1775

I received your Favour of the 5th of Novr and the Enquiries relative to Vessels suitable to be armed, Commanders and Seamen to man the same, secure places for building new Vessels of Force &c. are important in their Nature, and to have the same effectually answered I propose to submit them as soon as may be to the Court that a Committee may be raised for obtaining the Facts from the Maritime Towns.¹

I congratulate You on the Success of the Continental privateers which have lately brot in one of the ministerial store Ships and several other prizes of which You will doubtless have a List from the General. A privateer is fitting out by Private persons at New Port to mount 14 Guns and I hope soon to give an Account of several by the Government and many more by Individuals. The late Act and Resolve for fitting out armed Vessels in this Colony,[2] I apprehend will have a good Effect, having already animated the Inhabitants of the Sea-ports who were unable to command much property, to unite in Companies of twenty or thirty Men and go out in Boats of 8 or 10 Tons Burthen which they call "Spider Catchers". One of these the last Week brot in two prizes, the last of which was a Vessell of 100 Tons burthen from Nova Scotia loaded with potatoes and 8 or 10 head of Cattle. Two Days since I was at Marblehead and the Lively, prepared for a Decoy,[3] appeared about two Leagues off and so deceived one of the Continental Commanders then in the Harbour that he put to Sea after her. One of the Spider Catchers like a brave Fellow gave likewise *Chase* to the *Frigate*, and by the Time they had got within Reach of her Guns they found their Mistake and were obliged to make Use of their Heels whilst the Ship with a Cloud of Sail pursued and pelted them; they Ran with great Dexterity and like Heroes *escaped.*

The Situation of the Army at this Time is critical, the Men declining to inlist on the Terms proposed by the General. The Connecticut Forces are with much Difficulty persuaded to tarry 'till the 10th of the present Month, at which Time it is expected they will all leave the Camp. The Court have ordered in 3000 of the Militia and General Sulliven is gone to New Hamshire for 2000 more to be all in by the Time mentioned. The Men are dissatisfied at the Reduction of their Wages by payment according to Calendar instead of lunar Months while the Officers Wages are augmented. They likewise dislike the new Arrangement in which Officers are displaced and all the Field Officers belonging to some Counties are dropped—and No Bounty they say is offered. These are the Difficulties complained of, as far as I can collect and whether just or not I will not undertake to determine. I wish that a patriotic Spirit in the Men would outweigh such trifling Considerations, but since it is otherwise the Enquiry naturally arises, what must be done? To loose the Affections of so great a Number of brave Men, who perhaps are led to be pecuniary by Suspicions that they are not treated with the Genoristy exercised towards the officers and that ought to be exercised also to them, may not be that prudent; indeed however mistaken they may be, It may prove fatal to the Continent should their Affections be lost and I have

Reason to think it will be the Case if the Matter is not overruled by the honorable Congress before the last of the present Month. It will be peculiarly unhappy after a Series of the most happy Events in Favour of the Colonies, if a trifling Consideration compared with the Object of their Struggles should disaffect and defeat them. I have great Confidence in the Wisdom of the Congress and apprehend they will think it necessary to conciliate the Affections of the Soldiers and gain their Confidence, since without these an Army may be altogether useless. I hope this will be done and the Army reinforced in proportion to our Enemies and there will be little Danger of the Enemy's prevailing in this part of the Continent.

The military Stores are at the present Time all at Cambridge excepting what are wanted at Roxbury, but is this altogether prudent since a place may be fortified a few Miles in the Country and what are not wanted for immediate Use be kept therein. This is a Matter belonging to the General, but it is nevertheless wished here that it was otherwise regulated.

I hope the Army will in future be reinforced from the Southern Colonies since the Number of Men raised from this Colony has so increased the Burthen of Husbandry on those left behind that We found a Difficulty in apportioning 3000 Men only as a temporary Reinforcement to the Army, and as the Colony will probably be the Seat of War it will be expedient to have a powerful militia ready to reinforce at a short Notice. This We are destitute of at present as nothing is done to organize our Militia. Mr. Fessenden is waiting and gives me only Time to assure You sir that with much Respect I remain your most obedet. and very hum ser   Elbridge Gerry

P.S. By Mr. Sullivan from Biddeford We are just informed that another Store Ship is carryed into Portsmouth;[4] he Came thro that Town so that there is little Reason to doubt it.

RC (Adams Papers); docketed: "Mr Gerry   Decr 4. 75."

[1] On 9 Dec. Gerry submitted JA's request for information to the General Court, which referred it to a committee composed of Gerry, James Warren, and Azor Orne. When the three men reported on 11 Dec., the General Court resolved to request the seacoast towns to complete a blank form with the information wanted by JA and return it as soon as possible (Mass., *House Jour.*, 1775–1776, 3d sess., p. 32, 33–34). No record of the returns has been found.

[2] See James Warren to JA, 20 Oct., note 11 (above).

[3] Commas supplied.

[4] This may have been the schooner *Rainbow*, Capt. John McMonagle, containing potatoes and turnips for Boston that was captured by the *Warren*, under Capt. Winborn Adams, on 25 Nov. and carried into Portsmouth (*Naval Docs. Amer. Rev.*, 2:1152–1153, 1217; see also the *New-England Chronicle*, 30 Nov.).

From Samuel Osgood Jr.

Sir   Camp at Roxbury Decr. 4th 1775

I fancy such an Army was scarcly ever collected together before. What a Contrast do my Eyes behold every Day: in Boston an Army of Slaves!—on this Side the Sons of the respectable Yeomanry of New England. At Home we are Lords of our own little but sufficient Estates. Some of the worthy Committee from the Honble. Continental Congress were very uneasy, the Soldier's Pay being too high in their Opinion; and Men enough at the Southward could be rais'd for 5 or 6 Dollars per Month, and now the Season was such that our Men would be out of employ, if they should return Home; which is altogether a Mistake. A Farmer, Sir (if he does his Duty) finds very little Leisure in the Winter. His Wood, which he will certainly procure in Sufficiency till the Season revolves, his Materials, and Stuff for his Fences in the Spring and consider what an almost infinite Lenght of Fences (I mention this because I fancy our Farms are smaller and more Divided with Fences than the Southward Plantations) not less than eight or ten Million of Miles in this Province which must all be attended to in the Spring; removing Manure for his Land, and tending his Stock &c. Engage his Attention thro the cold Season. From my own Knowledge, I am sensible, that Farmers have little Leisure in the Winter, but if we should grant it to be the Case, yet the Enlistment is to be for twelve Calendar Months, which must include the Leisure and Busy Times, if it is allowed we have such. If we compare the Pay the Soldier is to have the succeeding Campaign, with what the Massachusetts Soldier had last War, it will appear to be eighteen Dollars less per Year. They were pay'd lunar Months at the Rate of 6 Dollars which amounts to 78 Dollars; and their Bounty was twenty Dollars, which equals 98 Dollrs. But their present neat Pay is 80 Dollrs. I do not desire, Sir, from the above, to infer that their pay is low, for it is certainly generous and noble, but they have a Precedent of higher pay. I find, Sir, the raising the Pay of the Subalterns, gives great Uneasiness to the Privates, whether they can have any Objection in Reason or not; that, with the Rate laid upon them by our Genl. Assembly, is supposed will prevent many Persons Enlisting. The Policy of Rating the Army at this juncture I submit to better Judgments than mine. It may have a Tendency to disgrace our Colony, and will as far as it prevents any from Enlisting. The General has good Reason to complain of the Unwillingness of our Army in General to tarry after their Time is out. A considerable Number of the Connecticut Forces went of[f] in a mutinous Manner, but the greatest Part have, by the Exertion and Perswasion of the Officers, been bro't back to Camp.

I wish to Heaven I could impress upon the Minds of all our Soldiers the pressing Importance of their continuing in the Service. Every Officer of true genuine Sentiments, will use his utmost Endeavors. But there will be some sordid Souls among them, (I mean of the Subaltern Kind) who will for the present, stay the Mens enlisting, flattering themselves, they are able to raise a Company, and are therefore entitled to a Captaincy which will after the Generals find the Wheels move heavily on, be conferred upon them. Such infamous Hirelings will sooner or later meet with a Punishment adequate to such mean, low lived Behavior. A good Soldier will eternally act with a great generous and open Soul. My Soul bleeds to hear even a Hint (*it is too much*) that it is in the Power of the southern Colonies to make their Terms of Peace and forsake us and that they will do it excepting we appear more spirited than we at this Time of raising a new Army appear to be. Gentlemen at the Helm here, say, they *know* it will take Place if as above &c. for our Militia are a damn'd pack of Scoundrels not that they *beleive*! I cannot express myself decently upon the above Assertions and therefore leave them to your Honor. But this I beleive (if I do not know it) that Newengland had much better stand out till the Earth is fertilized with the last drop of Blood in her Veins if she is forsaken by every other Colony nay if they all join against her—*than submit*. The Newengland Colonies may and probably will harmonize in the same Form of Government but no more, and therefore when we have finished this War with Credit (as I firmly beleive it will be) we may anticipate what may turn up afterwards. Forgive me!!! I am with the greatest Respect your Honors most Humble Servant   S. Osgood

RC (Adams Papers); docketed: "S. Osgood. D. 1775   Novr 30."

From James Swan

Sir   Watertown 4 Decr. 1775

By a resolve of Congress the 18th of Oct. last, I[1] perceive the Sufferers by fire and Seizures, occasion'd by the Enemy, are invited to lay their loss before them. For that reason I now trouble you, as one of the Committee.

You are doubtless acquainted with the General damage from the fire, which happen'd last May, in the Town dock of Boston,[2] caused by

Genl. Gage's 47s. or Tarring and Feathering Regiment, making Cartrages in one of the Stores, which was improv'd as a Barrack; and which might have been prevented from Spreading, had not he very lately before that time, taken the Command from the Fire Wards, appointed by the Town, and vested it in the persons of known Tories; fixed locks upon the Doors, and Centries at each of the Engine Houses: So that before the *people* cou'd go to Gage, be admitted to his presence for Orders to obtain the Engines; *who* were directed by him to the New Captains, and then the Captains to their respective Wards, that, I say before these things cou'd be done, the fire was communicated far, and the Soldiers wou'd not permit the Inhabitants to assist in extinguishing it; by which means I became a loser in about £100 Sterling by the distruction of the Store which I improv'd, leading down on Treats wharf. My loss was in merchandize. The Warehouse belong'd to A. Oliver Esqr, of Salem, who with the Honl. John Hancock Esq., Mr. Fairweather, Mr. Ben Andrews and E[l]iakim Hutchinson, were the principal Sufferers in the Buildings.[3]

I know not, whether it is meant to indemnify the Sufferers: nor can I say, that from the hopes of such indemnification I am now induc'd to write you, so much, as to comply with the desire of Congress.

If this is not sufficiently authenticated, I can send you the particulars. I am, with respect, Sir Your mo. obd. Sevt.   Jams. Swan

Depy to Treas. Gardner

RC (Adams Papers); addressed: "The Honbl John Adams Esqr Philadelphia"; docketed: "James Swan 1775"; in another hand: "Decr 4."; stamped: "FREE N*YORK*DEC: 11."

[1] James Swan (1754–1830) emigrated from Scotland in 1765 and soon became a member of the Sons of Liberty. He participated in the Boston Tea Party and the Battle of Bunker Hill. During the war, not all of which he spent as a soldier, he rose to the rank of colonel; using his wife's money, he invested heavily in loyalist property and speculated in western lands. He ended his career in France, first as an agent for the French Republic on naval stores and the American debt, then as an independent businessman. He died in debtors' prison in Paris (*DAB*).

[2] For another account of the fire which occurred on 17 May and a list of those suffering losses, see *Massachusetts Gazette* of 19 May and 1 June. Swan's account is similar to those in the newspapers, particularly that in the *New-*

England Chronicle of 25 May, which includes a letter from a Boston inhabitant describing the fire and efforts to prevent its spread. For Gage's orders after the fire, see French, *First Year*, p. 167.

[3] Andrew Oliver Jr. (1731–1799), judge and scientist, a founder of the American Academy of Arts and Sciences and member of the American Philosophical Society (*DAB*). Thomas Fayerweather and Benjamin Andrews Jr., both Boston merchants (Thwing Catalogue, MHi). Fayerweather was father-in-law of Professor John Winthrop (Winsor, *Memorial History of Boston*, 4:494–495, note). Eliakim Hutchinson (1711–1775), loyalist and wealthy Boston merchant (Sibley-Shipton, *Harvard Graduates*, 8:726–729).

From John Warren and Others

Sir   Cambridge Decr. 4 1775

As Surgeons of the continental Hospital we take the Freedom to address you upon an Occasion which though it does not immediately Concern our Department, yet as it relates to the Hospital with which we are so nearly connected, we thought called for our Attention, as being a Subject, upon which, we might be able to give some Information, which might perhaps be of some little service in assisting your Honour as a Member of the continental Congress, to determine upon the Matter when it shall be laid before that honorable Assembly, and which by Reason of the particular acquantance with Facts which Divers Circumstances have furnished us with, you might not perhaps be able to obtain from any other persons, for which Reason we would wish you to communicate this Letter to The honorable President, Mr. Paine, Mr. Samuel Adams and Mr. Cushing, and to any other Gentlemen Members of the Congress you shall think proper.

We have had some Intimations that there is one or more Persons soliciting of the Congress, an Appointment to the office of Apothecary to the Hospital. We are utterly ignorant of the Character of the Person who is making Interest for the place, and would not by any means suggest any thing against him—but as a very worthy Gentleman Mr. Craigie[1] must in consequence of such an appointment be superseded, we think it our Duty to make a Representation of Facts, as we think his merit intitles him to a Continuance; He has been employed in the Publick Service from the first Commencement of Hostilities, first by an Appointment of the Committee of Safety to procure Medicines for the Army, next by the appointment of the provincial Congress as Commissary of the medicinal Store, and from them he received a Warrant investing him with full power to act as such and lastly by the late Director of the Hospital Dr. Church he was appointed *Apothecary for the Hospital as well as of the whole Army* together, That he has discharged the Duties annexed to the Station which he has held, not only the Surgeons of the Hospital, but also those of the Regiments, as well as the whole Army who have in a great Measure been supplied with the most important medicinal Articles by his vigilance and Assiduity, can with Gratitude attest. It is needless to represent to you the Difficulties under which, whoever engaged in this Business at a Time of such general Confusion as existed when the Army was first formed, must necessarily have laboured, these you can better conceive of than we can describe, Mr. Craigie surmounted them all by using his utmost Exertions to procure Medicines wherever they might be purchased, for which purpose he put himself to great Expence and Infinite Pains when he found the Exigencies of an Army already begining to Suffer through want of Medicine so loudly called for it. These Motives induced him to run the Hazard of an Attempt to procure his Medicines out of the Town of Boston, the place of his nativity, and from whence he made his escape soon after the first Battle, having left the most valuable part of his Possessions there, and in this he so well succeeded as to get a considerable Quantity of the most valuable Articles safe to the Army having escaped the greatest Danger of a Detection by the Enemy; You will reflect that after having thus supplied the Army with all his own Medicines, he put it out of his power to pursue the Business upon which he depended for a maintenance, and therefore reserved no resource to which he could at any Time apply in case any thing of the kind now apprehended should take place.

It is also known by great Numbers that Mr. Craigies' Attention was not confined solely to procuring Medicines but extended even to Beding and Quarters for the wounded Soldiers particularly at the Time of the Battle of Bunker Hill. The Fatigues with which Mr. Craigies Office had till lately been attended, augmented by the procrastination of the appointment of an Assistant, had rendered him almost indifferent with Regard to his continuance in it, but after an Assistant was appointed, being enabled to perform his Business without Injury to his Health, he was desirous of remaining in it, especially as he had, after procuring a considerable Assortment of medicines, and born the Heat and Burthen of the Day, render'd the Task much more easy; He had not the least Suspicion of any probability of his being Displaced, but supposed that the Director had Power to confirm him, and therefore was much surprised when he was informed of an Intention to supersede him; more especially upon Consideration that a removal from so Publick a Station would afford reasonable Ground for a Presumtion; that some Misconduct in him had induced the Congress to disgrace him in this manner, and that thereby his Reputation might be affected in such a manner as would be infinitely injurious to him in his endeavours to procure a Subsistence in any other way: Your Honours Knowledge of mankind will point out his feelings upon such an occasion, and we doubt not it will suggest sufficient Arguments, (if these were the only ones) for giving your Voice in his Favour: The universal Satisfaction he has given, and that unblemished Reputation which he ever sustained, have interested all those who have had the pleasure of his Acquaintance in the success of any Applications in his Favour and particularly Your most humble Servants

John Warren
Samuel Adams
James McHenry
Charles McKnight[2]

RC (Adams Papers). This letter was probably enclosed in that to JA from John Morgan of 19 Feb. 1776 (below).

[1] On Andrew Craigie, see Dr. Morgan's appraisal.

[2] John Warren (1753–1815), a younger brother of Dr. Joseph Warren and a founder of the Massachusetts Medical Society, was a senior surgeon at Cambridge. After the evacuation of Boston he went with the Continental Army to New York. He returned to Boston in 1777 to become senior surgeon at the General Hospital, where he remained till the end of the war. He gave lectures on anatomy in the 1780s and became Harvard's first lecturer on medicine (Walter L. Burrage, *A History of the Massachusetts Medical Society*, n.p., 1923, p. 28–31). Samuel Adams has not been positively identified, for several men of this name were surgeons in this period; very probably this was not the patriot's son. James McHenry (1753–1816), trained by Benjamin Rush, was at the start of a career that brought him to the position of Secretary of War under Presidents Washington and Adams (DAB; this source says that he did not join the medical staff until 1 Jan. 1776, however). Charles McKnight (1750–1792), trained by Dr. William Shippen, served as a surgeon throughout the war (L. H. Butterfield, *Letters of Benjamin Rush*, 2 vols., Princeton, 1951, 1:163, note 6).

From William Cooper

Dear Sir   Watertown December 5. 1775

The letter you did me the honor of writing me dated October 19th. came to hand but a few days past.[1] The notice taken of me by the Committee of Congress appointed to collect an account of hostilities &c. I own myself indebted to you for, and you may be assured that I shall do every thing in my power to forward that business: A Committee of both Houses of which I am one has been appointed in consequence of the Committee of Congresses letter being laid before them,[2] and a circular letter is to be forwarded to the Selectmen and Committees of Correspondence in the several towns where hostilities have been committed, that we may be able to furnish your Committee, with a collected account of the damages sustained in those towns.

The Copy of the account of the Charlestown Battle I immediately procured, and the same will be inclosed.[3]

We are all obliged to you as a Member of the Continental Congress for your exertions in favor of your Constituents, and the common

357

cause of the Colonies. Are we still to hold up our alegiance, when we are not only deprived of protection, but are even declared Rebels; and by this absurdity forbid every Court in Europe afording us any countenance or assistance. Is a sea coast of above 2000 Miles extent from whence three hundred sail of Privateers might this winter by the way of foreign ports at least, be launched out upon the British trade, still [to] be held in a state of neutrality, under a notion that we are opposing Ministry and not the People of Britain; while our enemies are employing the whole force of the Nation to plunder and ruin us: If the Congress remain silent on this head, will they take it amiss if a Colony, the first in suffering, as well as exertions, should grant letters of Reprisal to those Persons only who have had their property seized and destroyed by the Enemy. I sometime ago volunteered a prophesy, that it would not be long before we realised our importance as a Maritim power; and the success attending our first Naval enterprises, are very encouraging presages of what is yet to come. But if weak nerves and large estates should opperate to the preventing the whole force of the Colonies being exerted against the common enemy, the issue of so unequal and unheard of a war, may be easily augur'd.

You will not be offended at these liberties, I revere the wisdom of the Supreme Council of the Colonies, and feel my obligations, and pray God to succeed all their endeavors for the preservation and wellfare of North America. My best regards to my good friends Mr. Adams and Mr. Hancock. I remain, with much esteem and respect, Sir, Your sincere friend & obedient humble Servt

William Cooper

Sir   Watertown Jany. 3d. 1776

The foregoing with an attested Copy of the account of the Battle on Charlestown Hill not meeting you at Philadelphia, was Yesterday delivered me by the Speaker, which I again send you.[4] Last Evening the House chose three Major Generals, vizt Generals Hancock, Warren and Orn. Pray make my Compliments to the worthy Mr. Gerry, and acquaint him that his Brothers Vessel is got in from Bilboa, and the Master informs that Mr. Gerrys Vessel was near loaded with Powder &c., and waited only for a few hands, and was expected to leave Bilboa within a Week. May a kind Providence give her a safe arrival. I am with the greatest regard, dear Sir Your most obedt. hum. Servt.   William Cooper

RC (Adams Papers); docketed in an unknown hand: "Mr Cooper   Dec 5th 1775."

WATERTOWN, November 18, 1775.

YOU have hereunder, Copies of two Resolves, one passed by the American Congress, and the other by our General Court, relative to collecting the proper Evidences of the Depredations made by the Ministerial Army and Navy in the American Colonies: Being a Committee for the Purpose aforesaid, we take the Liberty to request of you a full Account, agreeable to said Resolves, of the Hostilities committed by the Enemy in your Vicinity, since the Boston Port-Bill's taking Place; which you'll please to transmit to our Chairman, *Joseph Palmer*, Esq; at *Watertown*, with all possible Dispatch.

As you will immediately perceive the Utility and Necessity of this Measure, for the Justification of the Colonies, or obtaining a Compensation for Losses sustained, we think it needless to make any Apology for giving you this Trouble; and doubt not from your known Regard to the common Cause of your Country in these Times of Distress and Danger, you will readily afford us all the Aid in your Power.

We are,

Gentlemen,

Your most obedient humble Servants.

per Order.

In CONGRESS, Wednesday *October* 18, 1775.

RESOLVED, That a just and well authenticated Account of the Hostilities committed by the Ministerial Troops and Navy in *America*, since last *March*, be collected, with proper Evidence of the Truth of the Facts related, the Number and Value of the Buildings destroyed by them; also the Number and Value of the Vessels inward and outward bound, which have been seized by them since that Period, as near as the Number and Value can be ascertained; also the Stock taken by them from different Parts of the Continent.——Mr. *Deane*, Mr. *John Adams*, and Mr. *Wythe*, a Committee for this Purpose.

A Copy from the Minutes,

CHARLES THOMPSON, Sec'ry.

In COUNCIL, November 7, 1775.

READ and Ordered, That *Joseph Palmer*, Esq; with such as the honorable House shall join, be a Committee to collect a true Account of all the Hostilities committed by the Ministerial Troops and Navy within this Colony, and the Evidences of the Truth of such Account, agreeable to the above Resolve of General Congress; and that the Committee sit in the Recess of the Court for the above Purpose.

Sent down for Concurrence.

PEREZ MORTON, Dep'y Sec'ry.

In the House of REPRESENTATIVES, *November* 8, 1775. Read and concurred, and Mr. *Cooper* and Col. *Thompson*, are joined.——And the Committee are directed to extend their Enquiries as far back as the taking Place of the Port-Bill.

Sent up for Concurrence.

J. WARREN, Speaker.

November 11, *In* COUNCIL, Read and concurr'd, with the Resolve of the House.

PEREZ MORTON, Dep'y Sec'ry.

12. BROADSIDE ON BRITISH DEPREDATIONS, 18 NOVEMBER 1775

See pages xii–xiii

[1] See JA to James Warren, 18 Oct., note 5 (above).

[2] On 19 Oct. the committee on British depredations sent to the various colonial assemblies a form letter seeking information on the extent of damages (JA's Service in the Congress, 13 Sept. – 9 Dec., No. III, above). The Massachusetts circular letter is shown in Illustration No. 12.

[3] The Committee of Safety's Account of the Battle of Bunker Hill, 25 July (above).

[4] This letter, together with several others that did not reach Philadelphia until after JA's departure on 9 Dec., was probably enclosed in Samuel Adams' letter to JA of 22 Dec. (below).

The General Court to the Massachusetts Delegates

Gentlemen[1]   Watertown Decr. 5th. 1775

We are informed by his Excellency General Washington, that it is his opinion, the paying our Troops, by the Lunar Month, will throw the rest of the Army into disorder, as the Continental Congress have resolved, that it is the Kalender Month they mean to pay by; and that the difference between the two, must be consider'd as a Colonial, and not a Continental Charge.[2]

We are sensible, it is unhappy when there is any militation between the doings of any branch in a Society, and those of the whole, as it hath a tendency to produce a disunion and disorders consequent thereon; But such we consider may be the state of things, that fully to prevent a diversity, consistent with a due regard to the greatest good may be impossible.

The *Congress* have Resolved, that the Men shall be paid by the Calender Month. It may be unhappy for us, that previously we had taken a resolution diverse therefrom with Regard to our Forces. You are sensible, Gentlemen, that it hath been the invariable practice of this Colony, to pay their Troops by the Lunar month, and it was, with an expectation of this that our Men inlisted. For us to have attempted an innovation after the service was performed, which would have been the case had we adher'd to the resolution of the American Congress, we supposed would have produced such uneasiness in the Minds of the People, as could not easily have been quieted, and that it would have destroy'd that Confidence, and Esteem, which every person in the community ought to have of the justice, and equity of their rulers, a confidence never more necessary to be maintained than at the present day, for without this, it would have been extremely difficult if not impossible for us to have continued our Forces in the Field.

When these circumstances are taken into consideration, and that our establishment for the pay of the Men, was long before any resolution was formed in the American Congress to pay the Troops upon any Conditions, therefore cannot be consider'd as a design in this Colony, to involve the united Colonies in an undue expence in paying them, We trust that we shall meet with the approbation of the Honble. Congress; and if any inconveniencies shall arise, they will be attributed to the necessity of the case.

With regard to the expence arising by the difference between the Lunar, and Calender months being Colonial, and not Continental, after you have fully represented the matter to the Congress, we can safely confide in their determination, being assured that it will be founded in that Wisdom, and Justice, which hath ever mark'd their resolutions.

In the Name and by Order of the whole Court

Walter Spooner

RC (PCC, No. 78, XX); addressed: "To The Honble. John Hancock Esq President of the American Congress   Philadelphia Free"; docketed: "Walter Spooner   5 Decr. 1775."

[1] Despite the address, this letter was intended for all five Massachusetts delegates, whose names are individually listed at its close.

[2] The language beginning "will throw the rest of the Army into disorder" to "Continental Charge" is virtually verbatim from Washington's letter to the General Court of 29 Nov., including the spelling of "Kalender" (*Writings*, ed. Fitzpatrick, 4:129).

From Samuel Chase

Dear Sir   Annapolis. Decr. 8th. 1775

I am obliged to you for your Letter of 2nd. Instant.[1] I intirely agree with You in Sentiment as to the Propriety, nay the Necessity of assuming and exercising all the Powers of Government. Our Convention only met yesterday afternoon. I shall, if possible, induce our People to set the Example, and first take Government.[2]

We have no News here worthy of your Notice. I cannot but intreat your Correspondence. If any Thing material occurs, pray inform Your affectionate and Obedient Servant   Saml. Chase

I beg to be remembered to Messrs. Adams and your Brethren.

RC (Adams Papers); addressed: "To John Adams Esquire   Philadelphia Free"; docketed: "Sam. Chase Esqr. Decr. 8. 1775." This letter took up only one page of a possible four. Pages two and three contain a Dft in JA's hand of a letter to Washington that was sent on 6 Jan. 1776 (see below).

[1] Not found.

[2] The Maryland Convention, first called into being in June 1774 during the Port Act crisis, had taken formal possession of province government by July 1775. But the session that opened

on 7 Dec. failed to move in the direction that Chase hoped for. Although
it did vote to raise troops, it also passed
a resolution calling for reconciliation
"upon terms that may ensure to these

colonies an equal and permanent freedom" (Matthew Page Andrews, *History
of Maryland: Province and State*, N.Y.,
1929, p. 304, 310, 313–314).

From William Tudor

Dr Sir   Cambridge 11th. Decr. 1775

I seize a few Minutes before the Post sets out to send You a little
Information. Manley took two Prizes last Saturday, a large Ship of
more than 300 Tons with a Cargo of Coals (chiefly) a large Quantity
of Porter, some Wine and 40 live Hogs—destin'd for the beseiged
Troops at Boston. The Captain found Means to throw overboard every
material Letter. The other Capture was a large Brig from Antigua
with 139 Puncheons of Rum—some Cocoa—a handsome Present of
Lemons, Oranges and Limes for Genl. Gage's own Use.[1]

Above one half the Connecticut Forces are discharg'd, and are gone
or going home. The Massachusetts shew more Spirit, and in General
are determined on no Consideration to leave the Lines till the Army
is inlisted. Some Regiments have presented Addresses to the General,
with Assurances of this Kind, which have given great Satisfaction.
About 2000 of the Militia are come down and 3000 more are expected
every Hour. They are in high Spirits and look like an exceeding clever
Set of young Fellows. We shall do very well yet.

The pompous Display of Riflemen's Courage which fill half the
Papers of the southward—is ridiculous.[2] The Affair at Leechmere's
Point hardly deserved mentioning—and when read by Howe's Officers will make them laugh—at least. I will not by *Letter* make any other
observation on this Subject.

You would much oblige me Sir, to procure from the Secretary of
the Congress, an exact List of all the General Officers, and principal
Staff Officers in the Continental Service—and send it me.

The New Articles for the Government of the Army ought to be
sent as soon as possible.[3] The Judge Advocate should have been au-
thoris'd to have sworn the Members of Courts Martial, and ought to
have been under an Oath of Office himself. Your most obt. Servt.

RC (Adams Papers); addressed: "To the Honble: John Adams Esq   Philadelphia   Free"; docketed: "Tudor   Decr. 11. 1775"; docketed by CFA: "W.
Tudor   Decr 11. 1775."

[1] The ship *Jenny*, William Foster
master, and the brig *Little Hannah*,
Robert Adams master. Foster's attempt

to destroy papers failed, for the signal
book, manifest, and several letters were
recovered from the water (*Boston*

Gazette, 11 Dec.; Clark, *Washington's Navy*, p. 91–92, 231).

[2] Tudor may be referring to accounts, certain to anger people from Massachusetts, such as that which appeared in the *Pennsylvania Gazette* of 29 Nov.: "Extract of a letter from an Officer of distinction in the American Army near Boston, dated November 15, 1775." It stated that "We had a skirmish the other day on Litchmore point with General Clinton and a body of his myrmidons. Col. Thompson and his riflers acquitted themselves most nobly. OUR FRIEND MIFFLIN PLAYED THE PART OF HIMSELF—THAT IS OF A HERO."

Tudor was not alone in his dislike of the riflemen; see letters to JA from James Warren of 11 Sept., William Heath of 23 Oct., Samuel Osgood Jr. of [23 Oct.], and John Thomas of 24 Oct. (all above). For AA's account of the skirmish, see *Adams Family Correspondence*, 1:324–325.

[3] Although passed by the congress on 7 Nov., the revised Articles of War were apparently not ready for distribution until 7 Jan. 1776 (*JCC*, 3:331–334; General Orders, 7 Jan., Washington, *Writings*, ed. Fitzpatrick, 4:220).

From James Warren

My Dear Sir   Watertown Decr. 11th: 1775

Since my last[1] I have not A Scrip from you. Whether you Intend by withholding the Encouragement you used to give to get rid of the Trouble of my many long and Tedious Letters I don't know. However I am determined to write this once more at least not out of Spite, and malice, but to rectify some Errors I find I Committed in my last and to remove any Impressions of despondency the Temper I wrote in, and the Spirit of the Letter might make. Capt. Stevenson who was the Bearer of it left us last monday, and I hope will be with you this day, since which I find I was much mistaken in the account I gave you of the progress of saltpetre in this Colony. It is certainly makeing in great quantities in many Towns, and I believe we shall next spring have as much as we want. One man in Wrentham had a fortnight ago 50 lb. One at Sherburne about as much. Dr. Whittaker has 70 lb. Parson Whitwell 50 and in the County of Worcester great quantities are Collecting. All Agree that the process is as Simple and easy as Makeing Soap. Our Committee[2] too at Newberry Port have succeeded with some Improvements and make steadily 12 lb. a Day and as good as I ever saw. So much for Saltpetre. We have Assigned this afternoon to Choose A Committee to Erect as soon as possible A powder Mill at Sutton and Another at Stoughton.[3] Several Prizes have been taken in the week past, and among the rest A fine Ship from London, with Coal, Porter Cheese Live Hoggs &c. &c. and a large Brigantine from Antigua with Rum Sugar &c. All the Country are now Engaged in prepareing to make salt Petre fixing Privateers, or Reinforceing the Army. I suppose if the weather had been favourable 12 or 13 Privateers would have been at Sea this Day in quest of 7 Sail of Ships which came out with this Prize, and had similar Cargoes. Commissions are makeing out for 2 Privateers from Salem, two from Newberry Port one of them to Mount 16 Guns. I hear one is fixing at Plymouth and one at Barnstable. It will be in the power of the Congress another Year to Command the American Sea. We have here great Numbers of fine Vessels, and Seamen in Abundance.

The 3000 Militia called to Reinforce the Army, are all I believe in Camp, and I Conjecture some hundred more than called for, such was their Indignation at the Conduct of the Connecticut Troops, and Zeal for the Cause that they Immediately Inlisted and Arrived in Camp at the Time set, tho' the Traveling is Exceeding Bad. The New Hampshire Troops I am told are not behind them. The Small Pox is broke out at Cambridge and 1 or 2 other places among those late out of Boston. I hope good Care will be taken of them to prevent its spreading. The Inlistments in the Army go on rather better than they did. Upon the whole the Hemisphere is brighter, and the prospects more Agreable than they were A Week ago. Our Army Acknowledge they have been well Treated paid and fed, and if you had not raised the pay of the officers they could hardly have found A Subject of Complaint. I am sorry it was done [tho' if the Soldiers were] Politicians they might see it was an [Advantage to them . . . .] The Southern Gentlemen seem to have [taken a dislike to . . .] Equality among us, and don't seem [. . .] that Many of the Soldiers are [. . .] possessd of as much property as [. . .] The People of Boston by their Imprudence [. . .] Town so long have given us more trouble [. . .] the Ministerial Army and Navy. I don't [. . .] an Eighth part of our whole time since [. . .] been taken up about them people, and the [. . .] last perhaps ruin us by spreading [. . .] what shall we do determine not to [. . .] they die.

Adeu

I have no Letter from Mrs. Adams to Inclose. I may recieve one Tomorrow.

Just as I finished the Above I received your Short Letter of Decr. 5.[4] Shall Endeavour to reconcile the Troops as far as I have Influence to the Terms you mention. The greatest difficulty however is about Officers wages lately raised. Crafts I know is A deserving Man and fit for the Office you Mention. Trot I presume is by the Character you give him, but what is to be done with Burbeck. He is said to be a good Officer, is well Esteemed at Head Quarters, and is now a Leut. Colonel. Do you design there shall be 2 Lt. Colonels as well as 2 Majors in that Regiment. What Shall be done for our Good Friend Doctr. Cooper. He is A Staunch Friend to the Cause A grat Sufferer, and No Income to support him. Must he not be provided for in the Civil List. Do Devise something.

It is reported from Boston that they have taken one of our Privateers.[5] I fear it is True.

[...] it is [true they have] indeed got one of our [...] Brigantine the General fixed from Plymouth. She [...] double fortified six pounders, about 20 Swivels [...] we dont know who took her or any [...] about it. Tis supposed she made A stout [...] much fireing was heard in the Bay. [...] Head Quarters Yesterday but the General was gone [...] not see him. I met Crafts he says the [General?] offered him the 2d. Majority, and that A Man [...] formerly his Serjeant is to have the first [...] Accept it. Mason is the Leut. Colonel [...] wishes to be made Barracks Master, and I could [...] if it don't make A difficulty.[6] Brewer[7] is at present Appointed, and gave up his Regiment for it to Accomodate Matters, and facilitate the New Establishment. I had A Vessel Arrived on Monday from the West Indies. She has been at Almost all the Windward Islands. The Master is Sensible, and Intelligent. I Received A Letter from Home last Night. Shall Inclose[8] you A paragraph which Contains the Account he gives. It may do service tho' you no doubt have Intelligence more direct. My Son Met Mrs. Adams on the road Yesterday in her way to Weymouth. She was well.

RC (Adams Papers). The third and fourth pages are badly mutilated; words in brackets are supplied from *Warren-Adams Letters*, 1:192–195.

[1] Warren to JA, 3 Dec. (above).
[2] Dr. William Whiting, Deacon Baker, Capt. John Peck, and Jedidiah Phipps were members of this committee, which was appointed on 31 Oct. and 1 Nov. (Mass., *House Jour.*, 1775–1776, 2d sess., p. 215, 219).
[3] Formed on 12 Dec., the committee was authorized to use up to £600 in order to establish powder mills in the two towns (same, 3d sess., p. 36).
[4] That is, 3 Dec. (above).
[5] The armed brig *Washington*, Capt. Sion Martindale, was captured by the frigate *Fowey*, Capt. George Montagu, on the night of 4 Dec. (Clark, *Washington's Navy*, p. 86–87). The Massa-chusetts *Gazette* of 14 Dec., reporting the capture with obvious pleasure, stated that the crew was to be sent to England on the *Tartar*, which was to sail that same day.
[6] For what is probably the substance of this conversation with Crafts, see his letter to JA of 16 Dec. (below).
[7] Col. Jonathan Brewer gave up his regiment to Col. Whitcomb, who had been left out of command in the remodeling of the army, much to his men's disgust (General Orders, 16 Nov., Washington, *Writings*, ed. Fitzpatrick, 4:94).
[8] Enclosure not found.

From Thomas Crafts Jr.

Dear Sir   Cambridge Decr 16 1775

I ever thought thare was such a Thing as sincere friendship, and that some perticular Persons, with whom I had long been Intemate with And had made such great professions of it to me where possese'd with It. But I had given up the very Idea of such a thing, for the last three Months, and was become a perfect Infidel, Till yesterday Col. Warren shew me a Letter from you to him[1] in which you mention my being recommended to General Washington for a Commission, For which I return you my sincere Thanks; and am now become a Bleaver again. Even Mr. Cushing mentioned me in a Letter to Mr. Cooper. But how am I greaved not being thought off by him whom I Valued as the apple of My Eye.[2] Out of sight out of Mind. I cannot Express the astonishment, Mortification and Disopointment I was thrown into on hearing the Appointmet of Mr. Knox to the Command of the Train. On the 13th Instant was sent for by General Washington and offered the Majority in the Train—Under the following Officers, Col. Knox, Lt. Col. Burbeck, Lt. Col. Mason, First Major John Crane, which shocked me very much. Lt. Col. Mason was formerly Captain of the Train in Boston but was so low and mean a person, thare was not an Officer or private that would train under him In consequence of which he was oblige'd to retire. Major Crane is a good Officer and a worthy Man But Last June he was only a Serjant in the Company whereof I was Captain Lieutenant.[3] You certainly will not blame me for not excepting under such humiliating Curcumstances. I had the offer of the same place when you was down. I see of but one way to provide for me In that Department, As the Redjt. [Regiment] of the Train is to be Devided into two Battalions, appointing me to Command One, It will make only the Addition of One Colonel, thare being One Colonel, Two Lt. Colonels and Two Majors Already Appointed. I find Col. Brewer is appointed Barrack-Master General. I was in hopes if I failed in the other Department Should have been provided for in this. Will not the services that I Endeavourd to do my Country—The Werasome Days and Sleepless Nights—Loss of time and the expenses I have been at from 1765 to 1775 Make an Interest for me Superior to Col. Brewer. If not Sir I submit to my Hard Cruel Hard fate. I like that place and should be fond of it as it would be less likely to give offence to Two Officers in said Train. You may remember I mentioned that Office to you when at Watertown. I am now reduced from Comfortable Circumstances to a state of Poverty. An Ameeable

Wife (As you know Sir) and four small Children to provide for. I realy wish myself in Boston. I could support with firmness all the Insults I might receive from A Howe and his Bandity of Mercenaries, But to be negratted by those I thought my Friends, and my Country I cannot Support It.

The Connecticut Forces have in general gone home. Many of them I bleave will Enlist again. Our Militia have done themselves honour by the readiness with which they enlisted and came down to Man the Lines. They might have had double the Number had they been sent for. The Military Stores that was taken by Capt. Manly is a noble acquisition at this time. Ten Tons of Powder is arrived at Dartmouth.[4] The Militia is likely soon to be settled, Tho' I think it has been much two Long Neglected. They are pulling up the pavements In Boston in full expectation of a Bombardment. Bleave me to [be] with all sincerity and due respect your Friend and Humbl. Servt.

Thos Crafts Junr.

PS Pray spare so much of your precious moments as to write me one line.

Present my best regards to Honl. Saml. Adams Col. Hancock and Thos Cushing Esqr.

My mind is much agitated excuse bad speling and writing.[5]

RC (Adams Papers); addressed: "To The Honorable John Adams Esq at ⟨*Philadelphia*⟩"; in an unknown hand: "Watertown."

[1] That of 3 Dec. (above).

[2] Probably Col. John Hancock, the only member of the Massachusetts delegation with any military experience.

[3] By "Last June" Crafts probably meant June 1774, when both men were members of Capt. Adino Paddock's artillery company. Crafts' rank was what today would be called first lieutenant. In June 1775 John Crane (1744–1805) was a major in the Providence, R.I., train of artillery and retained that rank when he returned to Massachusetts and joined Knox's regiment (Thomas J. Abernethy, American Artillery Regiments in the Revolutionary War, unpubl. bound typescript, MHi, p. 4, 175–177).

[4] The port area of old Dartmouth is now part of New Bedford, Mass.

[5] JA did not receive this letter until after he returned to Philadelphia (JA to Crafts, 18 Feb. 1776, below). In JA's absence it may have been sent back to Watertown, since the address was altered.

From Lemuel Hayward

Honored Sir   Roxbury December 16 1775

By the hand of Dr. Morgan I had the Pleasure of receiving yours of Nov. 13.[1] and thank you not only for the Honour you did me in writing, but for your kind Disposition towards me discoverable in it. Agreable to your Advice upon the Arival of Docter Morgan I waited on him, and find him the Person you represented[2] a well bred Man of Sense. He appears pleased with those Houses under my Care and fully disposed to have me continued as Surgeon, yet informs me he can't at present establish me as he is limited to the Number four but would have me continue to act as Surgeon and further informs me that he has reccommended our Establishment to the General and that the General has recommended it to the Honorable Congress. I therefore take this Method again to ask for your Influence to my Establishment when the same shall be laid before the Honorable Congress. What I ask for myself I wish for Doctr. Aspinwall. He is certainly a deserving Gentleman.

The Town of Roxbury you must be sensible is torn to Pieces, my Practice in it of Consequence must be of little Importance to what it once was. Indeed I am rather urged by the common Feelings of Humanity to attend the Sick than by any Motives of Interest. Besides I am loth to leave so good a School as the Hospital is under the Direction of so great a Man in his Profession as Doctr. Morgan. You therefore can't wonder that I am a little importunate in the Affair.

As to the Necessity of our Appointment I cease to urge it since Dr. Morgan I trust has already done it, and of our Abilities he must be the Judge. I am with the greatest Respect your Honor's most obedient and most humble Servent.   Leml. Hayward

RC (Adams Papers); addressed: "To The Honorable John Adams Esqr Member of the Honorab Congress   Philadelphia   Free"; docketed: "L. Hayward."; in a second hand: "Decr. 16. 1775."

¹ Not found.
² For JA's opinion of Dr. Morgan, see JA's third letter to James Warren of 25 Oct. (above).

From Joseph Hawley

Dear Sir   Watertown Decr. 18th 1775

I received your favour of the 25th of Novr. as soon as I arrived at this town which was last friday and a very kind and generous return I esteem it to the few lines I sent you from Brookfield. I hope the lines will not be Abandoned. I hope an Army will be inlisted for the Next year before the Spring Advances but am clearly of Opinion that the Charge of Marching in the Militia their equipment and pay will amount to More Money than would have been Necessary by way of Bounty to have inlisted a new army by the last of this Month. But good fruit Will come of this Measure, Many More of our people will be Made Soldiers than could any otherwise been Made in the same time and I hope the

Encampments preserved. You will undoubtedly hear of the Flame blown up in Connecticutt by raising the pay of the officers and Not granting a bounty to the Privates. The Tories throughout the land do their utmost to highten the flame. The disturbance has Not been so great in this province but the complaints and noise has been very uncomfortable here.

But enough of this, and to go upon some other Tack—there are two or three Matters I will Just hint to you and hope some time or other to be able to treat upon them to you by detail.

I apprehended the difficulty of a bounty &c. arose from the different Ideas genius and Conditions of the inhabitants of the Southern Colonies from ours in N. E. and I have No doubt but the same Cause will operate greatly to retard and delay two or three other great events which must take place unless Britain imediately Shifts her course. An American Parliament with legislative Authority over All the colonies already or that Shall be united Must be established. Until that Shall be done we Shall be liable to be divided and broken by the Arts of our intestine enemies and cunning Menoeuvers of Administration. Undoubtedly the plan Must be when formed laid before each Several Assembly or provincial Congress on the Continent and be consented to by all. The Numbers of Members each colony Shall send to that great Council Must be Settled. The Same time of election Must be fixed for All, and the term or period for which the Members Must be chosen must be determined. May God prevent Septennial Parliaments. Nay I hope they will be Annual.

All the Colonies I hope will as soon as possible assume Popular forms of Government and indeed become several little republicks. I freely own Myself a republican and I wish to See all Government on this Earth republican. No other form is a Security for right and virtue. I hope an eye will be Steadily kept on Connecticut Model tho' I am sensible it May be Mended.

I know the hardness of Mens hearts will delay and retard this Salutary glorious work but Great Prudence, patience and fortitude, firmness and perseverance will effect it. The work will Meet with Many rebuffs but I trust will be as the Morning light which Shineth More and More unto the perfect day.

Soon very soon there Must be Alteration to the Paper Currency of the colonies. The Continental Congress or Parliament Must inspect Each colony and See that each one keep its faith otherwise the Medium will inevitably depreciate but if the periods for which the Bills shall be emitted shall be not too long and there Should be a punctuality in Sinking them We may get along comfortably with a paper Currency. High taxes can easily be paid in time of War. Money will then infallibly circulate briskly and if the Taxes keep pace with the emissions the Currency will not depreciate. But more of this at another time. All the colonies Must be brought to be equally honest as to the redemption of their Bills otherwise a discount and difference will imediately take place which will embarrass and tend to disunite. Surely this Matter is worthy the Attention of this great Superin-[ten]ding council of the whole Good. Civil polity and Government Must go hand in hand with military Operations.

We are somewhat alarmed with Dunmores ferocity but hope that he will be soon crushed.[1] The Surprising Success of the Privateers this way we hope will animate the whole continent to the like practice.

The art of making Saltpetre is well investigated here. But the exertions for the largest Supplies of amunition and arms through the whole Continent ought to be now Constantly as great as if all the force was in sight which they talk in Britain of Sending against us early Next Spring.

For God's sake let the river St. Lawrence, the lake Champlain and Hudsons river be impenetrably Secured against all the Attempts of Ministerial troops and Pray order Matters so without fail that the inhabitants of Canada may be refresh'd with full draughts of the Sweets of liberty. This has been my cry and prayer to you ever since the taking of Ticonderoga.

I am Sir with highest esteem Most faithfully yours

Joseph Hawley

RC (Adams Papers).

[1] Probably a reference to a report from Williamsburg, Va., dated 7 [i.e. 17] Nov., printed in the *Boston Gazette* of 11 Dec. It described a battle between 350 "Regular soldiers, sailors, runaway negroes, and Tories, . . . the *very scum* of the country," led by Lord Dunmore and 200 of the Princess Anne co. militia on 14 Nov., in which Dunmore was victorious.

From Jonathan Williams

Dear Sir   Providence Decr 20th 1775

I[1] have just heard of your return from Philadelphia, and am exceeding sorry I had not the pleasure of seeing you as you passed thro' Providence;[2] I want very much to consult you Sir, about entering into the Practise of Law, and the favour you did me when an Opportunity offered for my going into Business at Portsmouth, encourages me to make this Application.

I have for this some time past had a great desire to enter the Army, [and?] I find the Thoughts of it, affects my [Mother] so much, that I think it ungenerous to urge it farther; I have now turned my thoughts to the Practise of Law, and according to your advice, am determined to pursue my Studies. I think a favourable opportunity now offers, and I wish to take advantage of it. You know Sir, I have now been in the Study of the Law, above the Period, necessary for an Introduction to Court, and as the Court is to meet here the first Wednesday in Jany. I wanted to ask you, if you woud think it adviseable for me, to offer myself to be sworn—and if you shoud, whether it woud not be necessary for me to have some Credentials, or Recomendations from you. I am not determined to settle here, that I shall leave to a future day, but I think if I was sworn, I might perhaps get some Business, which woud relieve me from a state of Idleness, and have a tendency to fix me to a close application to my Books.

If it woud not be too much trouble, I shoud be much obliged to you for your advice.

Sometime ago you put Hawkins's Pleas of the Crown,[3] into my hands. I read him thro and have since read Finch, and Burns Justice and am now reading Plowden's Reports.[4] I have several of your Books in my possession which I will take good care off, and if possible prevent them from falling into the Hands of any one, that woud sacrifice them [because] they belong to you.

I am exceeding unhappy Sir that I cannot immediately pay you the price of my Education, but my Father's Absence,[5] and the embarrassment of our Family, woud make it at present difficult. Sir, if you shoud want a sum of Money I will exert myself to answer your purpose.

I heartily wish you Joy upon the honorable Appointment lately [assigned?] you, by your Countrymen, and congratulate you as a Patriot, upon the late acqui[sition?] to our Cause, in Cannada, and the success [...] prizes obtained at Sea by the vigillance [of] Manly and others.

My Respects to Mrs. Adams. I hope She, and all your Family are well. I am Sir your much obliged & sincere Friend

Jon Williams

RC (Adams Papers); addressed: "To The Honble John Adams Esqr in Braintree"; in another hand below the address: "To be delivered to Mr Tudor"; docketed in an unidentified hand: "J Williams to Jno. Adams Esqr" and in another hand: "Decr. 20th 1775"; in the lower right corner of the address portion: "Thos. Smith." The MS is badly mutilated, but relatively few words are missing.

[1] Jonathan Williams (d. 1780) had been JA's law clerk from Sept. 1772 – Oct.(?) 1774 (JA, *Legal Papers*, 1: lxxxi, cxiii).

[2] JA passed through Providence on either 19 or 20 Dec. (JA, *Diary and Autobiography*, 2:171).

[3] William Hawkins, *A Treatise of the Pleas of the Crown*, 4th edn., 2 vols. in 1, London, 1762 (*Catalogue of JA's Library*).

[4] Sir Henry Finch, *A Description of the Common Laws of England, according to the Rules of Art, Compared with the Prerogatives of the King*, London, 1759; or *Law, or a Discourse Thereof, in Four Books . . . Notes and References, and a Table . . . by Danby Pickering*, [London,] 1759. Richard Burn, *The Justice of the Peace and Parish Officer*, 7th edn., 3 vols., London, 1762 (*Catalogue of JA's Library* lists vol. 1). Edmund Plowden, *The Commentaries, or Reports of Edmund Plowden*, [London,] 1761 (same).

[5] John Williams, father of Jonathan, was a former inspector general of customs at Boston, who at this time was probably still in London, where in 1774 he had a number of meetings with Josiah Quincy Jr. and prevailed upon him to meet with several officials in the ministry (MHS, *Procs.*, 50 [1916–1917]:437, 438, 439, 441, 442, 443, 446).

From John Sullivan

Dear Sir   Camp on Winter Hill Decemr. 21st 1775

Did not the hurry of our affairs prevent; I Should often write you Respecting the State of our Army: but it has been my fortune to be Employed almost night and Day. When I had Winter Hill almost Compleated I was ordered to Plowed Hill[1] where for a Long Time I was almost Day and night in Fortifying. Since have I been ordered to the Eastward to fortify and Defend Pescataway Harbour[2] but unfortunately was oblidged to Return without an oportunity of proving the works I had Taken So much pains to Construct. This being over I was Called upon to Raise 2000 Troops from New Hampshire and bring them on the Lines in 10 Days; this I undertook and was happy Enough to perform otherwise the Defection of the Conecticut Troops might have proved Fatal to us: I might have added that 3000 from your Colony arrived at the Same time to Supply the Defect. This with the other Necessary Business in my Department has So far Engaged my time and attention that I hope you will not Require an apology for my not writing. I have now many things to write you but must Content myself with mentioning a few of them at present and Leave the Residue to another opportunity. I will in the first place Inform you that we have possession of almost Every advantageous post Round Boston from whence we might with great Ease Burn or Destroy the Town was it not that we fail in a very Triffleing matter namely we have no powder to do it with. However as we have a Sufficiencey for our Small Arms we are not without hopes to become Masters of The Town; *Old Boreas and Jack Frost* are now at work Building a Bridge over all the Rivers Bays &c. &c. which once Compleated we Take possession of the Town or Perish in the Attempt. I have the Greatest Reason to believe I Shall be Saved for my faith is very Strong. I have ⟨*the great*⟩ Liberty to take possession of your House. Mrs. Adams was kind Enough to Honour me with a visit the other Day in Company with a number of other Ladies and The Revd. Mr. Smith.³ She gave me power to Enter and Take possession. There is nothing now wanting but your Consent which I Shall wait for till the Bridge is Compleated and unless given before that time Shall make a Forceable Entry and leave you to bring your Action.⁴ I hope in Less than three weeks to write you from Boston.

The Prisoners Taken in our Privateers are Sent to England for Tryal and So is Colo. Allen.⁵ This is Glorious Encouragement for people to Engage in our Service when their prisoners are Treated with So much Humanity and Respect and The Law of Retaliation not put in force against them. I know you have published a Declaration of that Sort⁶ but I never knew a man feel the weight of Chains and Imprisonment by mere Declarations on paper and believe me till their Barbarous usage of our prisoners is Retaliated we Shall be miserable. Let me ask whether we have any thing to hope from the Mercy of his majesty or his ministers. Have we any Encouragement from the people in Great Britain. Could they Exert themselves more against us if we had Shaken of[f] the Yoke and Declared ourselves Independent. Why then in Gods name is it not done. Whence arises this Spirit of moderation. This want of Decision. Do the members of Your Respectable Body Think the Enemy will Throw their Shot and Shells with more force than at present. Do they think the Fate of Charlestown or Falmouth might have been worse or the Kings proclomation more Severe if we had openly Declared war; could they have treated our prisoners worse if we were in an open and avowed Rebellion Than they now do. Why then do we call ourselves freemen and Act the part of Timid Slaves. I dont apply this to You. I know you too well to Suspect Your firmness and Resolution. But Let me beg of you to use those Talents I know You possess to Destroy that Spirit of moderation which has almost ruined and if not Speedily Rooted out will prove the final overthrow of America. That Spirit gave them possession of Boston. Lost us all our Arms and Ammunition and now Causes our Brethren which have fallen into their hands to be treated Like Rebels. But Enough of this. I feel Too Sensibly to write more upon the Subject. I beg you to make my most respetful Compliments to Mr. Hancok and your Brother Delegates also to Colo. Lee and those worthy

Brethren who Laboured with us in the vineyard when I had the Honour to be with you in the Senate.[7] You may venture to assure them that when an oportunity presents if I Should not have Courage Enough to fight myself I Shall do all in my power to Encourage others. Dear Sir I am with much Esteem your most obedt Servt.

Jno Sullivan

RC (Adams Papers); docketed: "Gen. Sullivan. Nov. 21. 1775"; below this entry in JA's hand: "ansd. March 7." Because Sullivan neglected much terminal punctuation, it has been supplied.

[1] Both these hills command the Mystic River and the road leading northwest out of Charlestown to Medford. Then in Cambridge, these sites are now in Somerville (*Early Amer. Atlas*, p. 50).

[2] That is, Portsmouth, N.H.

[3] William Smith, AA's father.

[4] By his playful reference to JA's house in Boston, perhaps Sullivan was attempting to spur JA and through him the congress to action. The visit of the congressional committee in Oct. had left unresolved the question of mounting an attack on Boston. On 22 Dec. the congress did approve such an assault (JCC, 3:444–445). AA mentioned her meeting with Sullivan in her letter to JA of 10 Dec. (*Adams Family Correspondence*, 1:336).

[5] The crew of the *Washington*, captured on 4 Dec., were transported to England on the *Tartar*. Ethan Allen was captured in an ill-fated and somewhat foolhardy effort to surprise Montreal in September. The men of the *Washington* were distributed as "volunteers" among various ships of the British Navy, but the officers were sent back to Halifax, from where Sion Martindale, the captain, ultimately escaped. Allen spent the next two years as a prisoner at Pendennis Castle in England, at Halifax, and in New York until he was finally exchanged in May 1778 (Clark, *Washington's Navy*, p. 86–90, 184; John Pell, *Ethan Allen*, Boston, 1929, p. 296–298).

[6] On 6 Dec. the congress, in response to the King's declaring the colonists rebels, adopted a declaration that promised retaliation against British prisoners for ill-treatment of American prisoners by the British (JCC, 3:409–412). Being general in tone, it did not in Sullivan's mind meet the need presented by the situation of the *Washington* crew and Ethan Allen. In a letter of 18 Dec., however, George Washington told Gen. Howe that should the mistreatment of Allen continue, he would retaliate against Gen. Richard Prescott, whom Americans had captured at Montreal, and who was largely responsible for Allen's treatment (Washington, *Writings*, ed. Fitzpatrick, 4:170–171; French, *First Year*, p. 423–424).

[7] Sullivan had served in the First Continental Congress and in the first session of the Second. He left when he was appointed a brigadier general in the American Army on 22 June (Burnett, ed., *Letters of Members*, 1:xlix).

From Samuel Adams

My dear Sir   Philadelphia Decr. 22 1775

My Concern for your Welfare induced me carefully to watch the Weather till I conjectured you had got to the End of your Journey, and I have the Pleasure of believing it has been more agreable than one might have expected at this Season. I hope you found Mrs. Adams and Family in a confirmd State of Health. I will not envy you, but I earnestly wish to enjoy, at least for a few Weeks, domestick Retirement and Happiness. I dare not however, urge an Adjournment of the Congress. It would indeed be beneficial to the Members and the publick on many Considerations, but our Affairs are now at so critical a Conjuncture that a Seperation might be dangerous.

Since you left us, our Colony has sometimes been divided, on Questions that appeard to me to be important. Mr. C[ushing] has no doubt a Right to speak his opinion whenever he can form one; and you must agree with him, that it was highly reasonable, the Consideration of such Letters as you have often heard read, which had been assigned for the Day, should, merely for the Sake of order, have the Preference to so trifling Business as the raising an American Navy. I know it gives you great Pleasure to be informd that the Congress have ordered the Building of thirteen Ships of War viz five of 32 Guns five of 28 and three of 24.[1] I own I wished for double or treble the Number, but I am taught the Rule of Prudence, to let the fruit hang till it is ripe, otherwise those Fermentations and morbid Acrimonies might be produced in the political, which the like error is said to produce in the natural Body. Our Colony is to build two of these Ships. We may want Duck. I have been told that this Article is manufacturd in the Counties of Hampshire and Berkshire. You may think this worth your Enquiry.

Our Fleet, which has been preparing here will be ready to put to Sea in two or three days, and it is left to the Board of Admiralty to order its Destination. May Heaven succeed the Undertaking. Hopkins is appointed Commander in Chiefe.[2] I dare promise that he will on all occasions distinguish his Bravery, as he always has, and do honor to the American Flag.

General Schuyler is at Albany. By a Letter from him of the 14th Instant we are informd that "there had been a Meeting of Indians in that place, who deliverd to him a Speech, in which they related the Substance of a Conference Coll. Johnson had with them the last Summer, concluding with that at Montreal, where he deliverd to each of the Canadian Tribes a War belt and the Hatchet which they accepted; after which they were invited to feast on a Bostonian and drink his Blood, an ox being roasted for the purpose and a pipe of Wine given to drink. The War Song was also sung. One of the Chiefs of the Six Nations who attended that Conference, accepted of a very large black War belt with an Hatchet depicturd on it, but would neither eat nor drink nor sing the War Song. This famous Belt they have deliverd up, and there is now full Proof that the ministerial Servants have attempted to engage the Indians against us."[3] This is copied from the Generals Letter.

You will know what I mean when I mention to you the Report of the *Committee of Conference.* This has been considerd and determind agreable to your Mind and mine.[4] Mr. H agreed with me in opinion, and I think, in expressing his Sentiments he honord himself. I dare not be more explicit on this Subject. It is sufficient that *you* understand me.

I have more to say to you but for Want of Leisure I must postpone it to another opportunity. Inclosd you have a Number of Letters which came to my hand directed to you. Had you been here I should possibly have had the Benefit of perusing them. I suffer in many Respects by your Absence.

Pray present my due Regards to all Friends—particularly Coll. Warren, and tell him I will write to him soon. Your affectionate Friend

RC (Adams Papers).

[1] The congress voted for this construction on 13 Dec. The 13 ships were to cost no more than $866,666 2/3 and were apportioned as follows: New Hampshire 1, Massachusetts 2, Rhode Island 2, Connecticut 1, New York 2, Pennsylvania 4, and Maryland 1 (JCC, 3:425–426).

[2] Esek Hopkins (1718–1802) of Rhode Island was officially designated commander in chief of the navy on 22 Dec., but was unable to take his small fleet to sea until Feb. 1776 (DAB; JCC, 3:443).

[3] This passage describing a meeting between Guy Johnson and the Indians is, with minor differences, quoted from the original letter received by the congress on 22 Dec. Opening quotation marks are supplied (PCC, No. 153, I; JCC, 3:443).

[4] The report of the Conference Committee recommended that Gen. Washington be permitted to mount an attack on Boston (JCC, 3:444–445). John Hancock, who, according to Richard Smith of New Jersey, "spoke heartily for this measure," assured the general that he completely supported an attack, "tho' individually I may be the greatest sufferer" (Richard Smith's Diary, 22 Dec., and the President of Congress to Washington, 22 Dec., both in Burnett, ed., *Letters of Members,* 1:284, 285–286).

John Adams' Service in the Council

26 December 1775 – 24 January 1776

I. CALENDAR OF COUNCIL ACTIONS SIGNED BY JOHN ADAMS
II. REPORT OF A COMMITTEE ON FITTING OUT ARMED VESSELS, 11 JANUARY 1776
III. REPORT OF A COMMITTEE ON A LETTER FROM GEORGE WASHINGTON, 13 JANUARY 1776
IV. A PROCLAMATION BY THE GENERAL COURT, 19 JANUARY 1776

Editorial Note

Adams returned to Braintree from Philadelphia on 21 December 1775 and departed from Watertown for the Continental Congress five weeks later on 25 January 1776 (JA, *Diary and Autobiography*, 2:226, 227). Relatively little is known about his activities and thinking in this period, for he wrote few letters and made no entries in his Diary. The official record of his role in the Council at Watertown is comparatively meager, even his days in attendance being uncertain. Although Adams is not listed as present until 28 December, he may have begun attending earlier, for he signed a number of resolutions dated the 26th, and on the 27th he was named to a committee. He also signed two Council resolutions on 3 January and one on the 10th, when he was not recorded as present (No. I, below). Payroll records indicate that he was paid for sixteen days' attendance, but the clerk listed him as present on only fifteen: 28–30 December 1775, 4–6, 11–13, 15–19, and 24 January 1776 (Records of the States, Microfilm, Mass. A.1a, Reel No. 12, Unit 1, p. 402–497, *passim*; M-Ar:164, p. 269 gives the payroll record).

During that time he served on eight committees, the most important of which were those to form a plan for arming one or more vessels, to consider a letter from General Washington dated 10 January, and to draft a proclamation to open the courts (Nos. II, III, IV, below). The other committees, for which no information has been found to illuminate Adams' role in their activities, were those to respond to a petition from the Town of Harvard complaining of excessive wages paid to officers in the army, to investigate the character of Dr. Samuel Gelston, who was accused of supplying the British Army with provisions (see Gelston to JA, [19 Jan. 1776], below), to report on a letter about lead from William Williams of Connecticut, to wait on Washington with the response to the General's letter, and to consider the militia bill (Records of the States,

Microfilm, Mass. A.1a, Reel No. 12, Unit 1, p. 401–402, 425, 450, 452).

While carrying on this strenuous schedule, Adams, as a member of the Continental Congress, advised Washington on Gen. Charles Lee's plan to bring New York under American control and attended two meetings at headquarters (JA to Washington, 6, 15 Jan. 1776, below; DLC:Washington Papers, 22:101, 102). He was probably also consulting privately with various members of the General Court, as well as with Washington and his generals. Adams' last full day with the Council was apparently 19 January, the day on which the proclamation for opening the courts was accepted by that body (Records of the States, Microfilm, Mass. A.1a, Reel No. 12, Unit 1, p. 472–476).

His return to the Continental Congress, so far as the General Court was concerned, had been settled on 15 December, although the official appointment and instructions for the delegates were delayed until 18 January. The General Court gave Adams 126 out of a possible 129 votes. John Hancock was elected unanimously, and Samuel Adams got only two fewer votes than John. Robert Treat Paine, however, was chosen by the minimum number of required votes, 65, and Elbridge Gerry, with no vote count recorded, was selected to replace Thomas Cushing (same, p. 467, 371–372). The election brought to a climax the political controversy that had divided Massachusetts leaders into moderates and radicals on the issue of American relations with Great Britain (see James Warren to JA, 3 Dec. 1775, note 12, above, and Thomas Cushing to Robert Treat Paine, 29 Feb. 1776, MHi:Robert Treat Paine Papers). Adams' margin of victory and the election of Gerry, who would give the radicals so clear a majority within the delegation that the Massachusetts vote would no longer be indecisive, probably influenced Adams' decision to return to Philadelphia. He was also swayed by the urgings of James Warren and other friends and by his own belief that the courts could open effectively without his being present as Chief Justice given the proclamation (No. IV, below) that was to be read upon their opening (JA, *Works*, 1:192).

After a busy day in the Council on 19 January, Adams set out for Braintree. On 23 January he began his trip to Philadelphia, stopping in Watertown, where he had a last, probably brief, meeting with the Council and perhaps received the £130 voted by the General Court to each of the delegates to the congress (Mass., *House Jour.*, 1775–1776, 3d sess., p. 201). He also attended a meeting at Cambridge between Generals Washington and Gates and "half a Dozen Sachems and Warriours of the french Cocknowaga Tribe," to whom he was introduced by Washington as a member of the "Grand Council Fire at Philadelphia." The following morning, at about ten, Gerry called for him, and the two men set out on their journey to attend what was to be a momentous session of the congress (*Diary and Autobiography*, 2:226–227; JA to AA, 24 Jan., *Adams Family Correspondence*, 1:343).

I. Calendar of Council

Actions Signed by John Adams

26 December 1775. Resolution to pay post-riders. M-Ar:207, p. 311–315. PRINTED: Force, *Archives*, 4th ser., 4:1242–1243.

26 December 1775. Resolution appointing members to a joint committee to determine how bills of credit were to be signed and numbered. M–Ar:207, p. 316. PRINTED: Force, *Archives*, 4th ser., 4:1243.

26 December 1775. Resolution to pay John Davis a sum in behalf of Edward Johnson, a petitioning soldier. M–Ar:207, p. 317–318.

26 December 1775. Resolution to approve committee report recommending payment to the Committee of Supplies for its services, in response to its petition. M–Ar:207, p. 319–321.

27 December 1775. Resolution to approve appointment of a committee to assist the commissary general in procuring military supplies. M–Ar:207, p. 326.

28 December 1775. Resolution to liberate Henry Middleton and George Price, prisoners in the Plymouth jail. M–Ar:164, p. 228.

28 December 1775. Resolution ordering committee for purchasing saltpeter to deliver it to Richard Devens. M–Ar:207, p. 329.

28 December 1775. Recommendation to towns to promote the manufacture of saltpeter. M–Ar:207, p. 330.

28 December 1775. Resolution to approve payment to Committee for the Poor of Boston to assist those at Shirley Point (see Joseph Ward to JA, 3 Dec., note 1, above). M–Ar:207, p. 331.

29 December 1775. Resolution ordering the Milton committee to deliver Thomas Hutchinson's furniture to Mrs. Deborah Cushing. M–Ar:207, p. 332.

30 December 1775. Resolution concerning payment of military companies at Braintree, Weymouth, and Hingham (see Josiah Quincy to JA, 2 Jan. 1776, note 1, below). M–Ar:207, p. 337.

30 December 1775. Resolution approving a new levy of men for the seacoast forces. M–Ar:207, p. 351–352.

3 January 1776. Resolution to have copies made of military rolls for use of the treasurer. M–Ar:207, p. 366. PRINTED: Force, *Archives*, 4th ser., 4:1251.

3 January 1776. Approval of mittimus of Moses Wayman and Samuel Webb to Plymouth jail. M–Ar:164, p. 230.

4 January 1776. Message to House concerning the guarding of Hull and other towns. M–Ar:207, p. 369. PRINTED: Force, *Archives*, 4th ser., 4:1252.

5 January 1776. Resolution to supply the Continental Army with 4,000 blankets. M–Ar:207, p. 370–374.

5 January 1776. Resolution concerning mittimus of sixteen named men to Worcester jail. M–Ar:164, p. 231. PRINTED: *Naval Docs. Amer. Rev.*, 3:631.

6 January 1776. Order to Plymouth jail to release James Middleton. M–Ar:164, p. 234.

6 January 1776. Resolution directing the Receiver General to pay £8,000 to the committee for fitting out vessels for importing powder. M–Ar:283, p. 141.

10 January 1776. Resolution ordering Frenchman's Bay committee to deliver clothing to Neal McIntyre or to Charles Chauncy in McIntyre's behalf. M–Ar:207, p. 392. PRINTED: Force, *Archives*, 4th ser., 4:1258.

15 January 1776. Resolution to allow the accounts of the treasurer of Barnstable county. M–Ar:207, p. 405.

17 January 1776. Order to Worcester jail to release Thomas Mullin. M–Ar:164, p. 237.

19 January 1776. Order that blankets collected in Hampshire and Berkshire counties be retained there for use by troops going northward. M–Ar:207, p. 423–424.

19 January 1776. Resolution requesting accounts from towns of powder, lead, and flints supplied to the Continental Army. M–Ar:207, p. 426. PRINTED: Force, *Archives*, 4th ser., 4:1267.

19 January 1776. Resolution ordering commissioners designated to erect a powder mill to do so at Stoughton. M–Ar:207, p. 429. PRINTED: Force, *Archives*, 4th ser., 4:1270.

19 January 1776. Resolution for raising 728 officers and men in Hampshire and Berkshire counties to go to Canada. M–Ar:207, p. 430. PRINTED: Force, *Archives*, 4th ser., 4:1270.

19 January 1776. Resolution to approve choice of field officers for regiment going to Canada. M–Ar:207, p. 434. PRINTED: Force, *Archives*, 4th ser., 4:1270.

24 January 1776. Resolution approving appointment of a committee to call in misprinted bills of credit. M–Ar:207, p. 461.

24 January 1776. Resolution approving an order that bills of credit be delivered to the committee appointed to sign them and that it in turn deliver them to the treasurer. M–Ar:207, p. 465.

II. Report of a Committee on Fitting Out Armed Vessels

[11 January 1776]

The Committee of both Houses appointed to consider a Plan for fiting out one or more Armed Vessels for the defence of American Liberty,[1] have attended that service, and Report in the following Resolves, vizt.   John Adams Per order

⟨*In Council, January 10th. 1776*⟩

Resolved that two Ships be built, as soon as may be, at the expence of this Colony; One Suitable to carry Thirty-Six Guns, vizt., Twenty ⟨*Four*⟩ Guns carrying twelve Pound Shot, and Sixteen Guns for Six

Pound Shot; and the other Ship suitable to carry Thirty-two Guns, vizt., Twenty Guns for nine Pound Shott, and Twelve for Six Pound shot; and that these Ships be built in a manner best calculated for swift sailing, and of Timber and other Materials suitable for Ships of War of such a number of Guns and weight of Metal, and furnished with a Suitable number of Officers, Seamen and Mariners and that all kinds of necessary Arms, Ammunition and Provisions be furnished for such Ships.

Resolved, That   with such as the Honble. ⟨House⟩ shall join, be a Committee to carry the foregoing Resolution into execution as soon as possible; and that a Sum of Money, for that purpose, not exceeding   be put into their Hands, they to be accountable to this Court for the expenditure of the Same.

In Council Jany. 11th. 1776 Read and sent down,

Perez Morton Dpy Secry

In the House of Representatives Jan. 12th. 1776

Read and ordered to be recommitted, and the Committee are directed to report an Estimate of the Expence of building and Furnishing the Vessels above proposed to be provided.

Sent up for Concurrence,   J Warren Spkr

In Council Jany. 12th 1776 Read and concurred,

Perez Morton Depy Secry

In Council Jany 23d 1776

Resolved that Thos. Cushing Esqr. be of the aforesaid Committee on the part of the Board in the room of Jno. Adams Esqr. who is absent. Sent down for Concurrence,   Perez Morton Dpy Secry

In the House of Representatives Jan. 24 1776

Read and concurred. Sent up.   J Warren Spkr

FC (M–Ar: 137, p. 58); docketed, probably by Perez Morton, on a separate slip of paper bound in the volume: "Report to fix out 2 armed Vessels in Defence of American Liberty Jany 11th: Recd. Page 487"; also on the same slip but partially lost: "in Jany. 24 1776 [. . .]."

[1] Formed on 29 Dec. 1775, this committee included JA and Joseph Palmer from the Council and Col. Azor Orne, John Brown of Boston, and Col. Joseph Otis from the House (Mass., *House Jour.*, 1775–1776, 3d sess., p. 94; Records of the States, Microfilm, Mass. A.1a, Reel No. 12, Unit 1, p. 405). JA's membership on the committee and his apparent authorship of the report probably arose from his involvement in naval affairs at the congress, his correspondence with people in Massachusetts on naval matters, and his request to the General Court that he be supplied with information on the naval resources of the province (JA to Elbridge Gerry, 5 Nov. 1775, above). The report was the first formal step in the creation of the Massachusetts Navy as distinct from the force of privateers authorized on 1 Nov. It was not, however, the instrument by which the ships for the navy were actually built. That

resolve, probably drawn up by the committee of 29 Dec., to which Thomas Cushing had been added in the place of JA, was passed on 6, 7 Feb. 1776 with an appropriation of £10,000 to build ten sloops of war. By the following July the first ships, led by the

Tyrannicide, the *Rising Empire*, and the *Independence*, were ready for sea (Mass., *House Jour.*, p. 192, 253–254, 256–257; Records of the States, Microfilm, Mass. A.1a, Reel No. 12, Unit 1, p. 539; Paullin, *Navy of Amer. Rev.*, p. 324–325).

III. Report of a Committee on a Letter from George Washington

[13 January 1776]

The Committee[1] appointed to take into consideration the Letter from his excellency General Washington of the Tenth Instant,[2] have attended that service and beg leave to report. That a Committee of both Houses be appointed to wait on the General and to assure him that this Court are zealously disposed to do everything in their power, to promote the Recruiting of the American Army and to acquaint him that they cannot be of opinion that the public Service will be promoted by offering a bounty at the separate expence of this Colony, or any other encouragement beyond that which has been ordered by the Congress, that they are still further from an opinion that the same service can be promoted by any coercive measures, or any other expedient than voluntary enlistment. But that this Court is willing if his excellency shall approve of this measure, to recommend any further temporary draughts from the Militia, that may be necessary to supply the present deficiencies, to be Continued untill the first of April next, and also to exert the Influence of this Court by recommending to the Selectmen and committees of correspondence and others to exert themselves and employ their influence among the People to promote and encourage by all reasonable methods the Recruiting service in the several Towns.   John Adams per Order

In Council Read and Accepted and Ordered that John Adams Esqr. with such as the Hone. House shall join, be a Committee to wait on his Excellency General Washington for the purposes expressed in the above Report.

In the House of Representatives Read and concurred and Mr. Speaker and Major Hawley are joined.[3]

Tr (M–Ar:Legislative Council Records, 34:490).

[1] Formed on 11 Jan., this committee consisted of JA and Jedediah Foster from the Council and Capt. Josiah Stone, Dummer Jewett, and Maj. Eleazer Brooks from the House (Mass.,

House Jour., 1775–1776, 3d sess., p. 140; Records of the States, Microfilm, Mass. A.1a, Reel No. 12, Unit 1, p. 450).

[2] Washington expressed anxiety over

the strength of the army as shown in the returns of the previous day; moreover, he faced the prospect of the imminent departure of the New Hampshire militia after one month's service. He was also concerned about the number of men joining the provincial rather than the Continental Army in the belief that they would have easier duty and be closer to home. He complained further that officers displaced by the reorganization of the army were recruiting companies in the vain hope that they would be recommissioned. Their activities were interfering with authorized recruiters. Washington had become convinced that voluntary enlistments could not supply the needed number of men and wanted the General Court to devise a new system (*Writings*, ed. Fitzpatrick, 4:227–229). The re-

sponse of the General Court could not have been consoling, for it offered sympathy and little else.

[3] JA, Speaker James Warren, and Joseph Hawley conferred with Washington not only on the General's letter of 10 Jan. but on that of 13 Jan. as well, which dealt with a shortage of firearms. The legislative report on this second letter was prepared by a specially appointed committee, but it was thought that the committee conferring on the first of these letters with the General could also confer on the second. Washington took the occasion to invite this three-man committee to attend a council of general officers (*House Jour.*, p. 148; Records of the States, Microfilm, Mass. A.1a, Reel No. 12, Unit 1, p. 452, 458; Washington to JA, 15 [Jan.] 1776, below).

IV. A Proclamation by the General Court

[19 January 1776]

The frailty of human Nature, the Wants of Individuals, and the numerous Dangers which surround them, through the Course of Life, have in all Ages, and in every Country impelled them to form Societies, and establish Governments.[1]

As the Happiness of the People ⟨*alone*⟩, is the sole End of Government, So the Consent of the People is the only Foundation of it, in Reason, Morality, and the natural Fitness of things: and therefore every Act of Government, every Exercise of Sovereignty, against, or without, the Consent of the People, is Injustice, Usurpation, and Tyranny.

It is a Maxim, that in every Government, there must exist Somewhere, a Supreme, Sovereign, absolute, and uncontroulable Power:[2] But this power resides always in the Body of the People, and it never was, or can be delegated, to one Man, or a few, the great Creator having never given to Men a right to vest others with Authority over them, unlimited either in Duration or Degree.

When Kings, Ministers, Governors, or Legislators therefore, instead of exercising the Powers intrusted ⟨*to their Care*⟩[3] with them according to the Principles, Forms and Proportions stated by the Constitution, and established by the original Compact, prostitute ⟨*it*⟩ those Powers to the Purposes of Oppression; to Subvert, instead of Supporting a free Constitution; to destroy, instead of preserving the Lives,

Liberties and Properties of the People: they are no longer to be deemed Magistrates vested with a Sacred Character; but become public Enemics, and ought to be resisted. ⟨*by open War*⟩ [4]

The Administration of Great Britain, despising equally the Justice, the Humanity and Magnanimity of their Ancestors, and the Rights, Liberties and Courage of Americans have, for a Course of ⟨*Twelve*⟩ years,[5] laboured to establish a Sovereignty in America, not founded in the Consent of the People, but in the mere Will of Persons a thousand Leagues from Us, whom we know not, and have endeavoured to establish this Sovereignty over us, against our Consent, in all Cases whatsoever.

The Colonies during this period, have recurr'd to every [peaceable Resource] in a free Constitution, by Petitions and Remonstrances, to [obtain justice;] which has been not only denied to them, but they have been [treated with unex]ampled Indignity and Contempt and at length open War [of the most] atrocious, cruel and Sanguinary Kind has been commenced [against them.] To this, an open manly and successfull Resistance has hith[erto been made.] Thirteen Colonies are now firmly united in the Conduct of this most just and necessary War, under the wise Councils of their Congress.

It is the Will of Providence, for wise, righteous, and gracious Ends, that this Colony Should have been singled out, by the Enemies of America, as the first object both of their Envy and their Revenge; and after having been made the Subject of Several merciless and vindictive Statutes, one of which was intended to subvert our Constitution by Charter, is made the Seat of War.

No effectual Resistance to the System of Tyranny prepared for us, could be made without either instant Recourse to Arms, or a temporary Suspension of the ordinary Powers of Government, and Tribunals of Justice: to the last of which Evils, in hopes of a Speedy Reconciliation with Great Britain, upon equitable Terms the Congress advised us to submit: and Mankind has seen a Phenomenon without Example [6] in the political World, a large and populous Colony subsisting in [great] Decency and order, for more than a Year ⟨*without Government*⟩[7] under such a suspension of Government.

But as our Enemies have proceeded to such barbarous Extremities commencing Hostilities upon the good People of this Colony, and with unprecedented [Malice] exerting their Power to spread the Calamities of Fire, Sword and Famine through the Land, and no reasonable Prospect remains of a speedy Reconciliation with Great Britain, the Congress have resolved "That no Obedience being due to the Act of

Parliament for altering the Charter of the Colony of Massachusetts Bay, nor to a Governor or Lieutenant Governor, who will not observe the Directions of, but endeavour to subvert that Charter; the Governor and Lieutenant Governor of that Colony are to be considered as Absent, and their offices vacant; and as there is no Council there, and Inconveniences arising from the Suspension of the Powers of Government are intollerable, especially at a Time when Gage hath actually levied War and is carrying on Hostilities against his Majesties peaceable and loyal Subjects of that Colony; that in order to conform as near as may be to the Spirit and substance of the Charter, it be recommended to the Provincial Convention to write Letters: to the Inhabitants of the several Places which are intituled to Representation in Assembly requesting them to chuse such Representatives, and that the Assembly, when chosen, do elect Councillors; and that such Assembly and Council exercise the Powers of Government, untill a Governor of his Majestys Appointment will consent to govern the Colony, according to its Charter." [8]

In Pursuance of which Advice, the good People of this ⟨*Province*⟩ [9] Colony have chosen a full and free Representation of themselves, who, being convened in Assembly have elected a Council, who, ⟨*have assumed*⟩ as the executive Branch of Government have constituted necessary officers ⟨*civil and Military*⟩ [10] through the Colony. The present Generation, therefore, may be congratulated on the Acquisition of a Form of Government, more immediately in all its Branches under the Influence and Controul of the People, and therefore more free and happy than was ⟨*ever*⟩ [11] enjoyed by their Ancestors. But as a Government so popular can be Supported only by universal Knowledge and Virtue, in the Body of the People, it is the Duty of all Ranks, to promote the Means of Education, for the rising Generation as well as true Religion, Purity of Manners, and Integrity of Life among all orders and Degrees.

As an Army has become necessary for our Defence, and in all free States the civil must provide for and controul the military Power, the Major Part of the Council have appointed Magistrates and Courts of Justice in every County, ⟨*and this Court, giving others*⟩ whose Happiness is so connected with that of the People that it is difficult to suppose they can abuse their Trust. The Business of it is to see those Laws inforced which are necessary for the Preservation of Peace, Virtue and [good Order.] And the great and general Court expects and requires that all necessary Support and Assistance be given, and all proper Obedience yielded to them, and will deem every Person, who shall fail of his Duty in this Respect towards them ⟨*an Enemy to the Country*⟩ a disturber of the peace of this Colony and deserving of ⟨*strict and impartial*⟩ exemplary Punishment.

That Piety and Virtue, which alone can Secure the Freedom of any People may be encouraged and Vice and Immorality suppress'd, the great and general Court have thought fit to issue this Proclamation, commending and enjoining it upon the good People of this Colony, that they lead sober, religious and peaceable Lives, avoiding all Blasphemies, Contempt of the holy Scriptures and of the Lords Day and all other Crimes and Misdemeanors, all Debauchery, Prophaneness, Corruption Venality all riotous and tumultuous Proceedings and all Immoralities whatever: and that they decently and reverently attend the public Worship of God at all Times acknowledging with [Gratitude his merciful Interposition in their Behalf, devoutly confiding in Him, as the God of Armies, by whose Favour and Protection alone they may hope for Success, in their present Conflict.

And all Judges, Justices, Sheriffs, Grand Jurors, Tythingmen, and all other] civil Officers, within this Colony, are hereby Strictly enjoined and commanded that they contribute all in their Power, by their Advice, Exertions, and Example towards a general Reformation of Manners, and that they bring to condign Punishment, every Person, who shall commit any of the Crimes or Misdemeanors aforesaid, or that shall be guilty of any Immoralities whatsoever; and that they Use their Utmost Endeavours, to have the Resolves of the Congress, and the good and wholesome Laws of this Colony duely carried into Execution.

And as the Ministers of the Gospel, within this Colony, have during the late Relaxation of the Powers of civil Government, exerted themselves for our Safety, it is hereby recommended to them, still to continue their virtuous Labours for the good of the People, inculcating by their Public Ministry and private Example, the Necessity of Religion, Morality, and good order.

In Council January 19th. 1776

Ordered that the foregoing Proclamation be Read at the opening of Every Superior Court of Judicature &c. and Inferiour Courts of Common Pleas and Courts of General sessions for the Peace within this Colony by their Respective Clerks and at the Annual Town meetings in March in Each Town and it is hereby Recommended to the several Ministers of the Gospel throughout this Colony to Read the Same in their Respective Assemblys on the Lords Day next after their Receiving it immediately after Divine Service.

Sent down for Concurrence,[12]   Perez Morton Dpy Secry
Consented to
  W Sever
  Walter Spooner   Cha. Chauncy
  Caleb Cushing   J. Palmer
  John Winthrop
  [rest of names missing]

MS in JA's hand (M–Ar:138, p. 281–284). A number of passages have been crossed out and substitutions interlined, all in JA's hand. The bottom of one page, containing about four lines, is missing, and in two or three other places the MS is worn from creasing. Missing and illegible words are supplied in brackets from the printed text in Mass., *House Jour.*, 1775-1776, 3d sess., p. 189-192, which exactly follows the MS as corrected by JA.

[1] Initiated by the House on 18 Dec. 1775, this proclamation was intended "to be read at the opening of the several County Sessions, for the Purpose of inculcating a general Obedience of the People to the several Magistrates appointed under the present Government of this Colony." For the purpose of preparing a draft as part of a joint committee, James Sullivan, Samuel Phillips Jr., and Maj. Benjamin Ely were named by the House, William Sever and John Winthrop by the Council. Probably because of his position as Chief Justice, JA was chosen on 28 Dec. to take the place of Sever (*House Jour.*, p. 55; Records of the States, Microfilm, Mass. A.1a, Reel No. 12, Unit 1, p. 405).

The reason for proposing such a proclamation may have been the meeting of two Berkshire co. conventions in Stockbridge on 14 and 15 Dec., which showed that the members of that county's Committee of Correspondence were badly divided over whether to accept judicial officers appointed by the Council. A majority insisted that such officials should be nominated by the people for the Council's consideration, and they declared that they would not recommend that the people support the existing form of government. A counter-convention of the minority drafted resolutions condemning the stand of the majority (Robert J. Taylor, ed., *Massachusetts, Colony to Commonwealth*, Chapel Hill, 1961, p. 14, 16–17).

In seeking support for the appointees of the Council through a proclamation,

JA picked his words with great care and stated his argument in the broadest terms. His first eight paragraphs read more like a preamble to a declaration of independence than a plea for acceptance of appointed magistrates. He even notes that Massachusetts took the milder course of a temporary suspension of government rather than "instant Recourse to Arms"; in short, that as the Declaration of Independence would later argue, the people chose to suffer as long as evils could be borne rather than abolish the forms of government to which they were accustomed.

The tone of this introduction is quite out of keeping with congressional advice to Massachusetts that it operate as usual, with the office of governor vacant, until a royally appointed governor was willing to abide by the charter. That charter with its provision for royal disallowance did not vest sovereignty in the people. The wholly new government of its own creation that the congress had denied to Massachusetts, JA was here claiming in uncompromising tones despite his quotation of congressional advice. Over two months before, JA had sketched out for Richard Henry Lee some of the specifics he thought essential in any independent government (JA to Lee, 15 Nov. 1775, above); he was now helping to ready the minds of the people for that essential step. Yet JA carefully pointed out that, however free the forms of government might be, freedom depended upon piety, virtue, and knowledge—a theme that he was to sound again and again in his writings. It therefore behooved the people to worship God, eschew immorality, and obey the law as interpreted by Council appointees, who had been named through the system advised by the congress.

[2] This proposition was a favorite of those insisting that uncontrollable power lay with Parliament; JA gives it a different twist.

[3] JA's deletion suggests that he did not want to leave the *care* of powers solely to magistrates, even in trust.

[4] The phrase rejected here is used below, but there JA makes it plain that open war was begun against the colonies and brought forth a manly resistance.

[5] JA's second thought that the number of years should remain indeterminate was perhaps influenced by the debates in the First Continental Congress over whether to list grievances extending back beyond 1764.

[6] The passage "to submit: . . . Example" shows several words erased, two deletions, and three substitutions, all for merely stylistic reasons.

[7] On second thought, JA did not want to deny the legitimacy of the provincial congresses or the governments in the towns.

[8] JCC, 2:83–84.

[9] With the royal governor rejected and not likely to be reinstated, the less technical term was preferable, especially to one who did not want the royal

governor re-established. It has been suggested that "colony" still permitted those who could not accept separation to see some sort of dependence on Great Britain (Mass. *Province Laws*, 5:506). JA was careful not to alienate such people.

[10] The two deletions in this "who" clause show JA treading cautiously around a thorny issue. To say the Council *assumed* executive power implied what some House members had argued, that the Council arrogated powers to itself. The issue had become acute in the quarreling over whether the Council had exclusive power to name military officers. It was better just not to mention "military." JA himself believed that it was right for both houses jointly to choose military officers (JA to James Otis, 23 Nov., and to Joseph Hawley, 25 Nov. 1775, both above).

[11] "Ever" raised awkward questions. Massachusetts liked to believe that its first charter had given it virtually self-governing powers, and JA had argued in the Novanglus letters that the original compact with the king still held (JA, *Papers*, 1:xxv–xxxi).

[12] The proclamation was approved by the House on 23 Jan. and was printed in the *Boston Gazette* on 12 Feb. 1776 (Mass., *House Jour.*, p. 192). It was also issued as a broadside (Ford, *Mass. Broadsides*, No. 1973, with facsimile facing p. 272).

Samuel Hopkins to Thomas Cushing

Much honored Sir[1]   Newport, 29 Dec. 1775

The degree of acquaintance I have with you, through your indulgence; and your known candour, condescention and goodness, encourage me to address you on an affair, which, in my view, is very interesting, and calls for the particular attention of the honorable members of the Continental Congress.

They have indeed manifested much wisdom and benevolence in advising to a total stop of the slave trade, and leading the united American Colonies to resolve not to buy any more slaves, imported from Africa.[2] This has rejoiced the hearts of many benevolent, pious persons, who have been long convinced of the unrighteousness and cruelty of that trade, by which so many Hundreds of thousands are enslaved. And have we not reason to think this has been one means of obtaining the remarkable, and almost miraculous protection and success, which heaven has hitherto granted to the united Colonies, in their opposition to unrighteousness and tyranny, and struggle for *liberty*?

But if the slave trade be altogether unjust, is it not equally unjust to hold those in slavery, who by this trade have been reduced to this unhappy state? Have they not a right to their liberty, which has been thus violently, and altogether without right, taken from them? Have they not reason to complain of any one who withholds it from them? Do not the cries of these oppressed poor reach to the heavens? Will not God require it at the hands of those who refuse to let them go out free? If practising or promoting the slave trade be inconsistent with what takes place among us, in our struggle for liberty, is not retaining the slaves in bondage, whom by this trade we have in our power, equally inconsistent? And is there not, consequently, an inconsistence in resolving against the former, and yet continuing the latter?

And if the righteous and infinitely good Governor of the world, has given testimony of his approbation of our resolving to put a stop to the slave trade, by doing such wonders in our favor; have we not reason to fear he will take his protection from us, and give us up to the power of oppression and tyranny, when he sees we stop short of what might be reasonably expected; and continue the practice of that which we ourselves have, implicitly at least, condemned, by refusing to let the oppressed go free, and *to break every yoke*?

Does not the conduct of Lord Dunmore, and the ministerialists, in taking the advantage of the slavery practised among us, and encouraging all slaves to join them, by promising them liberty, point out the best, if not the only way to defeat them in this, viz. granting freedom to them ourselves, so as no longer to use our neighbour's service without wages, but give them for their labours what is equal and just?

And suffer me further to query, Whether something might not be done to send the light of the gospel to these nations in Africa, who have been injured so much by the slave trade? Would not this have a most direct tendency to put a stop to that unrighteousness; and be the best compensation we can make them? At the same time it will be an attempt to promote the most important interest, the *kingdom of Christ*, in obedience to his command, 'Go, teach all nations.'

A proposal of this kind has been entered upon, of which the enclosed[3] will give you some of the particulars. The blacks there mentioned are now with me, and have had the approbation of Dr. Witherspoon,[4] with whom they spent the last winter. They continue disposed to prosecute the design; and would be sent to Guinea in the spring, if any way for their being transported there should open, and money could be collected, sufficient to bear the expence. The proposal has met with good encouragement in England and Scotland, and more than £30 sterl. has been sent from thence; and we had reason to expect more: But all communication of this kind is now stopped. Application would be made to the honorable Continental Congress, for their encouragement and patronage of this design, if there were no impropriety in it, and it should be thought it would be well received. And I take leave, kind sir, to ask your opinion and advise in this matter; and desire you to signify it to me in a line by the bearer, Mr. Anthony, if not inconsistent with the many important affairs, which demand your attention. I am, honorable Sir, with much respect and esteem, Your very humble servant,   Samuel Hopkins[5]

RC (Adams Papers); addressed: "The Honorable Thomas Cushing, Member of the Honorable Continental Congress, Philadelphia. Favored by Mr. Anthony"; docketed in an unidentified hand: "T Cushing at"; in another hand: "29 Dec. 1775."

[1] Cushing probably passed this letter to other members of the Massachusetts delegation, and it wound up in JA's possession. Since up to this period there is very little in the record suggesting JA's attitude toward slavery, his preserving Hopkins' letter perhaps suggests no more than that he recognized it as important for the awkward question it raised about Americans' inconsistency in their treatment of blacks. AA, incidentally, had already declared that slavery had "allwavs appeard a most iniquitious Scheme" to her (*Adams Family Correspondence*, 1:162).

[2] As part of the Continental Association, which forbade the importing of slaves after 1 Dec. 1774 and the purchase of any so imported.

[3] Not found, but it may have been Samuel Hopkins and Ezra Stiles, *To the Public. There Has Been a Design Formed . . . to Send the Gospel to Guinea*, [1773] (repr., 1776, Evans, No. 14803).

[4] Rev. John Witherspoon (1723–1794), president of the College of New Jersey (now Princeton), leader among American Presbyterians, and signer of the Declaration of Independence (*DAB*).

Bristol Yamma and John Quamine, two free Negroes, had been sent to the College by the Missionary Society of Newport to be trained for missionary work in Africa (Varnum Lansing Collins, *President Witherspoon, A Biography*, 2 vols., Princeton, 1925, 2:217).

[5] Rev. Samuel Hopkins (1721–1803) went from Great Barrington to Newport in 1769, where he soon became active in opposition to the slave trade and slave holding. His views arose chiefly out of his Christian belief that slavery was against the law of God and had to be extirpated, as men had to strive to eliminate all forms of sin. Scholars disagree about whether he thought blacks were the equals of whites, but in any case, he did not expect the two races to live in harmony and was, therefore, an early advocate of colonization of former slaves in Africa (David S. Lovejoy, "Samuel Hopkins: Religion, Slavery, and the Revolution," *NEQ*, 40:227–243 [June 1967]; Stanley K. Schultz, "The Making of a Reformer: the Reverend Samuel Hopkins as an Eighteenth-Century Abolitionist," Amer. Phil. Soc., *Procs.*, 115:350–365 [Oct. 1971]).

Robert Treat Paine to Joseph Palmer

My Dear Friend   Philadelphia Jan 1st 1776

I arrived here the 28th ultimo from my journey as far as Ticonderoga, we proceeded no farther as we had some expectations when we sat out, partly because the season was too late to pass safely by water and too early to pass on the ice; and also because the object of our commission of most immediate importance could be determined at Ticonderoga—but a very great reason was because the Military situation of Canada would not admit of our receiving that assistance from Genl. Montgomery which was necessary to promote the chief purpose of our going there.[1]

At Albany we attended a treaty with the Six Nations and it appeared to be very serviceable to the cause that a Committee from the Grand Council Fire at Philadelphia attended it. The Indians were much elated and behaved with every mark of friendship; their speech contains matters of importance and I suppose will be published as soon as the report arrives from Albany to the Congress.[2]

You write in low spirits about salt petre making among you, but as your letter is of old date[3] I hope your spirits have been since raised by the production of considerable quantities in divers places, we are informed here that you have got into the right method and that you make considerable quantities. Pray use your influence to have people in different parts set up small works. This will spread and increase it and the Works will always be enlarged in proportion to the success. They make it at this time here in the city works from earth taken from the bottoms of Cellars where wood and vegetables have lain and they have good success. It is spreading also in the family way —I intended to enlarge on this subject but have not been here long enough to digest matter.

At present my mind is much agitated on the discovery of a malicious and slanderous correspondence between James Warren and John Adams respecting Mr. Cushing and myself[4] and on comparing what is written with the behaviour of some of my brother delegates it appears to me that while I have been exerting myself to the utmost in supporting the common defence of all that is valuable and by that means exposing myself to the vengeance of administration if I should fall into their hands some particular persons whom I considered as struggling with and supporting me in the same cause to my astonishment are undermining my importance happiness, and safety, so that not only if our common enemy conquers we shall be made miserable but

391

if our struggles are crowned with success I am then to be crushed and rendered unhappy by the very men, I have been endeavoring to support at the risk of every thing that is valuable. I have received a notification[5] of my appointment as one of the judges of the Supreme Court and a list of the whole set with the rank, of which the Hon. John Adams is chief Justice. By this opportunity I have sent my answer in the negative and have assigned one reason which I think of itself sufficient. I have had but little time to consider the matter and could have wished to know how the other gentlemen like their rank and wether they have accepted; I am far from thinking that the honorable board had the least intention of disparaging the merit of any gentleman but when we consider that the proposed chief Justice ranks the last but one in age and as a lawyer at the bar it looks to me as if some imperceptible influence had regulated the appointment of a chief justice upon political or other principles than what are usual in such cases; if I was not worthy of such a trust (as my former friend Col. Warren, suggests) why was I appointed; and if I am defective either in law, knowledge, integrity or political rectitude it certainly was wrong to appoint me; but if supposed sufficiently qualified in these respects, why am I degraded? I mourn the appearance of these and some other matters that are coming to light. I fear they spring from a fountain that will embitter the administration of our public affairs. Excuse my writing thus freely to you but it is to no purpose to disguise some sorts of uneasiness; if a junto of two three or four men are able to combine together, settle a test of political rectitude and destroy every one who will not comply with their mode of conduct, ⟨*if vanity arrogance and violance are primary qualities in a free state*⟩ I must confess things are like to take a turn very different from what I expected.

Inclosed is the extract but I have not time to explain the manner in which it came to light, but I have wrote it to Maj. Hawley who will explain the matter to you. I have no desire to incense you against particular persons, but if you think such conduct is wrong you will behave accordingly and give me that support you may think I deserve. Wishing the promotion of our common happiness and a deliverance from the perils of public enemies and also false brethren—I am with great esteem Your friend & humble svt   (Signed) R T Paine

Tr in an unknown hand (Adams Papers); Dft (MHi:Robert Treat Paine Papers). This letter was probably given to JA to keep him informed of the quarrel that had developed between Paine and James Warren.

[1] See James Warren to JA, 3 Dec. 1775, note 11 (above).

[2] The report on the conference with the Indians has not been found. In Schuyler's letter to the congress of 21 Dec. 1775 the general notes that the

"proceedings will be transmitted . . . in a few days" (Force, *Archives*, 4th ser., 4:375). But see S. Adams to JA, 22 Dec. 1775, note 3 (above).

[3] Joseph Palmer to Paine, 1 Nov. 1775 (MHi:Robert Treat Paine Papers).

[4] See James Warren to JA, 3 Dec. 1775, note 8 (above).

[5] Perez Morton to Paine, 28 Oct. 1775 (MHi:Robert Treat Paine Papers).

From Josiah Quincy

Sir   Braintree Jany 2d: 1776

A number of my Neighbours who are present, and in the Names of the rest who are absent, desire me to acquaint you, that, not withstanding Genl. Ward's Request, that the Companies stationed for the Protection of Squantum would tarry there till further Orders, they are all gone, and that important Place, and the valuable Farms in the Vicinity of it, are left exposed to the Ravages of the Enemy,[1] who must be under the strongest Temptation that the want of fresh Provision can create, to run every Hazard to supply themselves.

In short, such is our Apprehension of Danger, that some are moving their Families and Effects, and unless we are immediately relieved, we are in the utmost Hazard of losing our all. We, therefore, earnestly beg, that you would be so good (in Conjunction with Colo. Palmer and Colo. Thayer)[2] as to represent our deplorable Circumstances to his Excellency Genl. Washington, who we understand, has taken Squantum Neck under his immediate Protection; and will, doubtless, upon your *joint* Application send, a Force sufficient, and without Delay, to defend and effectually secure us. I am, Sir, in the Name of my destressed Neighbours Your most obedient and faithfull Servant,

Josa: Quincy

RC (Adams Papers); addressed: "To the honble John Adams Esquire   at Watertown"; docketed: "Coll Quincy   Jany. 2d. 1776."

[1] Four companies stationed at Braintree, Weymouth, and Hingham, although told to remain at their posts by the General Court on 30 Dec. 1775, had apparently deserted them. That those troops were outside the area Washington considered vital to the general defense and the maintenance of the siege had been reported to the legislature on 21 Dec. Further, Washington stated on 29 Dec. that he could not extend the guards under his command past Squantum and Chelsea (Mass., *House Jour.*, 1775–1776, 3d sess., p. 94, 63, 95; Washington, *Writings*, ed. Fitzpatrick, 4:192–193). Squantum was a neck of land at the mouth of the Neponset River. The General's decision meant that if the four companies were to remain, they would have to be put into the seacoast establishment then being created by the General Court, which, though the companies were deemed essential, did not include them because they were assumed to be part of the Continental establishment, paid for by the congress. Indeed, the question of finance lay at the bottom of the whole matter (*House Jour.*, p. 73, 77–79, 87–91, 94; *Writings*, 4:192–193, 195). Nothing indicates that this letter or representations made by JA or others had any effect on Washington, for on 30 Jan. in a letter to the President of

the congress, he was still holding firmly to his position (*Writings*, 4:289; see also S. Adams to JA, 15 Jan., below).

[2] After Joseph Palmer, originally elected to the House from Braintree, was elected to the Council at the opening of the General Court, Braintree replaced him with Ebenezer Thayer on 14 Aug. 1775 (*House Jour.*, 1st sess., p. 3, 6; *Braintree Town Records*, p. 463).

To William Cooper

Dear Sir   Watertown, Jany. 4. 1776

As some worthy Members of the Honourable House of Representatives may possibly be desirous of knowing the Cause of my return at this Time, I must beg you to inform them, that judging this the most favourable Opportunity which would probably present, I asked and obtain Leave of the honourable continental Congress to come home, on a visit to my Family, whose Distresses and Afflictions in my Absence[1] seemed to render it necessary that I should return to them for some short Time at least.

I have no particular Intelligence to communicate from the Honourable Congress, more than has come to the Knowledge of the Public, heretofore, only I beg Leave to say that as much Harmony and Zeal is still prevailing in that honourable Assembly as ever appeared at any Time, and that their Unanimity and Firmness increase.

I hope the Honourable House will soon receive authentic Intelligence of a considerable naval Force ordered by the Congress to be prepared, as I am well informed they have resolved to build Thirteen ships, five of Thirty two Guns, five of Twenty eight and three of Twenty four,[2] which together with those fitted out before, by the Continent, and by particular Colonies as well as private Persons, it is hoped will be a security, in Time to come, against the Depredations of Cutters and Tenders at least, if not against single ships of War.

I must beg the Favour of you, sir, to communicate the substance of this Letter, to the Members of the Honourable House in such a Way as you shall think fit. I have the Honour to be with great Respect to the Honourable House, sir, your most obedient sert.

John Adams

Tr in the hand of W. C. Ford (MHi:W. C. Ford Papers). In the upper-left-hand corner of the first page of this Tr, marked for printing, is a faint notation "MHS Misc." An old catalogue entry for this letter has been found, but the original is not in Misc. MSS. Although the nature or provenance of Ford's source is unknown, the letter's authenticity is not in doubt, for JA was in attendance at the Council in Watertown on this date, and he refers to information in a letter received from Samuel Adams.

January 1776

¹ AA was still mourning the death of her mother and had suffered some from illness, but JA was probably most influenced by his desire to turn his burden over to others and to be with his wife (*Adams Family Correspondence*, 1:325, 327, 331–332). Why he waited a week before explaining his presence to the House remains undetermined.
² See S. Adams to JA, 22 Dec. 1775, note 1 (above).

To George Washington

Dr Sir   Watertown Jan. 6. 1776

As your Excellency has asked my Opinion of General Lees Plan, as explained in his Letter of the fifth instant,¹ I think it my Duty to give it, although I am obliged to do it in more Haste than I could wish.

I Suppose the only Questions which arise upon that Letter are whether the Plan is practicable; whether it is expedient; and whether it lies properly within your Excellencys Authority, without further Directions from Congress.

Of the Practicability of it, I am very ill qualified to judge; But were I to hazard a conjecture, it would be that the Enterprise would not be attended with much Difficulty. The Connecticutt People who are very ready upon such occasion in Conjunction with the Friends of Liberty in New York I should think might easily accomplish the Work.

That it is expedient, and even necessary to be done, by Some Authority or other, I believe will not be doubted by any Friend of the American Cause, who considers the vast Importance of that City, Province, and the North River which is in it, in the Progress of this War, as it is the Nexus of the Northern and Southern Colonies, as a Kind of Key to the whole Continent, as it is a Passage to Canada to the Great Lakes and to all the Indians Nations. No Effort to secure it ought to be omitted.²

That it is within the Limits of your Excellencys Command, is in my Mind, perfectly clear. Your Commission constitutes you Commander "of all the Forces now raised or to be raised, and of all others, who shall voluntarily offer their Service, and join the Army for the defence of American Liberty, and for repelling every hostile Invasion thereof: and are vested with full Power and Authority to act as you shall think for the good and well fare of the service."³

Now if upon Long Island, there is a Body of People, who have Arms in their Hands, and are intrenching themselves, professedly to oppose the American system of Defence; who are supplying our Enemies both of the Army and Navy, in Boston and elsewhere, as I suppose is undoubtedly the Fact, no Man can hesitate to say that this is an hostile

395

Invasion of American Liberty, as much as that now made in Boston, nay those People are guilty of the very Invasion in Boston, as they are constantly aiding, abetting, comforting and assisting the Army there; and that in the most essential Manner by supplies of Provisions. If in the City a Body of Tories are waiting only for a Force to protect them, to declare themselves on the side of our Enemies, it is high Time that City was secured. The Jersey Troops have already been ordered into that City by the Congress, and are there undoubtedly under your Command ready to assist in this service.

That N. York is within your Command as much as Massachusetts cannot bear a Question. Your Excellencys Superiority in the Command, over the Generals, in the Northern Department as it is called has been always carefully preserved in Congress, altho the Necessity of Dispatch has sometimes induced them to send Instructions directly to them, instead of first sending them to your Excellency, which would have occasioned a Circuit of many hundreds of Miles, and have lost much Time.

Upon the whole sir, my opinion is that General Lee's is a very useful Proposal, and will answer many good Ends. I am with great Respect, your Excellencys most obedient humble Servant

John Adams

RC (DLC:Washington Papers); docketed: "From Honble. John Adams Jany. 6. 1776." Dft on second and third pages of Samuel Chase to JA, 8 Dec. 1775 (above).

[1] Gen. Charles Lee proposed to secure New York against British attack and to suppress or expel the tories on Long Island, using Connecticut volunteers together with whatever men he could raise in New York and New Jersey (NYHS, *Colls., Lee Papers*, 1:234–236). The plan had particular urgency, for a force under Gen. Clinton was preparing to leave Boston, reportedly for Long Island, but in fact, for the Carolinas. On 8 Jan., Washington, taking JA's advice, ordered Lee to proceed with his plan. On the day before, Washington had written to Gov. Trumbull of Connecticut asking his cooperation (*Writings*, ed. Fitzpatrick, 4:221–223, 217–219).

Lee set out immediately but, plagued by bad weather and gout, he did not reach New York with the troops recruited in Connecticut until 4 Feb. The delay was beneficial, since it allowed time for a committee from the congress to arrive, giving Lee's presence legitimacy and quieting the fears of local patriots. Carrying out Lee's plan meant taking a stronger stand than some New Yorkers thought advisable with elements of the British fleet in the harbor. Lee strengthened the city's defenses, ended communication with the British fleet, and subdued the tories on Long Island. The vigor with which Isaac Sears carried out the last caused local resentment and protest to the congress. Lee remained in New York only a month, not time enough to create a strong defensive position. Washington completed the work when he brought the main body of the army to New York (Alden, *General Charles Lee*, p. 95–103).

[2] The draft omits the explanation for New York's strategic importance.

[3] Closing quotation marks supplied; see Washington's commission, *JCC*, 2:96.

From George Washington

Sir   Cambridge Jany: 7: 1776

You will excuse me for reminding you of our conversation the other Evening, when I inform'd you that General Lee's departure for New York is advisable upon the Plan of his Letter, and under the circumstances I then mentioned, ought not to be delayed. In giving me your opinion of this matter I have no doubt of your taking a comprehensive view of it. That is, you will not only consider the propriety of the measure, but of the execution. Whether such a step, tho' right in itself may not be looked upon as beyond my Line &ca &ca.[1]

If it could be made convenient and agreeable to you to take Pott Luck with me today, I shall be very glad of your Company and we can then talk the matter over at large. Please to forward General Lee's Letter to me. I am &ca.,   G. Washington

Tr (DLC:Washington Papers).

[1] JA's and Washington's letters must have crossed in the mail; see JA to Washington, 6 Jan. (above).

To Mercy Otis Warren

Dear Madam   Braintree Jany. 8. 1776

Your Friend insists upon my Writing to you, and altho I am conscious it is my Duty, being deeply in Debt for a number of very agreable Favours in the Epistolary Way, yet I doubt whether a sense of this Duty would have overcome, my Inclination to Indolence and Relaxation, with which my own Fire Side always inspires me, if it had not been Stimulated and quickened by her.

I was charmed with three Characters drawn by a most masterly Pen, which I received at the southward. Copeleys[1] Pencil could not touched off, with more exquisite Finishings, the Faces of those Gentlemen. Whether I ever answered that Letter I know not.[2] But I hope Posterity will see it, if they do I am sure they will admire it. I think I will make a Bargain with you, to draw the Character of every new Personage I have an opportunity of knowing, on Condition you will do the same. My View will be to learn the Art of penetrating into Mens Bosoms, and then the more difficult Art of painting what I shall see there. You Ladies are the most infallible judges of Characters, I think.

Pray Madam, are you for an American Monarchy or Republic? Monarchy is the genteelest and most fashionable Government, and I dont know why the Ladies ought not to consult Elegance and the Fashion as well in Government as Gowns, Bureaus or Chariots.

For my own Part, I am so tasteless as to prefer a Republic, if We must erect an independent Government in America, which you know is utterly against my Inclination. But a Republic, altho it will infallibly beggar me and my Children, will produce Strength, Hardiness Activity Courage Fortitude and Enterprice; the manly, noble and Sublime Qualities in human Nature, in Abundance.

A Monarchy would probably, somehow or other make me rich, but it would produce So much Taste and Politeness, So much Elegance in Dress, Furniture, Equipage, So much Musick and Dancing, So much Fencing and Skaiting; So much Cards and Backgammon; so much Horse Racing and Cock fighting; so many Balls and Assemblies, so many Plays and Concerts that the very Imagination of them makes me feel vain, light, frivolous and insignificant.

It is the Form of Government, which gives the decisive Colour to the Manners of the People, more than any other Thing. Under a well regulated Commonwealth, the People must be wise virtuous and cannot be otherwise. Under a Monarchy they may be as vicious and foolish as they please, nay they cannot but be vicious and foolish. As Politicks therefore is the Science of human Happiness, and human Happiness is clearly best promoted by Virtue, what thorough Politician can hesitate, who has a new Government to build whether to prefer a Commonwealth or a Monarchy? But Madam there is one Difficulty, which I know not how to get over.

Virtue and Simplicity of Manners, are indispensably necessary in a Republic, among all orders and Degrees of Men. But there is So much Rascallity, so much Venality and Corruption, so much Avarice and Ambition, such a Rage for Profit and Commerce among all Ranks and Degrees of Men even in America, that I sometimes doubt whether there is public Virtue enough to support a Republic. There are two Vices most detestably predominant in every Part of America that I have yet seen, which are as incompatible with the Spirit of a Commonwealth as Light is with Darkness, I mean Servility and Flattery. A genuine Republican can no more fawn and cringe than he can domineer. Shew me the American who can not do all. I know two or Three I think, and very few more.

However, it is the Part of a great Politician to make the Character of his People; to extinguish among them, the Follies and Vices that he sees, and to create in them the Virtues and Abilities which he sees wanting. I wish I was sure that America has one such Politician, but I fear she has not.

[...] Letter begun in Gaiety, is likely to have [... conc]lusion while

I was writing the last Word [. . .] Paragraph; my Attention was called off [. . .] and most melodious sounds my Ears [. . . Can]non Mortars and Musquettes.

A very hot Fire both of Artillery and small Arms has continued for half an Hour, and has been succeded by a luminous Phoenomenon, over Braintree North Common occasioned by Burning Buildings I suppose.[3]

Whether our People have attacked or defended, been victorious or vanquished, is to me totally uncertain. But in Either Case I rejoice, for a Defeat appears to me preferable to total Inaction.

May the Supreme Ruler of Events, overrule in our Favour! But if the Event of this Evening is unfortunated I think We ought at all Hazards, and at any Loss to retrieve it tomorrow. I hope the Militia will be ready and our Honour be retrieved by making Boston our own. I shall be in suspense this Night, but very willing to take my Place with my Neighbours tomorrow, and crush the Power of the Enemies or suffer under it.

I hope Coll. Warren sleeps at Cushings[4] this night and that I shall see him in the Morning. Mean Time I think I shall sleep as soundly as ever. I am, Madam, your most humble servant, and sincere Friend,

[John Adams]

Mrs. Adams desires to be remembered to Mrs. Warren.

RC (MHi:Warren-Adams Coll.); docketed: "J Adams Esqr Jany 8th 1776"; in another hand: "Braintree." The signature has been cut from page four, mutilating several lines on page three.

[1] John Singleton Copley (1738–1815) had left Boston in June 1774 to take up residence in England and resume his painting there (*DAB*). JA saw some of Copley's paintings in 1769 (*Diary and Autobiography*, 1:340).

[2] Mercy Warren to JA, Oct. 1775 (above). JA wrote, but did not send, a reply on 25 Nov. (above), and even this letter of 8 Jan. was delayed, for Mrs. Warren did not report receiving it until Feb. 1776 (Mercy Otis Warren to AA, 7 Feb., *Adams Family Correspondence*, 1:343–345).

[3] Maj. Thomas Knowlton was leading a raid against the few houses that had survived the burning of Charlestown during the Battle of Bunker Hill. After capturing six men and a woman and destroying the houses to prevent the British from using them as firewood, Knowlton's force escaped without casualties despite heavy British fire (Washington, *Writings*, ed. Fitzpatrick, 4:223–224; *Boston Gazette*, 15 Jan.; see also a letter to a Gentleman at Philadelphia, 9 Jan., Force, *Archives*, 4th ser., 4:612–613). In reporting the event on 11 Jan., the *Massachusetts Gazette* minimized its importance, lamenting only that the performance of *The Busybody*, then being presented at Faneuil Hall, had been interrupted.

[4] Probably the home of William Cushing in Scituate, on the road from Plymouth to Braintree (Sibley-Shipton, *Harvard Graduates*, 13:28).

From Samuel Chase

My Dear Sir   Annapolis Jany. 12th. 1775 [i.c. 1776]

The Business of our provincial Convention draws to a Conclusion, and the Session will end in a few Days. I have Leave to visit my Family before I sett off for the Congress, and I expect to take You by the Hand before 1st. of Febry. I cannot omit in the mean Time to express to You my opinion on the present State of our public Affaires, and the Measures I would wish to be adopted.

The early attention and great Dependance of the Ministry on Canada evince the infinite Importance of that Country in the present Dispute, to obtain the Possession of that province is an object of the first Consequence. We must at all Events procure and keep Possession of that province. Quebec must at every Hazard be ours. No Succours can arrive there before 1st. May. I would have a chosen Committee go to Canada as soon as the Lakes are frozen hard enough, let them call a Convention, explain the Views and Designs of Congress, and persuade them to send Delegates there. Let a Body of 6,000 Canadians and 2000 Colonists be embodyed for the Defence of that province. I think the Success of the War will, in great Measure, depend on securing Canada to our Confederation. I would earnestly recommend Charles Carroll, Esqr. of Carrollton, of this province to be one of your Deputies to Canada. His Attachment and zeal to the Cause, his abilities, his Acquaintance with the Language, Manners and Customs of France and his Religion, with the Circumstance of a very great Estate, all point him out to that all important Service. My Inclination to serve my Country would induce Me to offer my Services, if I did not esteem Myself unable to discharge the Trust.[1]

I would have an Army in the Massachusetts encreased to 30,000. I would [have] 10,000 stationed in New York, and every proper place on Hudsons River strongly secured by Batteries of heavy Cannon and obstructions in the River. A Body of 3000 should be stationed in the middle Colonies. I would exert every Nerve to fitt out a Number of vessells from 10 to 30 Guns. I would cruise for the India and Jamaica Men. I would make prizes of every british Vessell whenever found. I would if possible destroy the army at Boston, tho the Consequence should be certain Destruction to the Town. The Colonies should either bear the Loss, or tax the Damages in the Bill of Costs. I would from Canada, if practicable destroy the Fur Trade on Hudson's Bay. In short I would adopt every Scheme to reduce G. B. to our Terms. Whether to open or to continue our Ports shut, I am undetermined.

To starve the West Indies, and to ruin the Sugar trade ought not to be easily given up.

I have this Moment seen the Kings Speech.[2] I am not disappointed. Just as I expected.

I shall always be glad to hear from You, direct to Me in Fredk. Coty.[3]

Make Me remembered to your worthy Colleagues. Your Affectionate and Obedt Servant,

Saml. Chase

RC (Adams Papers); a rectangular piece has been cut from the folded sheet in the lower left corner so that on the last page only an "S" remains for what was probably a docket entry: "S[amuel Chase]."

[1] Chase, Benjamin Franklin, and Charles Carroll made up the committee that the congress sent to Canada in early 1776, which failed to win strong Canadian support for the American cause (JCC, 4:151–152). JA's endorsement of the choice of committee members was enthusiastic (JA to James Warren, 18 Feb., below).

[2] That of 26 Oct. 1775, in which George III in opening Parliament referred to conspirators who "meant only to amuse, by vague expressions of attachment to the parent state, and the strongest protestations of loyalty to me." Their object was "an independent empire" (*Parliamentary Hist.*, 18:695–697).

[3] Frederick co., Maryland.

From Samuel Adams

My dear sir   Philada Jany 15 1776

Altho I have at present but little Leisure, I cannot omit writing you a few Lines by this Express.

I have seen certain Instructions which were given by the Capital of the Colony of New Hampshire to its Delegates in their provincial Convention, the Spirit of which I am not altogether pleased with.[1] There is one part of them at least, which I think discovers a Timidity which is unbecoming a People oppressed and insulted as they are, and who at their own Request have been advisd and authorizd by Congress, to set up and exercise Government in such form as they should judge most conducive to their own Happiness. It is easy to understand what they mean when they speak of "perfecting a form of Govt. *stable* and *permanent*." They indeed explain themselves by saying that they *"should prefer the Govt. of Congress* (their provincial Convention) till quieter times." The Reason they assign for it, I fear, will be considered as showing a Readiness to condescend to the Humours of their Enemies, and their publickly expressly and totally disavowing Independency either on the Nation or *the Man* who insolently and perseveringly demands the Surrender of their Liberties with the Bayonet pointed at their Breasts may be construed to argue a Servility and Baseness of soul for which Language doth not afford an Epethet. It is by indiscrete Resolutions and Publications that the Friends of America have too often given occasion to their Enemies to injure her Cause. I hope however that the Town of Portsmouth doth not in this Instance speak the Sense of that Colony. I wish, if it be not too late, that you would write your Sentiments of the Subject to our worthy Friend Mr. L—[2] who I suppose is now in Portsmouth. If that Colony should take a wrong Step, I fear it would wholly defeat a Design which I confess I have much at heart.[3]

A Motion was made in Congress the other Day to the following purpose, that whereas we had been charged with aiming at Independency, a Committee should be appointed to explain to the People at large the Principles and Grounds of our Opposition &c.[4] The Motion alarmd me. I thought Congress had already been explicit enough, and was apprehensive that we might get ourselves upon dangerous Ground. Some of us prevailed so far as to have the Matter postponed but could not prevent the assigning a Day to consider it. I may perhaps have been wrong in opposing this Motion, and I ought the rather to suspect it, because the Majority of your Colony as well as of the Congress were of a different opinion.

I had lately some free Conversation with an eminent Gentleman[5] whom you well know, and whom your Portia, in one of her Letters, admired if I recollect right, for his *expressive Silence*, about a Confederation, A Matter which our much valued Friend Coll. W.[6] is very sollicitous to have compleated. We agreed that it must soon be brought on, and that if all the Colonies could not come into it, it had better be done by those of them that inclind to it. I told him that I would endeavor to unite the New England Colonies in confederating, if *none* of the rest would joyn in it. He approved of it, and said, if I succeeded he would cast in his Lot among us.   Adieu

                                                                    Jany 16th
As this Express did not sett off yesterday according to my Expectation, I have the opportunity of acquainting you that Congress has just receivd a Letter from General Washington inclosing the Copy of an Application of our General Assembly to him to order Payment to four Companies stationed at Braintree Weymouth and Hingham.[7] The General says they were never regimented, and he cannot comply with the Request of the Assembly without the Direction of Congress. A Committee is appointed to consider the Letter of which I am one. I fear there will be a Difficulty and therefore I shall endeavor to pre-

vent a Report on this part of the Letter, unless I shall see a prospect of Justice being done to the Colony, till I can receive from you authentick Evidence of those Companies having been actually employed by the continental officers, as I conceive they have been, in the Service of the Continent. I wish you would inform me whether the two Companies stationed at Chelsea and Maldin were paid out of the Continents Chest. I suppose they were, and if so, I cannot see Reason for any Hesitation about the payment of these. I wish also to know how many others our Colony is at the Expence of maintaining for the Defence of its Sea Coasts. Pray let me have some Intelligence from you, of the Colony which we represent. You are sensible of the Danger it has frequently been in of suffering greatly for Want of regular Information.

RC (Adams Papers); with enclosure. This letter was forwarded by James Warren (Warren to JA, 31 Jan., below).

[1] These instructions, which appeared in an enclosed clipping from a Philadelphia newspaper, and from which Samuel Adams quotes below, intended a firm stand against independence and cited the bad effect that the precipitate assumption of government by the New Hampshire Convention would have because it would allow Britain to persuade its people that independence was the American aim (*Documents & Records Relating to the Province of New Hampshire*, cd. Nathaniel Bouton, 7 vols., Nashua, N.H., 1867–1873, 7:701–702).

[2] John Langdon, delegate to the congress from New Hampshire, had obtained a leave of absence on 2 Jan. (JCC, 4:23).

[3] Presumably independent governments for other colonies, which would lead in turn to independence from Great Britain.

[4] This motion was offered by James Wilson of Pennsylvania on 9 Jan. On the 24th a committee composed of John Dickinson, Wilson, William Hooper, James Duane, and Robert Alexander was appointed to prepare an address to the American people. On 13 Feb. the address, which was in the hand of Wilson, and which, according to one observer, was "very long, badly written and full against Independency," was tabled by the congress, never to be considered again (Richard Smith's Diary, 9, 24 Jan. and 13 Feb. in Burnett, ed., *Letters of Members*, 1:304, 326, 348; JCC, 4:87, 134–146, which contains the draft of the address).

[5] Benjamin Franklin; see AA to JA, 5 Nov. 1775 (*Adams Family Correspondence*, 1:320–321).

[6] James Warren, who had called for a confederation in a letter to JA on 14 Nov. 1775 (above) and in another to Samuel Adams, which, though not found, is referred to in Samuel Adams to Warren of 7 Jan. 1776 (*Warren-Adams Letters*, 1:197–200). "W" is identified as George Wythe in JA, *Works*, 9:373 and thus by Burnett in *Letters of Members*, 1:311. This identification is mistakenly based on William Gordon's *History* (3 vols., N.Y., 1794, 2:13), in which Gordon, quoting from this letter, identifies the person with whom Adams spoke as probably a Virginia delegate. Gordon makes no reference to Franklin, the central figure in the paragraph and in the controversy over the Articles of Confederation.

[7] Washington's letter of 31 Dec. 1775 was referred to a committee consisting of Samuel Adams, George Wythe, and James Wilson (PCC, No. 152, I; JCC, 4:54; see also Josiah Quincy to JA, 2 Jan., note 1, above).

From Jason Haven

Sir   Dedham Janry 15 1776

My Freedom in troubling you upon the Affair, which is the Subject of this Epistle, may need an Apology. Your Candor and Goodness will excuse it. The Design is benevolent to the Publick, as well as to a particular Friend. I partake in the general Satisfaction of this Province, in your being appointed chief Judge of our Superior Court. I doubt not the Publick will reap great advantages from the Improvement of your Talents, in that important Station, as well as in several others. I understand it is with you, and your Brethren on the bench, to appoint the Clerks. I take the Liberty to recommend *Mr. Joshua Henshaw* Jr.[1] as a Person I think well qualified for that office. He is Son to Colo. Henshaw late a Counsellor. He now lives at Dedham, is a Man of a fair and amiable Character, of liberal Education, of good political Principles, A very good Penman. *Mr. Samuel Adams* has a particular Acquaintance with him. He is put out of Business by the Troubles of the Times. If your Clerks are not appointed, your Influence to introduce him into that Office, would be acknowledged as a singular Favor by your most obedient humble Servt.,   Jason Haven[2]

P.S. Pray make my most respectful Compliments to your Lady. I should be extremely glad to wait on you at my House. You'rs ut Supra,   JH.

RC (Adams Papers); addressed: "For The Honble. John Adams Esqr. Braintree"; docketed: "Jason Haven   Jan 15th 1776."

[1] Joshua Henshaw Jr. (1745–1823) had been in business in Boston with his father, a distiller. When the siege began, the Henshaws moved to Dedham, where they met Rev. Haven. Although this letter failed to bring Henshaw the clerk's position, he was appointed a justice of the peace on 30 Jan. Thereafter he served in a variety of positions, notably as register of deeds for Suffolk co. (Sib-ley-Shipton, *Harvard Graduates*, 15: 400–403).

[2] Rev. Jason Haven (1733–1803) served as minister in Dedham from 1756 until his death (same, 13:447–453). For the remarks of JA and AA on Haven as a minister, see *Diary and Autobiography*, 1:14–15, and *Adams Family Correspondence*, 1:263.

From George Washington

Dr Sir   Cambridge 15th. Novr. [i.e. Jan.][1] 1776

I am exceedingly sorry I did not know that you were in this place today. Our want of Men and arms is such, as to render it necessary for me to get the best advice possible of the most eligeble mode of obtaining of them. I adjourned the Council of Officers today, untill I could be favour'd with your opinion (together with that of others of the General Court) on these heads. They meet again tomorrow at 11 Oclock (head Quarters) when I should take it exceedingly kind of you to be present.

I understand that the Speaker and Major Halley,[2] are to be of your party to Town at Dinner. Let me prevail upon all three of you to be with me at Eleven. To Make some attempt upon the Troops in Boston before fresh Reinforcements arrive, is surely a thing of the last Importance;[3] but alas! We are scarce able to maintain our own extensive Lines. If the Militia will not be prevailed upon to stay, I cannot answer for the consequences; longer than this Month we are sure they will not; as certain I am that our Regiments cannot be Recruited to their establishment in any Reasonable time; 'tis for these Reasons therefore, and without loss of time I am exceedingly desirous of consulting with you, and the Gentlemen before mentioned on the most efficatious method of collecting a sufficient Force to answer the valuable purpose we all wish to accomplish. In hope of seeing you at the hour appointed, tomorrow; I shall not now enlarge, but only ask that I am with sincere esteem and respect Dr Sr. yr. Most obt. servt.,

Go: Washington

RC in Washington's hand (Adams Papers); addressed: "To The Honble Jno. Adams Esq   Watertown"; docketed: "G Washington   1776."

[1] That Washington misdated his letter is evident from several others he wrote on 14 and 16 Jan.: to Joseph Reed, the Massachusetts General Court, Gov. Jonathan Trumbull of Connecticut, Gov. Nicholas Cooke of Rhode Island, and the New Hampshire Convention, all of which deal with the problem of filling out the regiments (*Writings*, ed. Fitzpatrick, 4:240–251). The letter to Trumbull mentions that the Council of General Officers "met at Head Quarters yesterday [15 Jan.] and to day [16 Jan.]," dates that coincide with those mentioned in the present letter (same, p. 248).

[2] That is, James Warren and Joseph Hawley. Whether the three men attended the meeting called by Washington for the 16th is not known, but JA and Warren did attend the Council of General Officers that met on 18 Jan. (DLC:Washington Papers).

[3] "Last" as used here is an idiomatic expression of the period. Today we would say "first."

From Samuel Gelston

Sir   Fryday 9 OClock [19 Jan. 1776][1]

Pardon me for the Liberty I take in Sending a Billet to a Gentleman of your exolted Station and Character, when I have not the Honour to be in the number of your Acquaintance. Had not my situation been Really distressed, I should not have done it. When the Council Rose

Yesterday p.m. I was Acquainted by one of the Members That they had come into sundry Resolutions on my Matters and that Business was to be finished in the afternoon by a comitte chosen for that purpose. Since which I am told the court have it under Consideration. How far that may be consistant with the present Constitution I dont pretend to say, but I'm sure it is widely Different from every Idea I have Formed of the Custom of Courts. Perhaps there may be something very extreordinary in my case to Require it.

For God's sake Sir take a View of my Situation, to be dragd from my family and Business upwards of an Hundred miles through thick and thin, mud and mire bearing the insults of the Missled and un-knowing for a supposed offence only—for I think no one in his sences can condemn me with Regard to the supplys.[2] As to anything further it is merely Information the wait of which can have no Enterence into the mind of a Man of your knowledge and candour especially in this day of Anarchy and Confusion. Pray Sir consider me and my situation and use your Influence to bring about a speedy Settlement of my Affair and Let me know my Doom, which Shall ever be most Grate-fully acknowledg'd by Sir Your most Obedt. and very Huml. Servt.,

Saml: Gelston

RC (Adams Papers, microfilmed under Jan.? 1775); addressed: "To The Honl John Adams Present Favour Cpt Palmer"; docketed: "Mr Gelston [Ja]ny [177]5."

[1] Since Gelston dated his letter Friday and mentioned Council resolutions passed "yesterday," and since the committee report on him was sent down from the Council on Thursday, 18 Jan., a date of 19 Jan. for his letter is indicated (Mass., *House Jour.*, 1775–1776, 3d sess., p. 163).

[2] Dr. Samuel Gelston (1724–1782) of Nantucket, described as "a bold and staunch friend to Government," was ordered by the General Court on 18 Dec. 1775 to be arrested and brought to Watertown. He was accused of supplying provisions to Capt. James Ayscough of the British sloop *Swan* (same, p. 53; Shubael Lovell to Ays-cough, 16 Nov. and Col. Nathaniel Freeman to George Washington, 12 Dec. 1775, *Naval Docs. Amer. Rev.*, 2:1044; 3:66; *Vital Records of Nantucket*, Boston, 1925–1928, 5:328). A joint committee, of which JA was a member, was formed on 4 Jan. to consider Gelston's case, but the Council and House could not agree on what course to take. The Council proposed to release him on his good behavior secured by a bond for £1,000, but the House wanted him confined to jail for the security of the colony. The stalemate resulted in the naming of a new committee. Meanwhile Gelston escaped with the help of a John Brown, whom he bribed. Both men were brought back to Watertown in February and confined by order of the General Court until further notice (*House Jour.*, p. 111–112, 163, 194–195, 202, 212, 234, 242; *Boston Gazette*, 5 Feb.).

From Perez Morton

Sir   Council Chamber Jany 19th 1776

Agreable to the Direction of the inclosed Resolution, I am to acquaint you that by a joint Ballot of both Houses of Assembly for the Colony of Massachusetts Bay You are elected one of the Delegates to represent that Colony in American Congress untill the first Day of January AD 1777 And the enclosed Resolve you are to make the general Rule of your Conduct.

By order of the Genl. Court,

Perez Morton Dpy Secr

ENCLOSURE

In Council Jany 18 1776[1]

Whereas John Hancock, Samuel Adams, John Adams, Robert Treat Paine, and Elbridge Gerry Esqrs. have been chosen by joint Ballot of the two houses of Assembly to represent the Colony of Massachusetts Bay in New England in the American Congress untill the first day of January A.D. 1777—

Resolved that they or any one or more of them are hereby fully impowered, with the delegates from the other American Colonies to concert, direct and order such further measures as shall to them appear best calculated for the Establishment of Right and Liberty to the American Colonies upon a Basis permanent and secured against the power and arts of the British administration And guarded against any future Encroachments of their Enemies with power to adjourn to such times and places as shall appear most conducive to the publick Safety and advantage.

Read and accepted, sent down for Concurrence,

John Lowell Dpy: Secy: pro tem

In the House of Representatives Jany: 18, 1776

Read and concurred, And the Secretary is hereby directed as soon as may be to signify to each of those Gentlemen their Appointment, with an attested Copy of this Order.

Sent up for Concurrence,

J Warren Spkr:

In Council Jany: 18 1776

Read and concurred,

John Lowell Dpy Secy: pro-tem

RC (Adams Papers); with enclosure, which is docketed: "a true Copy Attst   Perez Morton   Dpy Secr"; docketed by JA: "Morton   1776."

¹ Actual election of these delegates had taken place on 15 Dec. 1775, but over a month's delay occurred before the two houses agreed upon the form of instructions and commission; moreover, through oversight the list of Council choices does not include either Gerry or Cushing on 15 Dec. (Mass., *House Jour.*, 1775–1776, 3d sess., p. 44, 74, 83, 158, 164–165; Force, *Archives*, 4th ser., 4:1235–1236). The *Boston Gazette* of 25 Dec. 1775, however, lists the names of all five men as having been elected "Last Week." See JA's Service on the Council, 26 Dec. 1775 – 24 Jan. 1776, Editorial Note (above).

From Jeduthun Baldwin

Sir   Cambridge Jany 21 1776

Pleas to allow me the freedom of informing your Honour that in the year 1755 in August, I Received a Captains Commission in Col. Brown' Regiment[1] and marched with my Company by the Way of Dearfield, and Hoossock Fort,[2] thro the woods to Fort Edward,[3] and to Lake George. Soon after I got there I was employed in building Fort Wm. Henry,[4] under the direction of Col. Ayres.[5] In Decr. when the army came off, at the request of Genl. Johnson,[6] I inlisted a Company in Col. Bagleys Regiment,[7] and tarryed thro' the winter and Spring to finish the Fort, and Garrison it, and in the year 1759, I Received a Captain Commission in Genl. Ruggles[8] Regiment. After I arived at Fort Edward I was Sent to Halfway Brook, to build a Stockade Fort there,[9] under the direction of Col. Ayres. When we came before Ticonderoga, I had the direction in throwing up Som brestwork at that place. After we had got possession of this place, I was ordered to Crownpoint where I was employed as a director and Overseer, under Col. Ayres, in building that large Fort. When the Army came off, Genl. Amherst was pleasd to Thank me for my Service, and ordered that I should be paid 4/ per Day from the time that I went to Halfway Brook till I left the place In Decr. which was about 6 months, exclusive of my pay as a Captain. I have Served as an Engineer in the present Army before Boston, was at the Leying out the works on Charlstown Hills, was in Charlstown the whole of that memorable Day 17th June, gave all the assistance I was able, went directly to Prospect Hill, had the direction of the work there, and then to Sewels Point in Brookline.[10] I have had the principal direction and over Sight, Since the 17th of June in laying out and raising the works in Cambridge Cobble Hill, and at Lechmer Point all which I have done without having an Establishment equal to the Service. This Province made me a grant of 30£ for my Service to the first of August,[11] which was equal to a Colonel pay, and left the Establishment to the Honble. Congress.

It has been proposed that I should have a Regiment, but this was objected too, for it was, said, that I could be of more Service in the Army as an Engineer. Now Sir, all I request is Rank and pay Equal to my Service, which I Submit to your Honour' Consideration. I am Sir your' and the Publick' most Obedient Very Humble Servant,

Jeduthun Baldwin [12]

RC (Adams Papers); addressed: "To the Honble John Adams Esqr A Member of the Honble Continental Congress in Philadelphia"; docketed: "Jed. Baldwin. 1776 Jany 21. answered Feb. 18. 1776."

[1] Col. Josiah Brown (Nancy S. Voye, ed., *Massachusetts Officers in the French and Indian Wars, 1748-1763*, [Boston,] 1975, No. 806).

[2] Probably Fort Massachusetts on the Hoosic River, present site of Adams, Mass. (Howard H. Peckham, *The Colonial Wars, 1689-1762*, Chicago, 1964, p. 108).

[3] About fifty miles north of Albany at a bend in the Hudson River (Edward P. Hamilton, *The French and Indian Wars: The Story of Battles and Forts in the Wilderness*, N.Y., 1962, p. 162).

[4] At the southern tip of Lake George (same, p. 195).

[5] Col. Ayres remains unidentified. He may have been a British officer.

[6] Maj. Gen. Sir William Johnson, commander of the expedition against Crown Point (same, p. 161).

[7] Col. Jonathan Bagley (Voye, Nos. 195, 196).

[8] Brig. Gen. Timothy Ruggles (same, No. 4918).

[9] One of several fortified positions on the road between Fort Edward and Fort William Henry (Francis Parkman, *Montcalm and Wolfe*, 2 vols., Boston, 1905, 2:247).

[10] The site of Brookline Fort, which with a fort across the Charles River had the task of keeping British ships from going up the river (John Gould Curtis, *History of the Town of Brookline*, Boston, 1933, p. 150). Sewall's Point is approximately the site of modern Kenmore Square in Boston (Walter M. Whitehill, *Boston, A Topographical History*, Cambridge, 1959, p. 75, 101).

[11] Baldwin petitioned the General Court on 20 Oct. 1775, asking that he be paid from 20 May to the date of his petition. On 24 Oct. the General Court authorized payment of £30 for the period of 12 May to 1 Aug. (Mass., *House Jour.*, 1775-1776, 2d sess., p. 175, 192; Records of the States, Microfilm, Mass. A.1a, Reel 12, Unit 1, p. 256).

[12] Besides having served in the French and Indian War, Jeduthun Baldwin (1731?-1788) had been a member of the First Provincial Congress (Wroth, and others, eds., *Province in Rebellion*, p. 2829). Baldwin's plea had no immediate effect. JA did write to William Heath asking about Baldwin's career (18 Feb., below), and on 22 April, Washington reported to the congress that Baldwin, whom he described as an assistant engineer and "a very useful man in his Department," had refused to go to Canada because of inadequate pay (*Writings*, ed. Fitzpatrick, 4:500-501). Finally, on 26 April the congress gave him the rank and pay of a lieutenant colonel (JCC, 4:312).

From William Heath

Dear Sir   Camp at Cambridge Janry. 22nd. 1776

Being informed that you begin your Journey for Philadelphia this week, I would beg to recommend to your Consideration the Services of Colonel Jeduthan Baldwin, who Joyned the Army the Beginning of the last Campaign, and has Continued ever Since in the army as an Engineer on the works. He has received for the months of June and July from the Assembly of our Colony Colonels Pay. But as the Continental Establishment Stands, He Cannot receive for his Services Since that Time more than Six pounds per month, which he thinks to be so Inadequate to his Services that he Informs me He must Quit the Army unless Some further provision Can be made for him. He is Constantly in Business even in this Severe Season and the works at Cobble Hill and Lechmeres Point which you have Seen, (as well as many others) were laid out and Compleated under his Direction. I wish you would mention the matter to His Excellency, if you should see him before you leave the Colony, and if He should have the Same Opinion of his Services, That you would Use your Influence in Congress, that he may have an adequate reward.

Thus far I think it my Duty to endeavor to obtain Justice for a Servicable and Faithfull man. I am Dear Sir with great Respect your most Obedient and very Humble Servt.,   W Heath

RC (Adams Papers).

From Lemuel Hayward

Sir   Roxbury Janry 23 1776

Ever since your Arrival to the Camp my colleague Doctr. Aspinwall has been confined by a Fever, which has doubled my Service in the Hospital and hereby rendered it impossible for me to do myself the Honor of waiting on you. I hope therefore you will rather impute it to Necessity than to the Want of either Gratitude or Complaisance.

I sincerely thank you for the Honor you did me in writing, but more especially for your kind Disposition towards me.

You doubtless have conversed with Doctr. Morgan respecting the Hospital. It is therefore needless to inform you that I have his and the General's Recommendation. How far they may be complyed with, I trust depends much upon your Influence which if you had not in your Favor of Novr: 13th[1] kindly offered, I should again ask. I am with greatest respect your Honor's most obedient and most humble Servent,   Lemuel Hayward

RC (Adams Papers); addressed: "The Honorable John Adams Esqr: Member of the Honorable Continental Congress"; docketed: "L. Hayward   1776 Jany 23."

[1] Not found. See Hayward to JA, 16 Dec. 1775 (above).

From Humanity

sir   ianary 23–76

Whot doth thee thenk of thes trubelsom tiems. Is thar not a caus— ye sin no dout is the caus—but among the many sins that might be named I would naem on and that is slaves keepen. Whot has the negros the afracons don to us that we shuld tak tham from thar own land and mak tham sarve us to the da of thar deth. Ar tha not the work of gods hand. Has tha not immortel soles. Ar we not the sons of on adam. How than is it that we hold that pepel in slavery. God forbid that it shuld be so anay longer. O bretesh nasion the lord is angray with you for this and is sufering you to dash on part aganst the other, but amaracae let us se that all things be right with us. Than and not tel than ma we luk for beter tiems. But sir I hear of nothing don for thos captiefs. Are we claeming freedom fighting for it and practes slavery. God forbid. My fathars this mater belongs unto you. Se whot jugments god has brot upon boston that fust imported tham into this provenc, and charlstown that burned on of tham, and will he not do so to many moer plaseses except we reform.

Sir I ask the faver of you that thee would ues your influenc that somthing might be don for thos captiefs. I hear the gentelman that heads the army holds 700 of them in bondeg.[1] Thenk ye god will prosper the wor in his hand. Might he not as wall tak 700 bostonens and cary tham to his plantsions to the da of thar death. Nuengland bhold the hand of the lord is upon you and is about to bring your owen wa upon your had except ye reform this thing.   humanity[2]

This my nu yers geft.

RC (Adams Papers); addressed: "to the honrebl John Adams Esqr at the Congras at Phaledelfe"; docketed: "Humanity."

[1] The number of slaves that Washington held in this period is greatly exaggerated here. Freeman cites a list of 1774–1775 for the Mount Vernon plantations which shows a total of 106 (*Washington*, 3:397–398, note 25).

[2] No clue to the identity of "humanity" has been found.

From Joseph Palmer

Dear Sir   Watertown, 23d January 1776

To regulate the trade of the United Colonies, being a field of vast extent, far exceeds my present comprehension; and 'tis not likely I shall ever fully investigate that complicated System of Regulation, which will best Serve the trade of these Colonies;[1] however, I will venture to Suggest to you Several reasons which incline me to favour the following Regulation, which respects the importation of foreign Articles. I wou'd first premise, that I apprehend it necessary that we shou'd have a good Sumptuary Law, well adapted to our circumstances: This being Supposed, I think we Shall be best able to guard against Some breaches of this Law, by being our own Carriers; and by having all imports in our own Bottoms, we Shall have all the advantages of *Supplying* and *carrying*; this will also encourage Ship-building, and will be an effectual Nursery for Seamen; and will also prevent other Nations obtaining Such knowledge of our Ports, as may, in some future time, enable them to improve it to our damage, as our unnatural enemies have lately done. When this matter is contemplated; I shou'd be very fond, for the reasons mentioned, to Secure this point, even at a great expence (if necessary) in some other way. For as we don't want any Imports, as *necessary* to *Life*; and as our Exports of the *Provision* kind will be large, I think we may, in treaty, fair claim the proposed article. I have no time, but only at the Board, where many interruptions necessarily take place; if I shou'd have opportunity, will write more fully.

I have to ask the favour of you to buy me a Silver Hilted Sword; I wou'd willingly have one that is both Strong and hansom, with a Hilt that will well Secure the hand: Formerly I knew somthing about the backsword, and a little, very little, about the Small Sword, and therefore prefer one that wou'd Serve to push, or cut, as opportunity and occasion may present; my Nerves are unstrung, so that I cannot wish to meet an occasion, but shou'd the necessity arrive, I shou'd be glad to be prepared for defence: When I know the price, will pay it as you may order.

I have had some tho'ts about Government which I have not had opportunity to mention so fully as I cou'd wish. You know how much we are embarrassed for want of a Governor; how Slow our proceedings; and how difficult to have 15 always in the Chair.[2] We now see that our enemies are determined to push with all their might early in the Spring; how necessary is it then that we take effectual measures for reduceing both Que[bec] and Bos[ton] before the Spring arrives. But this is not all; may we not also attempt to divert the Storm? If the United [Colonies] shou'd declare for *independence*, and offer their Trade, in some general way, until treaty shall settle particulars, to Somebody else; would not our Enemies find themselves immediately involved in a War with that Sombody? and would not that involvement break the Storm, in some degree, for the present? and can anybody accept such Trade without such an involvement? And if these things must be done at all, prudence says that they must be done soon, without any delay, and that a better form of Government, at least a more compleat one, is necessary for expedition.

I mentioned[3] a Governor serving only 1 Yr., and then 3 Yrs. next after, not to be chosen; I have not expressed myself right, but you know my meaning. I could wish also that the Council may be reduced to 21; and 7 others to be assistants, or privy Council to the Governor; these, with such assistants, to be chosen annually, I wou'd willingly trust the Governor with a negative power. May God bless and prosper all your endeavours to promote happiness; so prays yr. affect: Friend &c., Borland[4]

RC in Joseph Palmer's hand (Adams Papers); addressed: "The Honble: John Adams Esqr: Philadelphia"; docketed, with part of entry cut off: "J. Bo[rland]." Palmer must not have expected to see JA at the Council meeting on the 24th.

[1] In the fall of 1775, JA had raised with several of his correspondents the question of whether trade should be opened and whether the Continental Association should be modified or abandoned. Perhaps when he was at the Council he broached the subject to Palmer, who had already expressed himself on trade and government to JA in his letter of 2 Dec. 1775 (above), which JA may not have received before he left Philadelphia in December.

[2] To consent to legislation, the Massachusetts Council needed the votes of fifteen out of its twenty-eight members.

[3] Palmer's use of the past tense here suggests that this letter is a continuation of a conversation between the two men. In his letter of 2 Dec., Palmer had expressed his willingness to do without both a governor and a council. JA may have persuaded him that three branches were necessary for a free people.

[4] Why Palmer should have signed himself "Borland" is uncertain. Perhaps it was a code name that Palmer knew would be recognized only by his correspondent, for Palmer had mentioned loyalist John Borland's widow in his letter of 2 Dec. Interception of letters, especially those on sensitive subjects like trade and government, posed a constant danger.

From William Judd

Gentlemen   Philadelphia Goal Jany: 24th. 1776

The Debtors Confined in this Goal have Prepared a Petition[1] to the Honourable Continental Congress, praying that they woud devise or Recommend some Measure to prevent Mens persons from being Arrested or Confined in Goal for debt, during the present unhappy Conflict—which by the desire of the Petitioners I have inclosed to the President desireing him to present the same to that Venerable Body, Also requesting he woud shew the same, to each of you Gentlemen and ask your kind Assistance to Effect the end therein Propos'd.

The small Acquaintance I have had the Honor to have with you has given me Assurance sufficient to ask your Influence upon the Subject Matter of that Petition hoping I Shall be happy enough to meet with your Approbation and Patronage in the Matter aforesaid.

Shoud think myself happy you woud make all the Interest in your power for the Releiff of the Distressed which will lay an Obligation upon your Devoted Friend and Hume: Servt:,   William Judd[2]

RC (Adams Papers); addressed: "To The Honourable John and Samuel Adams Esqs Philadelphia"; docketed: "Mr. Judd   Jany 24. 1776."

[1] Not found. On 30 Jan. the congress recommended to all creditors that they not have arrested any debtor who owed less than $35, and who had enlisted or would enlist in the Continental Army (JCC, 4:103). No evidence has been found to indicate that this petition moved the congress to act; and since JA did not arrive in Philadelphia until 8 Feb., he could have had no role in its action (JA to AA, 11 Feb., *Adams Family Correspondence*, 1:345–346).

[2] William Judd, who had been one of the leaders of an expedition of Connecticut settlers to the West Branch of the Susquehanna River, had been seized along with others by Pennsylvania forces and jailed in Philadelphia because he could not furnish bail with sureties who were Pennsylvania freeholders. Judd's expedition was a great source of embarrassment to Connecticut delegates Eliphalet Dyer and Silas Deane (Julian P. Boyd and Robert J. Taylor, eds., *The Susquehannah Company Papers*, 11 vols., Ithaca, N.Y., 1962–1971, 6:362–363, 373, 395).

From James Warren

My dear Sir   Watertown Jany. 31. 1776

I am Extreamly hurried this morning, and therefore have only time to Express my wishes for your Happiness. I hope by this Time you are not far from Philadelphia. I wrote in great haste to Mr. Adams this morning to whom must refer you for all the Intelligence I could give. I have received and Inclose a Number of Letters for you which I suppose have been once to Philadelphia. I have Another for you from Mr. Adams, which Curiosity, and a Confidence in your Excusing me have Induced me to open.[1] You will please to pardon this freedom under your hand. I Inclose it and also a Copy of a Letter, from your Brother Paine, a very Curious one indeed. A model of Invective and dulness. My next may give you the Answer to it.[2] You will be able without any Aid to satisfie Mr. Adams queries about Sea Coast Men. I am as usual Your sincere Friend.

ENCLOSURE[3]

Sir   Phila. Jany. 5. 1776

I wrote you Last from Hackinsack, dated Nov. 15 that I had put my trunk on board a Waggon bound for Cambridge, and had directed it to your Care; this Letter I think I Sent by the Post, but the Waggon and Trunk never Sett off from Phila. By this means you are Saved any further trouble and I the burthen of any further Obligation to you.

How far your malevolent disposition towards me, would have Suffered you to have kept up the external appearance of Good offices, I know not, tho' I believe another disposition would have prompted you to it.

I dare Say by this time you are trying to pretend to yourself a Surprise at this kind of Expression from a person whom you Supposed Considered *you* as his best Friend; but I dare appeal to your conscience which will at Some time do the Strictest Justice, that you deserve Severer censures from me; however it is not my design to take notice of your conduct towards me in any other way than expostulation and call back your mind to the first principles of our common opposition from which it seems to me you are widely Straying; Union is undoubtedly the platform of our opposition, upon this we Sat out, and whenever we depart from it there is an end of our defence; whoever directly or indirectly doth anything to break this Union, is so far an Enemy to American Liberty, whoever abuses, disparages or discourages a fellow Labourer, is so far an Enemy to the cause; without enlarging in this strain to which there would be no End, I must refer your contemplations to a Letter you Sent to Mr. John Adams dated Nov. 3. 1775;[4] Mr. Adams met this Letter on the Road home, and (forgetting what destruction, the discovery of traducing Letters has brought on Some others,[5] and how necessary it is that Such a Correspondence should be kept Secret, in order to answer the vile purposes of it) Sent it open to his brother delegates; I cannot describe the Astonishment, Grief and vexation I felt when I read it: if possible Explain to me wherein I deserve such treatment from you; in the close acquaintance of 15 years and more, did you ever find me unfaithful? Was I not watchfully observant of your Interest, Reputation and happiness? Has any person been more attentive to the Interest and welfare of the family with which you are connected your *Dulce decus et presidium*,[6] and that at a time when my Interest and promotion would have been much advanced by contrary conduct? I mention not these matters to upbraid, but to Give you an Idea of the reflections with which your conduct agitates my mind.

I know not what principle to derive your treatment of me from, unless it be that, to the opposing of which in other persons you owe all your Glory; could you not have "particular friends" without calumniating, ridiculing and degrading your other friends? "Paine I hear is gone to gratify his curiosity in Canada," did you "hear" this from any of your "particular friends"? Alass I fear what you call "Friendship," has for its object a very contracted monopolising System, for the Support of which many incumbrances must be cleared off! "A Good Journey to him he may possibly do as much good there as at Philadelphia," what apprehensions have you of the Little Good I do at Philadelphia, unless from the intimations of your "particular friends"? And pray Sir what good do you do at Watertown or Cambridge? Do you consider how far and to what Subjects, Such Questions may be extended? And do you know as well as I do what the answer might be? "Tho I find some people here would not have pitched on him for the business we Suppose he is gone on, and perhaps there are some who would not have done it for any." By all accounts if your machinations had Succeeded, I had not been chosen into the Councill,[7] and I could easily percieve when there Last, that the influence of one of your party in favour of one of your "particular friends" degraded me in point of Rank; and what other Plotts you have Laid against me you well know.

Pray Sir do you really think that when such important matters were to be consulted and determined respecting our Expedition in the North that I took that Fatiguing Journey at Such a season to Gratify my Curiosity? If you knew how I spent all the time I was absent in this Journey, and what report the Committee made, you would not think that curiosity either prompted or Engaged my pursuit: I certainly took Great pains to be Excused from the Service, but was Urged to it by one of your "particular friends." If I have not acquitted myself well in this and all other my political undertakings, let my Deficiencies be pointed out to me that I may amend.

That there are some in our Colony who would not have "Chosen" me to this or any other "business," may be true, but if you were not one of them wherefore this insidious, clandestine way of spreading the knowledge of it? Who these people are, and how many of them owe their Sentiments to your influence, you do not say: are there any, or how many do you think there are, who have the same opinion of you.

Do you really think I have done and do no Good here? Do you know how I have Spent and do Spend my time? I could Set this matter in a Light that would Sufficiently account for some things, but I have affairs of more importance to attend to.

That you are my Enemy, and have been Labouring my disgrace, I am Satisfy'd; that finding yourself detected, your implacable temper will urge you on to execute your Ill-will I have so much reason to think, that I must necessarily take care of myself. R T Paine

RC (Adams Papers); docketed twice: "J. Warren Jany 31st 1776." For enclosures see notes 1 and 3 (below).

[1] Samuel Adams to JA, 15 Jan. (above).

[2] No answer has been found to Robert Treat Paine's letter to Warren of 5 Jan., which is printed here.

[3] Tr (Adams Papers); Dft, dated 1 Jan. (MHi:Robert Treat Paine Papers).

[4] A mistake for 3 Dec., the mistake occurring also in the draft. The letter is printed above. There is no indication that Paine knew of the letter from Warren to JA of 5 Nov., which comments on Paine's appointment to the superior court; yet Paine's letter to Joseph Hawley of 1 Jan., mentioned in note 8 of Warren's letter of 3 Dec., indicates that Paine strongly suspected that other letters critical of him had been written.

[5] A jibe at JA for his criticism of John Dickinson in the intercepted letter of 24 July 1775 (above).

[6] Sweet pride and protection. Warren through his wife was connected with the Otis family. Paine may be referring to his support for James Otis in preference to Thomas Hutchinson for appointment to the superior court. Gov. Bernard's refusal of the post to Otis was important in alienating many from the royal government.

[7] Paine was elected to the Council when JA was, in July 1775 (Mass., *House Jour.*, 1775–1776, 1st sess., p. 6).